WE GO FAR BACK IN TIME

WE GO FAR BACK IN TIME

The Letters of Earle Birney and Al Purdy, 1947–1987

Edited by Nicholas Bradley

HARBOUR PUBLISHING

Harbour Publishing Co. Ltd.
P.O. Box 219, Madeira Park, BC, V0N 2H0
www.harbourpublishing.com

Jacket letters and photo courtesy of Eurithe Purdy. Top left front jacket image by Thinkstock.
Copy edited by Elaine Park
Text design by Mary White
Index by Stephen Ullstrom, Megan Ferguson and Brianna Cerkiewicz
Printed and bound in Canada

Harbour Publishing acknowledges financial support from the Government of Canada through the Canada Book Fund and the Canada Council for the Arts, and from the Province of British Columbia through the BC Arts Council and the Book Publishing Tax Credit.

Cataloguing data available from Library and Archives Canada
ISBN 978-1-55017-610-0 (cloth)
ISBN 978-1-55017-662-9 (ebook)

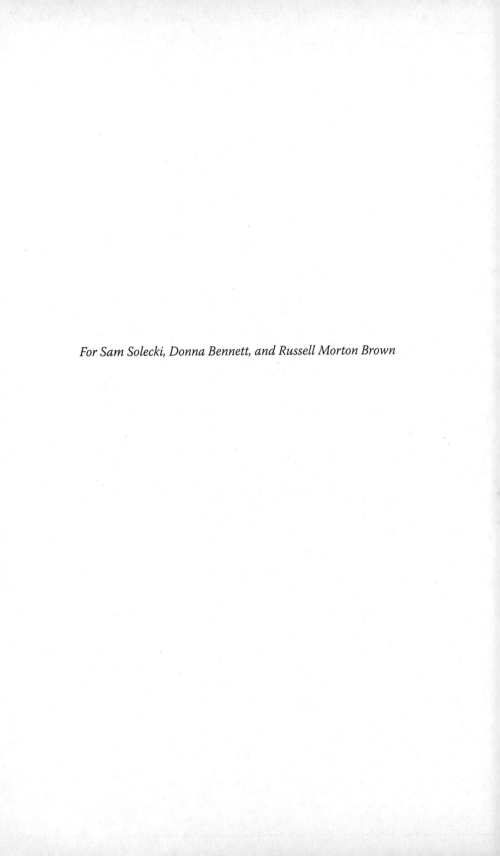

For Sam Solecki, Donna Bennett, and Russell Morton Brown

CONTENTS

Introduction: Reading the Poets' Letters   9

Note on Editorial Procedures   29
Editorial Abbreviations   35
Chronology: The Lives of Earle Birney and Al Purdy   36

In Purdy's Ameliasburg   *Earle Birney*   44

THE LETTERS   47

Earle Birney in Hospital   *Al Purdy*   435

Appendix 1: Undated Letters and Fragments   437
Appendix 2: Purdy on Birney   442

Glossary of Selected Names   446
Bibliography   457
Acknowledgements   463
Index of Titles   464
Index of Names   471

INTRODUCTION
Reading the Poets' Letters

For who can bear to feel himself forgotten?
— W.H. Auden, "Night Mail"

"The great masters of letter-writing as an art have probably been more concerned with entertaining their friends than disclosing their innermost thoughts and feelings; their epistolary style is characterized by speed, high spirits, wit, and fantasy."[1] So proposed W.H. Auden, in a review, published in 1959, of an edition of Vincent van Gogh's letters.[2] Auden wrote elsewhere of the impropriety of publishing the letters of writers and artists: "When we were young, most of us were taught that it is dishonorable to read other people's letters without their consent, and I do not think we should ever, even if we grow up to be literary scholars, forget this early lesson."[3] His sense is clear that literary scholarship is not altogether a noble enterprise; he admonished his readers that "The mere fact that a man is famous and dead does not entitle us to read, still less to publish, his private correspondence."[4] Auden allowed, however, that two conditions would mitigate the distastefulness of breaching decorum by making "epistolary style" a public matter. The first provision was the probability that the author of the letters would not have objected to their publication; the second condition was that the letters were of historical significance.[5] In the case of the correspondence of Earle Birney and Al Purdy, assuredly both requirements are met. Although the letters between the Canadian

---

1. W.H. Auden, *Forewords and Afterwords*, selected by Edward Mendelson (New York: Random House, 1973) 294.
2. The review ("Calm Even in the Catastrophe") is of *The Complete Letters of Vincent van Gogh*, published in London by Thames and Hudson and in Greenwich, CT, by the New York Graphic Society (3 vols., 1958).
3. Auden, *Forewords and Afterwords* 302.
4. Auden, *Forewords and Afterwords* 302.
5. Auden, *Forewords and Afterwords* 302–03.

poets are full of private material, from admissions of despair and bodily decline to unkind and occasionally obscene remarks about other writers, Birney and Purdy wrote to each other with a flair and sense of humour that, one suspects, they would have been pleased to share — even, perhaps, when their brio conceals genuine distress. They also wrote, as the years of their correspondence passed, with an increasing sense of having become part of Canadian literature and thus of being unquestionably public figures. The letters moreover supply an invaluable account of a remarkable literary friendship, a record of a vital period in Canadian literary history, and documentary evidence of the genesis of each author's poetry and prose.

Auden believed resolutely in the distinction between art and the life of the artist. He decried the publication of letters because he could not see, or claimed not to see, that "knowledge of an artist's private life" could illuminate the artist's works.[6] Although he and Birney were contemporaries — Auden, born in 1907, was younger by three years — he probably would have considered foreign, even improper, the intimate and almost transparent union of life and literary creation that characterized the careers of the Canadian authors, whose writing is often revelatory of and nearly always founded on experience, undisguisedly so. Birney and Purdy each made his life his primary subject. The correspondence between them allows the reader glimpses of the alchemy by which they rendered as poetry escapade and routine alike, although the transmutation inevitably remains mysterious. Are their letters also examples of "letter-writing as an art" — of the expression of style? They contain ample mischief-making, the "horsing around" that Margaret Atwood has identified as an essential element of Purdy's poetic style, as well as considerable divulgence: the letters repeatedly attest to world-weariness and professional frustrations.[7] The correspondence spans Auden's divide between "entertaining ... friends" and "disclosing ... innermost thoughts and feelings," and at times it does achieve epistolary artfulness, albeit in an idiom that might have seemed alien to the English poet (on whom American citizenship did not confer an American manner of speaking or writing). The letters exhibit doubts and foibles, too. They are utterly "human documents," although they are no less meaningful for their evident humanity.[8]

Purdy greatly admired Auden's poetry, but he probably would have guffawed

---

6. Auden, *Forewords and Afterwords* 302.

7. Atwood's review of Purdy's *Love in a Burning Building* (1970) was careful but ambivalent: "few of the poems are new: though most of the old ones have been revised, it's like eating leftovers — they've been warmed up but you know you've had them before." She wrote that "As always, one has to swallow Purdy whole, take the horsing around and the hyperbole along with the painfully-arrived-at honesties and the moments of transcendently good poetry" (*Second Words: Selected Critical Prose* [Toronto: Anansi, 1982] 97–98).

8. Auden, *Forewords and Afterwords* 294.

at any reviewer's prim consternation over the impropriety of publishing letters.[9] The publication of some of Purdy's letters during his lifetime indicates that he was willing to see his correspondence in print, or at least tolerated it. No volume of Birney's letters appeared while he was alive, however, and access to some of his archived papers, including boxes upon boxes of letters, remains restricted.[10] I begin with Auden's statements not to defend or justify the present edition of letters — his protestations were quaint even when he made them — but because they suggest, neatly and with some elegance, a divergence between a literary persona and an authentic self, and a distinction between entertainment and revelation. Such departures mark the Canadian poets' letters. Purdy's poetry is predominantly and notoriously autobiographical, although much artifice was required to create the belligerent persona on display in "At the Quinte Hotel," "The Horseman of Agawa," "Home-Made Beer," and other portraits of the artist as buffoon, some of which number among his best and most beloved poems.[11] His letters to Birney reveal differences between the poetic character and its episto-lary equivalent, but they also reflect his constant project of transforming the stuff of his life into literary material — into what Birney tellingly called "makings," a commonplace term, but one that alludes to the ancient Greek origin of the word "poet" and that evokes the artistry commanded by the skilful writer.[12] The letters

---

9. Several poems by Auden were particular favourites of Purdy's. In "Bestiary [II]," a reckoning of literary debts, Purdy praises "Auden for 'Lay Your Sleeping —' et cetera, / who was nevertheless anti-romantic, / a nay-saying man, a quiet torturer, / no spontaneity, decidedly magnificent" (*Beyond Remembering: The Collected Poems of Al Purdy*, edited by Al Purdy and Sam Solecki [Madeira Park, BC: Harbour Publishing, 2000] 394). Auden's "Musée des Beaux Arts" (1938) supplies the word "torturer" in Purdy's poem: "the torturer's horse / Scratches its innocent behind on a tree" (*Collected Poems*, edited by Edward Mendelson [New York: Vintage, 1991] 179). "Lay your sleeping head, my love" (1937), otherwise titled "Lullaby," is one of Auden's best-known poems. Auden himself did not allow his objections to published letters to prevent him from reviewing several editions of correspon-dence. Purdy owned a paperback copy of *Forewords and Afterwords*, in which some of Auden's reviews were collected.

10. The most substantial assemblage of Birney's papers is held at the Thomas Fisher Rare Book Library at the University of Toronto. The *curriculum vitae* described in the following pages is part of that archive.

11. Purdy typically went through numerous drafts in writing his poems.

12. The titles of two of Birney's books refer to poems as "makings": *Fall by Fury & Other Makings* (1978) and *Last Makings* (1991). Birney would have known that T.S. Eliot famously dedicated *The Waste Land* (1922) to Ezra Pound, "*il miglior fabbro*," or the better maker — the allusion is to Dante's praise of the troubadour Arnaut Daniel in the *Purgatorio*. And as a scholar of English literature, Birney would have known how frequently the notion of the poet as maker occurs in medieval and modern poetry. Thus there is some self-regard in his sly use of the everyday word to describe himself. Birney addressed at least one envelope to "Maker Al Purdy." In a letter (21 Feb. 1975) to Purdy, who had then embarked on travels to South America, Birney suggested that his friend was about to join a distin-guished literary group: "Glad you're going to see Peru — joining the Macchu Picchu poem-makers? (Neruda, Birney, Pat Lane)." Even this seemingly glib remark suggests Birney's commitment to the venerable conception of poetry as a form of making, and it reveals his sense that the best Canadian poets could be compared to great poets from elsewhere.

therefore stand in close relation to the poetry. Birney's own self-fashioning is likewise displayed in his letters to Purdy, which chart the various reinventions in the long duration of his career after his initial exchanges with Purdy in the late 1940s, when his reputation in Canada as an eminent writer was already secure.

The lives of Birney and Purdy extended through most of the twentieth century. The poets' youthful experiences — Birney's undergraduate days in Vancouver in the early 1920s, Purdy's riding the rails in the 1930s — may seem today almost impossibly remote, and the age of faithful letter-writing nearly as distant. In 1936 the General Post Office Film Unit produced *Night Mail*, a short film that documents the extraordinary (yet quotidian) complexity of mail delivery in Britain. Overcoming the logistical difficulties of conveying letters is cast as a meeting of ingenuity and modern technology. But in Auden's accompanying poem, the mechanized postal system remains in the service of sentiment as well as commerce. The northbound train crosses the border: "All Scotland waits for her: / In dark glens, beside pale-green lochs, / Men long for news."[13] They await "Letters of thanks, letters from banks, / Letters of joy from girl and boy," letters "Clever, stupid, short and long."[14] The letters between Birney and Purdy recount successes and disappointments as well as ordinary news and the interminable business of writing and publishing. They are evidence of a sustained literary friendship and of the seriousness with which the authors regarded the writing life and especially each other's commitment to the vocation. Birney and Purdy wrote letters with panache, but as they endlessly reminded each other, what mattered above all was writing poetry.

Earle Birney (1904–95) and Al Purdy (1918–2000) were two of the most significant Canadian authors of the twentieth century. Each was esteemed by critics and fellow-writers in Canada, and although neither poet was wholly satisfied with his book sales or reputation outside the country, each enjoyed a relatively broad readership. Birney, born in Calgary and raised in Banff and in British Columbia's mountainous interior, was a lifelong westerner, in temperament if not always in residence. (When he was born, Alberta was not yet a province.) At times he lamented and satirized the cultural backwardness of Vancouver, his home for much of his adulthood, but he rooted many poems in his intimate knowledge of the Coast Range, the Columbia Mountains, and the Rockies. "David" (1941), his most famous and possibly his most lasting poem, is not straightforwardly autobiographical, as he was seemingly always at pains to insist; its language nonetheless bespeaks his affinity for remote landscapes and his proficiency at travelling through

13. Auden, *Collected Poems* 132. "Night Mail" is dated July 1935 (133).
14. Auden, *Collected Poems* 132–33.

rugged terrain. Purdy, by contrast, made Prince Edward County, in Ontario, the centre of his world. Yet he too lived in Vancouver as a young man, and spent part of his last years on Vancouver Island. If western geography provided metaphors for Birney's sense of himself as an outsider, the village of Ameliasburgh offered Purdy an image of Canadian centrality. And if Purdy was, in Birney's phrase, "a Total Canadian," or appeared to wear this guise, Ameliasburgh, his home, was a necessary element of his identity;[15] the Canadian grain of his writing was made evident by his sedulous attention to local geography. Ameliasburgh was also the vantage from which Purdy observed the wider world. As Dennis Lee wrote, with an apposite hint of Joyce, Purdy created "a poetic cosmology focused concentrically around Roblin Lake, southeastern Ontario, Canada, North America, planet earth, all space and time."[16] The A-frame house that he built represented his connection to a particular place and allowed him to see himself in light of the lives of certain poets whose works he respected — it was a rough Canadian equivalent of Thoor Ballylee, William Yeats's tower in County Galway, and of Tor House, Robinson Jeffers's stone cottage in California. Yet while Purdy's house was a nearly mythical edifice in his poetry, it was also entirely real: as the letters indicate, it was the site of frequent visits by writers, Birney among them, and thus an important site of literary conversation, business, and mischief.

That Alfred Earle Birney and Alfred Wellington Purdy shared a name is coincidence, but — *nomen est omen* — the happenstance can be taken as a wondrous sign of other parallels in the poets' lives and works.[17] Each author was born into a family of farmers. They spent formative years in small towns: Birney in Banff and in Erickson, British Columbia, and Purdy in Trenton, to which town in Ontario his mother moved him after his father's death, and, for a short time, Belleville. But whereas Birney studied English literature at the University of British Columbia and received graduate degrees from the University of Toronto, Purdy had relatively little formal education; he left Trenton Collegiate Institute after the tenth grade. Their experiences of the Depression were different, but analogously important to their later lives. In the 1930s, as a graduate student in Toronto and as a university instructor in Utah and Vancouver, Birney was immersed in radical journalism and political activity, which he treated in his second novel, *Down the Long Table* (1955). His Marxist affiliations led to his meeting Esther Bull, a fellow Trotskyist, in 1934, while he was in London at work on his doctoral dissertation on irony in Chaucer's writing. (Birney met Trotsky himself in Norway in 1935.) Birney and

15. Birney, letter to Purdy, 30 July 1972.
16. Dennis Lee, "The Poetry of Al Purdy: An Afterword," *The Collected Poems of Al Purdy*, by Al Purdy, edited by Russell Brown (Toronto: McClelland and Stewart, 1986) 388. Lee added, however, that Purdy's focus on his home "does not invalidate visions of order centred elsewhere."
17. "I'm not Birney, despite the names' similarity," Purdy wrote to Birney (8 Apr. 1987).

Bull were married in 1940. Although he was involved with many women during the tempestuous marriage, his relationship with Esther was, for thirty years, a central element of his life. Purdy, meanwhile, spent the last years of the 1930s riding boxcars between Trenton and Vancouver and working at unremunerative jobs. This period would not be his last exposure to poverty; his descriptions of the "Bad Times" in his autobiography, *Reaching for the Beaufort Sea* (1993), convey vividly his desperation during the postwar years.[18] The trajectories of the poets' lives ran closer during the Second World War. Both men served, Birney in the Canadian Army and Purdy in the Royal Canadian Air Force. Neither saw combat, but their wartime experiences exerted an influence on their literary lives, most obviously in Birney's first novel, *Turvey: A Military Picaresque* (1949), of which Purdy was fond. Birney's poetry of the 1940s also responded to the war.[19] Purdy's desire to revisit the locations in northern British Columbia to which he was posted during the war provided material for his first successful books, *Poems for All the Annettes* (1962) and *The Cariboo Horses* (1965). His return to the West also set a paradigm for the mature phase of his career, in which he travelled widely in search of "places and situations that might incite a poem," as William Kittredge observed of Richard Hugo, an American poet whose works in some ways resemble Purdy's.[20] Also during the war, in 1941, Purdy married Eurithe Parkhurst, who would be his nearly constant companion in the decades to come.

Birney did not publish his first book, *David and Other Poems*, until 1942, when he was 38; his time had been consumed by politics, graduate school, and the first stages of his academic career. Purdy likewise did not publish his first significant volumes until relatively late in life. He printed *The Enchanted Echo* (1944) at his own expense when he was 25, but *Poems for All the Annettes* did not appear until he was 43 — roughly the same age that Birney had been when the two first corresponded. When Birney's career as a writer began in earnest in the early 1940s, Purdy was already a poet, but one with little sense of contemporary poetics: the minor poems that he placed in newspapers were amateur efforts, grossly outdated in style and theme. But the author of *The Enchanted Echo* perceived in Birney's poetry a powerfully modern quality. This recognition led to

---

18. Al Purdy, *Reaching for the Beaufort Sea: An Autobiography*, edited by Alex Widen (Madeira Park, BC: Harbour Publishing, 1993) 154–78. "At our worst times, even food was scarce. When our new neighbours ... ran over a rabbit, we made a stew with it. Eurithe's brother ... had the contract for removing garbage from an A & P supermarket in Belleville. Much edible food was buried in that rotting mess, and it was saved for us" (163). Purdy's "Ameliasburg Stew," a depiction of "the bad days" from *Wild Grape Wine* (1968), is based on the rabbit's demise. Poems such as "Bums and Brakies" and "Transient," both from *The Cariboo Horses*, provide accounts of Purdy's cross-country travels in the late 1930s.

19. Jeffers's poetry is again a relevant point of comparison.

20. William Kittredge, "Introduction: What Thou Lovest Well: Richard Hugo," *Making Certain It Goes On: The Collected Poems of Richard Hugo*, by Richard Hugo (New York: W.W. Norton, 2007) xxviii.

the first phase of their relationship.[21] Purdy sought aesthetic opinions from Birney, who was then the editor of the *Canadian Poetry Magazine*, a staid journal that he strove to modernize. Birney took an interest in Purdy's writing, and although Purdy was never simply an acolyte, the extended conversation between mentor and follower helped transform Purdy from an imitative poet to one with a distinctive, contemporary style. Birney meanwhile gained the acquaintance of an ardent reader of his poetry and a keen, sometimes brazen, critic. Purdy's letters to Birney in 1947 were those of an aspirant: he longed to be recognized as a legitimate poet but had not yet discovered the skill to match his ambition. Nor had he found the subjects that would lead to poems of real interest. Birney was a gatekeeper and a respected poet, already twice a winner of the Governor General's Award. He must have seemed to Purdy an epitome of the Canadian literary establishment. Several years afterward, when Purdy had achieved some limited success in publishing his poems in reputable journals, he wrote to Birney as a fan. A letter sent to Birney in 1955 by Purdy and Curt Lang, his Bohemian friend, is sycophantic in parts, but it also anticipates Purdy's later ambivalence about the merits of Birney's poetry. The gap between the brief exchange of 1947 and Purdy's pugnacious overtures of 1955 was followed by other fallow periods. But eventually Birney and Purdy were writing to each other regularly, as equals and as friends. In his letters Purdy greeted the senior poet as "Mr. Birney" or "Dr. Birney" or "Earle Birney" until the early 1960s, when he began to address him as "Earle" and started to sign his letters "Al" instead of "Alfred W. Purdy" or "Al Purdy."[22] The newfound informality was a sign of their emergent friendship.

Purdy revisited these beginnings in his introduction to *Last Makings* (1991), the final collection of Birney's poems published during his lifetime. (It was based on an incomplete manuscript from 1985.) Purdy noted both the length of their

---

21. The dreadfulness of *The Enchanted Echo*, Purdy's self-published first book, which he later disavowed, is part of the Purdy legend and an article of faith in studies of his works. A partial reassessment of the volume is provided by D.M.R. Bentley in "Unremembered and Learning Much: LAC Alfred W. Purdy," *The Ivory Thought: Essays on Al Purdy*, edited by Gerald Lynch, Shoshannah Ganz, and Josephene T.M. Kealey (Ottawa: University of Ottawa Press, 2008) 31–50.

22. A contemporary parallel exists in American poetry. A few months before Purdy wrote to Birney in 1947 to offer his opinion of *Canadian Poetry Magazine*, another noteworthy correspondence began when Elizabeth Bishop wrote to Robert Lowell. On May 12, 1947, she wrote to "Mr. Lowell" in care of his publisher to congratulate him on his having won several awards, including the Pulitzer Prize for *Lord Weary's Castle* (1946). Her second letter, of August 14, was addressed to "Robert"; she explained that "I've never been able to catch that name they call you but Mr. Lowell doesn't sound right, either." In her third letter (22 Sept. 1947), and at Lowell's prompting, she got the salutation right: "Dear Cal." (Elizabeth Bishop and Robert Lowell, *Words in Air: The Complete Correspondence between Elizabeth Bishop and Robert Lowell*, edited by Thomas Travisano with Saskia Hamilton [New York: Farrar, Straus and Giroux, 2008] 3, 4, 8.) On Bishop and Lowell as two of "Purdy's major contemporaries," see Sam Solecki, "Materials for a Biography of Al Purdy," *The Ivory Thought: Essays on Al Purdy*, edited by Gerald Lynch, Shoshannah Ganz, and Josephene T.M. Kealey (Ottawa: University of Ottawa Press, 2008) 14.

association and the antagonism with which it began: "I've known Earle Birney since the early 1950s. A young genius named Curt Lang and I scraped acquaintance by writing provocative letters to him."[23] Purdy and Lang also sent letters to Edmund Wilson and Roy Campbell — Wilson was an esteemed literary critic, having already published *Axel's Castle* (1931) and *The Wound and the Bow* (1941), and the poet Campbell was likewise highly distinguished. Only Birney replied with any enthusiasm. He invited Purdy and Lang to lunch at the University of British Columbia, where he was a professor of English: "Of course we went," Purdy later wrote, "and were rather tongue-tied facing Birney's tremendous vitality and a flow of energy strong enough to gag Mount St. Helens."[24] Purdy's own volcanic force is evident in his early letters to Birney, in which he bluntly gives his estimation of the successes and failures of Birney's works, whether individual poems or collections in their entirety. The bellicose dimension of the relationship never completely disappeared, and occasionally the letters suggest genuine acrimony. In *Reaching for the Beaufort Sea*, Purdy alluded to Birney's recalcitrance and temper:

Earle Birney and I were friends, despite the obvious differences in temperament and character. We got along well most of the time. Of course, there was a huge wall of reserve in him that you'd encounter if you pushed farther on some subjects than a tacitly agreed-on boundary. Birney was genial and expansive in the sense of a public man's expansive demeanour. And he growled at times. I think he did not suffer fools much, and could be very sarcastic.[25]

Purdy recognized moreover that he shared in these qualities: "At times I felt awe of Birney, sometimes impatience, perhaps even a little fear, but always respect. He was obdurate, stubborn, combative and occasionally unfriendly; all these things to the degree that he resembles descriptions I have heard about myself when young: and denied vociferously. He was a friend."[26] In writing to Birney in 1979, Purdy succinctly observed their essential yet curious similarity: "somehow you and I think alike in many ways" (22 May 1979). As the letters show, each poet mirrored the other, although not always without distortion.

Birney was patient in responding to Purdy's first letters. He saw that the hostility in the letter from Purdy and Lang was partly a function of intoxication. "Of course it's unfair of me to grope in cold sobriety with phrases you two

---

23. Al Purdy, introduction, *Last Makings*, by Earle Birney, edited by Marlene Kadar and Sam Solecki (Toronto: McClelland and Stewart, 1991) xi.

24. Purdy, introduction xi.

25. Purdy, *Reaching for the Beaufort Sea* 234.

26. Purdy, *Reaching for the Beaufort Sea* 234.

struck off in moments of winy rhetoric," he wrote in reply to Purdy, "So I take your disapprovals at the same discount as I took your praises."[27] He answered a litany of questions in considerable detail, and in that letter and others he encouraged Purdy, whose talent was yet unproven. Perhaps even then Birney discerned similarities between his life and that of his correspondent. Late in his career, Birney listed on his academic *curriculum vitae* various jobs that he had held before 1927, when he received his M.A. from the University of Toronto:

Newspaper boy.
Itinerant farm laborer.
Logger (bucker and faller).
Bank clerk.
Survey party chairman, axeman, rodman.
Assistant on palaeological explorations Canadian Rockies.
Mountain guide.
Mosquito control laborer and sub-foreman.
House painter.
Highway laborer (rock-driller).
Sewer man (pick and shovel).
Magazine salesman.
Door-to-door perfume salesman.

Birney — Ph.D., Fellow of the Royal Society of Canada, writer-in-residence at Massey College — clearly felt that these formative experiences were important elements of his professional record and had to be minded. Becoming a poet had been an arduous task. The support that he offered Purdy in the 1940s and 1950s was a tacit acknowledgement of the hardships, material as well as vocational, that Canadian writers faced. And if Birney understood Purdy's early literary and financial difficulties, he later shared with his friend an abiding sense that the writer's livelihood was precarious, that both inspiration and recognition were fleeting. The very paper on which the letters were written is evidence of the poets' thrift: Birney often wrote on stationery liberated from hotel rooms, while Purdy used whatever paper was at hand, sometimes typing on purloined letterhead or even on other letters.[28]

Birney tended to write to Purdy in the voice of a senior figure, and on some

27. Birney, letter to Purdy and Curt Lang, 15 Mar. 1955.
28. Purdy was amused by Birney's custom; the writers tried to outdo each other with particularly garish or tacky letterhead. In his introduction to *Last Makings*, he describes Birney as "both curmudgeonly and magnificent, close with money and wildly generous at the same time. A human being, that is" (xv).

occasions, his descriptions of physical afflictions throw into relief the difference in age between the two men. But the correspondence is largely one of peers. Birney and Purdy evidently enjoyed receiving each other's news. The postcards that they sent while travelling usually say little of substance, but their frequency suggests the extent to which each writer thought about the other. The letters often dwell upon trivia. The poets' endless accounting of the mundane details of their lives — appointments, expenses, the weather — forms a counterpoint to the salacious gossip and the serious debates over tradition and technique in which they also engaged. Birney had many romantic misadventures and travails — numerous affairs and perpetual battles with Esther.[29] Stories about Purdy's belligerence abound. Both writers drank heavily at times, although not as prodigiously as some of their contemporaries (such as Alden Nowlan, Patrick Lane, and John Newlove) or their mutual acquaintance, Malcolm Lowry, who was all but incapacitated by alcoholism. The ordinariness of much of the correspondence is therefore somewhat surprising. The letters are in general less concerned with flamboyant behaviour than with discussions of reading and writing, and of living day by day.

The correspondence spans a period of forty years and reaches across five decades. The letters of the 1940s and the 1950s help to illustrate Purdy's development as a writer, but they contain little personal material; the poets were not yet sufficiently close to abandon formality. The first gap in the letters coincides with the period of self-education that was crucial to Purdy's relinquishment of the archaism of *The Enchanted Echo*. As he wrote the poems collected in *Pressed on Sand* (1955), *Emu, Remember!* (1956), and *The Crafte So Longe to Lerne* (1959), and as he devoted himself to the study of the poetic past, his understanding of his literary ambitions and possibilities became far more sophisticated. His earliest letters to Birney are also notable for the views that they offer of his life prior to his success as a writer. They provide some details — although too few to satisfy the biographer — of his having met Lowry, his friendship with Lang, and his marriage to Eurithe. The letters of the 1960s are more candid and revealing. The steady exchange of letters in that decade and the next two provides a fascinating account of the writers' literary and personal lives.

From a strictly literary perspective, the most interesting letters, I think, are those of the 1970s, when Birney and Purdy wrote to each other frequently and at length about their own and each other's publishing activities. A melancholy strain runs through the letters of this period. They are increasingly full of references to ill health and impatience with the publishing world. Both writers were susceptible to malaise. Birney's rejuvenation during his relationship with Wailan Low

---

29. Birney's relationships with women are treated at length in Elspeth Cameron's *Earle Birney: A Life* (Toronto: Viking, 1994).

was accompanied by an acute sense of his mortality. And Birney and Purdy both evinced an awareness of the waning of their literary reputations. The letters of the 1970s are at times gossipy and cavalier, probably a function of the changed relationship between the friends: Purdy, by then a successful writer, had less cause to solicit Birney's opinions about matters of technique or literary history. Interludes between letters can partly be attributed to the full professional schedules of both writers. As they were preoccupied by writing and publishing and by protracted exchanges with other friends and colleagues, they went for periods without keeping in close contact. Both poets (and Birney in particular) remark that they misplaced or lost letters. The letters themselves also suggest that Birney and Purdy found other ways to remain in touch as the years of their friendship passed: they telephoned and visited each other. These encounters became easier once Birney moved from Vancouver to Toronto. Birney's heart attack in 1987 caused him a severe and permanent brain injury. Although he lived until 1995, the correspondence as it had been came to a close in 1987.

If the letters cast light on the intellectual and emotional lives of their authors, they also depict the business of poetry in Canada. As a poet without the stability of a permanent academic position, Purdy continually sought financial opportunities, including journalistic assignments, editorial duties, speaking engagements, and short-term teaching positions. Birney's posts at the University of British Columbia and the University of Toronto relieved him of some of the pressures that Purdy faced, but the time required to fulfill pedagogical and administrative obligations tormented him. The letters show that finding time in which to write was an incessant concern. Both poets wrote substantial amounts of prose, from book reviews and essays to novels, and they frequently expressed regret that doing so took them away from their poems. Indeed they often found themselves at an impasse: in barren periods for poetry, they wrote prose, further delaying, it seems, the return of the Muse. Letters too they sometimes viewed as a necessary evil. Time was also needed for travel, which they understood to be a precursor to writing as well as a source of pleasure. (Al and Eurithe also travelled for a more prosaic reason: to escape the winters of Ameliasburgh.) The letters are full of news of drafts and publications. Both poets were usually occupied with many projects at once. They wrote and revised poems almost compulsively, despite their claims to suffer from writer's block. Like Robert Lowell, Birney and Purdy "lived by revision," publishing several versions of poems in journals and books.[30] As a result, there was nearly

---

30. William Logan, *Our Savage Art: Poetry and the Civil Tongue* (New York: Columbia University Press, 2009) 49: "Lowell lived by revision and knew his poems sometimes withered because of it — revision was the vice of his virtues."

always some progress to report, quite apart from the exchange of scuttlebutt, of which there was seldom a shortage.

Birney and Purdy shared literary interests and friendships. E.J. Pratt — "Ned" to Birney — figures repeatedly in the letters, especially at first. Pratt's poetry was variously a technical model to emulate, an influence to refuse or deny, and an example of suitably Canadian writing. Neither Birney nor Purdy produced a national epic (or epyllion) in the mould of *Brébeuf and His Brethren* (1940) or *Towards the Last Spike* (1952), but their absorption in Canadian history and geography resulted in bodies of work that have a national scope that follows Pratt's template. Birney's and Purdy's recurring references to Lowry mark another convergence of their literary enthusiasms; their personal acquaintances with the author of *Under the Volcano* (1947) provided a lifelong subject of conversation and reminiscence. And of course Birney and Purdy knew many of the same contemporary Canadian poets, about whom they continually exchanged news and opinions.

The careers of both writers were sustained by grants, primarily from the Canada Council. Each had various affiliations with universities — Birney as professor first at the University of British Columbia and then at the University of Toronto, Purdy as writer-in-residence at several institutions — but they depended on grants to fund the travels in which they found topics and occasions for their poems. As a result, many of their letters concern applications and the appraisals that they wrote for each other. The earliest of such assessments are brief and reflect the insularity of the small world of Canadian letters at the time. In 1959 Birney wrote to the Canada Council on Purdy's behalf:

Mr. Alfred Purdy of Montreal has written me asking me to support an application which he plans to make to your Council this year, and I am very pleased to accede to his request. I think Alfred Purdy is one of the best of the younger poets writing in Canada today. In the last few years he has shown increasing range and vigour and productivity. His last letter to me outlined some of the projects he has in hand and others which he wants to pursue if he can finance himself meanwhile.[31]

Birney's more effusive letter to the Guggenheim Foundation in 1966 is a richer document. He offers a view of Purdy as a still improving but already prominent Canadian writer:

I have known Al Purdy's poetry for most of the 20 years in which he has been writing it. It has been both an astonishment and a joy to watch the way in

---

31. Birney, letter to the Canada Council, 4 Nov. 1959.

which he has shot into virtual leadership among Canadian poets in the last three years. There was always great promise, but his early work was very uneven and not well focussed in aim. Now he has found his own unique voice, and it has been heard both from platforms from one end of this country to the other and from the pages of his books and from journals both experimental and established. The best of his poetry to date is in *The Caribou Horses* [sic] but even better work is now appearing in journals and will shortly appear as a collection, *North of Summer* [1967]. These poems are the only good, authentic ones ever written about the Canadian Arctic, except by Eskimaux. They are also, apart from their subject matter, poems of remarkable vigor, originality and humour.[32]

The letters of support that Birney and Purdy wrote for each other are fulsome with praise, as befits the genre. But their mutual assessments, although they were written in part as favours and obligations, also demonstrate each poet's capacity to see clearly the other's literary aims. If "his own unique voice" is a platitude, Birney is nonetheless astute in suggesting that Purdy's poems aspire to be faithful to experience by deploying a comic persona. Birney mentions Purdy's "vigour" in both letters: he admired this quality immensely.

When Purdy was in his sixties and Birney in his mid-seventies, they wrote about their advancing age and their changing reputations. At this relatively late stage of the correspondence, the differences between the poets are as evident as ever. Purdy is reflective, at times sanguine and at other times seemingly morose. Birney, in contrast, relentlessly lists his latest triumphs, the details of his travels, and his many envisioned projects. Where Purdy is self-deprecating, Birney writes as if with his future biographer in mind. The energy with which he accounted for his days created a rich biographical record, but Birney suggested in the poem "Dear Biographer," from *Fall by Fury & Other Makings* (1978), that he was well aware of the unreliable nature of the papers left behind by writers. Purdy was a stern critic of his own work and that of others, despite the jovial tone of much of his correspondence and the praise that he frequently bestowed on his contemporaries. He remained at once appreciative of the achievement of his erstwhile mentor and free of illusions about its ultimate importance. A letter in 1994 to Elspeth Cameron, Birney's biographer, shows that Purdy had essentially abandoned his youthful assessment of Birney as a poet of the first rank. That his opinions should have changed over the decades is no surprise, but the letter suggests that in the end he held judicious evaluation of literary merit distinct from friendship. Purdy's late statements about Birney should not be understood as a betrayal but instead as a

---

32. Birney, letter to the Guggenheim Foundation, 28 Nov. 1966.

culmination of the critical acumen apparent even in the letters of the 1950s. After Birney's death and near the end of his own career, Purdy wrote letters with a sense that the practical concerns of the literary life — the chronically inadequate size of grants from the Canada Council, Jack McClelland's perennial inability to sell books in sufficient numbers — had finally ceased to matter. What remained, as time grew short, were the poems.

The Greek poet C.P. Cavafy wrote in "Sensual Delight" (1917) of the "memory of the hours / when I found and sustained sensual delight as I desired it."[33] Birney is largely a poet of remembered sensual delights — including erotic experiences but also the esoteric pleasures of mountaineering. His poems are especially concerned with the possibility that such elusive satisfactions, once encountered, could be regained. "David" depicts the tragedy that can occur in pitiless landscapes, but a more representative view of Alpine adventure is found in "Climbers" (from *Trial of a City and Other Verse*, 1952), in which the strange, fleeting joys of wilderness are placed in contrast with the banality of urban existence, to which lovers of the mountains must return:

and the climbers move under barred old snow
silently go beyond worn icefields
up the horny neck of desolation
till their hands bleed from the spines of the crest
and they lie at the end of thrust
weak in weak air and a daze of sight
on the pointless point of the peak
And this is the beginning of space
where there is nothing to say and
nothing to do and time only
for clambering back to the lean
pig of a streetcar squealing[.][34]

Birney's many poems about travel suggest a hope that new experiences could provoke longed-for pleasures and even moments of transcendence. Desmond Pacey wrote in 1958 that "No other poet has sought to describe so many of the

33. C.P. Cavafy, *The Complete Poems of Cavafy*, translated by Rae Dalven (New York: Harvest-Harcourt, 1976) 79.
34. Earle Birney, *Trial of a City and Other Verse* (Toronto: Ryerson, 1952) 69. The version of the poem published in *One Muddy Hand: Selected Poems* (2006) — that edition is based on Birney's *Ghost in the Wheels: Selected Poems* (1977) — is considerably different.

geographical areas of Canada as has Birney."[35] He made this observation before Purdy had established himself as a major figure, but Purdy eventually matched the example of his mentor. In his autobiography Purdy explains the appeal and importance of writing from a wide range of Canadian places: "[I] felt I was mapping the country, long after those early cartographers ... saying I was there, adding something personal to the map's cold nomenclature of heights and distances."[36] Birney, the restless cosmopolitan, ever fearful of parochialism, also travelled outside Canada whenever he had means and time. Purdy, too, ventured abroad in search of *materia poetica*. Both writers were highly aware of the literary contexts of their journeys. Neither could travel to Mexico, for instance, without thinking of Lowry and D.H. Lawrence, whom they viewed as guiding precursors.

Purdy's reputation as a blustery, accidental poet endures, but his letters to Birney, especially those of the 1970s, show a deep capacity for self-scrutiny. In his poems, letters, autobiography, essays, and even his novel (*A Splinter in the Heart*, 1990), Purdy's recurring subject is himself. He used autobiographical specificity as a strategy for avoiding the impression of pretentiousness, one of his great writerly fears, and to ground his broad range of concerns, from historical events to national politics to geological time, in particularities. (He tolerated abstraction in the works of other poets, however, including those whose writing he read in translation.) *Reaching for the Beaufort Sea* includes versions of many of the episodes imparted in the letters to Birney. The facts remain generally the same in Purdy's versions of his life — and he was prone to comic exaggeration in all genres — but the letters are strikingly different in tone. Purdy's dour and cynical tendencies are most apparent, I think, in his letters. The boisterous persona cultivated in his poems and prose is certainly sometimes visible, but the dismal missives from Winnipeg, for example, foreground Purdy's propensity for introspection and his inclination to despair about his productivity and talent. As writer-in-residence at the University of Manitoba in 1975–76, he found that the Prairie winter was not conducive to happiness.

In his introduction to *Last Makings*, Purdy wrote that Birney "has been a very large presence in Canada, one that extends backward in time, and into the future, for I'm sure that his work will remain alive for a long time to come. My admiration for him also reaches out in many directions."[37] The evaluative statement is accurate enough, yet the magpie nature of Birney's poetry — he flitted between styles and forms — makes his precise influence hard to detect. Sam Solecki has suggested

---

35. Desmond Pacey, *Ten Canadian Poets: A Group of Biographical and Critical Essays* (Toronto: Ryerson, 1958) 294.

36. Purdy, *Reaching for the Beaufort Sea* 249.

37. Purdy, introduction xiv.

that although Birney's presence in Canadian literature was powerful, the effect of his poems on those of other writers was fairly limited:

Unlike Layton's, or Purdy's, Birney's influence is more diffuse, less easily defined. With the exception of Purdy, I can't think of another important poet whose work shows his presence. On the other hand, there's little doubt that his editing on *The Canadian Forum* and *Canadian Poetry Magazine* helped shift the direction of Canadian poetry at mid-century. Similarly his creative writing courses shaped a generation of writers coming out of the University of British Columbia.[38]

Even in Purdy's case, Birney's "presence" can be hard to detect. Purdy's habit of undercutting serious poetic moments with an offhand remark, aside, or digression resembles Birney's similar penchant. Some of Birney's poems and Purdy's are linked by theme and perspective, particularly when they depict equivalent landscapes. The first lines of Birney's "North of Superior," for instance, find a complement in those of Purdy's "The Country North of Belleville." First Birney:

Not here the ballad or the human story
the Scylding boaster or the water-troll
not here the mind   only the soundless fugues
of stone and leaf and lake[39]

Then Purdy:

Bush land scrub land —
    Cashel Township and Wollaston
Elzevir McClure and Dungannon
green lands of Weslemkoon Lake

---

38. Sam Solecki, "Editor's Foreword," *One Muddy Hand: Selected Poems*, by Earle Birney, edited by Sam Solecki (Madeira Park, BC: Harbour Publishing, 2006) 12. Purdy's own influence in contrast has been repeatedly acknowledged. Dennis Lee suggests that "During this period [1970–85] the strongest vernacular influence has been the poetry of Al Purdy" and that Purdy is one of "the pre-eminent Canadian influences on this generation." Purdy's characteristic style — described by W.H. New as the "rhythmic skill with laconic idiom" of "an ordinary intelligent working-class traveller," by Lee as a "hinterland idiom," and by George Woodcock as a "colloquial exuberance" — was widely imitated. (Dennis Lee, introduction, *The New Canadian Poets 1970–1985*, edited by Dennis Lee [Toronto: McClelland and Stewart, 1985] xxix, xlii; W.H. New, *A History of Canadian Literature* [1989; Montreal: McGill-Queen's University Press, 2001] 239–40; Lee, "The Poetry of Al Purdy: An Afterword" 391; George Woodcock, *Northern Spring: The Flowering of Canadian Literature* [Vancouver: Douglas and McIntyre, 1987] 16.)

39. Earle Birney, *One Muddy Hand: Selected Poems*, edited by Sam Solecki (Madeira Park, BC: Harbour Publishing, 2006) 23.

where a man might have some
      opinion of what beauty
   is and none deny him
         for miles —[40]

The poems' rhythms and settings are different, but they comparably take absence
as the defining aspect of the landscape. The sense of place is founded on negation,
yet in a paradox North is, as again in Purdy's *North of Summer: Poems from Baffin
Island* (1967), a site of creative possibility. (In that Arctic volume, of course, the
North is much more distant.) Another resemblance consists in the poets' breadth
of interests. As George Bowering observed, "Purdy's poetry is characterized by its
sudden veering back and forth between classical references and domestic appe-
tites."[41] The same is true of Birney's writing, which, as "North of Superior" shows,
draws upon his considerable erudition.

   More significant perhaps are the poets' similar senses of the relative merits
of the literary past and present — the subject of extended epistolary conversations. But to a great extent Birney and Purdy remained different writers, as the
contrasts in the styles of their letters demonstrate. Whereas Birney as correspondent was laconic and often guarded, Purdy was digressive and anecdotal.
Birney's letters are summaries of his days; Purdy's are rambling accounts of his
thoughts. Purdy's self-deflating manner is as evident in the letters as in the poems.
Serious or sentimental passages about poetry, depression, frustration, even friendship and happiness are accompanied by jokes (usually crude), teasing, and mere
complaining. This mode is well illustrated by a letter that Purdy wrote in 1974 on a
ship in the Gulf of St. Lawrence, where he was gathering material for a journalistic
assignment. It begins with a blunt remark about the circumstances, shifts almost
immediately into a reflection about life itself, and then expands into a self-ex-
amination, colloquially expressed but attuned to the literary past, that leads to a
statement about the purpose of writing poetry:

   I haven't been so bored in years. Hope to escape in the next day or two. There
   sometimes seems no end to this sort of thing — the ordinary tissue of life is
   permeated with boredom, then unexpected bright places difficult to predict. I
   was highly interested the first day or so of this trip, now phut! Sure, I should
   be able to extract and feel maximum enjoyment from all situations, but reality
   is somewhat different than that rose-coloured philosophy.

---

40. Purdy, *Beyond Remembering* 79.
41. George Bowering, *Left Hook: A Sideways Look at Canadian Writing* (Vancouver: Raincoast,
2005) 230.

I suppose one's ego should be large enough to say that what one has written is important, therefore one is justified, and that the bright places make things worthwhile. But I'm not at all sure that I've written anything very important, just human stuff locked in a physical and temporal strata [*sic*]. Perhaps that should be enough. And the "bright places" are only worthwhile at their occurrence, so that one feels on a ski jump from high to low and back again. The existentialist business of inventing the world and oneself each day [is] easier said than done. Rilke kinda puts me off in that respect. And after you've written poems for years, you see that many of the things you write fall into a "knowing how" category, this way will make a poem and another way won't. So you take the way that will because your mind works naturally in that direction. Rilke is sort of "accept, accept!" which I don't like. (I'm fucked if I'll accept a lot of things.) A kind of roseate look at depression and death. One accepts, but dammit one doesn't have to like it, stoicism is too damn Greek for me. I want to be the cat yowling on the backyard fence sometimes.[42]

Kenneth Rexroth, an American poet who like Purdy had a profound interest in the history and literature of classical Greece and Rome, wrote in a short essay on Edward Gibbon's *Decline and Fall of the Roman Empire* that "the subject of all tragedy" is "the defeat of the ideal by the real, of being by existence."[43] Purdy shared this tragic sense. His writing often depicts, and is itself an attempt, to stave off mere existence. His poetic and epistolary "yowling" is at once protest and affirmation.

As Auden understood, by making public originally and essentially private documents, editions of letters can bring to light feelings or foibles that the writer might have preferred to keep unseen. The publication of Philip Larkin's *Selected Letters* in 1992 revealed that poet's predilection for racist humour (especially in his correspondence with Kingsley Amis), a taste for pornography, and a hostility toward the modern world. It made obvious what Andrew Motion, his biographer, calls Larkin's "eventual roll-call of right-wing prejudices," in which he "would make sure that blacks, women, children, trades unions, socialists and academics all got it in the neck."[44] If Birney's and Purdy's letters are unlikely to cause the scandal of

---

42. Purdy, letter to Birney, 5 June 1974.

43. Kenneth Rexroth, *Classics Revisited* (Chicago: Quadrangle, 1968) 231. Rexroth corresponded with George Woodcock, a fellow anarchist and a friend of Birney's and Purdy's, and with Birney. Numerous connections exist between Rexroth and Birney, from the textual (compare the titles of Birney's *Big Bird in the Bush* [1978] and Rexroth's *Bird in the Bush* [1959]) to the personal (Ikuko Atsumi, with whom Birney had an affair, collaborated with Rexroth on translations of Japanese poetry).

44. Andrew Motion, *Philip Larkin: A Writer's Life* (London: Faber and Faber, 1993) 65. Larkin's letters are gathered in *Selected Letters of Philip Larkin 1940–1985*, edited by Anthony Thwaite (London: Faber and Faber, 1992).

Larkin's, the authors' weaknesses and biases are still manifest in their letters. Thus reading once-private correspondence requires an ear for tone. Purdy is not truly at his most insightful when he suggests that an illustration of Birney as mountaineer reminds him of Birney as lover; nor was Purdy then writing, I assume, with his letters' public life in mind. Yet in context the joke shows not merely his scurrilous sense of humour but also his closeness to Birney, which licensed the teasing:

A while back someone sent me a dozen or so pictures of [Canadian] writers, you among them, of which I decorated my wall with four. You, [Margaret] Laurence, [Roderick] Haig-Brown and [Pierre] Berton. I'm just noticing now a peculiarity about your poster which I can only think is deliberate.

There is a mountain climber, presumably you, clambering around inside what looks very much like a woman's vagina. Did you ever really get in that far, is the question I've wanted to ask since noticing? What's it like?[45]

Is there genuine critical value in such a passage? Perhaps not much, but even apparently inconsequential moments offer views of the complexion of the friendship and thus of the lives from which the poetry emerged. If some letters are ribald, others are simply unflattering. Birney at his least appealing is jealous, obsessive about his reputation, and extraordinarily vulnerable to the slights of reviewers and critics. His tendency to become outraged is evident in a letter from 1969. Purdy had abandoned work on a book about Birney and had given his taped interviews to Frank Davey, who would write the book instead. Birney wrote to Purdy in a state of high pique to forbid the sharing of the tapes and to express his general displeasure at being made a critical subject: "The whole thing leaves me sick. I was glad *for your sake* that you quit on the job and glad anyway, since *I don't want a book about me*. I'm fucking well not dead yet."[46] But palpable in other letters are his affection for Purdy, his support of Purdy's career, and his dedication to poetry and the literary life. The assembled letters portray both poets as complex, contradictory figures who remain enigmatic despite the revelatory nature of the correspondence. Birney and Purdy were prominent authors, yet their private lives even now, as their papers come more fully into public view, can be seen only through a glass, darkly. What is clear, however, is the poets' ardent struggle to create an art that would outlast them, and to discern what a life could bear.

The deaths of Birney and Purdy led naturally to reassessments of the poets' literary achievements and their places in Canadian literary history. If they once enjoyed — and claimed for themselves — central positions in Canadian letters,

45. Purdy, letter to Birney, 20 Aug. 1979.
46. Birney, letter to Purdy, 4 Sept. 1969.

their works are now seen increasingly in historical context. Both poets have suffered a remarkable reversal in critical fortunes: the great enthusiasm with which their works often were received during their lifetimes, and the general acknowledgement of their significance, have been replaced by neglect. In the years since Purdy's death in 2000, there have been relatively few scholarly accounts of his writing or of Birney's in the major journals devoted to Canadian literary studies.[47] But if Birney and Purdy are perhaps not the iconic figures they once were, their poems retain appeal and power. At their best they have significant aesthetic as well as historical value. The letters suggest the vitality of the poets' writing: they are important biographical and literary-historical documents, but they also reflect the allure, diversity, and accomplishment of the poetry itself. If *We Go Far Back in Time* illuminates the poems and serves to sustain interest in them, then the edition will have met its goal.

47. Solecki's *The Last Canadian Poet: An Essay on Al Purdy* (Toronto: University of Toronto Press, 1999) is the chief exception to the rule of indifference. *The Ivory Thought: Essays on Al Purdy* (Ottawa: University of Ottawa Press, 2008), a collection of essays edited by Gerald Lynch, Shoshannah Ganz, and Josephene T.M. Kealey, is a recent critical reassessment of Purdy's works and influence.

NOTE ON EDITORIAL PROCEDURES

Birney and Purdy were prolific authors. Jonathan Kertzer has noted that Birney "was an epic writer of letters — 1200 correspondents, he once counted — who from an early age kept everything he wrote, received, recorded and thought."[48] *Yours, Al: The Collected Letters of Al Purdy* (2004) runs to nearly six hundred pages, yet gathers but a fraction of the extant correspondence.[49] The scope of the poets' archives presents a critical challenge. Birney's and Purdy's papers have been accessible to scholars, at least in part, since the 1970s, but they have not been studied comprehensively. Birney's letters in particular have received little notice, although some studies have made use of them.[50] The major exception is Cameron's biography of Birney (1994), which draws heavily on his voluminous papers, including his letters. In 2005 a selection of Birney's correspondence with Desmond Pacey was printed, but most of the letters remain unpublished.[51] Purdy's papers have attracted more attention; *We Go Far Back in Time* is one of several collections of his letters. Volumes were published during Purdy's lifetime of his correspondence with Charles Bukowski, Margaret Laurence, and George Woodcock.[52] *Yours, Al*, the most significant collection of Purdy's correspondence,

---

48. Jon Kertzer, "Teasing Birney," *Canadian Literature* 150 (Autumn 1996): 155.

49. Al Purdy, *Yours, Al: The Collected Letters of Al Purdy*, edited by Sam Solecki (Madeira Park, BC: Harbour Publishing, 2004).

50. For an example of the critical use of the unpublished letters, see Sandra Djwa, "A Developing Tradition" (*Essays on Canadian Writing* 21 [Spring 1981]: 32–52). The first accession of Purdy's papers at Queen's University is from 1971; the first of Birney's at the University of Toronto is from 1976.

51. See Tracy Ware, ed., "The Lives of a Poet: The Correspondence of Earle Birney and Desmond Pacey, 1957–58" (*Canadian Poetry: Studies, Documents, Reviews* 56 [Spring/Summer 2005]: 87–119).

52. Charles Bukowski and Al Purdy, *The Bukowski/Purdy Letters: A Decade of Dialogue 1964–1974*, edited by Seamus Cooney (Sutton West, ON: Paget, 1983); Margaret Laurence and Al Purdy, *Margaret Laurence-Al Purdy: A Friendship in Letters: Selected Correspondence*, edited by John Lennox (Toronto: McClelland and Stewart, 1993); Al Purdy and George Woodcock, *The Purdy-Woodcock Letters: Selected Correspondence 1964–1984*, edited by George Galt (Toronto: ECW Press, 1988).

includes a selection of Birney's letters to Purdy, particularly from the early part of their epistolary history. The present volume is primarily curatorial rather than archaeological: as a complement to *Yours, Al*, which newly published many of the manuscript letters, *We Go Far Back in Time* emphasizes the continuity and breadth of the Birney-Purdy correspondence.

This edition was prepared with two audiences in mind: readers of the poems of Birney and Purdy who wish to know more about the lives of the poets and the friendship between them, and specialist commentators on Canadian literature, especially those with interests in the relations between the published poems and their biographical and historical contexts and in the material history of postwar Canadian poetry. The two readerships will inevitably have different requirements and expectations of an edition of letters, but I have attempted to balance accessibility with scholarly usefulness and reliability. In practice I have sought to provide sufficient explanation to make sense of the letters — they are often opaque and predictably full of private references — and at the same time to avoid unduly burdening readers with editorial intrusions. In short, I have tried to present accurate, readable versions of the letters without overdetermining the significance of their contents. *We Go Far Back in Time* aims to provide a fuller picture of the accomplishments of Birney and Purdy and of the significance of their writing — the work of editing the letters serves the purpose of contextualizing the poetry.

The edition includes over three hundred letters, most of which are not contained in *Yours, Al: The Collected Letters of Al Purdy*, edited by Sam Solecki. The letters, from a period of forty years between 1947 and 1987, constitute much but not all of the correspondence between the two poets. The selection is in my view representative, but it is not definitive: more letters remain to be collected. The collection is an editorial making, as Birney would have said, but it is not the last making. There are in addition to the letters a few undated fragments and related documents that complement the primary correspondence, including letters to other recipients. Absent from this edition are letters lost, destroyed, and, of course, never written — not all outgoing letters received replies, while others were answered with telephone calls. Thus the record of correspondence is unavoidably incomplete. In the later years of the correspondence, Birney was the less dutiful respondent. There are extant letters that I found but excluded, principally because they seemed to convey little of significance, and undoubtedly there are extant letters that I did not find. Many of the poets' papers await thorough cataloguing.

The original letters, postcards, and aerogrammes are held in the archives and special collections divisions of the libraries of the University of Toronto, Queen's University, the University of Calgary, and the University of Saskatchewan. The text of this edition was created from copies of these holdings, variously print and digital. I have also drawn on related documents held at other libraries. Each poet made copies of outgoing letters, sometimes by retyping or rewriting them instead of by making carbon impressions; the copies are not always identical to the letters sent, whether because of simple error or because only the outbound version was corrected by hand. I have worked from these copies in various instances, but I have not conflated copies and letters sent. The text of Purdy's letters generally follows that of *Yours, Al* when the letters appear in both books, but I have made some corrections and clarifications, and in a handful of cases I have included the full text of letters that are abbreviated in Solecki's edition. The restored text often refers to business or personal details that are not of obvious literary interest, but for the sake of completeness the letters are reproduced in full; perhaps some biographical relevance will be found. Some of Purdy's letters to Birney that are not collected in *Yours, Al* are brief and important primarily to demonstrate the continuity of the correspondence. Others are more genuinely significant. No edition of Birney's correspondence yet exists, but several of his letters to Purdy are included in *Yours, Al*; I have made minor departures from the text of Birney's letters as presented in that volume. For reference, letters in this edition that also appear in *Yours, Al* are keyed to the relevant pages of the earlier collection.

The guiding editorial principle has been to balance fidelity to the original documents with the need for a readable and critically useful text. I have silently corrected some obvious (and presumably unintentional) spelling mistakes and other typographical errors, but I have usually retained the authors' frequent orthographic idiosyncrasies. (Birney spelled the name of Purdy's principal place of residence "Ameliasburg." Purdy favoured "Ameliasburgh," but he used both forms — at least once even in the same letter.) I have not attempted to achieve an absolute consistency of style at the expense of the spirit of the letters. Birney and Purdy typed most of their letters — neither poet had easily legible handwriting — and both were highly prone to errors. Purdy was an especially poor typist who used only two fingers. Birney typically, although not always, corrected his letters before sending them; Purdy did so irregularly. (Some of Birney's letters were typed by secretaries.) I have tended to incorporate such corrections without noting them. Where corrections or deletions are clearly meaningful and not simply the result of errors, I have included the original as well as the revised text. Some insertions are marked with carets (∧) or asterisks (*); others are simply incorporated into the text if the sense allows. In some cases deleted text is marked as struck out (~~like so~~). I have added, in brackets ([ ]), words to clarify the sense of particularly cryptic passages. Occasional instances of indecipherable handwriting are noted. Moments of true editorial uncertainty are marked as such: [?]. Birney employed a kind of telegramese, increasingly so after the first decades of his correspondence with Purdy, omitting words, foregoing regular punctuation, and relying on dashes and blank spaces in lieu of commas and periods. He also frequently declined to use capital letters. Birney's approach to punctuation in his letters mirrors his habit, especially in the 1960s and 1970s, of punctuating his poems with white space. The results are unnecessarily laborious to read, so I have introduced capital letters (changing the personal pronoun "i" to "I," for example) and regularized the essential punctuation for the sake of clarity while attempting to preserve as much of Birney's distinctive style as possible. When the sense is highly ambiguous, I have let stand the original punctuation (or lack thereof). Neither Birney nor Purdy wrote letters with any sense that conventions of spelling and grammar should be followed. Spelling and punctuation are thus not standardized throughout the edition, but reflect instead the inconsistency of the original letters. Purdy's characteristic colloquialisms ("coulda," "woulda," and "hafta," for "could have," "would have," and "have to," "on accounta" for "on account of") form part of his style and are retained. Both poets often chose to spell "poem" "pome." I have made titles of works consistent, putting those of poems in quotation marks and those of books in italics. I have indicated that postscripts were written by hand on otherwise typed letters only when the postscript is substantial. In general I have tried to keep alterations to a minimum as sense permits; yet clarity and a desire for minimal editorial intervention have often been at odds.

I have omitted sections of the letters only in a very few cases, such as when Purdy discloses somewhat sensitive medical information about his wife, and when the poets express views that seem to me gratuitously offensive, tactless, or cruel about people who are not public figures. The many disparaging statements about public figures remain. Omissions are marked with ellipses within brackets: [...]. The many other ellipses are those used by the authors.

For reasons of space, a table of emendations is not included, but substantive changes are indicated in the letters themselves. (An exhaustive editorial apparatus will have a significant place in a critical edition of the complete works of Birney and Purdy — a scholarly project that remains to be undertaken.) It is worth bearing in mind that both poets had a somewhat cavalier attitude toward editorial details. As Birney wrote in the "Author's Foreword" to his *Collected Poems* (1975), "Minor orthographical changes and word-substitutions ... I leave to Canlit students to track down or ignore without let or hindrance from me."[53] Nor were they always scrupulous about facts, as readers of the letters as well as the poems may note.

---

53. Earle Birney, *The Collected Poems of Earle Birney*, vol. 1 (Toronto: McClelland and Stewart, 1975) 5.

I have not included the full addresses that Birney and Purdy typed on their letters, but wherever possible I have noted the location of the writer and the destination of the letter. Often letters were sent to home addresses while the recipients were on extended travels. Purdy routinely included his Ameliasburgh address on letters even when he was not at home, making it difficult at times to tell precisely where he was. I have regularized the dates of the letters but noted a few instances where the date is ambiguous, absent, or apparently incorrect. Dates supplied are usually the dates of composition indicated by the authors; postmarks indicate that the letters were not always mailed immediately. The original letters naturally have various physical features that cannot be reproduced here. If Birney used a Canadian stamp with a portrait of Queen Elizabeth, for instance, he often affixed it to the envelope upside down.

The running notes to the letters are intended to provide contextualizing information, chiefly biographical and bibliographical. They also provide commentary on the letters when clarification or explanation is warranted. But they contain only partial information. Because some of Purdy's share of the correspondence is available in *Yours, Al*, in which the letters are extensively annotated, I have tried not simply to duplicate information but to provide additional explanation. Readers may wish to consult the notes in *Yours, Al* as a supplementary resource. Most personal names and titles of publications are glossed when they appear for the first time. Some people who are mentioned only incidentally are included in the glossary of names that follows the letters, as are those of literary figures who do not need introduction (e.g., Shakespeare, Cervantes, Milton). The glossary of names also provides basic biographical information for those figures whose significance is explained at length in the notes. Several names appear so frequently in the letters that repeated annotation or clarification would be unwieldy: "Eurithe" is Eurithe (Parkhurst) Purdy, Al's wife; "Esther" is Esther (Bull) Birney, Earle's wife until 1977; "Wailan" (also "Lily" and "Wai-Lan") is Wailan Low, Birney's companion from 1973 until his death; "Jack J" is Jack Jensen, a friend of Birney's — the initial distinguishes him from "Jack" (sometimes "Jack McC" or "Jack McStew"), who is Jack McClelland, both poets' primary publisher; and "Ron" is Ronald Everson, a poet and mutual friend of Birney's and Purdy's. "McStew" is Birney-Purdy shorthand for their publisher, McClelland and Stewart. Basic biographical information about Birney and Purdy is provided in the chronology and as necessary in the notes to the letters. Cameron's *Earle Birney: A Life* is the indispensable source of further information about Birney. Wailan Low's "Biographical Note" in *One Muddy Hand: Selected Poems* (2006) is also helpful. The salient details of both poets' lives are given in the useful entries on Birney and Purdy by Larry McDonald and Paul Matthew St. Pierre, respectively, in the *Encyclopedia of Literature in Canada*

(2002), edited by William H. New. (Full references for the biographical essays are provided in this volume's bibliography.)

When referring in the notes to poems by Birney and Purdy, I have followed the text of individual collections as indicated. Otherwise I have used Birney's *Collected Poems* (2 vols., 1975) and *One Muddy Hand: Selected Poems* (2006), edited by Solecki, and Purdy's *Beyond Remembering: The Collected Poems of Al Purdy* (2000), edited by Purdy and Solecki. I have provided page numbers when referring to these volumes, as well as to *Reaching for the Beaufort Sea: An Autobiography* (1993), edited by Alex Widen, and to *Starting from Ameliasburgh: The Collected Prose of Al Purdy* (1995), edited by Solecki. This group of books may be thought of as the necessary companions to *We Go Far Back in Time*.

Some trivial errors of fact in the notes to *Yours, Al* have been corrected. Preparing this edition has also allowed for the clarification of certain ambiguities, including the dating of individual letters. Any errors, of course, are my own.

EDITORIAL ABBREVIATIONS

Letters:

AA	Autograph aerogramme
AL	Autograph letter
APC	Autograph postcard
APS	Autograph postscript
CTS	Corrected typescript
TA	Typed aerogramme
TL	Typed letter
TPC	Typed postcard

People:

AP	Al Purdy
EB	Earle Birney

Works:

BR	*Beyond Remembering: The Collected Poems of Al Purdy*
CP	*The Collected Poems of Earle Birney*
OMH	*One Muddy Hand: Selected Poems*, by Earle Birney
RBS	*Reaching for the Beaufort Sea: An Autobiography*, by Al Purdy
SA	*Starting from Ameliasburgh: The Collected Prose of Al Purdy*
YA	*Yours, Al: The Collected Letters of Al Purdy*

Complete information for these volumes is found in the bibliography that follows the letters.

Other:

CBC	Canadian Broadcasting Corporation
UBC	University of British Columbia

CHRONOLOGY
The Lives of Earle Birney and Al Purdy

1904 Alfred Earle Birney is born (May 13) in Calgary, in the District of Alberta, to William G. Birney and Martha Robertson, who farm land outside Calgary. Also born are the poets Pablo Neruda, C. Day Lewis, Louis Zukofsky, and Patrick Kavanagh.

1908 Esther Bull is born (August 19) in London.

1911 Birney moves with his family to Banff, Alberta and attends school there.

1918 Alfred Wellington Purdy is born (December 30) in Wooler, Ontario, to Alfred Wellington Purdy, Sr., and Eleanor Louisa Ross, farmers. The Birney family moves to Erickson, BC, where William Birney has purchased a small farm.

1920–21 Birney, after finishing high school, works as a junior clerk in banks in Creston and Vernon, BC.

1921 Birney moves to Banff, where he holds various jobs. After Purdy's father dies (in 1920), Purdy's mother moves to Trenton, Ontario, where Purdy is raised.

1922 Birney moves to Vancouver to study engineering at the University of British Columbia. He soon abandons engineering and studies English literature instead. His summers are spent working and climbing mountains in the Rockies.

1923   Birney begins working as a reporter for *The Ubyssey*, the campus newspaper at UBC. He later becomes editor-in-chief (1925–26).

1925–33   Purdy attends Dufferin Public School, Albert College (a boarding school in Belleville, Ontario), and the Trenton Collegiate Institute.

1926   Birney graduates from UBC with a B.A. (Honours) in English Literature. He begins graduate school at the University of Toronto.

1927   Birney receives his M.A. in English from the University of Toronto. He begins a Ph.D. at the University of California, Berkeley.

1930   Birney takes a teaching position at the University of Utah.

1932   Having withdrawn from the University of California, Birney pursues doctoral studies at the University of Toronto.

1933   Birney marries Sylvia Johnstone; the marriage is annulled in 1937.

1934   Birney departs for London on a fellowship from the Royal Society of Canada. He studies at the University of London. He meets Esther Bull (b. 1908).

1935   Birney travels from England to Norway to meet Leon Trotsky.

1936   Birney returns to Canada. He receives his Ph.D. from the University of Toronto with a specialization in Old and Middle English and a dissertation on Chaucer's irony. He assumes a teaching position at University College, Toronto, and becomes an editor of *The Canadian Forum*, a position that he holds until 1940. He meets E.J. Pratt.

1936–37   Having left high school after Grade 10, Purdy rides the rails from Trenton to Vancouver and back.

1939–45   Purdy serves in the Royal Canadian Air Force. He is posted to several locations in Canada, but does not serve overseas.

1940   Birney marries Esther Bull (March 6). Purdy meets Eurithe Mary

Parkhurst, who is from McArthur's Mills, north of Belleville. Birney begins to write "David."

1941   Earle and Esther Birney have a son (and their only child), William Laurenson Birney. Birney revises and publishes "David." Purdy marries Eurithe Parkhurst. They move to Vancouver, where Purdy has been posted.

1942   Birney's first book, *David and Other Poems*, is published by the Ryerson Press. He enlists in the Canadian Army, in which he is made a Selection of Personnel Officer. He will leave the Army with the rank of major.

1943   Birney wins the Governor General's Award for *David and Other Poems*. He travels to England and continental Europe on military duty with the Army.

1944   Purdy publishes his first book, *The Enchanted Echo*, at his own expense.

1945   Birney, rendered invalid by dysentery and diphtheria, returns to Canada and is discharged from the Army. He works for the CBC until 1946. His second collection of poetry, *Now Is Time*, is published by the Ryerson Press. Al and Eurithe Purdy have a son, Alfred Alexander (Jim) Purdy.

1945–48   Purdy and his father-in-law, James Parkhurst, operate Diamond Cab in Belleville. Al and Eurithe Purdy are divorced for a time.

1946   Birney becomes editor of *Canadian Poetry Magazine* and an assistant professor at UBC. *Now Is Time* wins the Governor General's Award, Birney's second. As editor of *CPM*, Birney rejects poems that Purdy had submitted to the magazine.

1947   Purdy makes direct contact with Birney, writing to him at *Canadian Poetry Magazine*. Birney meets Malcolm Lowry.

1948   Birney publishes *The Strait of Anian: Selected Poems* and resigns from *Canadian Poetry Magazine*.

1949   Birney publishes his first novel, *Turvey: A Military Picaresque*. Dylan Thomas visits UBC.

1950–55 Purdy and his family move to and live in Vancouver, where he works for Sigurdson's Lumber Co. and Vancouver Bedding. During this period he meets Curt Lang and embarks on his self-education in modern poetry. With Lang, Purdy meets Malcolm Lowry.

1952 Birney publishes *Trial of a City and Other Verse.*

1953 Birney spends the year in France on a fellowship from the Canadian government.

1954 W.H. Auden visits UBC. Birney reads with Theodore Roethke (whom he disliked) in Vancouver. He is elected a Fellow of the Royal Society of Canada.

1955 Birney publishes his second novel, *Down the Long Table.* He separates from Esther. Purdy travels in Europe, visiting France and the United Kingdom. He and his family move to Montreal, where he writes radio plays for the CBC. In Montreal he meets several noted writers, including Irving Layton, Leonard Cohen, Louis Dudek, and F.R. Scott. He publishes a chapbook with the Ryerson Press, *Pressed on Sand.*

1956 Purdy publishes a chapbook, *Emu, Remember!*, in the Fiddlehead Poetry Books series issued by the University of New Brunswick.

1957 Purdy and his family move to Trenton, where they live in his mother's house. Al and Eurithe buy land at Roblin Lake in Ameliasburgh and build the A-frame house in which they will live year-round until 1986, after which they will spend winters in British Columbia. Later Purdy will describe this period as "The Bad Times."

1958 Birney makes his first trip around the world, travelling from Vancouver to Hawaii, Japan, Hong Kong, Thailand, India, Iran, Syria, Greece, Italy, Switzerland, and France. He ends the trip in London. Al and Eurithe Purdy work at Mountainview Canning Factory. Purdy's mother dies.

1959 Purdy publishes *The Crafte So Longe to Lerne*, another volume of apprentice-work.

1960 Purdy receives a Canada Council grant of $1,000. He travels to Vancouver by train and then by car through BC. This trip provides the material for some of the poems that he will publish in his first significant books.

1962 Birney publishes his first book of poetry in a decade, *Ice Cod Bell or Stone*. He travels widely in the next years, including a trip to the Caribbean and South America on a Canada Council Senior Arts Fellowship. Purdy publishes two volumes, *The Blur in Between: Poems 1960–61*, and *Poems for All the Annettes*. The latter, which appears with the Contact Press, marks a new beginning for Purdy's career.

1963 Purdy meets Margaret Atwood. The Vancouver Poetry Conference is held, bringing to UBC poets including Allen Ginsberg, Robert Duncan, Margaret Avison, Charles Olson, Robert Creeley, and Philip Whalen. The event is a signal moment in the development of avant-garde writing in Canada, of which Purdy generally disapproves, objecting to American influences on Canadian poets.

1964 Birney publishes *Near False Creek Mouth*, a new collection of poems. Purdy travels to Mexico and Cuba. On the plane to Cuba, he meets Pierre Trudeau.

1965 Birney finally succeeds in establishing a Department of Creative Writing at UBC. He retires from UBC, and moves to Toronto, where he is writer-in-residence at Scarborough College, University of Toronto. He is a Canadian delegate to the Commonwealth Arts Festival in London and Cardiff. Esther Birney initiates divorce proceedings, which are later suspended; Esther and Earle are not divorced until 1977. Purdy travels to Baffin Island. He publishes *The Cariboo Horses*, his first book with McClelland and Stewart. It will win the Governor General's Award.

1966 Birney publishes his *Selected Poems 1940–1966*. Purdy begins his substantial correspondence with Margaret Laurence.

1967–68 Birney is writer-in-residence at the University of Waterloo.

1967 Purdy publishes *North of Summer: Poems from Baffin Island* and travels to Newfoundland.

1968   Birney publishes *Memory No Servant* and holds a professorship at the University of California, Irvine. Purdy publishes *Wild Grape Wine*.

1969   *The Poems of Earle Birney* is published in McClelland and Stewart's New Canadian Library series. Purdy travels to Athens, Rome, and Pompeii, and stays with Margaret Laurence in England.

1970   Birney is named an Officer of the Order of Canada. Purdy publishes *Love in a Burning Building* and *The Quest for Ouzo*. He travels to Turkey.

1971   Birney publishes *Rag & Bone Shop*. Purdy travels to Japan.

1972   Birney publishes *The Cow Jumped over the Moon: The Writing and Reading of Poetry*. Purdy publishes *Hiroshima Poems* and *Selected Poems*. He travels to South Africa.

1973–74   Purdy is writer-in-residence at Loyola University in Montreal.

1973   Birney meets Wailan (then Lily) Low, an M.A. student in English at the University of Toronto. He publishes *The Bear on the Delhi Road*, a British edition of poems, with Chatto and Windus. He also publishes *What's So Big about Green?* He suffers a heart attack. Purdy publishes *On the Bearpaw Sea* and *Sex & Death*.

1974   Purdy publishes *In Search of Owen Roblin*.

1975   *The Collected Poems of Earle Birney* is published in two volumes.

1975–76   Purdy is writer-in-residence at the University of Manitoba.

1976   Birney publishes two volumes: *The Rugging and the Moving Times: Poems New and Uncollected* and *Alphabeings & Other Seasyours*. Purdy publishes *The Poems of Al Purdy*, a selection, and *Sundance at Dusk*, a new collection.

1977   Earle and Esther Birney divorce on grounds of adultery. He publishes *Ghost in the Wheels: Selected Poems* and *The Damnation of Vancouver*. Purdy travels to the Soviet Union with Ralph Gustafson. He publishes *A Handful of Earth* and *At Marsport Drugstore* (both books of poetry) and *No Other Country*, a collection of journalism.

1977–78 Purdy is writer-in-residence at the University of Western Ontario.

1978 Birney publishes *Fall by Fury & Other Makings* and *Big Bird in the Bush: Selected Stories and Sketches*. Purdy publishes *Being Alive: Poems 1958–78*.

1979 Birney receives an honorary D.Litt. from McGill University. Purdy travels to Peru and the Galápagos Islands. He publishes *Moths in the Iron Curtain*.

1980 Birney publishes *Spreading Time: Remarks on Canadian Writing and Writers* and *The Mammoth Corridors*.

1981 Birney is writer-in-residence at the University of Western Ontario (1981–82). Purdy publishes *The Stone Bird*.

1982 Purdy publishes *Birdwatching at the Equator: The Galapagos Islands Poems*. He is named an Officer of the Order of Canada.

1983 Purdy publishes *Morning and It's Summer: A Memoir*.

1984 Birney receives an honorary D.Litt. from the University of Western Ontario. Purdy publishes *Piling Blood*.

1985 Birney publishes three volumes: *Copernican Fix* (poetry), *Words on Waves: Selected Radio Plays of Earle Birney*, and *Essays on Chaucerian Irony*, the culmination of his doctoral research of a half-century earlier.

1986 Al and Eurithe Purdy begin to spend winters in Victoria, BC. (They will buy a home just outside Sidney.) They travel to Turkey and visit Troy. *The Collected Poems of Al Purdy* is published.

1987 Birney receives an honorary D.Litt. from UBC. He suffers a serious heart attack that results in permanent brain damage. *The Collected Poems of Al Purdy* wins the Governor General's Award.

1987–88 Purdy is writer-in-residence at the University of Toronto.

1990 Purdy publishes *The Woman on the Shore* (poetry) and *A Splinter in the Heart*, a novel.

1991   Birney's *Last Makings* is published. The book, based on his manuscripts, is the final volume of his previously unpublished writing to be published during his lifetime.

1993   Purdy publishes *Reaching for the Beaufort Sea: An Autobiography*.

1994   Purdy publishes *Naked with Summer in Your Mouth*.

1995   Birney dies (September 3) in Toronto, in the same year as George Woodcock, Stephen Spender, and James Merrill. Purdy publishes *Starting from Ameliasburgh: The Collected Prose of Al Purdy*.

1996   Purdy publishes *Rooms for Rent in the Outer Planets: Selected Poems 1962–1996*.

1997   Purdy publishes *To Paris Never Again*, his final book of new poetry.

2000   Purdy dies (April 21) in Sidney, BC, in the same year as the poets R.S. Thomas, A.D. Hope, Karl Shapiro, and Gwendolyn Brooks. *Beyond Remembering: The Collected Poems of Al Purdy* is published.

2006   Esther Birney dies (July 20).

2012   Jim Purdy dies (September 25).

Earle Birney
IN PURDY'S AMELIASBURG
(first visit, 1965)

But Al   this round pond man —
        where's Roblin Lake   I mean the real one?
        where's that great omphalos I know
        corpsegray below apocalyptic skies?
    this cosy girl's-belly-button
    brims with rosewater
    from one of those frilly May sunsets

Dont get me wrong   I'm grateful to be here
    after Toronto
        still hairy from a long winter
    after Trenton
        that raped that hustled town
it's good here it's peace the blackbirds
are setting off their own springs in the air
    but the air's too bright
it could be I've come the wrong time
    too soon for those horsecrap-fattened peonies
    you reddened the shores with
    too late for skulldeep snow
    stubborn in the fence zags
man there's only dandelions
barring the way to the privy

But no what's wrong is place as well
it's anybody's church across the lake
    the spire shrank
    and that carpenter who fixed it once
    against the sky is off in Trenton
    banging thumbnails and wallboard
    is you in fact
and you're not here   your mouse is hiding
quote representative of an equally powerful race unquote
that heron   the cosmic crying rays
    where in Roblin are they?

In this Ameliasburg a backyard of stones
is where they trucked off Roblin Mill
        declared historical enough
        for reassembly in Toronto
by god they'll whisk your own shack away
if you dont stop writing
        (and Eurithe too the ferocious wife)
        and the very cowpads before your eyes

Al I think they have
I think Somebody's cleaned up
        after your picknicking glaciers
they've raised the roof on the shack
        ringed it with Summer Homes
        told Ptolemy to leave town
        made your spouse patient and young again
it's the Same People of course
        who took the wolves away
        from Malcolm Lowry's woods
        sent Eliot's London Bridge to Arizona
        smoothed Jeffers' headlands back
        into Californian hills
so though it's fine here of course
        it's not Ameliasburg

But wait
        what's popping up when I sweep the kitchen?
        half an envelope
        with half a poem scribbled
and from behind the battered wood-heater
        yet another empty bottle
        smelling absolutely of wild grape

Next morning I drift down a nebulous way
        to the village hardware
        like a madman's tiny museum
        Can-opener   yep   got one
        got one all right   You in a hurry?

yeah   got mislaid some time back
I'd have to look   drop in nex week mebbe

I return under the ancient clouds
    the Lake is hazy   endless
what bird is flapping away?
the shack's doorknob turns planetary in my hand —
    Al that's your mouse on the floor bowing![54]

54. The poem was published in the Spring 1966 issue of *The Tamarack Review* — it was followed by a selection of Alfred Purdy's "Arctic Poems" — and collected in *Rag & Bone Shop* (1971). A version was included in the second volume (141–43) of EB's *Collected Poems* (1975). The present version is that of the *Collected Poems*, which was reprinted in *One Muddy Hand* (134–35). The version in *Rag & Bone Shop* is notably different.

THE LETTERS

To Earle Birney (Vancouver) from Al Purdy (Belleville, Ontario)
October 20, 1947   TL⁵⁵

Dear Mr. Birney: —

Just a note to let you know the verse I sent you has not been published before, nor will it be except in *C.P.M.* [*Canadian Poetry Magazine*].⁵⁶

I sometimes wonder when I read *C.P.M.* at the change of editorial policy that seems to accompany each new editor. In my own mind I have you labelled as an extreme liberal and Watson Kirkconnell as a progressive-conservative.⁵⁷ When I write poetry, I consciously strive for beauty as well as something that makes a person think a bit. Some people say that the poetry of a nation closely resembles its conversation. I thought that point was particularly true of your long poem "David."⁵⁸ Yet the trend of most modern poetry seems to be away from this principle and toward hyphenated words and phrases that you would think a bit odd found in prose. I notice this tendency in part of yours and all of Anne Marriott's for instance.⁵⁹ Don't think I'm acting the part of a critic but rather an observer with somewhat more than an ordinary interest. I would like very much to know whether it's a permanent trend — this swing to the ultra-modern. Well I guess I've used (if not wasted) enough of your time.

Sincerely Yours,

Alfred W. Purdy⁶⁰

---

55. *YA* 19–20. As EB noted in his letter of 6 Nov. 1972, he and AP had already corresponded briefly about poems that AP had submitted to *Canadian Poetry Magazine*.

56. *Canadian Poetry Magazine* was published from 1936–63. EB was editor from September 1946 to June 1948. The first poems of his to appear in *CPM* were "Dusk on English Bay" and "Monody for a Century" in issue 5.1 (Sept. 1940, edited by E.J. Pratt). AP's first appearance was in issue 8.2 (Dec. 1944, edited by Watson Kirkconnell), with "Dramatis Personae." The first issue that EB edited (10.1, Sept. 1946) included AP's "Dust." AP became a regular contributor to *CPM* in the late 1940s and early 1950s.

57. Watson Kirkconnell (1895–1977): Canadian poet (*Centennial Tales and Selected Poems*, 1965), anthologist, critic, and translator; professor of English at United College (Winnipeg) and McMaster University; and president of Acadia University (1948–64). He was the editor of *CPM* immediately prior to EB.

58. "David" (published in the Dec. 1941 issue of *The Canadian Forum*) is EB's single most famous poem and the subject of AP's continued interest, as subsequent letters demonstrate. *David and Other Poems* was published in 1942.

59. Anne Marriott (1913–97): Canadian poet (*The Wind Our Enemy*, 1939), journalist, and script-writer. With Alan Crawley and others, including Dorothy Livesay, she founded *Contemporary Verse*, an important literary journal published from 1941 to 1952. Marriott won the Governor General's Award in 1941 for *Calling Adventurers!*

60. EB's handwritten note on the letter: "ans. EB. Nov. 6." Almost all of the letters that he answered have similar notes.

To Purdy (Belleville) from Birney (Vancouver)
November 5, 1947   TL[61]

Dear Mr. Purdy,

The difference between me and Watson Kirkconnell editorially is not so much that of an "extreme liberal" as against a "progressive-conservative," as a very ordinary liberal against an incipient fascist.[62] In Kirkconnell's regime only a limited group of very traditional writers ("traditional" in a mid-Victorian sense) were welcomed; all others were attacked, lumped together as "reds," etc. In my regime, both you and the "ultra-moderns" as you call them, have a chance, as I believe in giving any craftsman a chance if he is a good enough craftsman. As for the strangeness and stylistic differences which you ask about in my verses and others — wouldn't it be more surprising, and a good deal duller, if everybody wrote the same all the time? Every poetic generation has had to fight against the people who wanted to keep things just the way they were in grand-dad's day — that's true of all art, and all life. I'd rather be on the side of the present, the creative, the changing — but I'll still give a place in *CPM* for the good writer in the old forms, so long as he *is* good in them and has something to say. And I demand as much, if not more, from the experimentalist.

Sincerely yours,

Earle Birney

To Birney (Vancouver) from Purdy (Belleville)
November 22, 1947   TL[63]

Dear Mr. Birney: —

(Sounds very formal doesn't it?) You must understand that whatever I might say that I certainly mean no offence in any way and actually feel quite cordial. I don't think a discussion like this will ever come to mutual agreement but none the less I feel impelled to add an explanatory million words or so to my first letter. First of all I was quite aware that Watson Kirkconnell was definitely conservative having discussed him with Joan Buckley but I didn't know that he was "hidebound"

---

61. *YA* 20.

62. In an essay (1981) about his experience of editing *Canadian Poetry Magazine*, EB described Kirkconnell in similar terms: "... the only really hostile review *Now Is Time* [by EB] had received had been written by the incumbent editor of *CPM*, the proto-fascist Watson Kirkconnell, who had taken over when [E.J.] Pratt resigned." The essay, "Struggle against the Old Guard: Editing the *Canadian Poetry Magazine*," was published in *Essays on Canadian Writing* 21 (Spring 1981); it complements the "Retrospective" (dated 1963) on *CPM* published in EB's *Spreading Time: Remarks on Canadian Writing and Writers* (1980).

63. *YA* 20–25. EB's note indicates that he replied on 13 Dec. 1947.

enough to exclude something really good from *C.P.M.* in modern form because he didn't approve said form.[64] I don't dislike modern verse because the term "modern" is applied to it. After all the most desired quality of poetry is that it be good regardless of date, period or anything else and some present day writers write very good verse without belonging to any particular class or school. I shouldn't have used the term "modern" at all because it can't be classified that way. Perhaps I sound a little mixed up. I hope not. Frankly I like *C.P.M.* better now under your editorship than before. There is more variety, more of the unexpected but I do have to disagree with some things. I noticed a radio play in one issue. I didn't read all of it but I didn't think it was exactly in a proper environment. Of course I have to allow that some people probably like it but unless the magazine intends to become the medium for several forms of literature, I thought it out of place. My idea of poetry is that it has no date, form or special identifying feature, it is a higher form of entertainment or enjoyment by the mind but nevertheless should be couched in the language of its own time. I believe anything that is stilted or grotesque in language is doomed to swift extinction UNLESS the message or beauty presented is so striking as to preclude this happening. Further I would say that anything stilted or grotesque militates against beauty. My whole contention is that poetry should use not everyday but natural English. I have no doubt that you can marshal your words together and shake my arguments at their foundation because I have left many loop-holes. Perhaps the reason is that I don't state my case in enough detail. I'm fully aware that because I don't like a thing does not signify that my opinion is universal. I believe that the only excuse for obscurity is if it adds something to the value of a poem which it may in the hands of the proper writer but obscurity coupled with the grotesque does not make a good combination. Here's a line from a recent issue "Disentangle lush water-lily cables, Thick as a wrestler's arm ... ."[65] In the first place I dislike the word "lush" and the comparison of water-lily stems to a wrestler's arm is grotesque to my mind or to say the least unlovely. Of course that's far from the best or worst example. I'll have to admit I like the rest of the poem. Also I like most of the verse in *C.P.M.* so what am I arguing about? Here's something I don't like ...

He had passed, inconscient, full gaze,
The wide-banded irides [*sic*]

---

64. Joan Buckley: Editor of the poetry section of *The Vancouver Sun*, in which AP published poems in the early 1940s. AP: "over a period of about two and a half years, I appeared in the *Sun* poetry page over forty times" (*RBS* 103).

65. The lines are from Ethel Kirk Grayson's "Summer's End," published in *Canadian Poetry Magazine* 10.3 (Mar. 1947), an issue edited by EB: "Disentangle lush water-lily cables, / Thick as a wrestler's arm, and trophy-bound / With starry pearlbursts of fair-glimmering bloom."

And botticellian sprays implied
In their diatasis;

Which anaethesis, noted a year late,
And weighed, revealed his great effect,
(Orchid), a mandate
Of Eros, a retrospect.

Beautiful, isn't it? Pound![66] If I got a dictionary and looked up the words I might understand. Here's one of my favourites ...

Spanish Johnny

The old West, the old time,
The old wind singing through
The red, red grass a thousand miles —
And, Spanish Johnny, you!
He'd sit beside the water ditch
When all his herd was in,
And never mind a child, but sing
To his mandolin.

The big stars, the blue night,
The moon-enchanted lane;
The olive man who never spoke,
But sang the songs of Spain.
His speech with men was wicked talk —
To hear it was a sin;
But those were golden things he said
To his mandolin.

---

66. Ezra Pound (1885–1972): American poet, one of the most influential writers of the twentieth century, whose *Cantos* (published in parts beginning in the 1920s) is a landmark of literary modernism. The quoted passage is from the "Mauberley" section of Pound's *Hugh Selwyn Mauberley* (1920). AP committed several errors in transcription: "diatasis" should be "diastasis," "anaethesis" should be "anæsthesis," and "effect" should be "affect," for instance. AP was ambivalent about Pound's writing; he admitted its importance but did not see in it a model for his own poetry. In Canada, Pound's influence has assumed various forms. Louis Dudek, for instance, had a notable correspondence with Pound. In the early 1960s, the Vancouver-based poets associated with the journal *Tish* (including George Bowering, Frank Davey, Daphne Marlatt, and Fred Wah) were highly influenced by Charles Olson, Robert Creeley, and Robert Duncan, American poets whose works derive in part from the poetics of Pound and William Carlos Williams. AP was dismayed by such developments, which epitomized what he understood as undue American influence on Canadian poetry, as his letters to EB and others make clear.

The gold songs, the gold stars,
The world so golden then;
And the hand so tender to a child —
Had killed so many men.
He died a hard death long ago
Before the road came in —
The night before he swung, he sang
To his mandolin.

— Willa Cather[67]

You might call that symbolic of my point of view but I don't mean it that way. I simply like it. I have a definite dislike of hyphenated words generally speaking because they are nearly always ugly or grotesque coupled. Among modern Canadians (there's that word again) I would single out Anne Marriott to bear the brunt of my opprobrium. Of course I wouldn't tell her so. I'd remain non-committal. If you care to answer this I'll be glad to hear from you. I won't expect it but if you don't I'll assume that my arguments are unworthy of consideration and what kind of a spot does that put you in. You understand, of course, that I'm not presenting my own verse as a model of my viewpoint. You can and will take that or leave it as you undoubtedly will. I merely have an idea and try to live up to it. Lucidity and modern usage (not slang) are the main points. I enclose a poem finished a minute before I wrote this letter. If you do write let me know what you think of it then.[68]

Sincerely
Alfred W. Purdy

67. Willa Cather (1873–1947): American writer now recognized primarily for her novels (*O Pioneers!*, 1913; *My Ántonia*, 1918). "Spanish Johnny" was collected in *April Twilights and Other Poems* (1923). AP's transcription was not accurate: his punctuation (retained here) did not always follow that of the original, he typed "moon-enchanted lane" for "moon-enchanted plain," and he missed the capitalization of the noun in "Before the road came in." In *April Twilights and Other Poems*, every other line is indented.

68. In *YA* the poems "Version" and "Invocation" are appended to the letter of 22 Nov. 1947 (23–24). The filing of the early EB-AP correspondence in EB's papers at the University of Toronto makes it difficult to determine precisely the sequence and dates of documents. I have included the poems in the first appendix.

Dear Dr. Birney:

This is a letter from two poets, to which there is no particular point, nor any particular reverence for your own undoubted status as a great poet. Has anybody told you that? I suppose they have not since your friends would think it too obvious a statement. But to get to this particular point in a letter without a dominating motive for being written, we think you are the greatest poet in Canada today. Better than Pratt, A.J.M. Smith, Klein etc, and almost as good as Birney.[71]

That should dispense with the flattery. Because you haven't written anything good since *Strait of Anian*, which contained "Mappemounde," a large masterpiece.[72] I meant to say in the previous paragraph that I regard you as better than any English poet such as Empson et al.[73] Nevertheless you will never be known beyond the confines of Canada, at least I don't think so, since a book has to be published outside of Canada in order to receive critical acclaim. It would seem that we are still a colony therefore. I regard that as a special tragedy that such poems of yours as "David," "Slug in Woods," "Vancouver Lights," "Mappemounde,"

---

69. Curt Lang (1937–98): AP described Lang as "a precocious teenager I had met at a science-fiction fan club gathering. Curt was one of those preternaturally brilliant youngsters who antagonize their elders by being too obviously intelligent. He was also a science-fiction buff. Curt admired my rather puerile poetry, which doesn't really speak well for the aforementioned intelligence" (*RBS* 135). Lang published very little, but in the 1950s he was a notorious presence in Vancouver's art world and literary scene. His friendship was important to AP's literary development. Malcolm Lowry appears to have admired Lang's poetry; see the notes to AP's letter of 17 Mar. 1955. AP's elegy "For Curt Lang" appears in *BR*: "Curt died of cancer in Vancouver / two months back and I am now 80 / unfit for all but literary endeavours" (587).

70. *YA* 26–29.

71. E.J. Pratt (1882–1964): Canadian poet (*Newfoundland Verse*, 1923; *Brébeuf and His Brethren*, 1940; *Towards the Last Spike*, 1952), professor at the University of Toronto, and a notable presence in the literary lives of both EB and AP, who debated in their letters the nature of Pratt's achievement and influence. One of the major figures of modern Canadian poetry, Pratt edited *Canadian Poetry Magazine* from 1936 to 1943, publishing some of EB's poems; see the notes to AP's letter of 17 Mar. 1955. EB's *Strait of Anian* is dedicated to "Ned Pratt." A.J.M. Smith (1902–80): Canadian poet (*News of the Phoenix and Other Poems*, 1943), critic, and anthologist. With F.R. Scott and Leo Kennedy he edited *New Provinces: Poems of Several Authors* (1936), an important anthology of modernist Canadian poems. AP owned copies of Smith's *Masks of Poetry: Canadian Critics on Canadian Verse* (1962) and *On Poetry and Poets: Selected Essays of A.J.M. Smith* (1977). A.M. Klein (1909–72): Canadian poet (*The Rocking Chair and Other Poems*, 1948), novelist (*The Second Scroll*, 1951), and lawyer. A technically superb writer and a central figure in Jewish Canadian literature, Klein was a significant influence upon Irving Layton and Leonard Cohen, among others.

72. AP's assessment was uncannily accurate about the direction of EB's career. After *The Strait of Anian* (1948) and *Trial of a City and Other Verse* (1952), the latter of which is mostly devoted to the eponymous verse-drama, EB did not publish another collection until *Ice Cod Bell or Stone* in 1962.

73. William Empson (1906–84): English literary critic (*Seven Types of Ambiguity*, 1930; *Some Versions of Pastoral*, 1935), poet (*Collected Poems*, 1949, 1955), and professor. His ingenious critical analyses had a transformative effect on literary interpretation and poetic fashion.

"Reverse on the Coast Range" and others should not be known and acclaimed as the very best.[74] You will notice that in the last sentence "we" is abandoned since I am speaking for myself.[75] But the world will lose much richness because it knows not Birney.

New paragraph. Lest the preceding flattery should go to your head, your later stuff is just ordinary. I dislike saying that, but think it true. *Trial of a City* was uninteresting to me, and you may put me down as an unperceptive pseudo intellectual if you like.[76] My likes and dislikes are honest, however. The tragedy is that you could still write great poetry under certain conditions and locale[s].

Poet number two now wrests the keyboard from resisting hands. What does the established poet think? Is he established even to himself? You are of course established, entrenched quite firmly, even, to coin, betextbooked. I speak recklessly you may see, but I am young, and a little in wine, so damn my hidden censor. But it seems to me that most poets do write their best before good taste does rear itself, for instance Donne and Eliot.[77] Certainly their later work is more responsible, more finely turned, but what can I say, you either know what I mean or you do not. Still, I wonder.

Yes, he is young, a malady not without remedy. I am fairly old. I am 36. If there was a subject and motive for this letter it was that we would like to talk to you, but I doubt that is possible. We can talk to anyone but I doubt that you can. It seems to me that a professorship or doctorate makes too much difference. I don't know if your classes are accessible to my friend and I; but in any case we are too lazy to go out to U.B.C. Do not mistake me. That is not indifference. You do not

---

74. "David," "Slug in Woods," "Vancouver Lights," and "Reverse on the Coast Range" are from EB's *David and Other Poems* (1942). "Vancouver Lights" appeared again in *Now Is Time* (1945). "Mappemounde" is from *The Strait of Anian* (1948), in which were reprinted "David," "Reverse on the Coast Range," "Slug in Woods," and "Vancouver Lights."

75. "I am speaking for myself": This section was evidently written by AP. Although the letter does not indicate explicitly which sections were written by whom, AP is clearly the primary author. Lang's contribution is the fourth paragraph.

76. *Trial of a City and Other Verse* (1952), by EB. *Trial of a City* was first performed at the Frederic Wood Theatre, in Vancouver, on 6 Dec. 1952.

77. T.S. Eliot (1888–1965): Poet (*Prufrock and Other Observations*, 1917; *The Waste Land*, 1922; *Four Quartets*, 1943), playwright (*Murder in the Cathedral*, 1935), and literary and cultural critic. Born in St. Louis, Missouri, he was naturalized as a British subject in 1927. Perhaps the most influential writer of the twentieth century, he won the Nobel Prize for Literature in 1948. John Donne (1572–1631): English poet, celebrated for the erotic themes and technical sophistication of his early poems and for the religious poems and meditations (*Devotions upon Emergent Occasions*, 1624) of his later life. Donne was championed by T.S. Eliot ("The Metaphysical Poets," 1921), whose praise caused a resurgence of interest in Donne's writing that has endured since Eliot's time. AP's *The Man Who Outlived Himself* (2000, with Doug Beardsley) includes commentary on Donne's works. AP's "For Ann More (1584–1617)," one of his last poems, is about Donne's wife: "I can't write about her / without a peculiar kind of love" (*BR* 581).

know if either of us can write poetry or are worth talking to. You may have seen my name, if not you very likely will. My friend may take longer.

But aside from that I'd like to see you write some good poetry again. Are we impertinent? I suppose it takes some special provocation to speak seeming truth even to oneself, in this case wine. Therefore you may ignore this missive, saying to yourself such words as may suit the situation, and letting it fade into the sea of hight time.[78] In your case perhaps I should.

Al Purdy

Curt Lang

To Purdy and Curt Lang (Vancouver) from Birney (Vancouver)
March 15, 1955   TL[79]

Dear Alfred Purdy and Curt Lang,

Glad to hear from you. By coincidence I'd just got *Pressed on Sand* out of the University library — mainly as a result of liking some of your pieces I'd seen in the *CF* [*Canadian Forum*] and *SN* [*Saturday Night*], Mr. Purdy.[80] Confess I don't know your work, Mr. Lang, but I should like to. I think we ought to have a get-together soon. A lot of the questions you raise take too long to spell out on paper. I'm in the last two weeks of readying a novel for shipment to a publisher so I won't propose a date till that's over with.[81] But maybe then we could extend this discussion over a beer wherever you like drinking beer, if you like drinking beer. Meantime, a few haphazard reactions to your joint assault.

First of all, if you'd been quite sober you wouldn't have called me a great poet, because on sober thought I'm not. I doubt I'm any better than Smith, Klein, etc., though I'm certainly different from them. I haven't the bulk of Pratt, and I'll never be the personal legend he has been. Sometimes I think P.K. Page is a much better poet than I am.[82] And I wouldn't be surprised if Jay Macpherson and Phyllis

---

78. In *YA* (27), the "hight time" of the original letter is transcribed as "high time." But AP was in all probability invoking the eleventh line of EB's "Mappemounde": "That sea is hight Time   it hems all hearts' landtrace" (*OMH* 46). EB's "hight" is an archaism used to mean "called." EB would have known the word from his studies of Chaucer's works; or perhaps he gleaned the phrase from Edmund Spenser's *The Faerie Queene*: "there sate an hory / Old aged Sire, with hower-glasse in hand, / Hight Tyme." AP misunderstood the word but evidently he liked EB's use thereof.

79. *YA* 29–32.

80. AP's *Pressed on Sand* was published in 1955 by the Ryerson Press. Only "Chiaroscuro" was retained from that volume in the *Collected Poems* of 1986; none of the poems appears in *BR*.

81. EB's *Down the Long Table* was published in 1955 by McClelland and Stewart. The British and American editions were published by Abelard-Schuman.

82. P.K. Page (1916–2010): Canadian poet and painter who was known first as a modernist (*As Ten, As Twenty*, 1946) but who had a long and varied career that lasted virtually until her death (*Coal and Roses*, 2009). As later letters suggest, EB and AP regarded Page as among the most accomplished Canadian poets.

Webb turned out to be the best Canadian poets yet.[83] But that's all just Canadian poetry anyway — not that I want to condescend to ourselves — leave that to the Americans and the British — but I do want to keep a perspective. I think there are half a dozen of us in Canada who are as good as hundreds of American poets who get published and praised, while we can't even get published in London or New York. (But that's nobody's fault very much except the people who caused boundaries and help to preserve them.) But there aren't and there never have been poets in Canada in the same street with Dylan Thomas or Auden or Eliot or Browning or Emily Dickinson or or etc.[84] Let's keep those names in mind when we use the word "great." Occasionally some of us put up a good poem; it seems hard to put up enough to make the sound of a poet. Frankly, of the poems of mine you were kind enough to list as good, I can stand only "Mappemounde" now. Chicago *Poetry* turned "David" down as "melodramatic"; I was sore at the time, but now I think they were right.[85] It's well-constructed, it's metrically sound, it tells a story, etc. But it's two-dimensional where it should be three. Most of my stuff that's got into anthologies and school texts is in them precisely because they are secondrate. My best stuff continues to be misunderstood or ignored, even by you two (except, I'm glad and grateful to see, "Mappemounde"). My best poems, I'll tell what they are —

83. Jay Macpherson (1931–2012): Canadian poet (*The Boatman*, 1957) whose writing was highly and influentially praised by Northrop Frye. Her works are characterized by religious and mythic themes. Phyllis Webb (b. 1927): Canadian poet (*Naked Poems*, 1965; *Wilson's Bowl*, 1980). At the time of the letter, Webb's poems had been published by Contact Press in *Trio: First Poems by Gael Turnbull, Phyllis Webb, and Eli Mandel* (1954), but her later works, for which she is best known, show more clearly her engagement with Buddhism and the Black Mountain poets. Like EB and AP, Webb has strong connections to British Columbia.

84. Dylan Thomas (1914–53): Welsh poet (*Twenty-Five Poems*, 1936; *Collected Poems 1934–1952*, 1952) whose works were very important to AP, especially during the development of his style in the years after the publication of *The Enchanted Echo* (1944). Thomas was infamous for his bardic persona and his heavy drinking; AP's "At the Quinte Hotel" and similar poems owe something to this model. In *RBS*, AP writes that he "snapped out of [his] lost soul condition in the air force during the war years; and found new prosodic mentors in Vancouver in 1950. Dylan Thomas, of course, was the foremost of these" (286–87). AP wrote a review ("Dylan") of Constantine Fitzgibbon's *The Life of Dylan Thomas* for *The Tamarack Review* 38 (Winter 1966), which was reprinted in *SA*. He paid tribute to "the wild futile man from / Swansea" in "Dylan," in *The Cariboo Horses*. W.H. Auden (1907–73): English poet (*Poems*, 1930; *Another Time*, 1940; *The Shield of Achilles*, 1955), playwright (*The Ascent of F6*, with Christopher Isherwood, 1936), and essayist (*The Dyer's Hand and Other Essays*, 1962). Born in York, he left Britain in 1939 and became an American citizen in 1946. AP considered Auden to be, after Yeats, one of the most important poets in English of the twentieth century; the poems contain numerous references to Auden and his works. Robert Browning (1812–89): English poet (*Men and Women*, 1855; *The Ring and the Book*, 1868–69) and playwright; a preeminent Victorian literary figure, he was especially renowned for his command of the dramatic monologue (*Dramatis Personae*, 1864). Emily Dickinson (1830–86): American poet (*Poems*, 1890), largely unknown during her lifetime but now generally regarded as a major figure in American literature.

85. More than a decade after this letter, EB returned to the rejection of "David" in the preface to his *Selected Poems* of 1966, in which he wrote that "'David came back to me fourteen times, because it was 'mere melodrama' (Chicago *Poetry*) ... or for reasons kindly unstated." The poem was eventually published in *The Canadian Forum* in Dec. 1941.

and don't tell me I don't know because I wrote them. I've had to live with them as well as write them, recite them from platforms, revise them, etc. You know what I mean. "War Winter," "Introvert," "The Road to Nijmegen" (these last two rejected in Canada, by the way, and published by John Lehman [*sic*] in London,[86] despite what I said about English publishers). From *Anian* volume, beside "Mappemounde," I'll stand on "Montreal," "From the Hazel Bough," "The Ebb Begins from Dream," "Pacific Door" (first published in *Harper's*, and I think a solid poem where "Slug in Woods" is only a tour de force), "Young Veterans," "Ulysses." (Not "Vancouver Lights," which is faded with its own topicality, and not "Reverse on the Coast Range" which had a merely pretty and sentimental ending.)[87] However, I'm willing to throw all those away if you'll let me keep the *Trial of a City* book, esp. "Bushed," "Images [in Place of Logging]," and "St. Valentine [Is Past]," and certain sections of the title-piece.[88] The whole book represents for me a deepening in meaning and intention and a widening of technique. It's still not a good book, but it's the best book I've done yet.

Of course it's unfair of me to grope [*sic*] in cold sobriety with phrases you two struck off in moments of winy rhetoric.[89] So I take your disapprovals at the same discount as I took your praises.

Curt Lang trots out the old bugbear used so often to discourage a poet when he's no longer "young" (what the hell *is* "young"? I'll bet Lang is older than Denys St. Garneau was when he died, or Chatterton or maybe even Keats — but I don't think he should feel his case is hopeless for all that).[90] Well, I don't think I'll ever improve enough to be a great poet, but I'm quite sure I go on improving, in my little way, just as Yeats did in his big way, and Chaucer in his. Chaucer's finest work he did in his fifties, Spenser in his forties, Shakespeare between 35 and 50, and Herrick perhaps also.[91] Milton *began Paradise Lost* when he was fifty, Browning

86. John Lehmann (1907–87): English literary critic and founder and editor of *New Writing* (1936–41) and *The London Magazine* (1954–61).

87. "War Winter," "Introvert," "The Road to Nijmegen," "Young Veterans," and "Vancouver Lights" appeared in *Now Is Time* (1945). These and the other poems were included in *The Strait of Anian*. At the end of "Reverse on the Coast Range," an avalanche "drown[s]" a forest "In implacable rocks and ice / In the valley's vast obliteration" (*David* version).

88. The "title-piece" is *Trial of a City: A Public Hearing into the Proposed Damnation of Vancouver.* In EB's *Selected Poems* of 1966, the title was changed to *The Damnation of Vancouver: A Comedy in Seven Episodes.*

89. "Grope" is typed clearly in the original, but possibly EB meant "gripe": the "i" and "o" keys are adjacent.

90. John Keats (1795–1821) died at age 25, Thomas Chatterton (1752–70) at 17, and Hector de Saint-Denys Garneau (1912–43), a Québécois modernist poet (*Regards et jeux dans l'espace*, 1937; *Poésies complètes*, 1949), at 31. AP knew Keats's poetry well and visited the pertinent landmarks in Rome. He wrote that "At an English-language bookstore near the Spanish Steps, I found two books by Earle Birney and Purdy. I bought them both, thus depriving the Romans of Canadian culture" (*RBS* 207).

91. William Butler Yeats (1865–1939): Irish poet, playwright, and essayist. By general agreement he is one of the major figures of twentieth-century literature, a view held strongly by AP. Yeats won the Nobel Prize for Literature in 1923; AP wrote that of the poets who were Nobel laureates, "only Yeats,

wrote *The Ring & the Book* in his middle-fifties. Hardy was in his sixties before he learned how to write good verse, Amy Lowell wrote juvenilia till she was forty, and Frost till almost that vintage, and Robinson Jeffers.[92] Ransom didn't write a good poem till he was 36.[93] Housman — some of his best stuff in his fifty-first year, de la Mare in his forties, D.H. Lawrence likewise (and dying), Edith Sitwell in her fifties, Robert Graves likewise. Jesus, you fellows have it all ahead of you, barring radioactive fallout ...[94]

So you can "talk to anyone" and I can't. Because I'm a professor?! What a quaint Victorian concept of a professor. Of course if you are "too lazy to come out to UBC" and drop in on my creative-writing class, 3–6 Thursday afternoon, that does erect a minor obstacle. And I *am* busy, but at a lot of things, radio, tv, public lecturing (I've just got back from talks at the Universities of Oregon and Washington, and some good stag parties thrown in), square-dancing, studying marine shore-life, starting to get up some Spanish for a trip to Mexico this summer, gardening, writing letters, working on the novel, on articles, playing table

---

whose work could not be refuted on any grounds whatever, was full value as best in the world" (*RBS* 289).

92. Amy Lowell (1874–1925): American poet (*Sword Blades and Poppy Seed*, 1914) associated with Ezra Pound and the Imagist movement. Robinson Jeffers (1887–1962): American poet (*Tamar and Other Poems*, 1924) much admired by AP. Jeffers's poems typically combine a profound reverence for the natural word with a philosophical outlook that at times verges on misanthropy. AP wrote that "There are no *great* poets in this era, but many who are excellent. Despite abiding pessimism, I think Housman and Jeffers came close with their large vision just slightly before our time" (*RBS* 288). In "Bestiary [II]," AP wrote that Jeffers "glimpsed another reality: dams broken / high in the mountains; after the bombers, / animals returned; earth grown bright" (*BR* 395). AP's library included Jeffers's *Selected Poems* (1965). EB's "Looking from Oregon" begins with an epigraph ("And what it watches is not our wars") taken from Jeffers's "The Eye" ("this is the staring unsleeping / Eye of the earth; and what it watches is not our wars") *OMH* 126. (The poem was published in the *Atlantic Monthly* in Nov. 1964 and collected in *Ghost in the Wheels: Selected Poems*.)

93. John Crowe Ransom (1888–1974): American poet (*Chills and Fever*, 1924), influential literary critic (*The New Criticism*, 1941), and professor at Kenyon College.

94. A.E. Housman (1859–1936): English poet (*A Shropshire Lad*, 1896; *Last Poems*, 1922) and classicist. The most brilliant philologist and textual critic of his time, he is known especially for his editions of Manilius and Lucan. AP greatly admired Housman's poetry; in "Bestiary [II]," he wrote that Housman was "aware of a moment coming / when human face and death's skullface / stare directly at each other, / and listened to what they said beforehand" (*BR* 395). Housman and Robinson Jeffers (who follows Housman alphabetically in AP's "Bestiary [II]") are major influences on what may be thought of as the misanthropic strain in AP's poetry. AP owned a 1979 printing of *The Collected Poems of A.E. Housman* (1939). Walter de la Mare (1873–1956): English author who wrote in various genres, from poetry to horror stories. *Collected Stories for Children* (1947) was notably successful. D.H. Lawrence (1885–1930): English novelist (*Sons and Lovers*, 1913; *Women in Love*, 1920), poet (*The Collected Poems of D.H. Lawrence*, 1928), essayist, playwright, and critic (*Studies in Classic American Literature*, 1923). Especially in his later life, AP was highly interested in Lawrence's writing. AP and Doug Beardsley published *No One Else Is Lawrence!*, a selection of Lawrence's poems with commentary, in 1998. Edith Sitwell (1887–1964): English poet (*Street Songs*, 1942); her brothers, Osbert and Sacheverell Sitwell, were also noted writers. Robert Graves (1895–1985): English novelist (*I, Claudius*, 1934), poet (*New Collected Poems*, 1977), autobiographer (*Good-bye to All That*, 1929), and mythologist (*The White Goddess*, 1948).

tennis with my kid, partying with my wife and friends, just going on living like anybody else. And when the novel is over I'm getting back to verse and I hope to write better than I ever have, again without too much hope that I'll ever write anything really first class. But maybe.

I like most of your poems, Alfred W. Purdy, and I'd like to talk about them with you sometime. So I'll drop you a note when, as I said, the bloody novel is off my chest.

Sincerely,

Earle Birney

To Birney (Vancouver) from Purdy (Vancouver)
March 17, 1955   TL[95]

Dear Dr. Birney: I mean Earle:

I stand corrected on several counts. But I will not retract on the poems of yours I like. Incidentally, I'm sober now, worse luck; just got home from work which makes it difficult to get out to your class 3–6, just a working stiff, 3 years high school and lots of reading, and varied other experiences. Europe: Spain, Italy, France etc next Sept, along with Curt and another chap. Curt is 19 by the way. Dunno how old Denys St. Garneau was when he died, don't know him either.

Incidentally, I'm very glad to hear from you. I remember reading about Dylan Thomas being surrounded with worshippers in the Van. Hotel, and being a little bored with it all. I don't at all feel like that, but I still regard your stuff as the best Canadian poetry written, Pratt or no, and the hell with what the author thinks (if he thinks they are not).

Ever read Cary's *The Horse's Mouth*?[96] The phrase "stabbed awake" comes to me recurrently because up till a year and a half ago I didn't like any of your poetry, even though I had *David*. (Did like that title poem.) Then I discovered your stuff. Life must be a continual growth and widening of horizons. At one time I could never have liked Thomas. I do agree with you about Thomas. There was only one Dylan Thomas, and when we [AP and Lang] have a few drinks we read "Lament" ["When I was a windy boy and a bit"] aloud or "Fern Hill," and others; just about drive my wife out of the house. She mentions feebly from the bedroom that the youngster has to sleep.[97]

So "Vancouver Lights" is topical: admitted, but it is conceivable that much the same circumstances could occur again; beyond that there are few endings that

---

95. *YA* 32–37.

96. Joyce Cary (1888–1957): Anglo-Irish novelist (*Mister Johnson*, 1939; *The Horse's Mouth*, 1944). AP's library included Cary's *An American Visitor* (1933) and *Selected Essays* (1976).

97. Alfred Alexander (Jim) Purdy was born in 1945.

stick in my mind like "There was light."[98] I can read that too! I have read *Strait of Anian* from the Library, but don't remember *Now Is Time* at all.[99] I'm still growing despite my 36 years, and I have no doubt that when I read *Now Is Time* again I shall appreciate it much more. I shall particularly look up "From the Hazel Bough" and "The Ebb Begins from Dream." *Trial of a City* I read cursorily and you shame me a little. *Turvey* I thought magnificent; perhaps comedy cannot be more than two-dimensional.[100] Do you think Leacock's stuff is?[101] It swims back from childhood now that it is two-dimensional. That doesn't matter. I am a solemn person while reading, but in *Turvey*, especially in the part where Turvey was getting an anima [enema]?, a hypodermic? I forget, I roared. But "Flight across Canada" in *Trial of a City* left me cold.

I have a confession to make. Before I read "Mappemounde" I wrote a poem with the cumbersome title "For 'Richard Hakluyt and Successors'" which depicts somewhat the creatures on the old ocean maps that you described in "Mappemounde." It was taken by *Sat. Nite* and will appear shortly. As I said, this was BEFORE I read "Mappemounde," and I thought I had a theme no one ever had written about. But when I read yours I felt like tearing up the poem, almost. This is it:

From the whales broaching on the stenciled coast
Of Terranova, cherubs with puffed cheeks
Blowing, and coloured cormorants like spikes
Of malachite balanced thoughtfully on a ship's mast:

These were voyages conceived in queens' bedrooms,
Mentioned in old documents and discussed
By doubtful ministers with stiff perukes pressed
On furrowed brows. The awkward captain comes,

Bows, hesitates and opens in the slow, warm fall
Of words; fingers a black eye patch perhaps;
And pours a fervoured [*sic*] flood on the still
Listening ears, on the held, momentary lips.

---

98. "O stranger / Plutonian   descendant   or beast in the stretching night — / there was light" (*OMH* 41). (The punctuation differs from that of earlier versions.)

99. *Now Is Time* (1945), by EB.

100. *Turvey: A Military Picaresque* (1949), EB's first novel.

101. Stephen Leacock (1869–1944): Canadian writer of gently comic fiction (*Sunshine Sketches of a Little Town*, 1912; *Arcadian Adventures with the Idle Rich*, 1914), political scientist and economist, and professor at McGill University.

Saliva ran in the captain's mouth, and spilt
Over his gold moustache; and the tall
Candles guttered. Dolphins intoxicated by a richer salt,
And birds sang on the antique coast of Hy-Brasil.[102]

As you see, this poem differs materially from yours, and I have a sanctimonious horror of being imitative. Although I have been. I'll enclose a few of my later poems for your cursglance.

Do you mind my thinking you've written better stuff than Pratt? Do you say "he has not reached the stage of proper appreciation for Pratt, the fact that he likes me (Birney) denotes a shallowness and lack of insight; no doubt he is a half-boiled pullet's egg, not yet turned over." You may think that. But I stick to my opinion. Birney: my hero. Pratt wrote "the grey shape with the paleolithic face / is still the master of the longitudes." That's great! Also, hell I've got to look it up:

But in the sound of invisible trumpets blowing
Around two slabs of board, right-angled, hammered
By Roman nails and hung on a Jewish hill.[103]

Magnificent. No one ever wrote any better. But the fact remains that Pratt is stiff, perhaps a concomitant of his style and verse forms. Not in "The Cachalot," and a few others.[104] But I can't read him as I do Birney. So I'm a moron. Don't get me wrong, to coin a cliché; if I didn't like Birney I'd say so. In fact I wouldn't bother writing him. The little of P.K. Page I've read I've liked, but admit I cannot fairly judge on that amount. But Finch judged on "Scroll-section" and "The Statue" and a few others is better than Page.[105] That's a bad way to judge, I know: say one poet is better, not appreciate each on his merits. As a matter of fact I like Malcolm Lowry better than anyone but Birney.[106] Again I am prejudiced. I spent two drunken

102. The poem was published in *Saturday Night* (19 Mar. 1955).

103. The first (and slightly inaccurate) quotation is from Pratt's *The Titanic* (1935); AP's "is" should be "Was." The second quotation is from Pratt's *Brébeuf and His Brethren* (1940).

104. "The Cachalot" was published in Pratt's *Titans* (1926).

105. Robert Finch (1900–95): Canadian poet and professor of French literature at the University of Toronto. He received the Governor General's Award for *Poems* (1946) and *Acis in Oxford and Other Poems* (1961). "Scroll-section" and "The Statue" appear in *Poems*.

106. Malcolm Lowry (1909–57): English novelist (*Under the Volcano*, 1947), poet (*The Collected Poetry of Malcolm Lowry*, 1992) and writer of short stories (*Hear Us O Lord from Heaven Thy Dwelling Place*, 1961). He lived in Canada from 1939 to 1954, primarily in Dollarton, British Columbia (part of North Vancouver). He was not a Canadian writer, strictly speaking, but EB and AP seized upon him as an important local literary figure. EB was Lowry's most important Canadian literary acquaintance. They met in 1947, when Lowry wrote to EB on the recommendation of an editor at McClelland and Stewart. EB edited two volumes of Lowry's writing: *Selected Poems of Malcolm Lowry* (1962) ("with the assistance of Margerie Lowry") and *Lunar Caustic* (1968), co-edited with Margerie Lowry, Malcolm's

evenings at Lowry's on the North Shore along with Curt Lang, drinking gin and orange juice, eating anchovies and copying Lowry's stuff by damnable lamplight.[107] Lowry knew [Dylan] Thomas as did his wife, repeated some scurrilous gossip about Thomas' wife being Augustus John's mistress at one time.[108] And we chuckled at the vitality that must reside in the unwithered frame of the old boy (John). Lowry was glassy eyed and imitated Roy Campbell outside the Oxford Hotel playing the barrel organ and Lowry did a clog dance on the wooden floor "dee, dah, deedle de dah etc" and later went swimming like Proteus with massive belly thrusting aside the water, and no doubt scaring all marine life for miles.[109]

I've been writing all this on memory from your letter and now will have to

---

widow. He also published a dozen of Lowry's poems in the *Northwest Review* 5.1 (Winter 1962); in the foreword that he contributed to the selection, he included an anecdote of "the times when I knew him personally." In addition to performing various editorial duties after Lowry's death — a role that brought him into conflict with Margerie Lowry, about which (and whom) he complained in letters to AP — he served as a link between Lowry and the Canadian literary world. Lowry was grateful for the contact, as he felt that Canadian readers were largely uninterested in his writing: "In fact, apart from a few kind words by Birney and Dorothy Livesay, all I have heard was from my royalty report, namely, that the sales in Canada [of *Under the Volcano*] from the end of 1947–49 were precisely 2 copies" (letter 6 Mar. 1950). In letters Lowry also made clear his admiration for EB's writing, noting, for instance, that he considered "several of his newest poems in the Straits [*The Strait of Anian*] among the finest in the English, or indeed, any, language" (1 July 1948). Lowry wrote a perceptive, enthusiastic review of EB's *Turvey* (*Thunderbird*, Dec. 1949), in which he referred to the author as "perhaps our richest poet." EB was sufficiently friendly with the Lowrys that he used their house in 1948 while Malcolm and Margerie were in Europe. EB greatly admired Lowry's writing. In the introduction to the *Selected Poems*, he wrote that Lowry's "life was a slow drowning in great lonely seas of alcohol and guilt" but claimed that his works "carried an eloquence such as no other artist has ever shaped for such experience." With an echo of the last lines of Layton's "The Cold Green Element" ("I am again / a breathless swimmer in that cold green element"; Layton wrote his poem in 1954), EB wrote of Lowry that "The world he could not live with is drowning in its own element. The self-drowned poet survives here in his."

107. AP and Curt Lang visited Lowry in Dollarton, a meeting that Lowry recalls twice in his letters. Writing to his friend Downie Kirk (Dec. 1956), Lowry mentions "Al & Kurt [*sic*], those wild & memorable poets." In a letter (29 Apr. 1957) to Ralph Gustafson, the Canadian poet, Lowry included a long section about AP and Lang: "Two wild western poets came to see my wife & I in the bush on Burrard one stormy night some years ago." Lowry was especially taken with Lang's poetry, but praised AP's as well: "The work of his [Lang's] friend on that occasion, whose name I've unfortunately mislaid, is also worth looking into: his name is Al something or other." AP paid tribute to Lowry in "About Pablum, Teachers, and Malcolm Lowry" (*The Craft So Longe to Lerne*) and "Malcolm Lowry" (*The Cariboo Horses*). AP wrote several memoirs of Lowry: "Dormez-vous? A Memoir of Malcolm Lowry" (1963), "Lowry: A Memoir" (1974), and "Let He Who Is Without Gin Cast the First Stone" (1974). In a review of the *Selected Letters of Malcolm Lowry* ("Turning New Leaves," *The Canadian Forum*, May 1966), AP called Lowry's "The Forest Path to the Spring" "as clear and lucid a master minorpiece as I have ever seen." (He signed the review "Al something or other.") In his autobiography AP noted his unexpected sadness at hearing in 1959 of Lowry's death (in 1957): "I was a mere acquaintance of Lowry's and he of mine. But he had touched me under the carapace we face the world with" (*RBS* 220).

108. Augustus John (1878–1961): Welsh painter. As a war artist in the First World War, he was attached to the Canadian Army.

109. Roy Campbell (1901–57): South African poet (*Collected Poems*, 1949, 1957, 1960) infamous for his support of Franco in the Spanish Civil War. The reference is to A.J.M. Smith's "The Plot against Proteus": "Old saltencrusted Proteus treads / Once more the watery shore."

look at it. Quite agree there's never been anyone here like Thomas, Eliot, Auden, Dickinson, Browning etc. But you know Auden's cold, too damned intellectual. Poetry needs more than that. But how many of the aforementioned poets are there? It is no disgrace we have none. Of course publishers are blind idiots most of the time. "David" should have been published anywhere it was sent with the exception of *The Ladies' Home Journal*. You would have to elaborate on that two-dimensional idea re "David." As I see it, your use of the phrase means that David was not a fully developed character, nor the poem itself. No, I'm wrong. But you couldn't see all of the man in the poem? Even if you were right I wouldn't care. But I wish you'd elaborate. "Slug in Woods" has a shining end "So spends a summer's jasper century" which Joan Buckley also thinks water soluble. "Eagle Island" is not great poetry but it gallops; it can't be read aloud (by me) but it chuckles in the mind. I wrote a poem about the Icarus myth which I'll quote. Your matter of fact manner in that, also Valentin Iremonger's "Icarus" helped muchly.[110] Do you think "waxen vanities" sentimental? I see your point, but it doesn't matter. "Anglosaxon Street" employs a device, I know, but "Hoy! with sunslope / ... / or lope to alehall, / soaking bleakly in beer, skittleless."[111] Don't make me feel that I have to apologize for my likes. Okay, I'll read *Trial of a City* pronto. Till then I keep quiet about it.

As you say, Curt and I were both quite high when we wrote the letter, and the "old" was meant to be insulting. It's like saying "hell" to old ladies which is not a good simile. But we both said Birney will throw this in the wastebasket, so what? Well, he didn't. But you see our feeling? Speaking of juvenilia, I wrote a verse play for radio about childhood called "A Gathering of Days" and sent it to CBC a month ago.[112] They received it Feb. 18. No word yet. Say to myself, they're sure to reject it. Is that the attitude to take? Graves, you mention. He's a peculiar poet (and novelist). I'd like to know something of his philosophy and yours.

About "we can talk to anyone," well I can't. I'm liable to be tonguetied sometimes, not often, but once in a while. I might with you, but not on paper. But give me a few drinks and I'll roar with anyone. The idea of you not being able to talk to anyone is more difficult. Can you talk to laborers? Some are intelligent and can be talked to. Of course it doesn't matter. I'm being very diffuse and cloudy. You're busy as hell, no time to breathe, and you don't want to talk to anyone at all. Let's just drop it.

Curt is studying Spanish for our trip to Spain this summer. Picked up Smith's

---

110. Valentin Iremonger (1918–91): Irish poet (*Reservations*, 1950), translator, and diplomat.
111. "Slug in Woods," "Eagle Island," and "Anglosaxon Street" appeared in *David and Other Poems* (1942).
112. *A Gathering of Days* was broadcast in 1955 and 1959.

latest.[113] Couldn't resist. Disappointment. Reprints "Plot against Proteus" but not "Like an Old Proud King."[114] He should be better. I hope you do improve, muchly. And I hope you can find time to come along to my address and drink beer (love it) or wine (love it) even rye or Scotch (don't like em). Here I have 50[-]odd books of poetry, plus a first ed. of Godwin's *Lives of the Necromancers* I picked up at the Antiquarian bookshop on Broadway where you go sometimes.[115] Don't expect a reply to this what with tv etc. I might say that I expect to be a better poet too, I have no greater interest in anything unless it is finding out what makes these odd two legged creatures act as they do, and getting my own idea where they're going to end up. Present time I think they'll end up next to a dead dog in an unmarked grave.[116] I've got no phone. Curt's is De 5287 R.

But I disagree with "without too much hope that I'll ever write anything first class." A poet should always think he will, so long as it doesn't dull his critical faculties. What else keeps him writing? I expect to write something first class, and I will. Advice to Dr. Birney: go ahead and think you will. Sound like Edgar Guest?[117] Sure, I've many faults, much to learn, but to offset that I know damn well I'm going to write something good. Good to me, anyhow. Is that enough? I've written verse since I was 12, a matter of 24 years. And I've been very slow in learning, but it's a continuous process. If I sound like a braggart, I'm not. But anyway ... We'll buy some French wine anytime (weekends preferred but not mandatory) you have free time.

Sincerely,

Al Purdy

P.S. Curt has written only two good poems in my opinion, but I think one of them very good. He is being very obstinate about one phrase, "one is dead." I say it should be "one dead," adds force etc. I mention this since if we do meet you and he or I read this poem, you might deliver a pontifical opinion. AWP

The following poem is Curt Lang's. All the others are mine.[118]

---

113. *A Sort of Ecstasy: Poems New and Selected* (1954).

114. The poem's full title is "Like an Old Proud King in a Parable." AP's "Post Script," from *Emu, Remember!* (1956), contains a related phrase, "like a proud queen."

115. William Godwin (1756–1836): English philosopher and novelist (*Things as They Are; or, The Adventures of Caleb Williams*, 3 vols., 1794). *Lives of the Necromancers* (1834) is subtitled "An Account of the Most Eminent Persons in Successive Ages, Who Have Claimed for Themselves, or to Whom Has Been Imputed by Others, the Exercise of Magical Power."

116. It is possible that AP here alluded to the last line of Lowry's *Under the Volcano*, which describes the fate of the protagonist, Geoffrey Firmin: "Somebody threw a dead dog after him down the ravine."

117. Edgar Guest (1881–1959): American poet (*Just Folks*, 1917; *Life's Highway*, 1933) and newspaper columnist whose sentimental writing was very popular.

118. The exact sequence of the poems is unclear from the original documents.

The Beachcomber's Lying Song

Here where the great clouds lie, the great sea does not remember us.
That sea that swallowed lovers, land, mapmaker's sight,
A ship loaded with oranges, the holds stacked with suns,
And went down far from port, with it went Portuguese sailors,
A dog, a trunk of books, a yellow haired girl, and five green cockatoos.
To this, no point, but that we know it.

Now here we stand, watching the gulls carry our wishes to sea.
They, tough, winged brethren, fly with the ships —
A lying, shifting constellation, not to be steered by.
And we stand, desperate as locked gates;
Cursing their wings and jealous of their flight.
Out go the lighted ships, at dawn, at noon, at any hour,
And we are there to watch:
Standing among the rocks and kelp whips,
Or high, high on the shore among the pines and cedars.
Watching till the ship dissolves in the sky-sea-merging white
Or till the last clear, winking port light is swallowed
By the kraken-sliding night.

It is true we have our relics and our secrets.
The two stony vertebrae of some prehistorically beached whale
Dug from an inland hill.
The Indian masks, the bundles of dried kelp,
The great sized skeleton of a strange crab.
Our beachwood, twisted, pungent when burning,
Our knowledge of the winds.
Our wondrous sea meals, and our watchings
Of the insidious, still, green-windowed bay.

But they are lies, all lies, contrived for our amusement.
Proofs and credentials, foolish things —
Only the tides tell half the truth,
The whole story lies beyond.

Strange how the sea does make us think ourselves immortal,
Consider ourselves as fit for such a trip —

Think on the legend of my forbears:
Two in prison, one is dead, the other lost at sea.[119]

— Curt Lang

Cantos[120]

He cries his sickness

Nostrum, specific, physick, have
Tempered the malaise somewhat.
Methinks the witch would let me live,
But I would not.

Ague in bone, night risings, plaguey fever,
Staked out in daisy field
To nourish flies, let ants discover,
And various beetles geld.

He discerns the cause

Albeit, the maid is fair beyond all need,
But shrewish, spiteful, deaf
To pleas, shouts of anguish. God
Will punish her, but not enough.

Meanwhile she scourges me: plumps
Herself in chair, smiles, arranges
Skirts, claps hands, glitters under lamps
Forsooth, while poor moth singes

Wings, moans, gulps to her giggles; lover
Of oddment she once wore.
Oaf, lout and churl, in fief forever
To barony of yellow hair.

He decides to live

---

119. AP added a note in reference to "one is dead": "should be deleted?"
120. "Cantos" was included in the 1962 *Poems for All the Annettes*.

Hark'ee now, the mildewed beldame in
High Street hath cured all ill;
I shout, I sing, I laugh at the wan
Woesome dog's lopped tail

That was I, howl hard to full moon's
Morion, lie drunk in ditch, or
Dream of beldame's daughter, the rich, ripe, roan
Mare — and the shining of her.

Postscript[121]

I say the stanza ends, but it never does,
There being something continual,
Apart from the blaze of man, in a woman.
After a parting grimly convivial
Nostalgia comes like an old shaman,

Says, "alley oop," and there like a proud queen,
(Somebody sang about surely) she
Sits with a wronged look in her drawers,
Or circulates naked in a dream,
For purely Freudian reasons; gay
As the now dust once started wars.

But she is not snow mountains, or green shimmer
Of mind-evergreens, the liquid insomnia
Of pre-natal memories in day-sky,
Being perishable and flesh; but in her was clamor
Of voices, the structure of music, the diamond flaw
Of regret that beautiful intricate things must die.

To —

We are not foreigners whose
Faces are light and dark.
Yours is white and has
Only the first mark

---

121. A version of "Postscript" was published in the 1962 *Poems for All the Annettes* (*BR* 36–37). Another version of "Postscript" was published in *The Cariboo Horses* and is also retained in *BR* (93–95).

Of sorrow, knowledge, death,
Endless multiple wrongs,
Words I broke in your mouth:
Mine has all these things.

The evil man who smiled
Cupped a breast in his hand,
Glimpsed when his heart was stilled,
And smiled into the wind.
And fumbled around in his mind.

Knowing it useless to speak,
Opened tall gates for her,
Silently letting her look
At the troubled country there.
And the half-light compassed her.

Seeing tall men fall flat,
Women with tragic eyes,
Smiled and seemed to forget.
But an old man knows.
The stone breaks under the plow.

The Dead Girl

Winged in words' transit, a kind told tale
Without immediacy of passion: swift foot passed,
Breath broke, and little loin-heated animals
Looked out from darkness, heard new bird calls,
Paeons and orisons of trumpets sennet and lost,[122]
Forlorn in a cooling sunset on once warm hills.

But still hidden crickets noted the notable things
In a rustle of music; locusts ground their leg armor
In sound of alarums and excursions; patrols went out,
Came back and reported nothing, no enemy that
They knew of; drank and sang stirrup songs,
Listened to weather reports: dark sky, no warmer.

---

122. The unusual word "sennet" later appeared in EB's "Cartagena de Indias," from *Near False Creek Mouth* (1964): "a sennet of taxi horns" (*OMH* 120).

Melt into dust the sculptured soap bubble brightness of her
In youth shining reasonless, remotely inhuman
Already, become what no man can understand:
Alive because she was waitress, car hop, store
Clerk, a live apparatus of useful hands,
But dead now because she was woman.

(Story about this one)

To Birney (Vancouver) from Purdy (Vancouver)
March 1955   TL[123]

Dear Earle Birney:
I find I disagree with your judgment of "Pacific Door." "Atlantic Door" is better.[124] Certain lines, of course, are the same, but it is the differences that do it. "Whalehalls" for me is the perfect name for the sea.[125] It at once limits the picture and widens it. "Lymph" meaning the poetical clear water and also the clear fluid from a human body fits exactly the lines that follow about the red infusions of sailors and lascars etc that still make no difference in the hue of the waves which "fracture white as a [the] narwhal's tusk."[126] You'd better revise your judgment. Of course, I don't suppose you will. I realize that a philosophy is wrapped up in the sentence "that there is no clear Strait of Anian [/] to lead us easy back to Europe" and it's good. But nevertheless, that single idea is all that is really added to the poem. Whereas in "Atlantic Door," many images are added, "scattered twigs on a green commotion."[127] What about it?

Your letter has aroused my interest in your poetry; I suppose it is natural that if you have even a tenuous knowledge of a writer, a papery echo of himself, then the more human interests are aroused. I've been reading your stuff several times and find much missed previously. Some people might read and find all on first reading, but one of the delights of poetry to me is the continual discoveries bobbing up over the worldcurve. Your "dazzle of folders," and the simple uncomplex image of

---

123. *YA* 37–39.

124. "Atlantic Door" and "Pacific Door" were both published in *The Strait of Anian* (1948), as were the other poems to which AP referred in the letter.

125. From "Atlantic Door": "Come, by a limbo of motion humbled, / under cliffs of cloud / and over the vaulting whalehalls." Later the phrase was changed to "gargantuan whalehalls" (*OMH* 47).

126. From "Atlantic Door": "In this lymph's abyss a billion / years of spawning and dying have passed and will pass / without ministration of man." Cf. *OMH* 47.

127. From "Atlantic Door": "the great ships are scattered twigs on a green commotion." Cf. *OMH* 47.

"brown as whiskey."[128] What makes a poem race like "Quebec May" is more than I can tell, except perfect iambic. It sounds incanted. "Eochromes" leaves me a little puzzled. I had to look up separately. "Eo" having to do with early geologic ages: "chrome," yellow and other pigments from lead compounds. But again mental stirrings give me an idea, but am still not certain where "eochrome" fits in. Unless it is that these early pigments and mineral formations might have told a story rowelled away by icecap and snowwild wind? "Scylding boaster" is mythology of course that I am too lazy to look up.[129] And "provender the luminous young" is a particularly felicitous description. You, I suppose, have only one language, in the sense that you speak the words you write in classroom. That is an advantage perhaps. But I have two languages. In most company I would not use such words as "paresis" or "pelagic," since they would not be understood.[130] Hence I am familiar with many words pronounced seldom, which makes emphasis difficult at times. In "Winter Saturday" I have not seen anywhere a better phrase than "[H]atch from their car like trembling moths," but on reading it alone, the phrase must be in context. Then the magic is complete. Also "they trip two tittering girls [/] in their whistle's lasso."[131] I am knee-deep in Ezra Pound at the moment; but his images are literary for the most part. An odd blend of simplicity and erudition. But at the present time I simply cannot read *The Cantos*. They are not coherent enough or continuous. But I revel in the Faber ed. of *Selected Poems*, the one with the Eliot preface.[132] A friend is sending *Strait of Anian* for last Christmas and when it gets here (she's taking a helluva time) I shall probably try and get out and get you to place your signature, also to mark the changes in "Mappemounde." I don't mention that poem because it's perfect of its kind. You say you haven't written anything first class. Which means that you think the subject has much to do with its "first classness." I don't. Eliot or no one else ever wrote a poem like "Mappemounde" and can't now because it's been written and cannot be bettered. I am perfectly subjective in this statement as I must be. I am not a critic but a poet, and do not hold it up beside other great poems. This is not necessary. It stands alone without company, beautiful-odd, old-Saxon-jargon that is queerly imminent as death. It brings all the old maps and youthful stories of explorers floating back on your tide

---

128. From "New Brunswick (Post Sir Charles G.D. Roberts)": "Glance from your dazzle of folders and leap / to a truth beyond Tantramar's loops." From "Quebec May": "Telesphore ... Sees the creek brim brown as whiskey."
129. "Scylding" and "eochromes" are from "Laurentian Shield."
130. "Pelagic" is from "The Ebb Begins from Dream": "the rolling politicians flow / to welter in the one pelagic motion." "Paresis" is from "Remarks for the Part of Death": "come with paresis and psalms."
131. From "Prairie Counterpoint."
132. Pound's *Selected Poems*, edited and introduced by Eliot, was first published in 1928. Another edition was issued in 1948.

to emplume the present with Tyrian purple.[133] Extravagant? Can't I be? "Fardel" is an archaic word meaning "burden," but I can't find "farded."[134] I suppose it means impregnated with the remains of a man's body in "Invasion Spring."[135]

To Birney (Vancouver) from Purdy (Vancouver)
April 1955   TL[136]

Dear Earle Birney:

I knew about "whalehall," having been curious enough to ask a lot of questions of various people about the language used in "Mappemounde." The thing absolutely fascinated me when I first read it, still does. Have also read Pound's "The Seafarer." He calls it the "whale-acre," also I suppose swiped from the old boys. But some of your words, most of them, I would judge, were personally invented. "Heart's [sic] landtrace" is peculiarly magic. I could wait no longer for the Christmas laggard and bought a copy of *Anian*. Have read the poems in *Trial* only a couple of times, but imagine it is myself at fault. Generally I do not have patience to go over and over a thing, push myself till I'm word weary. But so often I have to make a re-assessment of poetry once disliked, and since your own letters have roused a good deal more interest than normal, I shall get a copy and try again. You may say, or I say, "Bully for you." I realize that sounds as if I were in such a position of eminence myself as to be giving you special treatment, almost condescending. I assure you it is not. All your discussion of sources and special words brings several to my own mind. Those in skiing, of which you have used "herringbone," but "Christiana," "telemark," "bull-fighting," "veronica" and "media veronica." Also came across a lovely word in Joyce "pavan" or as I prefer the French version where the accent is on the last syllable "pavanne."[137] It could be used in countless ways. Your own grounding in words and literary references is an enormous leap ahead of me in writing poetry. I got out the encyc and looked up Laurentian Shield. You will think me a collector of coloured words, and I am, but "plumbage" is good. Curt Lang came across "phototropic."

---

133. EB quoted this passage of AP's letter in his own commentary on "Mappemounde," published in *The Cow Jumped over the Moon: The Writing and Reading of Poetry* (1972). (EB's quotation is not exactly congruent with the text of the original letter as I have transcribed it.)

134. The word appears in EB's "Anglosaxon Street," from *David and Other Poems* and *Now Is Time* ("farded, flatarched / bigthewed Saxonwives"), and in "Invasion Spring," from *Now Is Time* ("The ants have citified the farded earth / above the airman's bones"). See *OMH* 42.

135. At this point the page is torn, and the end of the letter is missing.

136. *YA* 39–42.

137. From James Joyce's *A Portrait of the Artist as a Young Man* (1916): "And he tasted in the language of memory ambered wines, dying fallings of sweet airs, the proud pavan ..." In "Cartagena de Indias" (published in *Near False Creek Mouth*, 1964), EB writes of "three gaunt mulatto ladies / circling in a pavane of commerce / down upon spotlit me" (*OMH* 122). "Christiana" [sic]: see "Skier's Apologies" ("performing Christianias in / the powdered snowslopes of your chin"), dated 1938 in Volume 1 of the *CP* (34).

The advantage of education is you know such words ordinarily on sight. I should think one disadvantage would be that it is more difficult to be in the mainstream of life and not an observer. I am told by a friend that Thomas was a participant and I am an observer. That's arbitrary, but partly true, I think, perhaps you're in the same neat pigeon-hold. Disgusting, isn't it? I presume you are not writing poetry now from your letter. I'm sorry. But you will. If you're like me you can't help yourself. In poetry as nothing else the sense comes on rare occasions when your mind feels projected beyond its own capabilities, some *rara avis* of thought, some exultation of words, that says what could never be said in prose. I work away at prose occasionally, but I am very bad. Paradoxically, I feel that prose has too many limitations that I lose in poetry. Most people would say otherwise. I hope you don't stay at UBC too long for the sake of your writing, that is. I think the mind settles comfortably into a groove as mine has here. Mexico should help. Who was the eastern Eng-born prof.-poet who went to Malaya to teach Lit. and came back with some records for CBC about adopting a monkey? Looked him up. Patrick Anderson.[138] I think I should have written much from that experience. Some critic said Anderson was much affected by Dylan Thomas and copies his rhythms. Can't see it. Ever read Irving Layton whom Smith reviewed last Sunday?[139] "In the Midst of My Fever" is a beautiful evocative title. And the absurdity of "The Long Peashooter."[140] When I was a kid I used to fire pease [*sic*] across the wide road onto a Biblical neighbour's window, frantically stubborn, and day after night. Dunno if he ever heard the hard dry sound of peas but he must have … Layton sounded good in Smith's excerpts. Privately printed, though, and hard to obtain. Here's my last verse:

To Candace
(Which is not her)

She hath placed sandals outside her door,
So that the heart clenched at seeing them,

---

138. Patrick Anderson (1915–79): Canadian poet (*A Tent for April*, 1945) associated with the *Preview* group of poets in Montreal in the 1940s. Anderson and F.R. Scott edited *Preview*, a notable literary magazine.

139. Irving Layton (1912–2006): Prolific and distinguished Canadian poet (*Love the Conqueror Worm*, 1953; *The Cold Green Element*, 1955; *A Red Carpet for the Sun*, 1959) and professor at Sir George Williams University and York University. AP met Layton in 1955. As Sam Solecki has noted, "they remained competitive friends, each seeming to recognize the other as the only serious challenger in the game of who is king of the castle of Canadian poetry" (*YA* 45). The published form of Smith's review appeared in *Queen's Quarterly* 62.4 (Winter 1955–56). "Last Sunday" refers to a version broadcast on CBC radio on 17 Apr. 1955. Based on that fact, AP's letter can be dated more accurately than it is in *YA* ("April"), if still approximately: it was most likely written between April 18 and April 23.

140. Layton's *In the Midst of My Fever* was published in Spain by Divers Press in 1954. *The Long Pea-Shooter* appeared from Laocoon Press in Montreal in the same year.

Moving apart aways, and there
Considereth a rarity without name.

She hath plucked flowers in Landseer
That lieth under the mountains of Ale:
And seemeth by ordinary to smile
For sadness like blue larkspur.

Let no more be said but must fade
Beyond traverse the part that is her.
Wall up with silence this certitude.
Add nothing, not argent nor vair.

That poem is about a girl who may or may not have committed suicide. You might be interested in hearing the story. Loretta had a sister who was divorced from her husband and committed suicide. Loretta herself grew ill as a result and was sent to a sanitarium. A friend tells me she died just two weeks or so ago, and the implication was that she probably took her own life. Her sister shot herself in the head with a revolver. Loretta had been married herself but was divorced in 1946. Her husband was a sports fan and she was a writer, fiction and undistinguished poetry. Loretta was a peculiar person, difficult to talk with and impossible to penetrate very deeply. But she was deeply sensitive, and my friend tells me she found a man necessary to direct her life for her. I don't imply she was a nymphomaniac which was my first thought. But in this day and age it is vaguely moving to come upon a person who is dependent and still intelligent. About a year ago Loretta and I walked in Stanley Park looking for the emu, while I tried vainly to penetrate the aforementioned shell. I talk in an ambiguous manner sometimes, and it seemed to me that she purpose[ly] drew the wrong meaning from things I said. In the end I was frustrated. I drove her home and reduced my conversation to monosyllables. Yet she was a person of some physical beauty, intelligence, sensitivity (which I have not at all illustrated). She wrote me a letter later in the form of a poem (now lost) calling me "the searcher for the emu." I think now that letter was one of her rare efforts to a greater understanding. My friend tells me that if she had known Loretta longer "it would have been only to learn the sum of things she could not know about Loretta." And I say to myself, if I had answered the letter, what might not have happened? If you are a fatalist, she would have died anyhow. But then I might have penetrated that carefully erected defence against the world, that private universe. But she had no means of communicating her feeling at the death of her sister to anyone. Her husband was a sports fan. She died. Is that too cut and dried? Dependency in a self-sufficient world. Or rather, a particular and definite sort of dependency. I tried to put that in a poem without saying it, but probably I failed. But I try. I hope you'll write again.

Best wishes,

Al Purdy

To Birney (Vancouver) from Purdy (Vancouver)
April 1955   TL[141]

Dear Earle Birney:

Strait of Anian makes me wonder where you got the term, if you read Howay and Scholefield's *British Columbia*, but I suppose it recurs in all writing on the subject.[142] Have read *Trial of a City* twice since I wrote the letter to you. Aside from comments on another page it is difficult to place this play in the category of Fry, Sinclair etc.[143] And not alone because it's Birney. Only nominally is it a play at all, and I notice you do not call it a play. The reader or listener cannot make the customary identification with any of the characters in *Trial of a City*; perhaps you feel they should do so through Mrs Wuns, or Powers. This reader-identification business you may or may not agree with, but generally the reader must fasten himself to a sympathetic person in the play. Of course qualities of you and I and all of us are scattered through all characters in *Trial*. Therefore I suppose it is a cross-section of human qualities and characteristics. But I will not regard it as a play ... it's poetry. Legion (who was one of Lowry's characters in "Sestina in a Cantina"; and please don't tell me that of course Legion is not only one character) has the trite rhetoric of a car salesman and a bad preacher which is what you intended, Mrs Wuns is a hedonist, an idealist and a materialist all in one, Long Will of Langland (lovely name) saw only the bad things through the eyes of his own era; Gassy Jack I loved stranded in his saloon in the past; the Salish chief had the sadness of his race and the world-view of the Indian in regard to other people.[144] Is it a good thing or bad thing that the Salish blood, the

---

141. YA 42–43.

142. *British Columbia from the Earliest Times to the Present* (4 vols., 1914), by E.O.S. Scholefield and F.W. Howay.

143. Christopher Fry (1907–2005): English playwright (*The Lady's Not for Burning*, 1948). Lister Sinclair (1921–2006): Canadian broadcaster, playwright (*The Blood Is Strong*, 1953, published 1956), and writer for the CBC.

144. Lowry's "Sestina in a Cantina" was published in *Canadian Poetry Magazine* 11.1 (Sept. 1947), when EB was editor. EB later wrote, in his introduction to Lowry's *Selected Poems*, of his editorial role: "It was, I think, because his verse was so innocent of defenses, that he was chary of publishing it in his lifetime. With Margerie's help I pried a few out of him, in the year the *Volcano* appeared [1947]; they were published in some Canadian journals and anthologies, but remained unknown to his international following."

blood of the chief goes careening and singing down the years in white veins? I think you said something in this verse drama that you wanted to say, and felt needed to be said. Have read the poems you mentioned as being your best. "From the Hazel Bough" reminds me of the early Yeats' "I went out to the hazel wood / Because a fire was in my head."[145] I know, I know … It is unlike but it pleases me to think so … I admire your knowledge of words, specialized words. "The Ebb Begins from Dream" is a beautiful poem. I had to look up "pelagic" in Oxford, as I did "paresis" in another poem. Ever think of bull-fighting terms, "veronica," and "media veronica," "muleta" etc? Notice "Mappemounde" is revised to the extent of two words from the first ed. in Smith's anthology.[146] Deleted "all" in "hems heart's landtrace." Much better. Also approve "towards" instead of "to" in last line. "War Winter" has the same modern-archaic language as "Anglosaxon Street" which you should have included in your best. Poems can be panorama without obvious "message" and still be very good???? Where'd you get "peltwarmer"? "Introvert" is not a success to me, although the lines "Some float like sloops of all his wish, / flow and flower his lost delight" — read the mind of a man while I think of [Dylan] Thomas' "[The] Hunchback in the Park" which portrays with words. "The Road to Nijmegen" is magnificent. Some of the thought in Spender's "I think continually" but "we remember the gentle and true as trees walking, / as the men and women whose breath is a garment about us."[147] A poem like this says things that cannot be analysed or even thought of except in another poem. The strong sense of belonging to a good race who "left the vivid air signed with their honour." "Pacific Door" does not reach the greatness of "The Road to Nijmegen," but the Strait of Anian motif about there being no easy road to Europe I like. "Bitchy" is a lovely word in a poem ["Ulysses"], belongs no other place. Of the poems in *Trial of a City* I liked "Bushed." Have more difficulty understanding them than earlier poems, and I fear my own limitations stand between myself and the poems. Have read so much of your poetry lately I'm a bit dizzy.

Best Wishes

Al Purdy

All witnesses want Vancouver as it was in their time, want no change. Prof Seen's

---

145. Yeats's poem is "The Song of Wandering Aengus," from *The Wind among the Reeds* (1899); it was first published as "A Mad Song" in 1897.

146. *The Book of Canadian Poetry: A Critical and Historical Anthology*, edited by A.J.M. Smith, was first published in 1943. It included a selection of EB's poems. Other editions followed.. The line from EB's "Mappemounde" as it appeared in the 1948 edition of Smith's book is "That sea is hight Time, it hems heart's landtrace."

147. Stephen Spender (1909–95): English poet (*Poems*, 1933), critic (*The Struggle of the Modern*, 1963), and autobiographer (*World within World*, 1951), associated especially in the 1930s and 1940s with the poets W.H. Auden, Louis MacNeice, and C. Day Lewis. He was editor of *Encounter* from 1953 to 1966. "I think continually of those who were truly great" (included in *Poems*, 1933) is almost certainly his most famous poem.

rhetoric nicely contrived, but witness[es] give impression they are spring boards for such rhetoric. Difficult to get in the mind the limitations of this sort of play. The characters are stationary in time, only minds rove back and ahead. Joycean language of Powers good. Makes me think the thing was written straight and then words and phrases changed. Intricately put together as a mile square jigsaw[: "] Pow — But do you know why you defy me? / Wom. — That you might also be[.] / Without my longer Will, my stubborn boon, / You'd have no mate to check with but the cornered moon. / It's my defiant fear keeps green my whirling world["]. Think it's wrapped up in above. The sword of Damocles idea, the woman who brings forth life and her fear and joy in the battle with extinction; there is no exultation in safety, danger and the promise of something beyond are more ... Through the play the idea recurs that people do not want physical change in their good green world, but a change in themselves. Difficulty is to keep the characters alive, the language to some extent does that. But the reader or listener knows it's a tour de force, not real, has no connection with possible events; therefore what's real and intimate and immediate has to spring from unreality. That's damn difficult. It becomes obvious in the end I think that the survival of one city makes little difference, since all cities are the same in the evils pointed up in the play, but the human race must go on for its merest promise of good to come.[148]

To Purdy (Vancouver) from Birney (Vancouver)
April 14, 1955   TL

Dear Alfred Purdy,

Maybe you're right that the Atlantic one is better — though "whalehall" is really pinched from Old English verse; it was one of the standard scop words for the deep sea. Glad you like the rhythm of "Quebec May" (which by the way is trochaic, not iambic). Jean Coulthard set it to music a few years back but for a chorale [1948], and I think she lost the simple, racing effect I was trying to get.[149] "Laurentian Shield" is a bit of an academic *tour de force*; its overtones strike me now as too pedantic. I was trying to reinforce the historical emptiness of the landscape by tentative references to *other* wild landscapes that do have human-literary associations. The English-Scottish border country has some wild empty spots but when I saw them I remembered this was the country of the medieval ballad and also, perhaps, of Beowulf (who was of the Swedish Scylding tribe, but who is described as if he were moving around in the moors and tarns of Northumberland). He fights

---

148. These remarks are probably but not certainly the "comments on another page" to which AP referred in his letter. The early documents resist precise classification.

149. Jean Coulthard (1908–2000): Canadian composer and professor of music at UBC. She later set EB's "Vancouver Lights" to music (1980).

a water-troll in the depth of a tarn supposedly in Denmark but Denmark never had such scenery. Eochromes, as I understand them, are surviving pictures or symbols on rock, from eolithic times; on the Laurentian Shield there are intricate yellow stains on exposed rocks which look like human work but are only the weather's. And nearby may be a pool looking like something out of *Morte Darthur* — so the last 4 lines of stanza 3 are echoing themes from the last book of Malory. The Ayrshire kirk reference is of course to [Robert Burns's] *Tam O'Shanter*, but Wirral is a less familiar reference.[150] In the middle ages there was a big forest, the Wood of Wirral, running down from about where Liverpool is now into Shropshire and south. Gawain, in *Gawain and the Green Knight*, goes lonely through its wildness in search of the big green fellow. Wirral is still a place name in Wales. The Den of Error of the *Faerie Queene* seems to me to [be] set in similar scenery, and could have been set in northern Ontario if Spenser had lived there. The Titania reference is to the wood of the *Midsummer Night's Dream*, as I don't need to tell you, and the "broken bough" to the Golden Bough legend that Lister Sinclair reworked so dramatically in that radio verse drama of his.[151] "No heart to harden ... dews" is an echo of some relevant passage in the Old Testament, but at the moment I can't remember where![152] The next stanza tangles up Milton, Gray, and Browning, as you can see.[153] The last stanza begins with the negation of a phrase from Wordsworth's *Prelude* (Cumberland — the English wild north again), and goes on to another reference to the Arthurian matter (the sword in the stone) and the last line is a straight steal from Malory, in the Excalibur-Lady of the Lake passage.[154]

"Fard" is in my *Webster's Collegiate* — "paint for use on the face" — and as a verb, "to paint; gloss over." I wanted a word that suggested harsh color that [was?]

150. "Scylding," "eochromes," "Ayrshire kirk," and "Wirral" are all references to EB's "Laurentian Shield," from *The Strait of Anian*. Wirral is also the name of the English region in which Malcolm Lowry was born.

151. Sinclair's radio play is *Encounter by Moonlight* (1948). It is based on *The Golden Bough: A Study in Magic and Religion* (2 vols., 1890; 12 vols., 1906–15), by the Scottish anthropologist J.G. Frazer (1854–1941). EB and AP were both interested in adaptations of myths. AP owned Joseph Campbell's *The Hero with a Thousand Faces* (1949; AP's edition was from 1968), an archetypal study of the heroic journey in mythology.

152. The lines in EB's "North of Superior" ("No heart to harden or a god to lose / rain without father, unbegotten dews") allude to Job 38:28 ("Hath the rain a father? or who hath begotten the drops of dew?") and perhaps to Psalm 95:8 ("Harden not your heart, as in the provocation, and as in the day of temptation in the wilderness") and Proverbs 28:14 ("Happy is the man that feareth alway: but he that hardeneth his heart shall fall into mischief"). They also echo G.K. Chesterton's "The Wife of Flanders" (*Poems of the Great War*, 1914) ("You have no word to break: no heart to harden") and resemble images and phrasings in several of Robinson Jeffers's poems, including (faintly) "To the House" (*Tamar and Other Poems*, 1924) and "The World's Wonders" ("I have hardened my heart only a little"; *Hungerfield and Other Poems*, 1954).

153. Thomas Gray (1716–71): English poet whose reputation rests primarily on his "Elegy Written in a Country Churchyard" (1751).

154. EB's "No sounds of undistinguishable motion" "negates" William Wordsworth's "sounds / Of undistinguishable motion" (from the *Prelude* of 1799, 1805, and 1850).

glossed-over. I remember being struck with the evilly pretty way the earth and stones had been colored (fired, perhaps) around a crater in Surrey, in 1944, made when a Lancaster bomber fell and exploded into almost-nothingness, shot down near us by a sudden "sneak raid."

It's very warming to have someone reading one's poems with so much thought and sensitivity. You almost persuade one to try writing poetry again! Anyway, whether that Xmas gift comes through or not, you must come up and see us — soon. I'll give you a ring in a few [...]

Next day (Fri.)
I'd forgotten I hadn't answered your second letter. "Strait of Anian," or rather "The Streights of Annian," is marked on Gulliver's map of Brobdingnag, and Swift got it probably from Drake's voyages.[155] It remained on the maps of Cook and others until Cap Vancouver showed, by putting a longboat up every inlet from here to Alaska, that it didn't exist ... *Trial of a City* shouldn't be judged as in the same formal area as Fry because Fry is writing for the stage, and this is a radio play. It happens that it has been staged, in a kind of way, but, as I predicted, it was too static — lacking the action you need on a stage and which I carefully excluded for radio. You certainly got what I intended about the characters. I hoped for some listener-identification with the housewife, but I think now I brought her in too late; the play has to pivot too sharply around her, and this weakness was reinforced in the radio production by a miscasting of the housewife's part; it was given to an actress with a hard aggressive sophisticated voice.

Once again, I appreciate very very much your interest in my work and your careful reading of it. And, as I say, I hope for a get-together soon when I can show you that I am also interested in yours.

Earle Birney

To Birney (Vancouver) from Purdy (Vancouver)
Summer 1955   TL[156]

Dear Earle Birney:
Sorry to hear about your physical condition, hope Mexico will help. I saw you when you were reading poetry at the art gallery several months ago, and thought at the time that you needed something, whether a woman or a rest I couldn't say at the time. Very probably I will have left by the time you return. I shall probably

---

155. The Strait of Anian appeared on a map (1562) by Giacomo Gastaldi; it was possibly the first depiction of a northern passage between Asia and the Americas.
156. *YA* 44. EB's handwritten note on the letter: "Not answered."

leave Vancouver at the end of August and damned if I know whether I'll come back. Unless my judgment changes in some respects I won't. But in any case I am glad to have heard from you by letter. And your poetry will go with me wherever I go. *The Strait of Anian*, that is. Reminds me of Roy Campbell carrying Baudelaire through Provence and Spain. Campbell must have been a romanticist and may even have liked Baudelaire. He translated him anyhow, but it turned out to be more Campbell than Baudelaire from my reading ...

O worms! black friends, who cannot hear or see,
A free and joyous corpse behold in me!
You philosophic souls, corruption bred,

Plough through my ruins! eat your merry way!
And if there are yet further torments, say,
For this old soulless corpse among the dead.[157]

Isn't that a cheerful quotation to speed a poet to Mexico. Shall take beside *Anian*, Pound, Eliot, Dylan Thomas, *Oxford Modern Verse* and perhaps Yeats. Noticed an article in Van. *Prov.* [*Province*] about Granville. Think you called it Gastown in *Trial*, but forget. Will rip out article in case you're interested.

Drink enough not to stay entirely sober, sleep enough to be rested and fornicate as occasion offers. And I shall not be forgetting "Mappemounde." Please write more poetry.

Best wishes for renewed health on your part.

Al Purdy

To Birney (Vancouver) from Purdy (Vancouver)
Summer 1955   TL[158]

Well, here I sit solitarily drinking the last of the home made wine, poems copied, nearly ready for bed, a six foot, 200 pound splinter of discontent. What do you think of Curt's poetry? I think if he keeps going, which is problematical, he will be far better than I. Who is to say? Now that wine has removed inhibitions it has produced a lethargy that will end in sleep. Tell me, how do I write better poetry? You can't? I'm not surprised. You can write it yourself but damned if you can tell someone else how, your classes to the contrary. All this white paper to use

---

157. The lines are from Campbell's translation of "Le Mort joyeux," "The Joyous Dead," in his *Poems of Baudelaire: A Translation of* Les Fleurs du mal (1952). (*YA* 44 n.1). Cf. *SA* 331–34.

158. *YA* 45.

and I don't feel like using it. I could talk now, but no one's here. But what could I say? How can I say. Ah, the uses of wine, which leads one naturally to the uses of cocaine and heroin. Would I then write better? We are great readers Curt and I, under the influence to paraphrase the WCTU [Woman's Christian Temperance Union], come along and let us inflate your ego by our rendition of "Vancouver Lights," "Mappemounde" etc. See you, perhaps.

Al Purdy

To Purdy (Trenton, Ontario) from Birney (Vancouver)
January 26, 1958   TL

Dear Al Purdy,

I'm glad you thought of me for your *Emu* list, and grateful.[159] It's come at the right time for me as I've been asked to do some poetry readings both on the campus and downtown next week (opening of the new Public Library auditorium) and I wanted to read some pieces of yours in a group of poems by B.C.ers. Normally I don't give a damn where poets live or write but this crappy Centennial is ignoring all poets and poetry, and the parallel International Art Festival is interested only in Great (i.e. non-B.C.) artists, so it will give me some pleasure to be blatantly B.C. in the one field that no B.C. culture-vulture will spit at, poetry.[160] And I can make up an amusing list: P.K. Page, Livesay, even Lister Sinclair, Hambleton — since by Centennial practice anybody who once set even the most reluctant foot in B.C. is a Native Son, especially if he departed quickly to Make Good elsewhere.[161] Like you, maybe, but I don't know how long you were around before you fled. I do know that I'm damned annoyed with myself that I never got off my fanny and got together with you in at least one good beer-and-poetry session when you were here. Maybe we'll cross paths yet.

I'm going to read "Here I am [*sic*] at six o'clock" & "Indictment" & "In

---

159. AP's *Emu, Remember!*, a chapbook of sixteen pages, was published in 1956 in the University of New Brunswick's Fiddlehead Poetry Books series.

160. British Columbia became a British colony in 1858; the centenary was marked by government-sponsored celebrations, as EB wrote. But he protested rather strenuously here; his "Pacific Door" was included in *British Columbia: A Centennial Anthology* (1958), edited by Reginald Eyre Watters.

161. Dorothy Livesay (1909–96): Canadian poet (*Green Pitcher*, 1928; *Collected Poems: The Two Seasons*, 1972), critic, and editor who was born in Winnipeg but who lived much of her life in BC. In a highly influential essay, "The Documentary Poem: A Canadian Genre" (delivered at a conference in 1969, and then published in Eli Mandel's *Contexts of Canadian Criticism* [1971]), Livesay suggested plainly that "David" stemmed directly from EB's experience, and that the character David was based on a real climbing partner of his. EB was incensed by what he understood as an accusation of murder. Ronald Hambleton (b. 1917): Canadian poet and novelist who edited the important modernist anthology *Unit of Five* (1944).

Mid-Atlantic" & "The Cave Painters" — half the book, in fact.[162] Hope you don't mind, especially as I can't pay you for reading your poems, as I don't get paid either.

Cheers,

Earle Birney

I forgot to say I *like* your poems, these especially, you get better all the time.

To Birney (Vancouver) from Purdy (Trenton)
February 1958   TL[163]

Dear Earle Birney:

Many thanks for your letter and kind words. I should like to think I was getting better myself, instead of perhaps merely changing and becoming more complicated. The stuff in that chapbook is all at least two years old, written just after the Ryerson one.[164]

I am amused by your description of the Centennial. Is it as bad as all that? Actually I have some right to be classed as a B.C.-er. Spent part of the war there and then from '49 to '56, and will likely go back sometime. I gather from a bookseller friend out there that they're spending lots of money on culture. Wish I could get in on it, but understand they commissioned Sinclair to do a play about B.C. I admire Sinclair (at times) but rather think it should have been an open competition. I'd have sent in an entry myself. I'm writing doggedly and persistently for CBC now, with poor to fairish luck. Had four plays on since '55, two this last year, but adaptations. However, have two tv deals ready to go ... The thought occurred as soon as you mentioned this Centennial business, what about *Trial of a City*. Why couldn't it be expanded, adapted to another medium etc. Generally a courtroom drama, in the ordinary *Caine Mutiny* sense of the word, has a lot of inherent drama.[165] I do not compare *Trial* with that, please believe me, but ... here's a radio drama on a B.C. subject, a courtroom drama, which sort adapts readily to TV ... I'm probably way off base, but still ...

My own last was about Spartacus and the Roman slave rebellion of 73 B.C. I hope it takes, but some bad spots may kill it. High drammer and tragedy.

I'm sorry we didn't have a beer myself, or several. Curt Lang, a friend of mine, said he had quite a chat with you at the art gallery about two years ago. He's been

---

162. EB listed poems in *Emu, Remember!* "Here am I at six o'clock" is from the first line of AP's otherwise untitled "Poem."

163. *YA* 49–52.

164. "That chapbook" was *Emu, Remember!* (1956). The "Ryerson one" was *Pressed on Sand* (1955).

165. The film version of *The Caine Mutiny*, starring Humphrey Bogart, was released in 1954. Herman Wouk's novel was published in 1951.

sort of a catalyst for me. His character is such that people are liable to be fully occupied liking or disliking him, and I sneak into the conversation when it's fully developed, like making a contribution to the snowball ... I spent a year in Montreal recently and the writers who can write, intend to write and will write some day are all over the place. Of course Layton and Dudek make quite an atmosphere all by themselves; you've probably seen the diatribes in the [*Canadian*] *Forum* and those in Dudek's new mag. *Delta*.[166] Layton and his wife just separated, by the way, and now I read his erotic poetry with a chuckle, being well versed in the situation ...

Chap named Acorn and I have a book coming out with Contact Press, the Dudek-inspired outfit.[167] 20 pages apiece. Will send along a copy ... Two titles; Mine: *The Crafte So Longe to Learne* [*sic*].[168] An open invitation to anyone who reviews it, but what the hell.

What about your own stuff? Dried up or still dribbling. Acorn tells me your "Anglosaxon Street" is shit, and I tell him he has no critical sense for a poem except his own narrow point of view. But then paradoxically, he thinks you're one of the top poets in the country ...

You still think Pratt is the legend you thought he was at one time? I'd disagree now, even more strongly than then, despite Sutherland's attempt to ascribe religious motifs to Pratt's poems ...[169]

Someday I'm going to dramatize *Down the Long Table* for CBC if you don't do it first ... also interested in Winnipeg General Strike, march on Ottawa in 32 or 33, but damned if I know how to do those for a visual medium.[170]

I enclose a couple of poems with this, later stuff, though not the latest. The Great Man is, of course, Layton.

I'm building a house at Roblin Lake near Trenton, doing it myself for monetary reasons. Between that and writing I keep busy. Acorn, who is a communist carpenter and poet, is here with me for a while. (I hope he can put in window sashes and doors.)

---

166. Louis Dudek (1918–2001): Canadian poet (*Collected Poetry*, 1971), critic, and professor at McGill University. He founded Contact Press with Layton and Raymond Souster in 1952 and *Delta* magazine in 1957; the magazine was published until 1966. AP's *The Blur in Between: Poems 1960–61* (1962) is dedicated to Dudek.

167. Milton Acorn (1923–86): Canadian poet (*I've Tasted My Blood: Poems 1956 to 1968*, 1969) who was an important influence on AP. He was briefly married to Gwendolyn MacEwen. AP's "House Guest," published in the 1968 *Poems for All the Annettes*, comically describes a visit to Roblin Lake made by Acorn.

168. The first edition of *Poems for All the Annettes* (1962) was published by Contact Press, but no earlier volume appeared with Contact. Ryerson Press published AP's *The Crafte So Longe to Lerne* (1959) and Acorn's *The Brain's the Target* (1960). Contact published Acorn's *Jawbreakers* in 1963.

169. John Sutherland's analysis of Pratt's poetry is found in *The Poetry of E.J. Pratt: A New Interpretation* (1956). Sutherland (1919–56) was a poet as well as the editor of *First Statement* and the *Northern Review*. His volume on Pratt reflects his recent conversion to Catholicism.

170. *Down the Long Table* (1955) is EB's second novel.

I'll look you up for a few beers and jawing session when I go back to Vancouver. I'm noted, by the way, for my beer consumption. For some reasons it seems to strike lesser mortals (i.e. two beers and sick) with awe. Address 134 Front, Trenton, Ont. if you find time to write.

Al Purdy

The Great Man

Wife
Five minutes once in the early morning
Under the words was someone —
Before and after even the discerning
Saw no one. ...
When outside opinions reached him
He altered and became them.
Only words reached and touched
On my life — and the children,
Not finding him anywhere but
In poems, must soon have known.

Friend
Sure, I praised him in the journals.
I think he deserved it.
But I became part of his furore
And poet's equipment:
One of the eyes that upheld him,
Raised the scaffold for
His footing on clouds that seldom
Have a good anchor.
Paradoxically, I talk to him, his voice
A sonorous echo among the galaxies.

Critic
Sex among the first editions,
Advice to the sick and childless ...
I must admit
He's almost a Canadian Catullus
With Freudian guilt. I'm convinced
His supersonic voice

Conceals a child in time once
And still afraid of noise ...

Himself
I am that Prince from Serendip
Who was what his mind held:
An Asian goddess, the Greek in Kishinev,
A conservative in Montreal.
Fifty years into the future
My poems will be read and loved;
Among the old books and authors
I shall sin-metrically live.
Pay homage (girls) because of this:
I am that Prince from Serendip.

Not published, of course.

Palimpsest[171]

The continuous excitement is done.
Back to the tired, old trade of words,
Where shades of meaning are constant once achieved —
No flicker over the featureless message runs,
On facial adjective and body verb:
An arranged sorrow, a mathematic grief.

Turn away with an ashamed face,
My mistress maybe and your hangdog love,
With dramatic dolour (saying made it so).
And this easily satisfied mood makes
False echoes mumble on the rain drubbed roof,
Describing a woman, reiterating slow,
She is beautiful as you ......

---

171. "Palimpsest" was included in *The Crafte So Longe to Lerne* (1959) and the *Collected Poems* of 1986.

If Birds Look In[172]

If birds look in the window odd beings
Retaliate and birds must stay birds.
If dogs gaze upward at yellow oblongs
Of warmth, bark for admittance
To hot caves high above the street,
Among the things with queer fur,
The dogs are turned to dogs, and longing
Turns to tolerant bitterness.

Clouds must be clouds always even if
They're not really, as we look up;
Trees trees, stones stones, when noticed.
But we're shapes, shades, silhouette,
Light, dark, or colour — they shoplift
Abstract variables of and and if and but,
Impose upon our negative another photo
Unknown through all our life as death.

To Purdy (Trenton) from Birney (Vancouver)[173]
April 7, 1958   TL

Dear Al,

Meant to reply long ago but have been busy on various things, including a Pratt lecture I gave at Carleton University last month. Expect it will be published in the series by Bissell and would like to get your reactions.[174] I agree with you about Sutherland on Pratt and tried to shift the emphasis back to Pratt's importance as a great craftsman in the neglected *genre* of heroic narrative. I think the fashions in poetry are changing in a way which will increase Pratt's reputation abroad.

Are you serious about wanting to dramatise *Down the Long Table* for the CBC? They have never approached me but I have often thought it ought to go. Have been too busy myself and expect to remain busy with other things for quite

---

172. The poem was included in *The Crafte So Longe to Lerne*. A revised version, with the title "Whoever You Are," was published in *Love in a Burning Building* and subsequent collections, including *BR* (27).

173. AP made a variety of notes on his copy of the letter: "fagged out," "rid=rode," "fit=fight," and others, largely indecipherable.

174. Claude T. Bissell (1916–2000): Canadian critic, biographer (of Vincent Massey), and professor at the University of Toronto, of which he was president from 1958 to 1971. The "series" was *Our Living Tradition*, a series of books containing lectures on eminent Canadians given at Carleton University; it was initially edited by Bissell. See the note to EB's letter of 1 Dec. 1959.

a while as I am going to London for a year this fall to work on a Chaucer book.[175] Perhaps *The Table* would go more easily on radio than t.v. Why don't you sound the CBC out and let me know their reaction.

I keep reading your verse in various magazines and I think you get stronger all the time as I said before. I haven't yet seen your Contact Press book and am looking forward to it. I enjoyed the poems you sent and would like to return the compliment with some new work of mine but I am afraid I have done very little lately. A couple of things are coming out in *Pan* and in *American Letters*, and a verse sequence in the April issue of the Royal Architectural Institute of Canada's journal. In the current *Canadian Forum* you will find my reactions to the Centennial, about which you asked. I have a couple of Mao translations in the next *Queen's Quarterly*. I agree with you that my *Trial of a City* had some aptness for the Centennial but the Cen. Committee turned it down and so also has the CBC, to whom I had sold a t.v. adaptation of it. I also asked them to revive the radio form this year but nothing has come of that either.

I hope your house is going well at Roblin Lake and that you will get some real writing breaks this year. If you happen to drift over to Europe this winter or next summer don't fail to look me up through Nuffield House, London.

All the best,
Earle Birney

To Birney (London, England) from Purdy (Ameliasburgh, Ontario)
May 24, 1959   TL

Dear Earle Birney:
Just a note from the colonies to express the hope that you and Mr. Chaucer are congenial drinking partners. How is the ivory tower of scholasticism — equipped with air conditioning and bar I hope?

I envy you most sincerely the drama and atmosphere of London, I mean stage-drama. I hope to be over there myself within the next year. A friend, Curt Lang, whom you met once or twice in Vancouver is there now.

Hope also you write a poem or six while there.

Best wishes,
Al Purdy

---

175. EB travelled to London to hold a Nuffield Fellowship (1958–59), ostensibly to be used to finish writing his study of irony in Chaucer's works. *Essays on Chaucerian Irony* was not published until 1985.

To Purdy (Ameliasburgh) from Birney (London)
June 15, 1959   TL

Dear Al,

Just got back from a week of knocking around Cornwall (when I should have stayed here and worked) to find your welcome note. By coincidence I had just been reading the latest *Delta* [April 1959] and your two poems and thinking I ought to write Al Purdy, if I knew where he was, and tell him I liked "The Dutch Masters," and that his "New Year Resolutions" set me thinking of the necessary special British Columbia footnotes e.g. line 3, for "except kilowatts" read "including kilowatts, buses, bridges, ferries and forests, but excluding all developed females between Hastings and the harbor for one mile extending east from Carrall" — line 6, for "Canada's" read "British Columbia's" — line 7, for "north" substitute "west" — line 8, for "Peace" read "Prosperity" — line 10, for "healthy children" read "parochial easterners" — line 11, for "the pipe line" read "Wenner-Gren," and so on; you can finish the emendations better than I can.[176] Glad to see you are writing, and hope maybe to see you over here before September, when I have to get back. Hope to run into Curt Lang in some pub or other but haven't so far. I've been working hard on Dan Geffrey but have little to show for it except a genuine desire to teach him all over again and differently; guess I'm trapped in my own pedagogic compulsions.[177] Play season has been pretty good, despite the critics. Got up to Scotland and had an evening with old Hugh MacDiarmid, holed out in a biggin in the Lanarkshire hills, polishing his Burrrrns bicentennial lecture which he is this week delivering to the stunned official translators at the Universities of Sophia and Bucharest; his Lallans is twice as thick as Robbie's ever was and I can picture those Balkan culture boys tearing up their Moscow *English-Made-Easy*s in despair.[178] Also had a fine long day-night's session in Edinburgh with Norman MacCaig, or however he spells it, Sydney Goodsir Smith, Alex Muir & Bingo Mavor (James Bridie's son), arguing poetry & nationalism and damning the Sassenachs over three bottles of white Highland whiskey,

---

176. "Canadian New Year Resolutions for 1959" was included as "Canadian New Year Resolutions" in *The Crafte So Longe to Lerne*. The Swedish industrialist Axel Wenner-Gren (1881–1961) was an ally of Premier W.A.C. Bennett in the economic development of northern British Columbia, which was founded on massive resource-extraction projects.

177. Dan Geffrey: Geoffrey Chaucer, as in Edmund Spenser's *The Faerie Queene*: "old *Dan Geffrey* (in whose gentle spright / The pure well head of Poesie did dwell)" (7.9.3–4). John Lydgate and Thomas Hoccleve, among other late medieval authors, wrote in praise of "Maister Chaucer." EB's poem "For Maister Geffrey" was published in 1969 in *Pnomes, Jukollages & Other Stunzas* and in 1970 in the *Red Cedar Review* (7.1, July issue), and collected in *Rag & Bone Shop* (1971). EB dated the poem to 1959 (*CP* 1.182).

178. Hugh MacDiarmid [Christopher Murray Grieve] (1892–1978): Scottish modernist and nationalist poet (*Collected Poems*, 1962) who wrote in both English and Scots (Lallans).

supplied by Bingo on the film royalties from his father, rest him.[179] Am writing a few things myself; have a minute piece in the current *Atlantic*, one probably out by now in *LHJ* [*Ladies' Home Journal*], and some coming in *Western Humanities Review*, etc. The sound barrier is thicker over here but have just wangled one on BBC and another into *Times Lit Sup.*

Let's have your news sometime. When are you coming back to B.C. if ever? Best of everything, salud y pesetas,[180]

Earle

To Birney (Vancouver) from Purdy (Ameliasburgh)
June 30, 1959   TL[181]

Dear Earle Birney:

Good to hear from you, and about your bustling hither and yon in the culture soaked little isles.

Amelia was probably some sprig culled from the root and branch of English nobility back in the days when the U.E.Ls [United Empire Loyalists] were being loyal. Place used to have the honest name of Roblin's Mills for an old small-time capitalist here. He died at 97 just after the turn of the century and his sons rapidly dissipated his substance. There is a fine old five-storied stone mill in the village with walls two feet or so thick which I've explored betimes and searched out history. Built in 1842 succeeding another mill. Will Roblin (grandson) rented the mill before 1st war; got dissatisfied with his earning and demanded more. Miller refused and mill closed, village declined all to hell as a result. Interesting little capsule portrait of life and death of a village which I've explored etc. (Place used to be 500 pop., now 200 or less.)

I get lonesome for B.C. sometimes. The place-names you mention are all familiar and nostalgic to me. Did you ever go to a place called the New Station café? The police go through there by twos every hour on the hour. I heard they discontinued the ferry services to North Van. Too bad — it was the best dime's worth I ever got. Wenner-Gren will probably be next premier of B.C. since he's the

---

179. Norman MacCaig (1910–96; *Far Cry: Poems*, 1943; *Collected Poems*, 1990) and Sydney Goodsir Smith (1915–75; *Collected Poems, 1941–1975*, 1975) were Scottish poets. Ronald Mavor (1925–2007): Scottish theatre critic, playwright, and physician. James Bridie (Osborne Henry Mavor, 1888–1951): Scottish dramatist (*The Anatomist and Other Plays*, 1931).

180. As EB and AP would have known, "*Salud y pesetas*" is a recurring phrase in Malcolm Lowry's *Under the Volcano*: "M. Laruelle returned to the table where he poured himself and drank a glass of Tehuacan mineral water. He said:
'*Salud y pesetas.*'
'*Y tiempo para gastarlas,*' his friend returned thoughtfully."

181. *YA* 52–54.

biggest property holder, and Robert Summers (spelling correct of last name??) will handle his timber interests.[182]

I know just enough of James Bridie to be interested, but that doesn't take much — just a few reviews in the *New Statesman*. And that's some time ago. If I could get to London I wouldn't be very critical of what was offered at the theatres, not for a time anyhow. Very interested in Ustinov — have book of his called *Plays for People*, but it's early stuff.[183]

Curt Lang passed through here on his way to B.C. He had a guitar and a fund of Rabelaisian stories. Once we were simpatico, or so I seem to remember. But gone now I'm afraid. How the hell does it happen? But I mourn the past. He was sent back at the expense of the government because of some contretemps or other. Smuggling on a boat in the Med., ball bearings and so on, he said. Also skin-diving for an archaeological expedition and coming up with amphorae of wine from old Roman ship. How did a Roman ship have Greek containers of wine, the name I mean — or do we call all such containers amphorae?

I think poetry here is in danger of being taken over by the Macpherson-Hine School.[184] The latter writes about original sin and makes me sick to my stomach. The former about Jung[ian] mythology and archetypal myths (whatever they are), but she has some passion, I think. Met her once — an exceptionally nervous and learned young lady with a tic.

Glad to hear you're writing — no poetry I suppose?? Why the hell not? Another book of poems and you could get a C.C. grant to explore B.C. forests, Driftwood Valley etc.[185] I wonder if they give grants to go to Tahiti. Alex Muir no relation to Edwin?[186]

Have you met Christopher Logue and the H-Bomb disarmament boys in the London pubs, or are they too serious to frequent such places?[187] English verse as exemplified in the *New Statesman* doesn't appeal to me at all right now — or is it just *N.S.*-type verse? Doesn't seem any guts in it at all. Or is it me?

I'm marooned here in the bucolic countryside for the last two years, but with occasional expeditions to Toronto and Montreal in search of work. Without success. Has compensations, of course. At this time I'm making strawberry,

---

182. Robert Sommers (1911–2000): Minister of Forests in British Columbia who was jailed in 1958 for accepting bribes.

183. Peter Ustinov (1921–2004): British actor, dramatist, and filmmaker. *Plays about People* was published in 1950.

184. Daryl Hine (1936–2012): Canadian poet (*The Carnal and the Crane*, 1957; *Selected Poems*, 1980) and literary editor (*Poetry*, 1968–78).

185. Theodora Stanwell-Fletcher's *Driftwood Valley* (1946) was a popular account of the author's life in northern British Columbia and of the natural history of the region. AP had a copy in his library.

186. Edwin Muir (1887–1959): Scottish poet (*Collected Poems, 1921–1951*, 1952).

187. Christopher Logue (1926–2011): English poet (*Selected Poems*, 1996) and translator of Homer (*Patrocleia*, 1962; *Pax*, 1967; *War Music*, 1981; and other volumes).

dandelion, orange, rhubarb and pineapple wine. Drinking the dandelion at this moment. Fairly powerful too. The exotic (for wine) ingredients of the others come via my brother-in-law who delivers for A&P store. Last fall I made about 150 bottles of wild grape wine and managed to maintain a slightly pickled state for the cold months. But the dandelion wine I make offends my pretensions to dilettantism ...

Yes, I'm writing too. Have a book out with Ryerson this fall called *The Crafte So Longe to Learne* [*sic*] — ought to be an invitation to critics.[188] It's 26 pages, but still a chapbook I'm told. I'll send you a copy at U.B.C. You ought to be back then???? Also stuff in *Queen's Quarterly*, on *Anthology*, and probably *Tamarack Review*. Robert Weaver asked me to send stuff for that.[189] I'm still changing and watching myself change, like diving into successive pools of water and seeing your own reflection in each. But damned if I know where I'm going, or whether my stuff is any good. I can see some difference in what I write now and what's in the Ryerson book, and that's just 2–3 months ago.

Did an adaptation of Peter Freuchen's book, *The Legend of Daniel Williams*.[190] On suggestion of C.B.C. producer John Reeves I wrote ballades (to be sung) for between scenes instead of music (radio of course), and "based" it on the book.[191] That means I used the characters, but re-wrote the story. It's corn, but may have some merit.

I still own a house (with mortgage) in Vancouver, so will have to go back there some time. My wife is in Montreal supporting me very inadequately — so I would[n't] be sure what address to give as home residence. Anyhow, I'm bound to be out in B.C. sooner or later and I'll hope you have time for a beer. You pedagogues are always so damn busy.

Best
Al Purdy

---

188. *The Crafte So Longe to Lerne* was published by the Ryerson Press in 1959.

189. Robert Weaver (1921–2008): Canadian broadcaster and literary editor. He founded *The Tamarack Review* in 1956.

190. Peter Freuchen (1886–1957): Danish explorer and anthropologist. *The Legend of Daniel Williams* was published in 1956.

191. John Reeves (b. 1926): Canadian composer and radio producer who worked for the CBC from 1952 to 1987. EB's papers at the University of Toronto describe his professional involvement with Reeves at the CBC; Reeves and EB had comparable philological interests.

To Purdy (Ameliasburgh) from Birney (London)
August 20, 1959   TL[192]

Dear Al,

If I don't answer yours now, god knows when. Am pushing out the last Chaucer article for a journal, and getting ready, as well as I can, for Vancouver again, the academic squirrel-cage, bigger and noisier than ever. It's sixteen months since I was in Canada and though I've by no means become English, I'm in some pleasant limbo of just being someone who lives in London — and with this supernaturally sunny summer, it's hard to leave. Also the plays, museums, parks, pubs, and even some of the people.

I have your reactions to the Macpherson-Hine stuff. Hine, I hear, is in hospital here; has a book of poems he's been peddling unsuccessfully. I saw some of it — trying to be "beat" all of a sudden. The only smart one hereabouts is Christopher Logue, who recites his new English beat verse with four jazzmen over BBC for a fat fee and publishes the most synthetic tripe I ever read, all over the place. I knew him in Paris six years ago when he was writing more "difficult" poetry than any other expatriate, and a great snob. Now he is the new English Man of the Peepul, full of shit (asterisked in the better journals only) and libertarianism. But when you meet him he is as limphanded and uppish as ever. The only one who outsells him is that royalist Edgar Guest, Betjeman, who has never looked back since he was photographed with Princess Margaret in the *Tatler*.[193] I've been buying or reading all the British poetry mags, and I really think we're doing as well in Canada these days. The liveliest stuff is still American, though, as Graves says, most of it is written for an expendable economy.

Glad to hear you have a chapbook coming out. Will look forward to a copy. My *Selected Poems* should be out next year — Abelard-Schuman here & possibly New York, & McC&S in Toronto.[194] Will have some new ones. Have done a few out of travelling in Asia last summer. One coming out in London mag., a Mao translation in *New Statesman*, and something last week in *Times Lit. Supp.*, but an old one. Trouble is I keep revising old stuff when I should be trying new ones. Hope CBC is going ahead with your Freuchen script.

Maybe I'll see you in Vancouver this winter. I'm flying back via the pole so won't be stopping in eastern Canada. Phyllis Webb is back in Toronto; a good poet, though not much of a producer yet. And a nice girl. Do you know her? Give

---

192. *YA* 54–55.

193. John Betjeman (1906–84): English poet (*John Betjeman's Collected Poems*, 1958), journalist, and architectural preservationist. He was Poet Laureate from 1972 to 1984.

194. Abelard-Schuman published the British edition of *Turvey* in 1958. The McClelland and Stewart *Selected Poems* did not appear until 1966; other volumes appeared with M&S meantime.

her a ring at WALnut 5–2913 when you [are] next in Toronto and say hello from me. She has friends, who are also friends of mine, on the Island — Bill Roedde, etc.

Your title — Robinson's edition spells it "The craft so long to lerne" — anyway I don't think Chaucer ever spelled it "learne," but a small point.[195] You know, of course, that he was talking of Love not Art. Maybe you are too. It's a toss-up which is the more "dredful joye."[196]

Cheers,
Earle

To Birney (Vancouver) from Purdy (Montreal)
Autumn 1959   AL[197]

Dear Earle Birney

Greeting — on your return to mountains (overlooking the city) and mud flats (False Creek & environs).[198]

Look forward to your collected ed — but hope it is no signal to cease & desist —

Logue comment interesting. His verse is crappy jingle — but I do endorse the anti-H-bomb testing — for which I understand he & Priestley & Russell etc are the main props —[199]

Oct 21 my first play re-broadcast on *CBC Wed. Night*.[200] About childhood if you listen — Sentimental shit in spots too — I have to admit. Originally done Sept 3, '55 — The money I can use.

Regards
Al Purdy

---

195. F.N. Robinson's edition of Chaucer's *Works* was published in 1933. A second edition followed in 1957.

196. AP's title is provided by the first lines of Chaucer's *Parliament of Fowls*: "The lyf so short, the craft so long to lerne, / Th' assay so hard, so sharp the conquerynge, / The dredful joye alwey that slit so yerne: / Al this mene I by Love."

197. *YA* 55–56. The letter is dated "October 1959" in *YA*, but the exact date is unclear.

198. EB's "November Walk Near False Creek Mouth" (in *Near False Creek Mouth*, 1964) contains descriptions of such landscapes: "into the sunblazed living mud / ... and I on the path at the high-tide edge."

199. J.B. Priestley (1894–1984): English novelist (*The Good Companions*, 1929), playwright (*Time and the Conways*, 1937), and critic (*Literature and Western Man*, 1960). Bertrand Russell (1872–1970): English mathematician (*The Principles of Mathematics*, 1903), philosopher, historian (*A History of Western Philosophy*, 1945), and essayist (*In Praise of Idleness*, 1935).

200. *A Gathering of Days*; see AP's letter of 17 Mar. 1955.

To Birney (Vancouver) from Purdy (Montreal)
November 1, 1959   TL[201]

Dear Earle Birney:

I'd like one of those Arts Scholarships from Canada Council. Would you write me a letter of recommendation?

I'm asking E.J. Pratt and Milton Wilson for the other two, and with a line-up like that (if they come through) I don't see how I can miss.[202] Jay Macpherson says Pratt is always generous with people who want recommendations, and I hope his health is good enough in this case.

If I get a scholarship I intend to go to the upper Skeena and see what I can find out about the Tsimsyans there, and perhaps from thence to the Queen Charlottes and the Haidas. I can't help writing poems — but I'd like to do some more plays for CBC, or what the hell. Then I'd like to go to Mexico when the cold weather hits, and do my writing there. Live as long as I can on the money I get (if I get it), then get a job as night watchman for B.C. Forest Products in my old age.

I've got a play with CBC which they contracted for right now. About an American negro, Daniel Williams, who came to Canada's Peace River country after the American Civil War, lived with the Beaver Indians there, killed two Mounties and was executed for murder in Mar., 1880. Songs between scenes instead of the conventional music. I'd like to do more about the Indians, Tsimyans, Salish, Haidas, or any of them that take my fancy and will make a play. What are they doing now, how adjusted to coeval Canada. … You know … you did it yourself in *Trial of a City*.

May have a chapbook with Jay Macpherson … recent poems in Montreal … title I think, *Montreal Poems* … enclose the best of them here to give you the idea I'm worth voting for.[203] But of course, for Christ's sake don't vote for the candidate unless you think he'll do something about the present corrupt administration …

I enclose a poem by Logue which surprises me. First one of his I've liked. Does it support the character of his you know? Bit like Reaney?[204] Most of his are chopped prose made to look more than it is. Is he changing and becoming more

---

201. *YA* 56–59.
202. Milton Wilson (1923–2013): Professor of English at the University of Toronto, anthologist of Canadian poetry, and scholar of romantic poetry (*Shelley's Later Poetry: A Study of His Prophetic Imagination*, 1959). He corresponded with AP as the literary editor of *The Canadian Forum*. His "Poet without a Muse" (*Canadian Literature* 30 [Autumn 1966]) remains an important statement on EB's poetry.
203. The chapbook was published in 1962 as *The Blur in Between: Poems 1960–61* by Macpherson's Emblem Books.
204. James Reaney (1926–2008): Canadian playwright (*The Donnellys*, published 1975–77) and poet (*The Red Heart*, 1949; *A Suit of Nettles*, 1958) whose strongly regionalist works are typically set in southwestern Ontario.

(or less) than his clammy handed self? Or is this the mark of an unhinged mind? Send it back if you have a copy. I haven't.

Anyhow, I'm sending my application forms to Canada Council within a week, and I think supporting letters are supposed to follow as soon as possible. So if you think C.C. should squander its money on me give me your vote: a laudatory letter. If not, what the hell. Maybe I can get one later. A scholarship that is. But anyhow, please let me know if you can or cannot write this letter????? I'd like to get out to B.C. again and will if I get this thing ... rather lonesome for the smell of Hastings St. and False Creek and mountains over all ... was stationed (in RCAF during war) in upper Skeena country, but didn't have brains to take advantage of opportunity at the time.

Please drop me a line. Sometimes I think of the Birney of "Vancouver Lights" and wonder where he is. The same? No, of course not. Or *Trial of a City*, or "Mappemounde"? All the goddamn Birneys wander over the globe looking for poems as I do ... Do they?

Layton here is selling in the stores like Billy Graham or Norman Vincent Peale.[205] 5000 copies of this ed. of *Red Carpet*.[206] Christ, the stuff'll be popular next. Ever meet him? Wonderful experience to see the naked ego like an unruptured maidenhead floating in the living room void. ... and he knows, he just knows, that he is the great one, the poet who will top Milton and Blake and Yeats and who do you like? He said so ... and there you are. But in a sense I love the guy, so improbable, grotesque, and despite his ability somehow wrong. Why? It's all too bloody trite and rehearsed ... so much assurance and so little doubt. ... he says to himself, this is what is popular so I go dead against it. He looks in the mirror and what does he see? Not a little fat man who will die soon, but a bloated haloed and immortal genius ... and this precludes searching and looking and wondering to my way of thinking. Or does the opinion of self detach, and look dispassionately at the poems? Somehow I think the opinions of self and poems are cut from same cloth. "The immortal claptrap of poetry" is too designed.[207] ... But I assign him a large status in my private Tussaud's, and think to myself I should not bloody well have this uncertainty. I should know he's good (as I know he is) and great ... well ...

205. Billy Graham (b. 1918): American evangelist and religious author (*Peace with God*, 1953). Norman Vincent Peale (1898–1993): American minister and author (*The Power of Positive Thinking*, 1952).

206. *A Red Carpet for the Sun* (1959) is one of Layton's most important volumes. Primarily a selection of works from his first collections, it won the Governor General's Award.

207. The phrase is from Layton's "Seven O'Clock Lecture": "Filling their ears / With the immortal claptrap of poetry, / These singular lies with the power / to get themselves believed ... I see their heads sway at the seven o'clock lecture."

Ever see Lowry's wife out there? I'm told the chap who translated *Under the Volcano* to Fr. is thinking of writing some bio. stuff on Lowry ...[208]

Run out of words.

Regards,
Al Purdy

And We Shall Build Jerusalem
** — in Montreal[209]

From the factory at noon with fifteen minutes
in my pockets to spend:
the Church of the Nativity at St. Germain
and Ontario (not listed in Betjeman's parish churches);
the streets full of school children,
matrons and tradesmen and traffic continuous. ...
Standing under the giant stone-grey
monster, looking upward till things blurred.

The white marble virgin benign and vacuous
(no strain or effort required for blessings),
treading out the life of an evil reptile
with its red mouth gaping (which I took
to be a harmless lizard). No doubt it's impressive,
has even a gathered crushed beauty
caused by so much weight falling into the sky.

All afternoon,
among the monotony of doing meaningless things,
my hands kept up their industrious trivialities —
I thought of the tawny
sunlight on temple roofs in the Land of Two Rivers,
stood on a jungle delta
when the priesthood originally
and willingly forgot their own clever origins,
as the land grew fat with waste gold.
But I could not forget myself

---

208. AP mistakenly referred to Downie Kirk. See the notes to EB's letter of 1 Mar. 1974.

209. "And We Shall Build Jerusalem — in Montreal" was published in AP's *The Blur in Between: Poems 1960–61* (1962).

and the centuries' umbilical cord
that binds me to a fat imaginary god
with a seven day epic creative itch
that shrinks to a jingle my last best poem.

But I forgave him at five o'clock
the weariness of my limbs, the castrated
effigy of myself in a window — because
I saw between pale faces of travellers
going nowhere forever in busses
and motor cars, the tall church tower!
toiling into the sky its human filigree,
permitting the heavy bells to blaze
over the old town their passionate cries
of jubilant silver hypocrisy —
a tawdry embroidered magnificence.
Almost I forgave him the pale travellers
on busses, hid from the light a long time
between the sweating breasts of their women.

At the Yacht Club
(corner of Drummond & St. Catherines)

This is the entry on my litmus mind tonight:
I have become a puritan.
Through a "literary evening" of windy decadence,
Stale words piled to ceiling height ...

All my fathers, all the old men
Lurking behind me come and glare
Through my eyes: the Roman gods,
Their intolerance blistering clear,
Disapproving the effete young men
With nothing to do but talk
About their own discoloured psyche,
Spawned in a festering sick world.
Ramrod straight from stony fields,
Full beards and bristling mutton chops
They march into the room and glare silently,

Gloom with Presbyterian distaste —
The grey exponents of Mendelian law.
Big headed Millers of Dundalk,
Doon River Mackenzies from Ayrshire,
Tall Rosses from Ross and Cremarty
and the Purdys with my face.

Contempt for the age and the time,
But not the world, our only world,
Spinning out of now and the human mess
Into starlight and hard green fields.
The waiters sweep floors, lift tables,
Grin at each other maybe,
And go home in the cool night of their day,
Go home tired to their beautiful wives.

To the Canada Council (Ottawa) from Birney (Vancouver)
November 4, 1959   TL

Dear Sirs,

Mr. Alfred Purdy of Montreal has written me asking me to support an application which he plans to make to your Council this year, and I am very pleased to accede to his request. I think Alfred Purdy is one of the best of the younger poets writing in Canada today. In the last few years he has shown increasing range and vigour and productivity. His last letter to me outlined some of the projects he has in hand and others which he wants to pursue if he can finance himself meanwhile. He proposes, among other things, to spend some time in Northern British Columbia familiarizing himself with present-day Indian life as well as the traditions of several of the tribes. I think this is an exciting and worthy project and one that he could do well with, judging from his dramatic work on CBC and his poetry, both what has been printed and what I have seen in manuscript. He speaks also of a plan to go later to Mexico and work there. My own experience in that country leads me to think that it provides an environment where a young writer, if sufficiently self-disciplined, can work with a low expenditure and in a stimulating atmosphere. I have only a slight acquaintance with Mr. Purdy personally but what I know of him leads me to think that he would take responsible advantage of an opportunity for a year's steady work on his own if the Canada Council were able to make it possible for him. Certainly I think he would do a great deal of writing, and the evidence of his last few years of work convinces me that he would produce poetry and other writing of very good quality.

Sincerely yours,

Earle Birney

To Purdy (Montreal) from Birney (Vancouver)
November 4, 1959   TL

Dear Al,

I have written a letter in your support to Canada Council and am very pleased to do it. Thanks for your letter, which I hope to answer when I get a little more time. This is simply a note to assure you of my support and to wish you success in your application.

Sincerely yours,

Earle Birney

To Birney (Vancouver) from Purdy (Montreal)
November 17, 1959   TL[210]

Dear Earle Birney:

Many thanks for the recommend ...

If I get this award I should be looking you up next summer for a beer, maybe ...

At the moment I am afflicted by that bane of poets, namely work, physical, comparatively unremunerative, monotonous in the extreme, and with the added danger: I may get used to it. Helluva thing!

Note the piece in *Sat. Rev.* by Ciardi.[211] Cites you and Layton. ... Doesn't seem to like Pratt. So what about your "Pratt as legend" thesis — and "Birney will never be the legend Pratt is" ...? No, I don't think so either, but why the hell should he? I mean, you lose sight of the poetry in the legend. Wade through *Brébeuf* (or however you spell it) and find that beautiful ending.[212] But is there anything else

---

210. *YA* 59–60.

211. John Ciardi (1916–86): American poet (*Selected Poems*, 1984) and translator of Dante's poetry (*The Divine Comedy*, 1977). Ciardi's essay on contemporary Canadian poetry ("Sounds of the Poetic Voice") in *Saturday Review* (24 Oct. 1959) critiqued Pratt and praised EB, F.R. Scott, Robert Finch, A.J.M. Smith, Wilfred Watson, Louis Dudek, James Reaney, A.M. Klein, R.G. Everson, and Irving Layton. EB's "Canada: Case History" was published in the same issue.

212. Pratt's *Brébeuf and His Brethren* (1940) ends with these lines: "Near to the ground where the cross broke under the hatchet, / And went with it into the soil to come back at the turn / Of the spade with the carbon and calcium char of the bodies, / The shrines and altars are built anew; the *Aves* / And prayers ascend, and the Holy Bread is broken."

but? And: "the grey shape with the paleolithic face / was still the master of the longitudes" ... with the one or two preceding lines ... and a few others.[213] Apart from your own personal friendship with him, do we need someone like Pratt in our past (for that's where he is)? I always have the feeling he's slightly inhuman, his poetry, I mean. What about Reaney's dictum that we start with a clean slate, that Can. poetry is all to be written — or something like that?

Just sent *Turvey* to a friend of mine studying medicine in Geneva. When will you write another? Not necessarily like that, of course. What about the bum who gravitates from one job to another, is a catalyst in every situation ... goddamn it I'll be giving you plots if I don't shut up — and that's an old one.

Best,

Al Purdy

To Purdy (Montreal) from Birney (Vancouver)
December 1, 1959   TL[214]

Dear Al,

Hope the Can. Council thing goes through. Hope also you're getting some time free for further poetry. I'm not. Last thing I wrote was on the island of Porquerolles off Toulon, in September — perversely a poem about a Himalayan dancing bear in northern India; anyway the *New Yorker* have surprised me by taking it; maybe this means I'm slipping, but at least it's nice to slip on a fifty dollar bill rather than a one dollar; actually I don't know what they pay, never having tried them with a poem before except once unsuccessfully.[215]

Things are looking up a bit on this coast so far as poetry readings go. There's a Vancouver Poetry Centre, very indigent and inefficient but still willing to sponsor George Barker — we had him all last week — and soon Richard Eberhart.[216] Robt.

---

213. AP quoted the envoi of Pratt's *The Titanic* (1935): "And out there in the starlight, with no trace / Upon it of its deed but the last wave / From the *Titanic* fretting at its base, / Silent, composed, ringed by its icy broods, / The grey shape with the palaeolithic face / Was still the master of the longitudes."
214. *YA* 60–62.
215. "The Bear on the Delhi Road" was published in *The New Yorker* (22 Oct. 1960) and collected in *Ice Cod Bell or Stone* (1962). EB published various poems in important American journals in addition to this success with *The New Yorker*, including "Conference of Heads" (*Antioch Review* 20.1, Spring 1960), "Mammorial Stunzas for Aimee Simple McFarcen" (*Massachusetts Review* 2.1, Autumn 1960), "Actopans" (*Massachusetts Review* 2.4, Summer 1961), and "Cartagena de Indias" (*Chicago Review* 17.1, 1964). But he was not always successful in placing his poems. For example, in 1964, he submitted "Caracas," "Meeting of Strangers," and "Prosperity in Poza Rica" to *Poetry*, all of which were rejected. The brief covering letter shows that EB, by then a highly distinguished poet in Canada, was rather modestly still sending his poems to the slush pile: "I submit herewith three poems together with biographical sheet and stamped air mail, self-addressed envelope. I would be grateful for an early decision."
216. George Barker (1913–91): British poet (*Collected Poems*, 1987) also remembered for his affair

Duncan is coming up from S.F. in a couple of weeks and will read somewhere.[217] I found Barker a complicated guy; Chelsea veneer over a wild Irishman. Drinks as hard and morosely as Dylan [Thomas] but manages to get sober again for appointments and readings. Like Dylan, his innate fertility in image-making is a curse as well as a strength and leads him to theoretical insistence on the absolute value of form in poetry which his own poetry only exemplifies occasionally and after enormous struggle; but perhaps it's the struggle that makes even his bad pieces interesting. He had along a copy of his *True Confession of George Barker* (published only in England in a limited edition, after Sir Geoffrey refused to include it in the Faber Collected edition); it has some of his best satirical-autobiographic writing; a pity it isn't circulating over here.[218]

I'm going to read my own stuff in Seattle, at their Poetry Centre in February and go on down from there to read at Reed College, Portland, and at the San Francisco Poetry Centre — first time the latter has ever asked a Canadian. I think there is a definite upswing of interest in Canadian poetry below the line, at least on this coast. Seattle has a new *Poetry Northwest* mag, have you seen it?[219] Run by Dave Wagoner and Carolyn Kizer, both of whom were up here in October reading at the U. [UBC], and very successfully.[220]

I'm afraid I think Ciardi is right about all the pre-Pratt stuff and partly about Ned, though my own article in the new *Our Living Tradition* makes me look inconsistent.[221] The trouble is that article was written as an address at Carleton

with Elizabeth Smart, which she recounted in *By Grand Central Station I Sat Down and Wept* (1945). (AP owned a copy.) *The True Confession of George Barker*, a volume of verse, was published in 1950. Richard Eberhart (1904–2005): American poet whose *Selected Poems, 1930–1965* (1965) won the Pulitzer Prize. In a review of EB's *Selected Poems* (1966), Hayden Carruth describes "Dusk on the Bay" as "third-rate Eberhart, fifth-rate [Allen] Tate. It is pretty awful" ("Up, Over, and Out: The Poetry of Distraction," *The Tamarack Review* 42 [Winter 1967]). The Vancouver Poetry Centre was organized by Warren Tallman.

217. Robert Duncan (1919–88): American poet (*The Opening of the Field*, 1960; *Bending the Bow*, 1968) associated with the Black Mountain school and the San Francisco Renaissance.

218. Geoffrey Faber (1889–1961): Founder of the publishing firm Faber and Gwyer, later Faber and Faber.

219. *Poetry Northwest* was founded in 1959 by Errol Pritchard. Carolyn Kizer, Richard Hugo, and Nelson Bentley were co-editors. Kizer was editor of *Poetry Northwest* from 1964 to 1966, a position that David Wagoner held from 1966 to 2002. EB corresponded with Kizer and Wagoner, who were important points of contact for him in the Pacific Northwest.

220. David Wagoner (b. 1926): American poet (*Traveling Light: Collected and New Poems*, 1999), novelist (*The Escape Artist*, 1965), and professor at the University of Washington. Carolyn Kizer (b. 1925): American poet (*Cool, Calm and Collected: Poems 1960–2000*, 2001).

221. EB's "article" was "E.J. Pratt and His Critics," in *Our Living Tradition* (Second and Third Series) (1959), edited by Robert L. McDougall. EB concludes by placing Pratt in a line of comic writers: "Pratt is old-fashioned mainly because his literary art, his prodigious virtuosity in the craft of story-telling and the structural use of image, language, and rhythm happen to have been expended not in the dominant Jamesian tradition of the prose short-story and novel but in the Chaucerian tradition of poetic narrative. ... [H]e is in Chaucer's tradition in his devotion to the great art of heroic verse narrative, whether grave or comic, a very long and rich and varied tradition that in our literature began with

[University] on the occasion of Pratt's 75th birthday, with the expectation he would be in the audience, and though I didn't say anything I didn't believe, I left out a lot of things I'd rather say after he's dead, since he's stopped writing and nothing said critically would do anything to him except make him feel unhappy and betrayed by an old friend. The truth is none of us who write poetry should allow ourselves to make public critiques of the others, not in a small country like this where we know each other too well.

I like "so much weight falling into the sky" and the passage about the church bells very much. Interested to glimpse your Celtic ancestry; are there any really Saxon poets? My mother was a Robertson from Aberdeenshire via the Shetlands.

Wish I'd heard your play. Had to go to a goddamned psychiatric lec at the Arts Club — Madness & Poetry or something. I was mad enough, in listening to it when I could have heard you. I understand it was ...[222]

Phyl[lis] Webb lives here now, and I find her a welcome variation from the almost unbroken non-poet front of Vancouver. All the rest of you have abandoned us.

In my letter to the Can. Council I stressed that Mexico was a sensible part of your plan, since I'd lived there & knew it was cheap, etc. Do you know Mexico? I have a lot of theories about how and where to live that I can bore you with sometime.

If you work on Indians out here, you should get to know, if you don't already, a couple of the Anthropology profs here — Carl Borden, who has made some spectacular carbon-datings and archaeological finds and pushed back the early Indians' dates in B.C. several thousand years.[223] Then there's Suttles, who is a Salish authority.[224] Also there's Bill Reid, a Haida himself and a sculptor, totem pole re-carver, etc.[225] He's in charge of the setting up of a set of Haida poles on the campus at present.

I share your contradictory feelings about Irving [Layton]; I think he's heading for some enormous gloom if ever he faces the possibility that poetry, his poetry

the *Beowulf* and has been passed down by the authors of *Gawain and the Green Knight* and *The Nun's Priest's Tale* and *The Rape of the Lock* and *Paradise Lost* and *Tam O'Shanter* and *The Ancient Mariner* and *Childe Roland to the Dark Tower Came* and *Sohrab and Rustum*, to the author of *The Witches' Brew* and of *Brébeuf and his Brethren*."

222. The text at this point becomes unclear.

223. Charles E. Borden (1905–78): American archaeologist, specialist in the prehistory of the Lower Mainland of BC and the Pacific Northwest generally, and professor of archaeology and German at UBC.

224. Wayne Suttles (1918–2005): American anthropologist (*Coast Salish Essays*, 1987; *Musqueam Reference Grammar*, 2004) who taught at UBC from 1952 to 1963. EB's papers contain correspondence with Wayne and Shirley Suttles from at least as early as 1951.

225. Bill Reid (1920–98): Haida sculptor, jeweller, and writer (*Solitary Raven: Selected Writings of Bill Reid*, 2000). His works figure prominently at the Museum of Anthropology at UBC, the development of which EB alluded to here.

even, may not be the answer to everything after all. But meantime he's a shot in the arm and very necessary to have in Canada.

Margerie Lowry, about whom you asked, is in California so far as I know, though haven't heard from her for a couple of years. I heard a rumour she was bringing out a second novel from the manuscripts.[226] There was masses of unfinished stuff left at his death and I think much of it could have been published as fragments or even as short stories — but it's her problem and not one I'd like to have to decide. Malcolm scarcely ever wrote an undistinguished sentence, but the connections between them is another matter.[227]

Let me know when you hear from the CC.

All the best,
Earle

To Birney (Vancouver) from Purdy (Montreal)
February 14, 1960   TL[228]

Dear Earle Birney:

Greeting. I hope you received the mimeo thing I sent.[229] No cover, had trouble with an artist who changed his mind. But we're getting Betty Layton and a couple of others to do something for future issues.[230] Mimeo work is also terrible, but will do better with that too. Anyhow, object, if any, is to get away from deadly dullness it seems to me pervades most mags, with possible exception of Dudek's [*Delta*]. Also no U.S. stuff unless we think it's wonderful and can't be ignored. But the *Fiddlehead* is a horrible object lesson in that regard.[231] I notice Acorn spelled "metaphors" "metaphores" and made a mistake in my piece on Lowry — but what the hell.

Anyhow, have you got anything, article, poems or what have you, pontificating on the Canadian scene? Article ought to be two full length foolscap sheets or less, but could run up to three if you need more space. I'm thinking of something along

226. "A second novel": i.e., a second novel after Lowry's first, *Under the Volcano* (1947). In fact, *Under the Volcano* was already Lowry's second novel. The first was *Ultramarine* (1933). AP owned a copy of the Penguin reissue (1974) of *Ultramarine*.

227. Margerie Lowry (1905–88) published several volumes of her late husband's fiction: *Hear Us O Lord from Heaven Thy Dwelling Place* (1961), a collection of stories; *Lunar Caustic* (1968), a novella; and *Dark as the Grave Wherein My Friend Is Laid* (1968) and *October Ferry to Gabriola* (1970), both novels. EB published, in collaboration with Margerie, the *Selected Poems of Malcolm Lowry* (1962).

228. *YA* 63–64.

229. The "mimeo thing" was the first issue of *Moment*, a short-lived magazine produced by AP and Milton Acorn.

230. Layton married Betty Sutherland, a painter, in 1946. The marriage was Layton's second. See AP's letter of Feb. 1958.

231. *The Fiddlehead*, founded in 1945 and published by the University of New Brunswick, is one of Canada's most venerable small magazines.

the lines of say, RELATION OF POETRY TO THE TRENDS OF THINKING —
I mean, does it have any influence on people. Or RELATION OF POETRY TO
POLITICS and THINKING BEHIND POETRY — I mean philosophy there.
Those titles are bad, but you get what I mean. Layton makes claim to Nietzsche,
Macpherson [Jay], Jung. Yours is a more personal way of thinking, to me anyway,
that aims at a deeper fulfillment of the individual, a breaking out from national
boundaries, a sadness at our violence etc. Anyway, that's part of what you are to
me. However, I don't suppose you enter into what you write about others. Another
title: DO CANADIAN POETS (ANY OF THEM) DESERVE A WIDER WORLD
CIRCULATION THAN THEY GET? Or THE PRECIOUS AND INGROWN IN
MODERN POETRY. One thing about the poetry we're writing now is that it has
nothing in it (or I don't think so) that bespeaks the feeling and longing of your
Strait of Anian — there is no clear and easy road to Europe — I know that's a
misquote — I should have said back to Europe even in a misquote.[232]

So are we always longing for the Good Land of Temlaham that lies behind
in the past?[233] Umbilical cord to Europe? I suppose ... There ought to be a positive virtue in living in what is still really a new country. But we make all the old
mistakes here and some new ones. What about THE CLIMATE NEEDED FOR
POETRY ...? Eliot says a poet should be a bank clerk or something similarly
sedentary.[234] Does this mean they should take no part in world events and express
no opinion in their work? I think not. I mean, the poet is a whole man and has an
opinion (or should) about nearly everything.

Anyway, I expect you'll have ideas on the things that interest you, without
my suggestions. But it's my nature to do that anyway. I'd certainly like something
from you if you're so inclined, in the mood now or in future, have time in the
midst of students crying for knowledge and enlightenment, ... AT WHAT DATE
DOES CANADIAN POETRY BEGIN, SHOULD EVERYTHING BE DISMISSED
BEFORE PRATT? OR CARMAN-ROBERTS-LAMPMAN?[235] WHERE IS

---

232. AP referred to EB's "Pacific Door," published in *The Strait of Anian*: "there is no clear Strait of
Anian / to lead us easy back to Europe" (*OMH* 58).

233. Temlaham is a village on the Skeena River in Tsimshian and Gitksan mythology. Marius
Barbeau's *The Downfall of Temlaham* (1928) was reissued by Hurtig Publishers in 1973, as AP may have
known. AP's elegy for the Canadian ethnographer, "Marius Barbeau: 1883–1969," was gathered in *To
Paris Never Again* (1997).

234. Eliot worked at Lloyd's Bank in London from 1917 to 1925.

235. William Bliss Carman (1861–1929), Charles G.D. Roberts (1860–1943), Archibald Lampman
(1861–1899): Canadian poets of the so-called Confederation group, which flourished in the 1880s
and 1890s. Roberts and Lampman are major figures in Canadian literary history; Carman's place is
less secure, but AP was unabashed about his youthful enthusiasm for Carman's poetry, which is typically ethereal and mystical: "I find the early poets boring, despite an adolescent attraction to Carman"
(*RBS* 288). AP's poetry of the 1930s and 1940s bears obvious signs of his having been influenced by
Carman's writing. Roberts was also a writer of stories about animals, as AP knew — he had a copy of

POETRY GOING IN THE MATTER OF FORM AND INTELLIGIBILITY? IS THERE A MAJOR FIGURE IN THE WORLD TODAY? And etc.

All the best,

Al Purdy

To Purdy (Montreal) from Birney (Vancouver)
March 5, 1960   TL

Dear Al,

Thanks for your letter and for *Moment*. I read it right through and found it full of kicks. Way out there cool, man. Liked your part in the GREAT SOUSTER DEBATE.[236] Seems to me Canadian critics are at the same old game — first they ignore, neglect (as they did both Layton & Souster); then they blow em up like dirigibles. Didn't FRScott have something to say about crows and swans?[237] Very interested in your piece on Malcolm [Lowry]. A few piddling emendations: his shack wasn't "across Howe Sound from Vancouver" but up Burrard Inlet just where the North Arm begins to separate off. He fractured not a limb but a vertebra, I think, and some ribs not rebounding against trees but falling off his pier at low tide onto the rocks while drunk and despairing because Margerie had flown to L.A. to see her sick mother. About his poems, the interesting thing I've always felt about them is that they are mainly notes for his prose, trial sections for the novels. It's a cliché that all good fiction tends toward the condition of poetry, but here was a man who conceived of a novel as something like super-poetry, for which simpler poems were only dry runs.

Had many inquiries about Malc when I was down the coast last month; interesting how his ghost still stalks; many didn't know he was dead.[238] I've been on a combined lecture & poetry reading tour, juggling all 3 of my balls: a public Chaucer lecture at Reed College, Portland; a talk & reading of contemp. Cdn. poetry at Eugene (U. of Oregon) & elsewhere; and readings of my own verse at the Seattle and the San Francisco Poetry Centres. But I've just written Louis Dudek, with all this narcissistic crap, and won't repeat.

Kings in Exile (in the 1947 Ryerson edition) in his library, among other volumes. Roberts wrote to EB (7 Apr. 1943) to congratulate him on *David and Other Poems*.

236. Raymond Souster (1921–2012): Canadian poet (*Collected Poems of Raymond Souster*, 10 vols., 1980–2004). With Louis Dudek and Irving Layton, Souster founded the influential magazine *Contact* in 1952. He helped establish the League of Canadian Poets in 1966. The first issue of *Moment* included a section titled "Raymond Souster. Extempore Debate: Dudek and Acorn versus Purdy."

237. F.R. Scott (1899–1985): Canadian poet (*Overture*, 1945) associated with the Montreal Group of the 1920s, and later professor of law at McGill University. Perhaps EB had in mind lines from *Romeo and Juliet*: "Compare her face with some that I shall show, / And I will make thee think thy swan a crow."

238. Lowry died in Ripe, England, on 27 June 1957.

A New Zealand professor has written some lowpower thoughts about literary colonialism, including Canadian, which he had mimeographed & has sent me. Some of his points are provocative; I hope to get round to quarrelling with them, & will send you the result for *Moment* if I do.[239] Afraid that's all I can think of just now, as the grizzly end of term approaches, and exam marking, term papering, etc.[240]

Will keep in touch. All the best,

Earle

To Birney (Vancouver) from Purdy (Montreal)
May 3, 1960   TPC

Dear Earle Birney:

Quit Job. Going to Ont. to see if I can get any writing done.

New address: R.R. 1, Ameliasburg, Ont.

Re. Lowry: Always did get Howe Sound and Burrard Inlet mixed. Another issue [of] *Moment* soon. Contribs solicited. No pay but appreciation. ??

MacLennan fairly interesting last night on *Fighting Words* — Children of Defeat — Highland Scots, U.E.Ls and French?[241] What legacy etc.

Best,

Al Purdy

To Birney (Vancouver) from Purdy (Ameliasburgh)
July 11, 1960   TPC

Dear Earle Birney:

I had hoped to say hello at that Kingston Conference. I came down from Montreal with Louis Dudek when it was starting, but I had my 14 year old youngster along and had to take him on to Belleville. Imagine you saw in the papers I got an award from C.C. Thank you very much for your letter. I'll be out to Van. in the next couple or three weeks. Legal business here first. At this time I'm adapting an Eskimo novel called *The Knife* for radio — in a pretty free adaptation.[242] Can't use much of the dialogue from the novel and have to write my own and rearrange the

---

239. The "New Zealand professor" was possibly Allen Curnow. See EB's letter of 25 Jan. 1975.

240. EB's expression echoes lines from his "Time-Bomb," published in *Now Is Time*: "O men be swift to be mankind / or let the grizzly take."

241. Hugh MacLennan (1907–90): Canadian novelist (*Barometer Rising*, 1941; *Two Solitudes*, 1945) and professor at McGill University. *Fighting Words*, a panel-discussion show, aired on the CBC from 1953 to 1962. EB appeared on the program on 19 June 1960. "U.E.Ls": United Empire Loyalists.

242. *The Knife* (1955), by Theon Wright (1904–80). The CBC commissioned the adaptation by AP. It aired in 1960, according to George Bowering's bibliography in *Al Purdy* (1970).

time sequence etc. It's hack work in a sense I suppose, but with something solid before me in the way of a plot etc. much easier than original. Hope to have a beer with you in Vancouver and hope you can give me your ideas about the Skeena country.

Best

Al Purdy

To Birney (Vancouver) from Purdy (Prince George, British Columbia)
August 22, 1960   APC

Dear Earle Birney:
Sitting right now beside a big fire & writing by its light just beyond Williams Lake. Bought a cheap car to go to Hazelton.[243] Read your Chinese poems two-three times again. That contemplative quality odd in Mao — much more than a pretty turn of phrase.

Al Purdy

To Birney (Vancouver) from Purdy (Trenton)
"Oct 5 or 6," 1961   TL[244]

Dear Earle Birney:
Have been talking with a Mr. R.S. James at CBC who is ass't supervisor of radio drama re. possibility of dramatizing "David." The CBC series *Cameo* "did" Pratt's "The Cachalot" recently, and Mr. James tells me it came off well.

The idea is to add dialogue and music to the poem which a narrator reads. I happen to be quite fond of "David" as a poem and would like to dramatize it. Would you be willing to negotiate with the CBC script dept concerning the poem?

In case you are willing for me to go ahead with it, would you send along a short analysis of what you were trying to say in the poem? I don't mean to sound like an undergrad here, but I want to see how it jibes with my own ideas. I see "David" and "the Finger on Sawback" as similar to your theme in "Bushed" — and I think you read my perhaps inept analysis of that poem when I was in Vancouver last year.[245]

Up till two months ago I was writing poetry frantically and almost compulsively — but now I seem to have stopped. Have about 50 pages if I could find a

<hr />

243. Hazelton and Kispiox are villages on the Skeena River in north-central British Columbia. The poems "Hazelton, B.C." and "Kispiox Indian Village" were included in AP's *The Blur in Between: Poems 1960–61* (1962). Williams Lake is a small town in the Cariboo region of British Columbia; AP's "The Cariboo Horses" (*The Cariboo Horses*, 1965) is set in 100 Mile House, roughly ninety kilometres southeast.
244. *YA* 65–66.
245. From "David": "But always we talked of the Finger on Sawback, unknown / And hooked" (*OMH* 36).

publisher who doesn't mind four-letter words which, I assure you, are necessary in their context. J.R. Colombo says no "reputable" publisher would take a chance on it. However, I suppose this is irrelevant —[246]

So anyway, could you let me know about "David"? I can assure you that I'd like to dramatize the poem in a manner of which you would approve — but apart from you, the indubitable author, I'd just like to do it. What else can I say?

Sincerely,

Al Purdy

To Purdy (Trenton) from Birney (Vancouver)
October 13, 1961   TL[247]

Dear Al,

I'm complimented that you would like to dramatize "David" and I wouldn't think of telling you how to do it. It has already had at least one musical setting.[248]

I've had to "expound" this poem on too many occasions, some of which probably got into print here or there, but I think it's better for you to set down what you want to do with it, send me a copy, and I'll tell you if I think you've really got off the track. And you can stay off it still, if you want. Seems to me you would have to write your own "David" in a way, to do this job, and the more you do that the better it will be. So far as the extremely simple structure of the poem is concerned, and the meaning of technical words (which you would know anyway), I've talked about them in a series of questions directed to high school students in the back of my *Twentieth Century Canadian Poetry*.[249] But I was also fumbling with a much larger and cloudier symbolism which I'd rather not talk about since if it isn't there it isn't there, and if it is you'll have seen it.

Everything of course is subject to CBC willing to pay a decent permission fee. They gave Pratt a quite sumptuous one some years back, but I won't hold them to an equality with Ned, bless him.

Hope you get a publisher for your fifty poems, four-letter words and all. Would it help if you made them five-letter, say by spelling "fuck" "phuck" and "shit" "schit" or even "schitt"; looks more learned and cosmopolitan that way don't you think?

All the best,

Earle

---

246. John Robert Colombo (b. 1936): Canadian poet (*Abracadabra*, 1967; *Selected Poems*, 1982), editor, and anthologist.

247. *YA* 66–67.

248. The Canadian composer Lorne Betts (1918–85) set "David" to music in 1949; Betts also scored other poems by EB and other Canadian poets.

249. *Twentieth Century Canadian Poetry: An Anthology* (1953), edited by EB. "A series of questions": EB typed "serious" for "series" — a telling mistake?

Dear Earle Birney:

Got your note today, and will tell CBC in another letter this evening to start nego-
tiating with Dr. Birney. That was the phraseology used by R.S. James in the radio
drama dept.

I have your *20th Century [Canadian] Verse [Poetry]* by the way and will look
at the back. Milt Acorn was here for two weeks recently and read it. He hadn't
before. Said there were poets in it he hadn't seen.

I'm a little afraid of what you'll think of anything I do with "David" since
it's your baby, but I've loved the poem since I had enough sense to do so. About
1950, I think, before that my own ego stood in the way. Much more difficult to
do than "The Cachalot," and a much more sensitive poem in all ways. No, I'm not
worried about technical words. My grasp of language is probably a strong point. I
think intuitive as well as lexicographical if there is such a word. I'll get your notes
right now and read them before I go on. Okay, I cry quits, "bergschrund" and the
accented "Neve" are outside me, but I'll look em up.[251] But I see you've provided
definitions ... That business may be hard to get across in drama; the ordinary
listener won't know what they mean, unless I provide very graphic description and
action —

Certain bits of dialogue in the poem I would delete, because they would duplicate the dialogue in the descriptive drama.

I'm scared to hell about not pleasing you, because I'd feel I'd in some sense
ruined the poem if I don't make it come across clearly. About the symbolism, I
want that to be more explicit than in the poem, and hope you agree. One simple
thing the poem does is replace David with Bob in the living world, perhaps giving
the world many of David's qualities, the best ones.

But I can't get away from "Bushed." However, I don't want to go into it too
much right now or I'll lose something that I intend to store up for the actual
writing, if you and CBC agree to terms. I don't want to trigger ideas now, and
uselessly, since I have a sieve of a memory unless I get ideas on paper right away.
Reading "Bushed" at this moment I'm rather awestruck at this poem, pay you what
I think is the ultimate compliment: I'd like to have written it. Tho I'm so different
I never could in a million life times. Also, I suppose you know the revolving sun
in "Dusk on English Bay" is mindful of MacLeish's poem or vice versa — "You,

---

250. *YA* 67–69.

251. From "David": "I remember / Only the pounding fear I would stumble on It // When I came
to the grave-cold maw of the bergschrund ... reeling / Over the sun-cankered snowbridge, shying the
caves / In the névé ..." (*OMH* 39).

Andrew Marvell" — I've always come under the spell of your poetry (in the last ten years or so) in a way I never could with Layton's.[252] Why, I wonder. I guess I think of Layton as a marvelous virtuoso, but I can never believe, not quite, that he really felt that way. And hence I can't either, not quite. By the way, I'll enclose one of Acorn's that I also envy. I'd like to have written it too, but there again Acorn is alien to me.

I'm getting a bit incoherent I see, drinking wild cherry wine while I type. Acorn incidentally, has a social sense unmixed with sadness, that is fierce and unrelenting. The poem I enclose is a marked exception to this fierceness. You, to me, have a social sense that includes sadness and history. Queer as I think of it. Time will have a stop for you and I, but never for Acorn. I don't think he'd admit it even if he knew for sure. That indomitable quality I admire. But he's naive in a way I have never been, nor yourself I suspect. He still isn't sure about the sexual behaviour of homosexuals, for instance. I gave him Havelock Ellis to read.[253] And yet he writes SUCH poems. If you do another anthology — Oh well, I suppose you won't. Why don't you edit one of the series Ryerson is putting out? [A.J.M.] Smith wants to I hear from Colombo. I wish you would.

Best
Al Purdy

To Birney (Vancouver) from Purdy (Ameliasburgh)
December 3, 1961   TL[254]

Dear Earle Birney:

Just got a letter yesterday telling me you'd come to terms. I thought the thing had fallen through, and Mr. James at CBC apparently thought he'd written before to say go ahead. But he damned well hadn't. They tell me it's scheduled for New Year's Day, so I am working like hell this week. Through their own failure to communicate with me in time there won't be opportunity to even ask you any questions and consult you before the thing goes into rehearsal.

Have written the first scene, which comes after the first two verses of poem, and it's GOOD — I made David centre of a humorous incident to take off the curse of philosophy later. Also, I intend to give it an upbeat at the end, tho of course your verses will end the play. Way I'll do it is anticipate the ending in a

---

252. Archibald MacLeish (1892–1982): American poet (*Conquistador*, 1932; *Collected Poems 1917–1952*, 1952), playwright, essayist, and critic (*Poetry and Opinion: The Pisan Cantos of Ezra Pound*, 1950). His famous apothegm about poetry, "A poem should not mean / But be," appears in "Ars Poetica." "You, Andrew Marvell" is mentioned several times in AP's letters.

253. Havelock Ellis (1859–1939): English author of the seven-volume *Studies in the Psychology of Sex* (1897–1928).

254. *YA* 71.

prose dialogue scene. So if you have one single word of advice please send bloody quick.

Tonight is Sunday, oops, early Mon. morning. I expect to be working most of the night. Have a wood fire in my Quebec heater here and water boiling for coffee.

By the way, Milton Wilson and Louis Dudek kindly gave me short analyses (is that plural correct?) of poem. Wilson says the ending does have an upbeat despite the words, partly due to change of tone. Dudek calls it "flunked Nietzsche" and a "Canadian failure" — I disagree strongly, at least, why the hell bring in Nietzsche? And I just can't see it as a portrait of failure. Maybe I WON'T see it that way.

Any final word?

Best
Al Purdy

To Birney (Vancouver) from Purdy (Ameliasburgh)
February 1, 1962   TL²⁵⁵

Dear Earle

Pleased you liked the script in general, and of course keep the carbon. I had made up my mind, re. the "possible addition," not to use it on discussion with CBC people. Would have been just too too —

Didn't wish to imply homosexuality at all — tho it certainly had occurred to me. Can't there be a male relationship without that getting into the act? In my experience there can, and I don't think it's necessarily in the interests of "reality" to push sex into a poem like yours. One or two people have said there is homosexuality implied in the poem itself, but I don't see why. Anyhow, it could have no bearing on the story itself as you told it in the poem. Male friendship or male "love" certainly can exist without having that in every case. Sometimes I think Freud's influence has got us hypnotized as hell.

Why don't you make a tape of the tape before you have to return it? Set up your two recorders in an empty room and close the door on it for half an hour. Extraneous sounds ought not to be too bad.

Looking forward to your book — Hope new poems go into it, and *Trial of a City* is not deleted because it's a play.

The older Bobbie, to my mind and thought, was to make the separation between "now" and "then" more pronounced. I guess I made Bobbie a somewhat stronger character than the poem did, but if Drainie read the poem like I think

---

255. *YA* 72.

he may have (I didn't hear it) he made the younger Bobbie much too smooth and strong.[256] Oh well —

Very best to you

Al Purdy

To Purdy (Ameliasburgh) from Birney (Bowen Island, British Columbia)
June 22, 1964   TPC

Dear Al,

Thanks for that good letter. You should see the letter I never sent Skelton![257] The bastard has decided he can get attention by attacking me (in B.C., anyway). So now Lowry's poems, he finds, are crap, & Lowry not really a sensitive alcoholic but just non-U English. I've been busy setting up a large Creative Writing Dept. here; now handing over admin to Zilber, & Bob Harlow, & hope to get back to writing.[258] Come west again soon. Don't see you often enough.

Earle B

To Purdy (Ameliasburgh) from Birney (Vancouver)
August 25, 1964   TL

Dear Al:

Many thanks for sending "Cancel All My Appointments," and for your letter. The latter I hope to answer in a few days. The poem I am holding until I get your reaction to a couple of puzzlements of mine about it. First let me say I like it very much and want to use it, but I do not understand the section beginning "uncautious love" down to "legendary innocence."[259] Does this passage refer to the father or is it a continuation of the message "to the girl"? At the end why do you repeat your disparagement of your own work? To say "this awkward music" is charming and modest. To come back and say "These inconsequential verses with emphasis

---

256. John Drainie (1916–66): Canadian radio and television actor.

257. Robin Skelton (1925–97): English-born poet (*Collected Shorter Poems, 1947–1977*, 1981; *The Collected Longer Poems, 1947–1977*, 1985), critic, anthologist, and co-founder and editor of *The Malahat Review*. He started teaching at the University of Victoria in 1963 and was, like EB at UBC, instrumental in establishing a Department of Creative Writing.

258. Jake Zilber (1924–2012) and Robert Harlow (b. 1923) were colleagues of EB's at UBC who assisted him in developing Creative Writing as an academic unit independent of the Department of English. Harlow was the first Head of Creative Writing, a position he held from 1965 to 1977. A novelist (*Royal Murdoch*, 1962; *Scann*, 1972), he was a writing student of EB's at UBC. Zilber was editor of *Prism* from 1966 to 1973. The interesting correspondence between EB and Zilber suggests that the two were important allies at UBC, and friends.

259. "use it": i.e., publish it in *Prism*. See EB's letter of 15 Oct. 1964.

on all the wrong syllables" is to protest too much and appear falsely modest, even though I know this is not your intent. And *please* explain your title!

I would appreciate a quick reaction if you have time.

Yours sincerely,

Earle

To Purdy (Ameliasburgh) from Birney (Vancouver)
c. October 15, 1964   TL[260]

Dear Al,

Haven't had a chance to answer yours of Sep 24 till now. However, I did send a chit to the CC. I hope it helps. I thought you might like to see what I wrote, and attach a copy.

The Poetry Ed. liked "Mr. Green[h]algh's Love Poem" which you sent on Sep 15 but wasn't too happy about the way in which the associations get so loose at the end; most of the way, he says, they're exciting and free; at the end, for him, just free.[261] Well, it's a criticism, though I suspect if the poem had been shorter it would have passed more easily through his needle's eye. There wasn't time for it or the other one, for this *Prism* anyway, so I am returning them both so that you can feel free to get them in somewhere else earlier than we could now plan for.[262] You asked me whether I think "On a Park Bench" is a poem. Of course I do, though for me an incomplete one, one that leaves the essence unexplored, the mysterious moment of communication between poet and mother-on-bench: what happens to it? How did it start, finish, or didn't it happen at all, didn't her nerves quiver at all in the poet's? I want to know more, and a poem for me isn't just a titillation, it's a satisfaction, an orgasm not a belly rub.

You have a review in the Sep *CF* [*Canadian Forum*] containing, in the opening of its 2nd para., one of the more remarkable misstatements of the year. "Twenty years ago young poets," you tell us, "imitated Bliss Carman (in Canada anyway), Eliot, Auden and the 19th century romantics."[263] Jesus! What "young poets"? Name

---

260. *YA* 89–91.

261. "Mr. Greenhalgh's Love Poem" was eventually published in *Delta* 25 (Nov. 1965) and collected in the 1968 and 1973 editions of *Poems for All the Annettes* and in *Love in a Burning Building* (1970).

262. *Prism*, a literary journal published at UBC since 1959, was conceived by EB in opposition to *Canadian Literature*, which also started at UBC in 1959, but which was (and is) devoted to criticism. Jan de Bruyn was the first editor of *Prism*. EB's first issue as editor-in-chief of *Prism* — previously the title had simply been "editor" — was 4.1 (Summer 1964). Beginning with that issue, too, the journal was called *Prism International*.

263. In a short essay ("Who's Got the Emphasis?") in *The Canadian Forum* (Sept. 1964), AP reviewed books by John Newlove, Roy Kiyooka, and Gerry Gilbert. The essay in large part concerns the influence of William Carlos Williams on contemporary writers. The offending passage is as follows: "Twenty years ago young poets imitated Bliss Carman (in Canada anyway), Eliot, Auden and the 19th

ONE in Canada (you certainly couldn't outside of Canada) who was imitating Bliss Carman in 1944 or indeed in 1934 or 1924, anyone who was, is, a *poet* by any honest definition, and who was young, or even not really young, say under forty.[264] NAME ONE! Do you know who was writing poetry in 1944 in Canada? I'll tell you, and I'll tell you who I think they were imitating, insofar as they were imitating anybody:

Anderson at age 29: Dylan Thomas

Bailey at age 39: Eliot, Pratt[265]

Avison at age 26: Marianne Moore? Yeats[266]

Daniells at age 44: Eliot[267]

Dudek at age 26: Pound, Auden

Finch at age 44: French symbolistes

Gustafson at age 35: Hopkins[268]

Klein at age 35: Eliot

Le Pan at age 30: Lewis[269]

Livesay at age 35: Auden, Sitwell, Symbolistes

Lowry at age 36: Aiken, Melville, Elizans [Elizabethans][270]

century romantics. Today the model has narrowed down almost exclusively to just one man: William Carlos Williams. Williams supplies the speech idioms, Charles Olson provides a theory; and sometimes I think a few of their worshippers supply little but echoes."

264. As EB would later recall in *Spreading Time: Remarks on Canadian Writing and Writers* (1980), as a young man he met Carman: the illustrious poet visited UBC when EB was a student there. According to EB's account, he was assigned by Garnett Sedgewick to be Carman's chaperone; the latter nonetheless got lost in the woods on campus and had to be retrieved by EB prior to his reading.

265. Alfred Bailey (1905–97): Canadian poet (*Songs of the Saguenay and Other Poems*, 1927; *Miramichi Lightning: The Collected Poems of Alfred Bailey*, 1981) and distinguished historian (*The Conflict of European and Eastern Algonkian Culture, 1504–1700: A Study in Canadian Civilization*, 1937). Bailey, Roy Daniells, Robert Finch, and EB met at the University of Toronto in the late 1920s.

266. Margaret Avison (1918–2007): Canadian poet (*Winter Sun*, 1960; *No Time*, 1989; *Always Now: The Collected Poems*, 3 vols., 2003–05) with links to Canadian modernism and American postmodernism but whose style is highly idiosyncratic. AP admired her writing, despite the Christian dimension of the later poetry. Marianne Moore (1887–1972): American poet (*Collected Poems*, 1951) and essayist (*Predilections: Literary Essays*, 1955).

267. Roy Daniells (1902–79): Canadian poet (*Deeper into the Forest*, 1948) and professor of English at UBC, where he was EB's colleague; they clashed frequently. Daniells and EB were roommates as graduate students at the University of Toronto.

268. Ralph Gustafson (1909–95): Canadian poet (*Collected Poems*, 3 vols., 1987–94) and professor at Bishop's University (1963–79). His *Fire on Stone* (1974) won the Governor General's Award for poetry. Gerard Manley Hopkins (1844–89): English poet (*Poems*, 1918) and Jesuit priest. Hopkins's poetry, mostly on religious themes, is technically ingenious. AP wrote in 1992 that he "could never learn from Hopkins or Eliot, the former too radical, the latter too world-weary" (*YA* 476).

269. Douglas LePan (1914–98): Canadian novelist (*The Deserter*, 1964), poet (*The Net and the Sword*, 1953), diplomat, and professor at Queen's University and the University of Toronto. Cecil Day Lewis (1904–72): English poet (*Collected Poems*, 1954) and translator (*The Georgics*, 1940; *The Aeneid*, 1952). He was Poet Laureate from 1968 to 1972.

270. Conrad Aiken (1889–1973): American novelist and poet. In the introduction to his edition of

MacKay at age 43: MacNeice, the Greek poets[271]
Page at age 28: Anderson, Thomas, Barker
Wreford at age 29: Auden, Lewis[272]
Whalley at age 30?: Lewis[273]
M. Waddington at age 27: E. Sitwell[274]
Souster at age 21: Whitman
Wilkinson at age 34: Dickinson[275]
Smith at age 42: Yeats, Eliot

There isn't one damn poet, old or young, worthy at all of the name, none writing & appearing in the mags and anthologies, who was being influenced 20 yrs ago by one damn nineteenth century romantic or by Bliss Carman. No nor 25 or 30 yrs ago. Forty years ago, yes. Man, don't think everybody a little bit older than you is CGD Roberts vintage. You're half right about Eliot & Auden, if you have to make superficial generalizations, but the real truth is more like this column — all over the place. I left myself out because I KNOW how scattered & unconcentrated my influences were. Sure, they included Audenspenderlewis, & Eliot whom I always despised, but these influences were no more important than those of Cynewulf, Chaucer, John Skelton, Herrick, Homer, Hardy, Robinson Jeffers and Wilfred Owen. And of all these only Chaucer seems to have been abiding within me, and yet led to little I could claim by kinship with him. [...]

Earle

Lowry's poetry, EB described the young Lowry as a "teen-age weight lifter and guitar-strummer who claimed Conrad Aiken as his spiritual father and wrote, while still an undergraduate, a novel under the influence of *Blue Voyage* fictionizing [sic] his seventeenth year, when he had knocked around the ports of Asia as a fireman's boy on a freighter."

271. L.A. MacKay (1901–82): Canadian poet (*The Ill-Tempered Lover and Other Poems*, 1948), professor of classics at the University of California, Berkeley (*The Wrath of Homer*, 1948), and commentator on Canadian literature. Louis MacNeice (1907–63): Irish poet (*Autumn Journal*, 1939; *Collected Poems*, 1949, 1966), playwright (*Out of the Picture*, 1937), translator of Aeschylus and Goethe, and critic (*The Poetry of W.B. Yeats*, 1941). With Auden he wrote *Letters from Iceland* (1937).

272. James Wreford Watson (1915–90): Scottish geographer and poet who moved to Canada in the late 1930s and then returned to Scotland in 1954. He wrote as James Wreford. *Of Time and the Lover* (1950) won the Governor General's Award.

273. George Whalley (1915–83): Canadian poet (*No Man an Island*, 1948), critic (*Poetic Process*, 1953), translator of Aristotle, and professor of English at Queen's University.

274. Miriam Waddington (1917–2004): Canadian poet (*Green World*, 1945; *Collected Poems*, 1986), editor (*The Collected Poems of A.M. Klein*, 1974), writer of stories (*Summer at Lonely Beach*, 1982), and professor at York University. She was a student of EB's at the University of Toronto.

275. Anne Wilkinson (1910–61): Canadian poet (*Counterpoint to Sleep*, 1951), biographer (*Lions in the Way: A Discursive History of the Oslers*, 1956), and literary editor (*Here and Now*). She helped found *The Tamarack Review*.

To Birney (Vancouver) from Purdy (Ameliasburgh)
October 19, 1964   TL[276]

Dear Earle:

That's a blockbuster of a letter. Before I get nasty want to thank you for CC missive. You hit what's nearly the crux of the whole thing in your comments about the travel allowance. On accounta I don't suppose very much "lateral" travel is possible in the north, and I'd likely have to go back south in order to go east or west. By plane anyway. Tho of course I'll take whatever transport is available. Anyway, it's a good letter, with, I think, very accurate judgments and estimates throughout.

I wish the rest of the letter was as close to the mark.

Naturally, I disagree about the "Love Poem." However, you either get and like such a poem or you don't. No amount of explaining makes it better if you (or whoever) don't get it themselves in the first place. And you certainly know what I mean here. I could talk about this one all night, and hope to do so on some later date with you. In the meantime I think your Poetry Ed. is full of shit.[277]

Okay — re review. In the first place, what I worried about in this was the whole business breaking in two at the middle, on accounta the Williams bit is tough axe grinding.

Anyway, you challenge me to name a poet who was influenced by Carman. That's easy. ME. He was the first reason for my writing poetry, and no snide comments please. I got over him eventually as you know, but "Arnoldus Villanova, 600 years ago (not 20) / said peonies have magic and I believe it so."[278]

Your list is damn impressive, and gives me info I didn't have before. I could have guessed some of it, but not nearly all. However, one of the things it demonstrates very strongly to me is that the poets with good models improved, and those who imitated (or were influenced by) Carman didn't. Moral: Imitate the best. I may say (modestly) that Birney too at one time was one of my influences. Still, despite this severe handicap, I survived. No kiddin tho, there is a point here. And don't you remember Carman's vogue at that time, and earlier?

You say none worthy of the name was influenced. Of course you're right. Except me. And I wasn't worthy [of] the name at the time. But there were also

---

276. *YA* 91–93.

277. The first associate editor of poetry during EB's tenure as editor-in-chief of *Prism* was Maurice Gibbons (first included in the masthead of issue 4.2 [Autumn 1964]). He was succeeded by Dorothy Livesay in issue 5.2 (Autumn 1965).

278. "Peony" (from *Later Poems*, 1921) by Bliss Carman: "Arnoldus Villanova / Six hundred years ago / Said Peonies have magic, / And I believe it so." (The poem's epigraph is from Villanova, the medieval alchemist: "*Pionia virtutem habet occultam.*") In his essay "On Bliss Carman," AP claimed to have read the poem for the first time when "I was thirteen in the early 1930s" (*SA* 321). He wrote that "The words hummed through my head like hydro wires in winter" (322).

the CAA [Canadian Authors Association] type (generalization) of poets who go nowhere. You know damn well they were influenced. Carman was worshipped among some of those people, just as Williams is now, he and the BM [Black Mountain] boys.[279]

Still, I'll give you best somewhat, since it isn't a precisely accurate generalization. If I'd written 40 pages tho would have done better. But I will not agree when you say that Carman had no influence. 20 years ago and farther back.

I went thru most of the influences you name in that table, except Eliot. But I went from Carman to Chesterton, W.J. Turner, Hardy to Yeats.[280] Then Dylan Thomas. The Americans I didn't even know about a few years back.

Among your particular influences, Auden and Jeffers have been strong. Hardy a little less so. The others not at all. Donne and Marvell to some extent. Even Kipling at one time. Yourself and Layton tho, in Canada. Eliot, beyond admiring somewhat la something or other and Prufrock, not at all. I can't even understand *The Waste Land*, nor very sure there's much to understand.[281]

Interesting to me that Jeffers is included on your list. In the last five years I've developed a helluva respect for him. "Hurt Hawks" for instance. That image about eagles' wings as "folded storms at their shoulders."[282]

I deny absolutely the gaffe you attribute to me re Oedipus. Said dead Greek is now in the public mind a helluva lot more than just a symbol of a son-mother incestuous relationship. I maintain very strong that he is a symbol of all incest. If you must be that specific, of course he had no relations with his daughter. BUT: he's still a symbol of ALL incest. Not to you apparently, but to very many people. Don't ask me to prove that tho, just as I'll not ask you to prove the opposite. Shall we go to the Gallup poll? Who, Mr. Man-in-the-Street, is the Canadian Minister of Defense?

Sharp or Helleur?

So — you busy bastard, I expect you to either disagree with this and not write,

279. William Carlos Williams (1883–1963): American poet (*Spring and All*, 1923; *Pictures from Brueghel and Other Poems*, 1962; *Paterson*, 1963), novelist (*The Great American Novel*, 1923), playwright, and physician. His writing was a major influence on postwar American and Canadian poets, but one that AP steadfastly resisted.

280. Gilbert Keith Chesterton (1874–1936): English novelist (*The Man Who Was Thursday*, 1908), poet, essayist, and writer on religious and philosophical topics (*Orthodoxy*, 1908). W.J. Turner (1889–1946): Music and theatre critic, novelist, and poet (*The Dark Fire*, 1918). Born in Australia, he emigrated to England; he befriended several Bloomsbury notables, including Virginia Woolf. In "Touchings" (*Naked with Summer in Your Mouth*, 1994), AP quotes (and misquotes) Turner's "Epithalamium for a Modern Wedding."

281. As Sam Solecki has noted (*YA* 93 n.2), "La something or other" is "La Figlia Che Piange," from Eliot's *Prufrock and Other Observations* (1917).

282. "Hurt Hawks" (from *Cawdor and Other Poems*, 1928) is one of Jeffers's most famous poems, but the line to which AP referred — it is correctly "cloaked in the folded storms of his shoulders" — appears in Jeffers's "Fire on the Hills" (from *Thurso's Landing and Other Poems*, 1932).

or disagree and write a year from now. However, I'm pleased to see some of the awe that seems to permeate the atmosphere these days (no kiddin) is not breathed in by you. Tho you've probably noted some of it. Eh? And are about to kick me in the egotistic balls. We could probably have a good argument under the "right" circumstances?

Next day — and where the hell was I?

Anyway, I find your graph damn interesting. For instance, whatever happened to Wreford? Or did he ever happen in the first place?

I see you have left out Pratt, perhaps thinkin he didn't imitate anyone.

What a nasty question. Do I know who was writing poetry in Canada in 44? I've written the stuff myself since I was 13 years old, and I've heard of or known most of them, including many who never got anywhere. Who weren't, as you say, "poets" — depending on the level of merit you have to achieve to deserve the epithet. But why worry about nomenclature, let the old ladies have their magic occupation. "Honest definition"? I've never seen a valid definition yet, one that would hold up, either of poetry or poets. Lots of stop-gap ones tho. And nearly everyone I know (who writes poems) just loves to make such definitions.

Anyway, before I stop, thanks again for your letter [to the Canada Council]. Really, I should think anyone who was so sharp and perceptive in such a letter wouldn't be the opposite in the accompanying letter. I'll give you about 50% of your points tho. Will you be that generous/dishonest??? No. Anyway, if I get this thing I hope to see you in Van, for I'll be out there before leaving for the north.

Best
Al

To Purdy (Trenton) from Birney (Vancouver)
November 26, 1964   TL + AL

Dear Al:

Thanks for yours of the 23rd. Glad you liked *Prism*. What you think about the early ones is no skin off my back since I never edited them.

There is no chance for anyone from W.H. Auden down, or up, coming reading here this winter unless they pay for everything.[283] We have a new dean who cut that item out of our budget. As soon as the situation changes, we will of course let you know, but the immediate future is grim.

---

283. EB corrected by hand his misspelling ("Oden") of "Auden," a mistake so egregious that he awarded it a marginal "!".

Peg Atwood has already been in to see me and I have asked her for some poems, and glad to know you think well of her work.[284]

Al — Sorry this was done in a rush, I'm swamped with mss — *Prism*, Creative Writing classes, etc.

Glad to know you're reviewing the book for *Fiddlehead.*

I like a lot of Lane's poem but it's too diffuse & long for us.[285] However, I intend to talk to him about it.

Hope you had a good reading. Those readings are of *very great* importance for the spreading of the knowledge of the *pleasure* of poetry.

Earle

To Purdy (Ameliasburgh) from Birney (Vancouver)
February 28, 1965   TL

Dear Al,

Good to hear, even if it's to learn you haven't any heat. So long as the scotch holds out. Thank *you* for being in Vancouver, and at such a time. Maybe I haven't many years left, so it's not such a Big Thing to say I'll never forget what you did for me, but anyway that goes for saying. Many other things go without, only because I'd only embarrass you trying to say them. That day I thought he'd strangled her! Wish things had gone better for you with *your* Miss A. though. I've seen little of her, except for a passing smile in the corridors, but this will interest you: STORY INDICATING SPEED OF ASSEMBLY LINE IN VANCOUVER GOSSIP FACTORY.

Rona Murray, one of our Creative Writing grad students & also a teaching fellow in the English Dept., came into my office in a great show of gravity and concern, said "I think you ought to know ... everybody knows that you and Ikuko are still *Seeing Each Other* ..."[286] I splutter the usual whaddyumeans. She says

---

284. Margaret Atwood (b. 1939): Canadian poet (*The Circle Game*, 1964; *The Journals of Susanna Moodie*, 1970), novelist (*Surfacing*, 1972; *The Handmaid's Tale*, 1985), essayist, and critic (*Survival: A Thematic Guide to Canadian Literature*, 1972). She is unquestionably one of the most prominent writers in Canada since the mid-1960s. In her foreword to BR, Atwood wrote that "I began to read Al Purdy's poetry about the same time it changed from being odd and ungainly to being remarkable — in the early sixties. ... I was somewhat frightened by it, and did not fully understand it. This was a new sort of voice for me, and an overpowering one, and a little too much like being backed into the corner of a seedy bar by a large, insistent, untidy drunk, who is waxing by turns both sentimental and obscene" (17).

285. "Lane" must be Patrick Lane, as Red Lane died in 1964.

286. Rona Murray (1924–2003): Canadian writer, primarily of poetry (*Selected Poems*, 1974), and teacher of writing. She was taught by EB, with whom she had an affair. (See EB's letter of 26 Mar. 1969.) A collection of her correspondence with EB is held at the University of Victoria. EB began an affair

"She was on a drinking party with you and Al Purdy last week, in his flat." So I say whotolyuhthatbloodynonsense etc. "O I can't tell you, but the English Dept. teaching fellows all know." So I tell her, O.K., so did Mr. Sato, it wasn't a drinking party, etc. But afterwards I try to think: who spread it? I know it wasn't you, or me, or Ikuko. And I very much doubt it was Peggy, who seemed friendly to both I. & me, & for whom I have done a favour (i.e. I got the UBC library to purchase a copy of her $125 book).[287] It was undoubtedly that wormy little Cohen who came and took her off at 10.30 pm. I'm just waiting to encounter him.

Well, as for Ikuko, things continue up and down, but presently somewhat up. Thanks partly to the discovery of a wonderful friend and counsellor, Giose Rimanelli, the Italian author who is on the staff here this winter.[288] He has established a sort of Neutral Territory of his house, where I. goes to get coaching from his wife, and where he propagandizes her on my behalf, with proper Machiavellian appearance of high disinterest. Also he has kept me from going stark mad by letting me talk myself out to him — as I did to you! And I think I would really be in a ward, if you hadn't been here that week. At the moment then there is a surface calm, I see her only in my office & for professorial reasons, but there seems some kind of hope we may see you in the east — but for god's sake breathe no word of it, for if it ever gets back here, I'll be a dead goose.

I hope good news comes soon about the northern safari. I've been talking to Dick Zuckerman, a local impresario for concerts, etc., who tells me the new streamlined mining towns up there have a much more sophisticated population than we might assume, and they would go "even" (he says) for poetry readings. So maybe you could pick up some extra cash while up there, if the CC pays up to start you going.

I've written quite a few poems to Ikuko, or about her, but they are too involved in the overdramatic tangles of the moment, I think. And I've no time to do more than slop out first drafts. However, I'm hoping. It's all or nothing for me this time, as you know, Al.

I hope things go well with you at home, the poems too; let me know as soon as you hear from the CC. And keep writing anyway, whenever you have the impulse.

---

with Ikuko Atsumi (b. 1940), a poet and then a visiting student from Japan, in 1964. It lasted until 1966, when Atsumi returned to Japan.

287. Atwood taught at UBC in the 1965–66 academic year. In her biography of Roy Daniells, *Professing English: A Life of Roy Daniells* (2002), Sandra Djwa notes that "While in Vancouver, Atwood wrote *Surfacing* on UBC exam booklets" (*Professing English*, 340). The book to which EB referred is probably *The Circle Game* in the limited edition (1964) made and illustrated by Charles Pachter (b. 1942), the Canadian painter and sculptor.

288. Giose Rimanelli (b. 1926): Professor of Italian and comparative literature at SUNY Albany, novelist (*Tiro al piccione*, 1953), poet (*Carmina Blabla*, 1967), and anthologist. His *Modern Canadian Stories* (1966), co-edited with Roberto Ruberto, contains a foreword by EB. AP had Rimanelli's *Modern Canadian Stories* (1966) in his library.

Prism I:3 is easy to send you; no. 4 is in very short supply, but I'll wangle one shortly and send the two together, with my compliments, please.

Earle

To Purdy (Ameliasburgh) from Birney (Vancouver)
March 28, 1965   TL

Dear Al,

I'm delighted the CC had the sense to give you the grant. Cheers! When do you start roaming again then? This is really wonderful — but I hope it doesn't mean we won't see you, IF AND WHEN we go east. The pot is still bubbling, but all may spill into the fire, any moment. *She* is firm, constant, determined; and so am I. But we seem pitted against the universe in this matter. The whole enormous mass of Canadian Squaredom is poised to crush us for daring to feel our obscene, comic, incestuous, tremendous, racially impure, determined unputoutable LOVE. We dare confide in no one, get help nowhere, just endure, fear, hope. The Marquis de Sato grows madder daily, an incredibly watchful jealous jailer who now will not even allow her to come up to the university and take my class (the only one she is now left with). The telephone is not answered, he accompanies her shopping, everywhere. I see her in a hurried stolen dangerous moment or two perhaps once a week. We read Donne's "Canonization" (once together, now separately, and mutter: "For God's sake hold your tongues and let us love!" — but the tongues go on waggling, the husband refuses ever to divorce, threatens suicide or other violences). Two more weeks must be endured, at least, before we can dare make a move, even if then any opportunity is granted. Pray for us, ~~unwilling martyrs of~~ and for all criminals, all round lovers in the world's square cells.

Al, that is a most marvelous kind appreciative review.[289] Thank you, my friend, for being so sparing, even silent, of my faults — and for writing with such ease of style and sense of sincerity and warmth. It's the most welcome of all the reviews I've had of this book, and doubly welcome coming from you.

If the miracle happens, you'll hear quickly from me.

Earle

---

289. "A Pair of 10-Foot-Concrete Shoes," Alfred W. Purdy's review of EB's *Near False Creek Mouth* (1964), appeared in *The Fiddlehead* 65 (Summer 1965). AP was enthusiastic: "The impression I want to leave in this review is that here's another chapter in the continuing wonder of being Earle Birney. It would be a good thing to read the other chapters too, for only part of the man is visible now unless you also look at the past. A more personal, human chapter: by reason of the process of addition and subtraction (change) which we all undergo."

Note left for Purdy at Ameliasburgh
May 4, 1965   AL

Tues. May 4, 1 p.m.

Dear Al —
Ikuko & I hoped to see you, on our way to Montreal, & sorry we didn't find you in. Will try on way back.

> Cheers.
> Earle

To Birney (Charlottetown, Prince Edward Island) from Purdy (Ameliasburgh)
1966   TL

Dear Earle:
A note for no reason, unless maybe to greet you in Charlottetown where there may be little to do but read letters. However, I expect there's your play to — what? — attend? — oversee? — or whatever you do.[290]

The damn truck, we find, may take us several more weeks to obtain, therefore may be stuck here for a while. But lots to do, mowing the lawn etc. all of which I let Eurithe accomplish, taking advantage of her reserves of energy released by Ontario Teachers' College. Myself, writ two poems last week, one a nasty anti-American piece —, about Charolais bulls admitted to Canada because of their large asses.[291] The rich man and the eye of the needle bit immediately follows.

Well, best to Esther, and do hope to see you later, tho not sure on accounta the damn truck biz.

> Salud,
> Al

To Purdy (Ameliasburgh) from Birney (Charlottetown)
July 3, 1966   TL

Dear Al
Good to find your note in the mail waiting me when we got here last week. But sorry to learn you've been hung up on getting that truck. Still you seem to be in

---

290. *The Adventures of Private Turvey*, an adaptation by Don Harron and Norman Campbell of EB's *Turvey*.
291. "Syllogism for Theologians" was published in *Wild Grape Wine* (1968).

command of the situation sitting/lying? on Roblin's shores watching Eurithe mow the lawn while you write down immortal damnation to the Yankees.

Wish I could feel on top of my situation here but so far I've been bogged down in helping Esther clean up this flat we rented. Fantastically cluttered & dirty. The reek of baby-piss rises from every carpet. We arrived ahead of time so can't really blame the landlord for the fact there's still no blankets or cooking pots. If these Atlantic fogs & rains wd stop rolling in we wdnt need blankets I guess.

Still PEI isn't all chilliness & piss. A green & quiet land. A green skin of grass & potato beds with a red soil-flesh showing through on the roads and beaches. No red showing thru in the politics however.

Theatre isn't as big as was reported to me. But does seat 900 odd & looks handsome. Rehearsals start in a few days. Meantime I'm catching up with gobs of mail, masses of bad verse & worse prose from applicants for my writing course (which begins in a week). Still hoping for time & sunshine to get a swim.

We do hope you'll make it here before we leave. The *Turvey* opening is Jul 25, followed by 18 further performances alternating with 2 other plays up to Sep. 3 — but I'll be pulling out for Toronto again about August 8.

Heard from a gal at McMaster U/Hamilton who's running an arts festival the students are planning for Nov. Wants me & Creeley & Olson & suggestions for others.[292] I said she shd try to get you. So you may hear from her. I gave her the Ameliasburg addr.

The motor trip here turned out to be hot, tiring but stimulating because of the people we met. Scarcely ever 2 nights in the same place: first one at a farm near a big waterfall near Lake Cayuga. Hosts were John Gill & wife.[293] He a young Amer poet starting a Cdn-Amer mag — think he's got some of yours for forthcoming issue hasn't he? Likable guy. Mag to be called *New* & has a good roster of names to kick off with. The Johnson govt. pays him (& 2 million other Amer. farmers) so much an acre NOT to farm the land. The decadence of empire ... Next day we visited another unfarmed farm rented by Philippe Thoby-Marcelin, the Haytian [*sic*] novelist who taught Malc Lowry voodoo (Lowry determined to believe, T-M determined to disenchant him — Lowry won of course). Had some good tales of Lowry's Haytian incursion. Tho good only in the drunken-horror volcanic way.

A third farmer-writer was Bob Chute, ed of *Small Pond* (Maine) where I also

292. Charles Olson (1910–70): Innovative American poet known in particular for his *Maximus Poems* (published in parts during his lifetime and collected as *The Maximus Poems*, 1983). He was an important theorist of experimental poetics and an idiosyncratic literary critic (*Call Me Ishmael*, 1947). Robert Creeley (1926–2005): American poet (*The Collected Poems of Robert Creeley*, 1982, 2006), editor, and professor at SUNY Buffalo. Like Olson, he was associated with Black Mountain College and the eponymous group of poets.

293. On Gill (1924–95) see AP's letter of 18 June 1969.

met John Wade, ed of *Northeastern Q* [*Quarterly*].[294] Both good guys & serious poet-editors starting up with handpresses & letting the weeds take over.

Stayed 3 days in Gloucester/Mass. Mainly seeing J.D. Reed,* a young Michigan poet who's moved down to the sea.[295] He took us over to Chas Olson's for an aft. He was very welcoming & in good form. A huge noisy manic talking-non-listening bawdy Swede of a man. His 15yrold daughter happened also to be visiting — she lives with his ex-wife in another part of the town — a sullen sexy piece who put on an enigmatic sideways look every time Olson made some remark about how big she was getting & how he wished the laws weren't so tough about incest.

Diverted our route up to N. Hatley [Quebec] & by chance walked into a party at the Gustafsons' where were the Frank Scotts, Glasscos & AJM Smiths.[296]

So quite a reunion & ball. Went on for a weekend.

But now all is quietness except for Esther rattling into filthy cupboards to look for an unleaking pot & me at this damned typewriter.

So let's hear what gives — truck   Nfld   Arctic   What?

Love to you & Eurithe from us both
Earle

* You met him at my place — he's bartending in a nite spot.

To Purdy (Ameliasburgh) from Birney (Charlottetown)
July 13, 1966   TL

Dear Al

Don't know if this will miss you at Ameliasburg. It's just to say I do like "The Drunk Tank" far beyond the re-creation of whatyousay ("piece of Purdy-hell") is the shuddery little parable of the big theme: "who goes there, friend or enema." The touch-me-not thing that's wrong with the human race it seems or so I drift from it, thinking of something I didn't quite get to say in "some things my loving never has convinced."

Don't let the Ravenscroft job bug you.[297] Take it from an old hand, it's always easy to do too much research — a substitute for writing directly what you think. You know the scene well enough. & he isn't paying enough to make you wear the

---

294. Robert Chute (b. 1926): American poet (*Uncle George: Poems from a Maine Boyhood*, 1977) and professor of biology. John Wade is the pen name of C.J. Stevens (b. 1927), an American writer.

295. J.D. Reed (1940–2005): American poet (*Expressways*, 1969).

296. John Glassco (1909–81): Canadian poet (*Selected Poems*, 1971), memoirist (*Memoirs of Montparnasse*, 1970), and translator (*The Poetry of French Canada in Translation*, 1970).

297. Arthur Ravenscroft (1923–89): Professor of English at the University of Leeds and editor (1965–78) of the *Journal of Commonwealth Literature*, to which AP contributed an essay on Canadian poetry. (See AP's letter of 22 Sept. 1967.)

ass down about it. The motto is ILLEGITIMI NON CARBORUNDUM. Which in my Latin is "don't let the bastards wear you down."

Got the *Beaver*. Still in middle of reading it. Looks grand. Really, a fine mag & I'm going to subscribe at last. Man those poems are ALL good tho wd agree that "What Do the Birds Think" is the best.[298] Still you shouldn't keep up that intensity, lyrical high pressure, thru a *series* of poems on *same* general subject. So when you relax a bit, in the earlier poems here & there, it actually helps the over-all effect. The whole thing *North of Summer* is a unique success (long ago I daydreamed of doing something like this, maybe persuading an artist to take me along (the AYJs [A.Y. Jackson] seemed the only guys getting up there on an art kick) or hitching with Zuckerman's flying orchestra. But I never worked up the steam or freed myself from other things to really go & do it. No other poet so far as I know ever even thought of doing this but maybe Pratt & me & you). And you did it man & brought back a total composition in which the prose leads are as brilliant in their way as the poems — only reservation I'd make about them is that sometimes they anticipate the poems too much. This is ok maybe for *Beaver* readers. But I'd like to see your Arctic book with some of the prose interweavings left in, wherever it wasn't reducing the surprise & tension of the following poem — on other hand my nosiness longs for the filling-in of obvious gaps in the personal record like

how come you got to sleep in a room with both Tore & Jan?

did *both* Regally & Leah have new "living experiences" to tell their hunter husbands? what DID happen at home those 3 days? I can't wait for the next installment.

what did that bosom-loving Purdy say in what language to those Eskimo wives when they hauled out their baby-feeders.

Some lost poems in that prose too:

1. Guns booming ... "being at the centre of a seashell ..." Beethoven.

2. "The long stems of kelp floating up from seal towns below" — put me in memory of Johnstone Straits (Inside Passage), also once I was shore-netting with a crazy fish biologist at 2 a.m. in blackness under Lions Gate bridge at the lowest tide of the year. Terror of being halfway down to the Kraken somehow.

3. Those bergs cracking up outside your tent at night

Sounds like you've been having too damned many visitors. You'll be getting like Thoreau. Having to move from Walden.

---

298. EB's remarks refer to works of AP's in *The Beaver*, a magazine published by the Hudson's Bay Company. "What Do the Birds Think?" was collected in *North of Summer: Poems from Baffin Island* (1967).

Been exchanging letters with an incredibly naive undergrad girl at McMaster's who's trying to arrange this fall's "FESTIVAL" there — wants Olson Creeley me, asked me for more suggestions. I suggested you among others. She replied today saying you'd been there last year & were much enjoyed etc, but they want a new crop this year. She concludes: "James Reaney is coming, and we are also going to ask Gertrude Stein."

I wrote & said I didn't think Gertrude wd be able to make it, but would certainly think it *worth* trying if McMaster's had a ouija board.[299]

You're right to insist on 5 gr from Sask. Meantime why not write Howard Gotlieb (Dr.), Chief of Special Collections, Boston University Libraries, 725 Commonwealth Ave., Boston, Mass. 02215. He just wrote me inquiring about my stuff. You might just get a 10 grand offer from them. Who knows? Depends to some extent on bulk of material of course. But not too much in yr case. If Newlove can get 5 you shd get at least 10 anywhere.[300] I got a lot more than that from U of T.

Now you got the truck & the camper. Get those goddamned articles tossed off & make it for Charlottetown & the beeg opening July 25. Hurry hurry.

Love to Eurithe & you from us both

Earle

To Purdy (Deer Lake, Newfoundland) from Birney (Fredericton, New Brunswick)
August 9, 1966   APC

Dear A & E,

Leaving for Tor. tomorrow a.m. with so much musical *Turvey* stuffed in me I play "Look over Yr Shoulder" when I fart.

Nat Cohen's reviews were encouraging but critical (for the most part, shrewdly I thot).[301] N.Y. *Variety* man saw it last nite & seemed to like it, but then he liked *Anne [of Green Gables]* too! — It was grand having you both, & very lonely when you left — I think Halifax hasn't got you because you're so popular they can't keep you in stock — what about Deer Lake? Doc. says my rib still cracked, but mending. Let's hear the end of that poem.

E.

---

299. Stein, the American modernist writer (*Tender Buttons: Objects, Food, Rooms*, 1914; *The Autobiography of Alice B. Toklas*, 1933), died in 1946.

300. John Newlove (1938–2003): Canadian poet (*Lies*, 1972, won the Governor General's Award; *Apology for Absence: Selected Poems 1962–1992*, 1993), editor, and civil servant. He was the poetry editor at McClelland and Stewart from 1970 to 1974. Several of the references to Newlove in the correspondence between EB and AP pertain to his editorial duties.

301. Nathan Cohen (1923–71): Canadian theatre critic (CBC, *Toronto Daily Star*) and radio and television broadcaster with the CBC.

Dear Al

Got yrs of 13th. Hope you got one of mine that I guess crossed with it. Tho I doubt if I said a damn thing in it. & probably won't in this. But I did like hearing from you & abt those good Norwegians digging into their ancestral shards & bones. Must read [Helge] Ingstad's bk. Don't think Mowat is the type to be generous to rivals.[302] Hope you're getting lots (of material I mean. For pomes.). & Newfie screech.

Missed you at the Rosenblatt launching shindig.[303] Which was at Diagoneault's (sp??) with hordes & very lively till the booze ran out about one. I brot Alison & Pat Christmas.[304] Gwen was there with her big Egyptian whom I thot seemed an OK guy but maybe a little bewildered by the company & who'd blame him?[305] Elaine there mad & sexy as usual. The BM [Black Mountain] boys, Vic, etc there & Vic's precariously pregnant wife.[306] I was afraid to look at her on account of feeling already I had a whammy eye that nite of the sort to induce parturition because when I called for Pat there was her pregnant Siamese squatting on the floor & damn if she didn't start popping while we looked at her.

So we both shot tires. I blew one of my expensive Volvo originals somewhere west of Lévis & had to unpack every fucking thing in the car to find the one essential spanner while cars raged by within inches & the humidity was about saturation. No job for cracked ribs. Took me an hour even with yeoman work from Klarika. & 40 bucks for a new one, tho I got a slightly soiled one for less.

302. Farley Mowat (b. 1921): Canadian writer (*Lost in the Barrens*, 1956; *Never Cry Wolf*, 1963) and conservationist. AP's reviews (1967, 1985) for *Canadian Literature* of Mowat's *Westviking* and *Sea of Slaughter* were reprinted in *SA* (216–24). AP discusses Mowat and Ingstad, the Norwegian explorer, whom he met, in *RBS* (238–39).

303. Joe Rosenblatt (b. 1933): Canadian artist, poet (*The LSD Leacock*, 1966; *Poetry Hotel: Selected Poems 1963–1985*, 1985), and magazine editor (*Jewish Dialogue*, 1970–83).

304. Robert Daigneault illustrated *The LSD Leacock*. Alison: Alison Hunt, whom EB had met in Toronto in 1965 and with whom he had an affair that lasted until 1969. The poem "i think you are a whole city," collected in *Rag & Bone Shop* (1971), was written for Hunt. *Last Makings* (1991) contains two other poems written for her: "there are delicacies" and "i should have begun with your toes," included with "i think you are a whole city" in the sequence "Three for Alison." Hunt (b. 1930 in London, according to the *curriculum vitae* included in EB's papers) was a graduate student in English at the University of Toronto and worked as a schoolteacher.

305. Gwendolyn MacEwen (1941–87): Celebrated Canadian poet (*The Shadow-Maker*, 1969; *Afterworlds*, 1987) and novelist. Her "big Egyptian" lover's name was Salah. Her "Letter to an Old Lover," a poem in *Afterworlds*, is addressed to him.

306. Victor Coleman (b. 1944): Printer and editor at Coach House Press, and a central figure in Toronto's avant-garde literary world.

Got a note from Klarika saying she was on her way hitching to Vancouver. However the letter was postmarked New York City??

Joe's bk I forgot to say looks really good & apparently they shot all the dough on it so tho it sells for 2.50 Joe gets nothing. The [*Workers*] *Vanguard* boys started selling it for 3 bucks till Joe found out but they didn't offer him the extra fifty cents. I suppose Dowson figures Joe is now a capitalist enemy to be exploited.[307]

Enjoying ostensible bachelorhood while Esther is in Vanc. The flat is so virgin-white & carpeted & clean I have lapses of nostalgia for the old pad it once was. Also nostalgic for the old rental.

All these young girls you find who've never been home to their villages for 3 yrs. I'd like to be along helping them find the way. What you wrote reminded me of the summer I lived on a pre-revolutionary farm on Sourdough Mt N.J. & the old man on the next farm hadn't been to NYC (60 miles away) he told me "since Buffalo Bill was there." Appears Buff. B. took his Wild West show there as late as 1910 or so or maybe earlier (it was '38 when I was in N.J.). What capped it was that his wife, still alive, & born on the mt. had *never* seen NYC. (& probably never did. & maybe is still alive in consequence.)

I'm sweatin over these Imp Tobac briefs.[308] What a bunch of boring kooks want to write Orwellian novels. One guy thinks Montreal will be destroyed by earthquake in 1975 unless they blast away in other regions with atomic explosions to take the pressure off.

I'm seeing only 80 screened from over a thousand. Can't imagine how bad the other 920+ must be.

Also busy with letters & trying to sell my hunk of Bowen Is. & I've lost the bloody subdivision maps somewhere & can't make a deal until I find them or pay a surveyor to do the job all over.

Toronto is dull this month. But pleasant under the trees. Hope you'll come back thisaway before launching off for Guatemala or wherever. How long do you think you'll stand Nfld?

Cheers. & love to that fine cook & patient lady Eurithe.

Earle

---

307. Ross Dowson (1917–2002): Canadian Trotskyist leader who ran in several mayoral elections in Toronto. He was an editor of *The Workers Vanguard*.

308. EB was judging a Centennial writing contest sponsored by Imperial Tobacco.

To Purdy (Ameliasburgh) from Birney (Toronto)
September 12, 1966   TL

Dear Al

Welcome back to Canada & esp Upper C. Maybe you'll stop off in Ameliasburg long enough to read yr mail. But hope to see you soon here with or without skreech.

Story I heard about Acorn's pants was he cut off the bottoms jagged-like so they wd look like proletarian ones. But they still looked new.

So you're vetting your entry into *Cdn Who's Who*. They're on the level & right about their competitors, who are merely biographical racketeers. After *Cdn Who's Who* comes *Authors & Writers Yearbk*, *Who's Who in Ontario*, *Who's Who in Ameliasburg*. You gonna be fillin out them forms for years now.

That was a loaded & cryptical Delphi of a sentence you dropped about Woodcock's review of me.[309] Huh?

Hope the news about Nowlan is better than you first heard.[310]

Looking forward to seeing you both soon. Hope to be out from under a half-dozen deadlines in a few days. & will be ready to throw a party.

Earle

Liked yr "Correspondence." Wish I'd something to send in return but too busy with files & other crap.

To Purdy (Ameliasburgh) from Birney (Toronto)
October 4, 1966   APC

Dear Al,

Hope you had good trip back & will be here again soon. I checked my Purdy Goldhord. I found I have only *The Blur in Between* & *Cariboo Horses*. What have I got of mine you haven't? *From the Earle's Court*? *Prism* 4:2, 3, 4, & 5:3–4? [*Near*]

---

309. George Woodcock (1912–95): Poet (*Collected Poems*, 1983), literary critic, anarchist intellectual (*Anarchism: A History of Libertarian Ideas and Movements*, 1962), professor of English at UBC (beginning in 1955), and first editor of the critical journal *Canadian Literature* (1959). Born in Winnipeg but raised in Britain, Woodcock returned to Canada after the Second World War, by which time he was already a distinguished man of letters. He was a powerful presence in the Canadian literary world, and a friend to EB and AP.

310. Alden Nowlan (1933–83): Canadian poet (*An Exchange of Gifts: Poems New and Selected*, 1985), playwright, and writer of stories (*Miracle at Indian River*, 1968) and memoirs. Born in Nova Scotia, he was writer-in-residence at the University of New Brunswick from 1968 to 1983.

False Creek Mouth, hard & soft? 1966 nail-clippings? Wd. have got obscene if there'd been enough card. You like this old Jupiter?[311]

Love to Eurithe

Earle

Earle Birney
Draft Letter, "Re Application by Mr. Al Purdy for Guggenheim Memorial Foundation Fellowship"
November 28, 1966   CTS

I have known Al Purdy's poetry for most of the 20 years in which he has been writing it. It has been both an astonishment and a joy to watch the way in which he has shot into virtual leadership among Canadian poets in the last three years. There was always great promise, but his early work was very uneven and not well focussed in aim. Now he has found his own unique voice, and it has been heard both from platforms from one end of this country to the other and from the pages of his books and from journals both experimental and established. The best of his poetry to date is in *The Caribou Horses* [*sic*] but even better work is now appearing in journals and will shortly appear as a collection, *North of Summer.* These poems are the only good, authentic ones ever written about the Canadian Arctic, except by Eskimaux. They are also, apart from their subject matter, poems of remarkable vigor, originality and humour.

No Canadian poet has ranged his country as widely as Purdy, both in respect to landscape and to the human topography. Moreover his interest in the living forces of the past, in relation to the present, is as probing and poetically effective as is his attention to what is new or predictive.

The fact that Purdy is a "high school drop-out" has (given his personality) operated in his favour as a developing writer. He has continued to share the lives and work of the non-academic majority, while reading enormously and thoughtfully in an effort to ensure that he has caught up with his literary heritage.

He is a man of unflagging energy, habitually somewhat restless and roving, but he has the ability to concentrate his considerable powers on any literary project he takes up and a single-minded persistence in carrying it through.

I have the greatest confidence that the project he has outlined to your Foundation is a sensible one in relation to his experience and character. The remarkable quality of the poems he managed to write under very difficult circumstances in Baffinland last summer is evidence that Purdy is in fact challenged

---

311. The postcard shows a marble head ("Tête de Jupiter Serapis") from the Musée de la Maison Carrée, Nîmes.

and stimulated by conditions of hardship and by strange and even unpromising environments. In the Arctic he had only a few weeks to live in genuinely Eskimo conditions, since so much of his time was taken up in waiting for transportation beyond the usual "civilized" landing places. This summer, in northern Newfoundland, Purdy had a better chance to combine his interest in travel and his desire to understand himself by understanding other peoples and other ways of living. His latest poems confirm the value of such experiences in his development as a poet. In Newfoundland, also, Purdy visited the new Viking sites and got to know the archaeologists in the field there. This has quickened a natural desire to live for a while in a country such as Greece where the evidences of the past are richer and the conditions of [?] living more stimulating. Characteristically he is already reading widely to acquire a background of information on Eastern Mediterranean history and archaeology. I have no doubt therefore that if he gets to Greece he will write many good poems. They will be, as they should be, poems about Purdy and his Canadian identity as much as about the Classic past or about travelling in a country new to him. In short, wherever Purdy wanted to go, I believe that the cause of English-language poetry would be furthered by any foundation which gave him the money to buy the time to go. I very much hope that your Foundation will agree with me.

Earle Birney, Ph.D.
Writer-in-Residence, The University of Toronto
Massey College

To Birney (Toronto) from Purdy (Ameliasburgh)
December 25, 1966   TL

Dear Earle,

Helluva day for you to be stuffed up with a cold — However, you'll probably be over it by the time you get this missive —

Letter from Walter Herbert, director Canada Foundation, saying thanks for judgments on applications, one sentence making me a bit uneasy: "You will be interested in knowing that your assessments are very shrewdly 'in line' with the scores reported by our more experienced judges." The subjects of the judgments were newspaper writers and two old pros. However, I don't necessarily want to be "in line" with more experienced assessors. He adds "— we will be sending you applications from the younger group of writers, and you may find these more interesting."

Joe Rosenblatt showed up at hotel room, with the highly original idea of going to interior of B.C. to write poems. (You may recall I was there myself in

'60.) I mean under the aegis of a CC [Canada Council] fellowship for Joe. I told him I thought the thing to do in his application (next fall) was try to relate his poems already written with the suggested program, i.e. in his case move away from the abstract (butterflies etc) to the human — It being pretty obvious that there is no basis of progression and interest moving from one area of the human condition to another (except in his "working" poems), it might be a good thing to use and take advantage of this, to me, very obvious point — Also said Birney would have some ideas on all this and Joe should see him. And to get a general book on B.C. and read the thing, since he obviously knows little of the province. But I think Joe might write some very good poems if he got to the right place, whether in B.C. or wherever — Butterflies and eggs being a dead end as far as I'm concerned.

I enclose the piece I read over the phone. It has some pretty obvious shortcomings. The most obvious being: I don't like the poem's viewpoint much. The old tired man is talking about his youth. Also, the facetious element of "praying to / Allah there is no god but Allah Purdy" fucks it up slightly.[312] Besides which it's a goddam exaggeration, since I'm not quite so dead as all that. Still, writing that sort of thing makes me realize the necessity of movement and life etc. i.e. fellowships. The retrospective immediate being okay, but not going back all that far as if it were the only weapon (subject) in your arsenal or repertoire.

I am still working on the North Hastings County poem I mentioned. Have three lines in it which thicken and distract at the wrong time.

Best,

Al

To Purdy (Ameliasburgh) from Birney (Toronto)
April 27, 1967   TL

Dear Al,

Bleeding income tax finagled at last, now I can get down to important things, like Al Purdy. Tried to phone you today but was told by op. your phone was "discontinued at subscriber's request." Well, at least it wasn't at request of neighbours, Mounties, or/c. Just wanted to assure you, fast-like, the letter of reference had gone off to Waterloo, enshrining faithfully yr phrasing (except where I expanded it to cover things your modesty had not thought worth giving). I even kept the spelling

---

312. "Notes on a Fictional Character" was included in *Poems for All the Annettes* (1968). (In that book the poem was given the date of composition of 1964.) In the published version of the poem, AP's middle initial was included in the line (and the joke): "Allah / W. Purdy" (*BR* 133).

132

"Ameliasburgh," since it's plainly what you wrote, and you ought to know — but dammit I'd always thot it was "Ameliasburg" and so spelled it in that pome about yr place ["In Purdy's Ameliasburg"].

Feel guilty never answering yrs of last week enclosing yr noble defense of me before the bar of *Tamarack*.[313] Like the irony, most of the time, but it's a tricky weapon & I just wonder if it mightn't be better to drop the last sentence of your second para ("His poems were also dealt with") and maybe the whole of the last para., which, though it "rounds out" your letter, says little you haven't already said. Para 5 should begin (strictly speaking) "Hitherto Canadian poets and other Canadians of a ..."

Seems niggling of me to look such a loyal supporting letter in the horse's mouth, but you did ask me to "comment," & that's why I suggest these tiny changes (tho maybe dropping the last para. isn't so tiny a change). It is good of you, Al, to take time to bother about this guy [Hayden] Carruth, & I appreciate it. I also miss you, & wish I cd at least call you up on the phone. What's new? I don't know nothin.

Cheers & love from us both to you both

Earle

Alfred Purdy
Letter to the Editor, *The Tamarack Review* (1967)[314]

I'd like to commend *Tamarack* for its review of Earle Birney's *Selected Poems* in issue No. 42. I think it was an excellent idea to have a non-poet do the review.[315]

The important business of using spaces instead of punctuation in poems was treated with admirable brevity in a page and a half. The reader is also furnished with a definitive list of first lines from great poems as an illustration of the "objective correlative" and the "functionally revaluative language of coterminous mythopoeic commitment" which Birney has not got.

---

313. AP's "noble defense" in *The Tamarack Review* follows this letter.

314. First published in *The Tamarack Review* 43 (Spring 1967): 100.

315. The review (Winter 1967) was written by Hayden Carruth (1921–2008), a distinguished American poet (*Toward the Distant Islands: New and Selected Poems*, 2006), anthologist, editor, and critic. It was highly critical. Its opening sentence gives a sense of the tone throughout: "Normally when a reviewer is confronted by a book he does not like, but whose author is nevertheless a distinguished elder of the tribe, he is inclined to say nothing about it — in one thousand nice, ripe nothing-words." Carruth proceeded to observe that "The case of Mr. Earle Birney forces us, however, to take a harder view of our obligation." AP's letter was followed by one from Joe Rosenblatt, who also rose to EB's defence: "I have never read such a sniping review of a poet's work! It seems to have been written by a small-minded Yankee pedant and grammarian." AP's library included *The Voice That Is Great within Us: American Poetry of the Twentieth Century* (1970), an anthology edited by Carruth.

I am grateful to Hayden Carruth for pointing out the delicate shades of differ-ence between Birney being called the dean of Canadian poetry by "common consent" and T.S. Eliot as "the serious leader 'elected' by a serious society." I'm sure that in the great and serious democracy of America an elective office is more significant than common consent.

But the review's most valuable contribution comes in mentioning a poem called "Wendigo" ["Windigo," by George Bowering] (first published in *Tamarack* [Autumn 1965]): "that seemed at first, to us in the United States, just what we are looking for from Canada: fresh, clear, and natural in its formal elements, distinc-tively Canadian in its thematic elements."

Hitherto Canadian poets and other Canadians of a dissident nature have been rather in the dark as to what was required of them by the United States. There has even been some degree of cynicism in the matter, which Hayden Carruth has most happily disspelled. In a prose message at once logical and inspiring he tells us that what is required is good poems, "fresh, clear, and natural" that are "distinctively Canadian." Thanks to Hayden Carruth there is no longer any evading this ringing clarion call for the Canadian beaver, Canadian maple leaves and sugar, Winnipeg gold-eye, fiddleheads, wendigos (northern spirits), ookpiks, baked apples, Arctic char, and Quebec separatists. The formal and thematic elements of these, allied of course to the objective correlative and the functionally revaluative coterminous commitment, should ensure that great poetry is available for export in sufficient quantity. Of course this might affect stock market quotations on other exports, such as oil, iron, newsprint, and napalm; but it is a risk true Canadian poets will have to take.[316]

Alfred Purdy

To Purdy (Ameliasburgh) from Birney (Toronto)
May 3, 1967   APC

Al & Eu

"Isn't it strange how evil is never believable on canvas?" Or is this the excep-tion, where the "cause" shows too (in the masochistic Christ-face, inviting the crucifiers)?[317]

Have straightened out the difference between Al A. & Alfred W.

Can't come down this weekend because we have a lit. party for [illegible]

---

316. Cf. Dennis Lee's *Civil Elegies* (1968, rev. ed. 1972): "we will carry the napalm for our side, proud of our clean hands."

317. The postcard is illustrated by a reproduction of Hieronymus Bosch's *Christ Mocked (The Crowning with Thorns)*. EB's quotations were references to AP's "Notes on Painting," from *The Cariboo Horses* (1965).

(hiking thru from Vancouver) but will count on M&S [illegible] unless you hear contrariwise soon. Good to have yr phone # now.

Loved yr. *Digest* clip, Eurithe.

If you happen to be coming up to Toronto this weekend, then remember to come to our party Sat.

Love & soon-seeings
Earle

To Purdy (Ameliasburgh) from Birney (Toronto)
May 1967   TL

Dear Al

Glad to know you're both coming up next week & hope we can get together. You don't say anything in yr letter about our coming down on the 13th for the weekend. Maybe it's not convenient for you. Anyway we can talk about that when you come up.

As for the *Tamarack* affair, I'm rather sick of it all. In fact I wouldn't have bothered giving advice on yr letter if I'd thought Colombo would lay down the law, & cut out most of it. If you, & the other writers hereabouts, really stood up to this prick he wouldn't continue getting away with murder. But eastern writers are really hung up on the sacred *Tamarack*. They couldn't bear the thought of never getting into it, or offending whoever is running it. The fact is it's never been a good mag, a really good one, esp. considering all the public funds pumped into it (largely, I gather, for Colombo's salary!!). Certainly I'll never contribute or submit to it again. Since Colombo turned down a better-written review, from another & better American poet than Carruth, which he could have run along with Carruth's, for free — turned it down even after he had told *me* that he wouldn't publish Carruth's review if he could get a more favorable one from an American. The reality is that Colombo will maneuver & contrive to put down anybody that's up, if he can do it without harm to himself. Eventually he'll do it to you and all the rest of you here in the east, however much you go along with him now. I'll be writing & telling him this — once I can get the Poetry League files out of his greedy little paws (he's hanging on to them on the excuse of sending out the letters he long ago promised us to send out, and never has) — but I have no expectation he'll publish a word of any protest of mine. Joe [Rosenblatt] has sent in a letter too, I think, which I'll lay two to one will never see the light of *Tamarack*.

Unfortunately Colombo has been sitting, for 1½ years now, on a review he commissioned me to do of Walcott's poetry — since then another book of Walcott's has come out! — I'm trying to get my review back, as it will look silly appearing now, & in any case I don't want to appear anymore to be collaborating with *Tamaretch*.[318] But I can't get it back from Colombo (he promises to return it but doesn't).

Shit I'm really browned off tonight with the Cdn literary life! Forgive me — nothing personal — I'm grateful to you for trying to crack the Colombo front — but he's too cunning for all of us — see you!

Earle

To Purdy (Ameliasburgh) from Birney (Toronto)[319]
June 4, 1967   APC

Hey I saw you both @ the Country Club & never got thru the crowd until you'd disappeared (or I had — I left early — couldn't stand it).

Hope you & [illegible] worked out something good. When are you coming to Toronto again? I'll be here till June 30. Liked "Detail."[320] Your anthol. sounds much better now. Must send you something.

Is your Commonwealth anthol. out yet?[321]

Earle

To Birney (Waterloo or Toronto) from Purdy (Ameliasburgh)
July 11, 1967   TL[322]

Dear Earle,

Nothing much to say. Just got back from Trenton last night, after having meant to sleep there, but too damn hot. And how's that for inconsequential yak —

Have been writing poems pretty plentifully here in the last few weeks, but don't have a very high opinion of what I've written. I suppose I channel what vitality I have into poems, which means that I'm not doing things that provide more grist — Of course not doing things is money too, for I'd be in Greece or Rhodesia if I'd got that Gug. Add gossip: Colombo says in a note that Atwood got

---

318. EB probably meant Derek Walcott (b. 1930), whose *Selected Poems* (1964) and *The Castaway and Other Poems* (1965) had been published in recent years, but he misspelled "Walcott" in two ways ("Wilcott," "Wolcott").

319. EB addressed the postcard to "Al & Eurithe Purdy (Patrons, Hotel Purdy)."

320. "Detail" was published in *Wild Grape Wine* (1968).

321. Although he wrote "anthol.," EB probably meant "essay" (or a similar term), with "Commonwealth" referring to the *Journal of Commonwealth Literature*. (See AP's letter of 22 Sept. 1967.)

322. *YA* 118–19. The letter is dated 1966 in *YA*, but the contents of the letter suggest the later date. The postcard of 15 July 1967 was postmarked in Toronto, but the postcard of 4 June 1967 suggests that EB was in Toronto only until the end of June. It is not clear to me to which city AP sent the letter of 11 July.

the Centennial poem contest, but that [he] received honourable mention.[323] He ends the sentence with an exclamation mark.

I suppose what I'm writing is more or less passable, but I think either you or myself would want to feel when we write the sort of lift and air bubbles in the veins that make it worth while — Incidentally, I took your suggestion re the Nor/west Passage poem,[324] and interjected three quatrains with the third line of four stresses having a double rhyme. However, I don't think that does it either. Came across some good prose by John Ross, the old captain (1777–1856) who commented:

> "— let them remember that ice is stone
> a floating rock in the stream —"

It's not verse but it oughta be.[325]

Also by Ross:

> The Eskimos
> "— being informed
> that we were Europeans
> they answered
> that they were men —"

Of course Ross finishes the last word of that quote by adding "Innuit" [sic] after, but it's better without.

I think I'll give the poem (Passage poem) one more try, with a different rhyme scheme in the middle, I should say different metric scheme, because I don't care whether it rhymes. Point about it is: if I could get one good thought in any damn rhythm at all, then I think I could carry that on thru — But jesus, it has to come out of my blank blank mind!

Have you heard of what Doug Jones calls a Frank Scott "love-in" later in the year?[326] Almost sounds like a free whorehouse.

---

323. Atwood's *The Animals in That Country* (1968; it had not yet been published) won the Centennial Commission Poetry Competition in 1967.

324. AP wrote two poems called "The North West Passage," the first published in *North of Summer: Poems from Baffin Island* (and retained in *BR* [97–99]) and the other published in *Wild Grape Wine*. The "North West Passage" in *Wild Grape Wine* takes for an epigraph the lines written by John Ross that AP quoted in this letter: "— let them remember that ice is stone / a floating rock in the stream —." In the poem AP writes of "Ross frozen fast in the Arctic / ice four winters."

325. John Ross (1777–1856): Scottish explorer who led three naval expeditions to the Arctic, the third of which (1850) was an unsuccessful attempt to locate the expedition of John Franklin (1786–1847).

326. D.G. (Doug) Jones (b. 1929): Canadian poet (*Under the Thunder the Flowers Light up the Earth*,

I'm beginning to feel exiled here, cut-off, trapped by wholesome woman-hood in the shape of my wife. She probably feels the same with the proviso, male. The currents of life are elsewhere from me right now, tho I hope to locate them again, or what I think they are for me. In the meantime I type here with Eurithe in the other room looking at a crappy tv movie. Last night tho, we saw *Who's Afraid of V. Woolf,* which was not crappy.[327] All Eurithe's brothers, sisters, relatives of any kind, didn't like it, so I was almost sure it would be good. How's that for snobbishness? But god, something to see the snarling snappy stuff of a bad marriage whipping into your eyeballs like healthy poison — If I didn't think such plays a dead end I'd think Albee was the next Williams or Miller.[328]

When you have some idle time let me know what's goin on —

Best,

Al

To Purdy (Ameliasburgh) from Birney (Toronto)
July 15, 1967   APC

Al —

It ain't Pang [Pangnirtung] — something standing more on end — more Arctic for Conqueror Purdy — be patient with me, I have a long letter to write you & no time yet at all — got yr good letter of 11th, & earlier note.[329] AND THE BOOK which I am enjoying all over again really, more than ever.

Esther flew to Mtrl, saw Expo for 2 days, then to S Francisco — she'll be in Calif. till Sep., it seems, staying on for Bill's wedding.

Cheers, love, peace.

Earle

Thanx for good words on fly — remember that verse for next book!

E

1977), critic (*Butterfly on Rock: A Study of Themes and Images in Canadian Literature,* 1970), translator of Québécois poetry, and professor. Scott's *Selected Poems* was published in 1966.

327. *Who's Afraid of Virginia Woolf* (1962), by Edward Albee (b. 1928). The film adaptation was released in June 1966.

328. Tennessee Williams (1911–83) and Arthur Miller (1915–2005): American playwrights. Williams is probably best known for *The Glass Menagerie* (1944) and *A Streetcar Named Desire* (1947), Miller for *Death of a Salesman* (1949) and *The Crucible* (1953).

329. The postcard shows mountains — "something standing more on end" — in Alaska.

To Birney (Waterloo) from Purdy (Ameliasburgh)
July 21, 1967   TL

Dear Earle:

Received your card, for which thanks. I guess you're pretty busy with summer school these days.

I enclose a letter written to Peter Dwyer at the Canada Council, asking if any help can be given Joe Rosenblatt.[330] I got a letter from Joe recently in which he sounded pretty desperate, no job, no money, not writing. I hope C.C. can do something for him.

Also, the goddam Belleville income tax office has refused to regard the sale of manuscripts as capital gains. According to Harrison, the tax consultant, this Belleville taxation office is one of the tougher such offices in the country. In connection with this, perhaps I might profit by your own example re. income tax returns. Harrison wants to get examples of other people who've sold manuscripts. This of course without using names of anyone. Therefore I'd like to ask some questions, which I'll also ask Newlove, who sold his manuscripts earlier. Did you have any discussion with the tax dept. as to the taxability of the money realized by the sale?? Was the sale reported? If so, was it listed as capital gains?

That's what Harrison did with my sale, listed it as capital gains. And since it will be a thousand buck bite at my backside I don't like the situation. Do you think I should buy a shotgun and hold off the tax dept. with imprecations and buckshot?

I shall be seeing you at Expo in Sept., I notice by the news report Guy Sylvestre sent to me.[331] But hope earlier than that. I am not [i.e., now] all fucked up, immersed, half-drowned by the school antho for Ryerson.[332] Dick Lunn has done precisely and exactly nothing, so I am left with the whole thing. So that, along with the U.S. antho., leaves me feeling very put-upon, not to say persecuted, prosecuted etc., if not yet convicted of anything.

Best,

Al

---

330. Peter Dwyer (1914–73): A former British spy, Dwyer held various posts, including that of director, in the Canada Council. AP dedicated *Piling Blood* (1984) "To the memory of Peter Dwyer."

331. Jean-Guy Sylvestre (1918–2010): Canadian critic, anthologist (*Anthologie de la poésie canadienne d'expression française*, 1943), and National Librarian from 1968 to 1983.

332. The "school antho" was published in 1969 as *Fifteen Winds: A Selection of Modern Canadian Poems*.

To Purdy (Ameliasburgh) from Birney (Waterloo)
July 26, 1967   TL

Dear Al

I think it was a good idea for you to write Dwyer about Joe. Provided Joe doesn't repudiate you. And me. Since I've taken a leaf from yr book & written Dwyer. In my note I reminded Peter D. that he knew Joe's work from *The LSD Leacock* (which I passed around at the art advisory panel meeting when I was plugging for a grant for the Coach Hse [Coach House Press]) & I told Peter about Joe's hard luck with his search for welding jobs. I didn't go along with the idea that the interior of B.C. was necessarily going to be any help to Joe. Joe's much more a home-body than you & inclined to get panicky away from friends & familiar environment. After all you can get turned on by a couple of ice-floes but Joe needs a couple of miles of predictable pavement under him I suspect. I think Kitsilano might work, for a while. However Joe will or shd make his own mind up abt *where* he goes. But as to *when* that may be never unless he gets prodded enough. & I think yr letter to Peter may start the ball rolling.

I also put in a hurried plug for *Evidence* & Bevan & will send a longer letter when I've had time to correspond further about it with Al B. himself.[333]

This has been CC week indeed as I've also written letters in support of David Harris & his Fleye Press, & in support of the W.W.E. Ross *Coll. Poems* project of Longmans, & against the proposal of *Artscanada* to milk the Council for vast sums &c.[334]

All this plus a hell of a lot of other accumulated letters-to-answer has left me little time for writing the letters I enjoy writing. Like to you. & even now as I tap away in the office I have guilt feelings as I'm supposed to prepare a complete program of my lecture activities at Waterloo this winter, for my boss now. Ho hum.

The U of WO [University of Western Ontario], London, Ont., want me to read my pomes there the nite of Sun Sep 24. To share platform with Len Cohen.[335] They asked me if I wd share with Layton, if Cohen cdnt make it. I said, of course, yes but added that if Cohen didn't accept why not ask you. I gave yr address. There's probably $400 & expenses in it so I hope they do ask you.

I also gave yr address to Sylvan Karchmer, acting ed. of *Northwest Rev*, U. of

---

333. *Evidence* (1960–67) was a small Toronto-based magazine edited by Alan Bevan and others.

334. David W. Harris (1948–94): Canadian poet, known as David UU, associated with the experimentalism of bill bissett and bpNichol. W.W.E. Ross (1894–1966): A significant but somewhat obscure Canadian modernist poet. The "project" to which EB referred came to fruition as *Shapes & Sounds: Poems of W.W.E. Ross* (1968).

335. Leonard Cohen (b. 1934): Canadian poet (*Let Us Compare Mythologies*, 1956; *The Spice-Box of Earth*, 1961), novelist (*Beautiful Losers*, 1966), and singer and songwriter.

Ore., who wants to get bk revws of Cdn ptry for his mag. They pay a little. He wanted me to do some but I don't want to.

I looked up Nelson Ball the other night.[336] Nice kid with nice young wife (or maybe just girlfriend) Barbara Caruso (she has the best stuff in the current *Weed* I think).[337] They are moving to Toronto in Sep. Fed-up with isolation of Kitchener. Doesn't seem to be another soul poetically inclined, at least in his direction, for 60 miles around. Barbara asked me to come & meet her father so he cd see that there are *old* poets too. Her father thinks being a poet is just something some kids have to grow out of. I can't say that her request made me feel young & gay again but Nelson had already softened her blow to my vanity by mistaking me, in the gloom of the doorway, for Al Purdy. I said the resemblance was remarkable, of course, & probably due to my pure life, on the one hand, & yr aged-in-the-wild-grape sort of existence. I'm sure you agree.

Yr letter of July 11 says "add gossip: Colombo says in a note that Atwood got the Centennial poem contest but that received honourable mention." I have been brooding over this sentence periodically which doesn't seem to pinpoint the gossip in the way I like to have it. Is there some Contest of Contests, in which the Centennial poem contest got an honourable mention? Or is there a word, not to say a key word, left out after "that"? Who, then? My imagination is titillated. But then I don't know who was writing "Centennial" poems. You? Miriam Waddington? Please drop that other word so I can go to sleep.

Also tell me more about the GREAT SCOTT LOVE-IN about which I have been kept brutally in the dark.

Yr last letter (July 21) has the disquieting news about yr goddam Belleville tax office. I'm afraid to give info. about my own returns to a lawyer. Is Harrison a good friend of yrs? Can you trust him? He may furnish names, to make his point, & the result wd be the Inc Tax wd be down & into me for several grand.

However, strictly between you & me, I never asked for ruling or got one from the tax boys on the classificn of my book/mss sales but I did do a lot of rdg of fine print in the tax manuals & decided that selling old mss was like treasure trove or like worthless-old-postage-stamps-become-rare. *No* one reports that sort of thing surely! Anyway I didn't once I was advised how to report my inc. tax over the rental & later the sale of a house, & in the process learned that any appreciation of land value is not taxable. So why not of book/mss value? These accruements don't come as a result of my own activity either vocationally or avocationally. They are pieces of good luck (in the middle of a

---

336. Nelson Ball (b. 1942): Canadian poet, bookseller, and small-press publisher (Weed/Flower Press).

337. Barbara Caruso (1937–2009): Canadian painter.

lot of bad, also not accountable. I don't get a rebate from the tax boys when I fail to write a book).

Hope you can revive Dick Lunn to help with the anthol. Too bad if you were to get so involved in anthos, revs., etc that you had to turn off that good flow of poems. That's what's important. As you well know.

I think "The North West Passage" is greatly improved ... love that image of Parry's bottle-cork ship.

Some monotony of structure & language e.g. "Martin Fro ... finding ...

> And Luke Foxe who ...
> he turned back
> having found ...
> And John Ross ...
> And Parry who ...
> Belcher who
> John Franklin ...
> who ...
> And George Back who ...
> turned home
>
> ... what they were looking for
> might have been found elsewhere ...
> what they were searching for ...
> and open water appeared.
> And on expeditions ...
> that reappear

In general I think you overwork "but" and the loose participial construction. I say this knowing that these are devices you use consciously or unconsciously to create a part of the magic, the informality-yet-singing quality of your work which I very much admire. It's just that you mustn't get into parodying yourself, as you occasionally do, formally, that is, here.

Sec. ii has excellent build-up from the map-images, nautical words, then the bull skull & carvings, & the silences & the bosn.

Sec. iii. The switch of metre is abrupt but I think you carry it off. Though I'd like to see you maintain more of the duality of effect you get from the first two lines of sec. iii — those lines are invaluable as they set up a "voice" which is the historical composite of all sailors-seeking-the-passage — in the rest of the sec. it seems to be only the voice of the *early* sailors & so begins to take on a somewhat

Ancient Mariner tone — whereas one wants to hear a voice that might as easily come from the *St. Roch* as from the *Erebus* — (the difficulty is that yr metre *is* so close to Coleridge's).

Sec. iv. "ice mountains" you overwork — twice in sec. 2, twice again here, no 3 times.

The mythopoeic quality is good in "like cleaning stables" etc. But I'm a little troubled by the accuracy of the image in "booted out of the club sit drinking / whiskey sours in the back room." Back room of what? Of the club? You get booted out of a club you don't come back into any room of it. Sounds like a confusion between a club & a pub, as in the latter you cd be kicked out of the "saloon" or gentlemen's section & have to sit in the "ordinary."

Geez this is too long a letter. Sorry.

I'll be in Toronto briefly this weekend. If you are up phone me at Alison's or the Allens', as both will know where I am, if I am anywhere.[338]

Had a good weekend last week. Went swimming in a waterfall up near the Bruce Peninsula.

Miss you. When are you coming down here? No chance of a poetry reading for you till October, however — but maybe Western will ask you for that Sept. deal. Hope so.

Cheers. Love to Eurithe.

Earle

To Birney (Waterloo) from Purdy (Ameliasburgh)
July 27, 1967　TL

Dear Earle,

Re Joe, sure anything he likes, tho I don't think Vancouver good, because Acorn is a goddam depressing influence on Joe as he admits. Had a letter from him (Joe) saying good about the idea — But you could be right about Joe and the city, tho I deny me and the ice floes, and think you yourself are parodying the idea of Purdy on the ice floes etc., which is fine as a myth if it brings in a few bucks. Smith sends me a card with Eskimos and sleighs on it saying it reminds him of me. And one or two others done the same thing. Of course this is an old idea, our friends pick us up mentally by using the salient characteristic as a handle.

Jumping now to Colombo — I had the same letter earlier mentioning he got honourable mention. I'm not sure what he's talking about either. I know there was

---

338. Robert Greer Allen (1917–2005): Playwright and television and radio producer for the CBC. Rita Greer Allen (1918–2010): Broadcaster, writer, and artist. EB's *Trial of a City and Other Verse* (1952) is dedicated to "Bob and Rita."

a contest of some sort earlier for a book, and I ought to have entered it really, because I had enough poems even then for another book, but I didn't like a damn fool. I suppose this is what Atwood won — Or is it for just one poem? Colombo always does that in anything he writes or wins — mentions it in a letter. In correspondence over this Tammy tell me true antho [*sic*], Colombo says he just sold twelve poems to Trent Univ's *Mag* [*Journal*] *of Canadian Studies*, or a name nearly like that. Found poems of things well-known Canadians have said. One of them being (he says) about the John Macdonald quote I used in one of my Arctic poems. I didn't use it in an Arctic poem at all, tho it may be a misquote as he says.[339] Anyhow, I wonder if this is a form of oneupmanship Colombo employs, because he does it in nearly every letter or note of any kind. He does it with you too, which means that he regards you as a father image no doubt, tho I'd failed to see the incipient relationship before. He will no doubt ask your advice on his next mistress. In that regard, he had a girl friend in London, and as a matter of curiosity I asked him the difference between how he felt about this girl and how he felt about his wife. As I remember he said that the London girl was an affair of the flesh, i.e. profane, whereas his wife was true love, i.e. sacred. I didn't laugh at the time, but thought how fortunate he was to be able to separate the two clichés so easily.

And this is confidential absolutely, I have it on the best authority whose source I can't mention, that Colombo traded his way into a certain anthology in exchange for using the antho ed's poems in *Tamarack*. You might guess who all the various other people involved are if you think about it a little, including who told me. What gets me is I go on talking to the guy. I met him by chance in Toronto a while back and he said he was now the ed. of my book. I said could he get me 20 odd copies of it as [Len?] Cummings had said he would, since I needed em for personal distribution. He said he'd try. And the next thing he said was what about the antho of stuff about the U.S. I was doin. The implication was plain as hell. The same exchange method was about to be used on me. As it happens I may be short of material if guys like Birney don't kick in, and may have to use Colombo. I've got some good stuff from among others, Souster, Nowlan, Atwood, Newlove, C.J. Newman (a killer) and promises from others.[340] How about Birney?

So okay, I guess I can't use your bit with tax. div. of not reporting it, on accounta the damn accountant already did and I'm in the soup. (Why oh why didn't I send in a manuscript for that goddam Centennial contest?) Unless this guy comes up with something good I'm out a thousand bucks and I don't like it.

---

339. From "Canadian," published in *Wild Grape Wine* (1968): "old John A. looking thirsty / not having had a drink for 75 years / and his immortal quote / 'an Englishman I was born and ...'"

340. C.J. Newman (b. 1935): Canadian novelist (*A Russian Novel*, 1973).

I would think I could trust this accountant Harrison, but then one can't be absolutely sure, so will leave any mention of you out of it. The same thing is gonna come up over these tapes, and I'm gonna be doomed over those too on accounta the precedent with the worksheets. Fuckit tho, I'll make out my own damn forms. I'm not gonna lose there too, I just won't report the tapes as taxable income.

I could sure use that unlikely money from U. of W.O. Maybe I could take up the guitar and get a hairpiece? Learn a few songs Cohen wrote. Dance a few steps. But jesus, thanks for mentioning me to them, if they did come thru it would ease the tax bite a little. The anthos seem necessary to me, cause I'm not writin the best poems anyway, I don't seem to myself to be in any kind of groove, not breakin loose into anything, just repeatin myself in some way. Think I need outside stimulus, like that Gug woulda given me in Tiryns and Mycenae and Ottawa — but will apply CC and Gug this year — When I wrote my best stuff I knew or thought I was, now I retain perhaps the expertise (call it that) but not that final little opening door in the mind that circles around and binds the first half of a poem with the whole thing, doesn't homogenize it but makes the lumps palatable. I suppose what I'm really kickin about is I haven't made another break thru, which I did feel about [Poems for All the] Annettes and [The Cariboo] Horses. Of course the Arctic material was almost ready made for me, all I had to do was work on it. And I picked up the particular style I use now in other poems while writing the Arctic ones, and difficult to get loose again. I work like hell on poems, and the damn things seem unsatisfactory, not bad to me, but definitely unsatisfactory.

Here's the new part iii I wrote for Passage poem —

We came in steel ships and wooden ships of small tonnage
Bristol men mostly
green slime in the water butts and biscuits so weevilly [sic]
they crawled to us where we lay in our bunks

We were also Canadian and French French including the Scandinavian
and came to get away from one woman or find another
the press gangs found us drunk in waterfront taverns
or we listened soberlike while they talked away our freedom

And some of us still thought the world flat (it may have been)
and we'd drop over as a stone drops
over a cliff with a cry for God in heaven
to save our souls — but some scoffed at us

Sea unicorns came by and things with slack breasts like old women
our faces turned grey and the bone showed through
we didn't know why that was or believe what the officers said
about sin and prayed to Mary we might go home

Storms swept some of us over and others clung to the rails
blind things under the sea came and sucked us
into their arms and a darkness entered the ship through great holes
so that we mutined and cried to the captain
                                    TURN BACK you old bastard

We shall never go home we know that now
and have cursed God to Satan and said we'd broken His rules
and lied to God we'd been holy men and save us allow us
a few small sins scattered among the greedy port women
but the ice and cold was just too much punishment beggin His pardon
and we prayed to the God of Wisdom consent to the prayers of fools
We shall never go home

In the above as a loose scheme, I was tryin two non-stress to a stress, but not rigidly, so it wouldn't be too apparent. The rhymes are off and may be a coupla syllables back or after the end, and not match the previous rhymes — Anyway, this is where your suggestions get me — Worked on that most of the afternoon. It's there for the purpose of breaking up the rhythm of the main body of the poem, whether it succeeds in this. Also, it's there a little for its own sake I suppose, and I do like it better than the Coleridge metre. Incidentally I knew the other was somewhat Coleridgy, but didn't mind and aimed it that way slightly for obvious reasons. Besides it's damn easy to write metrical stuff, since I wrote Bliss Carman's poems for years that way. But it's not so easy when you start playin around with your metrics to make them do unforeseen things. Eventually, like Camembert cheese is it? — you're liable to have no metrics at all and no poem and nothin but holes in yr cheese. Will look at the other things later, and then revise this too. Who says a poet doesn't work? Your fault too.

The Scott love-in is at Keewaydin, and I get a note from Sheila, Doug Jones' new wife inviting me, say she didn't know if Doug told me but all poets are supposed to write a poem to be presented to Scott.[341] I said did she think I was a

---

341. Sheila Fischman (b. 1937): Canadian journalist and distinguished translator of Québécois literature.

short order cook and I only wrote poems for girls name of Sheila. Saturday. Word games next I guess. Maybe I get a little lonesome for people with these goddam anthos hangin over my head. No word from Lunn, so I shall ask Doug Jones since Birney is so busy. Re a collaborator, that is. Some real killer posters from Cuba, makes you wanta go bite LBJ.

Anyways, this is longern yours. I'd like to get down to Western, tho I tell myself I need somebody to pay me to do things for the sake of my ego or something — But that's not really true either. I will get down if you have any room there, but you likely have a small apt. I have a reading at Queen's Sept 16, and the Expo thing early, which you're at too accordin to the sheet I got. Maybe if the Birney/Layton reading is after Sep 16, I can get down for that. Keep it erect in the morning.

Best,
Al

To Purdy (Ameliasburgh) from Birney (Waterloo)
August 1, 1967   APC

Gad, sir, those were the wine-making days![342] Look at the size of those grapes, or are they loganberries, back in the year 1500! Note the sly boy on the right slipping his bunch of grapes to the little beauty. Thanx for yr marvelous big letter & drafts of Sec. III. The drafts get better & better. (Small question — why does the narrator suddenly start dropping his "g"s? Why not all along?) You are definitely getting away from the rhythmic monotony of your first draft ... This apt. is big enough, & I have a sleeping bag plus inflatable mattress as well as a bed, & a small living room as well as a bedroom. So come any time, Al, & happy to see you. (I'll be away Aug 4–8 however.) See you at Expo anyway if not before.

Hope you make up your own income tax after this, or you'll have all us bards ruined ... Problem with Joe R. is to get him to actually fill out & mail an application. As for Acorn, Joe volunteered that Milton was the one person he *wouldn't* look up. Hope he means it!

Home phone: (519) 576–5935

---

342. The postcard is a reproduction of a harvest scene — "Les Vendanges" — from a French tapestry ("Vers 1500"). EB did not sign the card.

To Birney (Waterloo) from Purdy (Ameliasburgh)
August 7, 1967　TL

Dear Earle,

Was in Toronto Thurs. and tried to phone you at Waterloo, but didn't have the card with your ph. no. Wanted to ask you down if you're finally thru teaching for the summer. The operator couldn't get the right number then, but perhaps this belated invite will serve. How about coming down till Esther gets back, wherever she is.

I am in Toronto again in ten days, where I have to autograph books at the Classics, and hope someone shows up to buy the books. Feeling a little down over even reading poems these days, what with these two anthos —

Re. Joe, if he's lazy about filling out the forms, I really don't know what more can be done for him, one can't guide his hand when he writes. Other people are still other people and, as you tell me now and then in Joe's case, one can't write their poems or live their lives. I used to feel similarly helpless about Acorn, as if he'd walk off a cliff sometime while smelling a flower. I get pretty absentminded myself at times, so I know what it's like. Haven't heard from Joe since I sent him the forms, but I don't see what else can be done.

I enclose a clipping from local paper which is lovely. I didn't know people could be like that — no, I guess I did, but just the same — I tried to write a poem and flopped, so wish the idea on you. I'm sure you can if you feel like it.

As I said, at the present time I'm sick to death of poems. Reading so many bad ones I don't think I can ever write one again till I get some physical action of some kind under my mental belt. Incidentally, that was an amusing bit about Nelson Ball and his wife wanting to show her in-laws an "old poet" — You never did strike me that way, you have too much physical verve to give that impression. Tom Marshall, Mike Ondaatje and Stuart someone were down last night with accompaniment of drinking.[343] Tom stayed till tonight. Very serious and likeable young man, Marshall, which is a yardstick about my own age.

Best,

Al

---

343. Tom Marshall (1938–93): Canadian novelist (*Goddess Disclosing*, 1992), poet (*Dance of the Particles*, 1984), and professor at Queen's University. AP's "A Sorrow for Tom" (*Naked with Summer in Your Mouth*, 1994) is an elegy for Marshall, whose death is also referred to in AP's "Bits and Pieces," from the same volume, and in "Departures" and "The Names the Names," both from *To Paris Never Again* (1997). Michael Ondaatje (b. 1943): Canadian poet (*The Cinnamon Peeler: Selected Poems*, 1989, 1991) and novelist (*In the Skin of a Lion*, 1987; *The English Patient*, 1992; *The Cat's Table*, 2011).

To Purdy (Ameliasburgh) from Birney (Waterloo)[344]
August 16, 1967   APC

Dear Al,

Just a few companions to brighten the swimming out your way.[345] Heard from Joe he got the grant. Very happy for him, & he seems to be too. Says he's hitching down to see you this weekend at your "ranch." Hope you had a good reading & turn-out at the Classics. Wish I could come, but no car still.

Cheers. Love to Eurithe,

Earle

To Birney (Waterloo) from Purdy (Trenton)
September 22, 1967   TL[346]

Dear Earle,

Nothing specific to say, just wanted to write before leaving for Ottawa, which will be Sept. 30. I think we told you our address will be 173 Waverley, Apt. 3.

Both Scott Symons and Pat Lane descended on me for two days, one of them spent at the lake and the other here at Trenton (where, despite the address [Ameliasburgh], I am writing from).[347] Lane is likeable and unpretentious, Symons just the opposite, I don't mean that he's pretentious, but migawd, how complicated can you get! I believe you know him fairly well — Of course I am now going over his novel, partly as a result of his visit.[348] I am also sick as hell, having slept last night with a cold gale blowing in the open window on me, and sleepily not knowing enough to close the window but shivering and huddling and getting sicker — May I also take this moment to bring up, broach, mention delicate, the subject of antho — for which we now have a fine/bad Layton panegyric to the U.S. — and also pieces from Margaret Laurence and George Woodcock — where's Birney? —[349]

---

344. When addressing the postcard, EB added small letters to AP's name, so that it says "wALden PondUbaRDicY," i.e. "Walden Pond Bardic."

345. The postcard is illustrated by a reproduction of a sketch by A. Renoir for *Les grandes baigneuses*; it shows three nude women.

346. *YA* 151–54. The letter is dated 1969 in *YA* (151), but marked "1967" in AP's papers at Queen's University. If AP was sending a draft of "Joe Barr," a poem published in *Wild Grape Wine* (1968), then the 1967 date is probably accurate. EB's handwritten note on the letter: "answered by phone."

347. Scott Symons (1933–2009): Canadian novelist (*Combat Journal for Place d'Armes: A Personal Narrative*, 1967; *Civic Square*, 1969). Patrick Lane (b. 1939): Canadian poet (*The Collected Poems of Patrick Lane*, 2011) and novelist (*Red Dog, Red Dog*, 2008) whose early works, in particular, reflect his experience of violence and despair in small towns in British Columbia.

348. Sam Solecki has suggested that AP "probably read the manuscript of *Civic Square*" (*YA* 153 n.1).

349. Margaret Laurence (1926–87): Canadian novelist (*The Stone Angel*, 1964; *The Diviners*, 1974)

Fred Cogswell wrote me a scathing letter about my piece in *Com. Lit.* saying I had neglected to include Nowlan among the poets and list *Fiddlehead* and Dorothy Roberts.[350] Also accusing me of being "against" New Brunswick and being a member of the Ont. Establishment. I meekly admitted being guilty about Nowlan and *Fiddlehead* (in the list of mags) and that this was a bad mistake on my part. I said it was ridiculous that he should think me "against" N.B. and wasn't he getting a little paranoic to think that?[351] And establishment, me, by God? I suppose my status has changed somewhat in the last few years, but I can't see Purdy being regarded as a suave mover and shaker, recipient of favours from the most-high.

Read at Queen's [University] with Layton a week ago, to 500 frosh, mostly attracted by Layton I think — Irving was at his most charming for my taste, and when he wants to be can be the most likeable person possible to meet. He was at Kingston, and had Eurithe completely charmed. Incidentally, we drove to Kingston, encountered Irving in the hotel lobby at the La Salle, and he said he'd wait there and we'd all go to dinner after cleaning up in our room a little. So I go to our room, open the door and lo and behold it's Layton's room. There are all his poems and briefcase spread out before me. I'd got to the wrong room, but the key to our room had inexplicably opened the door to his room. Like lightning the Machiavellian Purdy-brain buzzed and whirred: I'll never never get this chance again with Irving, I said to the chuckling inner me who dominates such situations. I seized Irving's poems and briefcase, shoved them all under the bed. We went to our own room (after locking Irving's door with our key), washed, went down and to dinner with Irving, came back to get ready for the reading, then I went to call for him in his room. He was dirty gray-white beneath the tan. "Al," he said, "I left my briefcase in that restaurant." Of course he hadn't, since he hadn't taken it. But I couldn't hold out any longer, it wouldn't have been funny anyway. I told him where his poems were, with visions of frantic organizers of the reading scurrying around the restaurant etc. and poor Irving desolate at the loss of a fee.

Must stop, but will copy a poem on reverse, since this is the only one I have much use for lately. Note the strong rhythm, which I don't like but couldn't avoid. Tried to write it in loose speech-rhythms, but wouldn't work that way.

---

and writer of short stories (*The Tomorrow-Tamer*, 1963; *A Bird in the House*, 1970). AP and Laurence corresponded extensively from 1966 to 1987.

350. Fred Cogswell (1917–2004): Canadian poet (*Selected Poems*, 1983), professor of English at the University of New Brunswick, and literary editor (*The Fiddlehead*, Fiddlehead Books). The "piece" was "Canadian Poetry in English since 1867," by A.W. Purdy, in the *Journal of Commonwealth Literature* 3 (July 1967). Dorothy Roberts (1906–93): Canadian poet (*The Self of Loss: New and Selected Poems*, 1976) who was born in Fredericton.

351. "Paranoic" suggests the difficulty of reading AP's typed letters, riddled as they are with errors of typing and variations in spelling: did he mean "paranoic," "paranoid" (the "d" and "c" keys are adjacent), or possibly "paranoiac"? The sense in any case is clear.

Best to Esther, and remember our address when you're in Ottawa.

Cheers,

Al

Joe Barr[352]

In a grey town of seven-week days
during an eternal childhood
where I was so miserable sometimes
at being me that I roamed lonely
over the reeking town garbage dump
unable to talk to anyone
locked in my own body
captive of the motionless sun
in an eternal childhood

Old Joe went there too
happy as a young dog
pushing the garbage with his stick
grinning like a split orange
telling himself stories all day
the doors of his prison opening
into rooms he couldn't remember
places he couldn't stay
the river providing a green sidewalk
that bore his mind's feet lightly
his day like scraps of colour
and the night birds always teaching
him songs that because of his stutter
he never learned to sing

I could have learned from Joe myself
but I never did
not even when gangs of children
followed him down the street
chanting "aw-aw-aw" in mockery
children have for idiots
In a town that looked like a hole
torn in blue clouds

---

352. "Joe Barr" was included in AP's *Wild Grape Wine* (1968).

where I made-believed myself
into a moonlit grasshopper
and leaped the shadowed boundaries
that bore my mind's feet lightly
forty years ago
in the grey town of memory
the garbage dump is a prison
where people stand like stones
the birds are stuffed and mounted
a motionless sun still hangs there
where Joe is a scrap of crimson
when the sun at last goes down

Of course, Trenton is the town meant here, and having called it "that raped that hustled town" you get the idea yourself[353] — I will never get used to owning a house here, intend to sell the place as soon as we can get a price, but in the meantime we're stuck — Joe Barr is the actual name of the town idiot of my childhood, tho I've probably carried the parallel between us farther than it really was — But for some inexplicable reason I remember him, bearded, spittle dribbling on mouth corners, wild look — Poor bastard is dead long since. Trenton itself is a puzzle — why do I dislike the place so much? The obvious reason is association with an unhappy childhood, but I should be past that now, really should. But there it is, the place disgusts me.

To Purdy (Ottawa) from Birney (Waterloo)
October 24, 1967   TPC

Al

Just got yrs of 18th (have been up in sub-north, Earlton, New Liskeard, etc, distr. tchrs convention) & this instant sent off rave-support of AWP & his archaeological/poetical propositions. I'm sure you'll get it. I'll resign if you don't. I'll probably resign anyway. Too much work. (Kept carbon for record, but will write a different sort for Gugg.) Will phone Jonas re his book because I have uncomfortable feeling he signed one for me at the launching & I left it there or something.[354] I've just finished reading a 280-page TS [typescript] on parliamentary reform & decided you were wasting yr time attending Parl. unless you can get into Cabinet

---

353. The phrase is from EB's "In Purdy's Ameliasburg," published in *Rag & Bone Shop* (1971).

354. Probably George Jonas (b. 1935): Canadian journalist and poet (*The Absolute Smile*, 1967) whose early works were published by Anansi; his books of journalism (*Vengeance*, 1984) have been best-sellers. He was a script editor at CBC Radio and worked with AP (see *SA* 353).

meetins — real decisions are made there & in Fed/Prov. meets, secret stages of Committees, etc … Don't expect to be in Ottawa this year, alas; esp. sorry now I hear you have a winery …

Haven't seen Jim since I talkt with you on phone — heard once from Joe in Vanc. but I've never had time to answer it — re. anthol., can't you use my "Billboards" ["Billboards Build Freedom of Choice"] if you want something from me? I'm off Thurs. to Mtrl for the Imp. Tobac. contest.

Love to Eurithe, that Griselde among poets' wives!

Cheers,

Earle

To Birney (Waterloo) from Purdy (Ottawa)
October 26, 1967   TL

Dear Earle,

A guy named Gary Geddes of Copp Clark wants me to write a book on you — Birney really is a classic I guess, and Purdy is a goddam academic, or getting that way. I dunno, haven't time right now, tho Geddes says he can extend the time of preparation, and five hundred bucks would be welcome.[355] (When isn't money welcome?) If I did do it would get a tape recorder into your place and ask you to talk into it for a while —

Thought I'd let you know.

Best,

Al

Purdy

Or Layton alternately, Geddes says.

To Purdy (Ottawa) from Birney (Waterloo)
October 30, 1967   APC

Al,

Gary Geddes is a bright & responsible youth, who was in the U. of T. Grad School last year. He asked me to write a couple of books for this series but, for lack of

---

355. Gary Geddes (b. 1940): Canadian poet (*The Terracotta Army*, 1984; *Active Trading: Selected Poems, 1970–1995*, 1996), editor, anthologist, and professor at Concordia University (1978–98). Geddes edited the Studies in Canadian Literature series for the publisher Copp Clark, which included, in addition to George Bowering's *Al Purdy* (1970) and Frank Davey's *Earle Birney* (1971), *Hugh MacLennan* (1969), by George Woodcock; *Brian Moore* (1969), by Hallvard Dahlie; *A.M. Klein* (1970), by Miriam Waddington; and others. AP included a poem by Geddes in *Storm Warning: The New Canadian Poets* (1971).

time, I said no, but told him he should get you on his team. Please do consent. If you decide to write one on me, I'll of course be delighted, & we can do as much taping as you want. Let me know what you decide.

Cheers,

Earle

To Birney (Waterloo) from Purdy (Ottawa)
November 1, 1967 TPC

Okay Earle,

I'll take the book on, tho it will be January before I can do anything. Have a few forebodings of the work involved, but you and Layton are the only ones I'd be interested enough in to do said work. Thanks for the good word with Geddes. By the way, Bowering is doing one on me for another pub. and hasn't even asked me a question?[356] What the hell kind of book will that be? Anyway, I'll be after you with a recorder sometime in Jan, and also reading that thesis Nowel-Bentley or Bentley-Noel did.[357] Also asking people like M. Wilson about Birney, just to get some objectivity in there. I am finally writing a few poems here, one of which I think might be good. One on Dief too, whom I visited in his office yesterday.[358] Think P. Dwyer is a kinda good guy.

Best,

Al

P.S. Will be in Tor Nov. 7 at Westminster. Middle of week tho.

To Purdy (Ottawa) from Birney (Waterloo)
November 14, 1967 APC

Dear Al —

Glad you're going to do the hangman's job on me. I've a *revised* copy of Bentley's thesis (the only revised one, with bibliog. almost up to date).[359] Are you going to

---

356. George Bowering (b. 1935): Canadian novelist (*Burning Water*, 1980), poet (*Kerrisdale Elegies*, 1984), essayist, critic, and, from 1972 to 2001, professor at Simon Fraser University. Associated with the small literary magazine *Tish* in the 1960s and with Vancouver long afterwards, he wrote the first critical monograph on AP (*Al Purdy*, 1970).

357. "A Study of the Poetry of Earle Birney" (University of Toronto, 1966), by Peter Noel-Bentley.

358. John Diefenbaker (1895–1979): The thirteenth prime minister of Canada (1957–63). AP's "John Diefenbaker" was published in *Wild Grape Wine* (1968). "The Torn Country," in the same volume, also refers to Diefenbaker.

359. Noel-Bentley and EB published "Earle Birney: A Bibliography in Progress, 1923–1969" in the *West Coast Review* 5.2 (Oct. 1970). Noel-Bentley published *Earle Birney: An Annotated Bibliography* in 1983.

write a book on Dief too? Why not a popular series of paperbacks on the Senile Sixties, including Dief, Birney, Pearson, Ouimet & Charlotte Whitton?[360] Was in T. Thurs. & phoned your hotel, but you'd checked out. Yes, Peter Dwyer's a good guy, in fact a hell of a good guy.

When do I see your new poems?

Why don't you get a grant to go to Paris & write about C19 painters?

[Unsigned]

To Birney from Purdy (Ottawa)[361]
December 16, 1967   AL

Dear Earle —

I am saying in front of next book — "To Earle Birney, the youngest adult I know." Okay? My tenderest feelings will be hurt if you don't say yes. T'ain't accurate. Should be: "the oldest young man I know," or crap like that.

I am disturbed right now, Eurithe is in hospital ... As I say, I'm very disturbed, and it disturbs me just as much to be disturbed because I know I'm disturbed, if you can figure that out and I think you can.

In my view I've done what I came to Ottawa for — seven Ottawa poems — two more besides those.

And I am irritated with Birney, tho not Earle, on accounta he ain't writ me anything for antho. Course will use poem from book, but not the same thing. I don't care if it's only a few lines — six or five or four — it's you now and not then. But I know you I me they etc. can't produce the goddam junk just because somebody wants it, me in this case.

Not really much to say. Could talk more trivia, but it means little. Sorry you aren't in Ottawa — I've just had an inkling of what you go thru at Waterloo — at Carleton. Admirers make me feel hostile sometimes, then ashamed of myself for being so — Shit.

Hope to see you

Al

---

360. Lester B. Pearson (1897–1972): Prime minister of Canada, 1963–68. J. Alphonse Ouimet (1908–88): President of the CBC, 1958–67. Charlotte Whitton (1896–1975): Mayor of Ottawa, 1951–56, 1961–64.

361. AP's copies of this letter and the following two letters do not indicate whether they were sent to Waterloo, Toronto, or elsewhere.

Dear Earle:

Greeting and all that. Not much to say here, still so damn busy I can hardly turn around. What the hell, I suppose I'd complain if I weren't. Ten buck reviews for the *Citizen* too, but no more of them for a while.

Have writ seven political poems as well as a coupla others. Think that's enough. I think one might be good. Am getting them photocopied and will send you the works later.

Eurithe is back home and think she's okay. Cost me about two hundred for not having any hospital insurance. I never get sick myself, haven't been in hospital since RCAF days. Will know better from now on.

Re. the book for Geddes and Copp Clark, I don't think they'll cough up any advance; and while I'd like to do the book, I wanta do it well enough if I did take on the job so it would cost me some money. So let it go —

As I look at that inscription to Earle Birney for the book ("the youngest adult I know"), it seems possibly silly.[362] A 21-year-old could be the youngest adult I know. I'm rather sick of that damn book anyway, friggin around trying to get poems right. Oughta be fairly large tho, somewhat larger than first McStew book.

I will hope to see you in Toronto in Jan. or Feb., since I guess you still go there for weekends. I think I have Alison's number somewhere, but if that isn't valid right now please send me another, and I will drop you a line when/before I intend to go there —

Will try to pick a poem from the ones you listed in your letter to Hurtig, and am sure I can.[363] Would have preferred your own narrow focus aim new, not in a book, but both Hurtig and myself want you in it. I believe Frank Scott will likely be in, which is surprising because he kinda looked down his nose on the project when I wrote him some time back. But he phoned me a few days ago, saying he was working on a poem.

Best,

Al

---

362. *Wild Grape Wine* is dedicated simply "To Earle Birney."

363. Mel Hurtig (b. 1932): Canadian bookseller, publisher (Hurtig Publishers), and prominent nationalist.

To Birney from Purdy (Trenton)
January 8, 1968   TL

Dear Earle:

Greeting and all that crap. News: I signed the new contract Copp Clark sent for the Birney book, to take one year. Any chance you comin down for a week or weekend to Trenton? Alone or accompanied, singly or ensconced and balanced on female eyes. That way we could tape, drink, tape, talk, drink etc — and besides quite a while since I've seen you.

I hope to wind up this fuckin antho in the next month, and use what money we have to go to Mexico after, sometime in Feb. I guess. Whether you make it down here to the hustled town or no, I'll see you in Tor. or Waterloo and we can make some tapes? Say where and when you're gonna be anywhere. Antho manuscript has to be delivered in Tor. sometime next month, and will maybe stay in Tor. a week before driving to Mexico. So either then or later at Waterloo we can do some tapings? I wanta do a good book on you, therefore it'll take a few sessions and some talk. Wanta weave bio and your mental processes into the standard literary stuff —

Forgot to say: Copp Clark came thru with actual $250. advance, the money to come soon. Our offspring at Waterloo down for Christmas to Ottawa, and think he's gonna fail there too. Makes me wanta beat his goddam head in. Standard parental response, I suppose.

Best,

Al

Purdy

To Purdy (Trenton) from Birney (Toronto)
January 21, 1968   APC

Dear Al,

I hope your anthology will at least supply the answer to the Great [illegible] question of What on earth happened to Eurithe? That time I phoned you she was in hospital in Ottawa with an undiagnosed illness. I delayed writing you expecting to hear from you. Then it was January & though I got your change-of-address card, I didn't have your Trenton phone #, & still don't. Should have written you, of course, but had flu over Xmas, & very busy since. (I did send off a letter for you to the Guggenheim back in Dec.) ... Glad the Copp Clark thing is settled the way you want it. I talked on phone yesterday with Queen's. I can't go there the day you want to tape me. However, I'll be in Toronto next Thurs. (25th) at Lionel Kearns' reading @ Classics, & will stay on for Earle Toppings' party, so maybe we cd. do something on Fri. 26th?[364] Phone or write me to Waterloo.

Love to you both,

Earle

It's Quetzálcoatl, not Quetza ..., & he was God of many things. Nice pome, tho.[365]

To Purdy (Trenton) from Birney (Waterloo)
Early February 1968   TL

Dear Al,

Don't know where to send this letter as, if you gave me an address in Belleville, I lost it, and when I tried to get LD [long-distance] central to connect me via yr Trenton number, all I found was yr Ameliasburg one & she didn't think she cd connect me from that to yr bro-in-law in Belleville, esp. as I cdnt remember his name. However, maybe I'll send this to Trenton, if I can find *that* address. I'm stoopid, I admit it. And it's especially annoying to me right now as I want to tell you, in strict confidence of course, that you look a cert. for a CC [Canada Council grant]. Later, I can tell you some of the discussion, maybe when I see you. Of course, there's many a slip. In your case it could be that some mastermind on the CC itself might invoke some policy against more than X number of grants to any one person. This question came up, not necessarily in connection with yr application, in the Arts Advisory Panel, but I felt that Peter Dwyer is firmly of the opinion that if an artist is good enough it would be a pleasure to the CC to support him for life. Also, yr application had a very good reception, & compliments were made by some (& ignorance revealed by others (about which I may be able to tell you something after I've resigned from the Arts Panel!)).

I shouldn't like you to get too proud, however, so I will now turn to reviling you. Well, not exactly. But, having had to read & weigh the significance of various statements you have been in a sense badgered into making (I refer to these strange CC sponsor forms) I do want to talk with you about the curious results that happen (not just from your remarks about candidates, but mine, & everybody's who is trying to be honest in appraisal). In short, *don't* assume that your sponsorial remarks about a candidate are going to be read, necessarily, by intelligent

---

364. Lionel Kearns (b. 1937): Canadian poet (*Ignoring the Bomb: New and Selected Poems*, 1982) and professor of English at Simon Fraser University (1966–86). As a student at UBC, he was taught by EB and was part of the *Tish* group in the early 1960s. Earle Toppings (b. 1931): Editor at the Ryerson Press and editor, producer, and newscaster at the CBC.

365. The "pome" in question is probably "On the Avenida Juarez," from *Wild Grape Wine* (1968): "She has certainly been sacrificed / to Quetzacoatl [*sic*] / God of Civilization / whose lineal descendants are / Imperial Oil Co. / and Coca Cola."

& informed & contemporary-minded people. Some awful silly buggers (like for example, Guy Sylvestre, Roy Daniells & others even older & more hidebound) are detailed to read what you & I write in support of other writers. And invariably they interpret the slightest demur on our part from 100% Oriental Praise of the Candidate, as a warning that the candidate is in fact unworthy of an Award. This in turn forces me, as a member of the Panel, into the most belligerent defense of our Flock, etc. Will tell you more what I mean when I can, i.e. when we meet.

Earle

To Purdy (Trenton) from Birney (Waterloo)
March 15, 1968   TL

Dear Al,

A note in haste, as I leave tomorrow. I was delighted to get John Wain's autobiography from you.[366] Even though it wasn't my birthday it turned out to be Wain's the day the book arrived. I don't know whether you arranged this coincidence. I am taking it along to read in motels on the way. Keep in touch, both of you and don't lose my address.

Cheers

Luv   Peece

Earle

To Purdy (Trenton) from Birney (Laguna Beach, California)
April 1968   TL

Al my friend

How are you? Where are you? I will not ask *what* are you for I daren't ask myself that question. However, to start the ball rolling, I am on a cliffhouse on South Laguna Beach (the less fashionable one) having just watched a particularly improbable sunset over the rolling waves. Which are rolling more than merrily tonight perhaps as a result of last night's earthquake. Which shook the house &, since we hang on a cliff, agitated Esther but caused no damage except to human hearts (tho the big Alsatian up the hill, a fierce bitch, was turned into a craven whining pooch for a few hours). So that's where *I* am, on flower hung palisades as they say in the tourist pamphlets. Went swimming today & came out bruised, scratched & shaken. The surf is full of loose gravel whirling like a laundromat & equally dirty-looking, though only from good clean mud of course. I give one lecture a week, public, with color

---

366. *Sprightly Running: Part of an Autobiography* (1962), by John Wain (1925–94), an English novelist (*Hurry on Down*, 1953), poet, and critic associated, especially in the 1950s, with The Movement and the Angry Young Men.

slides & opaque projections too, concrete, audiovisual, mixed media, etc. — & I keep 2 office hrs a week — otherwise I have, I swear it, done nothing but sit & catch up with correspondence & write to Australians & do other nonsensical things. Have about 5 more letters to write & then by god I'm going to write some poems again.

Income tax also I've been groaning over & paying masses out on account of I'm too goddamned honest. My office (on the Irvine campus) is with John Woods, the Michigan poet. & across the hall is Charles Wright, whose first book Dave Godfrey intends to publish.[367] Tom Wayman is here as you know but having to leave to get a job, as he finishes his grad degree this spring — will probably go to Ft Collins Colo.[368]

Esther is fine & learning to play cribbage. Mel Hurtig sent me a cheque & hints at great events to come. Hope the launching of the anthol goes well & all yr various enterprises.

The trip here was a race against snow all the way to the Calif. border (the last big winter storm). But Calif. is of course vulgar with sunshine flowers trees birds. The works. Also with reactionaries. But the deptl [departmental] characters & students seem liberal at least.

When do you take off for Mexico? Or have you already? We have loads of room if you want to come thisaway. & you'd really enjoy it & we'd enjoy having you.

[...][369]

But dammit I need that $500 right now for somebody else. Specifically for Bill Bissett a guy who is a good editor/writer & will almost certainly go to jail for two years on a framed-up pot charge, unless the money can be found to pay lawyers & keep on paying them.[370]

[...]

Earle

P.S. Normally I'd have a cash reserve to send to Bill the Poet, but alas the U. of Calif. isn't going to pay me, as I haven't a visa & don't dare apply for one! Damn children! Esp. my own, & those of my friends!!

---

367. John Woods (1926–95): American poet (*The Deaths at Paragon, Indiana*, 1955) who taught at Western Michigan University for many years. Dave Godfrey (b. 1938): Canadian novelist (*The New Ancestors*, 1970) and co-founder, with Dennis Lee, of the House of Anansi Press. Charles Wright (b. 1935): American poet (*Country Music: Selected Early Poems*, 1982; *Bye-and-Bye: Selected Late Poems*, 2011) and professor at the University of California, Irvine (1966–83) and later at the University of Virginia. *The Dream Animal* was published by Anansi in 1968.

368. Tom Wayman (b. 1945): Canadian poet (*Did I Miss Anything? Selected Poems 1973–1993*, 1993), anthologist (*Going for Coffee: Poetry on the Job*, 1981), and teacher of creative writing. He received an M.F.A. from the University of California, Irvine.

369. Here EB turned to the matter of a loan that he had made to AP's son and that had not yet been repaid. I have omitted passages from this and subsequent letters that concern the debt.

370. bill bissett (b. 1939): Canadian poet (*Selected Poems: Beyond Even Faithful Legends*, 1980), artist, and publisher (Very Stone House, blewointmentpress). He is known especially for his concrete poetry.

To Birney (Irvine, California) from Purdy (Trenton)
April 1968   TL

Dear Earle,

Glad to hear you're in and settled down.

[...]

I'm sorry to hear Bissett is in trouble, and hope something can be done.

I picked up a copy of one of Douglas Stewart's first books, pub. in London (remaindered in Toronto) with you in mind.[371] Since you're going to Australia I wondered if you could use it? Nothing special as poetry, but you might wish to acquire my own autographed copies habit. Should I send it along?

I am working on the house at Roblin Lake, along with Eurithe, since it's necessary that we sell it to pay for other things. I'm sort of property rich and money poor right now, tho of course a long way from being broke. But can't afford to have so much money tied up in property with no return coming in. And I have plenty of callouses and a disgruntled nature to show for my work.

Yeah, the Hurtig book might do well. Re. my own new book at McStew, I saw the cover design by Newfeld — it consists of a bunch of blue commas in the shape of a bunch of grapes, and seems to me pretty good.[372] Jack McClelland also gave permission to do *Poems for All the Annettes* again as a selected poems, which Godfrey at House of Anansi will be publishing.[373] So I will have four books out this year, two poems and two anthos, one the school antho with Ryerson.

Not likely we'll be going to Mexico at all, since Roblin Lake house demands so much attention. Nor, I'm afraid, to Calif., but thanks for the invite. Things seem to press in on me sometimes, and this is one of them. Not many poems, but a long one on the Liberal Convention and Pierre Trudeau, whom [you] may recall I met in Cuba.[374] Don't want to write more rural poems for obvious reasons, but doubt not I'll write a great deal in Europe. Must stop.

Best to you and Esther.

Al

---

371. Douglas Stewart (1913–85): Australian poet (*Collected Poems, 1936–1967,* 1967*)*, critic, and anthologist — an important figure in modern Australian literature.

372. Although AP referred to Frank Newfeld of McClelland and Stewart, the illustrations in *Wild Grape Wine* are attributed to P.J. Moulding.

373. Jack McClelland (1922–2004): A principal figure in the publishing firm McClelland and Stewart from 1946 until 1985, when the company was sold to Avie Bennett. He was president of McClelland and Stewart from 1961 to 1982. McClelland was one of the most influential figures in Canadian publishing history. He published many works by EB and AP.

374. Pierre Elliott Trudeau (1919–2000): Prime minister of Canada (1968–79, 1980–84). A Christmas card sent by Trudeau to AP in 1977 alludes to the meeting in Cuba: "Dear Al, Joyeux Noël, Happy New Year, y Cuba si? Pierre." AP's "Liberal Leadership Convention," from *Wild Grape Wine,* describes the encounter.

May 16, 1968   TL

Dear Al,

[...]

My god you need money far more than I do, for, as you say, you've got too much tied up in property & not enough cash. I do hope the refitting of the Roblin Lake house hasn't cost too much in relation to what you can sell it for; also I hope you have a good buyer by now (though honestly I think the Fed. Govt. ought to invest in it as a Purdy Memorial Shrine, against the day, & may it not be till the 21st Century at least, when even Purdy proves mortal in the flesh, though by then the Canadian Immortal Memory, toasted on Confederation Day, in wild grape wine. No Mexico? But Europe now? When? I don't deserve a letter from you, having been so tardy & self-preoccupied in what messages I've sent you — but there, I would like to know all your news. Will you sell the Trenton house too?

I don't know what's happened about Bissett. His various pals, who were writing me or others about legal costs, have failed to answer my last cards & I can only suppose they've found enough money to go ahead with his defense. He doesn't reply either, & I'm out of touch with Vancouver news in general. Have you heard whether he ever came to trial or not?

I give a public reading every Wed. here, 4 p.m., when the afternoon sunshine lies golden on the campus & the lush overweight campus beauties are tanning their long thighs on the ranch grass, & only a score or more of compulsive learners, teaching fellows, or duty-joed [sic] faculty, have gathered to hear what nonsense I'm up to this week. Yesterday was mainly Purdy Day, though I was really supposed to be presenting a cross-section of the Cdn poets in the 30–50 age-group. We all had a ball with your cows & purple milk, & half a dozen others. Your work is a cumulating pleasure; I mean, the more I read your poems aloud to others the more & more they mean to me, which is quite different, alas, from the effect of reading most poets many times. When will the McStew and Anansi books of yours be out? And the anthologies?

Have been quite busy trying to get the Lowry *Coll. Poem* albatross off my neck. Margerie [Lowry] finally got too much for me, so I've unloaded the task of being agent for the poetry back on to her, & she promptly gave it to Tom Maschler, one of Heinemann's editors.[375] I expect now he will get some prestigious limey to write the intro., & make the notes, & I'll be lucky to get a credit listing on the Ack. page. I still have some control over the Lowry Bibliog., as I think she has given up

---

375. Tom Maschler (b. 1933) joined Jonathan Cape (not Heinemann) in 1960. EB's letter of 22 Aug. 1969 refers to Maschler as "the Cape ed."

trying to copyright it in her name behind my back. *Lunar Caustic* has been out some time now, for I see reviews of it, but no one has bothered to send me a copy, though it was I who persuaded Margerie it could be edited (out of the 3 jumbled versions) & did the main job of editing.

Been working, of course, on Anzac stuff, trying to sort out the poets, novelists, etc. I would like to meet, from those I'd like not; also writing letters all over the map to arrange dates & places for poetry readings of Can. poetry in both countries. Have a fair amt of work here too now, extra poetry readings, poets bringing in manuscripts. But I get some time to see a bit of the range & desert country behind. Don't do any swimming as the sea is still cold & the surf high & loaded with beach gravel. Looks beautiful from the window, however. Bob & Rita Allen are spending their holidays with us.

[...]

Get that house profitably sold, man, since it seems it must be sold; and then get off on your travels; but *write me first!*

As ever,

Earle

To Birney (Irvine) from Purdy (Ameliasburgh)
May 22, 1968   TL

Dear Earle,

[...]

Glad to hear you're settled in there. Say hello to Bob and Rita if they're still there. Also to Tom Wayman if you think of it. His poems in *Forum* impressed me a great deal. Yeah, the Lowry work must seem endless, and sounds a good idea to get out from under. I haven't seen *Lunar Caustic*, but will eventually, I suppose.

I am pounding nails, with Eurithe, and fixing up cottage, which I think I said before. The urgency of selling either or both the house at Trenton and cottage is now compounded, since we have taken an option to buy a far northern farm, with house and small lake. $3500.00, for which the money must come from the other two places. Not the CC [Canada Council] cash, which of course will be spent roaming around Greece and the Near East. The House of Anansi book will be out in June, amounts to a selected poems 1954–1965, in fact is a selected poems under the old title, *Poems for All the Annettes*. *Wild Grape Wine* is October. Incidentally, this year I have three poems in the Borestone Mtn. award book, the one you got a first prize from once. No money unless you win, which means they get a cheap antho. *The New Romans* is Sept., and I enclose Hurtig's advertising bookmark, if you haven't seen it.[376] He's advertised this, but without mentioning that I edited it, which rather got my hackles up. The [Toronto] *Telegram* published [Larry] Zolf's contrib., also without mentioning my name. But I'd expect that from Callaghan.[377] I wrote a — quite a — vigorous letter of protestation to Hurtig, and apparently hurt his feelings. He sent me a telegram saying "Tyro publisher forgives brutal editor" — something like that, to which I replied "Brutal editor accepts forgiveness meekly and hopes it won't happen again" (not verbatim, of course) —

Have also heard from Acorn in Charlottetown, asking my help in publishing another newspaper on the lines of the *Georgia Strait* or *Straight*, which he says he founded in Van. But I have no time to get involved in it really, tho I can send him five bucks instead.

Doug Fetherling, the rather likeable U.S. draft-dodger, poet, photographer, painter etc etc. was here last weekend, and says Bissett sold a Mountie half a pound of pot and is now in jail.[378] Migawd! Fetherling has 20,000 words of a novel that sounds hilarious, make me envious. I'm not even writing poems these days, but seem to keep revising and changing the old ones whenever I have occasion to copy them, immediately go off on a binge of re-writing. "Interruption" (one of the Boreston poems) was not immune either.[379] Dennis Lee, the Anansi ed., seems to want to re-write my poems too, à la Purdy-Rosenblatt.[380]

We won't get away to Europe until about Oct. McStew is talking of another poet univ. tour. Incidentally, I read at a Belleville high school last night, to these $35. a week adults re-training classes — two audiences of about 300 each, which is about the most I ever read to. I was sort of talked into that reading, got only a bottle of whiskey out of it. A mixture of flattery and talk did it.

Re the Birney book, I have transcribed the guts of those tapes, and that's all I have done. It weighs on me somewhat.

I will get back at it when Eurithe lays down her whip at the cottage, — where we are actually living, despite the Trenton address. Orioles and goldfinches, robins and chickadees (I think chickadees) in the trees. Trying to think of words to describe an oriole's song, five notes and rarely rarely six. The first a hesitant uh-clearing-of-the-throat, then full song. That goddam [Robert] Browning line

---

376. *The New Romans: Candid Canadian Opinions of the U.S.* (1968), edited by AP.

377. Barry Callaghan (b. 1937): Canadian author, editor, and journalist who then was the literary editor of the Toronto *Telegram*.

378. Douglas George Fetherling (b. 1949): Canadian author of poetry, fiction, biography (*The Gentle Anarchist: A Life of George Woodcock*, 1998), history, and memoirs. AP included Fetherling's poetry in *Storm Warning: The New Canadian Poets*.

379. "Interruption" was published in *Wild Grape Wine*.

380. Dennis Lee (b. 1939): Canadian poet (*Civil Elegies*, 1968, 1972; *Nightwatch: New and Selected Poems 1968–1996*, 1996) and critic (*Savage Fields: An Essay in Literature and Cosmology*, 1977), co-founder of the House of Anansi Press, and editor, notably for McClelland and Stewart. His works for children (*Alligator Pie*, 1974) are well known.

about singing each song twice over kind of throttles my own thinking of orioles.[381] But the minuscule world of birds seems very attractive to me — This morning no wind on the lake whatever, and a large school of fish, an inch long to a foot, sunning themselves in the shallows, all bass and sunfish, some shaped like spears (weapon imagery must creep in I guess), others like fisherman's lures. And a big bull muskrat pushing the lake ahead of him swimming to shore. Liken the fish to your campus beauties, which doesn't work.

Must stop. Say Hi to Esther if she's there. Will you be back east at all before Australia? If so we shall have a drink. Take care of yourself.

Best,

Al

To Purdy (Ameliasburgh) from Birney (Vancouver)
June 20, 1968   TL

Well Al here we are back & not far from where you were staying in the winter of 65–66 & my Ikuko days. Wonder have you sold the Ameliasburg cottage yet. I heard some kind of rumour you had bought somewhere else?? Must be the place you mentioned in your May letter "a far northern farm." Whatddyumean, Baffinland? Is yr *Sel. Poems* out from Anansi yet? My selected-selected, *Memory No Servant*, came out, 2 copies at least, from John Gill's press last week. & I'm expecting him out here in a couple of weeks with several hundred more copies, a wife, 2 kids, & a tent.

Any more word of Acorn's Charlottetown paper — sounds like a lead-balloon for sure, a hippy mag in Charlottetown, esp if edited by a politically committed nut like Acorn. Even with Ginsberg it couldn't go in PEI.[382]

Since I drove up here I've been unpacking, settling in, & trying (as ever) to catch up with letter backlog, esp. corresp. with Australia-NZ arranging what is turning out to be a fantastically tricky itinerary & lecture schedule. Won't bore you with the details. Anyway, what I started to say was I haven't literally seen one damned soul or even saved soul I know in this town yet or even phoned anybody — I *must* finish writing people before I can see them! Something wrong with that as a way of life, I admit.

Are you going on a reading tour, then, for McStew? For nothing, as usual? At least Belleville gave you a 5-buck bottle. I wish to hell you thought more of yourself

---

381. From "Home-Thoughts, from Abroad": "That's the wise thrush; he sings each song twice over."
382. Allen Ginsberg (1926–97): American poet (*Howl and Other Poems*, 1956; *Collected Poems 1947–1980*, 1984) and icon of the counterculture of the 1950s and 1960s.

than that as it makes it impossible for anybody else to charge, & so removes one of the few sources of income for really young poets (like me).

I'm hoping to be back in Toronto for about a week on July 2 or 3 — will you be in earshot? I hope so. Maybe by then I'll have dug the Vanc scene a bit & have news at least.

Will send you a copy of *Memory No Servant* for your colln [collection] (it doesn't have anything new in it, as Gill wanted to stick to the tried & true).

You got a new address now?

Mine, at top, is good until Sep., even though I push on to Australia at end of July, as Esther plans to stay on in this flat until the owner of it comes back in Sep. She's taken a social work job here.

I was glad to get out of the USA. The thickening atmosphere of violence, ignorance, hate, stupidity, mutual brainwashing. The day of Kennedy's funeral my daughter-in-law got us up at 6 a.m. to watch and weep on color tv, & so on thru the day (if I'd strung along). 2 days later, in Oregon, I stopped to visit old friends, a poet, & found myself in the midst of a family breakup & a suicide attempt by the wife which I was able to frustrate, without knowing, for a long 20 seconds, if I were going to get killed for trying. Well maybe it's only a time-lag of a difference up here & Trudeau's killer perhaps already has his gun.

Take it easy. Send me yr news.

Earle

To Birney (Vancouver) from Purdy (Ameliasburgh)
June 26, 1968   TL

Dear Earle:

[...]

I am very interested in your news, but will not comment on it much, since I am so goddam busy. Except for the bit about you being in Toronto. There will be a party for my book at Anansi right around that time. Send Toronto address quick, if any.

We bought a farm 20 miles from Bancroft — price $3,500., which includes a small lake, a house (about six rooms) and 200 acres with 40 cleared.[383]

Yep, I want my dog-eared annotated copy of Birney's new book.

I have undertaken to edit Acorn's selected poems for Ryerson and signed a contract with them. Acorn has amazingly given me carte blanche.

People from high school came to cottage when I was away with another 26

---

383. In "Hunting Season," from *Wild Grape Wine* (1968), AP writes of "Driving north / on the Bancroft road."

of scotch, and when I wasn't here drank some and left the rest. This is my full fee. Okay, I am a sellout. But they flattered the shit outa me, and as you know I am a pushover for flattery. (Same address ((above)) is valid.)

Eurithe is driving me with lash and goad and liberal applications of Mace to get the cottage repaired and otherwise fit for foreign tenancy.

I agree about Trudeau. I think some FLQ [Front de libération du Québec] or RIN [Rassemblement pour l'indépendance nationale] is liable to gun him down. I enclose my piece on Kennedy in *Star Weekly*, and mentally composing poem obit for Trudeau.[384] Jesus tho, I hope not.

I am also correcting proofs of *New Romans* at intervals. Also high school antho. Also *Annettes*. Also the McStew book. I am damn near crazy! Acorn yet to come. Birney book also.

Did you actually *feel* the atmosphere you describe in U.S.? The suicide thing is ghastly. Corpses being hit by typewriter keys. Turn over every red fallen autumn leaf and there is another dead man, still bleeding. A host of golden daffodils. I do not intend to start feeling guilty as a member of the human race, but still, won't the remnants after the next big bomb be complex and psychosis ridden?

Must stop. Best,

Al

To Purdy (Ameliasburgh) from Birney (Vancouver)
July 15, 1968 TL

Addresses: till 30 July: c/o Bk of Montreal, Fourth & Balsam, Vancouver 9

till 6 Aug: c/o High Commissioner for Canada, Canberra, ACT, Austrl'a

after 6 Aug: ditto, *please forward*

Dear Al

My letter, already belated, may get bogged down in the P.O. strike but I'm told it will go east if I post it tonite. So here goes. First, dammit I wish I were talking *with* you not writing *at* you. Very frustrated when I was in Toronto keeping getting messages from you & never having the luck to connect by telephone (I'd get another A. Purdy. No relation at all. Or just the wrong number or the wrong name entirely or no answer). & then I wanted very much to be at that party Anansi

---

384. "Lament for Robert Kennedy," published in the Toronto *Star Weekly*, was later collected in *Sex & Death* (1973). The revised poem was included in *The Collected Poems of Al Purdy* (1986) and *BR* (234–35) as "For Robert Kennedy."

gave (despite the fact I was never invited by the cove who was answering the Anansi telephone, whom I rang twice). But I wd have crashed it anyway. & I gather Alison got there with Joe! Oh good! Missing you is all my fault for not writing you quick, as you told me to, but I thought once I was in Toronto it wd be simple to reach you. However I was tied to the goddam Rare Bks Rm [at the University of Toronto] from 9 to 5, with 15 mins for lunch, from Tues. a.m. to Sat. noon. & over the weekend had to see & do a mass of other things & then hop it back to Vanc. because of flat-hunting-for-Esther here, masses of mail with Australia & N.Z. trying to arrange schedules & head off free-lecturer-organizations, & locate honest poets, etc. Also having typhoid & smallpox shots. Which always lay me low. & trying to make up in one month of reading for a lifetime's ignorance of Anzac kulchur, history, etc.

[...]

I have taken the cheque [...] & paid it into an account for Bill Bissett's legal expenses & fund to support his small daughter if & almost-certainly-when both Bill & his wife go to jail. I've also approached the U of T libr. to buy his mss for $3000 (they're worth every cent of it: stacks of visual-concrete stuff & art work & full typescripts in several stages for all his books, much correspondence around the world with poets, stuff used in *Blew Ointment* [bissett's magazine] etc). & I've also cottoned on to a Toronto businessman who feels sympathetic & may throw a good hunk into the pot. I have told Bill that the source of my hundred is partly due to your generosity to me but that your name isn't to be used nor is it to be assumed that you are necessarily approving of the fund-raising.

You seem to have got a bargain, to buy a whole lake & a 6-room house & 200 acres of farm for $3500. Incredible. I do hope it works out well for you all.

Gill is sending you yr copy of *Memory* from Trumansburg as he ran out of copies out here, apart from ones already committed to Australia for me. I cling to my one author's copy meanwhile.

I got myself your new *Annettes* at Marty's but gave it to A when I left without having had time to re-read it & compare yr changes etc.[385] Anyway it's good to see it in print again.

Yr "Lament for Robert Kennedy." You've got at the nub of it. That "the killers were ... privileged men slotted neatly into the power structure of a nation that will not alter or reform itself." Though maybe some of your best lines are when you are shooting off in yr own spaceship "three towns away across the belted planets." Jesus what a beautiful line! Tho speaking of Jesus the part I liked least of the poem was yr refs to Christ & Richard III, which are really refs. to legend or even historical

---

385. "Marty": Martin Ahvenus (1928–2011): Antiquarian bookseller in Toronto (Village Book Store), collector of literary manuscripts, and friend to writers.

falsifications, not to history, and I don't think you shd equate the real deaths of real Evers-King-Watkins with the alleged death of Jesus & the false account of the murder of the princes (Richard III never personally murdered them nor is it even likely he ordered or even wanted their deaths — this is a Yorkist canard to which Shakespeare fell victim & all English-Shakespeare-devotees since).[386]

[...]

Cheers. Keep in touch.

Earle

Been reading you in *Open Skull* — ??

To Birney (Canberra) from Purdy (Ameliasburgh)
August 1968   TA

Dear Earle,

Hope to hell this reaches you. Mail strike just ended so got your letter of Jul. 15 (long ago). I sent a copy of *Annettes* to you at the Vancouver address of your letter before that. Sorry as hell we couldn't contact when you were in Toronto. I should have dropped everything and gone to Toronto, as I realized later. When you were there I phoned three times, and left messages and our neighbour's number from here. Once Rita [Allen] said you were gonna be there at dinner between 6 and 9, so I phoned between then and of course some goddam answering service answered. I began to feel it was a bloody plot against me, or else that Birney had decided Purdy should be dropped, scotched and cut off —

Anyway, I feel terrible I didn't see you before you left — Not for any specific reason other than saying farewell for a few mos, which is specific enough. There are not too many people I do have any urgency about, and now I feel should have just gone to Toronto instead of waiting for the party which I hoped you'd be at — It wasn't much of a party by the way, one of those things that doesn't get off the ground for whatever reason. My guts were kicking up and still are, so I didn't drink and maybe that was it. Among the people there, Kildare Dobbs, Bob Weaver, Lee of course, Gary Geddes, and all the young poets in the book.[387] Dobbs is interesting, tho the more I see him (and he's very sharply intelligent) the more I feel his ego gets in the way of anything — Weaver you don't care for much, but as you know he's helped me in one way or another quite a bit. Joe [Rosenblatt] was there too, and

---

386. Medgar Evers was assassinated in 1963. Martin Luther King, Jr. was killed on 4 Apr. 1968 and Robert Kennedy died on 6 June 1968 after having been shot the previous day. But Hollis Watkins was not assassinated.

387. Kildare Dobbs (1923–2013): Canadian essayist, editor, poet, autobiographer, and writer of stories. His *Running to Paradise* (1962) won the Governor General's Award for fiction.

he's becoming a bit more articulate than he used to be. This new book of his poems is also better, and I contributed a blurb, one of those semantic traps, if you like the poems you're intelligent is the interpretation. Silly thing to write. Joe also asked Weaver for a blurb or a sentence recommending his book, just as I was leaving. Weaver rushed after me and asked about Joe's poems, which he didn't know very much. Anyway, he's gonna give Joe something he can use for the book also.

Re the hundred bucks I sent, this was Jim's money, not mine. After our real estate dealings lately I don't have much to spare anyway.

[...]

I'm deeply sorry about Bill Bissett. As you know, I don't have quite the high opinion of his writing ability that you do, which is beside the point in this situation anyway. Re fund-raising, of course I approve of it for Bissett, tho I wish to hell he'd grow up a little. But then I've been about as irresponsible as anyone several times in my own life, so I should talk. I have such a fixation about standing on my own feet tho, seem to deeply regard it as necessary to my own character —

Re Kennedy, yeah the Rich. III bit is a cliché, and the last part of piece best. The part I like is the: It is always morning it is always evening it is always noon.

Anyway, news. Geddes is using 10–11 poems of mine in that Oxford antho he is doing (down, ego, down!). More important, I've written about three poems or four, one of which I think pretty good. Did I mention three in that Borestone Mtn. best poems thing this year? Hurtig's advance sales are now 22,000 and he has scheduled a first printing of 30,000. Yeah, the ed of *Open Skull* asked for letters I'd got from Chas Bukowski and also, apparently, got my letters to Buk, also [Alan] Bevan's re myself.[388] Odd to see how I look to Bevan! You probably know Colombo replaced you on the CC council, and this seems to me a national calamity. Sammy Glick joining Schweitzer and Gandhi. Busted tape recorder working on your tapes, now at plant getting repaired. Plan to use your own words re your poems where at all possible. Tho can't use your words re say Beatrice, at least not without editing eh? Dunno if mentioned, but editing Acorn for Ryerson, with an iron-clad agreement from Acorn: no interference from him. Before strike received 8–9 page letters from him almost daily. One began: "Dear Al, I often think of the case of Mao Tse Tung —." I often think of the case of Milton Acorn. Also more or less completed the school antho did for Ryerson, and received $300. They rejected an anti-American poem by Dennis Lee, but would use it if there was a balancing poem. I'm now donning pseudonym of John Leander to write said pro-U.S piece.

---

388. Charles Bukowski (1920–94): American poet (*The Pleasures of the Damned: Poems, 1951–1993*, 2007) and novelist (*Post Office*, 1971). The correspondence between AP and Bukowski is collected in *The Bukowski/Purdy Letters: A Decade of Dialogue 1964–1974* (1983), edited by Seamus Cooney. Bukowski contributed "an appreciation" to AP's *At Marsport Drugstore* (1977). Douglas Blazek was the editor of *Open Skull*.

The *Annettes* is not quite a re-print, but a *Selected* prior to 65, and has new poems that I don't acknowledge as such. (To keep Jack McClelland's blood pressure down!) Dated new poems 1964, see Quinte Hotel piece ["At the Quinte Hotel"]. Do hope it got sent on to you. Wrote poem called "Married Man's Song" after which Eurithe accused me of chasing and catching other women! This poem is quite specific, but I proclaim my innocence. Hard to make her believe it tho. Also wrote an article called "An Unknown Canadian Genius" in which I took an 1880 poem and re-wrote it, and took a few shots at Colombo and Scott for their found poems. Look, take care of yourself in Aussieland eh? Let me know where you are etc etc.

Best

Al

To Purdy (Ameliasburgh) from Birney (Melbourne)
September 22, 1968   TA

Sun a.m.

Dear Al

I talked myself into a damn timeconsuming & exhausting job when I took on this Aussie tour. My letter-writing seems to be mainly frantic airmails back to Canada in reply to 2-months delayed letters sent to the wrong address over here. Or dashed-off thank-you notes to the kind poets, profs, hosts, etc. I've encountered so far. (The other kind just get the back of my arse, of course, & there's plenty of them too.) I confess I did get a letter from you a while back, though, which I've put off answering until I felt freer in time. But that day isn't coming so I'll just dash this off as usual — yours, by the way (dated Aug. 12) came in 3 pieces, somebody had really torn it, & then taped it together again & the Postmaster General's Dept of the Commonwealth of Australia actually attached a formal apology from them for "damage in transmission" — so if it isn't a strike in Canada it's a mad letter-sorter in Australia. I do wish some book of yours had come thru to me, I need esp. yr Arctic book [*North of Summer*] or the new *Annettes* at the moment. I HAVEN'T A SINGLE POEM OF YOURS TO READ TO ANYBODY! Airmail me a poem, & ask McStew to send AND BILL TO MY ACCOUNT one LIGHTWEIGHT book of yours — I mean light in avoirdupois dammit, you don't write them light in content, thank god. I can name a bunch over here who do. Have them airmail it (but a *paperback* not a heavy one) to me at address on other side of this letter [Wellington, New Zealand]. I was sorry to learn you were having to stay on the waterwagon when you wrote. Hope your internals are functioning properly again.

It's that wild grape, man! You remember what my chemist friend said. I don't want to see you drooping & having to write poems without liver-support. Interested in your comments about people at that party. I think you are dead right about Kildare Dobbs, whom I've known for some time: "sharply intelligent" & equally egoistic, & the latter gets in the road of the former — it's partly this Irish need to win verbal arguments & esp. by 100% contradiction (it's a Jewish folk-habit too, as I've noticed over the last 34 years). If Joe R. is still around for gossake tell him to write me & give me an address to write him. It's the only reason he hasn't heard from me is I don't know where to write not even what part of Canada. Hope his book goes well.

[...]

Don't know if he's [bill bissett] had his trial yet & what happened as I haven't had any news or mail from Canada for over 2 weeks now. I guess it's piling up for me in Sydney (I *hope* it is!) where I'll be in a couple of days, & stay till end of Sept., then a month in N.Z. After that I may come straight back to Canada (esp. if I'm still in the mood I'm in now) but a couple of Malaysian-Singapore poets I met at the Brisbane conference seemed willing to let me read poems at their univs. (Singapore & Kuala Lampur [*sic*]) provided I paid all my expenses up there. Since I've already spent the full travel allowance given by the Council (including a return ticket as far as Vanc., but directly back from N.Z.) I don't think I can find the dough for this extra jaunt. Anyway, as I've been intimating, I'm feeling damned browned-off. Of course all long tours are terrible — too much entertaining, eating, drinking, yapping, treading on hot conversational stones, meeting shoals of new people all of whom at once remember my name (except chairmen) & who all expect me to remember theirs & who they are, & are baffled I haven't read all their bloody books, & indifferent that none of them has read a line of mine, or indeed of any Canadian (I exaggerate a little, but damned little). In its literary life this country is just beginning to throw up a young-guard, but they are writing the way the young Americans were writing *15 years ago.* & as for the literature of ideas, liberal-socialist attitudes are either very oldfashioned or very much on the run, only the rare voice is ever raised about the Vietnam war, & the *complacency*! The assumption that Canadians are just secondrate Americans, that first rate Americans are the salt of the earth, the willingness to sneer at Canadians as being bought by the U.S. economy, & their own attitude of selling their souls to the Americans even before the Yanks have started buying their bootiful bodies. I hear *The New Romans* is out & more power to it! & to you. I was astounded at yr news that Colombo replaced me on the CC. I find it very unflattering to me, to say the least, & wonder if Weaver or you were asked & refused. (I suppose yr Mexican plans stood in the way.) It's indeed, as you say, "a national calamity." Alison (if you're ever in Toronto & seeing her) can tell you where I've been until latterly (Canberra, Sydney, Brisbane, Barrier Reef, Mt. Isa, Alice Springs, Melbourne, Adelaide, Perth, & now back here). More soon.

Love to Eurithe. Hope the new farm is working out, & all book commitments. Say hello to Jim. Write me!

Earle

To Birney (Vancouver) from Purdy (Ameliasburgh)
October 7, 1968   TL

Earle Birney, wherever the hell you are now —

Dear Earle,

You know damn well you love the tour, at least for the first two weeks. Right? I've just come back from one that lasted a month, and been yakkin at least sixty times to interviewers, radio, tv and newspapers, and it's terrible at the end of it, why I could hardly hold a glass of beer without spillin it all over my writing hand —

Re books, I sent the selected poems pre-1965 (*Poems for All the Annettes*) to the last Vancouver add., and despite your letter have no idea where you would be if I send another book. *Wild Grape Wine* is out (ded. to Birney) and quite a handsome book for a change, but I don't wanta dispatch it into the blue. You say send you a poem, so should I copy "Home Made Beer" on the reverse? Since you can't answer that question I shall — Let me know when you get back and will send *WGW* pronto —

Despite the gripes you sound as if you're having a great time, vitality issuing from loins of brown women and white, Birney forever etc. Hell, you don't wanta mess up your readings with Purdy —

New Romans has sold 32,000 copies, and as said, I completed this tour in aid of — Supposed to go to N.Y. and Chi. [Chicago] Oct. 21. Head of English, Simon Fraser asked me if I was interested in teachin CanLit there next year. Said I was, since by then will likely be no money comin in — Definitely can't ask CC for another and won't —

Saw Esther in Van. and Alison in Tor. and gave your love to both, 60/40. Also Joe R. in Van. Read at four univs, Simon Fraser, UBC, Univ. of Alta., and Prince of Wales [College] at Charlottetown. Hurtig had arranged for two of those as part of the tour with no pay dammit, so I grabbed the other two for money. I guess Ryerson Institute is comin up as well.

From the sound of it you're betraying the principles you've so often expounded sternly to me — by possibly reading for nothin at Kuala Lampur, tho it would be nice to say blandly to Dobbs or Weaver, "Now when I talked and read poems at Kuala Lampur there was this bushmaster who liked Birney and wound around my wrist listening —" Hey?

Yeah, I find that Colombo bit I mentioned a matter of some regret. He'll raise the standards quite a bit — of snobbery.

Will tell you more about *The New Romans* later, since there are things in connection I think interesting. Got called a communist five times in a row on a Wpg. hotline. Developed a kind of inarticulate fluency with one syllable words from interviewers at the end. Even wrote two poems on aeroplanes, which I haven't had time to type yet. Get back and find I've contracted to do an intro for a book, write two reviews and finish a long intro for the Acorn book I just edited. Met a lot of likeable people on tour too, and begin to respect students more and more as I talk and answer them — Even in Charlottetown, where they amazed me. I thought PEI would be backward, but jesus, all the intellectual females have a 38 inch bust. I am so damn sick of talkin about the U.S. tho, I sounded off continually about the damage to Canadian sovereignty from branch plants so I just wanta stick a lily in my mouth and lie down.[389] Also — migawd! — just got $750. for a poem from *Weekend Magazine*. I can see that I have sold out, "gone over" as I am told Gerry Gilbert of Vancouver thinks of me.[390] But really, I don't think that, but one's life does change, and it's how one acts after the environment alters. I sure did regret middleage as I sat next to a blonde chick in Charlottetown and some fat prof kept askin me questions. If her bust wasn't 38 it was extremely well arranged 36. I slavered a bit while answering the prof AND THOSE OTHER people. Eurithe was not along there, tho she was on the western jaunt. We had a violent quarrel in Vancouver and she took a three-hours-earlier plane ahead of me back east. Will now copy poem. So let me know when you get back, so I can send book. And where is the book of yours John Gill printed?

Al

To Purdy (Ameliasburgh) from Birney (Apia, Western Samoa)
October 22, 1968   TL

Dear Al,

A letter of yrs dated Oct 7 caught up with me a while back, in N.Z., & it was very welcome. & wd have been answered before this if I hadn't lost all energy &

---

389. "branch plants": AP contributed an article ("Why I Won't Let a U.S. Branch Plant Publish My Poetry") to *Maclean's* (Jan. 1971) in which he wrote that *Storm Warning* "was to have been published by Ryerson Press — at least it was until the United Church announced the sale of Ryerson to McGraw-Hill of New York ... I say no; *Storm Warning* will not be published by an American branch plant."

390. Gerry Gilbert (1936–2009): Canadian poet (*White Lunch*, 1964) and visual artist associated with Vancouver's literary underground.

ambition to write anything to anybody. The tropics has hit me, man. I once read an essay, by Aldous Huxley, I think, or was it Julian, called "Wordsworth in the Tropics," all about how W.W. wd have chucked up his pantheism/benevolent-teacher-naturism if he'd been brought up not in Cumberland but far enough south to realize that Nature for most of the world is full of poisonous snakes, sharks, man-hunting cats, tarantulas, stinging coral, & above all by simple enervating heat.[391] So, having escaped all the other tropical threats so far, I'm a victim, a placid willing victim, of a climate which never gets above 86, & only once, in a winter night many years ago, actually has plummeted to 62° Fahrenheit. However, a cool wind has started blowing from a suddenly black afternoon sky, blowing across the reef & the almost nude Samoan girls wading, picking sea urchins off the coral. And the wind is brisk enough to wake me up (soon it will be probably a zip-fast lightning & rain squall), after which I will really wake up & maybe at last walk up the 650 ft. "Mount" Vaea & throw hibiscus on the tomb of Robert Louis Stevenson. I can't possibly face accusing eyes of fellow Cdn bards, like Purdy's, if I've lived six days in Apia & never made it to R.L.S.'s tomb. Rupert Brooke ought to be buried here too, by rights. He was a sucker to go back to England & get himself wound up in World War One. It was Rupert who wrote about lying on a mat in a cool Samoan hut "and moonlight over everything. And then among it all, are the loveliest people in the world, moving and dancing like Gods and Goddesses. It is sheer beauty, so pure it is difficult to breathe it." Actually, it is the fine, evenly distributed harbor shit in the air which clogs the breathing, & I'm sure it was the same in Brooke's time, or Capt. Cook's, because the Polynesians have always shit just as much as anybody else (unless maybe Al Purdy in the Arctic) & they've always done it either on those white sand beaches Brooke loved in the moonlight, or, as they grew civilized, in 2-holers sited over the reef at the end of special catwalks, or (those who are now rich) in flush toilets which drain thru pipes that end frugally at high-tide mark on the beaches slap in front of the two hotels Apia claims to have. For the first 2 days this situation actually inhibited me from swimming, but now that *dolce far niente* has got me the only thing that keeps me out of the water is the hundred feet I have to walk to get into it. Those lovely people Brooke talks about? They're o.k., I like em. Almost any girl under age 14 is a beaut, as they say in Australia, but after that age she puts on a pound of flesh a week, until she has got to be 250, and is regarded at last as beautiful. The Gods are likewise in competition, enormous-beamed & bellied, slabsided, very dignified old men (I try to imagine what you would look like, old Tusitala Purdy, if you'd been born a Samoan & lived to be fifty. My mind ducks, the thought is too intimidating.).

---

391. The essay was written by Aldous Huxley (1894–1963), the English novelist and essayist, not his brother Julian Huxley (1887–1975), the biologist.

Well dammit I have to leave here on Friday (normal stay is 3 days; it took me 24 hrs maneuvering with govt. types in New Zealand, to get a 6-day visa) & will head back to Vanc., where I hope to find *All the Annettes* & *Wild Grape Wine* & *New Romans* & by then probably another couple of Purdy books, you wonderful fertile old turtle. Though evidently I won't find *you* anywhere short of New York or Palm Beach. I'm going on to Toronto in mid-Nov., & will be in Ottawa on Nov. 22, & hope to be around the east for some time, if Esther doesn't raise too much hell about it so maybe I'll see you east or, if I can live that long, when you join Simon Fraser (I'm very happy you have that offer & hope you'll try it on, who knows you may like it). Thanks for troubling to copy out "Home-Made Beer," which came in time to delight 150 members of Palmerston North Teacher Training College, New Zealand. You're getting around man, even into sheep country. Write me, but discreetly to the new "home" flat address

> apt 406
> 2030 Barclay St
> Vancouver 5

or, as indiscreetly as you want, in care of Alison, at 3025 Queen St E., Scarborough, Ont. (I'll have to arrange an address for her to write to, when I get back to Vanc.)

Hope it's been a good trip to NYC etc.

I'm absolutely pissed off with travelling, reading, partying, meeting new people, esp. Australians & New Zealanders — especially Australians.

Cheers and love to Eurithe.

Earle

To Birney (Vancouver) from Purdy (Ameliasburgh)
October 30, 1968   TL

Hey Earle,

For chrissake let me know when you land in Vancouver. I sent *Wild Grape Wine* yesterday, and sent *Poems for All the Annettes* when it first came out, so both should be there, Purdy being modest and sweet as usual.

Drop me a card pronto when you land so that if there's a chance we can get together briefly in Toronto before I leave. Just drop a card saying where and when you're gonna be anywhere.

Not a damn thing to say in this letter — I expect to be away about six mos, so I do hope to see you before I leave.

Write eh!

Al

To Purdy (Ameliasburgh) from Birney (Vancouver)
November 5, 1968 ("date of last Free American Elections")   TL[392]

Al   Soyez calme   j'arrive   je viens
Annette is here, her lovely face lifted but still beautiful. The *Wine*, however, has no
doubt been drunk by licentious postalworkers. You, the Author of *All*, will, I hope,
be trapped in Ontario till I get there — which will be Sunday Nov 10. I'll be busy in
Toronto, mainly in Rare Book Room [at the University of Toronto], & in Waterloo,
packing up stuff for shipment, but can be reached or can be messaged (be careful
of that word) at 691–0593 before 8.30 a.m. (but not too much before) or, sometimes, at suppertime.

Nov 22 I go to Ottawa & maybe on to Mtrl, & back to Toronto. So somewhere
sometime somehow man we gotta get together.

Haven't seen any *New Romans* either but have writ Mel [Hurtig] abt this.
Main thing is to see the old Purdy & the ever new Eurithe.

Cheers
Earle

To Birney (Vancouver) from Purdy (Athens)
November 26, 1968   TL

Dear Earle:
Greeting, and I feel that just saying that is some kind of achievement, after
winding thru Luxembourg, Germany, Austria, Yugoslavia & finally Greece. By
train of course. We (my wife and I) are installed in a three buck a night hotel room
on Athinas St., actually pretty damn good, and I have seen so much marble ruins
in the last few days that the dead are becoming more real than the living. If some
Spanish woman hadn't tried to pick me up in the lobby the other night I'd need
more reassurance as to which side of the Styx the Hotel Attalos is on —

We are waiting for some money here in Athens (from Mel Hurtig), and in the
meantime will go to Mycenae, and when the money arrives via Trent to Crete to
escape the weather. Bloody awful, rain and shit. Written a poem and some two
thousand words of prose so far (keeping a loose kind of journal with the idea
something might come of it later). Sorry didn't get to see more of you in Toronto.
My fault really, because I seemed [to] have so many last-minute things to do — but
you will know all about that.

---

392. EB's note in reference to the stationery from the Hotel Inter-Continental, Pago Pago, American
Samoa: "Pure swank. Thanks to the bungling of PANAM, who had to put me up for 2 nites waiting for
planes to go to less luxurious hostels."

Our friends the McDonalds are here, Bob [installed?] as a reporter for CBC, BBC and some other news agency, and has more or less forgotten about writing his novel. Old student or acquaintance of yours also here, name of Mike Welbank.

I am reading reading reading — [H.D.F.] Kitto's book on Greece [possibly *The Greeks*], a bio of [Heinrich] Schliemann, [Henry] Miller's [*The Colossus of*] *Maroussi*, an irritating but partially delightful book, and several others by Leonard Cottrell, a "popularizer," but I can't stand the dry stuff archaeologists write. And writing, and feeling very lucky to be here.

And at the moment, drinking some Greek wine not retzina, which I can't stand. Have your *Selected* also with the idea of working on that Birney book here, I should say in Crete, also notes of the tapes we made in Waterloo. I feel a little guilty about the Birney book, for I'll never get it done in the year deadline, which ends about Feb.

We have climbed the Acropolis, "done" the museum here, the big archaeological one, and all that marble is beginning to numb my senses, or is it the wine? Have wangled a free pass for any of the museums, tho poor Eurithe has to pay, I mean I have to pay for her. (Which I shall mention now and then to keep her properly grateful.) It's too damn cold to be very comfortable in Athens, so we want to find the sun again in Crete when Hurtig comes thru with some cash. Can't ask for second instalment from CC [Canada Council] for a while. Write when and if you have time eh?

Best,

Al

To Purdy (Athens) from Birney (Toronto)
December [9?], 1968   TA

Dear Al

Good to hear & I hope by now you got bread from Hurtig & you're both soaking in the Cretan sun in between bursts of prose in (by now) both Canadian & Greek. Don't remember who Mike Welbank is. As for reading what about Durrell *Reflections on a Marine Venus* or is that another Miller? [inserted: "PS It *is* Durrell (Lawrence)."][393] Anyway I remember it was a good book & maybe someday the poor memory of scholars, when I'm long dead, will pay off & they will credit me with some of your books. Be careful down in the Piraeus, a wickkked little port where the taxi-drivers make more from blackmail than from tips, they say. You shd drive out to Cape Sunion — well, take the bus, the way I did — & gaze at Byron's

---

393. Lawrence Durrell (1912–90): English writer whose *Alexandria Quartet* (1957–60), a series of novels, is his major achievement. His life and works are associated with Cyprus, Corfu, and other Mediterranean locales.

name, reputedly self-carved, in one of the best of the pillars. Bloody vandals, these English lords. & of course you won't pass up Delphi & Epidaurus (where the flowers, the March days I was there, were incredible). In other words come back from Crete as soon as you've had spring there, if they have spring there, because the mainland really busts all out with amaranth & hyacinth & whatever other Greek names you can match with flowers. I got a letter from Hugh McKinley, the Irish poet, yesterday, sent from the island he lives on.[394] His address is MCKINLEY — FILACA — SYROS — Greece (Don't you love that Hellenic simplicity, chaff-chaff.) He tells me [Óndra] Łysohorsky (the Slovakian poet) has survived the recent Czech troubles & that he (McKinley) has translations of his poems, & an article on him, in *London Mag.* I think McKinley might [be] an interesting guy to look up. Anyway drop him a card to his island & see what happens. I found it only took a couple of days to stop noticing the taste of retzina & it's so cheap & universal it's a bore not to be able to drink it. How are you with oozou or however it's spelled? The Pernod-like aperitif they have (but said to have a mite of absinthe in it).

I'm still in Toronto as you see but may fly back to Vanc next weekend as Esther is getting understandably a bit lonely & there is much work I must do out there too. I've at last got all my thousands of pix, photos, etc labelled & dated, & put my "restricted files" into order & made a list of correspondents & number of letters — you can understand how long it's taken me to straighten all this out when I tell you the restricted files, I can now tell them, contain 5,700 letters. I'd guess that the open files have about four times as many. I now understand why I've written so damned little in such a long life (well it seems long, right now).

I'm still halfcut from a huge party at Jack McStew's last nite where I missed you. Even tho there were 200 or more others, incl Richler, Brian Moore, Ludwig, Berton, Callaghan, McLuhan, Town, etc & the women got steadily more beautiful, intelligent, voluptuous, as the drinks wore on.[395] Farley Mowat in his sporran, the Cdn lit scene, & Jack stoned as an owl & half-weeping because his authors hated him, or so he said (some truth in it, sometimes, of course). The bugger won't bring out my paperback *Sel Pomes*, won't advertize [*sic*] or properly distribute the hard-cover, which has a thousand left, & won't even sell me the thousand, so he can

394. Hugh McKinley (1924–99): Irish poet (*The Transformation of Faust and Other Poems*, 1977).

395. Mordecai Richler (1931–2001): Canadian novelist (*The Apprenticeship of Duddy Kravitz*, 1959; *St. Urbain's Horseman*, 1971) and essayist. Pierre Berton (1920–2004): Canadian writer, journalist, and television personality, known especially as a popular historian (*Klondike: The Life and Death of the Last Great Gold Rush*, 1958; *The Last Spike: The Great Railway 1881–85*, 1971). Brian Moore (1921–99): Irish-born Canadian novelist (*The Luck of Ginger Coffey*, 1960; *Black Robe*, 1985) and writer of stories and screenplays. Jack Ludwig (b. 1922): Canadian novelist (*Confusions*, 1963) better known for his sports journalism (*Hockey Night in Moscow*, 1972). Ludwig contributed an essay to AP's *The New Romans: Candid Canadian Opinions of the U.S.* Marshall McLuhan (1911–80): Canadian literary critic, theorist of communications (*The Gutenberg Galaxy*, 1962), commentator on Canadian culture, and professor at the University of Toronto. Harold Town (1924–90): Canadian painter.

get on with the pocket ed. Impasse, esp. for a 64-yr old poet. You young farts can afford to wait.

Cheers anyway & keep in touch, as I will, & love to Eurithe. & watch out for minotaurs.

Earle

To Birney (Vancouver) from Purdy (Athens)
December 14, 1968   TL

Dear Earle:

Delighted to hear from you — and that Jack's parties are still going strong — I suppose this must have been for newly-arrived Richler. Will try and find the Durrell. Have read a lot, and written quite a bit too, could give you an enormous list: *Man & Time*, [J.B.] Priestley; *The Bull of Minos*, Cottrell; *The Naked Ape*, [Desmond] Morris; *Herzog*, [Saul] Bellow; *The Greek Stones Speak*, [Paul] MacKendrick; *The Greeks*, Kitto; *What Happened in History*, [V. Gordon] Childe (re-read); *The Lion Gate*, Cottrell; *The Immense Journey*, [Loren] Eiseley — as well as Earle Birney's *Selected* — you see what I mean — Oh yes, and Leslie Fiedler's *Waiting for the End*, which is pretty good, tho the guy is snobbish about some things —

I shall write to McKinley as you mention, tho later since I seem to have the Hong Kong or Athens flu, miserable as hell, may hafta get a doctor which I don't want to do —

Ouzo kills me dead, but Greek brandy is good, ten year-old bottle for 50 drachs, as you likely know, about $1.60, knock you on your ass and wipe it for you. I will have to give retzina another try, but drink brandy now hoping it'll knock the flu outa me, but it doesn't seem to, just gets me a little drunk.

Re Jack McStew and your *Selected*, I expect to go thru something with him myself in this line, since *North of Summer* sold some 1100 copies the first year and then stopped dead, so I figure he's gonna want to remainder them, a condition you won't be in. Seems to me there oughta be some deal you could make with him. Of course that last thousand will sell, but your point I suppose is to get a paper cover out soon — Now if you could just use the royalties on the paper cover to pay for the thousand hard covers — It's too bad you can't use Coach House or Dennis Lee for a lever of some kind, tho Jack doesn't push very well as I know —

No dough from Hurtig here, tho he has sent me a grand to Trenton, so it's just a matter of time getting it transferred to Athens by the bank. Ryerson sent the proofs of *15 Winds* here for me to correct, and I could only do it from memory. Incidentally, Frank Scott wanted $75. for each printing for his poems, twice as much as any other poet. I turned him down. Smith asked me when their *Blasted Pine* was comin out to let em have two poems for $15. each because their budget was short, and now Scott wants fives times that — !³⁹⁶ The highest poem now is your "Corridors" ["The Mammoth Corridors"] which is long and deserves it, but I can't get over Scott —

Have a very low opinion of the poems I've written here, but you might find this short one amusing:

St. Paul to the Corinthians

We decided some time back that
we were stuck with each other more
or less when I said "You bitch" it no
longer meant she was exactly
that but conversely not much
like a valentine either when she says
"You bastard" it means I may
be one but she forgives me
which is rather harder to bear
And I want the people to know

—Corinth, Dec. 3, '68³⁹⁷

Best,
Al

To Purdy (Athens) from Birney (Vancouver)
January 6, 1969   TA

Hi there Purdyman,

Ti kanete? Pos isthe? Me sihorite pu sas ékana na periménete me grama but I've been real busy coping with mountains of mail, shipments of books etc from Toronto to be unpacked, catalogued & if possible sold, to make room for more shipments etc. Well, anyway, eftihés to néon étos to you both.³⁹⁸ When you last wrote you had the gripi or something. I do hope you recovered quickly & Eurithe stayed immune. & also that yr bread arrived from Trenton & you're soaking [in]

---

396. *The Blasted Pine: An Anthology of Satire, Invective and Disrespectful Verse, Chiefly by Canadian Writers,* selected by F.R. Scott and A.J.M. Smith (1957). An enlarged edition appeared in 1967.

397. A version of the poem was published in *The Quest for Ouzo* and *Love in a Burning Building* (both 1970).

398. EB's Greek is reproduced here without correction.

the Cretan sun, unlike us, dunking in the BC rainsoup. Sometime or other I hope you'll have a look at Nafplion, if you already haven't, & take a swim at Tolo (Solon Hotel was cheap enough when I was there, but things change, yes, indeedy, change is what things do).

Had a talk with the (only) West End bookseller last week & she tells me she doesn't even bother to order a McStew book from the local rep (Jim Douglas) because he doesn't keep any stock here, since he no longer has a wholesale business of his own.[399] *If* there's a copy of my *Sel. Poems* in Vanc. it wd be with Harry Smith. But this bookseller (Pauline [Woodward]) says she is willing to *write* for *one* copy of my *Sel. Poems if* I wd guarantee somebody was ready to buy it. I'd say this is the general picture now throughout Can so far as my book goes. Seems to be that I'm really dead & just won't lie down. Because of course this same Pauline (old friend of Esther's, fellow Unitarian, dear sweet lady etc blah blah) has all the other Cdn poets represented right now on her shelf, whether they are McStew poets or not, even Pratt, who isn't exactly alive in the flesh, and various minor Macmillan poets, etc. So I can see that my *Sel. Poems* is definitely not going to get sold & McClelland will simply wait till the fine print in the contract allows him to remainder it. After all that's what he did with *both* my novels. As for Coach House, it doesn't exist any more, being absorbed by Anansi, which has never been interested in me or my work. I've had a 7-page letter from Jack McStew, saying how wonderful he is & his firm & how good of them to keep me on their list at all & how badly I sell, etc. So I say fuck em all now, I'll never publish another book unless I can get free of McStew, & since he won't free me, then I'll just write for my own amusement for the little while I have left. I can't be bothered even answering his letter. Anyway this means you can go ahead & finish yr obituary on me as I won't be screwing up the record with any more of my crap.

Local news: Joe Rosenblatt & Pat Lane took off last week for Mexico in Pat's Volks, & they are already back, having cracked up the car near San Francisco. The occasion for leaving was provided by Pat's wife who threw him out, saying she wants a divorce to marry another guy. Yesterday they were both looking for rooms & living in a hotel. I went to Bill Bissett's court case (he was to receive sentence) but his lawyer, Sid Simons, managed to get another postponement, & in any case is going to appeal the conviction. Some of the money for this is being provided by York U. Libr., as I've persuaded them to buy Bill's literary hoard. A little more was raised by selling some of his mags at public auction. Other poets on the scene

---

399. James Douglas (b. 1924) worked for McClelland and Stewart as a field editor and sales representative in Vancouver. In 1970 he co-founded, with Scott McIntyre, the publishing firm J.J. Douglas, which became Douglas and McIntyre. His daughter, Diana Douglas, mentioned by EB in another letter (Late November/Early December 1970), became the co-founder and owner of Self-Counsel Press. Douglas and McIntyre was sold to Howard White and Mary White of Harbour Publishing in 2013.

locally are Daphne Buckle Marlatt, Pierre Coupey, Robin Blaser, Lionel Kearns, Flo McNeil, Rona Murray (I mention all these somewhat maliciously, as none of them got a mention in that bloody article you wrote allegedly about West Coast Poets in that shrine of misinformation, *Tamarack Review*).*[400] Lionel is having a lot of family troubles, which is no news, I suppose, about any poet. I'm having them myself, of course. Daphne has just brot out 2 books, one in Toronto, one in SF. *Blew Ointment*, because of Bill's legal harassment, is pretty well folded, & Bill's wife has left him, & his current girlfriend is in hospital with pneumonia. So it goes. What's new with you? Sorry this is such a lousy letter. I do think lovingly of you both.

Earle

* Seymour Mayne is back but not likely to stay.[401]

Esther is out or she would want to send her love too to you both. Write when you can bear to. You've got many demands on your time these days.

To Birney (Vancouver) from Purdy (Athens)
January 1969   TL

Dear Earle,

Wanted to get that poem ["Hellas Express"] in and also get it in my copy-book as well. Have done some 5–6000 words of Birney book, very damn dissatisfied with all but my descriptions of your poems — If you haven't, why not look for Br. or U.S. publisher? I agree, this is rank injustice. Re. *Tamarack* west coasters selected by Purdy: this was limited to Can. poets never before in *Tamarack*, and I think this was stated. Kearns had been in already, Buckle was in U.S. Blaser is American, McNeill I never heard of, and Murray was rejected. Okay? Sorry about Bissett, tho apart from that I think he sticks his neck out, which you won't care to admit — Doesn't matter, he has too much trouble for any one man — Rosenblatt & Lane — migawd! Déjà vu, I too, I too — We are slowly going thru Greece, then Italy to

---

400. "West of Summer: New Poets from the West Coast," a group of poems "selected [and introduced] by Alfred Purdy," appeared in *The Tamarack Review* 45 (Autumn 1967). Daphne Marlatt (b. 1942): Canadian poet (*Steveston*, 1974) and novelist (*Ana Historic*, 1988) affiliated with the *Tish* group and known especially for her feminist politics and experimental techniques. Pierre Coupey (b. 1942) has published several volumes of poetry (*Bring Forth the Cowards*, 1964) but is better known as a visual artist. Robin Blaser (1925–2009): Canadian poet (*The Holy Forest*, 1993), editor, professor at Simon Fraser University. He was an associate of Robert Duncan's and Jack Spicer's and a notable figure in the San Francisco Renaissance of the 1950s and 1960s. Florence McNeil (b. 1937): Canadian poet (*Ghost Towns*, 1975).

401. Seymour Mayne (b. 1944): Canadian poet (*The Impossible Promised Land: Poems New and Selected*, 1981), translator, editor (*A.M. Klein: Selected Poems*, 1997), and professor of English at the University of Ottawa.

London — how be if I try to sell Birney to London pub?? My add. will be Canada House, Mecklenburgh Square, London — so on. Jack can't mind if a Br. pub. goes for a selected, can he? And I don't mean a tavern.

Will give it a try anyway — Re. *Tamarack* antho again, tried to get Coupey, but had no address —

Re my own poems, I have writ many, some 16–18, one may be the best I ever wrote, in euphoria can't be sure — By the way, I have feeling you're busier nor me, so don't interrupt things to write — Thing is, when I feel like writing letters I write em, and you don't owe me a damn one 26th of the alphabet — If you see Bissett say hi — it was a good deed to sell his stuff to York: "Now is the time for all —" Letter from Seymour, hope he gets the CC he applied for —

Best to Esther please — And to yourself, which also goes without saying —

Al

To Purdy (London?) from Birney (Vancouver)
February 7, 1969   TL

Dear Al

Liked the way you got the atmosphere of that train thru Jugoslavia & Austria. All trains a bit like that but European ones esp. This closed-in unreal feeling of not quite being alive. Just watching life staged outside.

Hope you've written lots more. Much more important than that guck about Birney even monetarily speaking. If the Vanc bkstores refuse to handle my *Sel. Poems* because they fear getting stuck with even a single copy, what hope for selling a book *about* such a book?? Even the magic Purdy name may come a cropper under such a saddleburden. What's new here?? Pat Lane & Seymour Mayne now apparently happily batching in an apt together while Mary Lane looks after kids alone (having been given the gate by the guy she threw Pat out to marry). Joe [Rosenblatt] living in a rattrap on False Creek but has a girl who intermittently loves him. Joe is writing a great deal, at least a poem a day, stories, plays, etc, a real kick he's on, some of it turgid but I think something good & new will come out of it all. He is really hung up on the primates & is considering changing his name legally to Joe Mandrill or Mandrillo, with which he signs all poems, letters, etc, now. Lane-Mayne-Very-Stoned-Press just brot out a group of wall poster poems, not bad at all, by themselves plus Joe, Marya Fiamengo.[402] Also active in town is the Intermedia crowd with a huge old warehouse on Beatty St & masses of expensive reduplicating machinery for multicolor jobs. Gerry Gilbert pretty well lives

---

402. Marya Fiamengo (1926–2013): Canadian poet (*The Quality of Halves and Other Poems*, 1958; *Visible Living: Poems Selected and New*, 2006) who studied creative writing with EB at UBC.

in their machine room. He & the old blackmountaineers (Tallmans, Hindmarch, Daphne Buckle) acted as solemn acolytes to a priesting job by Jackson Mac Low, latest San-Fran luminary to be given the purple crapet [sic] treatment (I like crapet).[403] Mac Low drops the concretist mask when he comes up here & is once again just one of the Olsonites, humorlessly gasping out short-line deadpannery with however bits of Michael McClure's grunts thrown in & the extra pitch of "random mass reading" which doesn't mean, as most of the UBC student audience thought, any involvement of the audience (how can blackmountaineers involve with such stupid people as audiences? Faugh!).[404] But means Gerry-Daphne-etc humbly & very rehearsedly reading bits & scraps of the great Mac Low's "found poetry" (i.e. bits & scraps of Xeroxes of mag. ads & timag [*Time* magazine] stories) while tinkling tinny yak bells as half the audience walks out two-by-two. Meanwhile the monstrously bearded Mac Low wanders independently thru the theatre aisles snorting & bellowing (but never, as he should have, farting). By mistake I arrived at this scene, on the UBC campus, an hour early & found the Tallman-Buckle crowd barring the way into the theatre because, as they explained to me, Mac Low had to have an hour's rehearsal with them — for what, I asked — for the random reading? O, yes, said Ellen Tallman, without a glint of humour. Apart from being a snide observer, about all I have done lately is (a) back Judy Copithorne in a venture to get her, I think, original art-poems published & (b) write such an eloquent 5-page denunciation of McStew to Jack McStew that he has capitulated, will bring out my *Sel Poems* in the New Cdn Libr within a year & meantime has given me back all foreign rights.[405]

So I'm free now to "look for Br or US publisher" to quote what you asked why I didn't do, in yr letter (untangle that syntax, brother!). So okay why not? But who shd I approach? You're in England, help me. Cape & Macmillan don't want me, or didn't. I note that Marg Avison got prtd [printed] by Routledge/Kegan/Paul — then there's Chatto & Windus (Phoenix Libr Poets) & Eyre & Spottiswoode. I shd think the best bet wd be Penguin Mod. Poets series, wh[ich] seems deliberately to

---

403. Warren Tallman (1921–94): American literary critic and, as professor of English at UBC, EB's colleague. Tallman was a champion of the Black Mountain poets (Charles Olson, Creeley, Duncan, Denise Levertov) and other avant-garde American writers, including Jack Spicer and Robin Blaser. He was a mentor to the student-poets at UBC involved with the magazine *Tish*, including Frank Davey, George Bowering, Fred Wah, and Daphne Marlatt. Tallman was the target of much invective from AP. Ellen Tallman (1927–2008) also taught for a period at UBC. Gladys Hindmarch (b. 1940): Canadian writer of experimental prose (*The Peter Stories*, 1976) and an editor of *Tish*. Jackson Mac Low (1922–2004): American experimental poet (*Representative Works: 1938–1985*, 1986) who collaborated with John Cage, among other musicians and artists.

404. Michael McClure (b. 1932): American writer best known for his involvement in the San Francisco avant-garde of the 1950s, including his friendships with Kerouac, Ginsberg, and others.

405. Judith Copithorne (b. 1939): Canadian poet (*Rain*, 1969; *A Light Character*, 1985) known for her visual poetry and associated with the small-press scene in Vancouver in the 1960s and 1970s.

have involved itself with Commonwealth poets (but perhaps provided only they live & lobby & cocktail in London, e.g. Peter Porter, ex-Australian, & Dom Moraes, ex-Indian, & David Wevill, very ex-Canadian, or, rather, anti-Canadian).[406] Who else? If you find me a Brit publisher for even a small selected-selected you will have my eternal blessing plus ten percent.

Bill Bissett got 2 weeks plus $500 fine. The York Libr. deal will pay off the latter. The former he's already served, in Oakalla (where they transferred him to solitary almost at once, no visitors, like some goddamned Bolshevik). You are quite right he sticks his neck out & has maybe been stoned too often to be quite "sensible" any more, tho one of the world's gentlest & most creative people, & being fuzz-buzzed beyond anything I had thot really could happen in Canada — he has only to walk down a Vanc. street to get picked up "for investigation" & doesn't dare have a town address or drive a car. At that he is luckier than about half the pop. of Oakalla these days, youngsters in for 6 mos or more merely for possession of an ounce or so of marijuana, while the attempted murderers & armed robbers hire expensive lawyers & go free.

So anyway I enclose shards of info. Maybe of use if you do approach anybody about my work (& I'm grateful to you, man, for thinking of it). Plus a coupla thises & thats.

You seem to belt out of Greece awful fast. You knock up one of those Spartan girls? Or make a pass at an evzone by mistake?? Sorry you didn't contact Hugh McKinley. Did you see his review of *Memory No Servant* (*Athens Daily Post*, Jan 12).

"News Reports at Ameliasburg" I have just discovered buried in a mass trench of bad poets in *Edge*.[407] But this a good poem, that builds to fantastic lines. I go around muttering "pike in the monocle eye of the lake ... ice in the conical eye of the Blake ... " But that whole last stanza is so good it's creepy, slides down my neck at the back. I liked the Roblin Lake one too. What by the way will you do with yr last year's "Armistice Poem" I read in *Weekend*?[408]

Tell me about yr trip up to Londontown & what it's like for you there now. I'd like to give you some addresses but you'd better tell me first if you want me to. There's Margaret Crosland, freelance London writer & very old friend of mine,

---

406. Peter Porter (1929–2010): Australian poet who was part of the British literary scene. Dom Moraes (1938–2004): Indian poet who lived for a period in England. David Wevill (b. 1935): Canadian poet and translator whose literary career began while he lived in England. He was married to Assia Wevill, who became involved with Ted Hughes.

407. "News Reports at Ameliasburg" and "Roblin Lake" were published in *Edge* 8 (Fall 1968). "News Reports at Ameliasburg" was included in *Poems for All the Annettes* (1968).

408. "Armistice Poem," which appeared in *Weekend Magazine* (9 Nov. 1968), was commissioned to mark the fiftieth anniversary of Armistice Day.

translator of Cocteau, etc. & Liz Cowley of BBC.[409] But you no doubt have plenty of lit. contacts of your own, much loftier or younger at least.

Don't jump if you see the Oct *Ptry Australia*. Has a big yellowsmellow pix of me on cover.

Best to Eurithe & to you from us both. Esther is on a drama pitch now & registered as full time student at City College (old King Ed. h.s. become a jr coll).

Next week I go east on a short reading trip (Castlegar, Barrie, all the cultural centres) but keep writing me, I'll be back here, tired & broke no doubt, considering the fees they are willing to pay me. Ah to be a Layton.

Earle

To Birney (Vancouver) from Purdy (Penn, Buckinghamshire, England)
March 14, 1969   TL

Dear Earle,

Sorry to be so long writing. As you see from letterhead we are in England, at Margaret Laurence's. Eurithe had an operation in London, in hospital 12 days, has to convalesce a month, then we plan to return to Greece. She is pretty well okay now, just has to take it easy. Cost me approx $750. tho, which hurts. If you come to England with the condition or ailment already, then the medicare scheme doesn't apply. So we pay — dammit!

Anyway, we stayed in Italy — Rome, Naples and Pompeii — about three weeks. I got sick and tired of lugging books around so I mailed em all home to Canada. Including, and here's the stupid thing, your own *Collected* — I mean *Selected* — *Poems*. I thought at the time, hell, I can tell em, the London publishers, about Birney. But that was bad thinking too, as you will readily agree. Purdy stupidity again. So I'm supposed to see an editor at Macmillan and will merely talk about Birney — and myself too — since they have expressed interest over the phone. We shall see —

Such is my state of confusion that I can't find your last letter at all, oh well —

Letter from Alison asking me to be on the staff of the Ryerson Polytechnic workshop, and around five invites to read, all of which should look after this hospital bill, which sounds gruesome, three hundred odd pounds sounds worse than $750.

Life is thrown into quite a jumble by Eurithe's illness. However, Penn village seems a good place for her to convalesce. Margaret has just finished two books,

---

409. Margaret Crosland (b. 1920): Prolific English author and translator who wrote a biography of Cocteau (*Jean Cocteau*, 1955) in addition to translating some of his works from the French. EB was being somewhat coy in referring to Crosland as simply a "very old friend."

one a novel called *The Fire-Dwellers*, out sometime in May, and a book of short stories called *A Bird in the House* out I don't know when. M. Waddington is also in London for a long stay, but I've managed to avoid meeting her up till now. Alice Frick, an old CBC editor of mine, is living not too far from here and hope to see her. My memory of her 12 years back as a very formidable woman, but she helped me a great deal writing plays and I'm not quite so awed of her as I was. There is a bookstore near here where I have unearthed a lot of Canadian books. Incidentally, in the one English book store in Rome I found Birney's [*Near*] *False Creek* [*Mouth*] and Purdy's [*The*] *Cariboo* [*Horses*] sitting cheek by buck teeth together, Birney softcover priced at $4. American, 2400 lira. Shows you it's a collector's item. How books get around!

I've written quite a lot, as mentioned, on this expedition, some eighteen poems, but not very satisfied with the overall quality. Two poems among the best I've done, whatever that is, and the remainder mediocre. Middleage spread is overtaking my poems —

I heard Bissett has a CC [Canada Council grant], and hope he makes out okay with it, altho I do consider him more in Layton's category as a showman, as a man who uses all the dramatic effects a poet supposedly has in the public mind for his own benefit. But that doesn't stop him being good, it just means he's kidding himself, at least it does to me. I know the respect, or call it belief, you have in him: but I find the dramatics so alien to me I have difficulty in believing such people are quite human in some ways. That's extreme, but I remember trying to pin Layton down on some of his beliefs once, he answering me as if I were an audience of five hundred.

Found your letter!!!!

Anyway, I see you are backing young poets right and left, i.e. communist and fascist? Copithorne, I mean. I am pleased about the re-pub of *Selected*. You mention Wevill, I see we have another guy here close to Wevill's non-resident category, Douglas Hill, who selected the Can. poets for this big history cum bibliography, at St. James Press.[410]

Glad you liked the poem in *Edge*, tho a bit surprised, because I felt I was getting into some sort of ruttish protesting non-valid stance or something. The Armistice poem in *Weekend* is crap, as you surely know. It will die an unnatural death. They gave me $750. for that, the most money I ever got for a poem. I cannot refuse that much dough, but despite it, and don't ask me why, I don't seem to have

---

410. Douglas Hill (1935–2007): Canadian writer of science fiction and literary editor who moved to Britain in 1959.

very much extra money. It's crazy, but we bought real estate, spent $3500. on a 200 acre farm.

I have no lit contacts in London whatever, only Macmillan's thru Margaret Laurence who publish her. But we are stuck about 40–50 miles from London in Bucks, so will have to go to London to see anyone.

I'm desolated I didn't see McKinley's review of *Memory No Servant* — christ, there I am right in the damn town — ! No Spartan fucking, just Eurithe ill, she fainting now and then to keep me on my toes. Menses — jesus! Birney on *Ptry. Aus.*? How come, you take out citizenship?

Must stop. I'm typing away in bedroom with Eurithe looking sleepy-eyed — And of course I am very tender and considerate as you know??? Ah well, you don't know then. Will give it my best try for Birney in London.

Affectionately,

Al

To Purdy (Penn) from Birney (Vancouver)
March 18, 1969   TA

7 Feb 69

Dear Al

That "7 Feb 69" was writ honest, but it's as far as I got. Now it's 18 Mar 69. I kept hoping to hear from you & almost afraid to write because Marty showed me yr letter to him (when I was in Toronto earlier this month) & I cd see clearly you had gone to England so Eurithe cd have English doctors.[411] I do hope the operation, whatever it was, was successful & she won't need more & is recovering quickly. Anyway you can see why I'm extra happy to have yr letter. Margaret Laurence's address sounds very cosy & even maybe genteel but a hell of a way from where the pulse of commerce & publishing & all is beating. Looks like you have to have an Ameliasburg as launching pad wherever. If you get to know the right guys, the London Colombos, you shd be able to pick up some readings in England. You might be the first Canadian to get paid to read to the limeys since Pauline Johnson wore feathers.[412] The pickings are so-so in Canada just now, at least for me, as I've just come back from a month of batting around: Vancouver (SFU), Castlegar (Selkirk Coll), Barrie, Ont. (Georgian Coll), Toronto (York), Mtrl (McGill), Sherbrooke (combined U. of Sh. & Bishop's), Toronto again (Vic. Coll), & Stevens

---

411. "Marty" was probably Martin Ahvenus.

412. E. Pauline Johnson (Tekahionwake) (1861–1913): Canadian/Mohawk poet (*The White Wampum*, 1895) and writer of stories (*Legends of Vancouver*, 1911). She was a popular performer of her works and a literary celebrity in Canada.

Pt., Wisc (Wisc. State U). After deducting over $370 for airplanes, & totting up other expenses, I cleared maybe $900 (thanks to living in friends' free rooms) and it took a month on the road to do it. Wisconsin, by the way, paid me more than McGill and Sherbrooke & Barrie combined. Had fun, sometimes, tho for reasons I won't go into here I kept hoping my plane wd fall far & fast.

Those *False Creek*s in Rome are undoubtedly some of the ones I lugged over when you & I went to Cardiff & I left them with Miles on Shaftesbury Ave. I bet they'll still be there when yr grandson visits the Last Pope.

You've got Bissett wrong. He's not at all like Layton. Layton, as you say, is a showman. Bissett is just a permanently stoned guy whom the fuzz have elected locally as the symbol of everything that must be put-down, socked, busted, spat at, etc. Dramatics is what people do to Bissett. & what Layton does to people. Neither one of them is publishing anything worth a damn any more, for opposite reasons.

I'm probably wasting finger energy sending you any London lit addresses since you apparently use my letters for arsewipe, if indeed you keep them long enough for the next shit. I'm really disappointed you never gave McKinley a tinkle. But anyhoo here (yet again) is Margaret Crosland's address. She in country too, other side of Lunnon. But comes up weekly for freelance business. Don't be put off by her delicate gentle scholarly air. She's a sweet woman who's had a mountain of trouble & still has to scrabble for her bread. But she does know lots of London lit types on a professional writer basis (she is a biographer of Cocteau, Colette, & other contemp. French authors whom she knew). Drop her a card & work out a time to have a beer together or something in London: Mrs. Margaret Crosland ((no husband)), The Red House, Hartfield, Sussex. She may have a copy of my *Sel. Pomes* if you really want to borrow one to show Macmillan's. However I think they are one of the huge congregation of publishers, British, American, etc, who have always turned and will always turn me down — so don't fuck up yr own chances by bringing in Old Jonah & his unfloatable whale.

New mag out here called *Ballsout* intends to be bawdy & take over from *Georgia Straight* which got busted for obscenity, libel, contempt of court, & what have you (but is out again on the streets, thanks to big sums raised by Allen Ginsberg & Phil Ochs when they came here last week & read/sang to audiences in — literally — the thousands).[413] A strange scene here. Very fine for outsiders. Indeed my only invitation to read in Vancouver for years came because the students at SFU thot I was a Toronto poet & wrote my agent there. I got a fairly decent turnout but by then the word had passed I was just a goddam native after all & certainly no American. The entertainment editor of the Vanc. *Province* made a special trip out to SFU to write the only full-length review I've ever had of my

---

413. Phil Ochs (1940–76): Politically engaged American singer and songwriter.

poetry readings. & wow it was a hatchet job. "Mechanical gimmicks ... accents & impersonations ... sounding older ... a quarulous (sic) dabbler in whimsy .... Birney in the past has tried to be [E.E.] Cummings, [Stephen] Leacock, and even Irving Layton" & now I'm trying to be a jeezly Entertainer, when I shd just keep out of sight & forget about "the performing arts." Well, they liked me in Castlegar. Good Doukhobor country, as you know.

Fifteen Winds came & it's a real honey of a book.[414] It does, so much better, what I tried to do 15 years ago, with that old ragbag Ryerson's brot out, i.e. to collect the poems I personally liked, without too much regard for age-levels, & yet with questioning notes that wd justify the book's use in senior schools (mine never was, of course, except in Perth, Australia). It's a neat way, too, of dodging critics, to say you publish only what appeals to you (so, bec. space is limited, who can blame you for leaving out Livesay, MacEwen, Waddington, Nichol, Kiyooka, McCarthy, Avison, Ondaatje, Finnigan, Gustafson, Mandel, Macpherson, Pratt, Webb, Page, Anderson, Roberts, Jones, Red Lane, LePan, Marriott, Anne Wilkinson, Heather Spears, Mervyn Procope & Edna Jacques [*sic*] (I hope it is evident by now that I don't intend *all* those names seriously — but I'll leave it to you to guess which ones I think are regrettable omissions).[415] I'm personally pleased to see "Mammoth Corridors" in an anthology, perhaps for the only time. & I *luv* your questions ("Do you think it should happen?" Damn you, of course it *should* happen, & I don't want you planting negative reactions to my possible approaches, in the minds of the lovely young girls I may meet someday yet before I die, propositioning me at the end of my readings).

Footnote: p. xv, [Peter] Stevens' title is "Waking Up ..."; p. 108, title is "Warming Up ... " Hell, I had so many things to say about this anthol., about the good stuff in it I had never even seen before, or had read & forgotten, e.g. all the poems of Wayman, Atwood, most of Acorn's. The D.C. Scott, [Robert] Service, [George T.] Lanigan, Lampman stand up. I think you select well for Bissett, Bowering, [Len] Gasparini, [Eldon] Grier, [George] Jonas, Lane, Lowry, [L.A.]

---

414. *Fifteen Winds: A Selection of Modern Canadian Poems* (1969).

415. Barrie Phillip Nichol (bpNichol) (1944–88): Canadian poet (*The Martyrology*, 6 vols., 1972–87) and publisher (Ganglia Press). Roy Kiyooka (1926–94): Canadian painter and poet (*Kyoto Airs*, 1964; *Pacific Windows: Collected Poems of Roy K. Kiyooka*, 1997). Bryan McCarthy (b. 1930): Canadian poet (*Smoking the City: Poems*, 1965). Joan Finnigan (1925–2007): Canadian writer closely associated with Ottawa. Eli Mandel (1922–92): Canadian poet (*Crusoe: Poems Selected and New*, 1973), critic (*Another Time*, 1977), editor (*Poets of Contemporary Canada 1960–1970*, 1972), and professor of English at the University of Alberta and York University. Richard (Red) Lane (1936–64): Patrick Lane's older brother, himself a poet (*Collected Poems of Red Lane*, 1968). Heather Spears (b. 1934): Canadian poet and novelist who was taught by EB. *The Word for Sand* (1988) won the Governor General's Award. Mervyn Procope (b. 1942): Perhaps the most obscure figure in EB's list; a volume of poems, *Energy=Mercy Squared*, was published in 1966. Edna Jaques (1891–1978): A minor Canadian poet who enjoyed some popular success; she is remembered for "In Flanders Now."

MacKay (did my anthol. put you on to it?), Newlove, Nowlan, Souster. I love that Szumigalski (who he?) "Victim," & Stevens' poem, & the joint [Annette and Jim] Murray.[416] What did you do to old [Alexander] McLachlan's poem? Haven't got the original here. Looks like a complete "modernization" or even translation? Can you do more of this with other old-timers?

Love to you both. Write soon.

Earle

To Birney (Vancouver) from Purdy (Penn)
March 21, 1969   TL

Dear Earle,

Eurithe had an operation [...], will be okay now, but has to take it easy etc.[417] Elm Cottage is not as cosy or cut-off as it may sound. 45 minutes from London. Not at all genteel either. She's turned out three books in the last six months, so it's a place where she can write and still be close to the whirling center —

You know goddam well I do not use your letters for ass-wipe. The only people I write to at all, I mean really write to as apart from necessary notes, are yourself and Margaret. I.e., I have few friends of this kind — possibly three or four, and my nature is very different from yours re the centres of things. I like to meet people, but it sometimes seems that this must happen by near-accident, for I rarely seek them out any more. I used to, and I think principally for lit. get-ahead reasons. I'm sorry I didn't look up McKinley, tho my lackadaisical nature is the explanation. But don't suggest I use your letters for ass-wipe, because you know it's not true.

I am envious of your readings, principally of the money. I arranged some sort of similar tour for myself three-four years ago by writing to univs, and came out with about $500. or so clear of liquor and meals. How did you do it? Write univs, the way I did? I am not known in England at all, therefore would have a helluva time getting readings for money here. You are, by comparison, a manor house to my tool shed on the landscape. [Arthur] Ravenscroft at Leeds, with whom you put me onto writing that article, is probably the only one with any memory of me. I don't mind that particularly, tho I'd like to pick up some reading bucks. Margaret says they don't pay at Leeds for readings, so that lets me out as well.

I will write Crosland, get her Birney book, then we shall see.

Okay, you know Bissett far better than I do. If you say he's a target he must

---

416. Anne Szumigalski (1922–99): Canadian poet (*Voice*, 1995, won the Governor General's Award) and an important figure in the literary community of Saskatchewan. She was born in England and came to Canada in 1951. In *Fifteen Winds* the poem "Victim" is credited to "A. Szumigalski" — thus EB asked "who *he?*"

417. I have omitted medical details.

be. My character, at least to myself, is that I would melt into the landscape, unless there were ethical or other reasons why I didn't want to. I mean, it's possible I might stand up for a principle (the U.S. makes me gnash my "few good mended teeth" as Layton describes them [in "Portrait Done with a Steel Pen"]). But as I grow older I tend more and more to channel energy only into writing. I am eclectic and discriminating, not in the aristocratic sense, but a purely selfish and inner-directed way — I'm pretty depressed by being here in these circumstances, where for whatever reasons apart from the obvious, I'm not writing. It kills me if I'm not writing something that interests me — or are all these obvious things to say?

Your comments on *Fifteen Winds* interesting? I said in intro that I picked only what interested me and with little regard for age levels, but I realize this was not entirely true. In view of your comments I stress now that I tried to put myself inside the kid I was at fifteen or so, and included only the more straight-forward poems where, if there are questions in your mind after reading, they are questions that lead outside the poem itself, that have very little to do with obscurity or complicated mental patterns of the poem. How explain? I read all those authors you mention except Jacques, and Red Lane and Wilkinson (I tried to get one of hers in at the end, but too late) are the only ones I would add. Still, if I had another year, I would do it somewhat differently. But you must realize, I didn't go by names, didn't say this poet should be in. Just chose the pieces that seemed right, without thought of exclusion as such. If we judged a poet "great" he still wouldn't be in there unless I thought the poem right. That's arbitrary, but it's bound to be that way. And yes, I did get the MacKay poem from your antho. The questions were written off the top of my head on the typewriter, I didn't mull over what I'd say since I don't like writing such notes. I couldn't read proofs, by the way, since I was in Greece then, had to rely on the Ryerson ed. Altho the mistake in Stevens' title must've been my original error. Scott, by the way, gave trouble over fees, wanted $75. each, more than any of the others. He settled for half that.

I will not fuck up my own chances by doing some publicity for Birney; if they wanta publish me fine, if they don't, well not so fine but it won't kill me. In Italy, we were lugging suitcases from hotel to hotel and town to town and books seemed unnecessary in Pompeii, they didn't read em in the whorehouse or pharmacy there. Trouble is I've since bought more in England, and now mailing them off to Canada as well. The wheel ruts at Pompeii were evocative to me, I had visions of rattling iron wheels and showers of sparks flying up, amused or shocked housewives leaning out of windows at the bad language: seemed to shorten time to a matter of a twitch and involuntary movement before death. Like Lowry, perhaps I'm "half in love with easeful death" tho I think that's from Webster isn't it?[418] The

---

418. EB corrected AP's misattribution in his reply to this letter (26 Mar. 1969).

Prov. ed (that Lorne Parton?) delivered the unkindest cut with you trying to be Layton. He's lost his ball bearings if he sees any resemblance. His remarks sound as if saying you were good would be old hat, that he was trying to be a sensational iconoclast. Such a performance confuses a reviewer, I think, since he has to judge poems as they come across in a reading and also judge the reader as a performer.

By the way, "Do you think it should happen?" was facetious; surely I, of all your admirers, would wish to aid and comfort your love-life — Well? Refer all lovely young girls before and after readings to me for brief briefings on Birney virtues right? Anyway, I emphasize again: there were no omissions *only inclusions.* Right! And if you have any magic formula for me to get readings here when no one knows me and make some money, do let me know. However, I shall be flummoxed if you have such formula. Miriam Waddington by the way in London, trying to meet other writers etc. I've carefully avoided being any place she might be or be going. If that sounds nasty, it is. Alison wrote about me being at Ryerson, then Colombo wrote suggesting we change classes after week

[The letter was not finished.]

To Purdy (Penn) from Birney (Vancouver)
March 26, 1969   TA

Al my friend,

Got your Mar 25 Blue with its cliffhanger ending — next time you write tell me why Colombo wants you to "change classes" with him at Ryerson's after a week. Where is *he* teaching that he can exchange with you? Sounds like a piece of Colombian nerve, whatever ... I'm relieved, as is Esther, that Eurithe's operation was successful and she [is] recovering OK. Give her our very best wishes & sympathies ... I fear you took my asswipe comment & other coarse jests too seriously ... My last letter was written in a mood of underlying despair, which I was trying to break by turning my mind to a good friend & trying to get in a mood of comedy again, as if we were drinking beer & talking — but it's one of the paradoxes of writers, I think, that because they try to write down the unwritable, express the unexpressible, they sometimes fail more drastically in communication than the guy who is writing only from the utilitarian surface of vocabulary (& that too is a failure of a sentence!). Anyway I wasn't really intending to be more than kidding with my assaults on you. I couldn't needle you if I didn't feel so close to you. You are the younger brother I never had, & wouldn't have been so kindred with you if I actually had been your brother (as real brothers acquire scars from family brawlings, & by reaction drift apart) ... You ask how I organized the reading tour: first there was a bid from Georgian Coll., over a year ago. I put them off, then wrote them when I got back from Down Under & got a Feb date. Meantime Castlegar wrote me (Rona Murray, on the staff there now, is an old doxy of mine) for a date, & I lined them up on the way to Barrie. Then I wrote Dudek at McGill, Gustafson at Bishop's (who rung in Ron Sutherland at Sherbrooke to share expenses), & [David] Steingass (a young American poet whose work I've helped to get into publisher's acceptance) at Wisconsin, & an ex-student on staff at York.[419] The Toronto date was offered me via Ludwig when he found I was coming to Toronto. So it goes. I could have got more if I had taken time ahead to write eastern Cdn collegiates & high schools — these places have budgets big enough to compete with the univs. now. By a little studying of the situation I bet you could go on almost perpetual touring of Cdn high schools, esp. once enough of yr work is in anthologies being used in the schools (my point of entry was "David" of course, but in earlier days the schools would pay nothing, or just expenses). In the 1950s I read my poems in over 25 Vancouver high schools — at $25 a head, by contract with the Vanc. Community Arts Council — this was spread over about 3 years, and was often very exciting, except that the dead hand of principals & supts. was on the project, parading the students like armies, & introducing me as if I were Fd Marshal Montgomery ... Forgot to say that Wisconsin State, in a town of 17,000 middlewesterners, paid me $350 for a single shot reading, as much almost as 3 of the Cdn places put together. Moral: take *The New Romans* down south & read it to them. They'll make you rich, esp. as poetry-loving Americans are even more anti-American than we are. Do let me know what you think of Marg Crosland & how you find her, if you do. She was once pretty & lively & sweet. God knows what middleage & unhappiness have done to her ... You should try not to feel depressed if the writing isn't coming quickly. Don't you realize how *much* you have done in the last few years? You deserve to relax, just enjoy being in Europe, storing away the new experiences of England in 69, Greece, etc. You'll write plenty from this eventually, & some of it may be all the better for stewing inside you for a while. Of course you have bread to think of, but nobody's going to let Al Purdy starve, believe it ... Your comments on my comments on yr anthology are revealing — "to put myself inside the kid I was at fifteen or so." Yes — good — but do you make this clear enough in your intro.? Now I know this was part of yr aim I must of course drop out the names of some poets I thought you might have been able to include, if it was simply a matter of yr adult taste here-&-now e.g. Dee Livesay's late (Indian Summer) love poems, which I think the best stuff she ever did, but

419. Ronald Sutherland (1933–2013): Canadian critic (*Second Image: Comparative Studies in Québec/Canadian Literature,*, 1971), novelist (*Lark des neiges [Snow Lark]*, 1971), and professor of English and comparative Canadian literature at l'Université de Sherbrooke.

the 15-yr-old is the last to accept such a theme. Personally it doesn't worry me as you didn't find any poems you liked very much in the work of La Waddington (her ex-husband Patrick wrote many poems better than any of hers) or MacEwen (obscure), Nichol (essentially a mixed media man, not exhibitable in a straight anthology), Kiyooka, Webb (strange fruit), Ondaatje & Finnigan & Jones & Procope (amateurs), McCarthy (only one good poem), Page, Anderson, Roberts, Pratt, Marriott, LePan, Spears, Mandel, Macpherson (writers in traditions already dead), Gustafson (always just misses the boat because he is so anxious to make it).[420] Well I guess that leaves just you & me ... Those chariot wheel ruts in Pompeii were the detail I carried off above all else, that & being taken short & having to shit in some ancient millionaire's patio (as also did Dudek, I discover, reading his *Atlantis*). (I've decided Dudek is one of the great. Am reading him like mad. No one thing really big but it all adds up to something unique in Cdn lit.) "Half in love with easeful death" was Keats, as he spat out his lungs ... Continue to avoid M. Waddington — also, for my money, A. Frick, an unsemitic, Albertan version of M.W. — As for readings in England, I don't honestly know any way you cd do it and make money — the English continue to regard it as a favor they do when they listen to Cdn poets, exc. sometimes on BBC. For that you should get in touch with another old sweetie of mine, Liz Cowley, on the *Today* programme TV — she is a UBC grad, a great reader, a tough sexy intelligent sensitive gal, now alas married with kids but still interesting & interested. Her married name is Mrs Michael Barnes & she lives at 14 Spencer Walk, London SW15. Gotta go. Keep in touch. I need to be hearing from you (you know that).

Earle

To Birney (Vancouver) from Purdy (Penn)
March 29, 1969   TL

Dear Earle:

Margaret has written her agents in London, A.P. Watt & Son, whom she says are the oldest agents in the country, and who have one of the best reputations. Michael Horniman of that company has written Margaret, suggesting that you send a selection of your best poems to him at A.P. Watt & Son, 26–28 Bedford Row, London, WC1, England.

Horniman's letter asks if you've ever had any poems (single) pubbed in England or reviews here or in the U.S. I'm writing today giving him a rundown on the Birney fame etc. But I suggest you airmail your *Selected Poems* to him (I know it's a bit costly, but what the hell) and then get together a selection for him. Or:

---

420. Patrick Waddington, a CBC journalist, was married (1939–65) to Miriam Waddington, the poet.

you may wish to let the McStew *Selected* speak for itself. I am also sending Watt, I should say Michael Horniman, the stuff you sent me re the U.S. ed. That book probably should go along to Horniman as well.

EARLE,
In my rush I started this letter on the other side. Read that first. Horniman says agents don't generally handle poets unless they also write other things said agents can make money from. You know that sort of talk. However, from the sound of it they're willing to take you on. And when I tell them about your novels etc. I think it might go better. Margaret has made me think it would be a very good thing and that the chances are pretty good of them finding a publisher. Who's to know. We'll just wait and see.

Must stop now, and write the letter to Horniman at A.P. Watt & Son, 26–28 Bedford Row, London, WC1.

All the best,
Al

To Purdy (Penn) from Birney (Vancouver)
April 4, 1969   TA

Dear Al
It's kind of you, man, & I'll play along with Mr. Michael Horniman & Watt & his Son, but I've the feeling This Is Where I Came In. Back in 1944–5 Margaret Crosland tried to help me get my 2nd book of poems (*Now Is Time*) launched, maybe in a combination with the *David* vol., in Britain, via a set of London agents named Pearn, Pollinger, Higham, etc etc, very snooty bunch, who made me tell my life story & submit bibliographies, curriculum vitae, reviews, the works — & then did nothing, but absolutely nothing, with any of it or with me, once I got back to Canada. Later, in 48, I sent them the MS of *Turvey*, & they did, if possible, even less about that. Eventually I took everything back from them, to their great relief, & when *Turvey* did get published in England it was thru my New York agent, ten years after the first Canadian edition. ... Another time, a Canadian medico in London, who was screwing Ann Faber, got her to read a copy of my *Twentieth Century Cdn Poetry*, which had just come out (this was 53, & [I] was back briefly in London); she thot it wd go in Britain, if T.S. Eliot, chief editor of Faber & Faber, would agree. So I was asked, cajoled, bullied into writing Eliot a letter asking for an interview. I got a curt note back from the Great Bard saying that he "did not feel that anything would be gained by an interview at this time." Then, in 1958, I was in London for a whole winter, & Abelard-Schuman brought out *Turvey* & even

had a cocktail party for me where I met masses of London literary shits, finks, etc. Ab-Sch. was going to bring out all my poetry — but somehow they never managed to send me a contract, kept putting me off, & finally stopped answering my enquiries. Sooo, you see, man, I don't believe anything whatever is going to happen in the U.K. for me or my poetry, but I do appreciate that you are making the try for me, & I'll go along with it & do my thing again. I've sent off *Sel. Poems*, & *Mem. No Servant*, & my curr. vitae, & bibliog, & lists of the 35 British mags & 70 US mags I've had poems in, & the dozen-odd lousy reviews I've had, & a clip from *Cdn Who's Who*, & all the other horseshit — at great expense, by airmail. Over to you! Or, rather, to Mr. Horny Man.

Hope you're having fun, & Eurithe again too, by now. Next letter, write me your own news.

Cheers,

Earle

ALSO PLEASE thank Margaret for writing her agents. & give her my best and also from Esther.

To Purdy (Ameliasburgh) from Birney (Vancouver)
May 24, 1969   TL

Dear Al

Welcome home. Yesterday morning this *Maclean's* ed phoned me to see if I'd go [to] the moon and write a poem or something. & he disclosed that you were already half way there after a stopover in Toronto for briefing. I look forward to reading all about it. Esp. if you were put in the same capsule with Peg Atwood.

I've been enjoying getting cards from you from all over the present planet. So don't stop sending them once you are on the Sea of Tranquility.

I didn't answer any of them because I couldn't aim a rocket fast enough.

Is Eurithe back with you? Well again, I do hope? Esther & I send her love (also to you too, natch). Did you get lots of work done after all? I've no doubt you did, one way or the other.

I'm working on the Lowry book & will be till end of June at least.

After that I can be footloose for a while.

When are you coming out here? Soon I hope.

Write me when you get time & a breather.

As ever

Earle

Just got a big cheque from your son. Can he afford to pay back at this time? I can easily wait if this is going to put him on short commons.

To Birney (Vancouver) from Purdy (Ameliasburgh)
June 2, 1969   TL

Dear Earle,

Greeting and all that. I hope to drive out to Vancouver some time this summer, Eurithe accompanying. She has recently got a yen for following me wherever I go, dunno if it's innate suspicion or compelling love. In either case she's generally there. I have somewhat missed the gentle Birney bon mots during last few mos., which is one reason for the drive west. Dunno exactly when, since doing a CBC program before leaving. Re. your reposing with A.P. Watt — I met Kevin Crossley-Holland before leaving England, mentioning you being with Watt.[421] Kevin knew the guy who was in touch with you, or I should say, with whom I was in touch (forget his name) and said he would phone him re your poems and give it a good word. Exactly how much help that is I dunno —

Re the book Purdy is doing on Birney — bad news. As mentioned before what I wrote was crap to me, and what I added to it was also crap. So my apologies about this, and I feel guilty, since someone else could have been writing the book in the time I've taken. You know all this well, of course, but there's little I can do except apologize. I'm sending Copp Clark's cheque back in this same mail, and apologizing to Gary Geddes. I fell flat on my face with that sort of writing. Found I could sustain a short article, say four-five thousand words, but when I get upwards from that I have no critical faculty to sustain it.

I hope you don't feel badly about this abandonment of the project, since you gave a lot of your own time in order to make it a success. So I worry a little over your own reaction to this news from me. I can just hear you saying "Purdy, that shit!" and I don't mean to be humorous. I am much too fond of you to abandon the book unless, as in the present case, I think it's crap. And I don't want to embarrass either you or myself by publishing something not up to a minimum standard.

I suppose I envy you the ability to write the Lowry book, envy you rather ruefully, if that is the word. I sweated in Athens — But enough. Hope tho, that Geddes can find a writer quickly to take the book on. I have your biblio stuff here, which will send to you quickly.

[...]

Two of the Acorn books were sent to me in England. I've asked Margaret

---

421. Kevin Crossley-Holland (b. 1941): English author, translator, and editor whose interests in Norse and Anglo-Saxon literature have something in common with those of EB.

Laurence to keep one and send the other direct to you in Vancouver. If you remember, this is the book I edited for Acorn.

Don't feel like saying much more till I hear your reaction to me not doin the Birney book.

Best,

Al

To Purdy (Ameliasburgh) from Birney (Vancouver)
June 5, 1969   TL

My dear Al

Set yr mind at rest! I don't *want* a book on me! So the only regret I have about yr dropping it is that it's bound to be a worse book, whoever writes it, than what you wd eventually, I'm sure, have written. But I thoroughly approve of yr dropping it. Man, you are here on this planet to write good — even GREAT — poetry. Anything else you write happens in spite of you & because of the fucking society we've been born into. So no apologies. & no envy! If you cd know how dispirited, bogged-down & quasi-suicidal I am about this Lowry book. We MUST get together soon & talk about the joint horrors, my being stuck with these Lowry poem-notes, etc. (& on a deadline ending first July next!) & you being stuck with a Birney-book. Shit I haven't yet written the really *good* poems I want to write, & these goddam publishers/editors & well-meaning but ambitious Gary Geddeses & attendant goddesses, are trying to BURY ME, ash me up into a neat urn so they can compose the appropriate niche-mottoes & get on to the next-for-vivisectional-immolation.

Thanx for everything with Watt, Watt-Ho, Watt-Holland & the other limey double-titters. Nothing will come of it but it was damned decent of you to worry and squander yr time on my lost cause. Curiously, I've appeared suddenly in an anthology of Faber & Faber, called _American_ Poetry, edited by that Acolyte of Black Mountain, Donald Hall.[422] You ain't in it on acct of yr too fucking young fellah. There are 5 Cdns among the 43 contributors (who start with Ann Bradstreet, d. 1672).[423] The others are the 2 Scotts (D.C. & F.R.), Pratt & Layton.

Yes you must come west pronto, Eurithe & all, as we have much to catch up on, esp. on acct of I cdnt write you & had to compose & throw away many beautiful pomes, odes, epistilia, etc. to you in response to yr missives from Scythia & god knows where.

---

422. *American Poetry: An Introductory Anthology*, edited by Donald Hall (b. 1928), a distinguished American poet.

423. Anne Bradstreet (c. 1612–72): Poet of colonial New England, usually considered the first published American poet (*The Tenth Muse Lately Sprung Up in America*, 1650).

Too bad you felt you had to send Gary back his cheque. I'll have to do the same, to Jonathan Cape, if I can't get the Lowry finished this month.

Joe Rosenblatt is still here but contemplating going to Mexico anytime now. He has recently been writing very good stuff again, after a long turgidity with the apes. A Vancouver spring, something he'd never seen before, really turned him on & he has written about 300 pages of flower poems, sexy tulips, etc, many of them, I think, better than anything he's ever done. He's been ill (sudden appendectomy, nearly a goner with peritonitis) but is well again.

I'm very much on the shelf now. See almost nobody. Even growl to myself. Esther, on the contrary, gets younger & goes out more which is the way it should be. However "it tikleth me about myn herte roote, / Unto this day it doth myn herte boote / That I have had my world as in my tyme."[424]

[...]

Thanx for thinking of me re one of the Acorn bks. Hope it goes well. Great oaks of royalties growing out of ... etc.

Suppose you heard of Pat Lane's latest crack-up. So keep off the junk while driving. Or better, let Eurithe drive & stick to grass.

E

I'll be here for sure till July 1st & probably forever. Hi Eurithe, hope yr all better.

To Birney (Vancouver) from Purdy (Ameliasburgh)
June 18, 1969   TL[425]

Dear Earle,

Could be you're right that whoever writes the Birney book will do a worse job than me — I hadn't realized this possibility very strongly till I looked at the new McStew series, McLuhan, Laurence, Pratt and some guy named Joe.[426] Yes, they are most jesus dull. I suppose also that the book Bowering is supposed to be writing about me may also be this bad, which gives me hernia of the ego or something —

We don't know when we're gonna drive west exactly. I have a stint at Ryerson

---

424. From "The Wife of Bath's Prologue" in *The Canterbury Tales*: "But – Lord Crist! – whan that it remembreth me / Upon my yowthe, and on my jolitee, / It tikleth me aboute myn herte roote. / Unto this day it dooth myn herte boote / That I have had my world as in my time. / But age, allas, that al wole envenyme, / Hath me biraft my beautee and my pith. / Lat go. Farewel! The devel go therwith!"
425. *YA* 145–47.
426. "new McStew series": McClelland and Stewart's series of critical studies of Canadian authors included Dennis Duffy's *Marshall McLuhan*, Clara Thomas's *Margaret Laurence*, and Milton Wilson's *E.J. Pratt*, to which AP referred, as well as *Frederick Philip Grove*, by Ronald Sutherland (all 1969); *Hugh MacLennan*, by Alec Lucas; *Leonard Cohen*, by Michael Ondaatje; *Stephen Leacock*, by Robertson Davies; *Mordecai Richler*, by George Woodcock (all 1970); and others. Cf. *YA* 147 n.1.

Polytechnic in August as Colombo's acolyte inna creative writing class, or seminar, or whatever it is. Also some CBC work, coupla readings — Re Lowry book, dunno whether to sympathize or not, since sympathy from someone who abandoned a Birney book seems obscurely insulting.

You mean you're right in there with Ann Bradstreet? — I thot she was Berryman's gal.[427] Incidentally, or not so incidentally, I never did get a copy of that book you had out with *New AmCan*, you got another copy to spare?[428]

I'm glad to hear Joe [Rosenblatt] is writin good stuff, tho I'm not sure what you think is good and I do too very often coincide in the case of Joe. As you've pointed out, I'm much too intolerant of poets who write in a way I don't approve. I sometimes even excommunicate them, that is don't buy their books. Letter from Joe re the Acorn book which he'd seen, saying something to the effect that I'd saved Acorn's life, which is a bit much. Acorn was a bit down tho, but he has bounced back since pub. of book, psycho, paranoid and schizoid as ever.[429] He was down here for a week, the first night of which he got up from bed at 6 a.m. and started to recite (loudly) poems. I mentioned in a penetrating whisper that I didn't appreciate his goddam shit at that time of the morning, whereupon he challenged me to fisticuffs which I refused disdainfully telling him to go out and get a reputation. But it was a fairly eventful visit. He just got a short term CC [Canada Council grant], and we went to a bank and got travellers' cheques, which he lost as soon as he came into the house here, which I expected him to do but forgot to expect it at the time he did it. Later (June 12) we read at Classic Book store, and had to be outside on accounta too many for store. So apt. owner called the police, which made it comfy. Acorn ranted, if you know what I mean. Never heard him do it quite the same before, actually ranted, emphasizing either vowels or consonants until you couldn't tell what the hell he was saying. Ah well —

You must be depressed to quote Chaucer like that — What is it, really, anyway? Age? Hell, I feel the same way a lot of the time, and Eurithe has taken off 5–8 pounds which irritates the hell outa me when I look at her, — and this surely indicates age, when you're irritated that your wife can take off weight and you can't, instead of appreciating the improvement in her figure. That's the goddam trouble with marriage as you know well — You look askance at yourself, as well as others whose condition is, as you say, "the way it should be" — I'm far too

427. John Berryman (1914–72): American poet of the "confessional school"; his major contemporaries include Robert Lowell, Theodore Roethke, Randall Jarrell, and Elizabeth Bishop. His works include *Homage to Mistress Bradstreet* (1956), to which AP here referred, and *The Dream Songs* (1969).

428. The book is *Memory No Servant* (1968), published by New Books, a small press in Trumansburg, New York, run by the poet John Gill. He also edited *New: American & Canadian Poetry*, a literary magazine — which is what AP meant by "*New AmCan.*"

429. Acorn's book was *I've Tasted My Blood: Poems 1956 to 1968* (1969), which was edited by AP, as would be Acorn's *Dig Up My Heart: Selected Poems 1952–83* (1983).

self-centred to think everything is as it should be unless everything serves all my needs and whims too — Morning after — Some people showed up from Kingston who'd (jesus, the road blocks on this paper!)[430] been reading my stuff and came along to see if the flesh equalled the fictional character created on paper. I don't think it did, since people generally make up their mind what you are beforehand from your poems anyway. Still, it was an afternoon of beer etc. Tom Marshall, whom I like, also came down with the others — Generally have the feeling that I'm expected to perform for such people, as Layton has it in some poem or other. They *want* to be impressed by the flesh, which is where Irving has an advantage, if one thinks it's important to impress them with more than poems.

I continually say to myself that poems are the most important thing, and yet there's a good chance that I'm obscurely and unfigure-outably lying to myself too — One part of one's mind thinks one should be golden boy, having the personality of Trudeau (who even before he got into politics had the personality to make everyone else in a room aware of him). (How did I get on this subject? Must be depressed this morning.) However, in my own mind I think a good poem says "Fuck you" to all the golden boys —

As you probably know, I growl at Eurithe too, having done it so long it seems a natural male condition of existence — generally my growling is not straightforward, has motives she doesn't know about. And to think another person is that important as to keep one's real motives concealed — well, it just proves the basic dishonesty of poets, Purdy in particular. However, I suppose the point of mentioning this is we've been together night and day almost continually for the last year, and I'm feeling very polygamous — either as a result or as a natural condition.

Well, off that subject. I wrote the moon-pome, not the "celebration" poem they wanted, but a rather sarcastic don't-care-much effort. Didn't like it myself, which bothered me that I didn't, so wrote another — and this too has goddam little to do with celebrating the astronauts landing on the moon and planting the U.S. flag which may wave forever the papers say — Called "Nine Bean-Rows on the Moon," and I give a Chaucer scholar one guess as to where that title comes from.[431] You see how straightforward I am?

---

430. AP typed his letter on a form, used upside-down, from the Javex Company Limited. His sentence was interrupted by a heading on the form: "SPEC. NO."

431. The moon landing occurred the next month on 20 July 1969. AP's "Nine Bean-Rows on the Moon" was published in the 1 Aug. 1969 issue of *Maclean's* and in *The Quest for Ouzo* (1970) and collected in *Love in a Burning Building* (1970). It was also included in *Inside Outer Space: New Poems of the Space Age* (1970), an anthology edited by Robert Vas Dias. The poem's title comes from W.B. Yeats's "The Lake Isle of Innisfree" (1892): "I will arise and go now, and go to Innisfree, / And a small cabin build there, of clay and wattles made; / Nine bean-rows will I have there, a hive for the honey-bee, / And live alone in the bee-loud glade."

Getting too long-winded. We don't know when we're gonna take off for the west. Will let you know tho, when we do.

Best,

Al

To Purdy (Ameliasburgh) from Birney (Vancouver)
July 30, 1969   TL

Al my patient friend

I know I know it is one hell of a time since you wrote me that good letter, and later the Acorn book came from Margaret Laurence. & nothing at all from Birney. It's been this fucking Lowry stuff. I hate him now, just as you would be hating me if you had stuck with that book on me, ruining Europe, your temper, Eurithe's health, etc. Anyway I got 225 pages of it of which HALF is apparatus, i.e. notes, bibliog., acknowledgments, index to titles, table of contents, et bloody cetera — and still I have a 20 page intro. to write. At least I got the main mess over to Cape's, exactly one month after the deadline![432] God knows what will happen now because, once Margerie Lowry sees those notes, all hell will break loose. Only because I've tried to be both honest and at times lighthearted, not taking too seriously what Malc wdnt ever have taken seriously either. Incidentally I found yr reminiscence of yr two visits to the shack most evocative — can you remember the year you heard him read the "Sestina"?[433]

I'm getting a laugh out of what the critics are doing to you, some of them that is, re. *Wild Grape Wine* — they are such fucking anxiety-driven bluffing knowitall nincompoops, our Cdn reviewers, that when they notice you dedicated the book to me they panic, thinking "jesus he's a friend of that old bastard, so maybe he was even INFLUENCED by him once." So they start frantically looking to see where the hell the influences are, & don't find any, & so they play it safe with guarded knowing allusions about the Pratt-Birney-Purdy tradition, etc.

Of all the things happening in Acorn's book what gave me most thought, pleasure, sense of gratitude, was your introduction and your "House Guest."[434] I

---

432. "Cape's": Jonathan Cape, publishers of several of Lowry's works, including the British edition of *Under the Volcano* and *Lunar Caustic* (1968), edited by EB and Margerie Lowry. EB was at this time preparing an annotated edition of Lowry's collected poems. The edition was not published: Cape objected to EB's lengthy introduction and Margerie Lowry objected to his having omitted some of Lowry's poems.

433. In a later essay, "Struggle against the Old Guard: Editing the *Canadian Poetry Magazine*" (1981), EB referred to Lowry's "Sestina in a Cantina" as "one of his best [poems], ... as fine a piece of writing, to my taste, as anything in *Under the Volcano*."

434. AP selected the poems for and wrote the introduction to Acorn's *I've Tasted My Blood: Poems*

say this not to put Milton down, but to affirm the paramount importance of your friendship, loyalty & persistent devotion to him as the most moving thing in the book; the book's very existence is the summation of that relationship.

In between agonizings over Lowry, I've proofed the "New Cdn Library poems of E... B...," catching &, I hope, scotching, the phrase in the publisher's puffs that I had "travelled expensively in many parts of the world" (how the critics & the Cancow [Canada Council] would love that).[435]

So the beautiful (and man, it *was* beautiful) Vancouver summer has been slipping away outside the flat windows.

When are you coming west??? Is Eurithe all better? Will you send me yr new poems, or bring them out with you?

Posting you today a copy of *Memory No Servant*. Sorry you didn't get one long ago as I intended.

Have you done yr CBC readings and all? As for you working with Colombo in August instead of coming out here, well man, you deserve whatever you get. You shd learn to stay away from that fucker.

Esther is well, workless but busy being an executive type for various artfarty & groupey-gropey outfits, when she isn't, poor girl, grinding out Lowry commentaries on the typewriter for me.

In case you haven't run into Joe [Rosenblatt] he's at 39 Roxborough St. W., Toronto 185.

I don't have any local news as I've been in my monkish cell all along. Newhouse dropped in one day & I hear occasionally from Jim Brown, Seymour Mayne, Dorothy Livesay, Judy Copithorne, John Mills but usually only when they want something.[436] Which is fair enough seeing as how I never try to get in touch with them, or anybody, anymore.

But you, I do want to hear from!

Earle

1956 to 1968.

435. *The Poems of Earle Birney: A New Canadian Library Selection* (1969).

436. EB might have had in mind Edward Newhouse (1911–2002), an American novelist whose *This Is Your Day* (1937) he reviewed in *The Canadian Forum* (June 1937). But EB probably meant to write "Newlove," as in John Newlove, the poet and editor at McClelland and Stewart. Jim Brown (b. 1943) started, with Seymour Mayne, Patrick Lane, and bill bissett, a publishing imprint, Very Stone House Press, in 1965. AP's review essay on the poetry of Mayne, bissett, Lane, and Brown appeared in *Canadian Literature* 35 (Winter 1968) and was reprinted in *SA* (349–52). John Mills (b. 1930): Professor of English at Simon Fraser University, memoirist, novelist (*Runner in the Dark*, 1992), and critic (*Robertson Davies and His Works*, 1984).

To Birney (Vancouver) from Purdy (Ameliasburgh)
August 3 ("I think"), 1969   TL

Dear Earle,

So, I thought you'd decided to ignore me forever, and wondered what had happened. I enclose a review I did recently on Lowry, my remark on the Lowry industry calculated to rouse your ire. Actually un-calculated. It was 53 or 54, since I believe Lowry left in '54 — that we did the drinking and Malcolm recited "Sestina." I mention this hastily in case you read the review first, for something called the *Five Cent Review* in Mtl.

Okay, you definitely do have my sympathy re the Lowry book, but far better you than me. I *couldn't* write the goddam book. I really did Epstein an injustice, but fuck the Cabbala, Jewish or otherwise.[437] However, I didn't call the writer fat and 56 or like personal remarks as someone did in *CanFor* recently to Layton. Letter from Mtl. says he's shafting me, and I wonder why the hell he would do that. Not that I really give a shit, for that's Irving.

Hey — I'm not workin with Colombo! Where did you get that idea? I am supposed to be teaching three weeks at Ryerson, as is Colombo with a different class in creative writing. And I fear and tremble as time approaches.

Re critics — of course they are not entirely off-beam re Birney influence, but there've been so many it's hard to pick out one more than others. I've liked and been influenced by thousands and millions. I really would deny Pratt tho, or even the tradition, since he seems entirely inhuman in his verse to me. Also, the "public poet" bit is disgusting and annoys me (I shall now write 88 love poems).

Thanks for your good word on the intro., and the friendship was very real once. Tho I am far too impatient and intolerant now to have many close friends. I am indulgent towards Acorn, and isn't that the ultimate insult? Condescension. Can't stand naiveté. Innocence, yes, that rare rare. If I do something I ought to be ashamed of, I want to know and realize it, and doubt if naive people do know. Ego is just as bad, the extreme said [side?] of it. Which is enough to bugger me completely, since I do have ego.

Congrats on the new *Selected*. Any new poems? Hope so.

Hafta wait till after this teaching bit, then try and work up some univ. readings to pay for trip west. Now writing letters to univs.

Later, plan to live somewhere interesting and write poems for winter, dunno where. Too lazy for it to be a place that would make physical demands on me, but thinking of an Indian reserve, tho may abandon that too. Any suggestions?

---

437. AP's reference was to Perle S. Epstein's *The Private Labyrinth of Malcolm Lowry: Under the Volcano and the Cabbala* (1969).

Doing a privately printed expensive art book here, local artist and woodcuts, some twenty poems, all new or just about. Probly sell for $20.–$25. if things work out. Send a copy later. Not done yet. Eurithe is okay, drives the hell outa me. Know any vacant mistresses?

I am serious about goin somewhere this winter, but all up in the air. Typing typing typing. Queen's has offered to buy worksheets, and since I'm peeved with […] will probably take em up on it, which means more work listing. Figure seven [grand] this time, since I hear Joan Finnigan got 4.5 from Queen's. I am also in a very […] state, the which I will relate to you when I see you. Real black night of the — […] love is hopeless. Aha, tho, it got me a coupla good poems! What shall I do […] girls when my old muse is dead? Sing we for love and idleness? […] Joe wrote me, will see him in Tor. You would not recognize me now, the carefree […] after beer, and I wear the bottom of my trousers etc. (Those goddam tags […] run thru your head!) And jesus tenants over in Trenton not paying their rent […] shit demanding it. Never own houses, except what you live in. […] sad, and I have visions of women. Helluva thing.

Best,

Al

Next day — are you spending fall and winter in Van., or elsewhere? Sun shining brightly, record player going, me drinking beer and it's still morning — I look forward to seeing you in leisure, i.e. not having to do something soon, a few days of nothing urgent to talk about etc. See you then —

To Birney (Vancouver) from Purdy (Ameliasburgh)
"Aug 5 or 6, '69"   TL[438]

Dear Earle,

I'm kinda lonesome for Birney, sitting in the midst of rural rural Ont[ario] with beautiful trees waving in the breeze etc. However, the delay getting west is for money's sake (not because I want to work at the same school with Colombo — incidentally, there's even a slight double-cross re this last antho he's doing with Hurtig, but then my paranoia and Birney's perhaps cancel out) — I have the last instalment of CC grant, and not a great deal more, since spent so much in Europe.[439] Therefore I am creating a lit agency called "E. Parkhurst Agency" of 91 Cannifton Rd., Belleville. This agency has already written thirteen letters on my

---

438. YA 147–48.

439. *How Do I Love Thee: Sixty Poets of Canada (and Quebec) Select and Introduce Their Favourite Poems from Their Own Work* (1970), edited by John Robert Colombo and published by M.G. Hurtig.

behalf to univs in Ont. soliciting readings at $150. per. More letters to western univs soon when I get all their names and places. Friend who's doing a book in Trenton (unbelievably in Trenton, with a Dutch émigré artist who's pretty good — sorta luxury item with about 15 woodcuts) printed up a few letterheads for the new agency. "E. Parkhurst" is, of course, Eurithe's maiden name.[440] I hope to bring you a copy of this book on the way west, since it will consist of most new poems.

Really tho, the place seems dull here, or else I'm dull — despite a coupla readings at Albert College (that one was incredible on accounta the Presbyterian principal, etc. It was the students wanted me to read there and paid the shot, and the principal snuck in in the middle of [the] reading, heard a bad word and departed hurriedly. We drank beer in the lit. teacher's quarters, he scanning students for over or under 21 years. Like being in a eunuchs' monastery.) Also Mtl. at Sir Geo. [Sir George Williams University] with time spent at [A.J.M.] Smith's, which was also hilarious. So many things about this trip were funny or sad, it's too long for a letter. Smith really is a goddam square tho, albeit a sad square —

The house here is much changed from time of your stay (no empty wine bottles, all beer now), I use one bedroom for workroom with new bookcases built there, office desk I picked up cheap, and posters all over the wall. Incidentally, you oughta get McStew to do a poster of you for the CanLib ed. of selected.[441] We even have water in the kitchen piped up from the lake, electrical appliances humming thru the night —

Bowering says he has 23,000 words done of a book on me, a book which I both welcome and feel apprehension about.[442] I.e. will there be any real insights in it, will it tell me anything about myself I don't know — both of which are doubtful, not to slight George at all. (His new book coming with Anansi, which I read for CC [Canada Council], is goddam good.)[443] However, it might help to sell Purdy and thus make me a buck. I thought I had a few insights about Birney while writing his book, but later it looked just bad. I seemed to say all the obvious things, Birney's compassion etc.

See you later,

Best,

Al

440. *The Quest for Ouzo* was published in 1970 by M. Kerrigan Almey, the "friend ... in Trenton." See AP's letter of 14 June 1970. The "Dutch émigré artist" was Tony Lassing.

441. *The Poems of Earle Birney: A New Canadian Library Selection* (1969).

442. *Al Purdy*, by George Bowering (1970).

443. *The Gangs of Kosmos* (1969).

To Purdy (Ameliasburgh) from Birney (Vancouver)
August 22, 1969   TL

Al man have patience with me friend.

This Lowry thing is a jinx, like all Lowryngs anybody ever tried. Haven't locked myself in a garage with the motor running yet, like Knickerbocker did, but sure have been feeling like it.[444] Incredibly difficult job, dragging itself out. In last fortnight I kept going only by Esther's patience & good letters from Maschler, the Cape ed., saying how everything I was sending was wonderful etc. Then I sent him the best part, the 47 page introd., sweatedout of my guts — & he writes back saying he was "embarrassed" because he wanted "only a page or two at most" and he didn't want a scholarly edition at all, etc. The sonofabitch has had almost 4 years of contact with me about this book, mainly letters of pressure from him to get the job done, & nothing said about wanting a simple pops. edition — in fact he made happy noises about the *one hundred pages of notes* I sent, & didn't even quiver when I warned him the intro. would be "at least 20 pages." Obviously Margerie [Lowry], or somebody, has got at him, because this is an honest edition & doesn't exactly pull punches about Lowry being a plagiarizer, liar, whiner, & all-time drunk, as well as a wonderfully funny & fantastically imaginative & sensitive cat. So I am left with a huge apparatus, that cost me some of my remaining eyesight & what could have been a wonderful sunshiny loafing summer to write, plus spare time over the last *ten years* to edit — which I can't market since most of it refers to poems I can't publish without Cape's & Margerie's consent — all I can do is offer a compromise (cut my intro. down from 47 to 20 pp) or take my junk back & tell them to get a new editor. What with all this & the usual depression when a book is (or is thought by its author to be) finished, & the pressure already from Holt R & W [Holt, Rinehart and Winston] to write crap for them, I am about ready to check out [of] this vale of tears.

I did enjoy yr Lowry "review" — the best kind of anti-review — I should have done an anti-edition. If I was smart like you instead of just over-educated, I'd have thought of it.

I hope yr experience with Ryerson Institute hasn't been too grisly. Doug Fetherling seems impressed with yr Patience* as a teacher, but I suspect that's just unnecessary awe of academia, desire to Make Good, and all, it can't last. Because academia isn't worth being patient with, in the long run. The young who get caught in its toils are worth being patient about, of course, but that's all. The universities should all be dynamited (except for the special collections depts that buy Purdy & Birney MSS). I'm sure you'd make a good teacher, of course, but what a waste of a good man, poet, potential anti-novelist, & all.

---

444. Conrad Knickerbocker committed suicide in 1966. He had been trying to write a biography of Lowry.

Only new poem in the new McStew paperback is the 1969 version of "Canada: Case History" printed in July *Sat Nite*. There wasn't room even for the best of the old ones, as I had to keep the size down or McStew wd raise the price — they tried to raise it anyway (from $1½ to $3), but I refused.

(Interruption!) Arrival of yr sisinlaw Judy with 3 other pleasant nursing wenches, for morning coffee, an hr ago. They had good trip it seems (by *car*, I mean — one must distinguish from acid, mescaline & other trips these days) — & I gather you & Eurithe are well, & that is good.

Hope you've got contacts worked up by now for that trip west. Otherwise I'll have to work up one going east, or maybe we shd plan to meet in Moose Jaw or Queen Maud Gulf.

Hope also you make something out of that 25 buck edition. It's a logical thing to do & have thought about it myself but never did anything — instead, have for the moment tied up with a young mixed media artist, Andy Suknaski, in the production, so far, of three books that are so damned exclusive they exist in only 3 copies of each edition.[445] They are mainly monoprints made off glass, with words by me & designs & execution (the big job, natch) by him. The largest of the three books has extracts from "November Walk [near False Creek Mouth]" built into "concretes" and measures 2 by 3½ feet. I can't wait to try it on the U of T library, which refused only one-foot high collages [Leonard] Brooks did for my *Sel. Poems* [1966] as being too large & unwieldy to handle, heh! Actually the edition of this big one will be reduced from 3 copies to 2 when Suknaski gets back to town from his summer job in Lake Louise, as he has designed a kite-form into which we will fold each page of one copy, & fly them into the Vancouver skies & let em go, to land in the saltchuck maybe, or in some bemused Lulu Island farmer's blueberry patch. He has also done some sand-candles with some word-designs we made up carved on them & we plan to light these on Third Beach some night & leave them for the tide. Anti-publication.

I am also serious about going somewhere this winter. What about Mexico? Or Apia, which is real cheap, lovely climate & girls & water.

How's Joe? Give him my very best & tell him to write me.

You are right about AJMS [A.J.M. Smith], a "sad square." Would have been more of a swinger if he had married a poor wife or none at all. He's had it too soft all his life, on the basis of about a year's creativity as an undergrad & a conscientious-conservative job as an anthologist/critic. But I do like him.

Damn I wish I cd talk with you &, as you say "in leisure; not having to do something." Wd like very much to be in Toronto next month for various reasons (paperback coming out, some "research" I gotta do into my own bloody letters,

---

445. Andrew Suknaski (1942–2012): Canadian artist and poet (*Wood Mountain Poems*, 1976) whose works often concerned western Canadian history, including Ukrainian settlement on the prairies.

at U. of T., for another book; recording to do) but above all to see you and one or two other old friends I miss all the time. If you don't come west soon, then expect to see me in the east! Or, as I say, maybe in Queen Maud Sound or San Miguel Allende (better the latter, since I can't speak Eskimo like you).

Say hello to Eurithe & tell her she's got a nice sister, which is only to be expected.

Cheers. Write.

Earle

* Note for Eurithe: this is not the name of another dame of Al's.

To Birney (Vancouver) from Purdy (Ameliasburgh)
August 29, 1969   TL[446]

Dear Earle, (gee whiz a letter) (!!!!)

Before I forget — and Geddes may have already written you — Frank Davey is onto the Birney book now.[447] He was down here copying the tapes I made at Waterloo and seems very enthusiastic. I don't think much of Davey's poems, but he is some kind of pedantic half-assed scholar, and I rather think he will do a good job on my failure. As a person he doesn't appeal to me either, but setting this aside he wants to make a reputation as a critic etc., which I expect may horrify you. But never fear, he thinks too much of himself to write a book he doesn't believe in somewhat more than himself — He is also very thorough-going, and I think will work hard and I hope quickly; especially since Bowering tells me he has $35,000 (jesus, what a typo!) on Purdy, words that is. And I still feel a little guilty about failure on Birney —

I forbear pointing out that the Lowry book is your own damn fault, and am too kind to gloat at your troubles with it, and editors. It's a bloody hard job, for your kind of writer, needs more of a pedant such as Mandel or Dudek etc. Of course I expect you were fond enough of Lowry to wanta take the book on for that reason mostly, and I strongly agree that the intro you wrote on the human side of Lowry — from what you say it appears to be on that side of him —should be included.

The teaching bit at Ryerson was grisly at first, and Colombo bugged me

446. *YA* 148–50.

447. Frank Davey (b. 1940): Canadian poet (*Selected Poems: The Arches*, 1980), critic (*Surviving the Paraphrase: Eleven Essays on Canadian Literature*, 1983), editor (*Tish, Open Letter*), and professor at York University and the University of Western Ontario. As the letters between AP and EB indicate, AP had abandoned the project of a critical study of EB's poetry. He gave his taped interviews to Davey, a former student of EB's at UBC, much to EB's displeasure.

whether he knew he did it or not, one snide remark about waiting for my drop-out students in his classroom down the hall which enraged me quietly, so that I was waiting for verbal opening with him later. However, I got back any dropouts later and some of Colombo's too when I figured out in the second week some sort of method. I just yakked away as a sort of M.C. about students' poems, got them to comment and set the comment against something else, got rebuttals for opinions etc. I.e., I worked it so the people there did much of the discussing. Nights I drank beer and stronger, got home to hotel late several occasions, hangovers in the daytime, tho not prostrating ones. As I did mention before, I believe, money was foremost thing, but I spent most of it on beer and hotel. But the secondary thing was I'd be able to say I taught at Ryerson if need money and the occasion arises again. At the end I felt all fucked out, mainly because my voice seemed to echo in my head, and mere act of speaking was tiring. I find lately that my voice on such occasions has grown much louder than it used to be, losing all my previous genius for sensitivity and delicacy of course, so that I feel like a goddam pipe organ or something. Among the students: an ex-nun, a private eye, and a girl who when I read her poems on request was so afraid of men that I could feel her ass (not really) edge away from me on the studio. Jesus, I thought, hope she doesn't get any friction burns from nylon.

Yeah, Judy is a pleasant gal, who yearns for a different sort of mental life than she has, and knows such exists.

Sure, I like ajms [A.J.M. Smith] myself, but a weathervane in conversation and a square in print.

You too on the de luxe bit — I shall withdraw my own (if it ever comes) from circ [circulation] until Birney gets his outa the way. But I've been payin so much money to this kid in Trenton I'm scared the profit will be rare and scarce rather than the book. Lesson to Birney: keep costs down to beer.

I think I'm joining Birney as a father-figure, since young poets keep writing about their troubles, asking advice etc. So many poets are out and out nuts, not sane sober like you and I, eh?

I like the idea of Birney poems, subversive I hope, landing in the saltchuck.

Spoke to Alison [Hunt] at Ryerson party end of classes, twitted her about "betraying" Birney with a nice guy when she could have had a genius, or almost had one. That's approximate, but you can guess. I knew this Harold Acker she married before (you did know she got married?) and he rouses great non-enthusiasm. And I must be getting crotchety, since that's two unenthusiasms in this letter. Eurithe promptly mentions that I shouldn't refer to Birney in Harold's presence, just isn't done, so must restrain myself I guess. Same party: James Farrell was up from N.Y., and Colombo not invited (joy joy).[448]

Best,

Al

To Purdy (Ameliasburgh) from Birney (Vancouver)
September 4, 1969   TL

Dear Al

I was glad to have a letter from you, & to know things didn't go too badly for you at Ryerson's. However, your opening sentence was a jolt and has left me quite dismayed at the turn of events. No-one had told me Frank Davey was going to write a book on me, & Geddes has never written me about it. Furthermore, as you must surely realize, I made those tapes with *you* and *for you*, at Waterloo. I was letting all guards down because I was talking with a friend whom I could trust not to use my frankness hostilely. They are a record of not too sober an evening which, as you will recall, began with the notion we were going to "cover the biographical part" on one tape, or something like that — & it turned out we had an enjoyable evening & got not very far at all, & you were dissatisfied with the taped result afterwards (and quite understandably) … what you must understand now is that I can't permit those tapes to be used by *anybody*. & Davey is just about "anybody" to me, since he was never at any time a friend, and for quite a while bore some unexplained hostility to me. He was a student of mine; I think he got firstclass marks from me; but he scarcely ever attended my lectures, & wouldn't speak to me in the hallways — and since he graduated I have never seen him! Add to that record of his knowledge of me, the one or two remarks he has made about me in print, and you don't come up with somebody likely to know or understand much about me or what I have been trying to do as an artist. You say he is "some kind of pedantic half-assed scholar." Is this the kind of guy you would like doing the book on *you*, from tapes I had made of *your* uninhibited conversations with me? The whole thing leaves me sick. I was glad *for your sake* that you quit on the job and glad anyway, since *I don't want a book about me.* I'm fucking well not dead yet. Let the "half-assed pedantic scholars" feed off my corpse not the living me. I know I can't *prevent* books being written by failed poets anxious to get a salary raise as professors, but I'm damned if I am going to help them along. The decent thing for Geddes' firm to have done was to have written me & asked if they could use your tape, *before* letting Davey go down to Ameliasburgh. I would have said "no" but at

---

448. James T. Farrell (1904–79): American novelist best known for his three *Studs Lonigan* novels (1932–35).

least I would have offered to meet Davey somewhere & give him his own taped interview with me & this is still possible but *he is not to make public use of your tape* nor is anyone else, except you, from now on. Will you please write Geddes & tell him this.

You say nothing about coming west. It looks as if I'll be in Toronto in October & will hope to see you then.

Cape have accepted my compromises, which means I must throw more than half the introduction back into the backpage notes, which will probably take up most of September.

As ever,
Earle

To Birney (Vancouver) from Purdy (Ameliasburgh)
September 5, 1969 TL

Dear Earle,

I've written Davey forbidding him to use the tapes made here, mention[ed] that this is by your instructions.[449] I've also suggested that he write to you immediately, and make whatever arrangements are to be made that way. I've told him to do this a couple of times before, but this is urgent enough for him to pay some attention I think. Geddes knows nothing about these tapes Davey made; however, will write him too.

I've got about six readings at univs lined up for Oct., therefore this trip west will end at Van. sometime in Nov. If you are going to be in Toronto then, I'd better have an address???

Up to my ass in work, so keep this short.

Best,
Al

To Purdy (Ameliasburgh) from Birney (Vancouver)
September 15, 1969 TPC

Dear Al,

Thanks for yours of the fifth. I've heard from Davey, though he doesn't say he's heard from you. His letter is O.K. and opens the way for dealing with him about

---

449. AP wrote to Davey (5 Sept. 1969), who was then writer-in-residence at Sir George Williams University in Montreal, to warn that his use of the tapes might result in EB's taking legal action. In an earlier letter to AP (12 Aug. 1969), Davey had inquired about the tapes. The letters are held in the Frank Davey Papers at Simon Fraser University.

the new book. Will see him in Montreal or Toronto next month. Won't know my Toronto address until I arrive but will let Mrs. Hodgeman know at McStew. Still can't get Lowry book finished because of eye-strain. This card is being typed by a beautiful girl who is now blushing.

Same to you,
Earle

To Al and Eurithe Purdy (Vancouver) from Birney (Fiji)
December 3, 1969　APC

Hi Friends!

[EB underlined part of the caption printed on the postcard:] "Soko the hula girl always has a smile for you!" Only a smile — but the weather is good to you too. At the moment, am in a "guest house" on a small island, while waiting for a copra schooner to take us towards some more skindiving and island hopping. ("Us" is Tony & I, not Soko.)[450] Hope you got that poem wrapped up as ordered, Al, & free to write what & when you want. Beat him when he's bad, Eurithe.

Love to you both,
Earle

To Birney (Fiji?) from Purdy (Vancouver)
December 7, 1969　TL

Dear Earle,

Hope you are sun-soaked and writing. I am, as usual, sun-lamped, and with a deadline. I think, as you surmised before leaving, that the trip will be a damn good thing for you, rest, isolation etc.

I've been offered a job with Simon Fraser [University], as "Visiting Associate Prof" for first four mos of 70, can teach more or less what interests me, since it has to do with my own development, long jaw-breaking title of course thought up by [Gerald] Newman [the chairman of English], work load nine hours a week. Despite the fact that I've wanted something like this a long time I may refuse, since I'm overwhelmed with thoughts like: how much time have I, and do I really need the $4,700. they offer?? Shit, I'm not that short of money, tho I could certainly use this, who couldn't? — but have a house and a few bucks comin in, so what the hell.

Maclean's magazine phoned, want a poem on nationalism, but give me lots

---

450. Tony Kilgallin (b. 1941): Professor of English at UBC and author of a critical study of Malcolm Lowry (*Lowry*, 1973). EB met Wailan (then Lily) Low through Kilgallin, who was her undergraduate thesis supervisor. The trip to Fiji that resulted in "Four Feet Between" and other poems was taken with Kilgallin, as the letter indicates.

of leeway and can write within that general area, which includes a lot of things for me. Also the CBC thing is done in first draft, tho I've worked at it only desultorily, and it may not be very satisfactory on typing.[451]

News: Mowat and Jack McClelland here Friday, former signing books, latter at a party at Bayshore Inn, which I attended with Esther, Eurithe and Pat Xmas … Usual sort of thing, Mowat with what I would judge to be an 18-year-old in tow. Jack looking a little weary of it all. Letter from Joe Rosenblatt in France, hentracks so bad I couldn't read.[452]

Think if I ever get to doing this McStew antho with Town portraits, will do a tough intro, since I'm a bit sick of pussyfooting reviews.[453]

Dinner with Phyllis Webb at her place at Whytecliff [in West Vancouver] yesterday. Think we shall leave for Vancouver Island next week, for as long as we feel interested. Have to get passport from Ottawa, since mine has run out, then Mexico if I don't take the Simon Fraser thing. From all this you can gather a great deal of indecision. The money is hard to turn down, but I would like to write a few more poems before leaving this mortal coil. Somehow working at SFU seems to be a positive deterrent, whether I'm right or not. I don't really like the yak-yak of such jobs, nor need the ego-food —

Anyway, I hope some tall seductive maiden strides toward you at this moment, and that poems are writing themselves in your mind.

Best,

Al

To Birney (Vancouver) from Purdy (Ameliasburgh)
May 18, 1970   TL[454]

Dear Earle,

Wanted to say hi before the mails get stopped.[455]

How is it with you, even if you can't answer? These being general good wishes

---

451. In 1970 the CBC published *Poems for Voices*, an anthology of commissioned poems by AP, Margaret Atwood, John Newlove, Phyllis Gotlieb, Tom Marshall, and Alden Nowlan. The following year the CBC broadcast and released *Al Purdy's Ontario*.

452. AP's letter to Rosenblatt of 5 Dec. 1969 begins on a similar note: "Dear Joe, If I could read your goddam writing I'd reply at more length" (*YA* 154).

453. AP intended to compile an anthology of poems by Canadian poets with portraits of the authors by Harold Town. The project was abandoned because of a dispute over the division of royalties between AP and Town. (See AP's letter to EB of 12 May 1972.) The dispute is recounted in *RBS* 245–47 and *YA* 194–99. *Love Where the Nights Are Long: Canadian Love Poems* (1962), edited by Irving Layton, was a model for the proposed collaboration. On Town, see also AP's preface to *Love in a Burning Building* (1970). Illustrations by Town (dated 1970) of EB appear as the frontispieces in the two volumes of EB's *Collected Poems* (1975).

454. *YA* 159–60.

455. There were several postal workers' strikes in 1970.

and questions, I say how did the tour go? How are your teeth roots? And what are you going to do now?

I believe I antagonized you over that Bromige thing, and want to say sorry over that.[456] Sorry to you, not to Bromige. Perhaps that isn't very generous of me, but I'm not always a very generous person.

But enough of such subjects. I went to Toronto for the Acorn shindig, and never saw so many people honouring a poet in my life.[457] People are really friendly to Acorn. And honestly, I think his book does and did deserve the award.[458] Not that I mean to put Bowering down with such a statement as Layton did with his ("there's more poetry in Acorn's dirty little finger nail than there is in the collected works of George Bowering": Layton). Still, Layton is generous. He phoned the premier of PEI to get money for Acorn, and got $200. Nice.

The party was loud, raucous and drunken, with me being not the soberest. Dave Godfrey, Gotlieb, Marty Ahvenus, Tom Marshall, Mandel, Layton and Aviva, Ron Everson, Dorothy Livesay (all the way from Edmonton), and dozens of others.[459]

I may have had the distinction of being involved in the only overt unfriendliness there (at Grossman's Tavern). Was escorting a Ryerson Press editorial girl (nice and blonde and sexy) to the can, and thru my own clumsiness caused her

---

456. David Bromige (1933–2009): Poet (*Desire: Selected Poems 1963–1987*, 1988) who was born in England and raised partly in Canada. He emigrated to the United States in 1962 and was associated with the American experimental poetry scene. In *RBS* AP describes an incident with Bromige, "whom I loathe wholeheartedly" (236). Bromige had reviewed AP's *The Crafte So Longe to Lerne* (1959) unfavourably in *Canadian Literature* 4 (Spring 1960); AP evidently thought that Bromige had reviewed *Pressed on Sand* (1955) as well as *The Crafte So Longe to Lerne*: "He keel-hauled and flogged them in his review, infecting them with syphilis and gonorrhea; he bastinadoed them with poisonous verbs on the soles of their feet. One might even suspect he didn't like my writing" (236). AP later reviewed two of Bromige's books (*The Gathering*, 1965; *The Ends of the Earth*, 1968) in *Queen's Quarterly* 76.4 (Winter 1964), to which Bromige and some colleagues objected. "Earle Birney had received one of the Bromige howls of protest, and it was the only one that concerned me even slightly. Earle wasn't sure of my literary morality in this instance" (*RBS* 237).

457. After Milton Acorn's *I've Tasted My Blood*, for which AP wrote an introduction (reprinted in *SA*), was overlooked for the 1969 Governor General's Award for poetry, a celebration in Acorn's honour was held at Grossman's Tavern in Toronto on 16 May 1970. The event is described in AP's autobiography as "half farce and half solemn event" (*RBS* 238).

458. George Bowering (*Rocky Mountain Foot* and *The Gangs of Kosmos*) and Gwendolyn MacEwen (*The Shadow-Maker*) shared the Governor General's Award. See the letter of 2 July 1970.

459. Phyllis Gotlieb (1926–2009): Canadian poet (*The Works: Collected Poems*, 1978) and science-fiction writer (*O Master Caliban!*, 1976). Ronald Gilmore Everson (1903–92): Canadian poet (*Indian Summer*, 1976) whose literary career remained secondary to his career in public relations. But he was not unknown: four poems by Everson were included, for example, in *Modern Canadian Verse in English and French* (1967), an anthology edited by A.J.M. Smith. The selection of poems for *Everson at Eighty* (1983) was made by AP. AP's poem "Fathers," from *The Stone Bird* (1981), is dedicated to Everson. EB's "Trawna Tuh Belvul by Knayjin Psifik," from *Fall by Fury & Other Makings* (1978) is dedicated to Ron and Lorna Everson. As a mutual friend of EB's and AP's, Everson is mentioned throughout the correspondence. Aviva Cantor was Irving Layton's third wife.

to fall flat among the beer-drinkers. Raised her to her feet apologizing feverishly and confusedly, and proffered her a cigar by way of recompense and absolution. Was about to light it when this guy I'd never seen before heaves in sight six inches from my left nostril and says with unmistakeable nastiness: "Fuck off!" Well, heavens to betsey, Earle, you know me better than to think I could possibly have done anything to offend him. Nevertheless the acrimony was strong, and I felt he wished me no peace of mind for the next few minutes. But with the peacefulness inherent in all the tribe of Purdys I questioned him re his intentions, only to have the same instructions repeated. Whereupon I shoved him vigorously around the scapula into a table full of beer drinkers. Then lit the lady's cigar, keeping a weather eye peeled to see his reaction to that. But the waiters, having seen me clasping a microphone previously and thinking I was Mayor Dennison, threw the other guy out as a gesture of courtesy towards high municipal office.[460]

It was a silly memorable evening, with Acorn making a speech, Mandel making a speech, and Layton the peroration, myself having said I wanted to drink beer only. Acorn got a large metallic object on a purple ribbon pinned to his throat — and what the hell! — you've been thru those shindigs yourself —

This may or may not get to you for a while. But good health and all that, and wishes etc. Also affection.

Best,

Al

To Purdy (Ameliasburgh) from Birney (Vancouver)
May 25, 1970   TL

Dear Al

Marvelous account of the Acoronation at Grossman's Tavern. If it isn't already whipped into poemshape I know it's going to be or ought to be. Good to hear from you. Would have written, myself, earlier but have been once more under the weather. It seems my good luck stopped when the Age of Aquarius began. It was May 2nd, a Sat. nite, I last saw you & Eurithe. Had a beer or two in that dark tavern after your reading. The next day I found I had a mounting infection from the place in the back of my mouth where the dentist's needle had gone in. (2 days before I saw you I had 8 fillings & various other things done, aftermath of the original accident.) The infection spread by the Tues. into my mastoid & my jaws slowly closed (again!) & I had to return to the weary round of doctors, antibiotics, clinics, painkillers, liquid diet, vitamins. This time with the addition of a Water Pik (very sensuous — shoots warm water between the holes in the clenched

---

460. William Dennison (1905–81): Mayor of Toronto from 1967 to 1972.

teeth). But nothing stopped the spread of the infection or the monumental ear-&-face aches so I got off back to Vanc. while I could still risk riding in a plane, as air-pressure-changes are hell for mastoiditis. So visited a new set of doctors etc here, like in Feb., & then went over to a cottage on Galiano [Galiano Island, BC] that Esther had rented for the summer. But had to come back after 3 days because of new symptoms. They decided I might be getting meningitis but didn't think there was anything they could do but wait till I had it, then bore a hole in my skull. Fortunately, 2 days ago, the turn came, the infection retreated somewhere under my neck, where it lies in ambush, a hard angry painshooting lump, and my jaws have actually opened up enough to slide crackers through. But the total experience is extremely debilitating (& boring, since alcohol is banned, or was). But I'm going to venture back to Galiano in a day or two now, & hope to begin the poem-writing I had planned to begin on February first. Can't see how I can make the McStew deadline now, for fall publication that is. Damn.

As for the Bromige affair, you didn't "antagonize" me, as you say, you just said things I don't agree with, which is fine, necessary in fact (how boring to be always agreeing with one's friends), but it happened that Bromige is also a friend, & put me on the spot by sending me a Xerox of his letter to the QQ [Queen's Quarterly] & asking me what I thought, so I had to be honest when I replied to him. The gist of what I said to him was that if I were in his place I wd also feel a little hurt & maybe indignant but that he shd know by now that reviews of his book were not something a poet can let himself get worried about, as they aren't directed at him but at the "public" that reads the mag. the review appears in, that reviewing is a nasty little game anyway but it's one a writer sometimes has to play, if he is, as Al Purdy is, trying to make his living as a professional writer (unlike Bromige). I went on to say to Bromige: "Al, as you say, is my friend, but I don't have to agree with what my friends say or do, just try to understand. I think I do understand Al's gibe at Bates & other profs because they come from a fine poet who has often been unjustly ignored or put-down by Can.lit. profs — & I understand the sort of highspirits, frankness & cussedness which leads him to tell his readers he feels malicious about you & so here goes![461] But understanding doesn't mean approving. I agree with you that he doesn't discuss your poetry fairly, clearly, or objectively, let alone sympathetically. So I think you have a right to complain, & to tell others you feel the way you do. But I don't know whether all this *gets* anywhere. Myself, I've had as much shit thrown at me as any Can. poet ever had, & most of it by college profs; I've generally tried to ignore it, just as I ignored the roses I got too, because neither are relevant *to me*; I know my own faults & virtues better than they do; & I

---

461. Ronald Bates (1924–95): Canadian poet (*The Wandering World*, 1959) and critic (*Northrop Frye*, 1971) who taught at the University of Toronto and the University of Western Ontario.

write to please myself first, & reviewers last. True, once in a while I get mad, when I feel a *personal* attack, & I fight back. It lets off steam but nobody wins these battles, & time-energy is drained off from what might have been real word-work. I think you deserved a better review. Maybe Al thinks so himself now, but that's for him to say. I'm sure you'll live to get better, & better ones. Cheers ... P.S. Almost forgot — about Black Mountain: just a Black Herring across this trail."

So now you know what I said & you can stop worrying that you "antagonized" me; it was Bromige who winkled me out into stating my own views — & I doubt that these will antagonize *you*, in return! Hope not, anyway. Don't give *me* up, just give up reviewing; the time you have to spend on it, & on scrapping with the reviewed, etc., is surely an "expense of spirit in a waste of shame" to quote, I think, the Old Man, Will Shaks. himself — who wasn't talking abt bkreviewing, because the Elizabethans were too smart to invent it.[462]

Keep in touch. & keep well. & write poems. & if you come out thisaway this summer, remember there's an island home, facing Active Pass, for you both to come to.

Love to Eurithe.

& even to you, you mean old flogger of the young poets,

Earle

To Birney (Vancouver) from Purdy (Ameliasburgh)
June 14, 1970   TL

Dear Earle,

Thanks for being generous, a quality I like to think I have but don't always. I know damn well that I probably (probably?) shouldn't be doing reviews, and I'm in the midst of one right now that illustrates what you said. Newlove's new book is not as good as it should be, and I have to say so.[463] I also have to say it justly and fairly, without wounding him if possible — something that perhaps (perhaps?) I didn't do with Bromige, and which he certainly didn't do when he reviewed me and others a few years ago. I suppose that last is the way I justify myself. However, reviews force me to read books carefully, which I might not always do if not for the job. I look for the writer's intent, and did he make it, why did he fail or succeed etc etc?[464]

What the hell. I enclose a poem ["The Horseman of Agawa"] I wrote after

---

462. From Shakespeare's Sonnet 129: "Th' expense of spirit in a waste of shame / Is lust in action."
463. The "new book" by Newlove was *The Cave* (1970).
464. AP's review of *The Cave* ("Calm Surfaces Destroyed") in *Canadian Literature* 48 (Spring 1971) was in fact fairly mild: "I remain dissatisfied with this book, despite its merits. Despair and bitterness are sometimes good material for poems; but some kind of magnificence and/or profundity has to come out of them." The review is reprinted in *SA* (340–42).

a week's trip to Nor Ont., took it to *Globe and Mail* mag ed. and he [inserted: "editor"] phoned the next day and is gonna use it with illos [illustrations]. That pleases me, for I think it's a good poem. I enclose it — feeling sentimental at the moment perhaps. It reassures me that I can still hit it once in a while, helps to alleviate the washed up feeling I get sometimes when doing too many reviews. Despite being a carbon it was typed for you, that is typed again earlier than it would have been otherwise. What I mean is, it's a sort of unburnt offering to Birney. (The treacle is dripping from typewriter's keys!)

Kerrigan fucked up the covers of my ltd. ed. book so it went to a pro bindery in Toronto, now back for more work from Kerrigan then to Toronto again.[465]

I will almost very-likely certainly be doing an antho of young poets under-30 for Ryerson P. Both text and trade. Andy Suknaski and Sid Marty (his friend) will be liberally included.[466] Have been corresponding with Andy — whom I like much. Title: *Storm Warning*, which tickles me. It goes with *Fifteen Winds* and also implies the younger generation etc.[467]

Oh, and not-so-incidentally, Ont. Arts Council turned me down last year for money to do poems on Ont., of which "The Horseman of Agawa" is one, and which I intend to use as a demonstration to them of what I could do (egotistic bastard!) ...[468] Gonna apply again and give em the full treatment, full outline, poem from *Globe* and letters from kindly friends such as Birney if he will hold still for yet another imposition. Dammit, such letters are impositions, for I write them myself quite a lot and know how I feel. So if Birney is feeling snarly or otherwise distempered, I snarl back and say okay all right for you you fucker, you friend. Really tho, if you're busy and all that crap. So how can you refuse such a request? I guess I can't myself so how can you? Which is a helluva spot to put you in and I am now working myself into a state of guilt, so fuck it. I want the goddam money —

Party at Ron Everson's in Mtl., where I stayed with Everson. He is a pretty good guy I think, of course square but heart of gold and all that crap. I'm square too in a different way. Layton there (had dinner with he and Aviva before party)

---

465. Kerrigan Almey printed a fine edition of *The Quest for Ouzo* (1970) in a run of sixty-nine copies. From a letter from AP to Almey (17 Mar. 1970): "I'm very disappointed and even angered that the book is not completed. ... At this point I wish you'd never started it." The friendship seems to have recovered from this episode. In addition to *The Quest for Ouzo*, Almey printed broadsides of AP's "The Horseman of Agawa" and "The Peaceable Kingdom" (both 1970). EB's copy of the latter is held in the Thomas Fisher Rare Book Library in Toronto. AP included one of Almey's poems in *Storm Warning: The New Canadian Poets* (1971).

466. Sid Marty (b. 1944): Canadian conservationist, park warden in the Rockies, poet (*Headwaters*, 1973), and author of non-fictional works about the Canadian West (*Men for the Mountains*, 1978; *The Black Grizzly of Whiskey Creek*, 2008).

467. The books were *Storm Warning: The New Canadian Poets* (1971) and *Fifteen Winds: A Selection of Modern Canadian Poems* (1969), both edited by AP.

468. "The Horseman of Agawa" was eventually collected in *Sex & Death* (1973).

and took the opportunity to say clearly at one point in party to Bowering: that you don't have to use one poet to put another down. Layton having said to newspapers that "there was more poetry in Acorn's dirty little fingernail than in all G. Bowering's collected works" — This being how I make friends and influence people the wrong way.[469]

Best love,

Al

To Purdy (Ameliasburgh) from Birney (Galiano Island, British Columbia)[470]
July 2, 1970   TL

Dear Al

Writing this on a roof looking at Active Pass. Eagles coast over every hour or so, looking for the same salmon I am. However, I beat them to a couple of five-pound coho this week — going out with an old friend & ex-rwy man, Ed Ketcham, who goes out alone (when he doesn't take me or etc) in a twin-engine motorboat with 3 trolls, sailing thru the 6knot tiderips, whirls, & all, & the old bugger is 81. Good for me to feel like a young tyro again, out with skipper Ed. I last fished with him in 1957 & said goodbye I thought forever.

I appreciate the superscription with the horseman poem, & all the more because you are right, it *is* a good poem, you catch hold of something very tenuous & individual as well as immemorial & I'm sure Eurithe must like it too.[471]

I've been writing quite a few but not too happy [with] them. Won't send any of the new ones yet, but did mail off to you today a copy of *Pnomes* in case you haven't yet got one from bp.[472]

Sorry about the further delay in your special book but glad you've got another anthology under way with Ryerson — hope they don't remainder *this* one too, after 5000 copies sold! I'm afraid I have a very low opinion of the savvy of [The sentence was left incomplete.]

Yes yes of course tell me where to write letter for Ont Arts Council, when, & what to say.

---

469. Bowering was one of two winners of the 1969 Governor General's Award for poetry (for *Rocky Mountain Foot* and *The Gangs of Kosmos*); the other was Gwendolyn MacEwen (for *The Shadow-Maker*). Acorn's *I've Tasted My Blood* did not win, to which Layton objected. Further fuelling the acrimony was the fact that one of the jurors for the award was Warren Tallman, who had close connections to Bowering. See the letter of 18 May 1970.

470. EB typed a note after "Galiano Island": "but use Barclay [St.] addr. after first Sep."

471. The poem is one of AP's most memorable portrayals of Eurithe, who is nimble where he is clumsy as they negotiate a tricky route to view a rock painting: "Wait for me, dammit" (*BR* 209).

472. *Pnomes, Jukollages & Other Stunzas* (1969), published by bpNichol's Ganglia Press.

Glad you have good words to say of Ron Everson as I've always liked him but I know that Frank Scott & others in Mtrl do not, & for reasons that have to do with racist ideas they say he expressed — but that was long ago, I think, if ever, & I never found him that way in person or in his poetry, which I think is good & getting better.[473]

Expect to be back in Toronto in mid-Sep & perhaps up to Ottawa at same time, to take over the Govt. Wd you like to be Poet Lariat? Just say the word to your friend.

Yours truly,

Napoleon Bonap$_\wedge$arte[474]

To Birney (Vancouver) from Purdy (Ameliasburgh)
"July 8 or 9 I guess, '70"   TL

Dear Earle,

Of course I don't wanta be lariated poet, but I want the money. (I write hastily, on accounta my theory translated concret[ely] — jesus just knocked bottle of beer over with typewriter carriage — is always take full advantage of your friends.) If it can be done, yes. Should mention Pacey turned me down once on proposal by Dwyer, also Ottawa U.[475] So might be tough, and I don't expect it. Don't expect either to write many pomes if I got it or be happy as hell. But could save a coupla thou to bugger off and maybe perhaps possibly then write poems. That's what I wanted to say right away.

I don't really believe the bit about Everson being racist. I saw a piece in *Time* years ago that implied it, but you know the climate of that sort of thing. For instance, I hear people carelessly, every now and then, say things like "nigger" — but these people are not on their mental toes re implications etc. More I see of Everson more I think he's a damn good guy, — with, of course, peevish moments, the kind we all have. Not racist peevish moments, I don't think, on accounta he knows what he's saying re that.

Along these lines, someone once said to me (I think it was Smith) that Frank Scott treated waiters very tough if they weren't on their toes. Nothing to be gained from this crap tho. I can, occasionally — even in bed — snarl with the worst of them: so I wanta hear it unmistakably before I believe the people I know well do this. The hell with it tho, for it's damn unpleasant.

---

473. See *YA* 391-92 for AP's later views on Everson's poetry.

474. Printed on EB's stationery was a cartoon of Napoleon and a valediction ("Yours truly, …") to which EB added his initial.

475. Desmond Pacey (1917–75): Professor of English at the University of New Brunswick and a prominent commentator on Canadian literature and culture (*Creative Writing in Canada*, 1952).

Slightly envy you your eagles and salmon (Lowry eagle? — oops, sorry, forgot Margerie!), seems so goddam "colourful" — Not Lowry, just does.[476] As a bird watcher I rush to the goddam book to find out if a scarlet tanager is — It is. (Two days ago.)

* (What did I mean there?) (The beer wasn't all spilled!)

Will send the Horseman poem from *Globe* if as and when. Idea is I want carte blanche to drive around Ont. with Eurithe and write poems. Carte blanche being five thou. They turned me down last year. So this year they give some money to publishers, of which I got some via Anansi, so I will say (solemnly presenting "Horseman"): if I could do this much with your measly piddling two bits worth of funny money, look what I could do with the whole bag. Not like that, of course.

I think the de luxe book might (might jesus just might) be done in next few days.

Al

* Now dunno what I meant —

To Birney (Vancouver) from Purdy (Ameliasburgh)
July 27, 1970   TL

Dear Earle,

The book Nichol printed looks fine — sort of good fun? I mean the typographical and "Campus Theatre Steps." I note also new poems I like, the poem for George and Angela — Like the picture of you particularly.[477]

My own book (*Ouzo*) is now finished after much blood and sweat.[478] Boxes are ordered, and will send a copy when I can get one.

But I write about something else. Can you send a short note recommending me for an Ontario Arts Council (151 Bloor St. West, Toronto 5, Ont.) [grant] of $3,500? I want to travel round Ont. by car next year and write poems. I enclose "The Horseman of Agawa" from the Toronto *Globe*, which I also sent to the Arts Council.[479] (Bought 30 copies of the damn thing, in order to send to people I want to write letters for me.) (What a sentence!)

Fucked up by work as usual. And Eurithe accusing me of shenanigans in

476. AP probably referred to Lowry's "Salmon Drowns Eagle": "The golden eagle swooped out of the sky / And flew back with a salmon in her claws."

477. Angela (Luoma) Bowering (1940–99): Canadian writer and professor at Simon Fraser University. She and George Bowering were married in 1962; their collaborative novel is *Piccolo Mondo* (1998). The poem "for george & angela in calgary" is "imageorge."

478. *The Quest for Ouzo* (1970).

479. The poem was published in the 25 July 1970 issue of the *Globe Magazine*. The copy that AP sent was inscribed: "For Earle with all the best. Al Purdy."

Toronto. Saw and hammer and nails. Jesus! And lit stuff I may never catch up with. Also doing another antho of poets under 30 for Ryerson called *Storm Warning*. If you know any good young ones tellem to send me some stuff.

Best,

Al

To Purdy (Ameliasburgh) from Birney (Galiano Island)
July 30, 1970   TPC[480]

Dear Al

Have banged off a note to Ont Arts C. [Ontario Arts Council] saying you are worth thousands more than that, but they ought to send a more scholarly character along with you to make sure you don't write your name on any of these old rock paintings or shit in anybody's spring on this trip. I've suggested myself of course, but only if you come too. Glad *Ouzo* is out but I want to pay for my copy. You can't afford to give *that* expensive a book away, only Pierre Berton or Sir John Eaton cd (& wdnt).[481] Got my ts [typescript] in for 64-page *Rag & Bone Shop* & writing still more.[482]

Thanx for *Globe* clip.

Love to you both

Earle

Will be in Toronto Sep. 13 on for a while.

To Birney (Vancouver) from Purdy (Ameliasburgh)
August 6, 1970   TL[483]

Goddam it Birney,

If I wanta give away a valuable work of genius that will undoubtedly depreciate to miniscule value in near future, stop trying to talk me out of it! You're welcome to say: I'll give Purdy my next hundred buck book, and I will damn well take it. Just try, I say, just suggest it, and watch out for the reflex leap I make in the direction of whatever it is. Okay?

Anyway, it's wrapped, boxed, sealed, fucked but not corded, on accounta I

---

480. The postcard was from the Hotel Wellington in New York. EB typed over the hotel's address: "never stay here it stinks."

481. John Eaton (1876–1922): President of the T. Eaton Company from 1907 to 1922; although he used the honorific, EB could have meant Sir John's son, also named John (1909–73), who held the same position.

482. EB's *Rag & Bone Shop* was published in 1971 by McClelland and Stewart.

483. *YA* 163–64. EB's note: "replied by card fr. Washington D.C. Oct 17/70."

got no cord. Only look, I'm only givin away two, you and M. Laurence, so please please don't show it to anyone who might think they deserve a free copy. Dunno who that would be, unless Andy [Suknaski] perhaps (and I'd like to give him one, but one must draw a line or something eh?) — This is, of course, to say forgive me for whatever I have to be forgiven for, to imply that I am a noble character and will not sign my goddam name on Indian rock paintings like you wrongfully stated and I am hurt, my feelings are wounded badly. Besides, the ballpoint I used wouldn't mark the iron oxide. The book box is not as good as I would like, on accounta glue didn't stick perfectly. If you have a bottle of red ink, dab the label's nose like it's supposed to be.

Just came back from Sudbury, Laurentian U., and a nice likeable square conservative English prof who felt he had to keep up with me drinkin, so fed me beer after beer, himself drinkin one for one, then we switched to scotch, and after three drinks he suddenly got glassy eyed, and Eurithe had to drive his car to the reading where 28 people showed up. Weep not, the next highest was 22. I assume the bit about him trying to be a hippie, as he may have thought I was, and tryin to keep up. But I kinda think it might be true. He got beer in esp. for me (which was nice of him — name of Ron Bates, poet too), soaked me in a Finnish steam bath where we all wore swim suits (that's why he's a conservative) — After the reading Bates is owl-solemn still drunk, but drives his own car, right up a one-way street in Sudbury the wrong way while everyone yowls murder in his ears — At this time I have survival-fears, and a milk shake is suggested for obvious reasons. So we see the red hot slag being dumped from the US mine (for which he has a pome I read of course) (makin noises like they're works of genius, which in a different sense they are) — and go home for more beer, Bates having forsaken scotch. We plight our troth by promising signed books to be sent later on accounta vows made to be broken.

Then drive to Cochrane, ride the Polar Bear Ex[press] to Moosonee and an Indian boatman from the little sticks (ha?) to Moose Factory,[484] where it rains and rains and I hate to get my hair wet on accounta then it looks like I got even less than I have and I know no swooning Indian maiden will consent to swoon for me ... But I don't write a poem, which grieves me.[485] I don't *feel* like writing a poem, and this unborn poem is not to be borne. I alibi I only write about things that are important, thus if I can't write them they're not important; but see thru my own sophistries and the result is hardly satisfying.

---

484. Perhaps AP gleaned the phrase "little sticks" from one of Jack London's Klondike stories, "Love of Life" (1907): "Farther on he knew he would come to where dead spruce and fir, very small and weazened, bordered the shore of a little lake, ... in the tongue of the country, the 'land of little sticks.'"

485. AP's "Tourist Itinerary," from *Sex & Death* (1973), describes this trip: "Then Cochrane and the train to Moosonee / over the soft spongy trappers' country" (*BR* 195).

English girl here right now, we met in Europe being chased by a love-mad Athenian, and I am intrigued by the way her ass wriggles goin up the loft ladder which I hafta hold on accounta she is more scared of the ladder nor me.

Luv,

Al

P.S. Thanks for *character* reference!

To Purdy (Ameliasburgh) from Birney (Washington, DC)
October 17, 1970   APC

dere al

thot yude injoi this luvlee pik of the nashnul capitul   i fergot to ask yu wot yu wuz doin in Moos Faktree   we wil get 2 gether b4 i go bak to bc   i hope books r selling like crazee for you

erl

[Dear Al,

Thought you'd enjoy this lovely pic of the national capital.[486] I forgot to ask you what you was doing in Moose Factory. We will get together before I go back to BC. I hope books are selling like crazy for you.

Earle]

To Purdy (Ameliasburgh) from Birney (Vancouver)
November 23, 1970   TL

Dear Al

Hope this reaches you b4 you split for Mexique Bay.[487] Dana swears she sent in her thing but I'm sure lots of other potes [*sic*] aren't being so prompt & perhaps anyway your switch to McStew from Ryerson's for the anthol means a delay in yr leaving Canada.[488] I shd hav writ sooner but had a great backlog of letters to saw up when I got back here after nearly 2 mos away. & also was up to Prince George, a John the Baptist belated, the Christ child having already got there & been crowned & all. Man the legends about The Purdy & The Bissett up in that there Cariboo are thicker than the ice in the Fraser — & no doubt thanks to Bissett & Purdy, not to

---

486. EB's note was written on a promotional postcard from a Holiday Inn in Arlington, Virginia. The picture is not of Washington but of the motel.

487. EB probably intended an allusion to Aldous Huxley's *Beyond the Mexique Bay* (1934).

488. Dana Fraser: One of her poems was included by AP in *Storm Warning: The New Canadian Poets* (1971).

speak of one McKinnon, the town itself is becoming or shd become a legend for Cdn poets, since I too had a full house in that 500-seat setup, & press interviews & students all over me from noon till midnight. After that it was Barry & his wife & the 2 girls next door & I drinking hot rums (on top of a lot of cold rye) till 5 a.m.[489] Then me getting up at 8 a.m. to make the goddam plane back to vankrs (which is how the CPA [CP Air, i.e. Canadian Pacific Airlines] spells Vancouver down on the South Pacific run anyway).

I'm here till New Year's since the book [*Rag & Bone Shop*], though it shd be & perhaps is "out," isn't "launched" till Jan 9 in Toronto, but is to be discreetly publicized here as soon as it arrives (which shd be in 2 more days time, unless there's a slide on the CNR). But I'll definitely be back in Toronto by the 6th of Jan. & maybe by the 3rd so I'm kind of hoping you can't get away before then (ouch, sorry, Eurithe) because, as you say in yr Oct. letter I've never answered (consider this an answer?) we don't seem to see each other on "a particularly casual basis any more" (good wording) & that is bad, not good for friends. It's partly that I've been distracted by the daily fuckups arranged by McStew (you really think we shdnt let the Yanks take over publishing?) & you've been doing 3 anthologists' work plus going on being a poet, broadcaster, lover, sage, & now political cavalry officer. However, in the same breath you regret this (as I do) you mention kind of casual like that you cd do with a half hour's reminiscing of mine ON TAPE. Man you want to talk with me casual you leave yr fucking taperecorder at home. You know what happened last time! If I only knew exactly when I was going to shuffle off this coil (what the hell did Shakespeare mean calling the earth a coil?) you'd be the first I'd send a smoke signal to, so you cd milk my pathetic little life for yet another Purdy book.[490] But until I *know*, you gotta let me hope I can write it all for myself. Though certainly I will need your corroboration for at least one quite improbable episode that happened in Kitsilano.

I have before me various lares & penates of Purdy.[491] Like York's Performing Poets Program wherein Bukowski calls you "one of the few very good poets since 1900" (why start there?) & I come along with a crashing anticlimax, no more than a sociological notation, of you being today in Canada, which reminds me that another of Bukowski's Greats gave a reading at UBC last week which I attended & which was really unforgettable, visually & audibly, & I mean that admiring-like, no shit. Basil Bunting read his Briggs Flats [*Briggflatts*] sitting on a bare stage

---

489. Barry McKinnon (b. 1944): Canadian poet (*Pulp Log*, 1991; *The Centre: Poems 1970–2000*, 2004) and publisher (Caledonia Writing Series, Gorse Press) — a central figure in the literary life of northern British Columbia. AP included two of McKinnon's poems in the first *Storm Warning* (1971).

490. EB's reference was to Act 3, Scene 1 of *Hamlet*: "For in that sleep of death what dreams may come, / When we have shuffled off this mortal coil, / Must give us pause." Cf. AP's letter of 7 Dec. 1969.

491. The Latin phrase appears in AP's "Ballad of the Despairing Wife," published in *The Cariboo Horses* (1965) and again in *Love in a Burning Building* (1970).

(semicircled, however, by the GREAT POETS & CRITICS OF U.B.C.) beside a small plain table containing a glass & a large bottle of wine (& another bottle *under* the table but in sight) with a beautiful silent maiden in a maxi sitting beside the table pouring the wine (you see what I mean by visual).[492] This was in the music bldg's auditorium with a pipe organ behind which was roaring out Scarlatti sonnets [sonatas] in between the sections of Briggs Flatts & Sharpps. But seriously old Basil is not only a bloody good poet he is a stagemaster & I shd suspect a horny old bugger who has thought up an act neither you nor I ever got around to, to wit: carting a young femme & TWO bottles of wine around to each performance. I swear he drank both bottles & in the process made me so goddam thirsty that as soon as I got out (with Dana & Geoff) we sped to a B.C. Liquor Store & got ourselves 2 bottles of B.C. Okanagan Vintage Sweet Ugh SAUTERNE & drank like mad while discussing who the hell the Elizabethan Nobles were ranged around the back of the stage. I recognized robin blaser, warren tallman, robert duncan, robert creeley, stanley persky — & thought it was meant to be an orchard arrangement or FRUIT BOWL.[493] But there was also huge Lionel Kearns with his tiny Maya & a lot of others who looked practically heterosexual. However all that's irrelevant to the experience of Bunting, who was really melodious & Thomas-Hardy gnarled & Hopkins-bizarre & himself-stately & I wouldn't have missed it. I did miss the party, however, mainly because I wasn't invited to it until 5 minutes before it was to start (though I'd heard of it a week earlier) so I got more lift out of telling the usual faggot-messenger from the UBC English Dept. to go screw himself.

So how did we get onto that? — all on account of Bukowski & the York program — anyway, my friend, you've got to believe that "most admired" from me is better than "very good poet since 1900" from Bukowski, but "better" for what is a good question, as Bukowski's opinion can undoubtedly set you soaring in Yankee circles, where mine will just help to keep you a prisoner of Canada — speaking of which I've been mailed a clip from the *Star* of Nov 11, just arrived today, a little late for you to be interested in my reactions which however you're going to get unless you quit reading right now. Anyway despite any kidding farther up in this letter I agree totally with your phrase "textbook contents that will express only friendliness to the American nightmare." Also with "we have a different history, environment, temperament" maybe 80% (we don't alas really have a different *social* environment anymore). I'm not so sure, however, that yr examples of what it

---

492. Basil Bunting (1900–85): English poet, an associate of Ezra Pound's, whose major poem is the autobiographical *Briggflatts* (1966).

493. EB left the names, unlike others in the letter, uncapitalized. Stan Persky (b. 1941): Canadian journalist, critic, professor, and writer of an eclectic range of books (*Autobiography of a Tattoo*, 1997). He belonged to the circle of Robert Duncan, Jack Spicer, and Robin Blaser in San Francisco in the early 1960s and emigrated to Canada in 1966.

means to be a Canadian cdnt equally be used by an American who was brought up in the Bronx & rode the rods [to?] the American Rockies in the Depression. Also I think this can be said without "selling out." You *do* exaggerate, & it doesn't reconcile me that Robin Mathews does too.[494] In fact I suspect that Robin Mathews makes more converts to the Cdn sellout, by his neurotic belligerence & egotism, than Standard Oil. But I do think yr ref. to the hitchhikers this summer has real meaning. I felt this pride too, in Canada, that had produced at last Canadians who wanted to experience it. & from then on in yr article, on the economic-political scene, & yr separation from FLQ "nastiness," I am in full agreement (not that it matters, if I am or not, I'm sure).

Enough enough. Write me from wherever you are & give my love to that saint, that foolishly-devoted enduring sybil & protectress, Eurithe by name. As well as to the old Belleville Newsboy Himself.

Esther sends her love to you both too.

Earle

To Birney (Vancouver) from Purdy (Ameliasburgh)
November 26, 1970   TL[495]

Dear Earle,

It did reach me before we left [i.e., leave] (today is Thurs.) next week, Wed. or Thurs. with Eurithe, I hope, remembering the names of places broken in and lubricated by Birney. As you might expect, I'm going nuts with work. Two articles for *TorStar* (the second is much better than the first, which was chopped) and one for *Maclean's* — me complaining like hell, but sorta enjoying it I guess ... But I sure will be glad to get away. Movement from here will be like mooring my brain and sailing my body — which is goddam poor imagery, but you know what I mean. Not that the body is inactive, in most of the ways a body is active, except for the extraordinary sports of skin and muff diving. (Do you know that last term?) ...

Yeah, Prince George is extraordinary, I think because of [Barry] McKinnon and the Eng. Dept. as well as populace. Isn't it really odd to see "a sea of faces" stretched out before you? I read at Loyalist College in Belleville to not more than 40 or so and it disgusted me, well not exactly, but I like an audience whose reaction you can feel when your head is down reading ... The kid who read before me — from Loyalist — had had a book out by Delta, Wally Keeler, and his poems

---

494. Robin Mathews (b. 1931): Canadian writer (*Canadian Literature: Surrender or Revolution*, 1978) and professor at Carleton University and Simon Fraser University, known especially for his strong nationalist views. Mathews was a student of EB's at UBC.

495. *YA* 169–71.

were mostly sex, tho not bad.[496] At one point, near the end of his period, he said "these poems are for my latest mistress and woman who is sitting in the front row" — and I had seen this modest looking gal before, all alone, who now betrayed no visible reaction to Keeler's words. Still, I had a reaction. I thought: The self-advertising prick!

Earlier I was on some sort of closed circuit tv the college has, wearing dark glasses for defense against the lights, girl student on one side and male on the other. Interviewing, that is. She asking silly questions like: does your brain work when you write poems? (Really very similar to that.) Or: You're a nationalist Mr. Purdy, why do you go to Greece? Me saying gravely, sure, my brain works when I write poems. And, I go to Greece cause it's the cradle of western civ. Should I stay in Canada honey? But I sure musta fucked up that interview for her, because she was nearly crying at the end and after. I hafta put my arm around her and reassure her she didn't bloop it up. But I look back at that interview, and see I could have worked harder and answered her questions more irrelevantly (as I did the guy on my right side), and possibly interestingly. Not "a pettiness to expiate" but a thoughtlessness on my part.[497] I probably should try and phone her still to make amends. Amends are always more difficult than the opposite, whatever the opposite is of amends.

Your Basil Bunting sounds like a showman who can't miss on any culture stage in the U.S. Even a good poet, you intimate. Do think the blaser, creeley, duncan, tallman lineup behind him sounds revolting, not to say throwupable.[498] I applaud you turning down the party invite, even tho you must have thought as I would: who are these pricks turning down me. On the other hand (I would've thought), these goddam in-groups don't know a good poet unless he's an actor like Bunting. Still, I don't think it sounds like a party you need mind missing, with the possible exception of Bunting.

I accept your stern decision re taped Birney with, if not equanimity, at least

496. *Walking on the Greenhouse Roof* (1969), by Wally Keeler (b. 1947). AP had a copy in his library.

497. AP here alluded to the final lines of D.H. Lawrence's "Snake" (1923): "And so, I missed my chance with one of the lords / Of life. / And I have something to expiate: / A pettiness." AP's "Elegy," in the 1962 *Poems for All the Annettes*, is a variation on the theme of Lawrence's poem.

498. AP had little patience for the *Tish* poets, in no small part for nationalist reasons — he objected to American influences on Canadian poetry: "The kindest opinion would be to say that the *Tish* people were 'influenced' by the Black Mountain movement in the US. The unkindest: they were slavish imitators" (*RBS* 232). Tallman, the professor of English at UBC who was a mentor to the *Tish* poets, was an American who, in AP's words, "never did get around to taking out Canadian citizenship" (*RBS* 232). Sam Solecki has suggested (*YA* 171 n.2) that the lack of capitalization in "blaser, creeley, duncan, tallman" was deliberate. AP's "Ballad of the Despairing Wife," from *The Cariboo Horses*, is subtitled "After Creeley." (Creeley wrote a "Ballad of the Despairing Husband.") When the "Ballad" was included in *Love in a Burning Building* (1970), "After Creeley" was omitted.

troubled calm. Knowing, of course, that you'll fuck around and waste all the good stuff on well-shaped, non-literary, but appreciative, feminine ears.

But don't give me that "pathetic little life" bit — At least when you're having me on I can tell once in a while —

Okay, re comments on article: don't we really have different social environments, even if perhaps not greatly different? Re riding freights etc. (which was included so I could talk more easily), sure an American might have done the same in the U.S. But what citizen of any country couldn't do something similar? And so what if they could? Doesn't it add up, the various parts, to a Canadian whole? You are certainly not going to give me, nor is any one, the components of a unique national identity, other than such memories, history etc. Perhaps the impression of the whole piece was exaggeration, but name me a specific item which I exaggerated. Oh sure, Mathews manages to antagonize more people than any fifty branch plant managers. He has real talent that way. But on the other hand, he speaks his mind, is not afraid to come out and say things. And there are so damn few people who will stand up and say things, that I admire him for that. Even if he does seem, at times, like something a bit nasty, and I'm afraid he does — at times.

I have another article coming in *TorStar* — been searching for a carbon and can find only the one destined for Douglas Library [at Queen's University] — which I will try to get some extra copies of, even tho I will be en route to Mexico when it appears probably. Also one in *Maclean's* that they cut the jesus guts out of by telephone. Incidentally, the *Star*, Peter Newman, that is, offered me a job in the ed. dept. at $13,000 per.[499] I'm flattered as hell, of course, but think I'd blow my mind at a job like that. What think you? I said I had no time, but was tempted. Newman asked me to write an article a month. In my weaker and more drained (mentally) moments, not sure if I'm capable of even that. I think it'd drive me nuts. Also offered me the book page, five columns a week etc. That too would knock me out, I'm sure. But maybe a column a month.

Earle, be sure and send me a copy of the new book when it comes. I'll drop you word from Mexico where we get to, tho I'm not really sure myself. Eurithe says Oaxaca, sounds like an Englishman saying Oxo. I suppose no chance at all of Birney getting to Mexico — Did I say I got the Ont. Council of the Arts cash? Well, did. Also, gonna try to go to Hiroshima on a short term in the spring. Might as well get around a bit, as long as travelling is all downhill. Well, we leave next week, after the last touches on antho are finished. Also a CBC date. Re antho, got the

---

499. Peter C. Newman (b. 1929): Author of several notable books on Canadian cultural and political life (*The Canadian Establishment*, 1975) and editor of the *Toronto Star* and *Maclean's*. AP's library contained several of Newman's books, including *Home Country: People, Places, and Power Politics* (1973) and *The Establishment Man: A Portrait of Power* (1982).

damnedest snivelling letter from Seymour Mayne and Bryan McCarthy wanting in. Makes me wonder if I ever whined like that —

Well, must stop. Work to do. Eurithe comments on your description of her in no very gentle manner, but also laughs. And may I direct similar sentiments to Esther, your "enduring protectress and sybil" —

Best,

Al

To Purdy (Ameliasburgh) from Birney (Vancouver)
Late November/Early December 1970   TL

Dear Al

Still don't know where to write you. Sent yr copy of *Rag* to Ameliasburgh & will do same with this (as you can see!). Wonder where you are. Hope you got yr work cleared off so you can relax a bit & turn to other things for a while — no not things — POEMS.

I'm going up the wall with the usual screwups from McStewup. No posters no books (except those I've bought & already so promptly got bills for). This Jim Douglas is a prevaricating Scotch fart who promises, fails to keep his word, hides behind his daughter, who knows nothing or lies too. Meantime Duthie's & other stores wanting copies of the books they ordered last June so I have to take my own copies around to them — while Douglas sits on a stack he admits has at least 150 copies in it, over in his West Van house.[500] By my own efforts I finally persuaded both radio & tv in this town to give me plugs but believe me this is the hardest place in the world for me to get a word publicly, even an unkind one. At least the book, apart from 4 proof errors, looks good.

That *Star* job is big dough these days but I think it would finish you as a poet if you took it for any length of time. Writing even 3 columns a week is very hard & creatively-draining work, I know from experience doing one a week! However, if you want for a while not to be a poet but some other kind of writer, there's no crime in that — provided you're sure you can pull back out again when you want to.

Best guide book to Mexico — by far — is Kate Simon's — a pleasure to read.[501] Places I liked best were (from north down): Zacatecas / Tepic / Guadalajara / Guanajuato / San Miguel Allende / Actopan / Pachuca / Tuxpan / Tepotzotlan / Teotihuacan / Acolman / Morelia / Toluca / Mexico C[ity] / Tlaxcala / Jalapa /

---

500. The Duthies chain of bookstores in Vancouver was founded by Bill Duthie in 1957. It remained in operation until 2010.

501. *Mexico: Places and Pleasures* (1963).

Vera Cruz / Puebla / Patzcuaro / Cholula / Oaxaca (with Mitla & Monte Alban) / & Salina Cruz — I mention only the places I've seen & which I know to have some archaeological interest as well as climatic or etc. I haven't been in the Maya country, still hope to get to it. No use my giving you any info about places to stay as my info is now 8 years old re. San Miguel & Mexico, & 14 years old as regards elsewhere.

Have fun anyway you two   & write

Earle

To Birney (Vancouver) from Purdy (Mexico City)[502]
December 19, 1970   TL

Dear Earle;

So how are you? It seems the first time I've had time for a letter in some time, even tho I did write before I left — I hope your jaw is now wagging in old-time form and the nerves are all fixed up by some wonder dentist — Sorry you aren't here at the moment, to help me drink the bottle of wine on one side and tequila on the other — In order to avoid Montezuma's Revenge I plan to subsist on a liquid diet of wine —

I believe we left Dec. 7, my time getting fucked up by lack of necessity to remember what day it is. Leisurely trip thru, over the raped U.S. countryside, visiting whatever book stores were handy along the way. I picked up the discoverer of Troy's (can't remember his name) excavations at Tiryns for ten bucks (U.S. ed.), which kinda elated me — oh yes, Heinrich Schliemann — how could I forget a character like that?[503] Down thru Cincinnati, Louisville to New Orleans, then west to Texas and down to Brownsville, the planned entry point, with Eurithe emitting tiny cries of ecstasy at the weather — Thru high mountains, tropic valleys with orange groves groping up the mtns., travelling the footsteps of Cortez Birney. At one Penex gas stn. the whole family of the Indian who ran the place so confused me that I paid 25 pesos for a wine bottle full of gas. Thereafter both Eurithe and I stood on guard together to watch the computor [sic] register litres — Jesus, it irritates me to be cheated. Then at Zimapan or something like that, we stay in a hotel with suits of armor in the lobby, and a Roman centurion in the shape of a retired U.S. naval engineer who'd graduated from M.I.T. for pleasant company. He being another skin diving enthusiast — now I call that term obscene tho have thought sometimes it's an apt description of Birney's activities above water. I explained to centurion [that] a nut of my acquaintance also

---

502. After indicating his location, AP added "(if that needs be said)."
503. AP's library included Marjorie Braymer's *The Walls of Windy Troy: A Biography of Heinrich Schliemann* (1960).

dived. Also a guy who runs a pipe organ factory, and was just returning from Puebla after installing one in the local cathedral there. By mischance Eurithe was with these people in our room with me absent and showed em some of my books, one of the latter being *The New Romans* — after which the centurion's manner grew noticeably colder after my return.

We are now installed at the hotel on the envelope, very luxurious place we get for ten bucks a night, the ordinary price being eighteen. My plans later in Oaxaca are to write a book (no nasty remarks, please, about my failure that rankles Birney still), and to do the notes on this new McStew book, *Storm Warning*. Your Dana Fraser sent me a prose piece that was unsuitable, as I expect she's told you I told her (so did two or three others), and the most dramatic picture of a female I've seen of a women's lib member in some time. As you know, most of the time they look like sixteenth century parchment. So I hafta admit the Birney taste in platonic friendship is still true and valid. (Sudden thought: what the hell volcano was Lowry under for his book?)[504] I sure as hell hadn't realized what phony bastards poets looked like until I see all the pictures they sent. Just about all of em must think poets look like poets — Sure, I know you're gonna say "we too have a right to mod clothes etc" — I grant you etc., but me an [*sic*] Souster, we're common men — and don't point out to me that the common man is affectation — Sure. Hey, I told you your book [*Rag & Bone Shop*] is marvellous! Newlove said you and he sat down together on it and toiled. Good result. I don't think I've seen you better, and that's saying a great deal.

Eurithe is champing to go out, so must stop and begin again.

Best,

Al

To Purdy (Mexico City) from Birney (Vancouver)
December 31, 1970   TA[505]

Can't let this old stinky year slink out without writing to wish you a fine new baby year tomorrow that will bring you masses of good poems (both your own & Young

---

504. From the first chapter of *Under the Volcano*: "Far to his left, in the northeast, beyond the valley and the terraced foothills of the Sierra Madre Oriental, the two volcanoes, Popocatepetl and Ixtaccihuatl, rose clear and magnificent into the sunset." The novel's principal setting, the town of Quauhnahuac, is based on Cuernavaca. "Iguana," from *Sex & Death*, refers to Lowry's volcanoes.

505. This letter was returned from Mexico to EB, who resent it to AP, who was by then back in Ameliasburgh, as subsequent letters indicate. EB wrote the following message (dated 9 Mar. 1971) on the front of the aerogramme: "So, my friend, you must have jumped your bill for that luxury suite in The Palacio, not realizing this might deprive you of a greater treasure — my New Year's Eve letter to you — but Birney is dogged — here it is again whatever it is." (The final words are unclear — the paper is torn.)

Unknowns) & time & energy for adventure, love, & just to sit and be peaceful. You too Eurithe.

From your letter I gather you didn't get one from me that I sent to Ameliasburgh in reply to yours from there dated Nov. 26. I also sent you a copy of *Rag & Bone* to same address & you mention knowing the book & you say nice things about it. So was the book sent on & not my letter? Or did you get a copy of the book from McStew before you left Can?

I'm well enough but bogged down with work & getting ready to get to Toronto next week for a fortnight of plugging the *Rags* over radio, tv etc, reading in Hart House [at the University of Toronto], & so on. Then back to Calgary by 25th Jan for a reading & back here for 2 readings (one a "showing") at Simon Fraser & then over to Lethbridge & then back here to UBC. Then over to London in late April for a couple of readings in London. I think the London people (Poetry Society) want to get you over too so I've sent Anne McDermid your present address in case they want to get in touch with you. I said you might be taking off for Japan so they ought to be in touch with you promptly if they were going to get you at all this spring. You wd have to find passage money from the CC or somewhere if you did want to do it, so first they have to get an invitation down in writing to you.

I hope you're not knocking Dana Fraser out because you didn't go for her crazy prose statement. Because I got her to write a second much more sensible & informational one, which was sent you same time as my letter, to Ameliasburgh. Jesus didn't you do anything about having your mail forwarded?! Shall I get her to send a copy of that second prose piece to you in Mexico or have you got the one she sent you by this time?

Esther is well & shuttling between babysitting for the Churchillian faced grandson & managing touch-groups and gestalts.

The Yankees in UBC creative writing dept have been doing hatchet jobs on my book here (Andreas Schroeder in *Province* & one Michael Finlay in *Sun*),[506] real slimy personal-attack jobs. But fortunately a beauteous young Swede girl, a free-lancer, came down & interviewed me in my own study for 2 hours & managed to sell her story (or part of it) to the *Sun* with 3 photos & a lot of throwing of flowers (you know that good Mexican expression: echar las flores?) which has somewhat

---

506. EB's marginal note in reference to Schroeder and Finlay: "both pupils of Yates." Andreas Schroeder (b. 1946): Canadian writer and teacher of creative writing at UBC, associated with a West Coast surrealist movement in poetry (*The Ozone Minotaur*, 1969) and known for his non-fiction (*Shaking It Rough: A Prison Memoir*, 1976). Although EB referred here to the "Yankees" at UBC, Schroeder was born in Germany and came to Canada in 1951. (Two poets with whom Schroeder was then affiliated, Charles Lillard [1944–97] and J. Michael Yates [b. 1938], were born in the United States.) Michael Finlay (b. 1949): Poet (*The Harpo Scrolls: Poems*, 1970) and journalist who received an M.A. in Creative Writing from UBC in 1972.

redressed the balance, weighed in with my being 2 hours on Jack Webster's Hot Line defending myself for not believing in God, the Bible & Wacky Bennett.[507]

Esther sends you both her love & so do I. We wish we were there too. Please keep writing. Send me new poems.

Earle

To Purdy (Acapulco) from Birney (Vancouver)
February 4, 1971   TA

Dear Al

Been so fuckin busy (but not busy fuckin) I got no time to write my friends. Packed yr Tehuantepec letter around for damnear a month now (take it out, read it fondly, think of old Al chasin the brown chiquitas on Acapulco beaches, put the letter away again, get back to writing editors, agents, contacts, bores, creditors, wish I had time to write old Al). Maybe you'll be back in Toronto in March. Seems there's a saturation campaign on yr *Storm Warning*, all the contributors being flown down from Cape Breton & Banks Island & Skookumchuck to the Park Plaza just to meet the nation's reporters & the OEA (& maybe you?). No expense spared by Jack McStew who could never afford the money, since 1966, to put errata sheets for my *Selected Poems* into the warehouse copies, & now that I've complained again, he's taken to writing me shit-letters instead of doing something about it. O well the One Canadian Publisher can't be wrong. Must be his authors. You say you met a woman at Oaxaca who was a French teacher from Vancouver who seemed to know me ...? Well — go on ...?

What prose book you workin on? I hope maybe a Purdyconfession novel (anti-novel?). Not criticism please. Not about me & Layton & Acorn & Lowry for Christ sake. Mind your own business you goddam stripling.

Nothing from my lawyers yet not even a letter.

Had 2 weeks in Toronto/Mtrl. About as hardworkin as any I ever put in since I swung a 12 pd sledge on a rockdrill crew in the bad winter of '22. One day I had a morning tv (CFTO 7.30, & an hour in a taxi in a blizzard before it) & back down with the blizzard worse to CBC for an hour's taping on *Ideas* & no time for lunch & off in a taxi to Scarboro Centennial Coll for a 1 o'clock slide-show-reading while the Ontario ETV did a filming of the whole scene. Then rapping with Harry Howith's students till 3, when I snuck off to the college firstaid station & got them to lock me in the emergency room so I could get a sleep on the stretcher table

---

507. W.A.C. Bennett (1900–79): Premier of British Columbia (1952–72) and leader of the Social Credit Party. Jack Webster (1918–99): Journalist and popular radio and television broadcaster based in Vancouver.

till 4, when Howith took me what seemed half way to Ottawa to pick up his new wife at her job & go back somewhere else in the wilderness to eat at his place & drink whiskey & then I had to bugger off to do a late writers workshop for Barry [*sic*] Nichol — all the days weren't that bad but many were.[508] However it must have been good publicity because *Rag* sold out & there'll be a 2nd edition (with errata corrections) in March. Good reviews almost everywhere, except Ottawa & of course Vancouver, where they really slayed me. So there's still plenty of books in Duthie's.

Calgary was a great scene. Science hall seating 500 & SRO [standing room only]. Over 2 hrs, & another hour yakking with people before I could get off to the party for me. Going back there in a couple of weeks, to Red Deer, Banff, Lethbridge & all.

Keep well you two & come back before you forget how to talk English. Love from us both.

write me

Earle

To Birney (Vancouver) from Purdy (Acapulco)
February 8, 1971   TL

Dear Earle,

Nice you decided the iguanas of Tehuantepec deserved a proxy letter. Also very pleased to hear *Rag & Bone* sold out, and jealous as bloody hell. Jack McStew keeps sayin to me he and I (he reverses the order) can make more money with hard covers, and don't I wanta make money? How can I reply to that question dishonestly? Your own lecture and reading activities are also fabulous, particularly in Canada. I am moved to get off the pot and reactivate the E. Parkhurst Agency for a triumphal last tour of the Maritimes afore demise.[509] (I keep learning how it's done from Birney, then find he's gone on to other ingenious ways of makin money and left me far in the ruck and surly something — What the hell's that line of yours about coming back from mountains and the lean pig of a streetcar squealing?)[510]

---

508. *Ideas*: A CBC radio documentary program started in 1965. EB appeared on one of the first broadcasts. Harry Howith (b. 1934): Canadian poet (*Multiple Choices: New and Selected Poems 1961–1976*, 1976) and instructor at Centennial College, Toronto. For a time he published books under the Bytown Books imprint.

509. See AP's letter of "Aug 5 or 6, '69."

510. The line is from "Climbers," from *Trial of a City and Other Verse* (1952): "time only / for clambering back to the lean / pig of a streetcar squealing." (Cf. *OMH* 66.) The "ruck and surly something" could be a misremembering of "the horny neck of desolation," but is more likely a reference to "David": "over the sunalive week-ends / We climbed, to get from the ruck of the camp, the surly // Poker, the wrangling, the snoring ..." (*OMH* 34). In "Regional Muses," his review in *Poetry* 86.2 (May 1955) of EB's *Twentieth Century Canadian Poetry: An Anthology*, Hugh Kenner quoted lines from "Climbers" as an

I am sorry to hear no fuckin, but then you do need a rest, surely a well-deserved surcease in order to recoup a supply of future generations. On the other hand, I suppose the shining admiration in the eyes of young gals is a sort of mass orgasm that must communicate itself somehow.

My sympathy re Jack McStew. I was so (probably) hard to get along with in connection with him and got nowhere at all that the One Canadian Publisher and I eye each other warily betimes, each knowing the other must be thinking nasty thoughts. Alas I have no pinup of Jack to stick pins into, tho he has mine in books. Strangely, when Gary Geddes runs down Jack very hard in letters I spring to Jack's defense. How can one explain that?

My prose book is 33,000 words of autobio (with, I admit sadly, some criticism here and there), lamentably Birney having to be left out on accounta no one would believe the Van. apt. episode anyway. Said Birney is mentioned here and there, even quoted from, but as a mere stripling I felt it takes a better man — such as Frank Davey, apparently — to do an intensive book. Any critical stuff I do is cursory and superficial. Parts are, I think, good, but I need other opinions than my own. It is not the tells-all sort of thing, but does come up with quite a bit. Plan to use photographs and relevant poems with it. Also wrote a few poems here, about which only one do I entertain proud poppa feelings. But I do think some of the prose is good. Despite having gone thru two revisions, it probably still needs work.

We leave here tomorrow, and between Feb. 20–28 will be at Ron Everson's in Florida. Then a slow trip up the U.S. east coast, visiting book stores etc., and to Tor. Mar. 13, where I hope Jack McStew will pay for a week's hotel room since he's doing it for everyone else.

Mr. R.G. Everson,
Box 296, 1001 Hill Street,
New Smyrna Beach, Fla. 32069, U.S.A.

And if you are so inclined and are not supervising theses on Birney — Incredibly, I am getting a little sick of sun and Mexico, tho when I hear of the Ontario weather it does much to alleviate sickness. I think the Mexico you knew and this present one are two different — It's swamped with tourists here, and garbage all over — The woman at Oaxaca was Edith Barton, seemed to react a bit peculiar to your name, so I didn't question her — Tact has always been — I note with interest that Lowry was in the Oaxaca jail, among others.[511] Has Margerie [Lowry] loosened up

example of EB's technique: "In the verse of Mr. Birney himself we discover the rudiments of a procédé. His trick is to *dramatize* his aloofness by providing the suspicious reader (who is then enabled to come into undisturbed possession of the entire poem) with a readily identifiable point of view."

511. In a poem on the subject of his brief imprisonment in Oaxaca, "In the Oaxaca Jail," Lowry

re the book you did [of Malcolm Lowry's poetry]? That is, precisely exactamente a bloody crime. And to Esther love,

Al

To Purdy (Ameliasburgh) from Birney (Vancouver)
February 27, 1971   TL

Dear Al

Okay so you can send me stationery from suites in Acapulco but I bet you never heard from a guy who's been living it up in the Park Plaza in Lethbridge?[512]

I had to choose between this letterhead & the Granada motel in Red Deer & the Mount Royal in Banff since I've just had a crazy week zonging around Alberta like a yo-yo: Calgary; Red Deer (jr coll); Calgary (taping at Riveredge Foundation); Lethbridge (U.); Calgary (autographing in book stores); Banff (taping for ARCHIVES OF THE CANADIAN ROCKIES no less) plus a 2-hr. intermedic [sic] happening with a photographer-teacher who has a color slide to match about every half-line in "David"; Calgary (Glenbow Foundation & Ranchmen's Club); & back for 2 days of yakkings & rappings at Simon Fraser.

So now I'm trying to catch up on mail, friends, while starting the book for Holt-Rinehart (Roy Bentley breathing down my telephone).[513]

Nobody's invited me to Toronto on account of I shd have invented a new name & sent you some of my new "straight" poems (maybe using Dana's address, or my doctor's) & so maybe got into yr anthology & got a free week in Toronto.

So won't see yew-all for a stretch, as I fly to London Apr 9 to read to Poetry Society. It made murmurings in one letter to me about inviting you at same time or later. Did you ever hear from them? I told them to write you via McStew as you were travelling in Mexico. I may stay over in Europe all summer if it looks interesting. Or come back to do a stint in a summer school.

Banff School of Fine Arts wants me to be a writer-in-res., but I haven't seen the color of their bread yet.

Are you going to "tour" Canada soon? (I'm apparently going to do an eastern stint for the League [of Canadian Poets] in Oct., if the Cancow [Canada Council]

---

turns to his constant themes of damnation and salvation: "In the dungeon shivers the alcoholic child, / Comforted by the murderer, since compassion is here too; / The noises of the night are cries for help / From the town and from the garden which evicts those who destroy!" (The last line is a version of a recurring phrase in *Under the Volcano*.) AP later wrote of his meeting Lowry in Dollarton: "I was nearly hypnotized from listening to Lowry talk: about his wanderings in Mexico, being jailed in Oaxaca" (*RBS* 137).

512. The letter was typed on stationery from the Park Plaza Motor Hotel in Lethbridge, Alberta.

513. Bentley, a professor at UBC, edited Aspects of English, a series of textbooks that included EB's *The Cow Jumped over the Moon: The Writing and Reading of Poetry* (1972).

consents again to be milked.) I do think you shd revive the E. Parkhurst Agency (or have E. Parkhurst — hi! you lovely enduring creature you! — revive A. Purdy).

A big cloud blew away off my back yesterday when I got a warm friendly letter from Jack McC (in the midst of all his woes — & maybe ours?). I hope to see him when he's in Vanc. briefly next week. It seems the 2nd letter he wrote was meant as an apology, but the letter didn't show the smile. You don't have to wonder that you spring to Jack's defense when he's attacked. So did I, & so I do still. He's the greatest publisher we'll ever know even if the most infuriating. &, now that he seems to be quitting, everybody in the goddam country is begging him not to. I think he should quit but for the sake of his own mental & physical health (also so he won't go completely for broke).

Your 33,000 twice-revised words of autobiog., knocked off between layings (lays? lies?) on Acapulco beaches, staggers me & fills me with hopeless jealousy. I can't get a damn word written in prose anymore except this sort of broken gibberish I inflict on friends like you in letters. I'm so envious I won't even read your goddam autobiog unless you supply an index so I can look up quickly what you've gone & said about me.

Hope you've had a good trip up to Everson's. I'm sure you'll have enjoyed the stay with him. A great guy & a fine poet not enough appreciated at all. (I didn't get yr letter in time to write you at Ron's, since I was away in Alta.)

Welcome home, Great Canadian, now that Ont. has fine weather again (& today we have 5 inches of snow in Vanc. & more coming down).

Never heard of Edith Barton. I think my son Bill had a girlfriend named Barton though come to think of it. Was she in the Oaxaca jail too?

Esther is off this weekend leading a Retreat of high school students studying Post-Existentialism somewhere near Squamish. She is snowed in.

Do send me your news if you can get the time, before April 9. Any chance you'll be in Europe this summer? I'll keep you in touch with my addresses over there.

Love to you both
Earle

To Birney (Vancouver) from Purdy (Ameliasburgh)
March 12, 1971   TL

Hi Earle,
Got your own re-sent letter, old news and welcome.

No, I didn't get mail forwarded, on accounta the danger of lost mail, a very real danger, since I lost some anyway. Also, lost quite a batch in Greece.

Jack Jensen gave me a copy of the new book [EB's *Rag & Bone Shop*], unsigned of course.[514] I'm pleased to get the signed one (you know my hobby-habits ...). On this point: how amazing that *David* is so scarce — I've never seen a copy in a used book store.

Anne McDermid mentioned in a letter before I left for Mexico, that she wanted me over there. However, I hate to ask CC [the Canada Council] for money, since I'm going to Japan at their expense shortly (a short term thing). I get nervous at all the lit charity, at least I want to keep my importunities scattered in time.

No, of course I don't knock Fraser. What made you say that? Her first prose bit just wasn't suitable, as you imply yourself. But most of those prose statements were cut to bits by Newlove after I left, in order to get the book into manageable dimensions. So Fraser may have a paragraph or two. Like all poets, Fraser will have to prove herself; I have few feelings on her, one way or the other; her poem being useable but hardly sensational.

I heard about the attacks on you via Andy, he rebutting the Finlay piece[515] ... The lit bit is sometimes nasty, as we both know — my own reaction to other people's nastiness being sometimes unjustifiably delayed, as you've pointed out.

When are you coming east again? I leave in approx. a month, but I might stop over in Vancouver. Are you gonna be there?

The snow here is sky-deep, so I'm staying in a friend's place until I can wade the long way home. Stopped at Ron Everson's place in Florida on the way north for a week. Ron very cordial and friendly — He went over my 33,000 word prose bio-crit thing, correcting and suggesting. Went to dinner with he and Lorna [Everson] and Jean Paul Lemieux and his wife at a fish place — You know Lemieux?[516] The painter, that is? Ron got a CC senior, which I think he felt sort of justified himself to himself, his poems that is. Also bought a lotta books in used and rare stores [on] the way north. Klein's *Poems*, 1944 being one of them.[517]

Write as soon as you get this letter and let me know your future whereabouts. A postcard only if you're busy, as I expect. (I have a sliver in 50% of my typing capacity, my right forefinger, this the legacy from Ron Everson Florida burrs ...) So if this screed is more than usually prone to typos and error, well ...

Best,

Al

---

514. Jack Jensen (d. 1997): Danish-born friend of EB's and AP's, who for a time worked as a sales executive at McClelland and Stewart and was involved in establishing *Books in Canada*.

515. In a letter to the *Vancouver Sun* (6 Jan. 1971), Andrew Suknaski objected to Finlay's "inane ramblings and spineless cliches" and praised EB's "experimental poems."

516. Jean Paul Lemieux (1904–90): Québécois painter and professor at l'École des beaux-arts de Québec from 1937 to 1965.

517. A.M. Klein's *Poems* (1944) was published in Philadelphia by the Jewish Publication Society of America.

To Purdy (Ameliasburgh) from Birney (Vancouver)
March 16, 1971   TL

Dear Al

Glad to hear you're back safe, if in deep freeze. You'd better hurry out here, where spring is springing (belatedly, however) & where I'll be leaving, Apr 9, via Wardair cheapjack jet Vanc. — Seattle — Reykjavik — London. Hope you are able to be here before I leave, just to have a glimpse of you anyway. It would be fun if you were going to be along to London with me. But maybe better for you to return there in solitary triumph, without the old relic tagging behind.

Cancow [the Canada Council] gave me price of a straight air ticket return, so by going by Wardair I hope to save about $400 & use that to move around Britain, begging to read at the tables of the Lords & Professors of Commonwealth Lit., etc. (if any exist). Then will waste my own savings perhaps hunting southwards for sun & swimming waters.

You say nothing about the great Get-Together of *Storm Warning* poets in Toronto — I saw the letter McStew sent out quite a while ago, to the contributors, preparing them for a week of publicity & all (it was this week they suggested) & telling them to await details of free fares, etc. They've heard nothing more (at least Dana [Fraser] hasn't, nor has Ken Belton [Belford], who's just come down from Smithers in hopes of picking up a ride back, or Barry McKinnon, who came down partly for the same reason last week & has gone back to Prince George).[518] When I saw Jack McC out here a week or so ago he told me they'd ask Air Canada to pick up the air tabs, but had got no reply, so probably the whole scheme would be off. Too bad. All part of the financial bog the firm is in, I guess — Jack & I made it up, by the way, after he wrote me another letter, & we had a drink & all. I do hope (a) that he personally does whatever will save him from physical & mental breakdown — which probably means getting out of publishing, if he can salvage enough money to afford to; (b) that Cdn. Capital comes to his rescue in time & generously enough.

There's a bed here if you want to stop over. Will Eurithe be with you? How long will you be away?

Glad to hear Ron got a CC senior grant. He doesn't need the money but he does deserve the public recognition.

I've seen an advance copy of *Storm Warning* & want to congratulate you on yet another original & constructive deed for Canadian poets — I wish only the paperstock, etc., had been better.

Was just kidding you about Dana Fraser.

---

518. Ken Belford (b. 1946): Canadian poet (*Fireweed*, 1967; *Ecologue*, 2005) and fishing guide.

Yeah the Vanc. lit scene is very hot, never cool. Schroeder attacked me twice, Finlay once — since they are both Creative Writing Dept. heavies, protégés of the Yanks who are now running that dept., it soon looked like a Yanks vs Canucks scrap, tho underneath it was really the usual struggle of fledgling operators to hold & extend their little powers & perquisites. Schroeder has contrived to become the *only* reviewer of poetry in the *Sun*, & the *only* advisor the Art Gallery has for selection of noon-day poetry readings (the *only* downtown regular readings in Vanc. now) — Finlay does *all* the local bookreviewing of poetry for the *Province*. Time after time these boys, and their friends, put down or ignore the local Canadians — whose letters of reply or protest are not published, & have to appear, symbolically, in the Underground Press, where the Canadians write, viz. *Georgia Straight*. There, recently, I was given a page-spread double review (Lionel Kearns & Judy Copithorne, plus a pref [preface] by Brad Robinson).[519] However, 2 letters from Andy Suknaski got into the *Sun*. And a freelance reporter got another spread for me, interview, in the *Sun*. So I can't complain — except about the grip the Yanks have got over mass communications in this town, & over the Engl. & CW [Creative Writing] Depts at UBC. The book [*Rag & Bone Shop*] has gone into 2 printings, the second being a revision, by the way — collectors note — & the reviews have been good almost everywhere except Vanc., the best & longest being in French in the Quebec *Soleil*!

Hope the new anthology is selling well & getting a good press. Do write me before I leave, & let me know if you will be here before that. If not, good luck in Japan, see you later this year, I hope.

Love to you both,
Earle

Hope you've got your autobiocrit. in the shops you want now.

To Birney (Vancouver) from Purdy (Ameliasburgh)
March 20, 1971   TL

Dear Earle,
Greeting. I could not keep track of all the things you were doing without the occasional letter. You mention Jack [McClelland] might have a breakdown, what about you?

Well, the drum-beating for *Storm Warning* still goes on. TV show Sunday, poets' reading at St. Lawrence Centre Monday, and undoubtedly other things.

---

519. Brad Robinson (1942–2009): Journalist and author (*Afternoon Tea*, 1986) active in Vancouver's literary scene, especially in the 1960s and 1970s. The reviews appeared in the 3–10 Mar. 1971 issue of the *Georgia Straight*.

About half the poets are getting to Toronto, one way or another, or so they tell me at McStew. I believe Jack is picking up at least part of the tab, perhaps all, since he is supposed to have borrowed money to do it. I dunno — kinda doubtful about all the business of McStew selling — Call me a cynic, but I wouldn't put it past Jack to make that announcement in order to get another loan.

I can't be sure when I go west, since it depends on getting the CC money then making travel arrangements — But if it's before Apr. 9 will certainly take you up on the bed offer, and thanks. No, Eurithe will be here, having tired of my company after three mos. (Incidentally, yes, I think the E. Parkhurst Agency oughta be revived too, and the money — but there are few univs east of Quebec, I think —)

Yes, I'm glad Ron [Everson] got the CC grant, for obvious reasons, but it does seem incongruous too ... I think he needs the literary reassurance tho ...

Re Jack again, is there any way he can avoid a breakdown, living the life he does? For no matter what business he was in, I think he'd have a frantic life. In the conference Thurs. re the St. Lawrence reading, Leon Major and all the actory boys there, find that Jack McClelland may be the M.C. for the tonight show, at which I suggest the two rock groups play "O Canada" when he appears.[520] (Yeah, they've got two rock groups lined up for anyone who doesn't like poets — and who does?)

I go back to Toronto tomorrow (which is Sat.). Had a long radio interview, then tv Sunday with the others, then the Monday thing at St. Lawrence. I have a reading at Frank Watt's class at Univ. College Wed., (for money), and undoubtedly more will be lined up.[521] After the holiday in Mexico, I guess I can take it, and besides one has to work to put this book across. I may even get some money (royalties) from the 15,000 copies of *Fifteen Winds* Ryerson sold up to last Nov. Have a letter from McGraw-Hill, sayin they pay after Nov. and Ryerson before. That must be three or four thou — jesus ... It just snowed here about five inches, which kinda numbs me ... Eurithe left the car lights on when she parked, so we have a dead battery for tomorrow (I made appropriate comments). Will let you know later what dates I'll be going west — I hope Esther is by now advancing at the high port.

Love to both of you, (and from Eurithe)

Al

---

520. Leon Major (b. 1933): Canadian opera and theatre director, general director of the St. Lawrence Centre for the Arts (Toronto) from 1970 to 1980.

521. F.W. (Frank) Watt (b. 1927): Influential critic of Canadian literature and professor of English at the University of Toronto.

Dear Earle,

I am feeling sad — which is perhaps not a very good reason to write you another letter so soon after the first one. Also feel ghostlike at the moment, nearly invisible to others — which will pass, of course. (The goddam tv shows in Toronto won't help tho.)

To another subject than myself, I liked the Town portrait that is now postered; you're fading out of life and into death, and death to life, dunno which. (Eurithe hates it.) There is a grisly horrible quality about that poster, totally unlike you, which yet hints at all of us ... The picture in the Geddes book is Moses of course, and the past several pictures of you have all been pretty different, which I like too.[523] Fading from metamorphosis to metamorphosis ... all any of us see is a stir in the spring air ... (If this goddam letter depresses you, throw it away!)

Have you ever read *Adolphe* by some obscure Fr. writer at the beginning of the 19th century?[524] I feel like him too. Except I also feel very strongly me, which I always have. (None of this fuckin no-identity stuff about Purdy, but ghostlike at the same time. How do you figure it?)

I'll have to read *Adolphe* again to verify how silly I am. My memory of the book ten years ago is much like the guy in Proust, chasing a woman thru the labyrinths of his own mind.[525] Also a physical chase, by stage coach and other ways ... Queer thing about love is that the mind is aware — or thinks it is — that there are certain ways to act and modes of conduct that give a certain appearance to the beloved, and which will ensure reciprocal feelings. But these rewarding ways of acting and conduct are impossible to discover, and one falls back on being one's self. Mostly a very unsatisfactory self too. But what is one's self? I find myself colouring myself to others — or at least one or two others — and can't be sure if the colours are real, or have become real because I used them.

Well, love calls me to the things of this world (Wilbur) or something[526] ... Guy

---

522. *YA* 175–76.

523. The "Geddes book" was probably *15 Canadian Poets* (1970), an anthology edited by Gary Geddes and Phyllis Bruce. EB looks wizened indeed in his photograph. EB and AP are the first poets in the collection.

524. *Adolphe* (1816), by Benjamin Constant (1767–1830).

525. The "guy in Proust" is, Sam Solecki notes (*YA* 176 n.2), "the eponymous hero of Proust's *Du côté de chez Swann*" (1913). A short poem entitled "Proust" appeared in AP's *Emu, Remember!* (1956): "In Proust one senses the intense clairvoyance / That shows the skeleton from a god's viewpoint."

526. "Love Calls Us to the Things of This World" is the title of a poem by Richard Wilbur (b. 1921), published in *Things of This World* (1956). Wilbur has claimed that the title originates in Augustine's *Confessions*, but it also has a biblical source: "Love not the world, neither the things *that are* in the world" (1 John 2:15).

coming out with a battery cable to start the car, battery dead now ... Snowed six inches, and have to go to Toronto ... Take a train I guess, for hear the roads are bad. Hope to see you before we both wander off to the opposite ends of the earth and Moses swims the Hellespont with an aqualung.

love,

Al

To Purdy (Ameliasburgh) from Birney (Aberdeen)
April 25, 1971 AL

Dear Al

Hear you didn't go to Japan in mid-April but maybe are there now — I got your 2 letters of Mar. 20 — since then I sat in on several Vancouver post-mortems about the week *Storm Warning* broke — hope you're making some bread out of it at least & that McGraw-Hill blow you dollars from all those fifteen winds.[527]

I flew from Seattle in a sleazy charter plane to Essex & London 2 weeks ago & have been dragging my ass around London ever since, until this moment when I have at last got aboard the express to Aberdeen & have time to scribble a few words to you. I give a "show" at the Aberdeen Art Centre tomorrow night & then drift around Scotland (Dundee, Edinburgh, Glasgow) doing readings & back via Leeds and other Midland rabbit-warrens to London again, where I am booked for 4 readings in late May. One of them is with a score of Brit poets in Bedford Sq., each reading a new commissioned poem (which I have to write by April 30!). Had a reading at the London Poetry Soc. which had a good audience response (about 75 there).

London is expensive, erotic, dirty, muddled, but probably still a fun place if I had the time & the money.

Are you coming over?

Lots of luck & whatever, wherever you are, man.

Earle

To Birney (Vancouver) from Purdy (Ameliasburgh)
July 27, 1971 TL

Dear Earle,

Just been reading *Rag & Bone Shop*, again, and enjoying it so much it prompted me to write ... "Sideburns have been sapping my strength" is, for instance, a great

---

527. EB's reference was to *Storm Warning: The New Canadian Poets* (1971) and *Fifteen Winds: A Selection of Modern Canadian Poems* (1969), both edited by AP. *Fifteen Winds* was published by the Ryerson Press, which was bought by McGraw-Hill in 1970. See AP's letter of 20 Mar. 1971.

comic line. And "Nearby Lions" — what sorta neighborhood was that anyway?[528] They're lovely poems, of the sort you must have enjoyed writing ... I may or may not have said before, but the design of the whole book strikes me as good. I believe you said Newlove and you whacked it out over beer or something like that.[529]

I've got about six readings lined up in the west for this Sept. and Oct. If energy doesn't fall flat (something other than sideburns saps my strength) I'll be out there come Sept., and see you then if you're not also touring. Tom Arnett, who with Gerry Lampert is arranging an unsponsored reading tour (that is, not by Poets' League [League of Canadian Poets] or C.C. [Canada Council]) because he wants to be an agent (Lampert does), talked to me about three poets going east, and who they would be.[530] Arnett asked me if you would come. I said for him to write you. But my own western tour is self-arranged, the E. Parkhurst Agency fallen by some wayside.

I may have said in Toronto: sent my *Selected* off to McS. George Woodcock writing an Intro, which Jack McC. doesn't like much.[531] Am also writing a few poems now and then, parts of which seem okay. One of them, "Temporizing in the Eternal City," has a verse you might like:

The women of course were women
I haven't yet seen any that weren't
which doesn't mean lack of appreciation
merely that when you take the gilding off a lily
all you really have is some gilding[532]

After the *Selected* I typed all the poems for another book later, I suppose a year later. About 85 pages, which doesn't seem a great deal. And I am very dissatisfied with the quality of some of them — but then, I guess I generally am. Figure I ought to do better, but can't quite. Also laying a hardwood floor in the living room here, which seems a pity. We bought this used flooring 14 years ago for fifty bucks, and just now putting it down, me sweating and cussing. But it seems like the end of an era, since the sub-floor was made from plywood boxes heisted from Mountain View dump (that's the airport dump) and painted with paint from the same source. Later Eurithe laid on surrealistic red and black, and we felt rurally stylish.

---

528. AP referred to the poems "Christchurch, N.Z." ("Sideburns") and "Loggia dell' Orcagna" ("nearby lions") in EB's *Rag & Bone Shop* (1971).

529. See AP's letter of 19 Dec. 1970.

530. Tom Arnett (1935–2008): Canadian newspaper editor, writer in various commercial and literary genres, and poet (*The Last Book of the Last Prophet*, 1976). Gerald Lampert (1924–78): Canadian arts administrator and novelist (*Tangle Me No More*, 1971; *Chestnut/Flower/Eye of Venus*, 1978).

531. Woodcock's "On the Poetry of Al Purdy" introduced AP's *Selected Poems* of 1972.

532. The poem was included in *Sex & Death* (1973).

I writ another Hiroshima poem here, to wind-up the small book.[533] I believe I said Jack Jensen and Mary Lu plan to publish it, if they ever get round to doing something concrete.[534] Both are so busy with other things, you know ...

Did I say anything about the C.I.C. [Committee for an Independent Canada] meeting in Ottawa? I asked Stanfield how he liked living in a mortgaged house.[535] He didn't understand.

Luve,

Al

To Purdy (Ameliasburgh) from Birney (Vancouver)
August 3, 1971   TL

Dear Al

You are always amazing me. This time because you somehow take time & energy to re-read books especially mine & furthermore then you sit down & write me a nice letter about it — nice is a lousy word for it. But then I am deep in a writing block & unable to pass anything but a few hard painful clichés — not even such as those, when it concerns the textbk I am supposed to have been writing since June — nothing but blank pages.[536] It's the worst writing block I ever had in a long life of blocking.

Have been fucking the dog by making up a new collection of old crap just in case, sometime in the 21st century, some lousy mimeo press in South Clapham actually wants to bring out a British edition. Hence a few spare Xeroxes of things you mightn't have seen but none of them worth a second reading except maybe "Small Faculty Stag."[537]

Hope to see you in Sep. In early Oct I go east to read for the League from Tor. to Nfld. At least that was the arrangement with Lampert, Souster et al, back in April. 2 "local" poets are supposed to join me at each of the 9 or 10 readings.

I can imagine Woodcock writing something categorical & eminently unimaginative about your work. Something patronizing like that solemn & harmful intro. he wrote for the NCL Turvey ...[538]

---

533. AP's *Hiroshima Poems*, a small chapbook, was published by John Gill's The Crossing Press in 1972. The poems were also included in AP's next trade collection, *Sex & Death*, published by McClelland and Stewart in 1973.

534. Mary Lu Toms of *Books in Canada*.

535. Robert Stanfield (1914–2003): Premier of Nova Scotia from 1956 to 1967 and Leader of the Official Opposition from 1967 to 1976.

536. *The Cow Jumped over the Moon: The Writing and Reading of Poetry* (1972).

537. "A Small Faculty Stag for the Visiting Poet" was written in 1968 and published in *Encounter* 36.2 (Feb. 1971) and in *The Bear on the Delhi Road: Selected Poems* (1973).

538. Woodcock's introduction appeared in the New Canadian Library edition of *Turvey*, published by McClelland and Stewart in 1963.

That's good, that you have 85 pages for a new bk next year. Great. Well I've got what I estimate as 92 printed pages of new stuff, at least half of which is godawful. I have masses of half-finished & maybe unfinishable others. So there's a half-block even with poems. & I'm not laying hardwood floors as an alternative but come to think of it the muscular female I have been laying lately could almost be hardwood.

No didn't hear nothing about the CIC meet in Ottawa. Well I'm on the shelf in Canada anyway. After giving 21 readings in Britain — a hell of a lot more than Pauline Johnson, though it's true she read to Q. Vic — I can't get a single newspaper in Canada even to mention the fact, or want to interview me about it — the only mention the Vanc. press has made of me since they attacked my *Rag & Bone Shop* was to compare me, once more, unfavorably vis-à-vis the great Pauline, who is being dug up for the Centenary — as for eastern Canada, I don't exist. Maybe I *don't* exist, maybe somebody else is writing you this. I wish it were somebody without a writing block.

Anyway I do hope to see yuh.

Earle

To Birney (Vancouver) from Purdy (Ameliasburgh)
August 7, 1971   TL

Dear Earle
I hafta believe you are the wittiest guy in the world, at least my world, the one inside my eyes. I can't believe a wittier poem than "Faculty Stag" has been written. The bit about the Czech and Hungarian profs is marvellous.[539] It's a beautiful beautiful poem. So good tears come to my eyes reading it. The John Audelay 1425 piece only slightly less interesting to me, for different reasons.[540] The Anglo Saxon English slows down my reading, and I am struck with the thought this slow-reading could be used deliberately, i.e. the reader could be made to read at the writer's pace ... sure, I know this is what various metrics could also accomplish, but A-S English makes it very very slow. Why don't you write the history of the world in ten lines, covering the Pleistocene only of course — or have you? History repeats etc. but this piece is grisly in its repetition. I like all of these pieces, like I said once, shall marinate Earle for a fertility symbol if I live long enough which I shan't ... Attached is my Hiroshima poems, an extra one written too late at the end ... the one not there is not a poem anyway, and nailing hardwood floors has tired me out too much to type it ... letters

---

539. "the Czech professor & the Hungarian / who dig everything / so civilised they're savage with disappointment / in us all ..." (*OMH* 142).

540. One of the sections of EB's "plastic plinkles for Gaudy Nite at HMF College, Yule 1966" (in *Fall by Fury & Other Makings*) is *"John Audelay's Hymn for Children's Day, c1475 /* (with one syllable added for updating." AP referred to "Anglo Saxon," but the poem was actually written in a version of Middle English.

I can do, but typing poems gets to be hard work if you're already — Dunno what to think about you not getting any attention from the press etc. Traditionally poets don't, but that's changed a bit, as we know. As well as being a terrific poet (as these poems demonstrate) I happen to think you're a terrific performer, by performer I mean the sort of guy who can stand up on a platform and hold an audience … i.e., when you can do that you should be able to do that when you want to … I mean have the opportunity … P. Johnson was an excuse for not having poets in her time, but now we do, or I think so, in fact certain of it — in fact think you should be travellin emissary of the country, on a slightly different basis than yr tours of Aussieland … I assume from yr blockage you don't really wanta write this text yr talking about, I mean really even if yr mind says yes …

I don't know yr full reasons for doing such a book, apart from the wish to keep busy (which I feel in myself sometimes too); but maybe you should look at the fuckin thing again: i.e., do I really wanta do this book? And reverting to the lack of attention re newspapers etc, I fully agree with you … and I don't mean to seem to go overboard for Birney in this, but those are marvelous poems … it makes me think of that Town/Purdy antho, and how there's no way of representing a good poet with two poems only. Re your schedule, I shall certainly see you in Van in the last half of Sept. Reverting back, maybe one reason you get some bad notices is that you are so goddam clever … reminiscent of Churchill not bein trusted because he was said to be too clever … but anyone with a tenth of one per cent of an iota of brains must appreciate "Stag Party" … To change subject have now seen Woodcock intro, and it *is* fairly solemn, but think it also has some insights, think also Woodcock has changed from the time he intro'd *Turvey*, has become a Canadian in other than name … and I like George, most odd com[bination] of stuffiness and likeability … Intro doesn't stress the freight train rider and all that crap, just as you are tired of the Birney who wrote "David," I reject the idea that other Purdys can't be interesting too as you reject the equivalent ideas … I'm very tired right now (from laying floors, when I can think of other things to lay) so won't correct the undoubted typos in this letter … You make your own muscular female sound more like gladiatorial combat than sex/love, but then each is peculiar to itself …

Al

To Purdy (Ameliasburgh) from Birney (Vancouver)
August 22, 1971   TL

Dear Al
I'm so "walwed and ywounde"* in this goddam book (half-way thru first draft) I'm not writing anybody but it's absolutely necessary to write *you* to send at least my

warmest thanks for the special and precious copy of *Satnight* you sent, with the extra poem clipped in and all the flattering, undeserved and lovely words writ by you. I'm very glad you like the "Small Fac. Stag." Well, we've both endured many varieties of it.

As for this book, it's only a Holt-Rinehart thing.[541] But the catch is I accepted an advance on it two (three?) years ago. They refused to take the money back. Been kindness itself. Waited while I went to Australia & New Zealand. Waited while I got over my busted face. Waited while I did two other books (*Rag & Bone* & Lowry Coll. Poems, which the widow [Margerie Lowry] has refused to allow me to publish). Waited while I went on several more reading tours. Now they're waiting for me to finish it. Meantime they keep getting orders, enquiries, etc, since they advertised it. All damned embarrassing for me. I MUST FINISH IT BEFORE I GO ON MY OCTOBER READING TRIP!

I should be writing a book about *sex in old age*. I keep discovering the damnedest things.

Your good words were necessary healing after I got thru the mail a copy of the San Francisco mag called *The Book Review*. I looked hurriedly through it for a review of *Rag & Bone*, copy of which I had sent them at my own expense (along with an honestly complimentary letter about their mag) back in Feb. Not a mention or a listing of it. Then I discovered this was an August *1970* copy, a year old — why had they sent it to me? I looked again & found an article by Douglas Blazek [inserted: "their poetry-book editor"] called "From the Small Press" and there was a big enthusiastic review of your *Wild Grape Wine* & *Poems for All the Annettes*.[542] *You* envy *me*?! This man Blazek is listing his favorite books of poetry and at the head are your two, "the best of the lot" & the lot includes Bukowski & a dozen other GREAT CONTEMPORARY AMERICANS but "Purdy, whether he is Canadian or not, it doesn't matter, is a most essential poet to read" and, like Abou Ben Adhem, leads the scroll.[543] Seriously, he is right, "whether ... Canadian or not." Me, I think I'm going back to Dublin and write shit-screams for the IRA and see if I can't be an Irishman. If, by the way, you hadn't noticed this review, I will at once send you a Xerox. He does really dig you and says percipient things, even if he is a fucking American — "whether he is American or not, it doesn't matter" — or does it?!

---

541. *The Cow Jumped over the Moon: The Writing and Reading of Poetry* (1972).
542. Douglas Blazek (b. 1941): American poet and small-press publisher associated with the San Francisco underground. The review, published in 1970, was of *Wild Grape Wine* (1968) and the 1968 version of *Poems for All the Annettes*.
543. The allusion was to the last line of the poet Leigh Hunt's "Abou Ben Adhem" (1838): "And lo! Ben Adhem's name led all the rest."

Looking forward to seeing you in Sep — & I hope to god I am freed from my bookchains by then so I can greet you with what is left of my free mind at least.

Earle

* v. Chaucer's "To Rosemounde" — tr. "wallowing and wound round." Ch. compares himself, in love, to a cooked fish swathed in sauce on a plate.

To Purdy (Ameliasburgh) from Birney (Vancouver)
September 9, 1971   APC[544]

Al —

After I wrote you, my copy of SN [*Saturday Night*] arrived. Liked especially the image of you bowing and leaning over that little Japanese girl — (sure she was only 10?) & the "Atomic Museum," congrats.[545] You keep up output, & sustain your voice & write about things that matter. Wish I were!

Love to you both
Earle

To Purdy (Ameliasburgh) from Birney (Vancouver)
November 21, 1971   TPC

Dear Al

I owe you many letters but always expected to be able to talk them to you. Howmsever our eyetinreeze as they say seem to got staggered. Never us 2 in th same place. Hope you found the maritime audiences as exciting as I did — when are we going to compare notes? Shall we safari in Mombasa? I've applied for a small travel grant to go to all the places Purdy aint goin to. Not because I doan wanna SEE you jus doan wanna comPETE thass all.

Anyway I'm so pissed off with hearing me reading me I doan really wanna read nowhere no more.

Love to you both,
Earle

---

544. Next to the stamp EB wrote "UP THE REPUBLIC."
545. The issue of *Saturday Night* (Aug. 1971) contained AP's "Hiroshima: A Poem Cycle" ("The Buddhist Bell," "Survivors," "Whose Mother?," "One Thousand Cranes," "In Peace Memorial Park," and "Atomic Museum"). The "image" appears in "In Peace Memorial Park": "Ceremonies continue all over the place / in the midst of which a ten- / year-old girl comes up / to me and says 'Please what's the time?'"

To Purdy (Ameliasburgh) from Birney (Vancouver)
December 4, 1971   TPC

Dear Al

Waking in the mornings & thinking where is Al & why haven't I heard from him & telling myself the answers: that I don't write him & only answer his marvelous letters with lousy postcards, lousy little postcards, I think well the least I could do dammit is send him a lousy *big* postcard so here it is, a double eye-assault in reeking pseudoriental kitsch but anyway by god "THIS CARD IS A 100% CANADIAN PRODUCT."[546] So don't knock it. Did you get your grant — a foolish question, of course you did, or will. The real question: when do you set off & what's your itinerary? I've got a $2950 grant to read Can. poetry wherever I can in east & west (central) Africa & parts of Asia — with that little money it will have to be a short straight-line tour. I plan to fly to Toronto & then as direct as possible to W. Africa, reading in Gambia, Ghana, Nigeria, Uganda, Kenya, Tanzania, & Sierra Leone, Liberia. Then South India, Ceylon, Malaysia, H.K. [Hong Kong], Manila, & home to Vanc. I'll start about Feb 20 — can we cross trails somewhere? Love to you both. Hope you had a good tour.

Earle

To Birney (Vancouver) from Purdy (Ameliasburgh)
"December 11 or 12, '71"[547]   TL

Dear Earle,

Congrats on yr grant — I kinda wanta go to Africa myself (South), but goddammit not to read. I did a dozen, and suppose you did many more than that. Too sick of it. Now doing real hack work at *Maclean's*, tourist come-on but pays so well couldn't refuse, now wish I had. Sick to death of. Went to work at *Maclean's* every morning at 9 or 9.30 for four days. Feature that, eh. And work ain't done yet. One good bit of news, poem into *Weekend* magazine, they say on "anniversary" but not sure what that is, whether of *Weekend* or Batoche, which is what the poem is about, one I showed you in Van.[548] My *Selected* [*Selected Poems*, 1972] also out in Jan. and been correcting proofs, also writing two *Globe* reviews, one on Layton and one on a Can. hist. book. You can see what I been doin — just so busy sometimes too tired to raise a hand, and with the flu besides. Well, it's money, but in this *Maclean's* stuff, I'm not sure it's worth it. One thing, tho, no more hack tourist crap for me, no matter how well it pays. Besides, the goddam stuff is *difficult* to write. To write badly is really

---

546. EB incorporated part of the postcard into his sentence. "Kitsch" was a reference to the postcard's depiction of the Century Inn, Victoria, BC.

547. EB referred to AP's letter of "Dec. 12" in his own letter of 7 Jan. 1972.

548. "The Battlefield at Batoche" was collected in AP's *Sex & Death* (1973).

difficult, and that's what they want. Always use clichés so everyone can unnerstan, unnerstan? Eurithe plans to go south alone this winter, and I may join her later if time. Readings and G.G. duties in Jan.[549] She plans to go south with Annette, and ... both oughta be good enough chaperone that each will ruin the other's life unintentionally. Well, I won't really be sorry to be alone for a change — that trailer trip is enough propinquity to turn me polygamous.

Luv

Al

To Birney (Vancouver) from Purdy (Ameliasburgh)
January 3, 1972   TL

Dear Earle,

Dunno if I answered your "long card" [4 Dec. 1971] or not, but this short letter anyway. We are taking off for Mexico again in a week to ten days. One or two small things to clear up first. *Maclean's* article finished, *Selected Poems* proofs corrected etc. I feel a bit lost without the pressure of work driving me nuts, i.e. I feel nuts anyway. But undertook to do a segment of Weaver's "The Bush and the Salon" series, which, after doing an Ontario tourist come-on for much dinero, I feel relieved and thankful to get.[550] One other thing that I'll tell you about later.

So how are you? Getting ready to leave for Africa, I suppose. If I get a C.C. I go there myself next winter. Dunno that I'd wanta read there, although if that was the only way to get there even that ... Don't think I actually *like* reading that well ... But it's a way to travel and get paid for doing it ...

Send you a card from Mexico. No, you'll be in Africa. Well, we get back in April, thinking of Yucatan this time.

Take care.

Best,

Al

To Purdy (Ameliasburgh) from Birney (Vancouver)
January 7, 1972   TL

Dear Al

A little puzzled by the combination of yr 2 letters — Dec. 12 says Eurithe going to Mexico with Annette & you might join them in Jan. — Jan. 3 makes no mention

549. AP was a juror (with Wilfred Watson and Ralph Gustafson) for the 1971 Governor General's Award for poetry and drama; he was also a juror for the 1988 and 1989 awards.
550. *The Bush and the Salon* was a CBC radio program that dramatized early Canadian life.

of this but says "we are taking off for Mexico again in a week or ten days" — I guess this means Eurithe changed her plans. Or you are going down with someone else???

I envy your fantastic writing energy, ability to turn out so much, so good, and not get tired of doing it. & all yr other commitments, including yr Establishment life handing out medals for the Queen and all, sitting in judgement on our Nobel Prize Prospect, Irving [Layton] himself, & other matters I don't even understand, like Weaver's "The Bush and the Salon." What the hell's that? Salon=Toronto, Bush=the rest of us?

Well I am glad you got the *Sel. Poems* readied — will it be out before you go? I think you are more sensible heading for one country, and a surefire one like Mexico, rather than me heading for 30 countries in about the same space of time — I don't really expect to survive it, but I'd rather die travelling than sitting in West End Vancouver.

You don't mention Davey's book on me. Nobody mentions it. I hope this means nobody reads it. I hope you relax. Have fun, both of you.

Safe landings & hope to see you somewhere by midsummer, if only as ghost.

As ever

Earle

To Purdy (Ameliasburgh) from Birney (Bombay)
March 29, 1972   APC

Dear Al,

Today I read your poem about that one-inch Arctic tree to about 50 Bombay literati; last week I was reading your Tomato Worm Culture in Nairobi (& your howling huskies echoed in Uganda).[551] So what Birney are you reading, & where? Goddam, let's be bi-lateral in this verse trade. Where are you? And Eurithe?

Love, wherever

Earle

---

551. EB was probably referring to "Trees at the Arctic Circle" ("They are 18 inches long / or even less" [*BR* 102]) and "Still Life in a Tent" ("and the huskies bark like hell / the huskies bark like hell" [*BR* 111]), both from *North of Summer: Poems from Baffin Island* (1967). *North of Summer* also contains other poems that describe the noise made by the "savage sled dogs / who sing at the top of the world" ("Dogsong").

To Birney (Vancouver) from Purdy (Ameliasburgh)
May 12, 1972   TL

Dear Earle,

You've been away so long I've forgotten your address, but Eurithe says this is the right one. Some photos you might care to have.

Supplanting you, I am now in a helluva fight with Jack McC. The Town Purdy book of course. Town wants 75/25 split in what money there is. One guess who gets the 25. Have just seen a lawyer, who says that Town is a bit nutty anyway, with which I agree.

You knew, of course, we just got back from Mexico? 80–90 degrees every day. Stopped on the way to see Leonard Brooks.[552] Not home, but [Scott] Symons and his wife were.[553] I writ some, not as much as would've liked. Sent you *Selected* thru publisher, hope you got etc.[554]

Goin to Africa this winter, CC grant again. Forgot whether you wrote me a letter this time, but you probably did so thanks much. Also to west coast again via trailer, two weeks teaching at Banff then on into nor. B.C., where I will write prose and poems. Really don't know whether you're there now, so I might be writing to someone who arrives next year and leaves next day. Day after next year, that is. But see you in west this summer, if you're there. Best from Eurithe and I —

Yours,

Al

To Purdy (Ameliasburgh) from Birney (Vancouver)
May 25, 1972   TL

Dear Al,

You posted your letter the day I arrived back in Vancouver and was wondering where *you* were. Glad you got some writing done in Mexico and that you got a C.C. grant to Africa. We must get together since I may have some contacts for you, depending on where you're going. I was in The Gambia, Sierra Leone, Ghana, Nigeria, Uganda, Kenya and Tanzania. Where are you going? I wonder if this will reach you before you leave for Banff so "I might be writing to someone who arrives next year and leaves next day" too. I do miss you and hope that we can really settle

---

552. Leonard Brooks (1911–2011): Canadian painter known for his works in watercolours and oils. He was a war artist with the Royal Canadian Navy during the Second World War, and lived in Mexico from 1947 until his death. EB and Esther Birney met Leonard Brooks and the photographer Reva Brooks (1913–2004) in 1938.

553. Symons was married to Judith Morrow from 1958 until the late 1960s.

554. AP's *Selected Poems* (1972).

down quietly and yak this time. Sorry you're having those problems with Jack and Harold. Hope the lawyer doesn't take *your* twenty-five!

My trip was very fast and crowded with readings, receptions, catching buses, taxis, trains, planes, catamarans, rickshaws, etc. In Nairobi I had to ride on the back of somebody's motor bike. I had a ball and did 43 readings and scattered the tropics with snow from your Arctic poems. Hope you and Eurithe are well and that you have a good trip out here. I expect to be around, or in and out, of the flat most of the summer. Do keep me posted on your dates.

Love to you both,
Earle

Thanks for pix of English Bay beachcombers

[APS, May 26:]
Your *Selected* has arrived from publisher — great to have — will have it read thru & massively notated for your arrival (AND SIG!?) —

To Birney (Vancouver) from Purdy (Ameliasburgh)
May 30, 1972   TL

Dear Earle:

Glad you're back home — altho I now get a typical picture of Earle rushing from country to country, reading poems, grabbing backs of motor bikes and asses (female), wind approaching the velocity at which airplanes remain grounded rushing thru sideburns. (Christ, I just saw an old picture of a beard you'd love, split at bottom and two pony tails belligerently pointing east and west —) I could simply not take 43 readings myself, particularly if I read my own poems. But gather you read others' as well, a kinda ambassador from the north wind.

Re my own troubles, the bastards are forcing me outa the book. Which is really *alright* with me, since it is a kinda pretentious bit of crap. However, I will not accept 25%, jesus, you know me better nor that Earle? I'm getting screwed not to mention other nazi and OGPU treatments. I'm fucked if I'll stand for it, *no matter what happens.* I don't know if Jack McC really understands that I won't yet, or if he cares in either event. The end result of all this is partly predictable: I'll settle for a lump sum for three years' off and on work — after which I don't want my name on the goddam book or [to] be included in it. Either one.

I am writing some, not too badly I think — which relieves me of the alternate despair of not writing and thinking I won't in future: or else writing and not thinking it's good enough. Esp. when I look at some of D.H. Lawrence in *Birds, Beasts* etc.[555] That guy was a great poet I believe firmly —

Anyway, "teach" at Banff last week in July and first week in Aug. Then supposed to write a piece for *Maclean's* on B.C. rodeos, one in particular if we can find the right mix of Indians and white, rural surroundings, colour etc. Maybe another on B.C. fishermen which Peter Newman would like if I don't spend too much for expenses.[556] Hope for Vancouver in Sept. Hope to ride out on a fishing boat for a week perhaps, if the union in Van. can be persuaded. But it's really poems I have in mind from both rodeos and fishermen. Now doing a long, strung-out fragmented piece on beginnings of Roblin Lake, which has turned into a lot more than that in process.[557]

See you in Van. Love from Eurithe and I —

Al

To Purdy (Banff, Alberta) from Birney (Vancouver)
July 30, 1972   TA

Dear Al,

Started to address this weirdo stationery to you at Ameliasburgh & then re-read your letter & realize you said that you plan to "teach at Banff last week of July & first week in Aug."[558] You didn't give an address but I suppose for even a Total Canadian like you, Banff is merely equivalent to the School of Fine Arts on the slope of Tunnel [Mountain Drive], so I'll take a chance & send this there. No great chance; nothing lost if you don't get it. It's only to send you a falsetto shout from the Barclay Old Peepul's Home.[559] I enjoyed yr letter & wd have replied to it long ago but I got the idea you had already set off from Ameliasburg & on the road, without an address. But then I heard you were in Ottawa, in Toronto, & other Ontarian villages recently, so went back to your letter, & so here's this — but with damned little to report. It took me a solid month to write the thank-you letters to all the Asians & Africans whom I knew expected them; & mailing off books; reading all the MSS by local poets wanting CC grants, & generally cleaning up on 3-months backlog from my strictly-postal life. I have no other now, apart from being the unpaid gardener for my son, or driving the occasional out-of-town-friend-of-my-wife's through

555. *Birds, Beasts and Flowers* (1923), a collection of poems.
556. AP's "Caught in the Net" was published in *Maclean's* (May 1974) and reprinted as "Lights on the Sea: Portraits of BC Fishermen" in *No Other Country* and *SA* (26–39).
557. *In Search of Owen Roblin* was published in 1974.
558. EB's letter was typed on stationery from the Nyali Beach Hotel in Mombasa, Kenya.
559. EB's address was 406–2030 Barclay St., Vancouver.

the Scenic Beauties hereabouts. (You, of course, being still With It, drive the Scenic Beauties with you.)

I hope by now you've won your battle with Jack about that book, one way or another. I hear nothing about it — but then I hear nothing about anything. Apart from Mrs. Tomkins' form letters, I have no contact with McStew any more. But I can't complain, since I owe them a MS, a new bk of poems, which I'll probably never send, & they will be happy not to get.

Hope also you are enjoying Banff, you & Eurithe. Hi, Eurithe! How does it feel to be living with the new Walt Whitman?[560]

Al, I do hope I thanked you for your *Sel. Poems*. They gave me the chance to re-read a lot of good poems I hadn't looked at for too long. I started "ticking" the ones I felt were Tops, & ended with about two-thirds of the book. So many of them I'd like to probe you about, & particular lines, refs., etc. But I doubt if I ever will. You'll never have time. I hope you will be in touch when you get to Vancouver, though. Also hope I'll be here.

Love to you both. Take care.

Earle

There's a new 2nd hand bkshop on Denman near Nelson. You'll have to visit.

If you see Andy Suknaski tell him Pooky says hello.

To Birney (Vancouver) from Purdy (Banff)
August 2, 1972   TL[561]

Dear Earle:

Great notepaper. Interesting how they identify the nationality of the board of directors.

Eurithe didn't make it this time, she deciding that the house being rented in Trenton (now empty) more important than coming. I am of course desolate.

I have managed to annoy my U.S. students, one in particular, with anti-U.S. poems, she saying twice she had no intention of going to bed with me. I really think she must have it on her mind at that rate. Indulged in a nose to nose shouting match with her. Also have offended the sensibilities of several others, to the point where I am now taking in my own poems for criticism since they're so delicate about their own. Not as hard-boiled as I sound however. It is tough to have your poems pulled apart by some guy with a loud voice.

---

560. "Why do I detest Whitman?" AP asked in a letter (26 Sept. 1973) to George Bowering (*YA* 231). "He's monotonous, long-winded and fulla shit. … He's boring to me. I'm intolerant of personal bores."

561. *YA* 207–08.

Met Trudeau in the Alpine library Sun.[562] Surprised he remembered me after so long ... I had kinda backed off from getting in touch since I thought he'd be so busy and important etc. To my surprise he said he hoped it wasn't something like that. By god, I have never found him as arrogant as other people say.

I will need you badly in Vancouver. This woman is writing me love letters, and has formed an undying attachment etc. Normally I would not object to this, thinking such admiration well-founded and deserved. But I don't like her looks (met her spring last year), and she may figure out what hotel I'm in — If I grow a beard do you think that sufficient disguise? Or maybe a trench coat and jodhpurs? May I enlist your help for male lib?

Come off that crap about McStew not wanting your poems! I mean I may be dumb, but not that dumb. No, my hoo-rah is not settled, and I'm afraid that fuckin lawyer *is* gonna get all the money as you intimated. Anyway, introduce me to the various "friends-of-my-wife" in order that I may have protective coloration and suitable bodyguard in case this woman catches up with me. (By the way, I have writ a pome on this situation. Me blushing shyly behind my modesty and protesting coyly. Hey?)

I too have no contact with McStew, having had a falling-out with Newlove, and only the p.r. people as dry grapevine.

As I may have mentioned, gonna go fishing on a fish boat in G. of G. [Gulf of Georgia] there. (I like "fish boat" instead of gillnetter or seiner, sort [of] more Purdy colloquial!) Seems that this Jack Ferry Associates is eager to show me the fishing industry. It's like the Martian who landed atop the Vancouver Hotel, didn't have to say "Take me to your leader," W.A.C. Bennett was already there to get his vote as a landed Martian emigrant. (All right, go ahead and kill me for that.) See you in Van. around the 19th.

Luv
Al

To Purdy (Ameliasburgh) from Birney (Vancouver)
September 25, 1972   AL

Dear Al

Hope the return tour went well for you — I'm not sure I can catch you with these letters anywhere west of Ameliasburg, you go so fast!

Do come to the League [of Canadian Poets] conference, Al — *we* need you. Hope all is well "back on the ranch."

Earle

---

562. AP probably meant the Banff Centre for Continuing Education, formerly the Banff School of Fine Arts, or the Whyte Museum of the Canadian Rockies (then the Archives of the Canadian Rockies), which housed the library of the Alpine Club of Canada..

To Birney (Vancouver) from Purdy (Ameliasburgh)
October 10, 1972   TL

Dear Earle:

Caught flu when I got here, still lousy, hope you are not the same. Also fucked up with work as you might expect, since you were in same condition on your return west. Now about to plunge into fishing piece, with slight bitterness at having to do it that would be worse if I didn't — if you see what I mean.

Anyway, I forgot what you said about "Beat Joe McLeod," your advice, that is; and it's been bothering me.[563] I send a copy to you to see if you can remember what you said. I think it had to do with the contrast of character between the two people. But at the time you said it, I knew exactly what I should do with that poem. Could you tell me again? Bothers me that I can't work on that poem until I find out what you said. That ought to flatter you, I guess, but that isn't the intent.

The *Hiroshima Poems* [are] out, and will send you a copy when I get some. My copy has about six typos, which is par I suppose ...

Actually, if I could think of another way to do that McLeod poem I'd try. Of course there are other ways, but to get that ending in as is, I dunno ... I know it's the contrast between those two men, but as I remember the key was what you said ...

luv

Al

To Purdy (Ameliasburgh) from Birney (Vancouver)
October 16, 1972   TL

Dear Al

Your letter's been around for a few days because I caught flu at the Edmonton conference & went about to make it worse by flying up to P.G. [Prince George, BC] on the 12th & back the next day to read at Simon Fraser. & all this weekend feeling lousy & trying to remember what the hell I *did* say to you about "Beat Joe McLeod" & finally this morning getting down to reading the poem over & over & deciding I never *would* remember what I'd said, but that what I say now is the poem

1. needs a little over-all polishing, pruning maybe's the better word e.g.

line 2   isn't "both" unnecessary?

4   can this "loaves & fishes" image stand up to analysis? If not, isn't it slightly spurious as an extension of "acts of God" or Jesus or Whomever?

---

563. "Beat Joe McLeod" was published in *Sex & Death* (1973).

8   "cloud in trousers" — since surely they're all in trousers, including Sadler, what's being said beyond the jingle?

22–24   syntax is complex. I know it works, when read twice slowly, but if you brought McLeod's name in again it would really run more smoothly & quickly here, & I don't know why you would want it to run so slowly as it does (asking oneself: whose hands? O yeah not Sadler's but McLeod's — & the first "I thought" is what Purdy thought about Sadler & the second what he thought about McLeod, & so on —)

27   "by indirection" — needed?

2. needs fixing about l. 47–53 — I think the chief trouble in the poem is here. I realize Joe McLeod has to reappear — but with the briefest glance, or we get impatient with this wholly shadowy figure — you don't even tell us what there was about McLeod's handshake that made you think him "insecure and arrogant" — we are as readers at too many removes from McLeod— neither you nor Sadler ever let us in on what he was like *to the 5 senses*, so he remains only a symbol of someone to beat. I'm not saying there's anything wrong about that, but if he's to remain only a symbol, then don't keep bringing him up or it becomes too obvious — my practical proposal is you throw out the 3 lines "but I'd say nothing of Joe McLeod … wholly remembered" because the line "but not absolutes …" is enough in itself to clinch the symbolic point of the title, & you certainly "say nothing of Joe McLeod," nor does Sadler, anyway. (So the reader will begin to think deprived.)

I hope you see that I do like this poem but you didn't ask me to say what I *liked* about it but what I thought was *wrong* (I *love* that Tyee Rainbow image & the way it builds in association with waterspout, thundercloud, into that apocalyptic womb & caul ending — magnificent & very Purdy). (I like the authenticity of the experience; you went out on a troller & by god it paid off in this poem, without your being demonstrable about it.) (I like "juddering" too, which I can't find in my *Shorter Oxford* after all — did Pratt invent it? — I haven't even a Coll. Pratt handy, but I do remember his phrase — in a later poem, perhaps the Great Panjandrum one — about "juddering over the airwaves" if I have it right — did you pick it up from him or did you re-invent it? Or do sailors actually use it on BC trollers?)[564]

I'm sorry you decided not to attend the League's conference — it was a good one & I think we lesser mortals enjoyed each other's work despite the lack of you Big Birds to lead the singing; Everson's wife was ill; so was Souster's; Atwood was presumably too busy; Nowlan & Lee & Nichol & Bissett not there; Bissett because

---

564. "The Truant" ("the Great Panjandrum one"), published in Pratt's *Still Life and Other Verse* (1943), does not contain the word. Perhaps EB and AP knew it from Alfred Bailey's "Miramichi Lightning" (1952): "Hurdling a hump of whales they juddered east, / and there were horse-faced leaders whipped the breath / from bodies panting on the intervales."

he said the League "hadn't asked him to read," which was an untruth — but he is really such an acid-head you can't get to him with truths any more. But many good people were there & the readings, I thought, were the best the League has ever given. I was especially impressed with Ondaatje's new stuff & Bob Gibbs's & glad to see P.K. Page active again — also hearing little Librarian Elizabeth Brewster breaking into a "fuck" that wowed the conference.[565] Ralph Gustafson's new stuff is his best yet I do believe. It was good to have Frank Scott there too, the REAL DEAN OF ETC standing up. Pat Lane is developing like mad both as a talker & as a poet. Barbour & Scobie did a great organizing job on the conf. & I'm glad they'll be doing the joe-jobs for the coming year.[566] Perhaps this all bores you. Certainly it will if you've lost interest in the League. I still think it has a service tó perform for all of us.

My flu's just about gone. Hope yours is long fled. Looking forward to the Hiroshima book. My *Cow* still pastured with the Toronto printers of HoltR&WCan [Holt, Rinehart and Winston].

Cheers. Love to Eurithe & to yousir.

Earle

To Birney (Vancouver) from Purdy (Ameliasburgh)
October 21, 1972   TL

Dear Earle:

Thanks for the précis on poem — you know more about poems, both past and present than I ever will, and I remember thinking how valuable those comments of yours were at the time ... Then forgot ... Jesus ...

As for that snide remark beginning, "I think we lesser mortals..." fuck that crap. It's a reverse put-down as you well know ... Cut it out.

I am all wrapped up in the fishing piece now, writing some 1,500 words of what I think is as good prose as I ever wrote, you know, characterization and struggle, all that, including of course the McLeod bit. Incidentally, the reason for the "cloud in trousers" bit in the poem was several, one of which I thought you'd know. Mayakovsky's cloud in trousers.[567] Two, the rhyming sound of cloud with

565. Elizabeth Brewster (1922–2012): Canadian poet (*Selected Poems of Elizabeth Brewster, 1944–1984*, 2 vols., 1985), novelist, and professor at the University of Saskatchewan. Robert Gibbs (b. 1930): Canadian poet (*The Tongue Still Dances: Poems New and Selected*, 1985) and professor at the University of New Brunswick.

566. Douglas Barbour (b. 1940): Canadian poet (*Story for a Saskatchewan Night*, 1989), critic, and professor of English at the University of Alberta. Stephen Scobie (b. 1943): Canadian poet (*McAlmon's Chinese Opera*, 1980; *The Spaces in Between: Selected Poems 1965–2001*, 2003), critic (*Leonard Cohen*, 1978), and professor of English at the University of Alberta and the University of Victoria.

567. Vladimir Mayakovsky (1893–1930): Russian Futurist playwright and poet. Herbert Marshall's

McLeod. Three, the fact that it seemed his (McLeod's) character ... (I have your letter pinned up where I can't miss it when I get back to that poem, as I will ...) You will have to stay at a better class of motel next time so you can get larger paper more suited to length of letter so you don't have to run over onto the advertising ... Myself, I make sure I get it all, at any motel ... Then have all sizes. You note yours is large ... Anyway, despite being very interested in parts of this fishing piece, I don't know whether to mourn because it takes me away from poems I probably wouldn't write anyway, or just gripe because it's so damn much work ...

Kinda agree about the Atwood novel [*Surfacing*, 1972], which I'm now reading, about halfway thru ... Think she's a better novelist than poet, which is sayin something ...

Dunno if Pratt invented "juddering" or not, thot it must be a word I'd heard somewhere else when I wrote it, if so I don't know where ... Sounds Prattish tho ... on accounta all his ships and seas and things ... But didn't he allus write about engine ships, and it goes with sail ships?

Sure, Scott was always the dean of things, he was born to be a dean, I think ... Glad you think Gustafson's new stuff is good, since I like him much but don't like his poems much ... Seems to me he's always been jest a leetle too chalky and consciously abstrusely intelligent and literate — Course the age itself is agin that, rightly I think, as I'm bound to, but time may roll around again for that sort of thing ... Brewster uttering "fuck" is too much, as if she might use more than the verb prior to her pension ... Letter from Fiamengo which indicates she thinks Lane and Newlove sorta spoiled brats ... Incidentally, her own (Fiamengo's) new poems, heard on tour, I thought very good, and she reads em like leviathan breathing fire underwater.

No, I haven't lost interest in the League as such, tho the business meetings do bore me and I feel and am useless at them ... I still go along with the League as a good thing, but reserve the right to my own feelings re its sleep-inducing proclivities ... Probably well on its way to being another CAA, which remark very common of course, which means little, since even the CAA did do some things ...

This letter with the Gill chapbook [*Hiroshima Poems*], and seem to have a helluva time communicating with him ... Have got a total of no letters to two I wrote asking how many copies he printed etc.[568] As I look at the book, and know what the Oberon book woulda been if I'd agreed to change publishers — I mean the Oberon *Hiroshima Poems*, which they would have published if I'd agreed to change — along the lines of Ondaatje's large animal book, that superimposes

English translation of Mayakovsky's poetry (*Mayakovsky*) was published in 1965. AP could have read that volume. AP referred to "The Cloud in Trousers" (1915). The translation in the letter of 9 Nov. 1972 is that of George Reavey.

568. On John Gill, see, e.g., the letters of 3 July 1966, 18 June 1969, and 27 June 1971.

over this one[569] ... But doesn't really matter ... If the poems are any good they'll find their own level regardless of format. Still, one does think of format. But Jack McClelland did come thru and pay me what I asked, therefore feel I can't do less than reciprocate ... Still have one niggling thot. Before lawyer Malcolmson's final meeting with McClelland, former asked me to indicate how I felt about McC. which he undoubtedly communicated to Jack, which was the purpose of the inquiry. I reserved the right to change, but admitted I'd be inclined not to if Jack came thru with the cash. Which he did. Still, that makes me wonder about Malcolmson's possible involvement with Jack, since Malcolmson hasn't sent me a bill even tho I asked him for it long ago when I was at Banff ... See what I mean ...

Your H. and W. [Holt, Rinehart and Winston] book in Tor. — I look forward to that — hope no more of those remarks about the sweet singer of A-burg eh?[570] In the book, I mean? Or should I pay you for a mention?

The Hiroshima poems now seem to me something I don't wanta read again, unpleasant to me, that is ... I wonder why ... Life also seems largely a matter of endurance these days, not unpleasant exactly, but beyond my powers to change to any other way that I certainly can conceive of ... Jesus, better motels for me too.

Luv,

Al

To Birney (Vancouver) from Purdy (Ameliasburgh)
November 4, 1972   TL

Dear Earle:

Fast note to straighten out if I got what letter or you got what letter. When I sent the *Hiroshima Poems* I sent a letter with it, which assume you got. The last letter from you was dated Oct. 16, (which I have up on the wall waiting till the flu aftermath allows me to go into your suggestions re McLeod) ... I've received nothing else but the card. Anyway, my last letter to you was in reply to your last.

Yeah, difficult to get printed in U.S., tho I haven't tried since that agent in London business a few years back. Did I tell you I had a manuscript at Random House with one Jason Epstein at one time?[571] Anyway, they turned it down. So I haven't sent anything since, except to mags that ask for poems. My attitude being if they want em they'll ask. I'd like book publication, but it will have to be done

---

569. *The Broken Ark: A Book of Beasts*, poems selected by Michael Ondaatje (1971). EB and AP worked with Oberon Press on several occasions. In 1970 Oberon published *The Cosmic Chef: An Evening of Concrete*, edited by bpNichol, in which appeared three poems by EB. In 1972 Oberon published *Four Parts Sand*, an anthology of concrete poems by EB, Judy Copithorne, bill bissett, and Andrew Suknaski.

570. *The Cow Jumped over the Moon: The Writing and Reading of Poetry.*

571. Jason Epstein (b. 1928): American editor and publisher who worked at Random House and co-founded *The New York Review of Books* and the Library of America.

thru whoever my Can. publisher is. On accounta you can spend too much time fucking around that way, too much preoccupation etc. In perhaps other words, I feel oddly that I'd be betraying myself if I worked too hard for U.S. pub. Okay, maybe that sounds odd, but there it is ...

Barry McKinnon commented on McLeod poem too, saying he thought "McLeod has to be clarified in some way. I didn't quite know how to feel about him ..." Which is in keeping with your own comments. But it puzzles me now to know what to do, since it seems I have been attacking a shadow in the poem itself, having set up a straw man etc. Actually, in person, McLeod was a long way from that, and I somewhere in my mind must have taken him for an inimical force without knowing or stating exactly why. I suppose what I'm really attacking is the quality of hero worship in Sadler which I both dislike and find appealing at the same time. All my own heroes turn out to be human from the knees up ...

Anyway, without the poem in front to stimulate or deaden me, it seems almost impossible to change. Perhaps that's because I feel lousy for last month, the flu hanging and hanging, until I decide to go to a doctor. The *Maclean's* article is now with them, incidentally, something over 6,000 words, and expect they will want changes. But the Gil Sadler/McLeod 1,000 words in that is [as] good prose as I've ever written (perhaps I can find a clue to the poem in prose) ... So I stare at this typewriter in foreboding of the work it still will have to do with a piece needing revision for Weaver and the *Maclean's* piece. And reading African travel lit. What I really must do is read a contemporary history of the country, a warts and all piece if there is one. Incidentally, I read at York last Monday, about 250 people, very uncritical audience someone remarked. Interesting way of saying it ... No one I knew there except Lampert and David Silcox.[572] Silcox used to be at C.C., now dean of arts or something.

Luv
Al

To Purdy (Ameliasburgh) from Birney (Vancouver)
November 6, 1972   TL

Dear Al

Your good letter of Oct 21 took a while in reaching me — some damned holdup-pings going on in the mail somewhere (a letter from Bishop's [University] took 10 days to come). (Things fall apart, the world is ending, etc.)[573] I'm relieved you didn't

---

572. David Silcox (b. 1937): The first Arts Officer for the Canada Council (1965–70), and later Associate Dean of the Faculty of Fine Arts at York University. He is a distinguished scholar of Canadian art (*Painting and Place: The Life and Work of David B. Milne*, 1996).

573. The allusion was to W.B. Yeats's "The Second Coming": "Things fall apart; the centre cannot hold."

find my comments on the McLeod poem useless — & I learn that I don't know Mayakovsky well enough (still don't — what the hell *is* the Mayakovsky ref?).[574]

Further to Gill (& thanks for the wonderfully signed copy of your Hiroshima poems) — Oberon has sent me one — did you know? — would you like me to send this second copy to someone else — I know it's a fairly small edition, so it won't go around too far — or give it to someone like Andy [Suknaski] (who's living in town here again)? But about Gill & his press — my experience was that he published a very limited edition [of *Memory No Servant*] — cd never find out how many, 500 perhaps — & then advertised it in more than one *Canadian* mag — & took orders from Canada (book-collectors, libraries, anybody wanting to "collect" me). This of course defeated the whole purpose of the book, from my point of view, which was to reach maybe a few thousand American readers, by the only way open to me. The same is at the moment roughly true for you, though I've no doubt you will eventually get a full book out with a good publisher in the States. This is something I always wanted for myself, not because I am an American-lover, but because poetry readers are good people anywhere & the percentage of them in the U.S. is maybe as high as in Canada, which makes for ten times as many extra readers. But I no longer believe I'll ever get to such an audience. But you can & more quickly if Gill & Co will really make an effort to *distribute* your Hiroshima book *in the States*. I don't think, however, they have even a rudimentary commercial distribution scheme, nothing comparable to what even our little mags do in Can. to reach across the country.

Had a letter from Scott Symons, in San Miguel Allende. Well ahead on a new novel, he says, tho all broken up with & about John [McConnell].

I came across a file card from my days as ed. of *Can. Poetry Mag* — it says

PURDY	Mr. Alfred W. 134 Front St., Trenton, Ont.
	Member CAA
Sep 46	printed "Dust …," prev. accptd by Kirkconnell
	Sent back 4 other poems in Kirkconnell's Hold File
	(which he had queried): "Sailor Legend," "Portrait," "Cave Man,"
	"Embarkation."
	Also wrote Purdy for reactions to new issue, & for sub.
	Note: Kirk. had given P. a minus rev. in Jun 45 issue, for
	The Enchanted Echo. Unfair. Try to get better poems fr. P.[575]
Sep 10/47	Acc. "Night Errant" & ret. 7 others.[576]

574. See AP's letter of 9 Nov. 1972 for his explanation of the reference.

575. In his review Kirkconnell wrote that "Haste has left its mark on all too much of" *The Enchanted Echo* (*Canadian Poetry Magazine* 8.4 [June 1945]).

576. "Night Errant" was published in *Canadian Poetry Magazine* 12.1 (Sept. 1948).

Nov 6/47.   Sent him letter re. my policy vs. Kirk's. Ret. his "Air Force Discharge" & briefly answered long letter.

I should have done you better than that. Who would return 7 Purdy poems these days in Canada? Or answer his long letter with a short one?

Love

Earle

To Purdy (Ameliasburgh) from Birney (Vancouver)
November 8 ("(wed nite)"), 1972   TL

Dear Al

Urgent. On Mon. I wrote you a letter (which has crossed with one from you dated Nov. 4). In it I said some silly things about John Gill. Complaints not really justified nor documented. I want you to forget about them. Above all don't quote me to him (I gather you may be going down there anytime). His edition of my poems was "limited" but I knew that in advance, that was the deal. & he may have taken only a *few* orders from Canada, & only before I asked him not to. & the advt. he placed (I saw only *one*) could have been done before he realized that I wanted the edition to circulate only in the US (that was Jack McClelland's stipulation [... Here the text becomes unclear.] distribution scheme — how could I expect so small a publisher to afford a distribution system? I don't know what was wrong with me when I wrote you that Mon. letter, bitching that way about John. He has been a good friend to me, even though he didn't include me in his anthol. of the 16 best Can. poets[577] — I guess that was what was sticking in my crop, & suddenly came out — I've no reason to complain, since I was the first Can poet he published in a separate book. He's really a nice guy & I would hate for anything silly I said in that letter to you to be repeated to him O.K. pal?

Sorry to hear you've had such a long bout of flu. It's great that you got a 6000 word article done, despite being sick. Are you alone? You don't mention Eurithe these days. Hope someone's looking after you.

As for reading "about Africa" it's not a country but a continent, an obvious fact that people don't really face till they get there. Read up on the countries you are going to stop in, you'll find that a complicated enough job. I couldn't advise you

---

577. Gill's *New American and Canadian Poetry* (1971) included works by fifteen Canadian poets: Milton Acorn, Margaret Atwood, Ken Belford, George Bowering, Douglas Fetherling, Ray Fraser, Len Gasparini, George Jonas, Patrick Lane, Irving Layton, David McFadden, John Newlove, Alden Nowlan, David Phillips, and Ian Young.

on S. African history as I've read only mag. articles on it but the Tor Ref. Library cd give you lots of help.

Keep in touch

cheers

Earle

To Birney (Vancouver) from Purdy (Ameliasburgh)
November 9, 1972   TL[578]

Dear Earle:

Your notepaper is making me envious. Have decided to lead with my ace — gunfighter I guess.[579] Top this one, unless there's a motel in the crater of Vesuvius.

The ills the flesh is heir to have sorta got me lately, so doing little but drink beer and moan about my sorry fate.[580] Well, a little more. Arranged the African trip today, Dec. 11, with stopover in Rio. Come back more or less when I feel like it. Movie named *Black Orpheus* was made in Rio years ago, and I hope to tromp over the poor section overlooking city where that was made.[581]

Re Gill. Yes, please give Andy that extra copy. He printed 300, then said they were shown in a book fair or arts exhibit at Trumansburg [New York], and a psychology teacher told his class to buy them or else. That took half, then he sold the other half to Can. stores, so none to U.S. at all, really. So Gill printed another 500, of which some must surely go to U.S. I made no arrangements with him at all re finances at the time he took them, which seems very stupid in retrospect. Now difficult to do so.

Of course I see your point about readers. Large countries, as we both know, tend in some ways to be even more insular than small ones. They believe the sun rises and sets on their own productions, for instance, associating art and literature with great power, and using the same adjective. Or so I think. Perhaps at least part of the time, the kinda manifest destiny sense a big country may have actually does help in the arts, just as ego is necessary for a writer to write well — Again, so I think, and these are not profound thoughts.

Still, when I think of your poems and you, and Layton and his, apart from nationality, particularly your best, I don't feel in the slightest bit that these are inferior. One can't permanently remain interested in inferior literature, can

---

578. *YA* 208–11.

579. The letter was typewritten on stationery from the Desert Haven Motel, Lovelock, Nevada. The background is a wood print; a large cartoon gunslinger appears in the top left corner.

580. From Act 3, Scene 1 of *Hamlet*: "The heartache and the thousand natural shocks / That flesh is heir to."

581. *Orfeu negro* (1959), directed by Marcel Camus.

one? Anyway, one part of the mind leaps the picket fence of nationality, decides these are fine poems whatever their origin. Except I don't think of origins at all times, only when it's necessary. And whether your poems or my poems ever get published elsewhere or not, I can't think yours are anything but good, and don't feel any inferiority in myself either.

I'm not at all sure mine will ever get published elsewhere. And while not precisely satisfied with this outcome, it's still too much trouble to worry about it or make more than a somewhat lethargic effort. I realize I'm taking the stance of an old lady in full flush of euphoria after having written a poem, and she believes it to be the greatest ever — all her friends tell her so. Perhaps we are like that old lady in a way (altho I doubt it), our friends (fellow Canadians) saying we are great etc. But you can make an argument for either side here, Rod McKuen or Emily Dickinson ...[582]

Before I forget (now we're in Mexico), Atwood's book [*Surfacing*], I agree, very fine. One thing troubled me, the complete switcheroo at the end. After heroine is back to nature, she suddenly turns round [and] goes back to city and her lover. That wasn't led up to far as I could see. There is a very shifty centre in a woman like that. Doesn't one want a modicum of persistence and permanence in the self?

Haven't read her handbook on lit, but hear the title is the key, and she takes poems of ours (yours, mine, Layton's etc) to demonstrate that theme.[583] Good enough, but at this point I've no doubt about survival, and doubt also I was thinking of it the way she seems to ... If I worried much about that it would be like worrying about death etc. All of these things have their place in a life, and we are preoccupied with all of them, more or less at one time or another.

Incidentally, re death, many years ago in Vancouver Curt Lang tried to get my poems published there, the publisher turned em down, saying they were about sex and death. Which I agreed with then and do now. Any writer worth his salt has them for subject matter, of course in degree. They also involve love and life. Anyway, thinking of using *Sex and Death* as title for book, with a note about that little anecdote above. Have a nagging thought tho, that Berryman used something similar before he said farewell cruel world.[584]

Anyway, reverting to Gill, I guess he's doing the same thing with me as with you, selling everywhere he can.

Re Scott Symons when I relayed your news, Eurithe says he broke it up himself. Which doesn't mean it can't be poignant anyway. But there's something funny about Scott weeping bitter tears over John, even if it is poignant.

---

582. Rod McKuen (b. 1933): Popular American songwriter and poet (*Listen to the Warm*, 1967).
583. *Survival: A Thematic Guide to Canadian Literature* (1972).
584. John Berryman committed suicide in 1972. AP alluded to Berryman's *Love & Fame* (1970).

Again reverting to ego-boosters like U.S. publication, I'm one down to practically everybody on another ego aspect, the writer-in-rez bit. Never had an offer in solid terms, tho U. of Man. did nibble last time thru ... I could use the cash as apart from ego-support.

But I gnaw away on this U.S. pub bit — I really think one can't waste time moping, you know the poems are there to be written, and it seems like hardly anything has been already written that cannot be bettered. I say that not as boaster or braggart or in excessive self-confidence, but as what I regard as simple fact. Every time your mind stretches a bit at some euphoric written instant, you realize this is so. Despite all the great things, very little comes within your peculiar orbit and registers as something you would like to have done ... Or so I feel. For it seems to me the best stuff is yet to be written, and while I may never even come close, no inferiority is gonna stop me from having a shot at it. Which is a kinda manifesto, except not so thundering, nor sad as all manifestoes [*sic*] are kinda sad ...

Jesus, we go far back in time, when you resurrect those old letters and poems. I remember only "Night Errant" or was it with a "d," "Errand," or is there such a word? That other self, so far back, and your other self ...

I've been tinkering with "[Beat] Joe McLeod" with your letter beside me, dunno if it's better or worse yet, but will be different. You have an eye for that sort of thing, whereas I was only uneasy about the poem. I'm really talking about myself in it, the business of gods and idols. One always expects too much of one's friends or women, the sandpapered burglar's fingers encountering an abrasive alien soul under flesh. Not only iconoclasm re Sadler's idol, but the fact that McLeod himself could probably never feel those things ... And it gets a bit similar to Hemingway I suppose ...

> What is Faust to me,
> in a fairy splash of rockets
> gliding with Mephistopheles on the celestial parquet!
> I know —
> a nail in my boot
> is more nightmarish than Goethe's fantasy!
>
> Mayakovsky

Surprised as hell you don't know him. Also came across this re sculpture of Aphrodite:

Aphrodite gazed down upon Cnidus, and said,
"Where on earth did Praxiteles see me naked?"[585]

That written 2,500 years ago! Or did the translator write it? But I'm reading Mayakovsky again as a result of this exchange, and more than ever enjoy him. Will send the book along to you if you want it, but quote some from "Cloud" for myself as well as you …

Your thought,
musing on a sodden brain
like a bloated lackey on a greasy couch,
I'll taunt with a bloody morsel of heart;
and satiate my insolent, caustic contempt.

No gray hairs streak my soul,
no grandfatherly fondness there!
I shake the world with the might of my voice,
and walk — handsome,
twentytwoyearold.

Tender souls!
You play your love on a fiddle,
and the crude club their love on a drum.
But you cannot turn yourselves inside out,
like me, and be just bare lips.

Come and be lessoned —
prim officiates of the angelic league,
lisping in drawing room cambric.

You, too, who leaf your lips like a cook
turns the pages of a cookery book.

If you wish,
I shall rage on raw meat;
or, as the sky changes its hue,
if you wish,

585. From the *Anthologia Graeca*. It is possible that AP read the translation in Alexander Eliot's *Greece* (1963).

I shall grow irreproachably tender:
not a man, but a cloud in trousers!

He's waiting for this girl:

The stroke of twelve fell
like a head from a block.
On the windowpanes, gray raindrops
howled together,
piling on a grimace
as though the gargoyles
of Notre Dame were howling.

Damn you!
Isn't that enough?
Screams will soon claw my mouth apart.

Then I heard,
softly,
a nerve leap
like a sick man from his bed.
Then,
barely moving
at first,
it soon scampered about,
agitated,
distinct.
Now, with a couple more,
it darted about in a desperate dance.

The plaster on the ground floor crashed.

Nerves,
big nerves,
tiny nerves,
many nerves! —
galloped madly
till soon
their legs gave way.

But night oozed and oozed through the room —
and the eye, weighed down, could not slither out of the slime.

The doors suddenly banged ta-ra-bang,
as though the hotel's teeth
chattered.

You swept in abruptly
like "take it or leave it!"
Mauling your suede gloves,
you declared:
"D'you know,
I'm getting married."

***

I,
the most golden-mouthed,
whose every word
gives a new birthday to the soul,
gives a name-day to the body,
I adjure you:
the minutest living speck
is worth more than what I'll do or did!

***

I spit on the fact
that neither Homer nor Ovid
invented characters like us,
pock-marked with soot.
I know
the sun would dim, on seeing
the gold fields of our souls!

I guess he's like olives tho — generally I don't like things quite so dramatic, but him I forgive. Well, this is long.

love,
Al

To Purdy (Ameliasburgh) from Birney (Vancouver)
November 20, 1972   AA

Dear Al

Dropped in [on] your friend McIntyre today & he tells me you're going to be Writer in Res @ U. of Manitoba, starting in Jan. ??[586] I guess this blew up since you wrote me (Nov. 9) — don't know whether to congratul- or commiser- ate you! Instead of a South African summer, a Winnipeg winter! But, as you write, you could do with the cash — provided it's a *real* writer-in-residency, and *no* teaching chores, then I do think it *is* wonderful, & right & all — but I do wish it were SFU [Simon Fraser University] or somewhere warmer, & closer to us!

Excuse paper and esp. handwriting — can't type at present — an attack of arthritis (left hand) — yes, old age — it gets you somehow — I enjoyed your letter & wish I could gas with you about it.

I *did* know Mayakovsky (before he killed himself, even) but had forgotten that passage.

Love to you both,

Earle

To Purdy (Ameliasburgh) from Birney (Vancouver)
November 29, 1972   AL

Dear Al

Sorry the U. of Man. writher-in-residence thing hasn't jelled yet. But the university deals take time & you may well get it yet — I hope it does, so you can write only what you want to, & when you want to, for a while at least.

You ask if I have any S.A. addresses you could use?? I've never been to South Africa or even within 1500 miles of it. The total English-speaking pop. of the whole so-called country is less than Vancouver's. I can't imagine any friend of mine living there, outside of jail. In fact, that's where most of the resident writers are living at present, so far as I know, the *good* ones (if they have off-white skins) — the ones of *our* color are dead or in exile — I attach an alphabetical list — afraid it won't be of much help — 66 names, no addresses, & info. out of date.

Heard from Jack Jensen — he hopes to be in Toronto this weekend (Dec. 2) so you may see him.

---

586. Steve McIntyre: A friend of AP's and Curt Lang's from early days in Vancouver, described by AP as "a Davie Street bookseller who liked good literature and sex" (*RBS* 135). "For Steve McIntyre" was published in *The Collected Poems of Al Purdy* (1986).

Joe Rosenblatt & Irving [Layton] & Marya Fiamengo have been here givin readings & departed. Life lapses back into sea fog.

Take care
Earle

To Birney (Vancouver) from Purdy (Ameliasburgh)
December 5, 1972   TL

Dear Earle:

I'm a little overwhelmed at the kindness on your part and consequent work compiling that long list of writers. Sure, I suppose most are in jail or fled the country, but maybe one or two … Thanks much.

Just read at Bishop's and Loyola, the prof there (Abrahams) is an ex-South African, a little too dark for the liking of authorities there.[587] Quite a nice guy. Said he'd try the writer-in-rez bit for me at Loyola. Mtl. would be more lively than Wpg. anyway. Maybe something will come thru …

Looking at your new book, the publishers sending me a copy, enjoying it. Note you placed Davey's bit next to me. Can understand why you're not fond of the Davey book on you, tho I haven't read it. He seems to have misjudged the poem entirely, since I never connected it with WW2 despite being written then, I mean even despite knowledge from you it's a farewell poem to a gal … Always seemed to me so much an expression of medieval sailors' fears as well as other interpretations …[588]

I am finishing off all sorts of work here. Managed to take on another poet from B.C. when I was there, to try and get him published. Peter Trower, and dunno if you met him.[589] Work uneven, but much good stuff. Feel like an elderly advising aunt, what with Trower and Sid Marty, whom I'm also pushing.

Maclean's article now in hands of editor there, scheduled for February. CBC poem-play also being worked on, producer John Reeves sounding very snotty in a letter. Eurithe didn't think so, but when he ended the letter by saying if Orson Welles could write 300 speeches for people talking in a movie, then "I'm not asking you to undertake a mammoth task —" which sounds damn snotty to me. I just had

---

587. Cecil Abrahams (b. 1940): Professor of English, scholar of African literature, and anti-Apartheid activist who has taught at several universities in Canada and elsewhere. In Montreal, where AP met him, he helped establish an office of the African National Congress.

588. The "new book" was *The Cow Jumped over the Moon: The Writing and Reading of Poetry* (1972), in which EB refers to interpretations of his poetry by AP and Frank Davey. The poem in question was "Mappemounde."

589. Peter Trower (b. 1930): Canadian poet (*Ragged Horizons*, 1978) and novelist (*Dead Man's Ticket*, 1996) whose works are largely based on his experiences as a logger in British Columbia.

VOICES, FADE B.G., THEN DOWN AND OUT. Life's minor annoyances I guess. Reeves used to be lauded as a poet, and it makes me wonder …

Will send you a card or letter from S.S.[590] Again much thanks.

Luv

Al

To Purdy (Ameliasburgh) from Birney (Vancouver)
December 16, 1972   AL

Excuse handwriting — still can't manage a typewriter with 2 hands.

Dear Al

I was just thinking, addressing your envelope (I always do the envelope first — it helps get steam up) how the P.O. has fucked up your image. That folksy address, absolutely right for the Canadian poet (nature's nobleman to Nobelprizeman), now has a super-urban code message tacked on — what does it mean? May your cock stay A1-O!?[591]

Hope Loyola comes thru with an offer. I found it a good place, both times I've read there — & there is, or was, a most beautiful & intelligent lady teaching English there, Elspeth Buitenhuis, whom I take it you met.[592]

I'm glad you haven't read Davey's book on me — not that I think it would make you think worse of me — but because I think it demonstrates a basic confidence between poets if they don't feel any need to read what the critics say about them — by the same token I bought Bowering's book on you, & have never bothered to read it!

Yes I know Peter Trower — got his *Moving through the Mystery* when it came out [1969], & lately was in touch & gave him what encouragement I could.

John Reeves — hmm — I recall a couple of times when he sounded peremptory & important on the phone or letter & later, when *I* became my usual screw-you self, he turned very 'umble & ingratiating. I think he has his own following in Toronto & likes to be a loud cockerel in a small barnyard, if permitted.

You end by promising "a card or letter from S.S." — a slip of the key, no doubt — the only geographical S.S. I know of is Spanish Sahara — if you get there, send

---

590. An error: AP meant "S.A." — he was departing for South Africa.

591. AP's new Ameliasburgh postal code was K0K 1A0.

592. Elspeth (Buitenhuis) Cameron (b. 1943): Biographer of EB, Irving Layton, and Hugh MacLennan (*Hugh MacLennan: A Writer's Life*, 1981); literary critic; and professor of English, chiefly at Loyola College/Concordia University, the University of Toronto, and Brock University.

me a sand-candle — but if you stay out of jail long enough in S.A. [South Africa] send me a real letter — in jail, they won't let you.

And come back hung with triumphs & poems.

Love to you both for Xmas & New Year's
& St. Swithun's & Richard III's Birthday.

Earle

To Purdy (Ameliasburgh) from Birney (Vancouver)
January 22, 1973   AL

Dear Al

Just a note to say I got your letter from Johannesburg — don't know if this will catch up with you — hope you found it cooler in Cape Town or wherever you went next — anyway you seem to be doing poems about it all, which is more than I've done about the whole of Africa & Asia so far! Guess I'm washed up — if you decide to go to Mexico do let me know as I'm thinking seriously of going down there myself again — that can't be till April however, as Gerry Lampert has worked out a reading tour for me that will take up most of Feb and March between here & Peterborough, Ont.

Keep well & out of trouble!

Love
Earle

I still have a bad hand & can't type.

Address me here to reach me before Feb. 23 — after that, via Gerald Lampert 106 Avenue Rd Toronto 180.[593]

[Verso:]

Have signed a contract with Chatto & Windus for a 64 page paperback selection of poems for the British & "Commonwealth" trade — probably out in early '74 — title *The Bear on the Delhi Road & Other Poems.*

(After 30 years! Poets like me *have* to live long to get anywhere at all.)

---

593. "here": EB affixed a label with his Vancouver address: 406–2030 Barclay St.

To Birney (Vancouver) from Purdy (Coatzacoalcos, Mexico)
February 27, 1973[594]

Dear Earle,

Mexico is getting to be a habit with me — us, for Eurithe is here too. Driving to Yucatan — Ron Everson will join us in Merida Mar 20 for a coupla days, then we head north. Stopped at San Miguel for a night and cordial visit with Leonard Brooks and Reva. We're supposed to call again on return trip, but dunno. Eurithe wants to go via Tampico —

Road death today a hundred miles north of here. Truck took a turn too fast & somersaulted over & over, hit a kid too — All this seen thru rear vision mirror, or so it seems now — Truck & cars stopped behind us. Don't think driver could possibly survive — Eurithe kinda went into shock, doesn't wanta talk about it — Very grim business —

Did some writing in Africa, but not satisfied, never am I guess — Stayed a week at Margaret Laurence's in England.[595] She's just finished another novel. We had a few drinks before I left, in fact quite a few —

Hear from Leonard Brooks you're dissatisfied with reviews of your new book — there aren't enough of them — Sorry to hear that — I enjoyed it.

Hope to see you in Toronto this summer. Our address until Mar 23 will be c/o American Express, Hotel Panamerica, Calle 59, No 455, Merida, Yucatan, Mexico. We'll be home about mid-April.

Love
Al and Eurithe

To Birney (Vancouver) from Purdy (Ameliasburgh)
April 6, 1973   TL

Dear Earle,

Got your letter written in Jan. in April when I got back from Mexico (Yucatan & Quintana Roo). Dunno if you'll get this or not since apparently it has to pass thru Lampert's hands, and you might be gone by this time.

Anyway, sincere congratulations on the English book of your poems. I think it was bound to happen, even if you didn't think so. This may work out to a "second career" or something, stimulate you to write like hell etc.

You sound gloomy with that "washed up" bit but don't think you should be.

---

594. *YA* 213–14.

595. Laurence lived in England from 1949 to 1950 and again from 1962 to 1973, although she spent stretches of that time in Canada. For most of the latter period she lived at Elm Cottage, Penn, Buckinghamshire.

As you well know, poems come at odd times when one doesn't expect it. Of course I suppose that's [an] uncomforting cliché, because I'm in much the same mood myself. Worried that I'm repeating myself, plus all the bad habits in poems, and now I'll be revealed as a naked charlatan. Which is the exaggerated part of it. Anyway, stop worrying, on accounta it ain't no damn use to worry. For example, I writ about three poems I regard as worthwhile in Africa, the others seemed like force-fed shit, things written on a descriptive basis that never did manage to achieve a point beyond words strung together.

We just drove some 5,000 miles in ten days, and I am dragged out. All around Yucatan, Quintana Roo as far as Chetumal which is the free port bordering Br. Honduras. Once a wrecked truck killed a kid as well as the driver while we watched, grisly thing — Since we put some thirty thousand miles on a car each year, or more, it scares one, like the pitcher going to the well — From Progreso we took a 75 year old woman who wanted to see Mexico other than from an aeroplane — to Texas, where she flew to Toronto. Had eight bottles of rum, of which could only take three thru the border, so had to drink five in four days. The old lady was a lush and kept drinking rum all day long.

Me bein the driver I couldn't drink till evening, but we finished all five bottles just in time, between the two of us since Eurithe doesn't drink. Again I writ several poems, about two any good at all. Ever see quetzal birds? At Chichen Itza they kept flutter[ing] purply over the sacrificial well. And on a dirt road in Quintana Roo parrots dive bombing the car ... Also got to Cozumel, walked for miles thru the jungle to find a Maya site, little narrow stone path built by the Mayas. An eighty year old man and his fat wife along with us. I was sure they'd collapse, and hurried ahead in case we had to get stretcher bearers for them. The jeep we started out with had to be abandoned when the trail got too rough and narrow.

Must stop maundering. Again, sincere congrats on the English book. I hope it sells a million, well at least fifty thousand à la Ginsberg.

love

Al

To Esther Birney (Vancouver) from Purdy (Ameliasburgh)
April 7, 1973   TL

Dear Esther:

Been away to Africa and Yucatan all winter. Home to find a mountain of mail. One from Earle, who appears to be on tour reading with Gerald Lampert.

Among the mail I find a manuscript of poems from Craig whatshisname, the psychiatrist I met at your place.[596] He sends me a manuscript of poems and asks me to help sponsor him at the poet's league [League of Canadian Poets]. Of course I'll be glad to, but I can't remember his last name. I can't even reply to his last letter, on accounta he signs it "Craig" only as if I'd remember and I *ought* to remember. Met him again at Brandon when he came to my reading there, but christ I just can't think of his name except Craig. If you remember it please drop me a note.

Good chance I'll be in Vancouver this summer, and will say thank you then. Especially for putting up with my secret cigars for a week or so. Tell Phil I will not do another tape for him.[597]

love,

Al

To Purdy (Ameliasburgh) from Birney (Vancouver)
April 10, 1973   TL + APS

Dear Al:

Welcome home. I suspect, if you read my letter again, you'll see I had already left for Vancouver again before you wrote Esther. Also, I wasn't *touring* with Gerry — he was simply acting as agent. As for Craig, his name and address are:

Dr. Craig Powell
Staff, Mental Health Centre
Box 420
Brandon, Manitoba R7A 5Z5

I've already written the League in his support. Glad you plan to do the same.

When will you be out here? I'll probably be leaving for a long summer in Toronto by mid-June. Let's stop dodging each other! Love to see you again. Hope you and Eurithe are in good shape.

Love,

Earle

PS Before I posted this your other letter came, via Gerry. What a 10-day drive that was! I did it from Mexico City to 100 Mile House in 10 days once, alone in an

---

596. Craig Powell (b. 1940): Australian poet (*Minga Street: New and Selected Poems*, 1993) who lived in Canada from 1972 to 1982. His poem "For Al Purdy," in *Music and Women's Bodies* (2002), depicts an encounter with AP: "Our first morning in your home you grumbled, / 'Your bloody kids kept me awake all night.'"

597. "Phil" was possibly Philip Thomas (1921–2007): Canadian musician and folklorist (*Songs of the Pacific Northwest*, 1979). Like EB, Thomas was taught by Garnett Sedgewick at UBC and met Malcolm Lowry.

old Chev — not much fun, esp. as I left my loving heiress behind forever in M.C. Thanks about the English book. What I gotta do now is get the *new* one finished for M&S. Have much much to talk with you about.

E

To Birney (Vancouver) from Purdy (Ameliasburgh)
April 15, 1973　TL

Dear Earle,

Thanks for your note. Let me know when you're gonna get to Tor. and how to get in touch. You probably know the phone here, but it's Belleville 968 8040 …

Just slight possibility of going to England if a friend there digs me up a hundred pounds or so for readings, but that would likely be May and early June. Slight possibility of writer-in-rez at Loyola, they're still tryin to raise the money. Also, I'm supposed to go to Banff in mid-July and early Aug.[598] But I haven't signed a contract yet, since they have me down for 25 hours teaching a week. I'd be a madman to take that on without knowing what I'm getting into. Also, I'd like you to take a look at a thing I wrote called "In Search of Owen Roblin" which is supposed to be published next year.[599]

Anyway, I expect to be seeing you shortly after mid-June. If anything happens will let you know.

love,
Al

To Purdy (Ameliasburgh) from Birney (Toronto)
June 23, 1973　APC

Dear Al,

I just phoned Westminster Hot. but you aint there tho Jack J. said you mite be. Wd much like to see yr Byronic face again. I'll be @ above flat starting probably Tues. (if not there, @ Anndore Hotel [Toronto] room 807).[600] Hope u & Eurithe [are] in pink. I'll be working in U of T RBR [Rare Book Room] most of July & Aug — do ring (flat phone is 923–1372) or write or telepath or something.

As ever
Earle

---

598. Banff: i.e., The Banff Centre for Continuing Education.
599. *In Search of Owen Roblin* was published in 1974 by McClelland and Stewart.
600. The "above flat" was 921–30 Charles St. W., Toronto.

r u going 2 Banff? England? Loyola? Heaven?

When do I meet Owen Roblin?

To Birney (Toronto) from Purdy (Ameliasburgh)
June 26, 1973   TL

Dear Earle:

Great to hear etc. (Byronic hell!) Hear you have a beautiful girl in TO (as usual) — this from Ron, I think —

Was there yesterday, but couldn't stay at all. Had a promised date with Angus Mowat's boat launching.[601] That sounds funny, but we promised.

Are you fucked to death or what? Or still climbing? I mean the slope of one pink nipple in the cellars of heaven?

The Loyola job is sounding kinda fucked-up. Ron might have mentioned reasons. Besides, I have a job for Mel Hurtig.[602] Besides, the idea of writer-in-rez gets more and more distasteful unless they offer me more money. Then it'll still be distasteful, but just the same ...

Tell me, how do you work this business of fascinating women? I know your conversation is marvellous and all that, and I want some lessons. (Remember when you talked the bird right outa bed with another guy and onto your lap in Van.?) I do not feel that true friends balk at revealing their secrets of sexual fascination to other true friends. So give, boy? How do you do it? I'm sure you use the poet bit, but what else? Perhaps being the wrong sex, I do not see these qualities in you abstractly. Can I bug your foreskin?

luv

Al

To Eurithe and Al Purdy (Ameliasburgh) from Birney and Wailan Low (Toronto)
October 15, 1973   AL

Dear Al & Eurithe

Here's a sedate family get-together on the shores of Roblin [Lake].[603] Doesn't do justice to any of you. But who expects justice in this harsh world?

---

601. Angus Mowat (1892–1977): Librarian and father of the author Farley Mowat (b. 1921). He worked in Trenton and Belleville and in 1937 became the Inspector of Public Libraries for Ontario.

602. The "job," as AP explained in a letter to Margaret Laurence (30 Apr. 1973), was "to write a history of Ontario, 150,000 words, taking two years, with an advance of living expenses for that time. [...] I am happy to sell out for money, unless ... On the other hand I'd wanta do a good job by my standards — which is liable to take a goddam lifetime" (YA 218–19). The project was never completed.

603. EB was referring to an enclosed photograph.

I'm sorry we haven't been in touch. My health has been up & down. & we tried to take it easy in between work. So didn't range far from Toronto when we could avoid it. Also spent much time flat-changing but we've got a place now that we like across the street from Maple Leaf Gardens & hope you'll be our guests there as soon as we get back.

From the way Stewart has bungled the invitations & finances to Books Canada I'm not expecting much next week.[604] If I hadn't the book out from Chatto, & invitations (as a result) from the Poetry Soc., etc, I wouldn't go at all, especially with hotel prices skyrocketed all over Britain.

I'm glad M&S got your book out at last — you're on my list, of course, but don't know when M&S will send it out.

Eurithe, I got a snap of you working hard on the lawn but it didn't do you justice either. Hope I can get another chance.

Take care, both. Watch those Jesuits, Al.

love

Earle

& Lily

To Al and Eurithe Purdy (Ameliasburgh) from Birney and Wailan Low (London, England)
November 5, 1973   APC

[WL:] Dear Al and Eurithe,
Hi! London is so much like "home" that I didn't feel as if I had gone away from home — and anyway, this is where E's heart has been all along. Don't feel bad about not being here for the Books Canada thing, Al; it was a good deal less than spectacular. How are those nocturnal train rides?

[EB:] Al — have much to tell you about the Books Canada shambles — you'd have hated it — have done 3 readings here since, & off Tues. for more (Glasgow, Edinburgh, Aberdeen, Wales, etc.) — back to Toronto 30 Nov. — Eurithe, I hope you've got that bonfire I built burned up by now!

Love to you both,

Earle & Lily

---

604. Sam Stewart was the director of the Books Canada showroom in London, which opened in October 1973 as part of a program to promote Canadian publishers and authors.

Dear Earle:

To welcome you back and say hello etc. I assume you are back. Apparently England was both pleasant and not, on accounta Sam Stewart and the marvellous indigenous culture of — this jesus isle set in a silver sea (or something — please correct when I see you)[605] — Course I never felt that way about the place, but I'm glad you did, altho it [leaves me?] wondering if it was the place or your mood. If, for instance, I am in a damn good mood for whatever reasons, whether sexual or sexual, I'd feel that way about any place. [Which?] accounts for all the poems I write, the down poems are sexual deprivation, the up poems are surfeit, no not surfeit but exactly enough. What about that — as a theory, of course.

My last class is Dec. 4 (I think), therefore Eurithe and I leave for Yucatan the next day from Mtl. to Merida. Have reading in Oakville Nov. 22, reading at New College, York, Nov. 28. Doubt Eurithe will be along either trip. But hope to see you (jesus, how conventional I sound) on one of them ...

As I grow old I think of myself as a slightly older Birney (discontent, cantankerous — and certainly the bit about grabbing the first bit of change that comes along is true, which you remarked about both of us the last time I saw you, and damn w[...] other points of similarity too). I.e. we're both a little nuts: I hug to myself the distinction of being a little like you, saving only the sexual potency of course. I've refused a coupla pieces of change since last seeing you tho, one Hurtig's Hist. of [Ontario] and several readings I coulda done, but shit, time, time, time ... Jack [McClelland] has now dug me a medium-size piece of change for doing a book on wine making which, if they let me do it as partly bio, I may write. Could be fun.

My own new book should [before?] long be with you; I look forward to your perceptive [...].[606] (Which means: I'm scared to death of em.) Reviews so far: one bad, one so-so, one very good. Where does that leave me? Now feel I am washed up for good, haven't written a [...] a week (except a short squib for a girl on reverse), so must aim myself like dandelion seed at the world to write more.

love

Al

[the "short squib":]

---

605. AP's allusion was to Act 2, Scene 1 of Shakespeare's *Richard II*: "This precious stone set in the silver sea."

606. Words in the original letter are illegible, but the meaning is clear enough.

I want to crawl
between her legs
all the way inside
stand up straight
among all the lovely machinery
and shout Hurrah

To Birney (Toronto) from Purdy (Mérida)
December 12, 1973   AL

Dear Earle —

We are not at the above high class joint, but a middle class place called the Hacienda Inn. We have not yet blown any fuses with electric frypan & coffee pot, where waiters & maids sniff the breeze outside in case of steaks frying.

Landed in Cozumel Sunday, missing one bag. When it turned up next day two cans of corned beef, one of ham & four sardines were missing. Eurithe duly complained to Mexicana. Norte blew for two days, so so did we to Merida, via ferry & bus. Misguided, we took a 2nd class bus, & had my feet stepped on, ears assaulted, dried corn & vegetables piled around me, small boys mistaking me for a stanchion & holding onto me — all for 8 hrs, some 250 miles to Merida. ...

Cold here too at night. I am imbibing the local rum for antidote. Also reading the two Lowry books I'm supposed to review. You know, I am jesus sick of Lowry. *Books in Canada* also asked me to do a short piece, and now I feel every time a new book about the guy appears I'll have to relate my two brief meetings. A nice simple guy like me having to deal with a complicated bastard like Lowry. [Douglas] Day (the biographer) makes all sorts of psychological etc interpretations, "oral-fix-ated" and the like, which are both interesting & repellent.[607] I can't write 4,000 words, 50,000 or nothing. Shit, I don't want to do either. But it'll keep me from dwelling on my blighted love-life & relatively unsober courtesy of "Ronrico Ron Oro." I am also bored with returning to Loyola, except for one thing, which I'll tell you about sometime. ...

Anyway, it's as if Lowry wrote truthful [illegible] & Day writes fictional Lowry.

love

Al

---

607. *Malcolm Lowry: A Biography* was published in 1973. As AP suggested, it is a highly psychoan-alytical study of the writer's life and works; Freud's influence is powerful.

To Birney (Toronto) from Purdy (Ameliasburgh/Belleville)
December 23, 1973   TL[608]

Dear Earle:

It's a damn fine book.[609] Just got back after very short ten days in Yucatan to find it. I pick out "Small Faculty Stag" as I did once before; regret using the word "poignant" re ending, but it is … Also the book has a vitality in all its poems … Dunno what to say about those Fiji cockroaches, except I'm jealous.[610] Good to find a villanelle too.[611] You're probly the only live man [who] writes villanelles now. It's a triumph, Earle!

How are the memoirs? I tried that for thirty thousand words and didn't make anything of it. Difficult to say everything, tell everything, so many people you might hurt or … what the hell … But you look at Garner and see one way of doing it — which is okay, but I'm sure it's not your way.[612] At the moment, I can't write poems, only reviews. Editor friend in Mtl. — as I mentioned — has me doin a long piece on Lowry. And I'm getting damn sick of Lowry.

Joe [Rosenblatt] and Susan Musgrave made it to Merida where we got together.[613] She being quite a skittish lady, as Joe may tell you if you see him. Both Joe and myself spent some time calming her. I liked her but didn't at the same time if that's possible, and it is. Joe is doing some quite marvellous drawings. I'm convinced that's where his future lies, and expect you to disagree. But the essential naïveté of his poems is not present in his art; the monsters are Thurberish as well as Rosenblattish.[614] Kinda sly monsters, so blatant they oughta be ashamed but aren't and brazen it out. When we left, Susan planned to go back to the Charlottes [the Queen Charlotte Islands, BC], and Joe to Vera Cruz and then Acapulco, or maybe it was vice-versa in Joe's case. Was interested in Susan's saying [Robert] Harlow was writing her a supporting letter, she afraid he would go into detail about her instead of just marking her in the slot supplied as "exceptional" — She

---

608. *YA* 233–35.

609. The book is EB's *What's So Big about Green?* (1973).

610. "Cucarachas in Fiji."

611. "Villanelle."

612. Hugh Garner (1913–79): Canadian writer of fiction (*Cabbagetown*, 1950) and autobiography (*One Damn Thing after Another*, 1973). *Hugh Garner's Best Stories* (1963) won the Governor General's Award.

613. Susan Musgrave (b. 1951): Canadian poet (*What the Small Day Cannot Hold: Collected Poems 1970–1985*, 2000; *When the World Is Not Our Home: Selected Poems 1985–2000*, 2009) and novelist (*Cargo of Orchids*, 2000). Musgrave and AP became close friends after he moved to Sidney, BC, where Musgrave resides when not in Haida Gwaii.

614. James Thurber (1894–1961): American humorist and cartoonist who was a long-standing contributor to *The New Yorker*.

did say that, and of course she may be exceptional, to some people. But it's interesting she thinks so.

I haven't seen the [Kildare] Dobbs review of you and myself. My own reviews (for *S. & D.*) are very mixed. Have had the worst review of my life from one G.S. Kaufman in *Chevron*, Univ. of Waterloo.[615] I do hope he's American, since he has no good word at all to say for me, and it would've been much more believable with one good word added for slight contrast. You might be amused by the beginning of review, (which McStew sent me):

> Al Purdy is one of the Canadian poets, right? And good old McClelland and Stewart are the self-proclaimed The Canadian Publishers, right? Then a new book of Al Purdy poems published by M & S must be the thing to get, right?
>
> Well, *Sex and Death* may be something but it's not good poetry, and the political and social insights contained here are too often embarrassingly shallow. Purdy is undoubtedly one of the most self-indulgent "poets" publishing on the commercial market today …

Etc. Please mention this to David Bromige if you're in touch.[616] If he thought I murdered him, I've undoubtedly been drawn and quartered, vivisected, and rejected as mulch for any self-respecting garden. I feel as if I'm getting what I deserve, only a little too much at once from one source.

Staying at a friend's apt in Belleville, since A-burg [is] an icebox inside a frig inside a cold storage locker. Drank a great deal in Yucatan, seem to be continuing here — having my own sense of failure I suppose, as apart from Lowry's. Altho what strikes me as Lowry's terror, I do not have. (We all transpose such feelings and situations from others to ourselves, at least I think we do, and I do.) … More a physical failure, as I think of it — than a literary one — A slow running down of the body, the impossibility of excellence other than momentarily; a feeling of futility that destroys even some of those moments; and being trapped by everything I say or do or even feel … Shit. That's getting depressing. When we got back from Mexico, Eurithe's family had heard Trudeau had been trying to get in touch with me. Everyone very curious. Why was Trudeau etc. I told em he'd intended to offer me the ambassadorship to Mexico job, but I meant to turn it down on

---

615. G.S. Kaufman's review of *Sex & Death* ("Canadiana for Christmas," *The Chevron* [23 Nov. 1973]) begins as AP indicated and further suggests that AP "seems to have arrived at that fatal point where an artist feels that everything topical around him deserves — nay, demands — his particular gift of insight."

616. AP reviewed Bromige's *The Gathering* and *The Ends of the Earth* in *Queen's Quarterly* 76.4 (Winter 1969). See AP's letter of 18 May 1970 and EB's reply of 25 May 1970.

accounta I wanted Brazil. They didn't know whether I was saying true or not. Actually, it was a party with that Russian poet Yevtushenko, I believe.[617]

love,

Al

To Purdy (Ameliasburgh) from Birney (Toronto)
December 24 ("Xmas Eve"), 1973   TL

Dear Al

Good to have yr letter from Hacienda Inn via Maya Excelsior notepaper. This comes to you from Toronto via Victoria Scotsman, the only Scotch place I could find enough stationery around to snatch.[618] I've heard of those Nortes driving motorists off highways onto ferries. But it must have been a hell of a wind to blow 4 sardines out of your baggage. Anyway some good poems will blow back north from it all, & the Purdys back with them, soon I hope, as I'd like to see you in the flesh again.

Know how you feel about writing about Lowry. I've just turned down yet another request (Mich. U.'s mag) to review Day's book.[619] Like you I was asked for approx. 4000 words, if I wanted it. Hell I'm so sick of the Lowry Industry I regret ever having known him. Although I don't buy this idea of you being "a nice simple guy" "having to deal with a complicated bastard like Lowry." It's true I've never thought of you as being illegitimate, but "SIMPLE"?! (You're right that Day writes finctional Lowry.) You wrote "fictional" but my bad typing improved on it.

To resume Instant Notes on *Sex & Death* & Purdy:

1. The Post Office hates your book. They stomped on it, twisted it, & spat something, tobacco juice I think, on the package. It don't matter, I still love it.

2. "Johnston's on St. Germain St."[620] "the body odour of race." *I* know that *you* know this is a famous phrase from a famous poem of Abe Klein ["Political Meeting"]. But its fame is largely Canadian. And maybe temporary. Wouldn't it be wise to put quotes round it?

3. I envy you for having written "For Her in Sunlight" among many other poems of yours.

4. Praise be also for "The Battlefield at Batoche" & "RCMP" ["R.C.M.P. Post"]

617. Yevgeny Yevtushenko (b. 1933): Prolific Russian poet, novelist, essayist, and film director. AP owned a copy of Yevtushenko's *Selected Poems* (first published in 1962; AP's copy was a 1967 printing), translated by Robin Milner-Gulland and Peter Levi.

618. EB typed the letter on notepaper from the Scotsman Motel in Victoria, BC.

619. The "mag" was probably the *Michigan Quarterly Review*.

620. The title in *Sex & Death* is "Johnston's on St. Germain" — without EB's "St."

& I like "Coffee with René Levesque" & "Beat Joe McLeod" & of course the Hiroshima Poems — I'm mentioning things I've mentioned to you before maybe.

5. I expect to like a lot more, when I've finished reading the book.

This is just a nonce word meantime. To reach you back at Ameliasburg & wish you & Eurithe health & energy & peace & love through all the year ahead.

Wai-lan is in Victoria for Xmas with her mother but I know she would send her love too.

Earle

To Purdy (Ameliasburgh) from Birney (Toronto)
December 30, 1973   TL

Dear Al

Great to know you're back, more or less intact, tho wish the mails had brought yr letter sooner — it's crossed with one of mine, by the way — as no doubt you've been up in Toronto & here I am sitting alone with a flat-full of room, beds, etc. Wai-Lan decided to have a dutiful Xmas with her Victoria fambly. A decision she is living to regret, from what she says in her letters. Anyway I've been batching it for the fortnight (she'll be back New Year's Eve, d.v.).

If I seem to have been chary in praise of *Sex & Death* it was, I assure you, only because I hadn't had time to read thru even a half of it when I last wrote you. (I'm talking about a card, or something, plus an Xmas Eve note I sent you to Ameliasburgh, which you may not even have got yet; the letter was in answer to your "Hacienda Inn" stationery letter.) I've been packing your book about, in fact, reading chunks to friends (Bob & Rita [Allen], etc). I hadn't got beyond p38 in *S&D*. "For Her in Sunlight" is one of several unexpected treats, unexpected because you had got quite away from the love lyric & it was hard to see how you could get back to it with your "voice" now so established, but what you've done is sort of sneak into it by an interweaving, with the pseudo-rambling philosophic-Purdy, the autopsyching Chaplinesque guy who suddenly Gets the Girl: it's great, & some of it so good I don't know what the hell it says, only how good it feels. "The Battlefield at Batoche" (known already) gets even better with re-reading, as so many of your things do, as all good poetry should. & jesus that's a good honest poem to write about the RCMP in the year of their sintennery. I like "Coffee with René Levesque" — the economy, balance, subtlety. If you weren't so goddamned bursting with words & ideas & need to get them out, you'd write more of these shorter bullseye pieces — but then we wouldn't get the lovely long rambling ones so often I suppose, like "Beat Joe McLeod" & that strange "Power

Failure in Disneyland," depressive yet not, the ending dares everything, & I think the poem makes good the dare. & speaking of longer ones, "The Double Shadow" is just something, just great.

"Flat Tire in the Desert." Yes, but one line bothers me. "the sky goes up millions of miles." Well it's either the *sky* (blue, with air, atmosphere, etc) which goes up scores of miles, hundreds at most. Or it's *space*. Which goes up millions of lightyears — I mean, "millions of miles" is weak.

"Hands." What those poor sods were asking for was food, or money to buy it — the poem didn't make me feel you knew about Mexican jails, how, in the small towns anyway, prisoners have to rely on friends, relatives, or passers-by to get enough to eat (or smoke). The state gives them less than a minimum to sustain life & counts on relatives to keep them alive till shot or booted out. That's why the old juzgado always had cells near the street & permitted prisoners to stand by the barred windows & beg for food or they unravel string from their sheets & dangle it down from the jail roof for you to tie a peso on (Guanajuato) — seemed to me that "asking for something we couldn't give," though true in the big sense (you couldn't give them freedom, a better life, etc) ignores the real situation, that they were "only" asking for bread.

"Iguana." Great, esp. "I broiled in the sun again the iguana / watched ... by ourselves" & that "great hunkered sun."[621] I never used "hunkered" in a poem. Now I can't, without being accused once more of imitating you — don't know that I like "gaunted."[622] It should mean "made gaunt" I suppose.

"Athens Apartment" I like, esp. "and god sits down at the morning comics" ... wow! I read it, & all your Greek pieces, to Rita, who's just back from Athens-with-curfew & Crete. She thought "Hallucinations of a Tourist" got the whole feeling of being a tourist there these days. I like especially "At the Athenian Market," which really gets a feeling about light & space & history, down there, which I was fumbling for in "Tavern by the Hellespont."[623]

"The Beavers of Renfrew." Still one of the tops. & the Hiroshima poems stand well.

"Portrait of Herman." This is a very original poem in its oblique exploring of practically all our contemporary hang-ups.

621. EB misquoted the phrase from AP's poem: "the great sun hunkered red in the sea waves." A different poem, also called "Iguana," appeared in *Piling Blood*. In it AP also used the word "hunkered," but he used it to describe himself observing the iguana: "Hunkered on hands and knees / then collapsing sideways / cheek on stony ground / in order to see close-up" (*BR* 370). The "Iguana" in *Sex & Death* is set in Mexico; the "Iguana" in *Piling Blood* is set in the Galápagos Islands.

622. From "Iguana," in *Sex & Death*: "while jewel-eyed iguanas stared at them / jaguars drooled over their gaunted bodies."

623. EB's "Tavern by the Hellespont" was published in *Ice Cod Bell or Stone* (1962).

"Chronos …" I envy you the poem & your having got to Quintana Roo, where I was always going to go & never did, & for using "et."[624]

"Hellas Express." Like the opening stanza very much, the feel of Jugoslavia both as reality & as myth, the feel of you at the page's bottom (Christ, what an ambiguous homosexual phrase!), & the call-up of run-sheep-run.

"Street Scene." Yes. & that remarkable & again very original "In the Foothills." Long but an unfolding *apologia* as artist. "[In] the Pope's [1968] Encyclical" is good language fun. You've brought more zest & language excitement than ever, with this volume. Super-Pratt (no, I'm not insulting you, you paranoiac middleaged man, I happen to think Pratt, for all his shortcomings, was our best till you on the score of *language*). One of the very top ones for me is "The Time of Your Life." You plumb right down thru the Wordsworth and the Dylan Thomas, themselves the great plumbers into the Child as Poet, & into the uniqueness of yourself as child and of the uniqueness of your Canada. There's a new You here (as Poet now) which is also in "Arctic Romance," "Observing Persons" & so many others I've mentioned. "Some mystery of ourselves in the huge land masses" & even more mysteries of your unique self.[625]

So don't worry about reviews. You should see the shit thrown all over me in that same Waterloo *Chevron*, by an English Dept teaching fellow (age 26) named Gale McCullagh: "Birney has made Canadian poetry a bad joke … he has traded in … nonsense … token rubbish … refusal to lie still now that the Muse has deserted him for a younger generation … should not be allowed," let the buyer beware, etc.[626] Or an equally vicious flinging of dung by some bastard named Blacky in the Carleton student paper. Or "Professor" Gary Geddes, who so recently was coming to me for help, advice, comfort for his own lousy scribbles, is now publicly re-writing my poems in the *Globe* in order to show how easily they could be made to sound better.[627] Or your friend Dennis Lee, who actually likes the book, it seems, but can only say so in a sentence which puts down everything

---

624. From "Chronos at Quintana Roo," in *Sex & Death*: "beans / they et under the eyes of Mayan gods."

625. "Some mystery of ourselves …": from "Arctic Romance."

626. Gale McCullagh's review of *What's So Big about Green?* ("Hegelian Cocktail") in *The Chevron* (9 Nov. 1973) contained many highly critical statements, several of which EB referred to in his letter: "Birney has made Canadian poetry a bad joke. He has not sold out; he has traded in"; "like McLuhan, the archetypal hypocrite to our literary culture, Birney continues to stamp over his past and present us with this token rubbish"; "Birney's refusal to lie still now that the Muse has deserted him for a younger generation is admirable by some. But it is humiliating to see him stumble"; "This book by Birney should appall critics. They should not allow him to play by ear, since we know the range of his past skill. Nor should he be allowed to sit on the keyboard to get attention or a laugh when our poetic culture is on such tenuous skids." McCullagh claimed that only four poems in the volume "warrant a second reading": "The Shapers: Vancouver," "Adagio," "The 21st Century Belongs to the Moon," and "A Small Faculty Stag for the Visiting Poet." (The titles are set entirely in lowercase letters in the book itself.)

627. Geddes's review of *What's So Big about Green?* in *The Globe and Mail* ("A Passion Thrives Unsated," 8 Dec. 1973) was not wholly unsympathetic. He noted that "There are a number of superb

else I've ever done.[628] I'm getting pasted for "my lengthening locks" (as McCullagh so politely puts it), which I can't do anything about, except at a barber's.[629] & you are getting your knocks because you are so good & have been good too long. Off with the old, or the recognizably good — on with: who-ever-is the reviewer's little bedmate of the moment. Criticism means exactly nothing, Al, never did, never will. So stop drinking, for jesus sake. Hang on to your brain cells. They are a limited stock, did you know? (Not just yours, everybody's.) Every drink permanently destroys hundreds of cells. Your poetry is what keeps you alive when alive, & after you're dead maybe too (if the world lives). Don't fuck it all up with alcohol.

Come to town & talk with me about Joe & Susan & Trudeau && ...

Happy New Year & all through it Eurithe, Jim, yourself.

Earle

To Birney (Toronto) from Purdy (Montreal)[630]
January 2, 1974   TL

Dear Earle:

Your letter of three weeks or so ago needs a reply. (You went over poems you liked and one you didn't in *S & D*.) You comment re "Hands" that what the prisoners wanted was food or money, and I didn't understand this. Wrong, I believe I did — but deliberately shut it out of my mind; no, not deliberately, but fooled myself for purposes of writing the poem. You understand that sort of action on my part, I expect. One part of my mind "probably" knew this but didn't admit it. At this point, tho, as a result of your comment, I wonder if the poem could be re-written?? I don't actually feel like rewriting, but the thing now bothers me.

I would defend "the sky goes up millions of miles" even if not perfect in conveyed meaning. You can't say space does, not right. So if there's a better way I don't know ... "Gaunted" is not a good word, I agree; nor do I like "jewel-eyed iguanas" — which I worked on but couldn't find anything but the fuckin gems. Incidentally also, there are many points in the poems you seem to like, that I don't like. Finally, tho, I guess you publish or work on em for years. "Hunkered" was a word I loved using. How did you know?

---

poems in Birney's new book" even if the collection is "uneven." Geddes praised "From the Bridge: Firth of Forth" but suggested that the poem would be improved by the elimination of three words.

628. In his review ("The New Poets: Fresh New Voices in the Land") in *Saturday Night* (Dec. 1973), Lee deemed *What's So Big about Green?* EB's "most attractive [book] to date." He also noted EB's age (69).

629. McCullagh asked "What can you expect of a man who now puts down 'Canada: A Case History' and rewrites it to comply with his lengthening locks, white beard, natty Eatons' clothes and 'right-on' outlook?"

630. AP was in Montreal as the writer-in-residence at Loyola College.

Incidentally, I am not "bursting with words and ideas" — wish I was tho. No poems at all — one about three weeks ago. Lunch with Frank Lowe of *Weekend* last Wed. and says write 500 words about your favourite place in Canada for a grand. I don't say jesus, I say yes. Also the pleasant job of talkin to Angus Mowat and writing a piece about him — so pleasant to spend time with him and Barbara — did I ever talk about those two?[631]

Re "Hellas Express," I think the ending breaks down somehow. I fumbled with that for weeks to "no avail" — And "[The] Time of Your Life" seems to me somehow a failure as a whole, but with good parts.

Re reviews, I love em, and so do you. (Judging from our talk at last lunch.) ... They are so silly, so bad, rarely say what one hopes for someone to say, and yet doesn't know what it is ...

Geddes is, of course, a lousy climber ...[632] A bad poet who nevertheless thinks he can criticise better ones, which is illogical but parts of 1973 ... I mean 4 ...[633] Lee chose a bad way to say your new book was good ... Your "lengthening locks" is, of course, a shitty way to say anything about anybody ... Again, re my knocks, unless they are very obviously stupid and silly, I've had it very good re critics for very long ... Atwood is the real star these days, and I think deserves much of her praise. Not quite all, for most praise seems exaggerated, in order to secure prominence for reviewer or reviewed.

The drinking bit surprises me. Migawd, square puritan Earle? No, not that, but what gives? I'm a semi-alcoholic at this date, I know, seemingly without much choice in the matter, altho ... well, yes, I do sometimes feel I'm drinking my vitality away ..., small as it is to an aqua-lung exponent ... I'm in a situation I see no way, know no way out of except death — life that is, to be facetious and end sentence resoundingly. But truly, I see no way out of where I am. Some situations are like that, given the detailed weaknesses of yourselves and others ... Greek tragedy without being dramatic is not just a bandied about phrase ... Christ, did I talk myself into a corner at the bottom of a page at the end of a life shit ... Well, maybe we can talk with you on coffee and me on beer sometime soon ...

How are you?

Al

---

631. AP's "The Old Man and the Boat" appeared in *Weekend Magazine* (27 Apr. 1974) and was reprinted as "Angus" in *No Other Country* and *SA* (88–94).

632. Geddes reviewed *Sex & Death* for *The Globe and Mail* ("A Victim in Darker Reality," 20 Oct. 1973). He found in AP's collection "a number of truly fine poems," including "The Horseman of Agawa," "The Beavers of Renfrew," "Tourist Itinerary," and "In the Foothills," but also registered several criticisms.

633. It appears that AP lost his train of thought.

To Purdy (Montreal) from Birney (Toronto)
March 1, 1974   TL

Dear Al

Have owed you a letter far too long now. Meant to write & thank you for sending me another copy of *Sex & Death* with its marvelously and justly insulting inscription (justly, that is, in respect to orneriness, but not as to the state of my testicles, I'm happy to say). There's also your New Year's letter lying unanswered beside me. Hard to write to you now you are such a celebrity, hobnobbing with the other Establishment Figures, the Mowats and all, & appearing in a dozen mags simultaneously. Still, I should do as you did, in 1955 [7 Mar.], when it was you who wanted to talk with me but you doubted if I would be able to engage you in talk because "a professorship or doctorate makes too much difference." Now here am I, having shed both those states, an old man in a cold month, wondering if you still maybe think I "haven't written anything good since *Strait of Anian*," and me the bashful one, with not even a young acolyte like Curt Lang to give joint sponsorship for a letter to the Great Man.[634]

   Enough of that bullshit, since I can't follow through on all the echoes to your own first letter to me, because I can't honestly say "I'd like to see you write some good poetry again" because you damn well go on doing it, and that's wonderful and so are you. I'm not so sure about your prose, however, having just finished reading your "memoir" of Lowry in the current *Books in Canada*.[635] O no nothing wrong with the style. But why compound the Lowry mythology? You make it sound as if Downie Kirk did the Fr. transl. of *Volc*. & it sold only 3½ copies.*[636]

---

   634. EB's "old man in a cold month" was possibly an adaptation, or perhaps a misremembering, of lines from T.S. Eliot's "Gerontion": "Here I am, an old man in a dry month, / Being read to by a boy, waiting for rain."

   635. AP's "Lowry: A Memoir" was published in *Books in Canada* (Jan./Feb. 1974). It describes episodes that AP would revisit in *RBS*. It begins with a passage that indicates AP's literary interests at the time and that contains the errors that offended EB: "Working in a Vancouver factory in 1954, getting involved with forcing a union into the factory against the wishes of management — reading Dylan Thomas on the bus going to work, more and more interested in Eliot rather than Chesterton, Ezra Pound rather than Oliver St. John Gogarty — I heard about this drunken novelist living in a squatter's shack on Burrard Inlet. Curt Lang, a 16 year-old who could talk the mood collar off a theologian, assured me the guy was good. Downie Kirk, who had translated the man's novel into French to sell 3½ copies, said the same." The same issue of *Books in Canada* included a review by George Woodcock ("Suffering Terminal Genius") of two studies of Lowry: Douglas Day's biography, *Malcolm Lowry* (1973), and *Lowry* (1973), by Tony Kilgallin, a friend of EB's. Woodcock treated Kilgallin's book cursorily but examined Day's at length — and savagely ("Day is a lumbering and myopic critic"). EB and AP probably read Woodcock's review.

   636. AP often wrote, in letters and elsewhere (as in *RBS* 136), of Downie Kirk as having been Lowry's translator. Kirk (1910–64) was a schoolteacher and friend of Lowry's. He did assist Lowry with minor matters of translation, but the primary translator of Lowry's works was Clarisse Francillon (1899–1976), a Swiss novelist. She assisted Stéphen Spriel with *Au-dessous du volcan* (1950) and translated the posthumous works as *Écoute notre voix ô Seigneur* (1962), *Lunar caustic* (1963), *Ultramarine*

And what will your readers make of the sentence "Among the nothing talk it was disclosed with bitter amusement that the novelist's novel ... had sold exactly no copies ... Translated into several languages, it sold in none of them ..." Did Downie Kirk really give you all that horsefeathers?[637] And did, do you, still believe it? If not, why mislead your readers?** Or, if you *do* believe it, you should study the Lowry Papers at UBC some day, or even look at the published Lowry Bibliog., & ask yourself how publishers in every country in western Europe had published, or were in process of publishing, translations of the *Volc.*[638] Just for fun? The Lowrys lived mainly from the royalties of the *Volc.* in the original (including Canadian sales, which were small, but not the mere two copies Lowry said) & in translations which sold even more widely than the original, esp. in French, German, Spanish, etc. Otherwise Lowry wouldn't have been able to replenish your liquor supply with 6 bottles of Bols on the way to church.[639] The Lowrys, with the help of some friends, must have drunk at least a hundred dollars worth of liquor per month, which was the entire monthly sum he got from his father — since they never starved, and went on several voyages to the W. Indies, Europe, etc., & paid large bills for being nursed in alcoholic wards, I think that it's time Canadian critics stopped weeping about Lowry's poor book sales.

Yes, Atwood is the moment's star & deserves a lot but not all the praise she's getting. I saw her play on CBC TV last night[640] — turned it on after the opening & didn't know whose it was, & guessed Mazo de la Roche or maybe Reaney in a bad moment — a really corny thing with dialogue out of *Wuthering Heights* or Bulwer Lytton.[641] But I bet all the Toronto Establishment praises it profusely.

Re the drinking. It's easy for me to be abstemious, though I still like the taste of liquor & the entrée the drinking habit gives into socializing with most of the world — but my heart simply won't function properly if I have more than an ounce or two of alcohol, or more than one cup of real coffee in a day. This is one of the

---

(1965), *Sombre comme la tombe où repose mon ami* (1970), and *En route vers l'île de Gabriola* (1972). The German translation of *Under the Volcano* (*Unter dem Vulkan*, translated by Clemens ten Holder, 1951) is dedicated to Margerie Lowry and to Kirk.

637. AP: "Among the nothing talk it was disclosed with bitter amusement that the novelist's novel, published in 1947, had sold exactly no copies but had received marvellous reviews. Translated into several languages, it sold in none of them; but everyone who read the free review copies said the thing was great. This was Downie Kirk's information."

638. The "published Lowry Bibliog." is probably Howard Woolmer's *A Malcolm Lowry Catalogue* (1968).

639. AP: "The novelist and I set out for Vancouver to buy more, me driving my little English [Ford] Prefect, hoping I looked sober. I wasn't, of course. At the liquor store near Main and Hastings the novelist bought six bottles of Bols gin."

640. Atwood's teleplay, *Grace Marks*, was broadcast as *The Servant Girl*, directed by George Jonas.

641. Mazo de la Roche (1879–1961): Canadian novelist (*Jalna*, 1927) and short-story writer who was once wildly popular. Many of her books were in AP's library. Edward Bulwer Lytton (1803–73): English novelist (*Pelham*, 1828; *The Last Days of Pompeii*, 1834), playwright, and poet.

real binds from cardiac ailments — smoking, drinking, coffeeing are the normal "dissipations" of contemporary life. If you don't indulge, as they say, so you get dropped. Or you don't get dropped, and get sick. Just the same, I've seen so many of my good friends lose their faculties & shorten their lives, & die miserably, from alcoholism. I think that's a worse fate than growing old & cantankerous & isolated like me — because I think just being alive is so wonderful. And I want you to live long and happily and healthily.

I do wish you would come & see me. I gather you come & go to Toronto. I don't get to Montreal — just passed thru airport last week, having to rush to Nfld & then Halifax & back here (gave a reading in Memorial & did some media yakking for M&S in Halifax). I also gather you are having some personal problems — you did mention once in a letter about them — "problems" isn't the word, of course — anyway, I do think of you often and always with affection & admiration, and I miss not seeing you.

I'll be here till the 28th, when I go to Windsor U., & on to Texas, & up to Banff (& back here by 8th April).

I delivered my *Collected Poems* to McStew — about 400 pages — & on the same day the TS [typsescript] of *David & Other Rocky Mt Poems with Photographs* — the latter contains one long uncollected bad poem, "Conrad Kain"; the former has 30 uncollected, all bad or halfbad, as well as about 200 from earlier volumes, most of them tinkered with.[642] Already McClelland, without even looking at the texts, is hedging on publishing them & I may have to go begging for a publisher somewhere else.[643]

Have you got my phone number? 923–1372.

Best to Eurithe too, from Lan & me
Earle

* Maybe he did one for himself & Malc as a private joke your readers wouldn't get.

** I *know* you say "the nothing talk" but if it was *nothing* why perpetuate it unless it's to be taken to characterize Lowry? Or Kirk? Or you? Or who?

---

642. Conrad Kain (1883–1934): Austrian mountaineer who moved to Canada in 1909. He was a major figure in the history of alpinism in Canada. EB published his poem of tribute to Kain in the *Manitoba Arts Review* 6.1 (Spring 1948). It was reprinted in the *Canadian Alpine Journal* in 1951 (vol. 34). It appears in *The Collected Poems of Earle Birney* (I. 114–20) but not in *OMH*.

643. *The Collected Poems of Earle Birney* was published in two volumes in 1975. EB's other manuscript was not published.

To Birney (Toronto) from Purdy (Montreal)[644]
April 5, 1974   TL

Dear Earle:

Can you favour me with about two paragraphs of your matchless prose?

I'm serious. Besides being serious, I'm writing a piece on Jim Foley for *Weekend*.[645] And Foley specializes in trying to get CanLit into secondary schools. Answers a thousand letters a month from teachers.

There's plenty of Canadian Studies, consisting of Can. geography, history and sociology in sec. schools, but CanLit tags along, if lucky, as part of English lit or whatever. There are three teachers' colleges in the country that have courses in Can. Studies, Toronto, London, Ont., and U.N.B.

Anyway, can you answer a question or two?

Should there be Canadian Literature courses taught in this country's secondary schools? If so, why, since many people seem to think CanLit is inferior to the literatures of other countries?

If you can give me a coupla paras on the above two questions it would be a big help. Margaret Laurence has sent something. Then I went to Vancouver for readings before I could get around to writing more letters. (You'll be pleased to know the city is still there, and had one or two queries as to your whereabouts — not, I hastily add, from Esther.)

I'm all through here [Montreal] next week, hence the A-burg address above. Despite some considerations that are attractive here, I'm not displeased to be going. Jesus, that's stilted, eh? Anyway, I'm a bit sick of Loyola. Maybe it's just as well you're not coming, you might feel the same. Write me at A-burg when you have a moment, esp. answering those questions if it's not much trouble.

luv

Al

To Birney (Toronto) from Purdy ("Aboard S.S. *Golden Hind* in Gulf of St. Lawrence")
June 5, 1974   TL[646]

Dear Earle:

I may quite possibly be going west near the end of this month without seeing you again before leaving. I may have mentioned that *Weekend* is arranging for me to

---

644. EB's note: "answered by phone 14 April."

645. AP's "piece" ("How the Salvation of Canadian Literature May Rest on the Good Deed of Three Toronto Prostitutes: Jim Foley's Unlikely Path to the Classroom") appeared in *Weekend Magazine* (15 June 1974). See *SA* 95–99..

646. *YA* 243–45.

talk to Dave Barrett in Victoria, and his press sec. wrote me to find out if I actually was a suitable character to talk to Barrett.[647] However, it will probably come off.

I've now been parked on 10,000-ton freighter in the Gulf here off the Quebec North Shore for the last four days.[648] Total time from Welland — I mean since Welland, eight days — five of which have been just sitting. Anchored. Seems there's a strike, or work-to-rule thing among the longshoremen at Baie Comeau — where we're bound with soy beans and corn — and we just can't get there, what with a coupla ships ahead, plus the workers' slowdown policy.

This is another *Weekend* article, of course. I figure on doing three or four more for them and maybe one for *Maclean's*. Sheer greed on my part, altho I like doing these things for *Weekend*. I guess you haven't seen either of the two already published, but will try to remember and send you a Xerox of one — I've written four so far, the last mostly done on the ship here, about my wine-making experiences and the history of wine and beer. Fascinating, some of the history. Did you know, for instance, that the priests in 16th century France brought down a curse and anathema on insects to prevent them ravaging the vineyards? Or that at the time of Classical Greece drinking postures changed from the vertical to horizontal, i.e., everyone lay prone on couches to drink around 500 B.C.?

That Persians and Goths discussed and argued questions when sober then again when drunk, to get both angles? And you might be amused by what B. Franklin said about the human elbow: "If the elbow had been placed closer to the hand, the forearm would have been too short to bring the glass to the mouth; and if it had been closer to the shoulder, the forearm would have been so long that it would have carried the glass beyond the mouth." Don't ask me what use such facts are beyond writing this article. I have also written eight or nine poems while parked here, of which one or two may have some merit. Since I haven't written many poems lately, this seems good. Also read the Penguin Rilke, and think Leishman must be a lousy translator, words shoved into slots to make all things metrical.[649] Still, I had neglected Rilke, and find some of him impressive. Also more than halfway thru *My Life and Loves* by Frank Harris, which is surprisingly interesting in spots ...[650]

---

647. David Barrett (b. 1930): Premier of British Columbia from 1972 to 1975 and leader of the provincial New Democratic Party.

648. AP's "The Rime of the Fledgling Mariner: Retracing the Route of Canada's Early Immigrants along the St. Lawrence" was published in *Weekend Magazine* (10 Aug. 1974) and reprinted as "Streetlights on the St. Lawrence" in *No Other Country* and *SA* (79–87).

649. *Selected Poems* (1964), translated by J.B. Leishman. Rainer Maria Rilke (1875–1926): German poet (*Duino Elegies*, 1923), novelist, and noted writer of letters, in whose writing AP became especially interested in the 1990s (see *YA* 464 nn.1, 2).

650. Frank Harris (1856–1931): Irish-born American journalist and publisher whose autobiography (*My Life and Loves*, 1922–27) was known for its accounts of sexual exploits.

I am beginning to go quite frantic from just sitting here tho. Of course *Weekend* is paying expenses (nine bucks a day, minimum rate, arranged by my wife's cousin), but that's not the point. Days drag by. It's 325 paces around the ship's deck, some two miles or so in twelve circuits, which I did last night. Ship 620 feet long. Relevant but irrelevant facts, I'm getting smothered by them right now. I now see why medieval seamen jumped ship. It wasn't because the world was flat at all. But the sea certainly is "hight time," haven't seen any flame-fanged bale-twisters tho. No nadders either.[651] I haven't been so bored in years. Hope to escape in the next day or two. There sometimes seems no end to this sort of thing — the ordinary tissue of life is permeated with boredom, then unexpected bright places difficult to predict. I was highly interested the first day or so of this trip, now phut! Sure, I should be able to extract and feel maximum enjoyment from all situations, but reality is somewhat different than that rose-coloured philosophy.

I suppose one's ego should be large enough to say that what one has written is important, therefore one is justified, and that the bright places make things worthwhile. But I'm not at all sure that I've written anything very important, just human stuff locked in a physical and temporal strata. Perhaps that should be enough. And the "bright places" are only worthwhile at their occurrence, so that one feels on a ski jump from high to low and back again. The existentialist business of inventing the world and oneself each day easier said than done. Rilke kinda puts me off in that respect. And after you've written poems for years, you see that many of the things you write fall into a "knowing how" category, this way will make a poem and another way won't. So you take the way that will because your mind works naturally in that direction. Rilke is sort of "accept, accept!" which I don't like. (I'm fucked if I'll accept a lot of things.) A kind of roseate look at depression and death. One accepts, but dammit one doesn't have to like it, stoicism is too damn Greek for me. I want to be the cat yowling on the backyard fence sometimes. In fact I ought to write some of this in a poem.

Love to both of you,

Al

To Purdy (Banff) from Birney (Toronto)
August 4, 1974   TL

Dear Al

This paper is about the only loot that Wailan brought away from three months of galley-slaving at McStew's.[652] How are you? Hope this gets to you before you

---

651. AP's allusions were to EB's "Mappemounde."
652. The letter was typed on stationery "From the College Department of McClelland & Stewart."

start back east. Because I do really want you to stop over in Toronto this time long enough to see us. Especially as we'll probably be taking off for London on Sep 15 & may not be back for a year if ever. Let me know when you're coming in.

How's Banff? I went to one of Sylvia Fraser's evenings & saw Jack Ludwig & his wife there.[653] Much talk of Banff & you & Andy [Suknaski] & Sid [Marty] & others. I was greatly pleased to see that Sid Marty got a CC grant. I wish Andy could get a goodsized one too. Give my best to them. I hear from Pete Trower, who didn't get one, & from Howie White, who wants (& deserves) a good grant for his *Chronicles* mag but probably won't get it.[654] I've applied for whatever aid they can give me for the trip I'm making but doubt if I deserve anything when so many young talented kids are needing help. Still I'd like to make this one last trip, revisit some places where I know now that I have an audience & good will (Sri Lanka, Singapore, Nairobi) & so update my existing notes — add a few new places for the stimulus — & work it all together into a retrospective travel book, the world of yesterday & today as I've seen it & tomorrow's world as I guess it. I've masses of travel essays, notes, etc from France & Mexico in the Fifties, & Britain going back to childhood, almost none of which has emerged into poems. I'd like to refer all this back to Canada & wrap it into one last book. Meantime I've been collecting & xeroxing & fiddling around with 4 prose ragbags — one of early political stuff, which Allan Safarik has taken, to bring out in a format something like your *Bearspaw* [*sic*] — & one of plays (including *Damnation of Vanc*, which won't be in the *Coll. Poems*, as there wasn't room for it) — one of lit.crits., mainly from the Thirties & Forties, when I was editing either the *CF* lit. or *CPM* — & one of short stories & skits & attempts at humour. At the rate McStew goes, I'll be dead before any of this comes out, but at least it'll be available if they want to print it.

I've lost track of your innumerable projects. Did you interview Barrett? (I should read the *G&M* I guess, but I can't even bother to read the *Star* any more). Maybe you'll send or lend me Xeroxes?? By the way, in your June letter you told me that the Greeks started the habit of lying down to drink. But what about those Egyptians in 2000 BC friezes, lying around & receiving cups from servants? I think lying down to drink started when lying down to fuck did. Hope to see those poems you wrote while marooned on that freighter.

I attach Xeroxes of 3 letters I got from Manitoulin which ought to give you a laugh. Did you get a bunch too? This Bruce character, who likes us both (because of the way we read: "Loud" period, etc.) but can't figure how we could like each other! Anyway I bet none of those girls wrote to tell you that you were their ideal

653. Sylvia Fraser (b. 1935): Canadian journalist, novelist (*Pandora*, 1972), and teacher at the Banff Centre in the 1970s and 1980s.

654. Howard White (b. 1945): Canadian author, publisher (Harbour Publishing), and editor (*Raincoast Chronicles*) — a leading figure in the literary culture of British Columbia.

grandfather. And then there's Mark Wilson: "Were you once like Al Purdy and picked up some finer points?" I think *you* ought to answer his letter. ... Anyway, Al I think you'll make a neat grandfather too, some day, and that you will keep on reading. Loud.

Wailan sends her love & so do I. Come & see us.

Earle

To Birney (Toronto) from Purdy (Banff)
August 9, 1974   TL

Dear Earle:

Good to hear ... etc. Will stop over in Tor. on return trip, may be anywhere from Sept. 3 to 10, damn hard to tell. Haven't seen Barrett yet, leave here to see him around 20 or 21 of this month. Then to Campbell River to talk to R. Haig-Brown.[655] I guess you don't see my pieces in *Weekend*, well, one Aug. 10 and another Aug. 17. The "drinking lying down" bit came from a history of wine-making. For purposes of article I take author's info as correct. Those Egyptians musta wanted no transition from drinking to fucking, maybe they did both at once.

You sound busy as hell, what with all these prose books, and the big *Collected* coming. I have no projects to compare. I am thinking of doing a mix of *Weekend* and *Maclean's* articles plus lit stuff, if Jack McStew will go for it. If he doesn't, maybe someone else will. I hafta assume these articles are good enough. I do enjoy doing them, until the time I don't. Of course the pay is not inconsequential, thousand bucks each.

I love that: "Were you once like Al Purdy and picked up some finer points?" But hell, it's too much trouble to do much letter-writing. I scarcely write personal letters at all except to you and Margaret Laurence. The very rare one to others perhaps. What I mean is, lessening vitality plus so much writing do take my time. I've done eight articles so far this year for *Weekend* and *Maclean's*, and two more coming up.

Eurithe has gone on to Vancouver to stay with Annette. She couldn't take me either typing, teaching or drinking beer. When I phoned tonight she'd gone to some resort with Annette to find a swimming pool.

---

655. Roderick Haig-Brown (1908–76): Canadian conservationist and prolific author of books on fishing (*The Western Angler*, 1939; *A River Never Sleeps*, 1946), of regionalist fiction (*Timber*, 1942), of children's fiction (*Saltwater Summer*, 1948, won the Governor General's Award), and of local history. He lived much of his life in Campbell River, on Vancouver Island, and was a notable figure in public life in British Columbia. AP wrote "In the Shoes of the Fisherman" for *Weekend Magazine* (28 Dec. 1974), which was reprinted as "Cougar Hunter" in *SA* (40–48) and in *Cougar Hunter: A Memoir of Roderick Haig-Brown* (1992), which also collects the correspondence between AP and Haig-Brown. Many books by Haig-Brown were in AP's library.

I've drunk much beer with Sid [Marty], Andy [Suknaski] and Jon Whyte.[656] And yes, I intend to do another antho for McStew, so there are some very good poets here who'll be in it. Handy for me. Jon Whyte told one of these best of them, several times, that I wouldn't like his poetry. Very nice of Jon. I am also writing an intro for Ron Everson's travel poems, first draft and probably the last one, done. Like fuck I'll make a neat grandfather, you look much more suitable and have the temperament. Besides, I bequeathed sterility to any chance offspring. Re Pete Trower, intend to include him in this antho. Trouble is, it's now weighted heavily towards the west, not a damn thing from Ont., Que. or Maritimes. Yes, I got a bunch of letters, I guess three, too.

You sound a bit final re your trip abroad. If you're gonna do that travel book and relate it to Can. you'll have to come back. What about the memoirs you were talking about? I look forward to those more than a travel book, tho obviously the one partakes of the other. No shit, the memoirs would be an historical document, you owe it to your friends to blacken their names. Like that Roberts anecdote you told me once, which I have nearly forgotten, but which you selfishly wouldn't allow me to use because of your own memoirs. Am I now to assume you're double-crossing both of us?

The student-poets here are interesting, but take up much time. They bust in at all hours of day or night. I give em all a beer and say they're great. Actually, some are, almost. Eli Mandel was here a week. I don't know whether to come back or not. Depends on whether I'm still writing for *Weekend* next year. In one sense it's a soft job, in another it takes much time. I like some people here tho — both male and female. Best to you and Lily — what's this Wailan bit?

love
Al

To Purdy (Banff) from Birney (Toronto)
August 1974   AL

Dear Al,

Glad you're stopping over here — there's a bed waiting, as you know — just phone when you get into airport — but if you decide you'd rather stay at a hotel, come & see us anyway — we leave on night of Sep. 15 for London, so we'll be moved out of the flat on the 13th — hope you had good interviews with Barrett & Haig-Brown.

---

656. Jon Whyte (1941–92): Canadian poet and writer on subjects of Alpine and ecological interest. He published two volumes (1983, 1985) of a long poetic work called *The Fells of Brightness*, which was unfinished when he died. He was a major figure in the literary community of Banff.

No great news — all's well here — take care, see you soon.

Earle

Will save a copy of Nesbitt's book (about me) for you.[657]

To Purdy (Ameliasburgh) from Birney (Cairo)
November 1974[658]   TL

We've "done" the usual museums, pyramids, Coptic churches & mosques, or Wailan has (I dooed them in 1958, & they look exactly the same in 1974, except maybe dirtier & more cluttered with French tourists). (In Dubrovnik it was Germans, in Paris Americans, in Vienna Viennese.) There are of course some Egyptians around — 30 million of them, I'm told — but they are all out on the streets either playing bullfight with motorcars or driving them. Cairo isn't as squalid as most African cities, but it still deserves a section in any Squalid Exhibition — the Dam has made the peasant work all the year round, by the same old handbucket system of irrigation & the amount of bilharzia, eye diseases, VD, etc is statistically just about unbelievable. So how are things in Ameliasburgh?

No doubt you are writing masses of new poems, & publishing books, articles, prose collections, handbills & handbooks to erotica. Ah it's great to be young. More power to you & blessings from a peaceful, declining ancient* (although perhaps I only decline because I'm not asked the right questions).**

I hope Eurithe is well & still tolerating you & that all that your heart needs is yours still.

Would be nice to get news from & of you. Just address your letter (packet, bundle) care of Anna P [Porter] at McStew for forwarding — & maybe I'll get it. So far, damn little has turned up at the various embassies.

That "Hellas Express" stands up to many readings — all travellers fumble in their breasts for things not stamped in passports, for sure.[659] In Athens the fear of the Generals lingers. I watched six workers in a taberna watching television showing Papadopoulos & his fellow conspirators being stowed on their island of exile — there were half-hid grins of savage pleasure, but scarcely a word said, though they'd been shouting & roaring at each other in fellowship up to that moment. Nobody trusts anybody politically any more in Greece — it'll soon be

---

657. *Earle Birney* (1974), edited by Bruce Nesbitt.
658. This appears to be the second page of an undated letter. I have not located the first page.
659. AP's "Hellas Express" was published in *The Quest for Ouzo* (1970) and *Sex & Death* (1973). The image to which EB referred appears at the end of the poem: "Greeks are lined up at every window staring / out at their homeland / at something not stamped on passports / when custom officials board the train / I fumble for it in my breast pocket." The train also appears in "On the Hellas Express," in *The Stone Bird* (1981).

like that in America, I think. I love that coin-image in "At the Athenian Market."[660] It's a poem that reads wonderfully. We had 3 days on Syros, with the Irish poet Hugh McKinley, & a week on Crete — I also began getting "bored with ruins" but never with the Cretans or the light and the shine.[661]

Wailan sends her love to you both & so do I

Earle

* and ** not true either. W.L. Low

To Birney (Toronto) from Purdy (Ameliasburgh)[662]
December 11, 1974   TL

Dear Earle:

Good to hear from you. I've mislaid your letter, but I gather the trip is enjoyable for both of you.

I am, as usual, doing quite a number of things. Incidentally, the article on you is supposed to appear in *Weekend* tomorrow.[663] Think I did quite a good job and hope you like it.

I'm stuck here at the lake in the cold and snow because of jobs taken on. Editing this book of young poets [*Storm Warning 2*] for McStew. Another piece for *Weekend*, this time on a hockey player. Makes ten this year. Also a company called Neilson & Fern has asked me to do a "treatment" for an hour-long tv piece on immigrants to Canada 1790–1830, which they are managing, and which Imperial Oil will sponsor. Payment $3,000. with an option for me to write it afterwards, I mean write the play as apart from doing the treatment. Which I suppose would mean at least an equal amount of money. Talking to Margaret Laurence about this after they approached me, she wanted me to turn it down, which she had herself, saying they were bad for the Can. ecology etc. I have no very high regard for ImpOil, but don't see that it hurts to take their money for something like this.

---

660. AP's "At the Athenian Market" also appeared in *The Quest for Ouzo* and *Sex & Death*. The "coin-image" is found in the opening lines: "You can see Sparta on bright days / the air is so clear they say / you can see old cities / spinning like coins / before the rain turned / them sideways / into dust." Later the lines were slightly revised: "You can see Sparta on bright days / the air so clear they say / you can see old cities / in the billowy upper air / spinning like coins / before the rains turned them / sideways into dust" (*BR* 184).

661. "Bored with Ruins" was published in *The Quest for Ouzo*. It begins: "What presumption to be dissatisfied with Greece?" "Chronos at Quintana Roo," from *Sex & Death*, contains the declaration "I HATE RUINS." AP's "Ephesus," from both *The Quest for Ouzo* and *Sex & Death*, concerns boredom during travels in Greece and Turkey. See also AP's "Depression in Namu, BC," from *Sex & Death*: "beauty bores me without the slight ache / of ugliness that makes me want to change things / knowing it's impossible" (*BR* 202).

662. EB's note: "Arrived by airletter from Rotorua, NZ 25 Jan 75."

663. See the notes to AP's letter of 3 Jan. 1975.

A while back, Allan Safarik, Pat Lane and Doug Brown phoned from Tor., wanted to come down.[664] They took 5–6 hours of drunken odyssey, ended up at a neighbour's around one a.m. six miles down the road. I went to pick them up, found them comfortably ensconced drinking beer with the guy. I kidded them about drinking somebody else's beer, that is, and mock-apologized to the guy. Then brought them to my place. Lane got mad at the kidding and walked out at 3 a.m. followed by Safarik. Doug Brown (editor of *Copperfield*) and I followed in his truck, since he had the wheels, wanting them to come back.[665] They wouldn't, so we said to hell with it. Left them walking down the road to A-burg. Eurithe phoning Annette in Vancouver, seems they told the story I threw them outa the house here, also boasted that I was the poet laureate of Canada, or would be after death. That annoys me. I never did have a helluva lot of respect for Pat Lane, but I didn't think he'd lie like that.

Eurithe is off to Grenada tomorrow, where we've rented a house for three months. I'm (interrupted — resumed Sat.) Now have Birney article, which I tear out and enclose here. It's badly cut, or I think badly. But as I look at it again, I'm quite dissatisfied with my own writing. I led up to the ending re the naked man, that leading-up is part of what's cut. Well, I guess I shouldn't write for *Weekend* if I don't want such things to happen but they happen anyway no matter who you write for — tho must admit, McStew never tries that with poems. Also, I'm slightly horrified at the title, which is just the thing you talked about at your apt. I don't do the titles, of course, but didn't expect that. Of course, if they mean it in the sense that an author killed one of his characters off, okay. But again, this just perpetuates the myth that David was a real person, etc etc. But it is complimentary too, in the sense that anyone takes that much interest in a poem you wrote.

I must get this off to Anna Porter, and maybe she can catch up with your addresses.[666] Eurithe phoned from Grenada. Ron Everson left yesterday for Florida (being at least partly recovered from his illness). Tom Marshall and [a] few others down here a while back. Andy Suknaski also. I've got all this work weighing on my mind right now, and feel dull. Not writing poems, obviously. I have two or three I do like from the last several months, will show when you get back.

Take care of yourself. Wailan too.

Al

---

664. Allan Safarik (b. 1948): Canadian poet (*The Naked Machine Rides On*, 1980), publisher (Blackfish Press), and memoirist (*Notes from the Outside: Episodes from an Unconventional Life*, 2006).

665. *Copperfield* was a short-lived "independent Canadian literary magazine of the Land & the North." It was based in Hamilton.

666. Anna Porter (b. 1944): Canadian editor, publisher, and author (*The Bookfair Murders*, 1997). She began working at McClelland and Stewart in 1969.

To Purdy (Ameliasburgh) from Birney (Colombo, Sri Lanka)
December 24, 1974   AL

Dear Al —

Looks like we're to eat turkey with the Cdn. High Commissioneress tomorrow. No news from you but the CHC did produce Xerox of the article you published on "The Man Who Killed David."[667] I appreciate the publicity you have given to the intrinsically fictional nature of "David," though I wish you'd written that "the poem's genesis derives *in part* from a newspaper story in the twenties ...," because the genesis was also in a later (30's) news story of the death of an American alpinist climbing in the B.C. Bugaboos (Mt. Eon), & partly in various climbs-without-accidents which *I* made in the mountains in both the Rocky Mt. Park & Garibaldi Park.

If Layton & I are the "2 best poets in Canada," where the hell are you living now? I suggest the sentence be revised to read, "Next to Purdy, — Birney & Layton are the most *evident* poets in Canada" — or maybe it should be "most vinolent." Some more real misinformation, of little consequence probably, is that I have blue eyes, entered the U of Toronto at 18 (it was UBC). I graduated in 1926 not 1934, took an M.A. in 1927 & a PhD in 1936 (both at U of T.). I became an instructor at the U of Utah in 1930, not 1934 (the year I left there). But I mention these *trivia* only in case you re-publish the article. I enjoyed most of it & am properly grateful to you for being so kind to me all the way through it. It's the only Xerox or clip involving me that I've seen since I left Canada. I don't even know if my *Coll. Poems* were ever published, let alone reviewed — just as well, I guess.

I did get indirect news of you from Andy including an account of the drunken visitation you had from Pat Lane & Safarik & their walk-out — also a very different account (& a much less probable one) from a friend of Lane's — how about answering my last letter & telling me the *real* version? I'm sure you were the one who suffered most.

Did you get a letter I wrote you last month?

I guess I never really get "bored with ruins" — at any rate I keep coming back for more. After Crete we went to Cairo for a week & then a week going up the Nile to the new Nasser Lake, "world's biggest" on the Sudan border & saw the rock tombs, temples, etc. We both got some kind of Nubian dysentery which we haven't quite got over yet, a month later. Then 2 weeks in E. Africa, mainly on safari in Kenya & Tanzania — saw masses of animals, went to Oldavai Gorge, Ngoro Ngoro crater, etc. — then 10 days soaking in the Indian Ocean, in an ancient ex-hospital on a remote beach in the Seychelles Islands, living dirt cheap & eating high on the

---

667. AP's "The Man Who Killed David" was published in *Weekend Magazine* (14 Dec. 1974).

hog (also battling flying cockroaches, "crazy ants" etc.) — now in Sri Lanka we've been looking at more ruins (old as Buddha) & some Ceylon game — I've given a reading here & in Nairobi & in Cairo — I begin with Purdy, Layton, etc. Then reams of Birney — I figure that Layton & Purdy don't read *any* Birney so I can read one of each & still look like a noble fellow.

I keep making scads of notes, in an even more illegible hand than this (no typewriter, except for 2 days in Cairo) but I haven't converted a damned thing into a poem or even a non-poem yet — I envy your ability to toss off a dozen a week & keep on travelling.

Wai-Lan is wonderful as ever — puts up with all my nonsense & keeps cheerful & bouncing, despite daily wounds from fleas, mosquitoes & all the other insects.

Give our fond greetings to Eurithe — & to yourself — & for sweet Christmas' sake, write!

Address c/o McC & S.

[Unsigned]

To Birney (Toronto) from Purdy (Ameliasburgh)
January 3, 1975   TL[668]

Dear Earle:

— Wonder if red is plainer nor black? Yeah, think it is. Anyway, I already writ you and sent article I wrote. *I did not write the title*, which I thought after seeing it was exactly the sort of thing you were peeved about. I really do sympathize with that feeling on your part now, and would feel like hysterectomizing D. Livesay if she could stand it.[669] And then to have me — supposedly — do much the same damn thing! Anyway, the culprit for that title is one Sheena Paterson, mg-ing ed. at *Weekend*.

What the hell color eyes do you have if not blue? Have noted the other info, since I may reprint that piece somewhere. It was cut rather badly here and there. Re the two "best poets," I don't include myself in any such assessments, hell I'd be silly to do that. Let others make judgments about me — which is why I was so damn annoyed with Lane.

I'm sure I told you about that in my letter, which you may get, have got,

668. *YA* 256–57. The letter (with the exceptions of "is plainer" and "black") was typewritten in red ink, as EB noted in his letter of 21 Feb. 1975.

669. EB charged Livesay with libel after the publication of "The Documentary Poem: A Canadian Genre," in which she wrote that "there is proof that this was no imaginary story. Birney's companion on that fatal mountain climb was a *real* David. His death was reported as being due to a rock slide" (in *Contexts of Canadian Criticism*, edited by Eli Mandel, 1971). See the notes to EB's letter of 26 Jan. 1958.

will get etc. Anyway, here's the story. Lane, Allan Safarik (the guy who printed *Bearpaw Sea*) and Doug Brown (editor of *Copperfield*) drove down from Toronto to see me.[670] Being somewhat stoned they took six hours and ended up six miles down the road. I drove there, found them comfortably ensconced at a neighbour's drinking his beer. I kidded them about that, mock apologized to the guy who was their temporary host for my sponging friends ... Then led them back to the house here. When here, Lane got mad at me for what I had said, walked out, followed by Safarik. Brown and I followed a minute later in his truck (he drove), since it was 3 or 4 a.m., tried to get em to come back. They refused. I said the hell with it, so we went back and kept on drinking ourselves. Where they got to at 3 a.m. I dunno. However, I hear from Annette later that Lane, in Vancouver, is saying I turfed them out at 3 a.m., boasted I was the poet laureate of Canada or would be after death. Which is bullshit. In the first place, I don't boast like that, in the second, I didn't kick them out, they went themselves for very flimsy reasons because they wanted to be angry at me, apparently. Anyway, as I may have said in earlier letter, I hadn't been so aware, or didn't know before Lane was such a goddam liar. Such a malicious fucking prick, that is. If you ever see him, tell him I said so. I had already gotten the rubber mattresses from the trailer we have in the backyard, so the three could sleep on them. To say I'm annoyed is very mild.

Reverting to my story, I think there's no doubt I made it plain that "David" was fiction, even tho, as you say, it derived from a newspaper story. I didn't expect it to have a title like "The Man Who Killed David" tacked on. Nor did you.

I've heard nothing of your *Coll. Poems*, except did see their listing in McStew cat.

Eurithe has abandoned me for the sweet south — or did I say that in the letter you ain't got? She's in Granada, I supposed to go there too later this month, but it will be Feb. before I go to Peru.[671] Did I say I had a short term CC? Well, it's for Peru, but so much to do can't leave.

That bit about me writing so many poems is absolutely inaccurate. I don't. Three or four in past several months. I expect you are much more prolific. Re you being "properly grateful" — shit, I expected you to be mad as hell when you saw that title. With some justice too. I talked to Sheena Paterson and said that was just what I was trying to convey: that Birney was sick to death and annoyed with being accused of murdering David. Her answer wasn't very satisfactory.

Guess I gotta call Lily "Wai-Lan" now — is this the Manchu or Hindustan usage? Anyway, I'm writing a filmscript, articles, editing book — and making

---

670. AP's *On the Bearpaw Sea* (1973, rev. ed. 1994) was published by Blackfish Press, which was founded by Allan Safarik and Brian Brett.

671. AP misspelled "Grenada," as he and EB determined in the following letters.

money therefrom of course. Come up with mucho poems on this trip — if you feel like it! There are times when it feels like a "duty" to write poems which is all wrong. Don't you think? Christ, I remember Peter Stevens saying something to me in a letter after I'd sent him some poems, words to the effect of "You've recovered your form" or "At your best again" or shit like that.[672] Makes you feel like a sausage machine, writing for writing's sake, rather than the thing's sake, whatever the thing or feeling is.

Okay — love to both of you,

Al

To Purdy (Ameliasburgh) from Birney (Auckland ["On a bus nr Takanini, N.Z."])
January 25, 1975   AA

Dear Al,

Got yr Dec 11 letter in Sydney, Australia. Hope meantime that my last letter(s?) have reached you. Am glad to get the real story of the Lane Visit from the Purdy Himself — NZ roads roll with the rolling hills, & the buses roll with the punches — & my writing just lies down & quivers. It's a cosy country, full of sheep & inappropriate place names (just passed Papatoetoe). Thanks for sending a copy of yr contributions to the Birn-Lie-say mythos. I don't have any comment beyond what I wrote you in my last letter except to say I'm an old journalist myself & long ago learned not to blame by-lines for the titles the weak-ended editors slap on their stories.

Wonder if this will reach you in Granada. Is this the W. Indies island? Maybe you can come over to San Miguel before you go back to Canada or wherever. Wai-Lan & I plan to reach Mexico City by Jan 30 & San Miguel Allende by Feb 5. Will probably stay in Mexico till August. Wd. be great to see you. Hope you can relax down there & get back to poems.

Wai-Lan sends her love to you both & so do I. We had good visits in Singapore & Sydney, seeing poet friends made on my previous trips: in Sydney, Bruce Beaver & some of the young poets organized a dinner-reading for 50 in 24 hours![673] Had to re-route out of Bali after Darwin blew away. Also we had to get two night guards with 15 foot bamboo poles into our bedroom at midnight to kill a goddam snake.

---

672. Peter Stevens (1927–2009): Canadian literary critic and biographer (*Dorothy Livesay: Patterns in a Poetic Life*, 1992), poet (*Swimming in the Afternoon: Selected Poems of Peter Stevens*, 1992), and professor of English, primarily at the University of Windsor. "Excelsior on the Prairies," from EB's *Fall by Fury & Other Makings* (1978), is dedicated to Stevens.

673. Bruce Beaver (1928–2004): Australian poet (*Letters to Live Poets*, 1969) whose works have been compared to those of Robert Lowell in terms of their union of life and art.

Tomorrow will be seeing Alan Cournow, & then flying to Fiji.[674]

Cheers,

Earle

To Birney (San Miguel de Allende) from Purdy (Ameliasburgh)
February 5, 1975   TL

Dear Earle:

Well, the odyssey progresses. I expect you are now in Mexico. I leave here Feb. 19 for Peru, and will be re-fueling in Mexico City around midnight on that day, probably flying over San Miguel shortly before. Haven't been able to get away because of work pressure.

Before I leave, may go with Armed Services overflights out of Halifax, overseeing foreign fishing trawlers etc. For *Weekend*. I expect to have a book of these articles out sooner or later, I hope sooner, for I must have nearly 50,000 words of more or less suitable stuff now. Next summer plan to take a boat to the Nfld outports, also for *Weekend*.

I'm just finishing off the "treatment" for film of/about early settlers in Canada, period about 1830 in Huntingdon County, Que., Scotch settlers there. I shall finish it just before I leave, so I don't get stuck with doing anything more on the subject. Also the antho of under-30 poets [*Storm Warning 2*] is coming along well, lists now closed, matter of getting photos, finishing one para. biogs etc.

Will stay in Peru some six weeks, more or less elastic sked, visit all the touristy places, write poems. I've written very few here lately, couple coming in *Q.Q.* [*Queen's Quarterly*], maybe two more in *CanFor* [*Canadian Forum*]. Never expected to get so involved with prose.

My new work room here is nearly finished, Lawrence my bro-in-law doing most of the work at minimal cost to me. So far it's cost me a thousand bucks, heaters installed, sheeting in and all. Bought used shelving from Belleville wine store being demolished for fifty bucks. That room is key to whole house here, takes pressure off the rest of the place.

Ron Everson may get down to Peru when I'm there, trying to keep him informed of movements there.

Fairly desolate picture here, surrounded by snow and ice. I'm lonesome for the warm sun. Wpg. will be a real icebox next season. Incidentally, that writer-in-rez

---

674. Allen Curnow (1911–2001): Poet (*Early Days Yet: New and Collected Poems 1941–1997*, 1997), critic, and anthologist (*The Penguin Book of New Zealand Verse*, 1960) — a major figure in the literature of New Zealand.

job is now confirmed, at much more money than Loyola.[675] Expect I'll see you in Toronto, come summer, both of you should be sick of travel by then.

Must get back to work again. Take care of yourself.

Love to both of you,

Al

To Purdy (Belleville) from Birney (San Miguel de Allende)
February 21, 1975   TA

Dear Al

According to yrs of Feb 5, just received (along with yr red-ink letter of Jan. 3) you are already in Peru, with Everson in pursuit. Well maybe you'll both come back via San Miguel & I'll see you before you read this, but it doesn't matter much since you mislay my letters anyway, & when you get back to Ameliasburgh you'll be too distracted & busy even to read this one. Which is a long alibi for making this one short. Glad you're going to see Peru — joining the Macchu Picchu poem-makers? (Neruda, Birney, Pat Lane.)[676] Glad to hear you plan a book of your articles, but hope you'll give me a chance to correct small factual errors in your one on me before you let the book go to print. I admire your skill & patience & persistence in getting that workroom finished, & at comparatively so little expense (albeit with broinlaw's help). That room is important for your work & everything else. Don't know if congratulations is the right word for that Wpg job. It's money, anyway, but jezus what a climate, but maybe you can arrange to commute from Fla. or Calif. or somewhere hotter, on the money from that UEL [United Empire Loyalists] film & the *Weekend* articles.

You were [one of] the few names on my list for [a] complimentary copy of my *Coll Poems*. Didn't you get it? I just got my copy this week. It seems a good printing & format job, but haven't had time yet to check thru for boobs.

Haven't written a single poem. Masses of notes. Probably come to nothing. However, Wailan has had the experience of a unique kind of education &, apart from bouts of tourista [*sic*] & insect bites, she has enjoyed it. I wrote you from Egypt & later from somewhere else, don't remember. Won't bore you with my travels except to say we hired a car in M.C. and did the Yucatan thing, down to the Belize border in Quintana Roo, then over the mountains (at night!) to Tuxtla-Gutierrez,

---

675. From AP's *RBS*: "I was writer-in-rez at the University of Manitoba in 1975–76. Eurithe and I had quarrelled rather violently over whatever it was before I drove west in the late summer of '75. She didn't come with me" (255).

676. Neruda's poem is "Alturas de Macchu Picchu," usually translated as "The Heights of Macchu Picchu." It forms the second part of *Canto general* (1950). Lane's poem is "Macchu Picchu," included in *Unborn Things: South American Poems* (1975) and subsequent collections. Birney's "Machu Picchu" was published in *Near False Creek Mouth*. AP's "Machu Picchu" appeared in *To Paris Never Again* (1997).

on around & up to Oaxaca, Cuernavaca, Taxco, & finally here: 5000 kilometros, 3 museums, 14 ruins, 10 hotels, in ten days — never again — ran out of gas once, had a flat in the desert, etc.

We've rented a flat here in an alley for a month & hope to get time to write something soon. But at present it's shopping, moving-in, catching up with mail, etc.

Good luck & good writing in Peru & drop me a line when you get back. Wailan sends her best. What do you mean Eurithe is in Granada? Spain?

love,

Earle

To Birney (Toronto) from Purdy (Ameliasburgh)
April 8, 1975   TL

Dear Earle:

Not sure where the hell you are, at Leonard Brooks' or on your way again. Got a letter from you from somewhere, when you were going to Brooks'.

The Peru trip wasn't a disaster, did write some poems. But jesus, had a hard time breathing in the Andes. Wrote nothing on Macchu [*sic*] Picchu, maybe too many others have already, viz Birney, Neruda and some I can't remember. And Lima was hot, jesus, we didn't go out until 4 p.m. finally to avoid the heat. Mad dogs etc. We didn't. (Eurithe, that is, who showed up in Lima two days late, me thinking she'd got kidnapped on the way across South America.) From Grenada, which is the West Indies island, not Spain.

I don't think the piece on you is very good, sad but true. Others I think more of. For I do plan a book of them. But one of my dearest ideas is fucked, since I wanted to go on a NorPat — Northern Patrol should say, with Argus aircraft, fly west to Yellowknife, then be handed to an eastbound Argus and taken the rest of the way west to Comox. Warned Sheena Paterson at *Weekend* somebody else might think of that for a piece, and they did. But I might do it anyway.

Your *Collected* is something to be proud of, both in content and format. It's a beautiful book in all ways. I'd like to have seen a younger drawing of you as well as the two by [Harold] Town, who's okay I guess, but jesus I've seen better of you than that. I note you wrote "Plaza de la Inquisicion" (or however you spell it) in Madrid.[677] So did I in Lima. And I have a strong feeling I imitated an ending of yours, my quote being "Father, forgive thyself." I see it's in "Letter to a Cuzco

---

677. EB's "Plaza de la Inquisición" (from *Near False Creek Mouth*) is dated "Madrid 1963" (*OMH* 125).

Priest," "Father forgive yourself ..." Well, great minds? Except, I was referring to God the Father.[678]

Everson has been having his troubles. He had meant to join us for a few days in Peru. But a letter from Ron says he fell down some fifteen times in two weeks, which sounds serious.

Look, phone me when you get back to Toronto, eh? It seems like a long time now.

love,

Al

To Purdy (Ameliasburgh) from Birney (Toronto)
June 12, 1975   TPC

Dear Al

Just to ask if you are back yet from the Land of the Midnight Sin, & if so when will you be back in Toronto with time to drop up to the new flat. Or have you dug in, wearing white to be invisible to the Inc T? [probably "income tax"]

I don't move in lit circles, or even semicircles, so have no news of you. Hope you've had time & inclination to get some more poems written. I got yr March & April letters finally. So my belated thanks. We are still busy with moving-in having a housewarming   answering months-old mail   etc.

Will have another house-w. special for you & Eurithe when you come to Tor. next. — Phone 489–8368.

— Earle

To Birney (Toronto) from Purdy (Ameliasburgh)
June 14, 1975   TL

Dear Earle,

Thanks for card. Yeah, I am obviously back, and will drop in tredidatiously [sic] at your new place.

North was good and bad — incidentally found out that — apart from 2–3 people the northern arranger asked for, myself, Atwood, Ondaatje — Frank Davey is behind the whole selection thru his wife Linda McCartney.[679] Now I know this raises your hackles — and I do agree with you about it, in fact sounded off at

---

678. The last lines of EB's "Letter to a Cuzco Priest" (from *Near False Creek Mouth*): "Pray to yourself above all for men like me / that we do not quench / the man / in each of us." (In *OMH* "man" is capitalized [114].) "Father forgive yourself" appears near the beginning of the poem.

679. Linda McCartney (1944–2000) married Davey in 1969. She was a literary agent and was involved in numerous other literary projects. She served on the editorial board of Coach House Press.

length to people in north. Forget I mentioned it: do not phone Davey at 2–3 a.m. breathing heavily.

I writ two poems in the north, have only typed one. Sounds awful. The other I'm afraid to type looking at the first.

See you later eh? Will ask Jack Jensen if it's okay to phone you?

love,

Al

To Purdy (Ameliasburgh) from Birney (Toronto)
June 19, 1975   APC

Dear Al,

Your card has me puzzled — quite apart from "tredidatiously," whose meaning is dark to me (nearest I can come is "trebuchet," a medieval French device for hurling stones to batter down walls), I'm at a loss to know why you feel you should ask Jack Jensen if it's "okay to phone" me! Wai-Lan thinks it must be because you think I have a mistress (about the last thing I need) but maybe you've just lost my phone number already, which is 489–8368 — stick it up somewhere, because Jack J. is in Copenhagen & it would be more expensive to phone him first — anyway there's a bed here for you &/or Eurithe anytime, with us; bring your new poems please & come soon.

Love,

Earle

To Birney (Toronto) from Purdy (Winnipeg)
September 14, 1975   TL

Dear Earle,

More or less settled at Wpg. now. An apt. in a big building near the univ., with a bubble in the middle where they grow palm trees etc. Miniature golf course and swimming pool. Place is a bit weird, as you'll gather from that description.

John Teunissen, the English chairman, seems a pretty good guy, and I have a great deal of freedom; in fact, with the exception of being there at unstated times, I have no duties at all.[680] Teunissen, I find out from Dave Williams was responsible for U. of Sask. buying my worksheets ten years ago, at a time when the money was very handy, as it always is of course.[681] Williams himself teaches 17th century

---

680. John J. Teunissen (b. 1933): Professor of English at the University of Manitoba. In *RBS* AP remarked that "In retrospect, it seems we disliked each other immediately" (256).

681. David Williams (b. 1945): Professor of English at the University of Manitoba, novelist (*The Burning Wood*, 1975; *The River Horsemen*, 1981), and commentator on Canadian literature

lit, but more important has a novel coming this month with Anansi. I've read one chapter in *Queen's Quarterly* and think it very good. Dave and I have had a few drinks and yakked a lot. However, my activity is cut down by a recurrence of arthritis that I had last winter, in only one knee but so painful I can't get around much. Very depressing too, as most physical disabilities are. At such times I think black thoughts about death and what the hell's the use of going on this way ... I'm sure you know exactly what I mean. I see a doctor Tuesday, but not a specialist whom you apparently can't get to see unless referred to. But there's no cure for arthritis, alleviation only.

I've been writing a few poems, about one a day for a week, and stopped now. Trouble is most of them, in fact all, are mediocre — maybe one has small merit. Which pisses me off, I don't like to do things I know are not worth doing. Trouble is you can't know that until after you do them.

Anyway, for ten days I slept in a sleeping bag (scrounged for me by Dave Williams), but bought a bed from a CBC gal leaving Wpg., then rented some minimal amt. of furniture, including of course tv for football and hockey etc. (I see they have a dramatization of Emily Carr's life tonight, which I am interested in.)[682] Incidentally, you were going to send me that poem about ants you mentioned when I was at your place. Don't do it if it means any trouble, but if you have one handy, I'd like to see it. I seem to have about a dozen readings between now and January, so hope that doctor can do something about this goddamn knee.

Thinking about all those notes you have for poems, but haven't been able to do anything about: is it possible to, say, look up the notes for one that sticks in your mind most and do some work on it? Must admit I think the poems far more important than prose, and you might be able to tinker and prod yourself into doing something. I really do think that is possible: dig out the notes and play around with them awhile.

You might be amused to hear I bought a signed Yeats for a large price, the collector's instinct again overcoming me.

Anyway, don't write if it's any work or trouble for you, only if you feel like talkin at a distance etc.

love

Al

(*Confessional Fictions: Portraits of the Artist in the Canadian Novel*, 1991). The University of Saskatchewan purchased AP's papers in the late 1960s.

682. Emily Carr (1871–1945): Canadian painter and writer known especially for her distinctive representations of coastal landscapes of British Columbia. *Klee Wyck* (1941), a series of autobiographical sketches, won the Governor General's Award.

To Purdy (Winnipeg) from Birney (Toronto)
September 19, 1975   TL

Dear Al

Good to hear from you. Sounds as if you got there ten days too early, what with having to resort to sleeping bags, & arthritis now — I hope you know these are all forewarnings of a Winnipeg Winter — consult your nearest insurance agent for sickness & life policies. I don't remember John Teunissen by name, but then I don't remember names, being the halfwit I am, & I've probably met him, also Dave Williams, maybe. Hope arthritis has gone away.

At least the poems are flowing, & maybe you'll like some of them better when you've given them a chance to sit & jell.

When I started looking for a copy of that ants poem I discovered all copies missing, except a draft & I can't remember now how I changed it, because I changed it so much. So I've phoned Joe Rosenblatt, who has a copy, & he'll send me a Xerox of his & I'll see if it's a good enough draft to perpetuate with further circulation. Yes, I should get to work on those poem-notes but the truth is I'm still in such perpetual pain in foot, leg, even thigh in that shrinking shank, so physically weak (still only 120 pds) & lacking in good sleep, that I find it hard to do more than write answers to letters, & those very slowly. But I must get back to real work or go mad.

I've cancelled the Russian trip, or rather asked them to postpone it till next April, as I have months ahead of going to therapy clinics before this leg can possibly get strong enough to move from crutches to canes. & I'm damnded [*sic*] if I'm going on a midwinter trip to Russia on crutches with a leg that shrieks every time the temperature falls 10 degrees around it.

Wai Lan is enjoying Osgoode [Osgoode Hall Law School] & so far is doing very well there but she has to work long hours on masses of dullness.

Am going to a hypnotherapist to learn ways of getting to sleep without pills. It helps a little & now I'm trying to line up an acupuncturist.

Keep in touch, have fun,

Earle

To Birney (Toronto) from Purdy (Winnipeg)
February 2, 1976   TL

Dear Earle,

Sorry to have to rush off like that from your place. Took me a little over half hour to get downtown, and did make it okay.

I thought you ought to have someone go with you to Mtl.; ice and snow and getting on and off trains is precarious the way that leg of yours is. Can't you get Wailan to go with you?

I'm in mid-winter Wpg. blues. Depressed as hell. Great time to write you, eh? Ron Everson has some kind of serious illness that he doesn't apparently recover from. (Let's all dance.)

I had been writing fairly heavily, one poem I like much and enclose it. Now I look at the new book, and think migawd I spent about three years getting this together and I'm not sure it's any good!⁶⁸³ When I'm writing I feel much better about the stuff, perhaps from the onward drive of writing itself.

I notice you're getting much notice and publicity these days, all the way from Jack Ludwig's piece in *Weekend* to [Claude] Bissell in the *Globe* — and the reviews I've seen of the *Collected* are very good.⁶⁸⁴ Does that cheer you, or is the foot too bad? My own NCL little book is out and you'll be sent a copy from McStew directly.⁶⁸⁵ *S.W.2* is imminently pending, and ditto that one.⁶⁸⁶ Expect also to have a small book of love poems with Barry McKinnon.⁶⁸⁷ Possibly also a book of articles (or essays as Jack McC. calls them) with McStew.⁶⁸⁸ So publishing goes on apace. Also have a book of poems ready, which can't be published until '77 according to Jack. Beating my brains for a title, *The Dreaming Skull* a tentative one.

Take care of yourself. When we're both in wheelchairs (me from arthritis) I'll race you down Yonge St. at 2 a.m., me drinking beer and you carrot juice?

love,

Al

[AP enclosed his "Lament" with this inscription: "For Earle — who undoubtedly has similar memories. With love, Al Purdy. Feb 2, '76, in forlorn sub-zero Wpg."]

---

683. The "new book" was probably *Sundance at Dusk* (1976).

684. In his article ("Sunny Walks in the Dark") in *The Globe and Mail* (29 Nov. 1975) Bissell wrote that "Of all the poets I have discussed, Birney is the one who has given us the most detailed and the most comprehensive view of Canada." "Jack Ludwig's piece in *Weekend*" could be Ludwig's favourable review of EB's *Collected Poems* ("Earle Birney, Poet and Pilgrim — Because He Returned Richer, So Are We"), published in *The Canadian* (29 Nov. 1975), a supplement to several Canadian newspapers, including the *Toronto Star* — AP and EB could well have read it.

685. *The Poems of Al Purdy: A New Canadian Library Selection* (1976).

686. *Storm Warning 2: The New Canadian Poets* (1976), edited by AP.

687. The love poems were published by Paget Press as *At Marsport Drugstore* (1977).

688. *No Other Country* (1977).

To Purdy (Winnipeg) from Birney (Toronto)
February 16, 1976   TL

Dear Al

Have been wanting to write you for some time but many things get in the way: health up & down, & more down than up; putting out energy writing ditties & sending them off, with just as little likelihood of acceptance as 35 years ago when I was peddling the *David* poems. O yes, I'm the "grand old man of Cdn" spittooetry, as says kindly Bob Fulford, but certainly not as grand or old as FRS [F.R. Scott] or as much a producing poet as AWP, & I have the infallible knack of writing what is wanted next year not today.[689] What else am I doing? Finishing the last piece for Marty Gervais' 32-page chapbook of my stuff (new or revised, & not in the *CP* [*Collected Poems*, 1975]),[690] & going on readings again: Queen's last month, then last week 4 colleges in 3 days. Loyola & John Abbott in the Mtrl area, Ottawa U & Carleton in Ottawa. I love the readings & the audiences are still really responsive, but what kills me is wading on crutches thru slush & snowbanks, or trying to walk with them over sheets of ice, or up stone academic steps & thru revolving doors — I've made Fulford's show at last — a hasty half hour today, not good — we waited 1½ hrs for the technicians to get the stage ready for my ½ hr recording, & Fulford, waiting too, and I talked it all out, with much fun and even a little wit — then the anticlimax of the recording itself — does it ever happen to you that way? Hugh Hood was kicking his heels in the wings, waiting his half-hour turn not very happily. I'm sure he did wonderfully being a rightwing yapper & monstrous egoist.[691] (I *think* — maybe I just instinctively distrust him, the poor fellow's never done me any harm, I *must* get mellower soon, or I'll end up a really ungrand old creep.)

It was good seeing you even so briefly. I miss you. Hope you're out of those Peg Blues — what the hell is wrong with Ron Everson? I can't get any facts. I must phone him but I'm afraid to.

Many thanks for the NCL selection, which awaits your inimitable inscribing. Look forward to the love pomes. I'm thinking of making up a book of my own, but Wai Lan won't let me put any in that were made for other girls. Women are really

---

689. Robert Fulford (b. 1932): Canadian journalist, broadcaster, and commentator on cultural affairs (*The Triumph of Narrative: Storytelling in the Age of Mass Culture*, 1999).

690. Marty Gervais (b. 1946): Canadian writer (*Tearing into a Summer Day: Selected Poems*, 1996) and founder of Black Moss Press, which published EB's *The Rugging and the Moving Times: Poems New and Uncollected* (1976) and several works by AP, including *Bursting into Song: An Al Purdy Omnibus* (1982). In *RBS* AP calls Gervais "One of the nicest publishers I've met" (283). AP included one of his poems in *Storm Warning: The New Canadian Poets* (1971).

691. Hugh Hood (1928–2000): Canadian novelist and short-story writer. His major achievement is a twelve-volume sequence of novels called The New Age/Le nouveau siècle (1975–2000).

possessive, even about the past they couldn't have affected, not being around. Well I hope soon to have enough made just for her. She's worth as many poems as a man could write out of love.

Are you sure it's arthritis? So many things are hastily diagnosed as arthritis when they could be something more quickly and surely cured (like bursitis, syphilis, etc).

All the surgeons so far have played chicken, don't want to operate, only 50–50 chance of helping, & some chance of killing me in the process, my heart being what it is. So they say "live with it" — if it weren't for Lan, I'd choose to die with it (the pain, that is). At 71 I can roll with the punch of being a semi-cripple permanently, what is permanence at 71? But pain that never ceases & gets worse with the exercise needed to keep the leg from stiffening up entirely, is a different matter — the drop-of-water torture, waking daily with the same pain I finally killed at 2 a.m. with booze & codeine, no fun. But I *do* love love, and still can make it, so what the hell, Archie [*sic*], as Mehitabel so poignantly put it.[692]

Thanks for "Lament." Were there brass spittoons still in the Hotel Europe in Skid Row, Vanc, when you were drinking there?[693] I remember them there & of course in my childhood in Banff, even in the "good" hotels, except the Banff Springs, where they spat over the balconies into the scenic panorama.

That's a good last stanza too.[694]

Tony Kilgallin was here for a few days & helped me back from Ottawa & Jack Jensen went down to Mtr. with me — Lan doesn't dare cut a class at Osgoode, they go at such a damnable pace — so I was well shepherded, despite my bellyaching in Para One.

Tony is separating from Donna, has a flat in downtown Vanc., & is off at present with some gal to the Yucatan.

Ah well, as the Wife of Bath said, (I translate) "But Lord Christ, when I remember my youth and all the jollity, it tickles me right to my heart's roots, and gives me joy to this very day, that I have had my world as in my time. Though age, alas, that eventually poisons all, has already stolen my beauty and my pith — farewell, let them go and the devil go therewith."[695]

---

692. Archy (a cockroach) and Mehitabel (a cat) were characters in newspaper columns (and later books) by Don Marquis (1878–1937). They firrst appeared in 1916.

693. "Lament" was published in AP's *Sundance at Dusk* (1976). EB's discussion of spittoons was in reference to the poem's first stanza: "They are gone the mighty men / they have vanished utterly gone the record-setters / once as a child I remember / the achievers of forty feet at a brass spittoon / — and it sang like the birds" (*BR* 274).

694. "When I lay in the grass staring at clouds / I imagined them up there sighting at planets / now the shoe-spattered targets and dead shot dowsers / blacksmiths horses teamsters all are gone — even at length / mouth pursed and ready my Uncle Wilfred" (*BR* 274).

695. See EB's letter of 5 June 1969.

So cheer up, you're still full of piss & vinegar & we all love you. & Lan says she wishes you were here.

Earle

To Birney (Toronto) from Purdy (Winnipeg)
February 24, 1976   TL

Dear Earle,

Reply quickly, since you ask about Ron Everson. (Please take your own time responding, since I know about these energy drains.) I believe his ailment is some form of heart trouble. I gather from Eurithe that — unlike you — he sits around all the time without exercise. Of course Lorna has to be pushed into anything besides bending an elbow. According to a note from him before he left Montreal to return to New Smyrna (Lorna was talked into flying down), he's better now but has been quite bad. How one translates that into his real condition I don't know. Eurithe has come back from Fla. along with her mother, is being visited at Belleville by Annette (who's just had a hysterectomy), and both of them plan to go to Barbados. Her brother phoned me yesterday re financing him on two town lots to the extent of $15,000., the lots to be kept in E's and my name. I resent this kind of banker status I seem to have with E's family, altho this doesn't seem a bad deal according to Eurithe. I.e., we make some cash out of it.

I can, to a degree at least, imagine the trouble you have getting around on those crutches. Kinda agree with you re the prospect of an operation, but think it takes more courage on your part to deal with all that pain than I'll ever possess. But booze and codeine as panacea? Jesus, I nearly killed myself taking 222s in Japan after drinking whiskey, being ignorant of the clash of those two drugs. In this goddam apt, tho, I'm drinking far too much. But a bottle helps get me thru the winter and Wpg, so don't knock it. And incidentally, that age 71 you mention, that ain't so old, not apart from the crutches anyway. Angus Mowat, whom you met, is now 84, and getting much outa life. Not sure of his sexual prowess tho, so maybe you're one up there.

As you'd guess from the paper, just came back from nor-Man. readings. Six in five days, Thompson, Leaf Rapids, Flin Flon and The Pas. Flin Flon high school was notable too. Dave Williams (novel: *The Burning Wood*) and I had to charter a plane at Lynn Lake, because the Transair flight couldn't land because of runway conditions. So we stagger into the air like drunks in a skating rink, after having waited four hours at the matchbox airport playing cribbage with Dave and a travelling salesman for toilets. Phone the principal, a stupid bastard named Rudd, who doesn't know if we should come to the school or not, but we arrive at 4 p.m. and turns out some forty kids have waited. So I read, and I read the easy funny stuff and the kids don't laugh — this is some twenty minutes after I started. So I say to them: "You little punks haven't got any sense of humor." At that very moment, as one transvestite little punk, they all get up and walk out on me simultaneously. My jaw musta dropped, didn't think a little plain language would do that. Hafta clean up the act, I guess. Turns out they all had a bus to catch at a certain hour, so they just left. Dave and I had some 500 kids at Thompson, all the way down to Grade 7. The mike didn't work right, so they ate sandwiches and talked in the back rows. Every town Dave and I got to there was someone to meet us at the airport with a bottle. We ended frazzled as hell. I started to write a poem at the Trappers Festival at The Pas, but it never got finished.

No syphilis, least none I know of. Dave says might be gout, and Peggy Atwood will look me up an orthopaedic guy near where she lives.

I met Hugh Hood, but have no opinion about him, except his ambition must be vast to attempt this 15-vol novel he's writing over his lifetime. But why get mellower? I guess one is mellow to one's friends, but hard to suffer fools sometimes. Far as I'm concerned you're mellow enough. In that connection, we had a reading at The Pas Library, and they had a book there in which visitors inscribed their opinions about what a magnificent edifice and facility it was. Opinions were unanimous. I noted my own in the book: AWFUL. I thought that was funny, but I hurt their feelings. Besides they were coercing me to say something nice.

Wailan shouldn't be so damn picky re those love poems of yours. I *hafta* keep mine secret from Eurithe, or she advances at full port with an ax. But don't see why Wailan should worry about the past. Tell her Can Lit will suffer or something? Tell her they were all nonentities compared to her magnificent performances? Me, I'm impotent now, she doesn't have that to worry about.

love

Al

To Purdy (Winnipeg) from Birney (Toronto)
February 27, 1976   TL[696]

Dear Al

Was just going to mail you this card when your letter came. I'll write him [Everson] to his Florida address. I don't know how you can lose buying Belleville town lots unless of course they find yet another radioactive fill somewhere close. … I hope

---

696. AP's copy of the letter was given a date of 27 Dec. 1975 by (in all likelihood) an archivist. This date is incorrect, however, as the contents of the letter make clear. The postmark is not entirely legible, but the letter was most likely mailed on 27 Feb. 1976 — the date that EB marked on his copy.

you make some money out of those h. s. readings, they sound pretty dreary apart from the dangerous flying conditions. It's the principals & school boards one would like to pin down by the ears of course, those kids must have as much inborn sense of humour as anyone else, but they are taught poetry not for pleasure, & certainly not for laughter, but as a new form of punishment — building character by intellectual cat-of-nine-tails. A girl in McGill told me she had hated "David" ever since she had to make a list of *every separate image* by next class — & she missed one, & got a C plus — Imagine the *attitude* they come to a reading with.

Thanks for writing so soon & fully. Hope you'll be in these parts again soon. No news that comes to me, except Fulford's ex-wife burned to death in a fire in her flat, a couple of days after Fulford interviewed me. No connection.[697]

Keep the mable lee flyin, our remnant dear.[698]

Earle

To Purdy (Winnipeg) from Birney (Toronto)
February 27, 1976   APC[699]

Dear Al,

I was phoning Rosenblatt & he said he saw you somewhere recently (in Collingwood or Great Bear Lake or somewhere) & you were feeling low. So this is to cheer you up. I've just re-read, for the umpteenth time, the pomes in your NCL selection, & they sound as marvelous as ever. This little book should sell for donkey's years. (I don't, of course, approve of giving Layton so much credit for your development. He's a good man but he didn't influence *these* poems much.)[700]

Cheers,

Earle

To Purdy (Winnipeg) from Birney (Toronto)
March 24, 1976   TL

Dear Al

Got two letters from Ron [Everson], one crossing with mine; seems he had some lung blood-clot which turned out not to be sinister & is clearing up, as also are other ailments. He says he & Lorna will be driving to Canada via southern Ontario

697. Jocelyn Dingman died on 18 Feb. 1976. She and Fulford were married from 1956 to 1970.

698. This parody of "The Maple Leaf Forever" was in the spirit of the subtitle of EB's "Can. Lit.": "*them able leave her ever*" (*OMH* 58). (In *Rag & Bone Shop* "them able leave her ever" is the title under which "Can. Lit." and "Our Forefathers Literary" are gathered.)

699. EB affixed a printed label to the card ("EMPHYSEMA, CHRONIC BRONCHITIS, ASTHMA") and added a note: "Just to make you feel better thinking of some of the disabilities you *haven't* got."

700. In his "Autobiographical Introduction," AP wrote that he had been "hypnotized by Layton."

& will look me up (next week, maybe). When are you going to be in Toronto again? Have you got any relief from your leg-foot-wherever pains or a clearer diagnosis yet? Your remark about being "impotent" I take as being merely rhetorical, some figment of the Winnipeg ice-fogs. If you are *really* then by god you should see a real doctor. Could it be you haven't been exercising the little fellow, for lack of yen for the Peg beauties? No, you must just have been depressed on Feb 24.

Since then you probably got my quite inadequate note of the 27th. Since I wrote that, I discovered I could move a tiny muscle in my foot, the one that raises & lowers it (in conjunction with the ankle) — I reported this to the Head Surgeon at Wellesley Hosp., to whom I'd been referred, & he gave me an examination & said that the nerve was definitely beginning to regenerate. He wouldn't say whether it would continue to, told me it would be still so slow a process that I didn't need to come back for three months! However, my morale has improved, though the net result is, in fact, increasing pain, as each week a tiny spot, somewhere between my balls and my big toe, will start to come alive again & complain at being re-born. (The balls themselves, thank the good god Pan, never quite gave up, except in hospital when I didn't need them anyway, but I had a hell of a struggle getting back into proper form — for a week or two I would concoct something I can only describe as a rubber erection — it could have been tied in a knot if long enough which it wasn't. And then when I got the old iron back into the fellah I found that it wanted to fuck forever without producing an orgasm, & I still never know when it's going to condescend to a little semen. The doctors fail to show interest, all doctors being basically puritanical moneygrubbers who don't see why I should want to fuck at all at my age. Most of them probably stopped at 45 ... anyway, I'm still on crutches & sleeping pills & codeine, but there *is* a chance of walking with a cane some day.

Thanks for *Storm Warning Two*. I haven't had time to digest it yet but I can see you have been really digging about in the national soil, tundra, etc. Interesting that a fair number of your new poets were born elsewhere: US, England, Ireland, Italy, Germany, Holland. PEI just made it through a Trail, B.C. boy; one expects nothing from the NWT or the Yukon but where the hell's Sask.?[701] My skipping eye has lit on Audrey Conard, very witty & promising poems — &, thumbing back, I see she's black — is this our first good black Canadian poet?[702] And there's this Banff boy, Gordon Burles, poems rather thin but enterprising in the subjects he tackles — including Bill Peyto, one of my father's buddies from the prospecting days, & also in World War I.[703] Peyto died before this kid was born but Burles catches

701. The "Trail, B.C. boy" was Wayne Wright (b. 1947; *The Girl in the Brook*, 1980).
702. Audrey Conard (b. 1943). Her photograph in *Storm Warning 2* was very dark.
703. Gordon Burles (b. 1949; *The Old Cabin: Poems from Banff*, 1984). Bill Peyto (1869–1943):

something of his spirit. Scott Lawrance was due for your recognition, & Jewinski, certainly.[704] I like Lawrance's "Prayer" ["Lord's Prayer"]. … Well, I shall keep the book bedside till I've gone through it.

Been on several radio/tv shows & more coming up. They have a choice of 3 books, my *Coll. P.*, the revived *Down the Long Table* or the Unexpurg *Turvey*. They *all* ignore the first two, & want me to explain why it's important to use the real "fucks" I wrote, but as soon as I open my mouth to explain, quote, or etc, they have to bleep me out. A great pretense in Canada that times have changed. In fact, on the mass media, things are more puritanical than ever. I had to go down & re-do an entire interview with Barbara Frum, when the Upstairs Brass killed the one we'd made.[705]

Enough. I still haven't my Northwest Foxe poem finished.[706]

Be well — & happy

Earle

Elspeth complained of not hearing from you & feels sorry that you couldn't "settle for being friends."

To Birney (Toronto) from Purdy (Winnipeg)
March 29, 1976   TL

Dear Earle,

Great about that foot muscle — and the complaint about being born again — I don't like congratulating you on pain, but in this case it calls for something. A drink? No, not sure if I [words missing] how my brain cells are doin lately.

Yeah, the impotent bit was rhetorical. On the other hand, I really don't know, since haven't used the unturning worm for months. And Masturbation Fantasy Card #647 isn't as effective as previously. Works, but not well. Sure, some depression, but what the hell. Peggy Atwood has dug up a specialist she thinks good; in Toronto for May, which is damn kind of her. As you perhaps know, she's gonna produce progeny — tho probably singular — in May herself.

Canadian mountaineer, guide, park warden, and an important figure in the history of Banff National Park.

704. Scott Lawrance (b. 1947; *Names of Thunder*, 1978; *In the House of the Great Blue Heron*, 1984). Ed Jewinski (b. 1948): Canadian poet (*The Cage in the Open Air*, 1979), professor of English at Wilfrid Laurier University, and author of critical studies of Canadian authors (*Michael Ondaatje: Express Yourself Beautifully*, 1994).

705. Barbara Frum (1937–92): Canadian radio and television journalist.

706. AP's "The North West Passage," from *Wild Grape Wine* (1968), a volume dedicated to EB, contains a reference to the same figure: "And Luke Foxe who called himself / 'North-West Foxe' to match his name with the Arctic." The poem called "The North West Passage" in *North of Summer: Poems from Baffin Island* (1967) refers to "Luke Foxe's cook" (*BR* 98).

Your comment about doctors, always felt that myself. Various things that go wrong with fucking-apparatus provoke reactions from indifference to distaste, like I'm all right Jack, why should you complain. Sotto voce, of course. Most of em look as if they need an enema anyway.

Didn't notice Conard looked black, have to examine again. Glad to have her either way tho. Recommend Conard to you, also whoever wrote "Maiden Aunt," plus Tom Howe — many others.[707] (Don't have the book with me now, everything packed but typer.) I'm quite high on this book. Trouble was when I accepted some poems, I found others later I liked better, but couldn't cut out the earlier acceptances. Just cut down on stuff I didn't like as well. Disagree with you re Lawrance. I like Jewinski, but strong element of trivia there too. If trivia can be strong. Yeah, Burles is — well, not completely capable of carrying thru those big themes. However, I'll be interested in knowing what you think when you've gone thru the book.

Fulford's first reaction to *Turvey* a little odd.[708] I thought it hilarious first reading, recognizing or knowing or feeling a tongue-in-cheek quality emanating from author. Altho I now object to the comment, "no more than a series of pratfalls" — Even if no more than that, those wild pratfalls would be plenty. But I think in this real-surreal fantasy that a picture of those days emerges, tough and tender and quite wonderful. Fulford can't see that I guess. Edinborough's comment — migawd, what's wrong with bodily functions?[709] Perhaps only if you haven't any except shitting on other people's books can you say that. However, Edinborough himself has justifiably sunk from sight, which is some kinda justice.

I can settle for bein friends with men, and maybe a damn few women. But not Elspeth. Besides, I'd be liable to say something nasty I didn't feel or mean; and besides she doesn't mean it. I am much alone here, despite having made a few friends; and that, along with the more recent bodily limitations makes me morose. Not morose when drinking beer with people, or necessarily on the surface, but morose nevertheless.

One of those friends, Dave Williams, has invited me to come along on a six day trip by canoe down the Sask. River this summer. McStew wants more length to article book before they publish, so I'll do a couple this summer, since I want the book pubbed. They'll advance me some money, expecting to get it back from mags on mag publication. Dave says I won't be completely dead weight, tho I'm not sure

707. "Maiden Aunt" was written by Anne Corkett (b. 1944; *Between Seasons*, 1981). Tom Howe (b. 1952; *Myself in the Rain*, 1979).

708. Fulford reviewed the reissue of *Turvey* in the *Montreal Star* (23 Feb. 1976).

709. Arnold Edinborough (1922–2006): Canadian broadcaster, writer on cultural matters, and editor and publisher (*Saturday Night*). In his review of *Turvey* in *Queen's Quarterly* 56 (Winter 1949–50), Edinborough wrote that "there is a Rabelaisian reliance on the bodily functions and the Army's treatment of them which makes the book in many parts a very unamusing affair."

of that. Camp along the river bank of nights, campfire and all that. Well, I hope it comes off.

I'm packed, mostly, to leave; car jammed and piled high. Go to hockey game Wed. night with people here, leave Thurs. My $25 bed gets given away, and I'm free. Can't wait to get on the road. Hey — ! Got thrown out of the dept. chairman's party. Got drunk on brandy, and apparently wolf howled in women's ear [sic], got told off good. Don't remember howling, which is alarming. Seems chairman thot me makin a pass at his gal in his apt. Reprehensible, very. Anyway, I sent the woman some roses as apology. Now Dave Williams, who talked to chairman, says latter thot this another pass at his woman. Jesus! What can you do and have it taken at face value. Sure as hell wouldn't send roses to that guy anyway ...[710]

No Sask poet I liked well enough to include. Can't have everything.

Won't be stopping in Tor. after long drive east. Hafta get to city for things later. See you then, and will try to dig up a bicycle tube which I'm told lengthens the penis as an exerciser. You twang end of tube with penis inside, and in self-defense penis erects. Should try it myself.

luv

Al

[AP's note on the envelope: "Earle, please send telephone # to A-burg — lost my address book AWP —".]

To Purdy (Ameliasburgh) from Birney (Toronto)
April 3, 1976 ("Washington Irving's Day")   TL

Dear Al

Yes, Tom Howe is about as good as anybody in the book ... Do you know the "All About Us" people and their latest anthology of "Young Canadian Writers": *It's Not Always a Game*?[711] I have a copy. Wonder if you're back. If you left Thurs maybe you'll be in Ameliasburg by now, driving thru States. Anyway my phone is 489–8368.

Without warning, Macmillan's dumped the galleys of Andy's enlarged *Wood Mt Poems* asking me for a blurb for the jacket.[712] Since Andy had never written even that it was coming out or existed, and since his acknowledgements suggested

---

710. Another version of the episode appears in *RBS*: "I misbehaved at a party in his apartment after drinking some rather potent Armagnac brandy. I have only vague memories of what happened, and have no wish for hypnotic aids to recollection. However, later on I felt I had to send Teunissen's lady, Evelyn Hinz, some roses to make amends to her" (256).

711. *It's Not Always a Game — Un Été d'illusions*, edited by Russ Hazzard and published in Ottawa by All About Us in 1974.

712. The original edition of Suknaski's *Wood Mountain Poems* was published in 1973 by Anak Press

that you [&] Dennis Lee were practically responsible for everything, & since I don't have time to write blurbs for Macmillan's, even when my friends try to stick me for it, I told them no. However, & of course, I've read the galleys & written a strong rec. for Andy to get the grant he wants from the CC for next year to write the Albertan sequel — which he ought to call *Mountain Woods*, maybe, esp. as he seems to be intending to dig into the Rockies Archives.

So when you coming up to Toronto?

We'll be here till 3rd week in May.

Take care
Earle

To Birney (Toronto) from Purdy (Ameliasburgh)
April 8, 1976   TL

Dear Earle:

Just got your note and phone #. Thought I'd mentioned Andy's book. Way it came about was: I offered to edit his manuscript for him. He sent me this huge collection, the same as previously rejected by Macmillan. As many as three versions of the same poem, no organization, no contents page etc. I cut the hell out of it, even altered it slightly (I know, I know your reaction to that!), the object being to get it published, establish order and coherence. When the script was sent to Macmillan Dennis Lee was the reader and recommended publishing. And that's his connection. I'm sure I've mentioned all this to you before, because I was pleased with myself for my work on that manuscript, and also astonished that Andy could have sent such a sloppy manuscript to Macmillan originally. But you seem to be irritated because Andy didn't mention the project to you? At least that's the way I read your note. Of course I can't comment on that, but do know how it feels to be continually asked for blurbs and suchlike. Woodcock asked for an Intro to his poems, and since he's written one for my *Selected* I didn't think I could say no to him.[713] Very awkward! I had to say what I thought and felt without offending Woodcock by criticism etc.

Expect to be in TO Apr. 15 and see you then or the weekend, depending on your own schedule.

Best,
Al

---

of Wood Mountain, Saskatchewan. The enlarged edition, with an introduction by AP, was published in 1976 by Macmillan.

713. AP wrote the introduction to George Woodcock's *Notes on Visitations: Poems 1936–1975* (1975). Woodcock wrote the introduction ("On the Poetry of Al Purdy") to AP's *Selected Poems* (1972). AP's essay is reprinted in *SA* (253–56).

To Purdy (Ameliasburgh) from Birney (Toronto)
April 9, 1976   AL

Dear Al

My phone is now in the (new) Toronto book & it's 489–8368.

   We are busy Easter weekend, at least Lan is, but I'll be home & expecting to see you. Also perhaps the Eversons, & Andy Suknaski, all of whom have hinted at making Toronto by Easter — phone & come up when you can — looking forward to seeing you, — & thanks for the explanation, Al — of course you'd mentioned Andy's book — my memory slips — & in any case it wasn't you I was annoyed at, — it was Andy who didn't warn me he was asking me for a letter to the CC for his next book, & Macmillan's for dumping this one on me for a blurb at the same time, & a very busy time for me — of course I sent off a rave letter to the Council & an "Excellent" rating — What the hell, we keep our rank firm against the Barons —

luv
Earle

To Purdy (Ameliasburgh) from Birney (Toronto)
April 29, 1976   TL

Dear Al

Went to *Books in Can* party mainly to see you & Eurithe again but found you'd already taken off. Undoubtedly a wise move. Not that the party wasn't full of nice bright kids & all but everyone squashed into narrow corridors of a refurbished building on Adelaide nr Sherbourne up 4 flights of stairs. They had to unlimber a rope-haul freight elevator to get me up & then somebody (Jack Jensen probably) had to find a chair, a real chair, & carry it over the heads of the standing quackery of editors/reviewers/artists/bums so I could sit down in a corner. Have you ever had to sit in a corner looking ninety — of course not — I felt already dead, observing from the unseen spirit world with perhaps only a sinister aura just visible enough to warn anyone approaching to make a deviation around my chair, eyes fixed elsewhere. True, some of these kids even knew I was a poet, or rather that I look like one of the Original Canadian Poets, long dead, but that wasn't their responsibility … I exaggerate as always. There were little angels of both sexes who brought me cheese (no, that was Jack again), & the EDITOR IN CHIEF himself brought me a beer, & I managed to keep my foot tucked underneath my arm (or maybe the chair arm) so it didn't get trampled hard enough to split up. & just as I was leaving a bright little girl told me she was the art editor of the *Can Forum* &

just loved "David" & even followed me out & down the freight elevator to[714] make sure I didn't break in two on the premises, & just then a beautiful lady arrived alone in a taxi & I helped her out & she told me she had just left her husband and ... but anything more would be betraying confidences, as well as lying.

So as I started out to say, I missed you both (Wai-Lan would have missed you too but she was back in the flat studying — flat-out flat-in.) — it seems only correspondence can reach you unless we come to Ameliasburgg or is it Ameliasborough? (To rime with Edinburgh, another literary shrine-city?)[715]

I mean omitting to have you both up & have a good talk & all. Lan's exams start next week & end on the 13th May after which we have two weeks for her to recover & us to get ready for our six-wk-special-cheap-holiday-deal in the Canaries. Will you both be in Ameliasburg any 2-days of those 2 weeks? If so, we'd like to make our long-threatened visit, coming & going by train (to Belleville, right?) & from B. by taxi unless it's a day you have to drive in to B. for something (if you know which day, tell us in advance). (I have dates in Toronto on May 16–20 May incl., otherwise we're free till 27th May when we take off.)

I hope you're both relaxing, feeling better, enjoying spring.

Much I'd like to natter about with you both.

As ever

Earle

To Birney (Toronto) from Purdy (Ameliasburgh)
May 1, 1976   TL

Dear Earle,

or dear long dead poet? —

be a while yet tho ...

From what you say, just as well didn't get there (to the party). Phoned you at noon day we left, no answer. Jack on the telephone said he'd phoned and both of you were out apparently.

So come to A-burg. You get to Belleville and give me a ring, and we'll pick you up there. Else let me know beforehand what time you arrive in Belleville, and will meet the train or bus. Much more room here now (think I've mentioned the large built-on room, 28' x 14'), tho Eurithe thinks it crowded already, and will want

---

714. Here EB was interrupted by the text of the letter, typed on Hollinger House Limited stationery, over which he was typing: "Thank you for your letter reporting that your purchase order number was not included on our invoice. Our reference number and yours are related as follows."

715. Another interruption gave rise to EB's odd phrasing at the start of the next paragraph: "We apologize for any inconvenience this omission has caused you." On his copy of the letter, EB wrote "Thanks for the ream of marvelous stationery!" But the note was not included in the letter that AP received.

to build a castle soon. My books proliferate, work room stuffed, a whole wall of shelves, some fifteen feet long by eight high in new room already filled. Why do I do it? Don't ask (you didn't). Must be some kind of craze or passion or sublimation under subjugation. However, there's still much more room than before. Guess I've mentioned the fireplace, towering some twenty feet into dull grey sky (right now anyway, it's grey), and smokes like hell.

No comment on the lady who left her husband and your own somewhat suspect relations with same. I remember well the male siren who talks this gal right outa bed with her boy friend to sit on your knee in the room's and your own middle? Remember that on Seymour St. or somewhere in Van?

I hafta be in Tor. May 25 and 28 for *SW2* [*Storm Warning 2*] thing and reading with S. Musgrave on latter date. Other than that May completely free. I'm expecting Dave Williams and wife near end of month, and hope he makes it. I've mentioned him before, guy who wrote *The Burning Wood*, somebody I'd like you to meet. (The ex-footballer prof, cum novelist next to my office at U. of Man.)

Think I've mentioned McStew will advance me $2500. to do more articles to make essay book long enough for pub., they faint hoping to get their cash back from articles sold to *The Canadian* or somewhere.

Anyway, come down and stay for a while. Weather is generally good here and we can sit around and talk ...

Al

To Purdy (Ameliasburgh) from Birney (Las Palmas, Canary Islands)
June 3, 1976   APC[716]

Dear Al,

Sorry I didn't see more of you — a great rush getting away — & an exhausting 28 hours from Toronto to here — [Thomas] Cook's booked us into a lousy hotel two miles from a beach (accessible by a trail over a lava cliff, scarcely suitable for an in-*val*-id, as the Spanish call me — so we came up to Las Palmas, which looks like this except the beach is empty — Too cold for swimming, no sun, & no fishing — thank god that still leaves f——g.[717] We will get back as soon as we can — probably June 19. Cheers (2) for us, poetry, etc.

Earle

---

716. The postcard shows the beach at Las Palmas, Gran Canaria.
717. The word was not spelled out in the original. EB's propriety was decidedly uncharacteristic.

To Birney (Toronto) from Purdy (Ameliasburgh)
June 15, 1976   TL

Dear Earle,

I'm leaving for Nfld this evening. But this note is for when you get back, whenever that is — I think you said mid-July? Well, that's around the time I'm back here for a week or two before going west.

I'm involved with hassles, did I tell you? [With] McStew ed Denise Avery over contents of new book. With ACTRA [Alliance of Canadian Cinema, Television, and Radio Artists] because they took — or rather, want to take — $127. out of a $400. CBC cheque, before taxes. After income tax is taken, that would be nearly 50% of my $400. to ACTRA. I'd rather work for nothing than give them 50%.

I'm in a helluva rush getting ready to leave this evening, since I just came back from the Blue Mtn. poets' thing at Collingwood yesterday. Very pleasant weekend, all the people I haven't seen in some time, including Gustafson. We (he and I) expect to be going to Russia in Sept. Have put down Samarkand as one place we'd both like to visit.

Must stop. Take care of yourselves.

love
Al

To Birney (Toronto) from Purdy (Ameliasburgh)
July 30, 1976   TL[718]

Dear Earle:

Mistake about the date I'm in Toronto. It's the 16th of August.

Got your book in this mail.[719] It's handsome. Like the "Six for Lan," also "Shotgun Marriage" and others. But the marriage, what a confrontation! Reminds me I should write a piece on the two or three times I've seen Layton and Dudek together, neither liking the other, and thinking: what effect would a remark of mine have? "one part iron, another clay" — jesus. This guy Todd was either a good writer, or else seized the occasion — and unless I see the original I don't know what Birney did to Todd.[720] I saw this in *Tamarack*, but my mind loses yesterday,

---

718. *YA* 269.

719. *The Rugging and the Moving Times: Poems New and Uncollected* (1976).

720. "Shotgun marriage without shotguns / the rugging and the moving times: *From the prose of John Todd, 1821*," also included (as "Shotgun Marriage without Shotguns") in *Fall by Fury & Other Makings*, is EB's rearrangement of a text by John Tod (1794–1882), a trader with the Hudson's Bay Company and a prominent figure in the colonial history of British Columbia. As EB's note explains, "John Todd [*sic*] was a member of the Committee of Management of the British section of the Hudson's Bay Company west of the Rockies and, after 1851, a member with James Douglas, of the governing

let alone three years.[721] Is it a "found" poem, or what do you call it? I guess it must be that.

The "Six for Lan" are the best love poems I've ever seen of yours. As if some bars to being personal had dissolved in yourself, and I think you have had such bars. But these, now, are lovely and delicate, they care about what they say.

I am struck by the differences between my own love poems and yours. I am wildly romantic, at least to myself; but you are delicate and tender, with an over-looking sort of love.

See you on the 16th.

Al

To Purdy (Ameliasburgh) from Birney (Toronto)
August 4, 1976   TL[722]

Dear Al

Your praise of the Lan poems is very generous & warming to me. It's so easy to muff any kind of love celebration, and seemingly impossible not to be laughed at for claiming mutual love, when the age difference is 46 years (not to mention the presumed race-gulf). It's only because it's really true, this relationship, that I can get up the nerve to write about it at all — & of course I'm just writing around the rim of it. You're right that I've had personal bars, but really more in relation to *publishing*, rather than to *writing*, love poems. I wrote a lot of them during the war, & published them in Canada under a pseudonym, which only one reader ever guessed (Pat Waddington, & he's dead) (no, they weren't to Miriam!). I wrote a lot of stuff to or about Ikuko [Atsumi], but was so disenchanted with her treacheries that almost none of it has been published.

I shortened Todd, without changing his words — & I rearranged him slightly, that's all. He was compressed & laconic enough, without me, to justify thinking of this passage as a sort of ironic prose-poem, & certainly only "found" by me.

Look forward to seeing you on the 16th. Better be prepared to do your smoking on the balcony, however, as Lan is coming back from Victoria via San Francisco on the 16th & I'll have to go out & meet her around 9.30 p.m. at Toronto airport. I'll certainly be glad to see her. I've been batching only 3 days & already I'm miserable.

Council of Vancouver's Island." EB also referred to Tod in *Big Bird in the Bush: Selected Stories and Sketches* (1978).

721. "Shotgun Marriage without Shotguns" was published in *The Tamarack Review* 60 (Oct. 1973).
722. *YA* 269.

Remember to remind me to give you a copy of the first issue of *Pulp 3¢* to carry a pome of mine.[723]

Earle

To Birney (Toronto) from Purdy (Kiev)
September 21, 1976   AL[724]

Dear Earle —

I am writing a poem about Kiev watermelons right now. We got a ticket for over-staying parking limits two minutes to buy melons & grapes today in Kiev. The cop timed us.[725]

Yesterday from Samarcand & Tashkent & Uzbek tribesmen outside Tamerlane's tomb; three days before that in Moscow at the Writers' Union (they talking about translating *The New Romans*) — (I am still winding down from writing my watermelon poem!).

About a dozen time zones are screwing up my sleep here, & we drink boiled water from our electric coffee pot. This is the Hotel Moscow in Kiev, and let me tell you the Kiev cops are tough!

All the best & see you & Wailan in Canada in Oct.

Al

To Birney (Toronto) from Purdy (Ameliasburgh)
October 18, 1976   TL[726]

Dear Earle,

Back from the Sovietskis. Marvellous time. Maybe I shouldn't say that, since you couldn't get there yourself. But having seen all the things we did see, I'm very sorry you couldn't make it. We landed in Moscow of course, then to Tashkent and Samarcand, then Kiev, Riga, Leningrad and again Moscow. With sidetrips to Yasnaya Poliana, Tolstoy's estate, and Novgorod.[727]

---

723. *Three Cent Pulp* (also *3¢ Pulp*) was a small literary magazine published in Vancouver from 1972 to 1980.

724. *YA* 271.

725. The poem that arose from the incident is "Make Watermelons Not Love," published in *Moths in the Iron Curtain* (1979). An abridged edition of the book was published by Black Rabbit Press (Cleveland) in 1977.

726. *YA* 271–72.

727. AP's *Moths in the Iron Curtain* (1979) consists of poems based closely on these travels. The trip to Yasnaya Poliana led to "Visiting Tolstoy," the Novgorod excursion led to "In the Fourteenth Century," and so on. The visit to Samarcand led to "Beyond the Mountains of Heaven," which was published in *The Stone Bird* (1981) but not in *Moths in the Iron Curtain*. Gustafson also published a book of poems based on the trip: *Soviet Poems: Sept. 13 to Oct. 5, 1976* (1978). In his introduction he noted that "Al

Gustafson saw dozens of operas and ballets, which I generally avoided them [*sic*] (Gus being much more cultured than me), and he had more energy than I had too, despite his operation of a while back. Anyway, I came out of it with eleven poems, including the enclosed plus one called "Colombo Was Here" — It seems he was Voznesensky's guest in Russia, having been Voz's host in Canada.[728] At Riga, at the Writers' Union there, a woman named Lalla said to me, "Colombo is a better poet than you, Purdy. He wrote a poem just for me." Well, I couldn't resist that one, so dashed off a long poem which I gave to Voznesensky when I met him in Moscow. Not very flattering to JRC, but he is not one of my favourite people. But the cordiality (for whatever reasons) was great; Eurithe (who came too) and Betty Gustafson got flowers on arrival and departure; we were wined and dined etc. Rode around in CanAmbas's great Lincoln, to be the cynosure of the local peasants and burghers — if they have any of the latter left. Damn thing must be sixty feet long — the car, I mean. Otherwise drove in a big Cheika, used habitually for diplomats etc. Never been treated so royally by non-royalists ever, and left with a good warm feeling for our hosts. Despite that, one poem I wrote (which won't be sent to S.U.) called "At Lenin's Tomb" is not one they would like.[729] Me bein kinda anti-U.S. tho, my feelings fitted in fairly well with those of our hosts. But the vodka toasts to everything but the kitchen sink began to wear on me, and the flowery speeches! And Voznesensky — well, I love his poems, despite them being in translation. He's a good likeable guy, which I hear (tho didn't meet) Yevtushenko is not. No matter, Voz was the guy I wanted to meet, and we had drinks (all of us) at the Hotel Russia for an hour.[730] One of those trips that leaves a great impression. I think you should try to get there if you possibly can, even yet. I think you'd love it. Please try. You'd come out with some great poems, that I know.

love

Al

Purdy was companion; Betty and Eurithe, indispensable." AP appears in one of the poems, "The Ride to Yasnaya Polyana," which describes the poets' being mistaken for Party officials while travelling in a limousine: "Bardship Kanuckski / Never so bowed to, / Erroneously erred to, / Stanza and senza, / Purdy, Gustafson, / Never so mutely, / Astutely proclaimed."

728. "Colombo Was Here" was published in *Moths in the Iron Curtain*. Andrei Voznesensky (1933–2010): Russian poet. As Sam Solecki has noted, "AP often contrasts Voznesensky and [Yevgeny] Yevtushenko" (*YA* 272 n.1).

729. "At Lenin's Tomb" was published in *Moths in the Iron Curtain*.

730. From "Possession of Monsters," in the same volume: "And look at poor Voznesensky / once respectable / as crackers and cheese / an architect if you please / now a poet-monster."

Monastery of the Caves[731]

Which should I remember?
— 11th century monks in deep caves
mummified to non-edible brown
blobs in glass cases
or the dog with a crushed paw
outside on the sunlit courtyard?
Not a choice between men and animals
the darkness seekers the non-Icarians
or one poor beast waiting to be kicked
because he can't run away fast enough
— nothing is quite that simple

Great men unburied here
from shadowy kingdoms
of long-ago Muscovy:
> O Redeemer of Berestovo
> & Yuri Dolgoruky
> founder of ancient Moscow
> you Anthony & you Theodosius
> co-founders of this underground rat-trap
> & you Nestor the Chronicler
> entombed in the 11th & 12th centuries
— wouldn't you trade all your greatness
your hope and heavenly ambitions
for a crushed foot in bright sunlight
among the tourists
and one moment of peace
before you escape back into darkness?

—Kiev

For Earle & Wailan
with love
from Al Purdy

---

731. "Monastery of the Caves" was published in *Moths in the Iron Curtain* and *Being Alive: Poems 1958–78.*

To Purdy (Ameliasburgh) from Birney (Toronto)
October 23, 1976   TL

Dear Al

I intended to welcome Eurithe back too, when I phoned you, but lost control when I passed phone to Jack J. So anyway, greetings & kisses, Eurithe, & I hope to get *your* side of the Russian story when next you are in Toronto. Should Wai-Lan & I attempt the trip at all? Well, Al says "marvellous time" & so says Ralph but what do Eurithe & Betty say, not being vodka fans?

I'm glad my itinerary worked out, i.e. so far as Tashkent, Samarcand, Leningrad, Kiev go. I hadn't thought of Riga, Novgorod, Yasna Poliana. It's great you have so many poems, & more maybe to come. We like your "Monastery of the Caves" very much, and also to have an inscribed copy to us. As you realize, the ending leaps home to this old man not yet quite dead, the answer "yes" to being alive even with "a crushed foot in bright sunlight." Look forward to seeing the one about Colombo too, & the Lenin's Tomb one.

Would a Chinese wife be welcome? One who drinks no alcohol at all? And I, who don't dare more than two drinks a day, & need 6 hrs good sleep out of 24, & can't walk a city block without energy-drain from pain? Still, I've come through 2 weeks in B.C. from Kimberley to Campbell River (where I saw Haig-Brown alive & looking very young & healthy; he was dead 5 days later)[732] — & 3 days of festivality [*sic*] in Sudbury, where I gave seven readings in 2 of the 3 days. I do want to try Russia, but it wd have to be with Wai-Lan, I can't manage alone, & don't want to be away from her 3 weeks, & we'd have to go in late May or June or July or early Aug. Well, I've told all this to Ford, but don't know whether he can swing it for that time of year.[733]

Do come & see me on yr way to or from Sudbury.

Love,
Earle

You'll enjoy the Sudbury kids.

---

732. Haig-Brown died on 9 Oct. 1976.

733. R.A.D. (Robert) Ford (1915–98): Canadian poet (*Coming from Afar: Selected Poems, 1940–1989*, 1990) and diplomat. He was ambassador to the Soviet Union from 1964 to 1980, a period that he described in *Our Man in Moscow* (1989), a memoir. *A Window on the North* (1956) won the Governor General's Award.

To Birney (Toronto) from Purdy (Ameliasburgh)
November 14, 1976   TL + AL (November 15)[734]

Dear Earle,

Sorry didn't make it to Toronto after Sudbury, but had much work here as I told Wailan on the phone. For instance, 2,000 words on the *Lit. Hist. of Can.* for *Books in Can.*, eight or nine hundred on Everson for *CanLit*, and some 3,500 article on the Russian trip.[735] To top off all that, Arlene Lampert asked me to go to the prairies for three readings, since the woman scheduled for the trip had gotten sick.[736] Therefore, I had to delay my coupla days in Toronto so I could catch up with all this. I said most of this to Wailan on the phone, but doubt if she remembered it all.

Anyway, I leave Tuesday for three readings out west.

It didn't occur to me when I sent you that poem ["Monastery of the Caves"] that it might have a personal application; rather stupid on my part, I guess. My own legs and general physical condition are giving me some trouble. I don't think that doctor in Toronto did any good at all, so I probably won't go back. However, I did want to talk to you about the Soviet Union — and I think the chief difficulty for you would be boarding and de-boarding aeroplanes. Still, it's a very worthwhile trip, and I'd like to see you take a chance and go over there. People get these chances once, generally, and I remember I felt the same way about going to Cuba. Some photographer (his name was Michel Lambeth) backed out, afraid he'd be blacklisted. I think he never made a bigger mistake in his life.[737] I am damn sure you'd write poems if you went. Why not ask Ford about it? Or just take a chance and go, then carry it as far as your physical condition will let you. I've no idea about Wailan, but agree that she ought to go with you. When I say no idea, I mean no idea how the Russians would go for a Chinese gal with you. But to hell with that, take a chance and go. You'll be royally treated.

I've been sawing wood and banging the typewriter here. The wood is for the fireplace, of course, and up to a foot in diameter. Christ, I forget what diameter is: around or through. But I mean through. Shows you you were right about alcohol destroying brain cells, I just lost a dozen or so.

I really will be getting to Toronto — sometime after this next western trip. Incidentally, Eurithe's father has cancer, and is in Kingston Hosp. Eurithe wants

---

734. *YA* 272–73. AP gave the date as "Nov. 14 or thereabouts ..."

735. AP's "Tribute to Everson" appeared in *Canadian Literature* 72 (Spring 1977). His review of volumes 1–3 of the *Literary History of Canada*, edited by Carl F. Klinck, Alfred G. Bailey, Claude Bissell, Roy Daniells, and Northrop Frye, was published in *Books in Canada* 6.1 (Jan. 1977). The long introduction to *Moths in the Iron Curtain* is possibly what AP meant by the "article on the Russian trip." See *SA* 146–57.

736. Arlene Lampert organized readings for the League of Canadian Poets.

737. Michel Lambeth (1923–77): Canadian photographer celebrated for his depictions of Toronto.

to go south and buy a trailer there, one of those big things that's permanently anchored somewhere. But she can't until her father has his operation. Also incidentally, my son just came back from Thunder Bay where he spent several months and had a job that paid him over $1,100. a week — as a steamfitter!!!!! The labourers shall inherit the earth? He's still as miserable as ever tho. Let me excerpt a line or so from Voznesensky, change the sex of the subject and make it male:

> You — people, locomotives, germs,
> Be as careful with her as you can —

I mean, be as careful with yourself as you can.[738]

love,

Al

Earle —
This goddam annoys me. See article by Fawcett in which I've marked your name & mine — Came today —

Al

To Purdy (Ameliasburgh) from Birney (Toronto)
November 23, 1976   TL

Dear Al

I'm returning you the *NMFG* shitrag (Not Much Fucking Good?) for your Spanish Collection. (I suppose you noted you're addressed as "Alfonzo.") There seems to be some conflict of opinion between Brian Pisstap Fawcett & the editor Gordon Lunkhead.[739] You may not have noticed that he doesn't think I'm on the Lunatic Fringe of the Chamber of Commerce along with you; no, he has declared me dead, with Dickey & Rosenblatt.[740] Well, so the Permanent Adolescents of the Poetry Family always look around for statues to deface, tulip beds to shit in. You are a

---

738. The lines are from the fourteenth section of "Oza."

739. Gordon Lockhead was a pseudonym of Brian Fawcett, the editor of *NMFG* ("No Money from the Government"), a small magazine in existence from 1976 to 1978. Fawcett (b. 1944) is a Canadian journalist and writer of poetry (*The Opening (Prince George, Finally)*, 1974), fiction (*My Career with the Leafs and Other Stories*, 1982), and cultural commentary (*Cambodia: A Book for People Who Find Television Too Slow*, 1986). Much of his writing concerns Prince George and the surrounding area of British Columbia. He has ties to writers associated with the Vancouver avant-garde (*Robin Blaser*, with Stan Persky, 2010).

740. James Dickey (1923–97): American novelist (*Deliverance*, 1970) and poet (*The Whole Motion: Collected Poems 1949–1992*, 1992). In *NMFG* (Oct. 1976) Fawcett wrote that "Poets like Al Purdy and Earle Birney, and more contemporarily Pat Lane and Artie Gold, are really functioning as a kind of lunatic fringe of the Chamber of Commerce. Their ethic, if not their goal, is the same."

flourishing garden now, complete with statue, & must expect to be the object of juvenilian delinquincy. *Don't* write them. Ignore it. What they want is to get a rise out of you or me, & print it with further insults, equally silly.

Thanks for your good letter. You do get into a lot of work. I hope you're making your first hundred-thou out of all this. Also that the prairie trip went well. At least the awful prairie winter hasn't set in yet.

You don't say why the boarding & deboarding of Soviet planes would be a hazard. Do you come off in a chute? Anyway, meantime we'll practise by a fortnight trip to Cuba, leaving the 18th Dec, the day after Lan's last exam. Stay on Varadero Beach, probably at the Kawama Sandpiper. Have asked External [Department of External Affairs] to get Cdn Embassy in Havana to arrange a meeting with a Cuban poet or two. Have you any suggestions about what writers would be approachable &, hopefully, bilingual? Did you meet any when you were there?

Sorry to hear about Eurithe's father. Is his cancer operable?

I think it's great that your Jim can make that much dough now. After all, it's only the rich who employ steamfitters, so he's not gouging the likes of us — & maybe he'll lend you enough to set up your own publishing firm.

We are busy these days. Keeping well.

I've been packing *Sundance at Dusk* around in the subways & busses. It's a *good book*, Al, as you must know, & no doubt are being told by countless reviewers, admirers, etc. You're breaking out, hopping fences, into a lot of new crops, grass, hay, woods. "Inside the Mill" is you being unashamedly lyrical but not as in *Emu* days, now you're singing in maturity. The title poem is one of many I like very much. Also you're telling a lot more stories, shaping them more, milking them for all sort of emblems. (Jeezus what a mixing of metaphors is happening on this page.) As I read, I marked the ones I wanted to come back to quickly. There's 6 in a row starting with "Pre-School"[741] — sometimes I find faint tracks of me, which of course pleases me, even if my eyes-ears are deceiving me out of my own vanity (e.g. my "fatal, pliant fish That first forgot the sea" swimming suddenly through in "Deprivations").[742]

I read poems to Lan. We liked the sound of "Sadness." & of course the Merida coyotes ["Coyotes in Merida Zoo"]. A wonderful longline tour de force, not quite like anything else I remember reading of yours. And the love poems, very moving

---

741. "6 in a row": "Pre-School," "The Children," "Ode to a Wornout Electric Stove in the Snow," "Transvestite," "Recipe," and "Deprivations."

742. EB's reference was to the final stanza of his "Young Veterans," from *Now Is Time* (1945) and *The Strait of Anian* (1948): "The soldiers merge and move with all of us / toward whatever mystery / bemused that fatal pliant fish / who first forgot the sea" (*OMH* 46). From AP's "Deprivations": "prototypes of that first one / definitely weirdo and oddball / who dragged himself painfully / away from the salt waves" (*BR* 282).

& honest & successful. & the Winnipeg ones & & ...[743] Wd like to talk about some of them if ever we two get time together again!

How you like my stationery huh?

Earle

To Birney (Toronto) from Purdy (Ameliasburgh)
November 28, 1976 TL[744]

Dear Earle,

What the hell is a sand cadger?[745] Yes, you surpassed all my stationery with this specimen — speciman? — no, specimen.

Your Cuba trip sounds fine. How come you use the English "fortnight"?[746] Is that a result of Chaucer?

Okay, the bit about boarding and deboarding planes: they don't have that inflated bicycle tube we have in North America, whereby you can walk on and off planes. You get into a bus that's generally crowded, then you climb the steps onto plane. Reverse when deboarding. Having been part of the sardine-mob in that bus made me think that might be tough for you. However, the translator who accompanied us everywhere, could easily ask that you be allowed to board first, therefore it would be a matter of all those steps only. But we can discuss any questions you might have in Dec.

Yes, *Sundance* [*at Dusk*], — thanks much for the good word on that book. I had such a hassle with Newlove and Avery over that book that the memory still leaves a sour taste. Both wanted to drop a lot of poems that are now in, including the first poem, the tobacco spitters' lament thing.[747] It was a matter of fighting both of them thru the book's production, and I did give way on some poems that I now regret, which last accounts for the slightly sour taste. It began to sound like a favour if they allowed me to keep some particular poems. Finally I simply made out a contents list of poems and said that's it, and I meant that's it. But I had deferred somewhat to their opinions, which I now regret in some instances.

Praise? Two reviews thus far, that I know of, both favourable. But as you

---

743. The "love poems" are "Uncertainties," "From the Wisconsin Glacial Period," "Antenna," "Stop Watching," "Paper Mate," and "Subject/Object." AP included a note about the poems: "The selection of love poems in this book ... was written from the possible viewpoints of several other poets; those poets were named in the original and somewhat comic titles. Those titles are now abandoned." The poems about Winnipeg include "Ritual," which contains an especially memorable line: "in any case Winnipeg is no town for T.S. Eliot." The sequence also appeared in *At Marsport Drugstore* (1977).

744. *YA* 274–75.

745. EB's letter of 23 Nov. 1976 was typed on stationery with an image of a man in traditional Scottish dress and the caption "19th Century Scottish Sand Cadger."

746. "Fortnight": see EB's letter of 23 Nov. 1976 and AP's letter of 30 Sept. 1977.

747. "Lament": see EB's letter of 16 Feb. 1976.

must know, you, Layton and Atwood get much more attention than I do from the media — what the hell is plural of media, or is it plural? But I get as much as I deserve, and mind you I'm not complaining. I ran into the awfulness of someone complaining with Gustafson in Russia, and it made me sick. Will tell you about that when I see you. But what I meant to say is: thanks for the good word on the book. I probably need some praise for this book more than the others, both because of Newlove and Avery and because I felt at the end of my tether as far as writing was concerned. See "Ritual" when I was at a very low point.[748] I was dubious about "Inside the Mill," which is, yes, lyrical, but I was afraid might be sentimental. Or too easy. I can adopt almost any rhythm — or conceitedly think I can — which made this poem seem a tour de force to me. I'm sure there's Birney in some of those poems, impossible not to be after knowing you and poems of yours such a long time. Think I read "David" not long after the book came out ...

Only met one Cuban poet, and can't remember her name. I wanted to meet Jorge Guillén at the time, but didn't manage.[749] Incidentally, have I recommended Voznesensky to you? If not, I do — think he's one of the most impressive poets I've read. Try to pick up *Anti-Worlds and The Fifth Ace*, two books in one, Schocken Books, N.Y. *Don't get the Grove Press Selected, trans Anselm Hollo.*[750] *Anti-Worlds* was pubbed originally by Basic Books, and later reprinted in the double volume, in paperback. This has Auden, Kunitz and others doing the translations.[751]

Yeah, you're right about not writing those people. But it's annoying to be told you have no social conscience etc.

Eurithe's father's cancer now being treated with some sort of radiation, periodically. It's in his face, and possibly that and his neck is a bad place to operate.

Yes, back from prairies a week, and quite a good three readings. Altho the Sudbury ones were more interesting. I went into a classroom before my scheduled appearance, and told the kids I was Layton, and not to come to Purdy's reading, that he was a half-assed poet etc. Then read one of Layton's poems with some panache. I guess a few saw thru the imposture, but Layton was supposed to be in Sudbury at the time; so I got a kick out of being Layton.

See you later —

Al

748. The poem, included in *Sundance at Dusk*, is a despairing self-portrait of the poet in exile: "A year in Winnipeg / and after some months my personality retracts."

749. Jorge Guillén (1893–1984): Spanish poet. Sam Solecki has suggested the possibility that AP confused Jorge Guillén with Nicolás Guillén (1902–89), a Cuban poet (*YA* 275 n.1).

750. *Anti-Worlds and The Fifth Ace*, edited by Patricia Blake and Max Hayward, was published by Oxford University Press in 1968 and issued in paperback by Schocken in 1973. The Grove *Selected Poems* was published in 1964.

751. Stanley Kunitz (1905–2006): American poet (*The Collected Poems*, 2000), translator, and professor at Columbia University. He was twice Consultant in Poetry to the Library of Congress.

To Purdy (Ameliasburgh) from Birney (Kitchener, Ontario)
December 3, 1976   AL[752]

Dear Al

Here I am in a draughty Kitchener hospice with no pen, & hoping to sell books — will have to borrow a customer's. Judging a Central Sthrn Ont Poetree Competition.

A sand cadger is an old guy who sells sand.

I use "fortnight" apparently unconsciously. My parents used it being British by birth. For same reasons I often hear myself saying "score" for 20 & "baker's dozen" for 13.

Wish I had something besides this pencil stub.

Yes — hope to see you in Toronto before 18th — I'll be back tomorrow.

Balls, you are the most publicized *poet* in Canada, even more than Layton now. Atwood is the sudden Authority in Cdn. Criticism. I am the Oldest-with-Beard, a fragile perishable Image.

Who is Avery?

Is Guillén still alive?

Yes, I've long believed Voznesensky to be the best unjailed Russian poet — Yevtushenko is the loudest rhetorician & spoiled suck.

I love your Layton-impersonation story — it gives me an idea — I'll try being Geo. Johnston — or shave & claim to be Purdy.[753]

See you
Earle

To Birney (Toronto) from Purdy (Ameliasburgh)
February 11, 1977   TL

Dear Earle,

How are you?

I'm getting ready for some readings in Ont., and the Yukon — where I've never been, hence hoping to extract one poem by placer methods. But be passing thru Toronto and maybe stay a day at the usual hotel, haven't gotten plans very firm yet.

Did I say on the phone that Eurithe's dad seems to have come thru his

---

752. EB enclosed a promotional bookmark from the Toronto Public Libraries that reprinted his "Can. Lit." To the slogan "Experience Canada!" EB added "& Al Birley." He also included a closing note: "from your friend Earle Purdy." The poem's subtitle ("or *them able leave her ever*") contained an extra word ("or *them able to leave her ever*"), which EB deleted. "No sense of rhythm, our librarians," he wrote.

753. George Johnston (1913–2004): Canadian poet (*The Cruising Auk*, 1959), translator of Icelandic sagas, and professor at Carleton University.

operation okay? But she, it turns out, has some painful arthritis, and is staying here in order to take physiotherapy at the Belleville hosp. Probably got the malady from Purdy association.

What's with the Russian trip? I'm anxious for you to go, then I can be dean when you're gone. Oops, forgot Layton, will never be dean dammit. I just think you'd like Soviet Union, and would write a pome or six.

I have writ about one poem I consider near-adequate since Russia. But also, to my immense mortification along with jubilation, have discovered a pome I wrote some eight or ten years ago, and the damn thing is good. Nasty shock, that. Overlooked it completely. Geriatric judgment is gone in second childhood. Missed it completely. It's the sideburns that are doin it, gotta let em grow and learn strine. What do you prescribe?

I touched it up a bit, and sent it to QQ, where it'll be mimeographed in QQQ — cut off that last non-Chinese q — sometime this summer. Send along it for you, since [I] see I got a carbon.[754]

Incidentally, Marty Gervais wanted a manuscript, so I sent him a buncha old stuff and a buncha new stuff too, says he likes and will pub. Title: *A Handful of Earth* (which is also title of a new poem).[755]

I do like these small books by small presses. In old age makes me feel I'm still goin, if not strong at least weakly. Marty did a good job on yours.[756] I thought it excellent, both as poems and book.

Hey, I got a sorta coloured catalogue from Lenoard and Reva Brooks. (Leonard, that is), very nice of them.

I get nostalgic for Mexico at times, like now. Feeling marooned in snow (altho that's not reason for Mexican love), lost in sub-lunary expanses, and the bitter trees and the bitter wind — You with that jesus apt.! Altho I expect you can't get onto the balcony lately eh?

My friend Rolf (the young poet I think you may have met) and his wife have busted.[757] He incarcerated for two weeks in the loony bin, probly as a result of

754. AP's "Starlings," "Running," and "On the Altiplano" appeared in *Queen's Quarterly* 84.2 (Summer 1977).

755. *A Handful of Earth* was published in June 1977 by Black Moss Press. The poem of the same name, dedicated to René Lévesque, was published in *The Canadian Forum* (Apr. 1977) and in *The Globe and Mail* (26 Nov. 1977). A revised version appeared in *Being Alive: Poems 1958–78*. The title of that volume was derived from "A Handful of Earth": "here I ask all the oldest questions / of myself / the reasons for being alive" (*BR* 312).

756. *The Rugging and the Moving Times: Poems New and Uncollected* was published in 1976 by Black Moss Press.

757. Rolf Harvey (b. 1947): Canadian poet (*The Perfect Suicide*, 1972). AP included a selection of Harvey's poems in *Storm Warning 2: The New Canadian Poets* (1976). Letters to and from Harvey appear with considerable frequency in AP's papers at Queen's University.

bustup), writes me, and meant to say that last outside parenthesis. Jesus, how the idylls end!

But leave us get one landscape pome outa the Yukon pretty please. Just one. I'll feel better if I can deceive myself it's any good.

(How are you?)

Amazing how Mexico gets hold of you. A poor dirt-poor country etc. Is it something in yourself mostly? I have feeling it's reality, and where I am now, my situation I mean, is not. And I think of those prisoners that I wrote the poem about, and which you mentioned I didn't understand their situation — and of course I didn't, tho with another part of me I did. What I'd really like to do some-time is meet you and Wailan there, say in Merida or Progreso or Oaxaca — altho I didn't like Oaxaca much. Too dry and grim. Did you get to Vera Cruz at all?? Sweatbox hotels at the sea's edge. And Tehuantepec was a bath on dry land — I kept thinkin of that sestina of yours about the place when I was there.[758]

I'm maundering, so stop. Hope to see you in Toronto.

Al

To Birney (Toronto) from Purdy (Ameliasburgh)
May 15, 1977   TL

Dear Earle,

Seems some time since the Poet's League thing. I've been so fiendishly busy since that I begin to feel like an industry. I went to Sask. after Toronto, rented a car at Regina, then drove to the Cypress Hills and ranching areas around Val Marie and Mankota. Talked to ranchers about the proposed grasslands park etc. At one point, after leaving a ranch house, I took a wrong turn, and was "lost" until I got turned around and retraced my steps. I saw this sleeping Hereford beside the trail — and it was a trail, not a road. When I got past, I saw daylight shining thru it; the beast was completely hollow, nothing there but hide, bones and hooves. It does give you a turn, and you see yourself there too, staring thru sightless sockets upward, surrounded by rattlesnakes and sagebrush.

Everyone at McStew thought the old piece I'd done on René Lévesque for *Maclean's* in 1971 wasn't very good. I agreed. I had to write another piece, finally,

---

758. EB's "Sestina for Tehuántepec" (later retitled "Sestina for the Ladies of Tehuántepec"), written in 1956, was included in *Ice Cod Bell or Stone* (1962), *Memory No Servant* (1968), *Selected Poems 1940–66, The Poems of Earle Birney: A New Canadian Library Selection* (1969), and *Ghost in the Wheels: Selected Poems* (1977). It is one of EB's most distinctive poems. It was published as "Sestina for Tehauntepec" [*sic*] in *Prairie Schooner* 38.2 (Summer 1964); that spelling also occurs in *Ice Cod Bell or Stone*.

in four days. I did it in three, feeling rather pleased with myself that I was able to meet a deadline like that.[759]

The book is skedded for Sept., altho it will probably be later as usual. The title at the present moment is *No Other Country*, scratching the terrible *Al Purdy's Canada*, which is too much of a much. The fact that all the areas of Canada are represented in the book, general areas that is, and the idea of some kind of a journey, — these give it a degree of unity. The title is from an old radio program I did years ago.

Now off to Ottawa, five readings in three days at sec. schools. On return I have to write a piece on the "mood" of Ont. for *The Financial Post*, of all places. I'm not sure how to go about this exactly, and perhaps "inexactly" will fit the piece eventually. I don't think anyone could write a piece about the mood of a place, perhaps a person, one person. Also, I'll probably be writer-in-rez at Western [the University of Western Ontario] this coming year. I don't like such jobs much, but it is money, handy stuff to buy things with.

And I meant to ask you: why did you say that poem of mine, "A Handful of Earth," would make me popular with the editors at *CanFor* [*Canadian Forum*]? I didn't write it for them; I wrote it for myself. I assume you feel cynical about Denis Smith and the others there. I'm not sure why?[760] The poem is no great thing, but it does express some of my thoughts on the country and Quebec.

Time to get ready for departure to Ottawa. Jack Jensen said he'd be down today, but if so there won't be much time for talk …

Al

To Purdy (Ameliasburgh) from Birney (Toronto)
May 31, 1977   TL

Dear Al

Your Canada book should really hit the bestseller list, in Canada of course. Even Berton complains his books don't sell in the States. But maybe yours will crash that barrier too. My selected, *Ghost in the Wheels*, is also slated for Sep, & also sure to be later. I haven't even got a copy of the contract yet. Hope the Ottawa readings went well. If you can heft the books, there's lots of sales waiting in the h. s. [high school] audiences. Nice to know you'll be in well-heeled Western this winter, & not too far to be dropping in & out of Toronto. Probably won't see you before August as we're off for Eire via Prestwick this Sat. & not back till July 19.

---

759. AP published "Lévesque: The Executioner of Confederation?" in *Maclean's* (Oct. 1971). A revised version of the article, "Bon Jour?," appeared in *No Other Country* (1977). The essay is reprinted in *SA* (100–08).

760. Denis Smith (b. 1932): Editor of *The Canadian Forum* (1975–79) and the *Journal of Canadian Studies* (1966–75) and professor of political science at several Canadian universities.

I'm also too damn busy, getting ready for the 6-weeks (to be spent mainly in Scotland, if we can find rooms there in the Jubilee Year), & have been doing flocks of readings — Newmarket, Holland Landing, Aurora, Blue Mountain (but never Black — v. attached).

Have a good June-July anyway.

Earle

To Purdy (Ameliasburgh) from Birney (Stirling, Scotland)
June 27, 1977   APC

Dear Al,

There's swans on that lake & perch in it, pipers in the hills & lovers in the woods.[761] I am sweating out a preface for the "new selected"[762] while Wai-Lan cooks (we're in student digs) & explores the Pictish ruins — we drove 1000 m. in Eire, saw Richard Murphy (The Second Yeats?) in Galway,[763] & then did another 1000 in the Highlands — at present recovering from five lost days with Aberdeen relatives — I suppose you have written a couple more books & a dozen articles since last I saw you, in between a Trip to Timbuctoo. — Hope all is well — love from Wai-Lan & me to you & Eurithe.

Earle

We'll be back July 20.

To Birney (Toronto) from Purdy (Ameliasburgh)
July 19, 1977   TL

Dear Earle,

Nothing to say, so I say it — in reply to your card from England. Suppose you're back now.

Oh yes, something to say: Eurithe and I would like you to come down here for a few days, if you can. I'll be here all summer, except for a few days after Aug. 11, when I'm in Victoria, BC. We'd love to have you. Why not? Why yes.

So hot right now one doesn't feel like moving. I sweat profusely merely from typing.

Incidentally, had a small fire on my desk (for which we collect mucho insurance), and address book burned. Please send me your phone number again.

I'm melting into the chair.

---

761. The postcard shows "Stirling University, in the grounds of the Airthrey Estate," Scotland.

762. The "new selected" was *Ghost in the Wheels: Selected Poems* (1977).

763. Richard Murphy (b. 1927): Irish poet (*Collected Poems*, 2000; *The Pleasure Ground: Poems 1952–2012*, 2013). His ties to Sri Lanka (then Ceylon), where he spent time as a boy, could well have interested EB.

To Purdy (Ameliasburgh) from Birney (Toronto)
August 25, 1977   TL

Dear Al

Intending to write for some time but have been preoccupied trying to write some more pomes, while Wai-Lan was away in Victoria seeing her family (for 2 weeks — guess you didn't run into her there). It was good seeing you & Eurithe in the new splendours of the Ameliasburgh home though it was a hectic time, trying to see & do too much in two days, & so not getting enough sober talk with you. At any rate I carried away *A Handful of Earth* & what a big handful & what rich soil it is. I should have written you about it long ago & I *am* properly honoured & grateful for your inscription.

Jack J told me you'd passed thru on yr way back to Ameliasburg from the West. How was it out there? & where next?

I like Eurithe's photo of you on the cover very much. Catches a lot of your strengths & it's also the guy who writes the poems.

I think your preface is over-kind to Frye & his "dictum that poems are created from poems" — "partially true"?[764] O.K. but what a small part of the truth, & Frye makes it everything. & you are right that literature hasn't yet caught up with "the expanding human consciousness."[765] I like the first two poems very much[766] ... the "Hub-Cap Thief" means nothing to me[767] ... "Funeral" is almost Laytonian in its (probably justified) paranoia, but it's so much better than the way Irving would have done it that I believe it, believe a preacher really did this to you, & I hate him too.[768] I like "The Shout" very much. It covers a lot of Greek ground, almost gets lost but comes back to base, home base, home run (metaphor mixed?). (I wonder

---

764. Northrop Frye (1912–91): Canadian literary critic (*Fearful Symmetry: A Study of William Blake*, 1947) and professor of English at the University of Toronto (1939–91). In his introduction (not "preface"), AP wrote that "Northrop Frye's dictum that poems are created from other poems seems to me partially true, in the sense that if other people's poems hadn't been written you couldn't have written your own. In that sense, what each of us writes balances and juggles the whole history of literature, and we are for that moment the 'midland navel-stone' of earth." His allusion was to A.E. Housman's "The Oracles": "And mute's the midland navel-stone beside the singing fountain." Frye's "dictum" — "Poetry can only be made out of other poems; novels out of other novels" — appears in *Anatomy of Criticism: Four Essays* (1957).

765. From AP's introduction: "Not that I believe there is nothing new under the sun, that everything has been said. Large as the field of created literature is, it scarcely touches the expanding human consciousness."

766. The first poems were "The Death Mask" and "Along the Ionian Coast."

767. "The Hub-Cap Thief" in full: "All our superiors perceive / our own merit if they merit / their own superiority."

768. The lines in question: "The preacher called beforehand / to make sure God / occupied a place in my heart / or somewhere nearby."

why "*sky* constellation" — isn't "sky" superfluous?)[769] "Fragmentary" is another favorite. ((I don't suppose you give a damn what my favorites are or indeed what I think in general, but old men have inner compulsions to natter (gnatter?) on.)) Love those last two lines — also the ending of the next one, "Infra-Red" & speaking of endings, I do very much dislike the growing habit among editors/compositors of omitting to signal when a poem is continued over-the-page.[770] O sure the really sensitive reader will *know* the poem isn't ended. But a reader like me, even if I *think* the poem isn't finished, gets held up trying to make it end, before I turn over to see if it has — this is the sort of confession no Geddes or Featherbrain or Clara Thomas would ever make, of course — but I'm just a guy who dislikes being held up even momentarily by a poem which is made to look as if it's ending when it's still in the middle.[771]

I don't know what the critics have been saying about this book, by the way, so probably I'm repeating the obvious, but I must say you have moved into a kind of tough lyricism out of deeper suffering, or that's how "Of Course You Can't" & several others hit me — a much sparer, more concentrated singing ... the Peruvian pieces are uneven, I think, but maybe it's just that I like "Llama" so much I find "On the Altiplano" not in the same class (the condor gets lost)[772] ... I like "Fiddleheads," wonderful chain of developing images (& I think your saurian nibbling ferns is better than my camptosaur who "nibbled weeds & ran," because now I think of it, there weren't any weeds till the humanoid gardeners appeared & invented the idea of them).[773]

I still love you both

Earle

---

769. "a flash of light bound for that other / Eridanos which is a sky / constellation known to astronomers / and not the gods that I am ignorant of." Although the poem is based on AP's travels in Greece, both he and EB would have remembered that "Eridanus" was Malcolm Lowry's name for Dollarton in "The Forest Path to the Spring" and other works based upon his life in British Columbia. EB described Dollarton in the introduction to Lowry's *Selected Poems* (1962): "Now there is an empty beach and beside it a Park with picnic tables and tarmac access; the sea air stinks with car exhaust. And the city that ignored him plans to cement a bronze plaque in his memory to the brick wall of the new civic craphouse."

770. The last lines of "Fragmentary": "the rare instant a word glints / disappearing in darkness." The last lines of "Infra-Red": "She brightens the room / as architecture / provides in space / a unity with itself / Better than Mondrian / or Moore's sculpture / and not so expensive."

771. Clara Thomas (1919–2013): Professor of English at York University (1961–84); scholar of Canadian literature; and commentator on the works of Margaret Laurence (*The Manawaka World of Margaret Laurence*, 1975). Thomas wrote about EB and AP in *Our Nature—Our Voices: A Guidebook to English-Canadian Literature* (vol. 1, 1972). Her accounts are generally accurate and full of praise for the writers' works. (She was gently critical of AP's *Wild Grape Wine*, noting that he has "never been loath to collect a little unemployment insurance to have time for his creative production.")

772. From "On the Altiplano": "the king condor floats / on fourteen-foot wings."

773. The poem describes a time "when the long-necked reptiles / thought they were emperors / of the trembling earth / with brains in their tails / and bellies like rocking chairs / they nibbled ferns."

To Birney (Toronto) from Purdy (Ameliasburgh)
August 31, 1977   TL

Dear Earle,

Thanks for your feelings on book. (Incidentally, how did Jack J. know when I passed thru Toronto, since I didn't even leave airport but caught a limousine there to Belleville?)

I'm not very fond of that photograph, since I like continual flattery, being eternally youthful and handsome and that shit. I have much better ones, one of which will be on *No Other Country*. Yeah, agree about Frye, but do think there's a limited amount of truth in that bit about poems from poems. I really haven't had any critical opinions or reviews of book yet, it's too new. Only some from people I know, notably Dennis Lee, whose opinion on one poem differed so strikingly from Ron Everson's — in fact, one line in particular — that it leaves me bewildered. Everson thinks the line a cliché, Lee that it's magnificent. How can you reconcile two opinions like that?

Where next, well, apart from being at Western I was planning a trip to Van. this fall. However, Ed Yeomans in the English Dept. told me UBC wouldn't look after my hotel or accommodations for a night.[774] Therefore I turned the invite down. Also told him that with Canada Council looking after some $400. in travel plus fee I thought it pretty small of UBC not to pay a hotel room. I'm sure they did for some of the many U.S. poets they've had there, plus the fee itself which I'm sure wasn't small for Creeley, Wieners, Spicer, Duncan et al.[775] I'm thinking of writing the CC on this one and sending a carbon of my letters to Robin Mathews. In short, I'm kinda stirred up by this shit.

As you no doubt gathered from my Intro to book [*A Handful of Earth*], the older things were/are borderline, with the exception of "Starlings," which I passed over unaccountably. Matter of fact, that poem "Funeral" is exactly true. I'll always remember that bastard preacher.

Of course I agree with the bit about the appearance of endings. But that was Inkster, the typesetter and compositor (what's a compositor? — must be impor-tant!).[776] I'm always a little surprised that someone/anyone, you in this case, likes more than about three poems in a book. I mean, I pick out the title poem,

---

774. William Edward Yeomans (1927–2009): Canadian professor of English at UBC, scholar of modern poetry, and poet (*The Green Dragon and Other Poems*, 1976).

775. John Wieners (1934–2002): American poet (*Selected Poems: 1958–1984*, 1986) who studied at Black Mountain College from 1955 to 1956 and was, like Robert Duncan and Jack Spicer, part of the San Francisco Renaissance.

776. Tim Inkster (b. 1949): Canadian printer and publisher (The Porcupine's Quill).

"Starlings," and "Prince Edward County," and the others rapidly descend in my mind, maybe due in part to time lapse.

I went to Victoria early, hoping to get to Campbell River and see Jack Jackovich for beer and say hi to Mrs. Haig-Brown.[777] But Jack was in Europe, so I didn't go north at all. I saw Norma, Eurithe's sister, whom you may recall. Nervous breakdown a few years back? I met her in a park, and she had come there with her sister-in-law for company, because she couldn't go there alone, or go anywhere alone. That is depressing to me, since I'm fond of Norma. I.e., she's worse.

Letter from Leonard Brooks, who says he'll be in Toronto in Sept. I expect he'll be at your place part of the time. Be sure and phone or write when he's there, and will hope to see both of you at that time.

Al

To Purdy (London, Ontario) from Birney (Toronto)
September 14, 1977 APC[778]

Dear Al

Congratulations on making Zena's cherry & passing the 200-book record set by Edgar A. Guest.[779] I hope despite this rise to the greatest eminence (or is there something greater even than being of planetary acceptance?) you will deign to call us on one of your processions between your London castle & the Ameliasburg estate. Meantime, wes hæl!

e. b.   Balliol Street's best[780]

To Birney (Toronto) from Purdy (Ameliasburgh)
September 30, 1977 TL

Dear Earle,

Thank you for the poultice of your own bad reviews. It was a good thought. They do reflect and reflect.

But I've been reading your poem ["Fall by Fury"] again. It is, I believe, by far

---

777. In "The Death of a Friend," a note on the death of Roderick Haig-Brown (*Canadian Literature* 72, Spring 1977), AP described Jack Jackovich: "I was at a 'health lodge' in Strathcona Park on Vancouver Island in 1974, writing a piece about Jack Jackovitch [*sic*], painter, ex-football player, fishing guide and high school teacher, etc. I intended to call it 'Jackovitch and the Salmon-Princess' (yes, I have a dramatic turn of mind), but the editor of *Weekend Magazine* destroyed my title. Anyway, Jack knew Haig-Brown ..." AP's "King Tyee and the Salmon-Princess" was published in *Weekend Magazine* (3 May 1975) and reprinted as "Jackovich and the Salmon Princess" in *SA* (174–82).

778. The postcard was addressed to "Alfred W. Purdy, Globe's Greatest Poet, Writer-in-Residence, University of Western Ontario."

779. Zena Cherry (1915–2000): Society columnist for *The Globe and Mail*.

780. EB's address was 2201–200 Balliol St., Toronto.

my recent favourite of all yours. And makes you so damn human, once more, again and still. I'd like to have written the poem without the fall. (Incidentally, don't for chrissake write "The Fall" into it.) I envy you the poem. But you had to live your life to write your poems, as I had to live mine for the same purpose. Still, it is beautifully and marvellously well-done.

I have some thoughts about it. I do not think "I slipped / forever from tree-tops" is sentimental. It should be there, just as a similar thing was said in "David."[781]

I question "cloven hip and thigh / with those I had cleft"[782] ... "Cloven" meaning separate or in two or broken. Your hip and thigh were broken, just as the limbs you had cut from the tree were. But I don't like that choice of words. "Cloven" is not good, reminds me of witches. "Cleft" is too much like an opening in rock or earth.

That's a picayune objection, I know; but it's such a good poem I'd like to make it conform to you, and does it really conform to you if you use those words?

I believe you agreed that the first verse is too slow (as I agreed with your comment about my first verse: both slow you down too much getting into the meat).[783] What about a commonplace title, like, "Pruning a Beech Tree"? That looks after the necessary exposition.

You know my objections to "fortnight" and reasons.[784] I know you can't say "two weeks."

There is a hint or two in the poem that the same guy wrote "The Mammoth Corridors."[785] That's not bad tho.

The last verse winds it up beautifully.

Congratulations. Should I say as Wolfe did, "I would rather have written that poem than take Quebec tomorrow"?[786] Or, "I would rather have written that poem than do anything except discover the meaning of things; in which case I should

---

781. The lines from "Fall by Fury" (published in *Fall by Fury & Other Makings*, 1978) could have reminded AP of the last line of "David" ("That day, the last of my youth, on the last of our mountains" [*OMH* 39]) or perhaps of the description of David's fall: "Without // A gasp he was gone" (*OMH* 37).

782. "my hard mother / crushed me limp in her stone embrace / stretched me still / with the other limbs / laid my cloven hip and thigh / with those I had cleft" (*OMH* 164). The lineation is slightly different in the version of the poem published in *Fall by Fury & Other Makings*.

783. "Now was the season / summer so high and still / the birds in the circling woods / held all the tale" (*OMH* 162).

784. "Shining ahead was the fortnight / given us here alone by our friends / to swim with the small fish in their pond" (*OMH* 163). (In *Fall by Fury & Other Makings* "their pond" is "the pond.")

785. "The Mammoth Corridors," dated 1965 by EB, was published in the *Northwest Review* 7.3 (Spring 1966) and in *Rag & Bone Shop* (1971). A book of the same name was published in 1980 by Stone Press of Okemos, Michigan..

786. James Wolfe (1727–59): British officer who died on the Plains of Abraham. "That poem" is Thomas Gray's "Elegy Written in a Country Churchyard." AP's "Dead March for Sergeant MacLeod," from *Sex & Death*, alludes to Wolfe's possibly apocryphal declaration: "does Gray's / 'Elegy' still seem very important now / to you in your pine box[?]" (*BR* 206)

be able to write poems after rigor mortis and before birth." Or should I be damn careful about whatever I say in case of your misinterpretation?

Al

To Purdy (London) from Birney (Toronto)
October 9, 1977   TL

Dear Al

I've re-arranged the opening sections of that tree-fall piece, & it's much better. Many thanks. But "cleft ... fortnight ..." etc will stay. These words I learned in childhood, they are part of me, as they are not part of the idiom of a young gaffer like you. I will lose some readers by clinging to my vocabulary. But I don't have any readers now anyway, only hearers, & not many of them.

I'm still reading your *No Other Country*. I can only read it in small chunks because I begin to run a temperature against McStew for publishing it without ensuring it was properly edited. A hard-cover ten-dollar book should not for gods-sake read at times as if it were a transcript from a tape-recorder. Your book is full of good things & full of bad things (I'm talking about style, thinking, organizing). The bad needn't have been there, because the bad occurs in phrases, mainly, which you could have cut or strengthened, given a little time — either you or your publisher didn't want to give the book that much time. & you are paying for it in reviews like that bugger Christy's[787] — Jack J. came around with his latest gal & we had a big argument, — Jack seemed to feel he had to defend Christy (Jack being Loyal to *Books in Can*). I haven't seen anyone else as yet who has read the review or the book. (Jack admitted he hadn't yet read the book, except as articles separately in the mags.)

I'm afraid you're right about "Wind over St. John's."[788] Such a waste of time writing it. This '78 book will absolutely be my last collection of poems. From now on: sober prose — which will give you a chance to tell me how bad *my* prose is. Well, I think we both write better than most, in whatever form — but we could both write better than we do.

There's always a bed here you know & chow. If you can stand my natterings.

Cheers. Hope Londonont & you are having fun.

Earle

---

787. Jim Christy's review of AP's *No Other Country* (" This Canadian's not the Weekend man he Maclaims." *Books in Canada*, Oct. 1977) was damning: "Al Purdy has gotten this collection published because he is, well, Al Purdy. Believe me — spare yourself! — it has nothing to do with good writing." Christy (b. 1945) has written books of poetry, fiction, and travel writing (*Rough Road to the North: Travels along the Alaska Highway*, 1980), among other genres.

788. "The Wind through St. John's" was included in EB's *Fall by Fury & Other Makings* (1978).

To Birney (Toronto) from Purdy (London)
October 18, 1977   TL

Dear Earle,

Hope I didn't lay that application on you too suddenly — just found not much time left and kinda panicked — if that's the word. If you by chance are applying yourself for anything, let me know.

I am feeling a little grumpy about the daily grind. Spoiled and pampered as I undoubtedly am, there's something about this sort of thing that stops poems for me. Not that I write that many anyway, but I have to be miserable in my own fashion, not somebody else's.

It does (the job) allow Eurithe to masticate travel folders by the bushel, and spit them out as recycled wasps' nests all bound for Mexico. She will have the Christmas break trip so planned and scheduled that we might as well stay home.

I've shown that poem of yours to several people here, and their reaction similar to my own. Of course if it hadn't been, I'd have tripped them or otherwise injured them.

Al

To Purdy (London) from Birney (Toronto)
October 19, 1977   TL

Dear Al

The ironies of life continue to beset me, you too. I had sounded out Kathy Berg [at the Canada Council] about a grant for me, in a letter I wrote her last month — she phoned me about it while you were in Ottawa (or at least the morning-after she'd had some drinks with you, as I recall her saying) — & it was she who gave me the idea of applying for the 3-year grant. Probably she didn't tell you this. So anyway I prepared a hell of a long application statement about my autobiographical plans, & banged it in. Then the mail came, with your Oct. 13 note — our turtle-footed postal service! — & *your* appraisal form for me to make out & I had the envelope waiting with my appraisal form for you.

I decided the sensible thing was to recommend you (as the alternative if I don't get it) & give you a chance to do the same for me, if you want to.

Here's what I've just written to the Council (I said nothing about whether your fee estimates were "justified" since you didn't make any).

"Although I saw Al Purdy last week, he did not tell me he had applied for the unique three-way [*sic*] English-language grant. Meantime I have sent in my own application for the same grant. I presume *he* did not know *I* was intending to apply. However, I see no reason why I cannot write in support of his application. He is now, next to Layton, Canada's most popular and prolific poet, and one of our most genuine and individual artists-in-words. If I am not granted the three-year award, there is no one I would rather see get it than Al — and I rather think he might say the same for me! He wants to continue roaming Canada and writing poems, activities no other Canadian has ever combined with such success and benefit to our literature." Rating: "Exceptional."

I do hope this is O.K. with you Al? In any case, you can call in another appraisal, to have three without mine.

By the way, did you know the deadline date for these applications has been extended to the end of October, so there's still time for me to find someone else if you'd rather not send in a "letter of appraisal" on me, in the circumstances.

I hope to see you soon. Would like to tell you about the things I really do like, very much, in your new prose book [*No Other Country*]. I saw another "review" by this Christy guy, putting down another writer (can't remember who, at this moment!). I think he's the new Andreas Schroeder.

& so *over to you!*

luv
Earle

To Birney (Toronto) from Purdy (London)
October 20, 1977   TL

Dear Earle,

Whaddaya mean, "young gaffer"?

Sorry you have such feelings about book, and may be right. I spent so much time on that book I don't wanta spend any more with it.

Sorry also Jack wants to defend Christy. The latter said, in effect and actually, there was nothing good about the book. (If so, I've wasted my time and a lot of other people's.) Therefore Jack goes along with the idea there's nothing good in the book. It was a hatchet job, for whatever reason, and may well have destroyed whatever hope the book had for any kind of readership. Reviews sometimes can do that.

You have no readers? That's a lotta shit! We are all going down the drain, soon or late, and I expect it, and don't have to like it. But the idea that you have no readers is simply ridiculous. Selah. (Whatever that means.)

"Wind over St. John's" is marvellously well expressed, images and all, but can it stand on that alone? I think it's too good, for the reasons I mentioned, to abandon, and hope you don't. I think you should look at your own circumstances of being in St. John's again, which I know is a helluva drag, since the impetus is partly gone. Can't you get yourself into that poem somehow, or some kind of spine and vertebrae?

London Ont is the shits, but it's money. The job bores the shit outa me. All young poets want is to be told they're geniuses. Certainly not criticism. How much money do I need? I dunno, guess enough for Mexico and a few more years. And I do owe other people who've done much for me some kinda return; and maybe keeping on writing and talking is helping to pay back some of the help I've received.

You sound sorry for yourself as hell. Maybe I do too. What's wrong with us?

Al

To Birney (Toronto) from Purdy (Ameliasburgh)
October 22, 1977   TL

Dear Earle,

Enclose the carbon of what I said to CC [Canada Council] for you.

I'll still complete my own application, since I believe one may still get a one-year grant even if not the three-year one.

In return for my extraordinary altruistic self-abnegation, I expect to receive in the next mail a hand-written copy of the falling from tree poem ["Fall by Fury"] in which you were showing off for Wailan and saying "Look maw, no hands!" and then fell. Mark you, the next mail! I'm waiting!

Good to see you and all that crap. I think you're getting more peevish as you grow older (unquote). I'd even speak to you if you didn't give me books. Would the reverse be true?

I hope you get the award, even if it's only one available.

Should be a sexy autobio ! ??

Al

To Purdy (London) from Birney (San Miguel de Allende)
December 20, 1977   APC

Dear Al —

I see it's exactly 2 mos. since you wrote me. Since then you've probably escaped the 5 ft. snow blanket to tropical paradises warmer than this, but I recommend the cloudless skies & dry warmth of SMA days in Dec — had a couple of weari-some days in the noise & aerial shit of M.C. [Mexico City] & have to go back there Jan 6 & take the plane back to ugh Toronto. I see you have been announcing 4 more books, after a dozen TV appearances & resting in the Ritz & feeling less pally with Lévesque & shafting Rosenblatt & being elected to the Academy of Can. Writers.[789]

Well, seasonal joys attend you & Eurithe — & our luv too.

Earle & Wai-Lan

To Purdy (Ameliasburgh) from Birney (Toronto)
January 12, 1978   APC

Dear Al

Apart from a few villages east of Aguascalientes or south of Tuxtla I doubt if you've yet found a place in Mexico I haven't been. But no doubt you're holed up in this Burrard St. palace already — it seems we were in Celaya when you were in Zacatecas.[790] Next week I'll be shuttling between Mtrl & St. John's. How about you look after those undamaged cells & have a good 1978, you & Eurithe.

Earle

To Birney (Toronto) from Purdy (London)
February 7, 1978   TL

Dear Earle,

Greetings. I wouldn't know about the places you've visited in Mexico, but since we've driven there four or five times by car, it seems likely we hit the same places. Think I sent you a card from Chapala, one of the more touristy places, where we stayed a month. I have ten days off mid-Feb., so we'll drive south again to Fla., drop in on Ron Everson briefly. Eurithe will stay there all of March, then drive back. I'll fly back at the end of Feb.

I hope to get out to Van. Is. in March, see some friends, do a coupla readings. Think I mentioned: turned down UBC because they wouldn't supply a hotel room. Very annoying: when CC [Canada Council] pays more than $500. in travel and fee for a single reading, the univ won't pay a twenty buck hotel.

---

789. EB's comment was probably intended to be facetious, but AP was in fact remarkably produc-tive in 1977 and 1978. In 1977 he published a book of journalism, *No Other Country;* two collections of poetry, *A Handful of Earth* and *At Marsport Drugstore*; and the American edition of *Moths in the Iron Curtain*. The following year *Being Alive: Poems 1958–78* was published.

790. The postcard was from the Hyatt Regency hotel, Vancouver (655 Burrard St.).

Damn sick of London snow (18 foot drifts here). But will see you in spring and summer. Take care of yourself and Wailan.

Al

To Purdy (London) from Birney (Toronto)
April 7, 1978   APC

Dear Al,

Looks like you don't know the right people, like I do. What can I say? Without your rec. I wouldn't have landed it — & with *my* rec. you were sabotaged — well, *next* year, you won't have to compete with indigent ancients & it should be plain sailing.[791]

Where are you? Still on a Florida beach? Or a Vancouver one? We'll be out there at end of May — then *maybe* England till mid-July — When do we see you?

Earle

To Birney (Toronto) from Purdy (Ameliasburgh)
April 14, 1978   TL

Dear Earle,

Glad to hear you got the three year thing.[792] I couldn't possibly compete with you for this or anything else. You deserved it. I hope the memoirs go well. Make sure you get that bit about meeting [Charles G.D.] Roberts, and all the women crowding round wanting to be the new Lady Roberts.[793]

Incidentally, I got the consolation prize, a senior grant.

Back at A-burg as you see. We may take a coupla weeks in Spain at the end of this month. Feeling better back here, except tired. Working on a new *Selected* with Dennis Lee as ed. for McStew. He's a tough ed, wants me to look again at poems that've been written for years. And being right sometimes, so that some poems are much improved. Has to have a title to differentiate from previous *Selected*, so *Being Alive: Poems 1958–1978*.

Will ring you in Toronto. I was there briefly for Gzowski show, then rush back to London.[794] And several readings at high schools — makes one feel like an industry.

Al

---

791. See AP's letters of 18 and 22 Oct. 1977 and EB's letter of 19 Oct. 1977.

792. See AP's letters of 18 and 22 Oct. 1977 and EB's letter of 19 Oct. 1977.

793. Roberts married Joan Montgomery on 28 Oct. 1943; he died nearly one month later.

794. Peter Gzowski (1934–2002): Canadian reporter and broadcaster who hosted the CBC radio program *Morningside* from 1982 to 1997.

To Birney (Toronto) from Purdy (Ameliasburgh)
October 1, 1978   TL[795]

Dear Earle,

Thanks for your new book.[796] As I've said before: I think the title poem is one of the best or possibly the best I've ever seen of yours, which is a pretty high standard. Of course I think the others are good too, because you never write a bad or mediocre poem, but the standard of the title poem is damn high, the sort of thing you (me) feel fortunate and lucky to write. Don't misunderstand me: I think you've written some marvellous stuff before, but this one is damn well great to me. I think finally I plump for both you and Layton as my best, and leave out Atwood. She's too damn cold for me, I guess; somehow doesn't seem human or enough human, as a poet ought to be.

Thanks also for your compliment about me, which not many people seem to share these days. No, I'm not paranoiac; it's just that people (such as Livesay in *CVII*) seem to think I am "roistering and self-indulgent" rather than anything else.[797] Same opinion in Ottawa *Citizen* re new book, quoting the Intro I wrote for the small NCL book.[798] Well, what can I say … I am sometimes roistering and self-indulgent.

Nobody's asked me to go to England or U.S., and I assume you're not in a position to anyway.

Just returned from west coast, and a trip to Q. Charlottes after three readings. Talked to some Haida carvers there, Davidson père et fils — Jesus, I now forget whether "fils" is son or daughter, but I think the former anyway.[799] But hope to do something with the trip. Incidentally, I see you are anticipating me with the Roberts' entourage bit, which I've mentioned a coupla times at readings or someplace. Which reminds me of the memoirs? Which are kinda equivalent of this kinda book of mine. A long *Selected*, which seems a tombstone on the sidewalk for me. There it is, the final nail.

love to both of you,

Al

---

795. AP dated the letter 30 Sept. but then corrected himself: "actually Oct. 1."

796. *Fall by Fury & Other Makings* (1978).

797. In her review of Ron Everson's *Indian Summer* (1976) in *CVII* 2.4 (Dec. 1976), Dorothy Livesay suggested that "The approach is reminiscent of Purdy, but the voice is much more subdued. No roistering or self-indulgence here." AP remembered the perceived slight, alluding to it in an interview published in 1981: "To me it's a virtue to disappoint Dorothy" (in *For Openers: Conversations with 24 Canadian Writers*, edited by Alan Twigg).

798. The "new book" was *Being Alive: Poems 1958–78*. The "small … book" was *The Poems of Al Purdy: A New Canadian Library Selection* (1976).

799. Claude Davidson (1924–91) and Robert Davidson (b. 1946): distinguished Haida artists.

To Purdy (Ameliasburgh) from Birney (Toronto)
December 31, 1978   AL

Dear Al

Last I heard from you you were living outside a cave in Purullena & renting your-self out as a burro. I hope this has been a fructuous experience, as De Quincey might have said. Anyway this is just to tell you & Eurithe that Wai-Lan and I are thinking of you on this auspicious Eve hoping we will see you somewhere sometime in '79, & in any case that you both stay healthy, creative, sober* & consequently as happy as mortals are ever likely to be, right thru from January to December.

Luv
Earle
&
Wai-Lan

* This of course refers only to Eurithe.

To Birney (Toronto) from Purdy (Ameliasburgh)
January 4, 1979   TL

Dear Earle,

I wrote you before leaving for England and Spain a couple of months ago, and phoned you on Christmas (no answer): so at this moment I'm wondering if you're not gallivanting out of the country somewhere. Which I plan to do myself, as soon as Eurithe recovers from the presumable flu, and the snow recedes from my shoulder blades then my ass. It must have snowed fourteen inches last night, twice the length of any good man's solar equipment or moon probe.

Yes, we plan on Mexico again, Lake Chapala (D.H. Lawrence's hangout in the 1920s).[800] (In fact, I have a story about Lawrence from someone who picked up his Spanish-English dictionary in Chapala under very odd circumstances.) Last time there we met some likeable people from near N.Y., saw them since in N.Y., and will see them again at Chapala. Too bad you're not coming down yourself. No possi-bility, I suppose? If you did it would be San Miguel and the Brookses ...

Anyway, as I may or may not have mentioned, we had planned on going to Scotland after landing in England in late Oct. But thought London cold and miserable, and expensive as hell: therefore, when Eurithe found one of those reasonable charter flights advertised, we went to the Costa del Sol: Torremolinos,

---

800. AP's "D.H. Lawrence at Lake Chapala" was included in *The Stone Bird* (1981).

in fact. Close to Malaga, where Sinclair Ross is.[801] I didn't have his address and tried to find him and couldn't. We rented a car in Torremolinos (half an inch longer than my knees), pedaled it up the coastal mtns, etc. Got to Granada and the Alhambra, Gibraltar and Algeciras, and most notably, Nerja, called "The Balcony of Europe" …[802]

Nerja has some paleolithic caves, dating from 20,000 B.C. to about 12,000, — I mean dates of their human occupation. Monster place, ceiling of one two hundred feet high, cave paintings, bones, etc. Cream-coloured stalactites and stalagmites, stone icicles — what a weird feeling. I wrote what I call a prose poem, first time I ever labelled anything like that. Overwhelming impression of an ancient man with a pine torch, venturing fearfully into that darkness full of gods and spirits, and maybe the odd reclusive cave bear. No wonder we're a superstitious lot still when we had ancestors who must have been half scared to death most of the time. Anyway, I tried to avoid using any modern words in the prose piece, even omitting stalactites and stalagmites, especially since I can never remember which goes up and which down. However, it was more a religious experience than anything, and my piece is slanted that way.

On return I tried to look up those caves at Belleville library. No dice. I'm sure larger libraries would have something, since the caves were enormous, altho only discovered in 1959.

So I am now trying to straighten out convoluted poems I wrote in Spain. And a later one about the desert north of Zacatecas, half-surrealistic I guess.[803]

Love to you and Wailan,

Al

To Birney (Toronto) from Purdy (Ajijic, Mexico)
January 27, 1979   TL[804]

Dear Earle,

I expect you are grimly enduring the Toronto winter, with the fortitude that does not permit you to cast yearning eyes westward or utter one syllable of mild dissent at the fates and Furies. You'll be pleased to know that it's 80 Fah. here daily, the sun always shines — or if not God is not in his heaven but working mischief elsewhere.

Anyway, we rented this three-room cottage for about $70. a month all found.

---

801. Sinclair Ross (1908–96): Canadian novelist (*As for Me and My House*, 1941) and writer of short stories.

802. AP's "Driving the Spanish Coast," from *The Stone Bird* (1981), refers to the Nerja caves. The next poem in the book, "Meeting," is about the caves. It is not a prose poem in its published form; otherwise it matches AP's description of his "piece" in the next paragraph of the letter.

803. The poem was probably "South of Durango," which was included in *The Stone Bird*.

804. EB's note: "answered by card from Vancouver 3 Mar 79."

Will use the above for a mailing address, do some wandering when the present rent is expired, then return here again in Feb., since here is the best climate we've encountered in Mexico.[805]

I managed to forget my jacket with passport inside at a motel in San Luis Potosi, and Eurithe forgot the car ownership at the border, both of which annoyed me considerably. Old age really deteriorates the brain cells as well as alcohol.

You're probably aware that: D.H. Lawrence lived in Chapala for about two months in 1923. Went down and took a look at the house, a peeling yellow-stucco two-storey place, with a large section of coloured tiles depicting a plumed serpent, the only trace of Lawrence evident. I wrote a coupla poems, which I'm still working on, one of which might turn out to be something.

Incidentally, if you feel like escaping Toronto cold, you and Wailan — why not come down here? We could pick you up at Guadalajara airport, about fifteen miles distant from here, and pretty easy to rent a place where we are ... It's a thought, if Wailan can escape school for a few weeks ...

Best from both of us —

Al

To Purdy (Ajijic) from Birney (Vancouver)
March 3, 1979   APC

Dear Al —

Would love to be down there in Ah-hee-hee (the "c" is silent as in Beaufort) but I'll just pig it out here with the wet-sea-trout or there with twenty below C.[806] Thinking of Eurithe & you (not me) down there in Ajijic with Lawrence & God (but no sea).

Luv from me & by proxy from Wailan back by the inland sea.

Earle

To Purdy (Ameliasburgh) from Birney (Toronto)
March 1979   TL[807]

Dear Al

Hope you're not still dragging your balls over all that snow. At Xmas we were off in the nearer snowbanks of Uxbridge & from there to Newburgh to spend a nite with Reg & Beth Watters on their chicken farm. Hope Eurithe is better & both

---

805. "the above": "General Delivery, Poste Restante, Ajijic, Jalisco, Mexico."

806. In "Ajijíc," a poem in *Ice Cod Bell or Stone* (1962), EB likewise wrote about the pronunciation of the name: "This hip gringo cant [*sic*] wait to tell you / it rhymes with tee-HEE."

807. The letter was undated. The references to the Nerja caves permit an approximate dating.

of you in shape for Mexico. Would like to see Chapala again. There was a night Len [Leonard Brooks] & I were staying on the lake & got restless & drove up to Morelia just to get drunk in the redlight distrito beyond — we nearly got shot in a cantina where a liquored Mexican was waving a pistol & looking for Americanos to kill because he'd just got word his kid brother had been machinegunned from the air trying to wetback across the Rio Grande at night. We got out fast and sobered for a friendlier bar but the girls there had to leave because of a curfew. So we got drunk all over again & Brooks drove at top speed over that mountain road back down to Lake Chapala. Next day we were both scared just thinking about that drive, let alone the mozo with the sixgun.

So I missed you in London. Ondaatje, P.K. Page & I were there reading in early Oct. Yes miserable weather but better there than farther north. The Lake District was entirely befogged & Newcastle was more like Alaska. So you were wise to get to the Costa del Sol. I put in part of a Spring up & down that coast & the Costa Brava, & driving around most of Spain. I prefer Barcelona or the Basque country. I missed those Nerja caves, though. Maybe they hadn't opened them up to the public in 1963? — Look forward to seeing your poems about Spain & Mexico esp.

I've put together a book of old radio plays & another of Canlitcrits & another of nonCanlitcrits. & then there's this one. What is it? Prose non-poems?[808]

Wailan & I send our love to you both.

Earle

To Birney (Toronto) from Purdy (Ameliasburgh)
March 25, 1979   TL[809]

Dear Earle,

Thanks for your note and the new book. (I hope to be sending *Moths in the Iron Curtain* to you in the next few weeks.) Dunno when you sent it, since no date on letter and I threw away envelope. I'm enjoying it, having read some before and others not. Esp. "Queen Emma." I can't write prose like that. Enjoyed also "Leavetaking," assume autobio.[810]

Tom Marshall was with us in Ajijic briefly with your book, and I read some of it then. Didn't expect him down and was away when he arrived. We drove him to the plane at Guadalajara a few days later, and had an engagement at Ajijic, so just

---

808. Three books were published: *Words on Waves: Selected Radio Plays of Earle Birney* (1985) ("old radio plays"), *Spreading Time: Remarks on Canadian Writing and Writers* (1980) ("Canlitcrits"), and *Big Bird in the Bush: Selected Stories and Sketches* (1978) ("Prose non-poems").

809. *YA* 296–97.

810. "Leavetaking" and "Waiting for *Queen Emma*" appeared in EB's *Big Bird in the Bush: Selected Stories and Sketches* (1978).

left him and hurried back. Turned out later his flight had been cancelled because he hadn't phoned to confirm, had to stay in Guad. a night. Now I feel guilty about it.

I wrote seven poems in Mexico, now dried up completely again. Drove to Florida afterwards, stayed with Ron Everson a week. E. [Eurithe] and I sat in the back seat of his Cadillac one day while other drivers cussed his bad driving, one yelling "Get offa the road, you old asshole!" — we trying to conceal laughter and embarrassment in the back seat. Migawd tho, he's goodhearted: wanted to loan me money when we were leaving New Smyrna, said he had a coupla hundred dollars not doing anything! E. and I were a little deafened from his flood of words, some of them damn interesting. I think he's a bit lonely in Fla. tho …

Didn't run into anything like your liquored Mexican waving a pistol, thank goodness. We were in Patzcuaro at one point, not far from Morelia, visited a volcano near Acuapan: Paricutin, and wrote a pome. (Send you a couple herewith from Mexico.)

Yes, I think the Nerja caves have been opened only in last ten years. Did I send you my prose pome about them?

I have readings in early April out west, but hope to see you both after that. I see we are both among Amiel's choice of five.[811] When I talked to her she wasn't gonna include Layton; musta changed her mind.

love from Eurithe and me,
Al

A coupla pomes for Earle & Wailan with a Neruda finale —[812]

love Al

Near Patzcuaro

Sun dominates:
a glass ball dashing back and forth
in the space between your eyes
It's like a disease you catch
but
  ∧ after exposure to fire-germs
a cure is effected
when the bugs begin to love you
Arriving from the 16th century

---

811. Barbara Amiel (b. 1940): British-Canadian journalist. In "Poetry: Capsule Comments on Canada" (*Maclean's*, 15 Jan. 1979), Amiel named Margaret Atwood, Irving Layton, Alden Nowlan, EB, and AP as major Canadian poets.

812. Both poems were published in *The Stone Bird* (1981). In *The Collected Poems of Al Purdy* (1986) and *BR*, "Pátzcuaro" has an accent (*BR* 350).

dugout canoes with fishermen
and the death-mask of Father Morelos
inside his 132-foot statue
gleams across Lake Patzcuaro
blessing damn near everything
which includes Indians market women
and near the Farmacia a dog
with arched back shitting
I have to learn how it is
to be alive here all over again
do as the brown people do
and their don'ts a dance step
I look out from a blind beggar's eyes
and see myself a northern myth
a tall grey gringo illness
and shudder away from me
Driving to Tzintzuntzan
Place of the Hummingbirds
ancient Tarascan capital
I learn how they defeated the Aztecs
in battle by shouting
Tzintzuntzan at them
reducing Tenochtitlan to a whisper
of many hummingbirds' wings
How to be alive again?
Did Father Morelos know
or Bishop Don Vasco de Quiroga
with their transplanted god?
— the flowers with their brilliant
rainbow faces turn
toward the mountain morning
— among the innocent mountains
unnoticed are the guilty ones
where 500 dormant volcanos shudder
whatever certainties there are
expressed in that shudder
— and love which is the inexpressible
turn to me in this place
and from my continual turmoil

grant me some knowledge of myself
and of my residence on earth

—Mexico

For Earle & Wailan
  Al Purdy

In the Garden

Poinsettias blaze red bougainvillea burn
the lake is a smooth blue plate
for sun-tongues to lick clean
Once maybe at the very beginning of things
everything was mud-coloured
you could look out and see only grey sand
you could see nothing to send messages
back from it to you
just dirty-coloured sea water
where rain had lashed things in fury
and wind had mixed everything up like soft porridge
and only the pole star shone like a white lever
for gods of the sky to shinny down
on long slender columns of light
and arrive on earth with a cry
Then we had blue and scarlet and silver
then we had vegetable love
whoever was looking for something dreamed it
then ^we^ made a wanting song of ~~whispers~~ SADNESS
then ^we^ made a finding song of joy
when the Moon said "Here I am Sun"
so he was
and went on sailing up there
all night for the first time

It must have been if you were watching
if you could have watched in the morning
a time to stand naked in rain
a time to feel the fingers of warm rain
touching your new human body

and stammer some praise for it
your thanks — and you had to thank someone
why not the earth?
Thank you earth thank you sea thank you sky
the beginnings of human love
when we said:
these things are dear
they are bought with your life
they are yours for only an instant
they are yours unconditionally
then you must give them away

To Purdy (Ameliasburgh) from Birney (Toronto)
May 17, 1979   TL

Dear Al

When you were here your mesmeric powers prevented me from remembering you had written me a good letter in March with two pendant poems. I've just dug them out of Drawer Two: PRIORITY ... Your Patzcuaro poem's ending is a fine surprise, not unprepared for, but suddenly very straight & moving. "In the Garden" is even more so, because the feeling has built earlier & been sustained longer. You are doing new things, growing less fearful of being thought sentimental & consequently not being sentimental — good. I hope the other 5 are like these.

I was in Mexico the year Paricutin came shooting up like a super-mushroom in some hombre's cornpatch. But the roads were sealed off.

Was out in Regina at a Regionalist Conf., subbing for [Mordecai] Richler.[813] Consequently learned, to my pleasure, how much money that slick bastard gets paid for a single "performance." (More even than *you* get, I bet.)

I take it your remark about assuming my "Leavetaking" was autobiographical is just one of your Birney-baiting jests.

Though I wasn't in good form when you & Eurithe were here, I did enjoy your coming. Since then I've had another goddam birthday & am plugging away at the Canlitcrits book. No time any more for pomes. Will be at McGill in June. Getting D.Littered ... July 5 we take off for Scotland. Back mid-August. Hope to see you before or after.

Have a good summer, wherever.

Love from us both

Earle

---

813. The Conference on Regional Literature was held at the University of Regina in early May.

To Birney (Toronto) from Purdy (Ameliasburgh)
May 22, 1979[814]   TL

Dear Earle,

Especially glad to hear from you right now, since I thought I had offended you somehow at your place and didn't know how. If so, you oughta hear Acorn on that subject: he was down here, dogmatic and thundering as usual. I said, at one point, "If I break the law and they catch me I gotta go to jail. So why shouldn't Claude Parrot go to jail?"[815] He says "I won't listen to you making slaves of the workers." I says, "When did I say I wanted workers to be slaves?" He says "I won't listen to you making slaves of the workin class." So we thundered at each other for hours.

Anyway, sorry if I annoyed you. I do that to people at times, viz. Acorn. Don't tell me what it was about if I did, then I'd have to explain and you'd have to explain and the conversation would be nothing else but that.

My mesmeric powers — in a word, Shit!

I never bait Birney — wouldn't dare!

I forget the mention of your "Leavetaking"????

Thanks for good words about those two poems. No, the others aren't as good. Or as bad or whatever. I did like "In the Garden," thinking that's the way I do feel about capital L Life. But I'm writing so much, so many — and I mean few — things that seem any good to me these days — so little at all really —

Of course Richler gets paid much, Cohen too. I get the CC rate only, surely you knew that. I quite agree that your — 500 bucks was it? — rate is justified, but I can't ask that — nobody would give it to me. What does Richler get, $2,000.? You're in a different position — apart from reverence from your vast age, and that you've managed to survive all those women — having written things like your despised "David," lapped up by so many schoolchildren (I happen to like it much still, despite your sneering remarks about your own wayward child), and the last marvellous piece about falling from the tree while showing off for Wailan …

Did you tell me about the Canlitcrits book? I don't remember.

Glad you like the Sylvia [Hotel], since I got their paper when in Van. too.

My own future activities are fairly limited. Coupla readings near Hamilton in June, a week at Canadore Col. [North Bay, Ontario] in July (yes, creative writing stuff), in fact damn near anything for money, since I have little comin in this year. I made the mistake of askin for last instalment of senior grant too soon and it was dated Dec. 28 last year, therefore taxable. And last year was my big year for

---

814. *YA* 300–01.

815. Jean-Claude Parrot (b. 1936): President of the Canadian Union of Postal Workers. The CUPW had not acceded to a government order to end its strike in 1978. Parrot was jailed in 1980.

earnings. So I get stuck because of bein stupid. This year, nothin from outside, I mean not CC, and damn little from anywhere.

Yes, Paricutin. I writ a piece in what I imagined might be the words and language of a Tarascan Indian about that —[816]

Odd thing — somehow you and I think alike in many ways (don't ask me how, just feel we do) …

love to both of you
Al

To Purdy (Ameliasburgh) from Birney (Toronto)
June 10, 1979   TL

Dear Al

Meant to answer your May letter but got tangled in deadline with Véhicule Press. Book will prob. be called *Spreading Time*. Still tangled but at least I got down to Mtrl for a day this week & worked out contract & now all I have to do is finish the damned intro. & extro. & inter-tros. before we take off for Scotland on the 5th July. Do you know Si Durdick [*sic*], Véhicule publisher?[817] Seems a good guy. Hope I get better treatment than I got from Seymour Mayne & his phony Valley-editions.[818]

No, I wasn't offended at all. But probably in a torpid state worrying about Getting Things Done (autobiog, etc).

In Sask Richler was to get 1500 plus everything.

Never heard of Canadore College — is it an adjunct of Anndore Hotel on Charles St.?

Wailan & I rode the night train to Mtrl last Wed. I was duly de-littered in a morning convocation at McGill & we were well lunched at the Union (target of so many Leacock shafts); then the aft. went in book-dealing at the Double Hook (I brought them some copies of *Fall by Fury* since McStew makes no effort to sell it any more, nor even to enquire why *Sat Night* won't review it even though they originally published the title poem you like) and 3 hrs with Véhicule Press going over the ms & the contract. Then supper with the Eversons & Dudeks (Aileen Collins has now moved in with Louis), then the night train back again in time for a Friday workday.[819] We would have planed down but that costs twice as much, & McGill doesn't pay any expenses for honorary degree recipients, though they

---

816. "At Paricutin Volcano" was included in AP's *The Stone Bird* (1981).

817. Simon Dardick (b. 1943) published EB's *Spreading Time: Remarks on Canadian Writing and Writers* in 1980. A revised edition was issued in 1989.

818. EB's *Big Bird in the Bush: Selected Stories and Sketches* was published by Mosaic Press/Valley Editions in 1978.

819. Aileen Collins married Dudek in 1970. She edited the small literary magazine *CIV/n* in the early 1950s.

require the recipient to attend their convocation in person. I suppose that McGill has damn little money for anything at all nowadays. But I was glad to go down and see Frank & Marian [Scott] & Louis & the Eversons & Hugh MacLennan who gave the convocation address. In fact, McGill is the only university in Canada I respect enough, as a *writer*, to accept an honorary degree from.

Maybe we'll hear from you on your way to Hamilton or back — if not, maybe when we get back from Britain &c in Sep.

Love to you & Eurithe from us both.

Have a good summer.

Earle

To Birney (Toronto) from Purdy (Ameliasburgh)
June 16, 1979   TL[820]

Dear Earle,

What's *Spreading Time*? Essays, or what?

I don't know if I'd have your restraint re Hon. Degrees, since I don't have any. Why is McGill so noble?

As time passes I find I like people like Frank & Marian, the Eversons and even Dudek much better'n younger people. Is that me, growing old? I guess so. Still, one doesn't have the sense of people striving all the time, at least not in the same way as the young tryin to put down the old because the old have done something.

Yeah, I agree re McStew, they don't make much effort to sell. I took a look at their stacks on the way thru Toronto (since I had no books to sell at Brantford and Dundas) and found they were nearly out of everything of mine. Even the last one. Saw two boxes of *Being Alive* only. Altho they may keep that in print.

I could not give you a high enough opinion of the title pome of *Fall by Fury*, because compliments begin to sound like shit if piled on too much. But it's a pome I'd like to have written, but not fallen from a tree while showing off for Wailan in order to write the poem. I guess I said I liked the delicate small love pomes too, and others as well. They, the love poems, avoid the alternates of wild despair and wild joy, find that place where one seems to scarcely touch the loved one (christ that makes me think of Waugh), the delicacy for which there seems so little time.[821]

I have some recent poems I'd like to show you, but I'd like to watch your face when you read them so I can read behind the poker face.

We have, incidentally, another bedroom here now, a private one, but it has

---

820. AP typed the letter on stationery from the Hotel López, Cozumel. He added a note in reference to a slogan on the letterhead ("paraiso [*sic*] tropical del Caribe"): "Grimy little tropical town, no paraiso, tho —."

821. Evelyn Waugh (1903–66): English novelist (*Decline and Fall*, 1928; *Brideshead Revisited*, 1945).

no floor yet. We hafta pour concrete for a floor this summer. Then can you come down again?

I may have mentioned some high school readings, and at a coupla them I mentioned Che Guevara, to find none of the kids knew him.[822] I felt deflated, time has passed me by I said to them, the wave of the future has expunged the past. (etc.)

Love to you & Wailan (say hi to her)

Al

To Purdy (Ameliasburgh) from Birney (London)
July 20, 1979   AA

Dear Al

No typewriter. You'll have to endure my script. I took yrs of 16 June along to "answer," as we say — what is to answer? Query re *Spreading Time*: Title of a Sarah Binks poem.[823] Essays? Yes, with autobiogcl intro. & linkings — my life wih CanLit etc — Trying to manure the Bush Farm with critical shit 1925–80 or maybe –79, as Si Dardick wants it out this year. But I'm still writing the links.

Not even doing that since July — 4 days packing, pulling all furniture from walls to centre — second time (first was for cockroach campaign, second so painters can decorate the flat while we're away) — then 7 days with a rented car in Burns country & The Border, then up east coast via Edinburgh, St Andrews, to Aberdeen & by plane to Shetland — had a good evening with Derry Jeffares (the Yeats man) & a day-trip into the Cairngorms with my Aberdeen cousins.[824] In Shetland we couldn't spend money; the islands are full of relatives; islands are incestuous places but very hospitable — we had only 3 days but saw a lot, from the billion-pound oil town to the puffins & fulmars on the thousand-foot cliffs.

Question — are you growing old, because you get fonder of older people? — Of course — older people, like me, are wiser, better-natured, funnier — there have to be *some* dividends to go with arthritis, insomnia & forgetfulness.

We are now in Herne Hill (London) with my old Trotskyist comrades from

---

822. Ernesto "Che" Guevara (1928–67): Argentine Marxist revolutionary and guerilla who figured prominently in the Cuban Revolution. AP's "Hombre," from *Wild Grape Wine*, describes him: "I remember his grip particularly / firm but perfunctory / for he had many hands to shake that day." AP met Guevara in Cuba in 1964. In a later version of the poem an additional line appears in this passage: "firm but perfunctory / half politician and half revolutionary" (*BR* 139).

823. Sarah Binks: "The Sweet Songstress of Saskatchewan" — the subject of a fictional biography (*Sarah Binks*, 1947) by Paul Hiebert (1892–1987), a Canadian writer and professor of chemistry at the University of Manitoba.

824. A.N. Jeffares (1920–2005): Irish literary critic and a major commentator on the life and works of Yeats (*W.B. Yeats: Man and Poet*, 1949).

the Thirties. Bert [Matlow] is 81, Roma [Dewar] 73. I am on my annual gardening spree in their back[yard] & loving it — also getting back some muscle health — Lan is bussing & tubing all over Greater Lunnon for the hell of it. Soon we'll take some trips together on our Britrail passes, ending up in Prestwick & back in Toronto Aug 17. Send me some poems to the Toronto address. Hope you are getting lots of concrete poured, also poems. I'm glad you liked some of those things I wrote for Lan — Love to you both from us both.

Earle

To Birney (Toronto) from Purdy (Ameliasburgh)
August 3, 1979   TL[825]

Dear Earle,

Since your letter took two weeks to reach me, I'll mail this to Toronto. I enclose the two most recent pieces I like best. The first two lines of "Spinning" come from a letter from Colleen Thibaudeau.[826] I had a week of most intensive writing six weeks back, then stopped completely.

"Fathers" contains a neurosis of mine that doesn't show, but certain ages have seemed to me like deathly watershed, which I contemplated with extreme dislike, didn't even want to mention the possibility of reaching sixty.[827] Then realized that all I was I still am, I contain everything.[828]

Moving around the places I've been and lived in, old buildings spring up in place of new ones, trees leap into the air from their dust and ashes, a phoenix geology joins the present, and people I knew jump from their coffins and walk and talk. Of course this was always so, but never more so than now.

I expect you're enjoying putting this new book together — I suppose connecting the essays with what you feel now as well as the autobio stuff. I thought of doing the same thing myself, then doubted if it'd be worthwhile for me, or that anyone would want to read it, or publish it.

Just returned from Cape Breton (Baddeck) where there was a gathering of Scots Gaelic poets, all of them gargling thru their porridge when reading poems. One Ian [sic] Crichton Smith, was pretty good tho.[829] Ron Sutherland was there

---

825. *YA* 305–08.

826. Colleen Thibaudeau (1925–2012): Canadian poet (*The Artemesia Book: Poems Selected and New*, 1991) and writer of short stories. Thibaudeau and James Reaney were married in 1951. She has been described by Stan Dragland (e.g., in his contribution to *Al Purdy: Essays on His Works* [2002], edited by Linda Rogers) as "Canada's least-known important poet."

827. "Fathers" was included in AP's *The Stone Bird* (1981). It was dedicated to Ron Everson.

828. AP perhaps intended to evoke Walt Whitman's "Song of Myself": "I am large, I contain multitudes."

829. Iain Crichton Smith (1928–98): Scottish poet (*Collected Poems*, 1992) and novelist (*Consider*

with his pipes and kooky kids. I bought all the Scots' books and they bought mine.

Birney is wiser, funnier — but better-natured? Well, maybe. I prefer to think of you as a bit acerbic, not to be pushed around much. You may have mellowed, but not much. And I just had a letter from Alan Twigg in Vancouver saying he thought I ought not to adopt my "crotchety old man" persona when reading poems.[830] Now am I that? I hope not in either case. But a little acerbic I regard as desirable; it prevents silly questions from an audience. Still, I do find myself growing a bit sentimental in some ways, and maybe "Spinning" is that.

I'm sitting in work room drinking the last of chokecherry wine, and it's so hot you wouldn't believe. In fact too hot to continue.

I hope to see you in Toronto on your return, if I don't melt down into my shoes in the meantime.

Yours
Al

Fathers

This year I realized my dead father
was sixty when he died and I am sixty
but it's a year like any other year

(The annuals in our garden
are only two months old
just babies in the arms of earth
our perennial peonies are fifteen years
and fifteen years I've watched them rise
in scarlet jets from earth
and still I wonder — what does it all mean?)

He was fifty-eight and suddenly
became an unexpected father
with a look on his face in old snapshots
as if he'd never enjoyed himself much
and two years later he was dead

---

the *Lilies*, 1968) who wrote in both Gaelic and English.

830. Alan Twigg (b. 1952): Canadian literary journalist, historian of literature in British Columbia (*First Invaders: The Literary Origins of British Columbia*, 2004), and author of books on various topics of regional interest.

In 1919 the year after the first war
there must have been several times
when the baby face and old serious one
looked at each other like blank coins
a thought registered a look stamped itself
something now forgotten was interchanged

There is a strength comes from fathers
(a different strength than women)
they are both annual and perennial
but unlike marigold and crocus
they dance under the skin of earth
with a clicking of ancient teeth together
the rattle of bare bones

For Earle & Wailan
with all the best
Al Purdy

Spinning
for Colleen Thibaudeau

"Can't see out of my left eye
nothing much happens on the left anyway"
— you have to spin around right quickly
then just catch a glimpse
of coat tails leaving the room
(lace doilies on the settee)
light foot rising and disappearing
the last shot fired at Batoche
or maybe it was Duck Lake
— thought I saw someone I knew
and turned faster and faster
said wait for me
it was my grandmother I never knew
before I was born she died
— sometimes I turned fast enough
and nearly caught up with the sun
it bounded like a big red ball

forward and then went backwards
over the mountains somewhere
— thought I saw someone I knew
she was young in an old summer
I tried to remember very carefully
balanced on one foot
and concentrated and concentrated
lightfoot white feet in the long grass
running to meet her lover
I couldn't stop turning then
wait for me wait for me

Al Purdy

For Earle & Wailan — a Proustian pome? — at any event, a fantasy

best
Al Purdy

To Birney (Toronto) from Purdy (Ameliasburgh)
August 20, 1979   TL[831]

Dear Earle,

I take it you're home now. Reason I drop you this note needs a bit of explaining. A while back someone sent me a dozen or so pictures of Can. writers, you among them, of which I decorated my wall with four. You, [Margaret] Laurence, [Roderick] Haig-Brown and [Pierre] Berton. I'm just noticing now a peculiarity about your poster which I can only think is deliberate.

There is a mountain climber, presumably you, clambering around inside what looks very much like a woman's vagina. Did you ever really get in that far, is the question I've wanted to ask since noticing? What's it like?

Most sincerely,
Al Purdy

To Purdy (Ameliasburgh) from Birney (Toronto)
August 28, 1979   TL

Dear Mr. Purdy,

Enclosed please find, ah, no seats left, sorry, Al, how are yuh? Found yr Aug 3

---

831. *YA* 308.

letter with pomes when I got to the bottom of my 2-pd. mailbag; while I was scrabbling, hoping for a cheque, another missive came darting through the mail slot from "most sincerely, Al." This second (& I thought not very sincere) message suggested that you are being beset by the sort of visual hallucination often occurring in *delirium tremens*. Prolonged, repetitive stimulation of the limbic system (v. Carl Sagan: *The Dragons of Eden*) stirs irrational fears followed by depression, sense of failure in comparison with the achievements of others (e.g. seeing in the poster of a good friend — one of wide and happy sexual as well as alpine experience — the taunting image of a mountaineer conquering a vast vagina).[832] All my self-portraits are packed away but I don't need to hunt them out to be certain you are simply using an innocent representation of me as a Rorschach Test & then giving way to neurotic terror at the sight of your own obsessional delirium.

How are you otherwise? It would be good to see you. When will you be in Toronto again?

Interested in your remarks about the Gaelic gathering, as I had the task of recommending (to the CC) the four who were imported for the occasion, after considering about a dozen others. I would have liked to have met them.

I'm surprised anyone thinks of you as a "crotchety old man" — crotchety middle-aged man, perhaps, except that you are too firmly rooted in a marvelously creative & hopefully permanent adolescence to be accused of any sort of oldness. Leave crotchets to piano-players like me, drink sparingly your chokecheerycherry & sing me, when next you come, the best of your woodnotes wild.[833]

I like "Fathers" & reproach myself I haven't written my fatherpome yet (will I ever? or a granmother [*sic*] one?). I get lost in "Spinning" probably my own fault. Perhaps the dedication gets me on a sidetrack. I think if I understood it I would like it very much.

I haven't written a fucking thing.

Thanks for inscribing the sheets to us. Wailan would say thanks too but she is away with her Plutonic family for the annual 2-week visit. Back on Lab[our]. Day. I batch & try to answer letters. Not very successfully. But I mean well.

Love to Eurithe too.

Earle

---

832. Carl Sagan (1934–96): American scientist, television broadcaster (*Cosmos: A Personal Voyage*, 1980), novelist (*Contact*, 1985), and writer of popular works about scientific topics (*The Dragons of Eden: Speculations on the Evolution of Human Intelligence*, 1977).

833. EB's allusion was to Milton's "L'Allegro": "Or sweetest Shakespeare, Fancy's child / Warble his native wood-notes wild."

To Birney (Toronto) from Purdy (Ameliasburgh)
September 14, 1979 TL[834]

Dear Earle,

Take a look at that picture of you in *Famous Canadians, Writers Series* thing —
you are definitely exploring somebody's vagina, on your way to fallopia.

I was in Toronto Monday, for lunch with Harold Engel, and had to rush right
back to have a tooth pulled.[835] Blood didn't clot right after return from Belleville,
and I bled profusely. Mouth fulla blood isn't very comfortable or conducive to a
serene mind. Had to rush back to Belleville again. Roots of tooth must've been
phallic as hell. (See what you bring on with your own explorations?) Coupla days
later seem okay, but sure did lose a lotta blood. A gusher, rather terrifying too.

Two-three days before that I had written a poem that keeps quoting itself
in my head, at least two or three lines. Very satisfying feeling, to have yourself
surprise yourself. Also wrote a short imitation of Gustafson, "Inside Gus," not a
parody, straight imitation.[836] Sent it to Ralph, whereupon he immediately sends me
one back, an imitation of himself. We really are getting inbred.

Yeah — heard a bit of this Carl Sagan — is he good? Saw him on tv once.

Yes, "Spinning": first two lines were in a letter from Thibaudeau, and since I
used em was duty-bound to dedicate it to her. When I read those two lines, immediately thought: okay, can't see much on the left, what if one turned right quickly,
what magical things in the past might be seen? And that's the poem, really. What
you can't see on the left you can just catch a glimpse of on the right, "of coat tails
leaving the room" … It's mental legerdemain of course, and also has to do with the
feeling sometimes that you just missed seeing something important to you, that if
your sight had been keener or you had been more perceptive, you might have seen
creation at work, apart from an old girl friend.

The Gaels were all understated, and Sorley MacLean was hypnotized by the
lectern, danced around it with eyes closed for some forty minutes.[837] One couldn't
understand a word he said either English or Gaelic. Iain Smith was probably best,
I thought. But I wasn't taken with any of them, really. Have their books, and in
their translations to English they seemed locked into that rigid English way of
writing poems, either metrical or seeming so even if not. I wouldn't know about

---

834. *YA* 311–12. EB's handwritten note on the letter: "4 Oct 79 answered by pc."

835. Howard Engel (b. 1931): Canadian writer of mystery novels and producer for the CBC.

836. "Inside Gus" was included in *The Stone Bird* (1981).

837. Sorley MacLean (1911–96): Scottish poet (*From Wood to Ridge: Collected Poems in Gaelic and
English*, 1989) who wrote primarily in Gaelic. In a letter to F.R. Scott (3 Aug. 1979) recounting his trip
to Cape Breton, AP wrote that "Gaelic seems to me gargling thru porridge, and finally strangling thru
excess of consonance. One Scot, Sorley MacLean, hypnotized himself, and wandered inside a three
foot circle of the lectern with his eyes shut" (*YA* 304).

their Gaelic, and they disclaimed their English versions as not equal, which always seems to me a nice out. Of course I was their exact opposite, being not under-stated at all, as you know. And Ron Sutherland was there with his pipes, and I love the pipes. Afterwards we went to visit the Percys in Granville Ferry [Nova Scotia] farther south, ate scallops, raspberries and lobster.[838]

Eurithe is off to Vancouver, nursing her sister, or rather looking after her, since the sister is taking some kind of treatment in Van. and needs help. That's Norma whom I believe you met. Agoraphobia is her ailment, means fear of the vagina.

I'll be in Toronto to tape some poems next month, and hope to see you then. Everything gets sandwiched between readings seemingly, some six or seven this fall. I'm writing very little myself, just the odd poem. All the drive I thought I had seeming to be dissipated in small everyday things, small concerns and uncelestial trivia.

love to you both,

Al

To Purdy (Ameliasburgh) from Birney (Toronto)
October 4, 1979   APC

Dear Al,

Hope no more gushing from roots — leave that to oilmen & Arthur [sic] Haley — hope you're not still eating your own cooking & Norma back now on her own wheels.[839] Also hope you will have time for non-CBC employees this time you come to the Big Crabapple. Give the old geezer on the Shelf a ring — someday you may be him.

This card is to be pinned where you can see it, and think about the Decay of Civilization in the West while sitting on your one-holer.[840]

Wailan very busy with crash courses & exams — the home stretch — What odds on the Bucs for W. Series?[841]

Luv

E

---

838. H.R. (Bill) Percy (1920–97): Canadian novelist (*Painted Ladies*, 1983), writer of short stories, and literary biographer.

839. Alex Haley (1921–92): American writer (*The Autobiography of Malcolm X*, 1965). EB's allusion was to Haley's *Roots: The Saga of an American Family* (1976).

840. The postcard, from Newcastle-on-Tyne, is illustrated by a reproduction of "Latrines at Housesteads Fort, by R. Embleton," No. 9 in the "Roman Wall Cards" series.

841. The Pittsburgh Pirates (i.e., the Buccaneers) defeated the Baltimore Orioles to win the World Series, four games to three. The first game was played on 10 Oct. 1979.

To Birney (Toronto) from Purdy (Ameliasburgh)
November 11, 1979   TL

Dear Earle,

Here's the letter form I asked you to write for me. I know it's an imposition on your time, and I hate asking people to write such letters. But what can one do?

I'm overdue with this supporting letter and application (I forgot about it, that it was due in Oct.), so I'd appreciate your attention.

Good to see you the other night. And I do expect to be following your lead re reading fees. Best to Wailan.

Al

Earle, a carbon — one line added. Does that make it more understandable? Al

The Dead Poet

I was altered in the placenta
by the dead brother before me
who built a place in the womb
knowing I was coming
he wrote words on the walls of flesh
painting a woman inside a woman
whispering a faint lullaby
that sings in my blind heart still

The others were lumberjacks
backwoods wrestlers and farmers
their women were meek and mild
nothing of them survives
but an image inside an image
of a cookstove and the kettle boiling
— how else explain myself to myself
where does the song come from?

Now on my wanderings:
at the Alhambra's lyric dazzle
where the Moors built stone poems
a wan white face peering out
— and the shadow in Plato's Cave

remembers the small dead one
— at Samarcand in pale blue light
the words came slowly from him
— I recall the music of blood
on the Street of the Silversmiths

Sleep softly spirit of earth
as the days and nights join hands
when everything becomes one thing
wait softly brother
but do not expect it to happen
that great whoop announcing resurrection
expect only a small whisper
of birds nesting and green things growing
and a brief saying of them
and know where the words came from[842]

To Birney (Toronto) from Purdy (Ameliasburgh)
November 14, 1979[843]   TL

Dear Earle,

Yes, I'm sorry too that Wailan was so busy.

It bothers me a little that you don't quite get that third verse. Take this proposition: if you have a brother who died before you were born, and whom you say influences your writing, isn't it also (il)logical that he should help you and that you should hear him in your travels? — on the Street of the Silversmiths, in Samarcand etc.???

Of course Plato's Cave is slightly different: I meant to refer to myself as a shadow of life, without carrying it any further — which I could do. But as the shadow in Plato's Cave, the shadow of his life if you prefer, I do remember "the small dead one." Does that help any?

Of course you have integrity: you are also cantankerous and all the other qualities that I have myself. I'd like to write a poem about you sometimes, but it seems tremendously difficult to me, or else I haven't got a concept that would work.

You are so stingy with your words I'm gonna be too. Incidentally, I'm sorry you don't wanta meet the gal I mentioned, whom I think you'd enjoy. It's your loss and hers too.

---

842. "The Dead Poet" was published in AP's *The Stone Bird* (1981).
843. *YA* 313. EB's handwritten note on the letter: "sent card from SF 17 Dec 79."

You know, for a while I was reading "Fall by Fury" at my own readings? (Credit to Birney, of course.) I still think that veddy English "fortnight" was wrong in the poem — or was it "fortnight"?

love
Al

To Purdy (Ameliasburgh) from Birney (Toronto)
November 15, 1979   APC

Well it was a pleasure to perjure my soul for you, as you have so often for me to our Holy Mother the Can Cow — I said you are the Undefeated Muhammad Ali of Canadian Poets, the Bob-Dylan-Thomas of our Reader Stars, etc. But you should have got it in on time. I hope very much, despite your tardiness & my dubious recommendations, that you will get it.

Love
Earle

To Purdy (Ameliasburgh) from Birney (Toronto)
November 29, 1979   TL[844]

Dear Al

Your letters deserve thoughtful answers. Forgive me if I don't really answer your last one till I get some real time — which may be in California, where we go for a break on the 15th, & where I'll be putting in some "research" too. Before I leave I have to finish proofing one book & finish writing another. In between house-keeping shopping trying to write a pome etc.

You know what it's like. Meantime have a good Winter Solstice you two & a glorious Hogmanay.

Love
Earle

To Purdy (Ameliasburgh) from Birney (San Francisco)
December 17, 1979   APC

We're in a Basque workers' hotel in Chinatown, & I'm hunting up friends &c of fifty years back. Expect to get down to San Diego for Xmas & in Vancouver for a few days after New Year's.

---

844. EB dated his note "29 XII 1979," but the contents and the following letter suggest that the date was an error. ("XII" probably should have been "XI.")

Back in Toronto on 7th.

I hear you are going to be the Archdruid at the next Eisteddfod. I suppose meantime you & Eurithe bask on tropical beaches. Have a wonderful 1980.

Love from us both

Earle

Yes, "The Dead Poet" is clear now, I think, & *good*.

To Birney (Toronto) from Purdy (Ameliasburgh)
January 3, 1980   TL

Dear Earle,

Just a note a few days prior to leaving here.

I am assailed by arthritis in right knee, so far less able to perambulate than you right now. Still, I'm writing a few poems, but nothing much that appeals to me.

I hear from Jack McC that he's gonna reprint *Being Alive* with a different cover, and *Selected* instead of *Poems 1958–78*. They allowed me to change one poem. I felt like sayin thank you very much to Jack on the phone. Doin me quite a favour.

We're gonna drive to Mexico first and soak my knee in the waters near Ajijic. I wouldn't be good for anything if we went to Galapagos first. We can fly from Mexico City to Guayaquil and Peru.

Been writin reviews for *TorStar*, one of Lawrence's letters, another on Layton and Lee, and a third on dirty songs from the last war. I'm still supposed to do an Auden bio if it gets here in time.

Yeah, the Welch thing — only way I could get to Britain without payin.[845]

Take care of yourself this winter, you and Wailan.

Love

Al & Eurithe

To Purdy (Ajijic) from Birney (Toronto)
February 18, 1980   TPC

Dear Al,

Maybe this'll reach you b4 you & Eurithe take off for those lizards & Darwinian finches. Hope you have fun, Eurithe, & that you write some reptilian pomes, Al — also that your arthritis is gone — don't get *TorStar* so I've missed yr reviews. We

---

845. See EB's postcard of 17 Dec. 1979. AP's "the Welch thing" was EB's "the next Eisteddfod."

spent 3 wks in SF & San Diego. Mainly looked up some pals of 50 yrs ago. Lan gets admitted to Bar in April but will start working even before that, middle Mar., so we'll be here if you happen back this way. You shd have great pix, suntans, pomes, memories, etc. I'm busy with my Canlittering book [*Spreading Time*], & articles for *BC Outdoors*. Love to both from us both.

Earle

To Birney (Toronto) from Purdy (Ameliasburgh)
June 1, 1980   TL

Dear Earle,

Wanted to say how much I enjoyed your piece in *Books in Canada*.[846] And you know, I still like "Drake's Drum."[847] Especially when I remember a cartoon with Davie Fulton and others of Dief's lieutenants pointing a cannon down the hatch of a fifteenth century ship saying: (to Dief) "Captain, art tha sleepin there below?"[848]

And Wilson MacDonald's ego is still visible today in Canada, in Layton especially. However, I do think the present situation a bit different, since there seems to be several poets here that if not better than Br. or U.S. poets, at least are not much worse. However, we still do a lot of tub-thumping for home-grown products; and other countries still pay us little heed. Still, I think a few of Layton's, a few of yours and some of Atwood's can hold their own. Probably Klein too, tho he is much more mannered.

I wonder if anyone remembers Garnett Sedgewick now, as you do? Fifty years ago?

It was pleasant to see you and Wailan in Toronto — when was it? — three weeks back now.

Al

---

846. EB's article ("Bliss of Solitude: How Carman Wandered Lonely as a Clod and Sir Henry Shot His Jingoistic Bolt when High Culture Came Hilariously to a West Coast, Cow College in the 1920s") appeared in *Books in Canada* (May 1980). It was adapted from *Spreading Time: Remarks on Canadian Writing and Writers*. In the article EB recalls "Drake's Drum," a "jingle" by the English poet Henry Newbolt (1862–1938), who visited UBC in 1922. EB wrote that "The Bombast of Sir Henry Newbolt and the turgidities of T. Sturge Moore left me cold." Wilson MacDonald (1880–1967), a Canadian poet (*The Song of the Prairie Land and Other Poems*, 1918) and popular reciter of verse, also came to UBC while EB was a student. EB was unimpressed: "MacDonald was even worse than Newbolt." In the article EB also described Garnett Sedgewick, whose course in English literature he took in 1923. Sedgewick (1882–1949) was a Shakespearean scholar (*Of Irony, Especially in Drama*, 1935) and Head of English at UBC from 1920 to 1948. A renowned teacher and campus eccentric, he made a tremendous impression on EB, who called him "the most brilliant and inspiring teacher I ever encountered, and one of the finest of human beings." Sedgewick supervised EB's graduating essay on Chaucerian irony.

847. AP appears to have typed "Drake's Drunk" and then corrected his mistake.

848. E. Davie Fulton (1916–2000): Conservative Member of Parliament for Kamloops (1945–68) and Minister of Justice (1957–62). After his political career he was a justice of the Supreme Court of British Columbia (1973–81).

To Purdy (Ameliasburgh) from Birney (Toronto)
June 6, 1980   AL

Dear Al

Where at's this Ridgetown? Seems they must have crossed a Percheron with a muskox.[849] Thanks for good words about *Bks in Can* article — did you see the stuff in *Q&Q*? (livelier, I think) & *CF*? (duller).[850] Your Hall of Fame (north annex) conspicuously lacks its biggest statue, engraved Purdy the Peerless ... As for the under-forty generation, there's considerable quality, but only a few have quantity yet. (Quantity might put some older ones into your Hall, too, if they ever produce it: Webb, Page, Newlove.) I think Lane & Ondaatje have made it already. No?

Sedgewick — Anybody still alive who took English from him up to 1948 remembers him with admiration & affection. That is, UBC students now over 50.

Got lots of Galapagodia? Submarine lizard books? Darwinnowings? Finchirrups? What's happening there in Ameliasburghundy?

Come & see us again — but not in July, when we're on the other side of that pond.

Earle

To Birney (Toronto) from Purdy (Ameliasburgh)
June 11, 1980   TL[851]

Dear Earle:

Never heard of Ridgetown. The hoss has quite a figure tho.

Didn't see *Q.Q.*, on accounta Belleville doesn't have it and I don't sub.[852]

I'd never include myself in any H. of F., up to other people to do that if they think I should be there.[853]

I doubt that Webb, Page or Newlove will make it. Page seems to have written her best before; Webb (and I love her) just seems doubtful; Newlove is paranoid and nursing a broken hip and a bottle out west. Ondaatje tho is writing very well,

---

849. The letter was written in a notecard from the Royal Ontario Museum, Toronto. AP commented upon the reproduction of a painting of a horse ("Sunbeam," by J.J. Kenyon) in his letter of 11 June 1980.

850. EB's "Canlittering with the *Forum*: 1936–42" appeared in *The Canadian Forum* (Apr. 1980). Excerpts from *Spreading Time: Remarks on Canadian Writing and Writers* were published in *Quill and Quire* (May 1980) as "Birney Recounts Growing Up with CanLit."

851. *YA* 326–327. The letter was typed on stationery from The Coach House Motor Inn, North Vancouver, BC. At the bottom of the page is a slogan: "old-fashioned hospitality at old-fashioned prices." AP circled "old-fashioned prices" and added a question mark.

852. EB's note on his copy of the letter: "Sent him a *Q&Q* [*Quill and Quire*] Xerox 23.VI.80."

853. "H. of F." was probably "Hall of Fame" (see EB's letter of 6 June 1980) or possibly "House of Fame," an allusion, as Sam Solecki has suggested, to Chaucer's poem of that name (*YA* 327 n.1).

but is a private poet only. *Billy the Kid* seems a tour de force to me.[854] Mike's private concerns are most important to him, which is fine. But to be a world poet, so-called, I think you hafta come from a country a place and a time, and be somewhat involved in those concerns. Of course you can easily refute that concept, but it's mine and I'm stuck with it.

Mentioning Sedgewick, I was thinking that fully half or perhaps more of the kids I went to school with are dead.

I have four poems deriving from the Galapagos, none of more than passing interest.[855]

Darwin's Theology

Stand under the great sky round
    circling these islands
where the absence of a god
leaves a larger vacuum
than a presence could fill
with a presence
sea and sky completely occupied
by the non-existent monster

                —Galapagos Islands

                    See you in Toronto
                           Al

To Purdy (Ameliasburgh) from Birney (Tangier)
July 14, 1980   APC

Dear Al,

I thought you'd like to see behind the veils (above) & me escaping from tourists in the Grand Socco.[856]

We'll be back come August & hope to see you, both. Thanks for note.

                           E

---

854. *The Collected Works of Billy the Kid: Left Handed Poems*, by Michael Ondaatje (1970).

855. "Birdwatching at the Equator," "Moses at Darwin Station," "Darwin's Theology?," and "Moonspell" were published in *The Stone Bird* (1981). In the letter, "Darwin's Theology" did not have the question mark in the title.

856. The postcard shows images of "Typical Morocco" — women in traditional dress and a market scene. The women are not wearing veils; a man in the market bears a passing resemblance to EB.

To Birney (Toronto) from Purdy (Ameliasburgh)
November 18, 1980   TL

Dear Earle:

Thanks for book [*Spreading Time*]. I've gone through it pretty thoroughly in the last coupla days. I like it, but I'm disappointed there isn't more personal stuff. I was hoping for autobiography. Personal adventures in the world and all that. But I sure do get a good idea what Birney has been doin literarily, his opinions, etc.

Me young? What shit! I'm now an abandoned old man, Eurithe off to Vic. [Victoria, BC] to be a nursemaid for her sister. But she's more a business partner than wife in most ways anyway.

I am pleased to see you getting all this stuff written, since it becomes the lithist [literary history] of the country. And presumably you will be writing more personal things later. What happened to you in the war, for instance? What about those stories about meeting the I.R.A. in Ireland; Roberts selecting his next lady at the pub of the Royal York or wherever it was?[857]

I applaud your work at *C.P.M.*, which I hadn't fully comprehended until I read your account of it, and all the difficulties. Gibbon and O'Brien particularly.[858] Of course the first chapter and the first part of the book really are more personal. But where's the girl you had the wrestling match with in the Kootenays?

Am I being too critical? I don't mean to be, for I do like the book, and think it a good thing to have written it. But there is a more colourful Birney that I know about, even tho I also know he can't say everything about his personal life. For instance, that time when we knocked on the door of Ikuko's apartment in Vancouver, when you said to the super, "I'm her professor, I'm responsible for her in this country." As it turned out, you sure were responsible. Or when you talked that gal right outa bed with her boy friend and onto your knee, while I gawked wonderingly. Yes, I know, some things can't be said.

Okay, it's good and interesting, one man's odyssey in the forest of clichés that was CanLit.

I expect to be leaving for Mexico around the middle of Dec., but hope to see you before then. Say hi to Wailan. Take care of yourself.

Al

---

857. See AP's letter of 14 Apr. 1978.

858. John Murray Gibbon (1875–1952): Editor of *Canadian Poetry Magazine*, publicity agent for the Canadian Pacific Railway, musicologist, and author (*Canadian Mosaic: The Making of a Northern Nation*, 1938). A.H. O'Brien (1865–1957): Lawyer in Toronto and business manager for *Canadian Poetry Magazine*. EB saw Gibbon and O'Brien as obstacles to the success of the journal; he described O'Brien as "senile" in *Spreading Time: Remarks on Canadian Writing and Writers*.

Dear Al

I want to thank you most warmly and sincerely for that letter, and for the trouble and time you took to go through the book [*Spreading Time*]. You probably read Fetherwit's [Douglas Fetherling's] *Satnite* rev or perhaps you just hoped I wouldn't stick so close to the limitations imposed by the subtitle (Fetherbrain, however, confessed he hadn't noticed there was a subtitle).[859] But you are pleased I wrote it, which is good — so often I've depressed myself thinking what a bloody waste of my time, when I have so little left. Yes, I do certainly intend to write more & more "personal things" once these peripheral books are out, if I'm still alive. I've thought about a war memoir & the Fisher has about a thousand pages of records I kept while a personnel officer overseas — copies of my interviews with soldiers — but I've despaired of using them, because the people might be identified, and if I start changing names, places, etc., I lose the documentary punch, the authenticity of the cross-section of Canadian youth in the Army in England, Belgium, Holland, Italy — my personal career in the war was nothing, but those records are unique.[860] (& even the personal stuff involves people still alive who might make trouble.)

The same is true of course of my amatory adventures. The Ikuko story, my side of it, is all down in a marathon letter I wrote Giose Rimanelli, & kept a copy, also in the Fisher (restricted section). It's a record of my own infatuation, & her elaborate "use" of me and everyone else who came her way. A novelette of my folly and ultimate misery.

The I.R.A. story will be in the Trotsky book (still unfinished), which will also have the Utah days (mine strikes, etc.), the Trotsky conversations, getting jailed in Hitler's Berlin, etc.

Some of the Roberts anecdotes should have been in *Spreading*. Believe it or not I just forgot to put them in!

The girl of the wrestling match appears in one of a series of reminiscences of my high school days, appearing in *B.C. Outdoors* mag — 4 installments, Sep-Dec 80. This is a MacLean-Hunter mag but seems to circulate not at all east of the Rockies. I'll send you a Xerox, as it will be a long time before I can get free to

---

859. The subtitle is *Remarks on Canadian Writing and Writers*. Fetherling's lukewarm review of *Spreading Time* ("Birney's Struggle to Find a Literature") was published in *Saturday Night* (July/Aug. 1980). He wrote that "the total effect is that of a missed opportunity." Fetherling's version of events is included in his *The Writing Life: Journals 1975–2005* (2013); it ends with a phone call to "soothe his [EB's] aged ego a bit."

860. "the Fisher": the Thomas Fisher Rare Book Library at the University of Toronto.

fatten those 4 articles out into the small book I intend (title: *Coming of Age in Erickson, BC*).[861]

Hope you are "eating well" — the standard solicitous wish for a grass widow. Send me your Mexican address, if you have one. How long will you be down there? We'd love to go down but Lan gets no more holidays till next summer. Will Eurithe join you down there or are you really "abandoned"? Do come and see us before you go. There's always the pull-out bed in the front room for you.

No of course you weren't being "too critical." Very sparing, in fact. Bill French was tougher but quite reasonable, I think.[862] The truth is I'm gambling on living (& writing) for another 5 years at least.

Am deep in the book for M&S, deadline is Jan., title: *Malc Lowry & Dylan Thomas in Vancouver*.[863]

The best from us both

Earle

To Birney (Toronto) from Purdy (Ameliasburgh)
January 4, 1981   TL

Dear Earle:

I wrote you a card from Florida, gave it to Eurithe; when we got back here I discover the same card unmailed. Ah well, it was nothing more than a greeting anyway. When we got to the hotel at St. Petersburg, Ron Everson and Lorna were already there. We drove with them back to New Smyrna for an enjoyable few days, then back to St. Pete's for departure. But the weather was awful, very little sun for me to disguise my dead white colour with. (I do hate being such a pale white colour — or lack of colour — and would like to have been born a nice mahogany or bronze, apart from the racial consequences that is.)

After the flurry of getting book ready last August I've written little or nothing, which I expect is the menopause of some kind. The contract for which you gave me advice has gone to a lady named Marian Hebb, who is a lawyer and works sometimes for the writers' union.[864]

---

861. Four articles were published in *BC Outdoors*: "Coming of Age in Erickson, B.C." (Sept. 1980), "A Chancy Venture" (Oct. 1980), "Hot and Cold" (Nov. 1980), and "A Camping Week" (Dec. 1980). The "small book" was never published.

862. In his review in *The Globe and Mail* ("Mosaic Biography: Earle Birney's Odd Look Back at 45 Years of CanLit," 22 Nov. 1980), William French called *Spreading Time* "an oddly unsatisfying book" that was "deficient as autobiography," even as it "provides a valuable look at the literary scene in this country in the thirties and forties."

863. The book was not completed.

864. Marian Hebb (b. 1939): Canadian lawyer specializing in copyright law and legal matters pertaining to the arts. As AP noted, she provided legal counsel to The Writers' Union of Canada.

On Tuesday we fly to Victoria, B.C., where we'll spend two or three months, instead of Mexico. Victoria because of Eurithe's sister, whom we both like, Norma (you've met her), who has agoraphobia, fear of Greek marketplaces. Sounds funny but it ain't funny. I hate to give up Mexico, because I wanted to write some travel essays there à la D.H. Lawrence. I regret now all the writings I didn't do in Mexico, since some experiences there were decidedly interesting. I wonder if I could write a coverall piece about Mexico, since my memory for specifics is partly fled? The impact of Mexico on me seems tremendous as I look back on it, the "foreignness" of it. Before one has travelled outside one's own country, the tendency is to take it for granted that all countries are more or less like your own. Whereas values and customs and mores are all different; it takes travel to sink that fact into your mind. And the Mexico I saw seems so different than the Mexico Graham Greene wrote about in *The Lawless Roads*, perhaps because of his fixation on Roman Catholicism.[865] And Mexico's impact on me similar to the feelings I had as a teenager, when I had such difficulty getting used to being alive, knowing what to expect from the strange world, learning to evade other people's fixed opinions and form my own. That may seem an odd comparison, but it was similar to landing on a strange planet where everything was completely different, and you had to act in a particular way to get by at all. Find out what was expected of you in order that you might or might not act according to those expectations. And the necessity for acting according to other people's expectations and custom is even stronger in a country like Mexico. People live according to some sort of fixed ritual. I would prefer, for instance, in hot countries, to dispense with clothes sometimes. Can you imagine the uproar if one did so. Or in Canada, say what one thinks about the weather or how one feels about almost anything. Such simple things, and yet one can't do it without creating disturbances.

I meant to just write a short letter about nothing in particular, and I see I've been maundering again. But reverting back to Mexico, I think of Tehuantepec — if that's the spelling — about which you have a poem. When I was there, and roasting nearly to death, I kept looking for those beautiful women you talked about in your poem, and didn't see any. Obviously they don't exist, eh? And there's a place in southern Cuba that's renowned for the same thing, green-eyed women. Oriente Province, if I remember right. What price romance? Or what about

---

865. Graham Greene (1904–91): English novelist (*Brighton Rock*, 1938; *The Heart of the Matter*, 1948; *The End of the Affair*, 1951), writer of short stories, playwright, and literary critic. Sam Solecki has identified Greene as one of AP's "favourite novelists": "He mentioned several times in conversations with me that he couldn't understand why Greene was never awarded the Nobel Prize" (*YA* 143 n.2). It is thus somewhat surprising that Greene's name appears only once in the correspondence gathered in this volume.

Tzin-tzun-tzan — Place of the Hummingbirds near Patzcuaro. And not a single damn hummingbird did I see.

love

Al

To Purdy (in Victoria, British Columbia, but the letter was sent to Ameliasburgh) from Birney (Toronto)
January 15, 1981   TL

Dear Al

Your good letter of the 4th has arrived as I was about to mail you *The Mammoth Corridors*. Both this note & the book should be waiting you when you get back to Ameliasburgh (you didn't give me your Victoria address or I'd send these west to you). The booklet is sent merely as a collector's item, as it contains nothing you haven't got. Sale is restricted to the U.S., edition of 500, copy no. 4. 80 copies went to U.S. friends & U.S. promotion or reviews. It's inconceivable there'd be a 2nd printing. So you should have something fairly scarce in Canada (copies nos. 1, 2, 3 went to me, Wailan & Marsha my d-in-law). Copy 5 to George Bowering. That leaves me with a hoard of half-dozen, for sale at some hugely inflated price or to mold on the shelf. However, since no more than 50 copies will ever be sold in the US, you'll eventually be able to buy handfuls of them at any Coles, Smith's, etc for 29 cents (price tag over "for sale only in the U.S.A.").

Anything you wrote on Mexico would be interesting but you have to remember that Mexican towns keep changing rapidly & you'll find yourself writing nostalgia rather than reportage. Those "fixed rituals" keep getting unfixed, except in our pomes, dreams, etc.

Greeting to Norma. Tell Joe Mandrillo [Rosenblatt] I'll be writing him. My best to Pat Page, Mike Doyle, Maxine Gadd & any other indigenous bards.[866] This in hope somebody's forwarding your mail.

And love from Wailan & me to Eurithe and you

E

---

866. Pat Page: i.e., P.K. (Patricia Kathleen) Page. Mike Doyle (b. 1928): Canadian poet (*Collected Poems 1951–2009*, 2010) and professor of English at the University of Victoria (1968–93). He has written about AP in various works, including "Proteus at Roblin Lake," an insightful essay in *Canadian Literature* 61 (Summer 1974). Maxine Gadd: (b. 1940): Canadian poet (*Lost Language: Selected Poems*, 1982) associated with the Vancouver art world and the experimental literary community.

To Birney (Toronto) from Purdy (Victoria)
January 20, 1981   TL

Dear Earle:

Many thanks for the new book. Seems to me a damn good selection for our bar sinister cousins. Glad you included "The Mammoth Corridors," even entitled the book that. The typos are annoying, I'm sure to you, but what the hell! — they don't interfere with enjoyment. It seems to me as good a selection, in fact a better short selection, as any others I've seen. (Now I see that I've fucked up the grammar of that last sentence by changing in mid-course.)

I'm sure I mentioned in my last letter why we came out here. But the new book is out; at least I've got an advance copy. I go back east Feb. 2 for a Harbourfront reading and probably some other drum beating. I haven't found any typos in *The Stone Bird*, but the cover sure isn't much. Half is an Eskimo carving, the rest my name in large letters and the title. My name unbalances the rest of the cover. A copy will go to you direct from McStew.

All the lush vegetation in this town makes my ascetic soul uneasy, somehow unearned increment for the eyes. In mid-winter yet. Few beers with Joe Rosenblatt at one time or another, a party at Robin Skelton's, some pool with bro-in-law, the extent of possible sinfulness here. The place is like calendar art, from which a lot of people with talent have fled and a lot of older people with money have replaced them.

At least I'm doing a lot of reading, for me. *The Old Patagonian Express*, by Paul Theroux; *D.H. Lawrence, Novelist*, F.R. Leavis (very tough to read, that last); *Life for Life's Sake*, Richard Aldington; a thriller by somebody, and one or two others. Now re-reading Birney. And bought a bunch of 1920s English poetry mags for two bits each, edited by Fowler Wright, in which Caresse Crosby had some poems. Only name I recognized. Remember Harry Crosby and Black Sun Press? — he committed suicide in N.Y. along with his mistress in 1929. Published Lawrence and Hart Crane.

Eurithe and I go to Campbell River next week for a reading at a local bookstore there. Friend, Jack Jackovich arranged it. Ex-football [player], painter, potter, fishing guide and sec. school teacher. Take your pick.

Anyway, I still hope to get to Mexico and do some travel writing, some damn thing anyway. Don't see that I'm doing any good here, since Norma (Eurithe's sister) remains about the same; besides, Eurithe is better looking after someone than I am. Hope to see you in Toronto, if Marta Kurc doesn't fill all my waking hours.[867]

Best to both of you.

Al

---

867. Kurc was a publicist at McClelland and Stewart.

To Purdy (Victoria) from Birney (Toronto)
January 23, 1981   APC

Dear Al,

Just got yrs. of 20th. Do make time to come & see me, have a bite, bed, whatever. But not on Feb. 2, when I'll be @ U. of Waterloo (back by aft. of 3rd).

Just got back from a good session @ UWO [University of Western Ontario] — had 150 out to a 2-hr. slide/talk on "concrete & audials" (intermedic [*sic*] stuff). & as many again to a straight read in the evening ... Hope *The Stone Bird* flies high (despite title, which sounds more like Phyllis Webb or Susan M. than Al P.).[868] I want to do one called *The Hoopoo Bird* (an Alabama fowl, I believe, that lays square eggs & shits tiles on the cotton pickers).

E.

To Purdy (Ameliasburgh) from Birney (Toronto)
February 5, 1981   APC

Dear Al

Apologies for not staying to see more of you after yr Harbour[front] reading — we'd been driven down there by the Allens, who had to leave right after, & we had to go with them — you had a good turnout — I liked the first poem best of all, as a reading poem, I think but it was good to feel you are still writing on top — thanks for your letter & I look forward to seeing the book — if possible, phone before you go back west.

Best from us both,
Earle

To Birney (Toronto) from Purdy (Ameliasburgh)
February 11, 1981   TL

Dear Earle,

Good to see you the other night in Toronto. I went on to Ottawa the next day and talked myself hoarse, then trained back here.

Did I mention that we bought a used car in Victoria, with the idea that we'd drive south to Mexico from there when I went back. Turns out the car isn't as good as we thought, and decided to sell it there. So Eurithe is out there tryin to do that. Presumably she will, and then we'll get out. But you remember we own this house in Trenton — well, there's been a drug bust there. So she has to look

---

868. "Susan M.": Probably Susan Musgrave.

after that too, decide about the tenants and so on. I don't take more than a passing interest or involvement in the place. Want to sell it and get it off our hands. Too damn old to both [bother?].

And I popped a guy in Victoria. He'd been insulting me all afternoon during the Super Bowl game at my bro-in-law's. Then he called me a piece of shit. So I hit him. No fuckin delay. Knocked him down, and was about to jump all over him when my bro-in-law pulled me off. No respect, that's what, my gray hairs mean nothing. Wished you were there so you could hit him with a crutch. But then you don't use em any more.

Anyway, expect you've got a book from McStew by now. I didn't know I'd be back east, so I gave Marta Kurc a list of people I wanted the book sent to.

Best to you and Wailan, in fact love,

Al

To Purdy (Ameliasburgh) from Birney (Toronto)
March 10, 1981   AL

Dear Al

Just a scribble — (busy with fucking book on Lowry etc.). Thanx for yours of 11th — hope you got the car sold & settled the Trenton house back into respectability — when will you get off to Mexico? — We're taking a 7-day holiday in San Miguel — flying out Mar 27, & back exactly a week later (cheap route by CP Air to MC & then hire a car & drive to SMA). Will be @ Hotel San Francisco on the Jardín, if you happen to come to SMA.

Your McStew book hasn't come yet — hope it's getting big sales.

I don't think I'll *ever* get this Lowry book finished.

O well.

Cheers —

Earle

Write us or come see soon.

To Purdy (Ameliasburgh) from Birney (Toronto)
June 15, 1981   APC

Dear Al —

Where & how are you? Have you written a hymn about Nazareth? Consider this [i.e., the postcard] a cue card —

Wailan & I got to an "exclusive" showing of the NFB film (Don Winkler, his producer, Lan & me in a cubbyhole on Adelaide) — the 20 or more hours they shot had been cut precisely to 58'17" & wrapped up so tight not even a syllable can be cut — take it or leave it.[869] You are in it, but no other poets — most of my friends are cut, & so are my son and grandsons & daughter in law — though the NFB spent 6 hours filming them. You'll see it all in Oct, maybe.

Earle

Eurithe not in, alas, nor Rita Allen (the crew spent a day shooting at her Uxbridge place!).

To Birney (Toronto) from Purdy (Ameliasburgh)
June 17, 1981   TL

Dear Earle:
Good the film is finished, sorry they cut it so much. Why don't you get the cuts (free, naturally), sell them to U. of T., and take a trip with Wailan around the world on the proceeds? But you've probably already thought of that, have the deal negotiated, and bought your airline tickets.

One word I can't make out on accounta the postmark. Have I *composed*, have I something about Nazareth? No, but why Nazareth? Also why 58'17", why not 59'5"?

Anyway, what a waste, all that film! You oughta get it.

I'm stuck here for the summer. Only visitor Norman Levine, whom I like.[870] Working on ten thousand word autobio thing, first ten years of life. Third draft now. Sick of it. Few poems.

McStew Sales told me *Stone Bird* was sold out. Then find they have "50 to 100" copies. So I ordered fifty. I am pissed off they didn't print more. Seems it was two thousand. I'd love to have it, the rights, revert back to me. Have visions of the thing sold out, and they not reprinting at all or else doing it a year down the road. When everybody's reading Birney or even D. Livesay. Couldn't stand that last tho. Too humiliating. But that's what happened to *Being Alive*, they reprinted after a year, when sales had lost all momentum. Why didn't I go to Oberon when I had the chance!

Did you hear any furrin poets besides the night you read yourself? I was interested to see what other people were doin, word games, surrealism, cover your

869. *Earle Birney: Portrait of a Poet* (1981), directed by Donald Winkler (b. 1940). Winkler also directed *Al Purdy: "A Sensitive Man"* (1988) and other films about literary subjects. He is also a translator of Québécois literature.

870. Norman Levine (1923–2005): Canadian writer known especially for his short stories and a travel memoir that is highly critical of Canada (*Canada Made Me*, 1958).

flanks with ambiguities, etc. Levertov, whom I admired ten years ago, seems to me repeating herself.[871]

Best to you and Wailan,

luv

Al

P.S. Come down. We're fixin a room for visitors.

To Purdy (Ameliasburgh) from Birney (Toronto)
September 25, 1981   APC

Dear Al

That film is on Oct 14, Harbourfront. I asked them to invite you & Eurithe to the 2nd showing (9 pm) — the first one is just for *hoi polloi*; the 2nd I read at & there's chow after. Hope you can make it, not because of the goddam film, but because it's so long since we've seen you.

I spend Mon & Tues. @ Londonont. or on train going/coming — except first week of Oct (Oct 4–9) when I'm reeding [*sic*] in BC.

Cheers

The Writher-in-Reticence

To Birney (Toronto) from Purdy (Ameliasburgh)
September 28 ("or so"), 1981   TL

Dear Earle,

Yeah, it seems a long time since we sat around with nothing to do but talk. And you don't write very many letters either. Also, taking advantage of your great age and infirm health, you won't come down here. Both of those are lousy excuses. You're younger'n I am, and could outrun me any day, esp. entering a bedroom.

By the way, we're going to U.K. on Oct. 4. Remember that Welsh exchange thing? Well, this is the Purdy half of it. I have various readings there, not sure of location of all of them. But apparently I'll work for my money. Anyway, we can't make it to see film, and see our shadows gabbing on the lawn at the bellybutton pond as you dubbed it.

Of all the odd things: I have a book coming in the Soviet Union. Seems they

---

871. Denise Levertov (1923–97): American poet (*The Jacob's Ladder*, 1961; *Selected Poems*, 2002; *The Collected Poems of Denise Levertov*, 2013) born in England and known for her association with the Black Mountain poets, her opposition to the war in Vietnam, and the Christian and ecological themes of her poetry.

just grab the poems and print em, no mention of money. Editor, guy name of Valery Minushin. Now you know damn near as much as me about it.

Another small book with Peter Brown at Paget Press, called *Galapagos Islands Poems, or Field Notes on the Great American Blue-Footed Booby.*[872] If there [is] any reflection of the character of our southern neighbours in that title, it's extremely deliberate. Will send along if and when etc.

I have an unsigned Birney book. I don't know how this strange thing did not come about. *Strait of Anian*, sitting demurely on the shelf here, blushing slightly on accounta its unsigned condition. I reckon the signed books here as around nineteen hundred at this point.

Did I mention selling work sheets to Queen's for quite a chunk of cash? I get four yearly instalments, which should take care of funeral expenses. Really, it does relieve one a little to have money coming, not that I've worried much for the last few years.

Dennis Lee was just down here. Seems he's in charge of the artistic at McStew. Jack must've unbuttoned his wallet to get Dennis. I am of course extremely unhappy with McStew, and a lunch with Jack didn't really help. I got a book back from Marty Gervais and sent it to McStew, figuring they'd turn it down and I'd be free. They accepted it, Jack did, not knowing it was scrapings after *Being Alive* was pubbed.

Dennis says it will conflict with that book (*Being Alive*), so they won't do it after all. Therefore, I am technically free, except there's this backlog of poems at McStew (*Being Alive* and *The Stone Bird*) which I can't take with me when I fly free into the sky. In other words, shit.

(I am continuing this letter in order to make you feel guilty about your goddam cards and non-communication generally.)

I've also just finished the fifth draft of an auto-bio thing called *Morning and It's Summer*, being an account of first ten years of life, wherein I escape with my skin after a disreputable beginning.[873] Jack McC. doesn't want it, so I must cast around for a publisher. Poems with it, including the one enclosed. Also old snapshots of various people in the narrative (it's 10,000 words).

Eurithe would like to go back to the Galapagos, and I guess I would too. Maybe we will this winter. Why don't you go in our directions sometimes, or vice-versa?

Love to both of you from Eurithe and I,

Al

---

872. *Birdwatching at the Equator: The Galapagos Islands Poems* was published by the Paget Press in a limited edition in 1982. The book, which contains seven poems and a short essay, is illustrated with photographs taken by Eurithe Purdy.

873. *Morning and It's Summer: A Memoir* was published by Quadrant Editions in 1983.

To Purdy (Ameliasburgh) from Birney (Toronto)
October 12, 1981   AL

Dear Al

Just so you won't "goddam" another card from me I write you on stationery I could never acquire (my legal partner brings this stuff back from consultative forays on Manhattan).

We are getting up courage to buy a car — if we do, & it lasts long enough, we'll no doubt drive it to Ameliasburg before the year is out — do let us know what weekend the Purdys will be receiving, before we set off as you didn't say when you'd be back from Wales. Are you returning by way of Galapagos or Baluchistan this time? Speaking of the former, I look forward to seeing your Paget Pr [Press] book (the sub-title is sort of wasted, tho — should be *the* title). Wish I had something coming up to promise in return, but my *Dylan etc* doesn't get finished, for various reasons. One of which is this 2-day commuting program to UWO [University of Western Ontario] (Mondays & Tuesdays from now till May, or ever to never). Another is a week in B.C. — just got back — Kwantlen, Kamloops, Kimon Fraser, Koobeesee, Kapilano, Krichmond etc. Read to Grades 3 & 4 in North Van (scraping the barrel in my old age) —

Did you call on the Arch-Druid in Cardiff this time? And can you pronounce Mynydd Eppynt now? And spell Llanarmondyffrynceiriog?

On 29 Oct, film will be @ John Abbott Coll. — maybe you can make it then.

Glad you made a good deal with Queen's — will be handy 40 years from now when you're writing your autobiog. Did you make an arrangement that gets you off the Income Tax hook? I understand this is now possible.

McStew is trying to remainder my *Fall* & *Ghost*, without using the dirty word of course — I can fight back only by buying more author copies & peddling them to high schools. If you've a chance to get out from that firm, take it!

Morning etc. sounds good — & the pix are almost *de rigueur* now — make sure you are getting McStew to make good reproductions.

Lan is with a new firm, a little more money, a lot more work. We had a great holiday on the West Coast — 31 days of August in sunshine — I gardened for my son, & for Lionel Kearns, & went swimming in the buff with the lovelies on Wreck Beach — & canoed beyond Sooke, & fished & picked Himalaya berries at Rona Murray's, & hiked up Capilano Canyon with Bill & Lan — saw the Woodcocks (they in great form), the Bowerings &&&.

Lan & I send you & Eurithe our love

Earle

To Birney (Toronto) from Purdy (Fort Pierce, Florida)
January 22, 1982   TL[874]

Dear Earle:

Thanks for your letter and invite. I will keep in mind that if I ever stay with you I'll be smoking cigars in outer darkness. It's good of you, and I appreciate it.

I had regarded the autobio stuff as rather special, the first ten years of my life, all those dream-things that happen and which you remember. Nothing at all to do with the literary life. I stopped at age ten. It doesn't seem to me that another section about writing and including Can. name-dropping would meld with that deeply personal first section. Anyway, no one except me seems to like it — at least no publisher. Basically, I'm interested in nothing but poems (which I'm not writing). I've written prose mainly because I wasn't writing poems. Although this autobio fragment did interest me. I had the unlikely illusion that I was saying something, but turned out to be only talking to myself.

"Old-age-depression" — I know it well. Similar and related to non-writing-depression and no-woman-depression and not-enough-attention-depression. Trouble is, Earle, you don't drink any more. Sometimes a release and balm of Gilead. And don't tell me it's a weakness. Of course. So is writing. So is fucking. I think of what a number of people have said, including John Glassco, that "it's better not to have lived at all," which I think is shit but can't prove it.[875] Life is largely pointless, even when you're titillated by flattery or others of the many things that divert one. Of course these grow fewer with age (wisdom of Purdy), and it seems to be a matter of trying to outwit one's self.

We went to Yucatan, and I was slightly bored. Maybe been there too many times. Heat was terrible too. I tried to write some poems, but didn't like them. Worse, they were bad, and I know that. But there's nothing to fill that gap in my mind if I don't write, and write what I think and feel is worthwhile.

Back in Florida, we bought a mobile home. Cheap. We own the home and rent the land it's on. Run by a power-hungry dictator, also money-hungry, whom the old people here don't resist simply because of age. I guess one loses the desire and ability to resist dictators when age comes. Not you, I think you'd resist. That's a good thing about you. (I can see you snapping at me when you're one hundred and I'm ninety-nine.)

That was a curious review of Scott's *Collected* by Woodcock. I mean at the end, where he said mediocre poems were forgiveable if included in a collected works.[876]

---

874. *YA* 345–46.

875. Cf. Ecclesiastes 4:2–3: "Wherefore I praised the dead which are already dead more than the living which are yet alive. Yea, better is he than both they, which hath not yet been, who hath not seen the evil work that is done under the sun."

876. At the end of his review in *The Globe and Mail* (2 Jan. 1982), Woodcock distinguished between

Bullshit! Mediocre poems are never forgiveable. But I expect Scott will get the GG this year because he's Scott.[877] I'd rather he got it for his poems. (This in *TorGlobe*) ...

Ron Everson seemed in good form a week ago, altho Lorna is pretty feeble except where food is concerned. Ron looks after her practically hand and foot, I'd say. He must have a tremendous affection for her, not that that's ever talked about. He is writing some too, I guess more than me, which is an indication that blood is flowing. We've invited them down here (New Smyrna is about 140 miles away).

Love to you & Wailan from E & me

Al

To Birney (Toronto) from Purdy (Fort Pierce)
1982 TL[878]

Dear Earle:

I wrote you some time back, when we had no return address to send. Now we do. However, we'll be leaving here in about three weeks anyway, which is the time it takes for letters to make return trips both ways.

We bought a mobile home here, quite cheaply; but rent the land it's on. And it turns out that the land owner is not so pleasant as we would like, in fact is quite a dictator. So we plan to sell the place again.

I've written a few poems, but only two are any good at all, and then not as good as they should be.

How's your autobio coming? Life, love and pursuit?

I think I mentioned we were in Yucatan; but I must be getting jaded: was somewhat bored. Marty Gervais is bringing out another *Selected*, taken from the stuff we couldn't pack into *Being Alive*. His title is *The Purdy Omnibus*, to which I have appended my own: *Bursting into Song*.[879] Which last rather tickles me. Marty and I will have a reading together at Harbourfront sometime in May. Anyway, I hope to see you then or sometime this summer.

Cheers and similar noises,

Al

---

standards for evaluating "an ordinary volume of verse," for which the salient criterion is "excellence," and those for evaluating a major collection: "in our judgment of a collection, we add the criterion of completeness, and in doing so we often find — as we do with Scott — that our final assessment of a poet depends on the power of his total achievement to carry its imperfections. There are not a few flat and discordant notes in *The Collected Poems of F.R. Scott*, but the final effect is one of undeniable grandeur."

877. *The Collected Poems of F.R. Scott* received the Governor General's Award. The other finalists were Barry McKinnon's *The The* and *Miramichi Lightning: The Collected Poems of Alfred Bailey*.

878. AP's undated copy of the letter is found in a sequence of dated letters sent in late February and early March 1982.

879. *Bursting into Song: An Al Purdy Omnibus* was published in 1982.

To Purdy (Ameliasburgh) from Birney (London, Ontario)
March 29, 1982   APC

Al,

This is good for overnight in Mtrl, if you can stand $40 (McGill was paying mine)[880] — I expect to be in Tor. all summer so hope you can come up & have a meal at least — finished here (UWO) Apr. 7 — but recording (with Nexus) all Easter weekend (the only time we can afford the studio) — are you going to LP [League of Canadian Poets] conf? WUC [The Writers' Union of Canada]? Hope to hear you read @ Harbourfront — good to hear you have a whole *Omnibus* to ride in.

Best from us to youse

Earle

To Purdy (Ameliasburgh) from Birney (Toronto)
June 11, 1982   AL

Dear Al

I've at last found time to read through your *Bursting*, & what a pleasure it's been to go back to fine poems already enjoyed, & to some almost forgotten & now back in the "canon." I don't have all your books in the flat now so couldn't check to see what the 4 new ones are you mentioned — this shames me, because I thought I knew & loved your poems, *all* of them, so well I'd never forget any — but hell, I begin to forget my own — maybe I wrote too many, or read too many, or both — old age is a bad joke — you'll never fall into it, but you may get pushed.

We're sorry we didn't see you & Eurithe apart from the rush of the LCP [League of Canadian Poets] first night. Life is getting to be too much.

Keep well. Enjoy the summer. Come & smoke on our balcony sometime.

As ever

Earle

& thanks again for *Bursting*.

Have made a ½ hr "David" record for OISE [Ontario Institute for Studies in Education], a one-hr "recital" record with the Fac. of Music @ Western, & 3 albums (= 3 hrs, 61 pomes, & 5 percussionists) with Nexus — in Aug. we go west (Banff, to make a "David" film, & the Coast to see relatives). And you?

---

880. The postcard was from the Hôtel Château Versailles, Montreal.

To Birney (Toronto) from Purdy (Ameliasburgh)
June 23, 1982   TL

Dear Earle:

Mislaid your letter so answering from memory of its contents, which is nil, the memory not the contents.

Your activities are awesome, all those movies, honours descending on you. I have no activity comparable. I did say I was editing an Acorn *Selected* for McStew???? I'm thankful he's in P.E.I — at least I *was* thankful, thinking it'd be too expensive for him to phone every half minute. But he has phoned anyway, several times. And left me gasping for oxygen, trying to think of some way to end the conversation without being very rude which has been a great temptation. Looking over his later poems: many of them refer to people the reader will not know, hence incomprehensible. Many of them are very mediocre and outright bad, or so I think. Therefore, I plan to homogenize the selection, mix early and late together with the hope that the early good will temper the later bad.

My own poems come slowly or not at all, the penalty of age I guess. If you'd stop yapping about your own age you'd realize I'm only a few years younger and not nearly so vigorous. All these furious activities of yours are a tribute to that log cabin by the Bow River and your virtuous abstemious life in which osculatory exercises served to keep your tonsils in shape. I.e., you're not so goddam old yet.

I seem to have become, without quite knowing how, a member of the Order of Canada. And note that Birney preceded me by a dozen years. I wonder who voted for me.

As I may have mentioned, did a ten thousand word chunk of autobio for the first ten years of life, not a lit name in the lot. And a friend, George Galt, keeps saying I should do a full scale job on Life, mine.[881] I feel very inadequate about it, since it seems to me that my life has been fairly ordinary. Therefore, how should it be of interest outside myself? The last twenty years have been excessively "literary" — which seems of small interest of itself unless I can inject some purple drama. Which seems doubtful. Or maybe I'm just trying to avoid the work.

As mentioned, some poems, but they seem to me of little merit. When I was writing the poems, esp. later ones, of *The Stone Bird*, I felt they were worthwhile things and they kept me stimulated (in fact it's the book I feel is my best, which somehow escaped without very much notice). Which is a fairly gloomy feeling about one's self. Perhaps if one primes the pump with some prose, then poems may come. As you know, when one isn't writing much there's a useless feeling.

---

881. George Galt (b. 1948): Canadian writer and editor who compiled *The Purdy-Woodcock Letters: Selected Correspondence 1964–1984* (1988).

Poems, good ones, are some sort of justification for existence and consuming all those mountains of food and newsprint over the years.

Hoping you are not the same, with fond memories of a balcony,

and best to Wailan,

Al

To Purdy (Ameliasburgh) from Birney (Toronto)
October 2, 1982   TL

Dear Al,

Never got a chance to talk with you at that charity ball for us scribblers. & I never answered yr June letter. I hope the writing (your own) is coming easier. I've just gone thru a block over an article on Geo. Lamming etc for Bill New (*Can. Lit*).[882] Thought I'd write it in 2 days. It took 2 weeks.

You should let the very young & foolish admirers of Milt Acorn do his editing. Your time is IMPORTANT.

I spoke to you about Peter Trower (trying to visit you in Ameliasburg) because he seemed anxious you should know he tried, and because Peter is a changed man, almost unrecognizable now, with a great woman who has him on the wagon and determined to help him write and write. He even *looks* sober and takes lots of sleep, she says. Anyway I like Peter a lot better sober and enjoyed their visit, and felt he has capacities for better writing and more of it now. They're doing a biog. of Herb Wilson, my late bk-robber friend.[883]

We still haven't bought a car but still talk of renting one for a weekend & paying you a visit. Who knows, it may happen. But so far I'm tied up with trying to flog the new albums, 3 of them. Because the Nexus group are in Europe on tour for a month, leaving all the initial pushing of records, publicity, sales, etc., to Wailan & me.

Which reminds me I'm sending you a record, compliments of the POTE.

I think you were the most sensibly dressed male at that shindig.

Cheers. Luv to Eurithe

Earle

May yr K0K stay 1A0.

---

882. The article was "Meeting George Lamming in Jamaica," published in *Canadian Literature* 95 (Winter 1982). W.H. New (b. 1938): Eminent scholar of Canadian literature, professor of English at UBC, editor (1977–95) of *Canadian Literature*, and poet (*Science Lessons*, 1996). George Lamming (b. 1927): Barbadian novelist (*In the Castle of My Skin*, 1953; *The Emigrants*, 1954).

883. "Gangsterquest: The Search for the King of Safecrackers," by Trower and Yvonne Klan, was never published.

To Birney (Toronto) from Purdy (Ameliasburgh)
October 5, 1982   TL

Dear Earle:

Greeting. Yeah, sorry we never got to talk. I had the GG's aides de camp at my table on accounta not enough Purdy subscribers. I drank fast to get the uniforms blurry.

What's this record stuff? You now a recording artist?

Yeah, Peter [Trower] phoned some time back, and I said (he in B.C.) come down. Didn't even know he was east.

I'm writing little besides autobio stuff. Got to 50,000 words and bogged down. What do I say, talk about, etc? Some two or three poems that seem worthwhile in last few months. Never get another book at that pace. And if I'm not writing stuff I think "decent" then I get depressed at myself. So writing is a kinda drug. You live your life doing it, and the withdrawal symptoms are terrible.

I didn't have dinner clothes, so my clothes were what they were. What'll I do at the Order of Can. investiture on the 20th? Rent clothes? Seems too much. Met Jim Houston before the Tor. shindig, and he rented clothes.[884]

Luv to both of you, and do get a car and come down,

Al

To Purdy (Ameliasburgh) from Birney (Toronto)
October 15, 1982   AL

Dear Al

Don't rent, don't worry about Jim Whoever, don't streak, just wear whatever you're wearing, & so uphold the uniqueness of Poets — I resisted all attempts by Aide-de-Campfollowers & wore my only matching coat & pants (dark & 10 years old) — at my shindig there was an Albertan cowboy in chaps & Stetson, & a missionary in sackcloth. Only poetaster finks wear monkey suits & medals — be Al Purdy for christ's sake.

E

---

884. Probably James Houston (1921–2005): Canadian author (*Confessions of an Igloo Dweller*, 1995) and artist with long associations with the North and with Inuit art.

To Birney (Toronto) from Purdy (Ameliasburgh)
October 21, 1982   TL

Dear Earle,

Thanks much for record. You did three of em? I hope they sell really well. Should've had your picture.

Just got back from Ottawa. Wore black jacket and charcoal pants, and bought a pair of black shoes for 25 cents from a thrift shop. I was not the most fashionably attired person present. However, I saw no cowboys nor sackcloth missionaries. Talked with Trudeau a coupla minutes, ate a lotta good food, and drank some good wine. I wore no medals. Think they're a bit ostentatious, especially if you don't have very many like me. I would say my jacket was much over ten years old.

Anyway, the investiture part was a dull and boring period.

I bought a book of erotic art that would make a dildo wilt.

We snuck out today (Eurithe was there too) into whimpering rain. Glad to be gone. And back to the goddam autobio, which sticks me in middle age and unable to grow old by more than a page at a time.

Oh yes, also talked with the guy — a lieutenant in the navy who's also an aide de camp — who printed Layton's unpublished poems in Valley Editions.[885] I haven't read them anyway. Man named Thomas, yclept David. (Beautiful word, yclept!)

Take care of yourself (and Wailan in some fashion)

Al

To Purdy (Fort Pierce) from Birney (Toronto)
December 29, 1982   TL

I see from the *Globe* you have a new book out which reveals your "granrled personality," accdg to John Bemrose — do you think this is an accurate description or will you sue?[886]

Wanna make a deal? Send me 1 copy of your $9.95 book & I will send you 1 60-min. album of me plus 5 John Cagey percussionists, suitable inscribed or inscrbled.[887]

Happy New Year Eurithe, & you too Purdy my friend

from Wailan & even from me.

[Unsigned]

---

885. *The Uncollected Poems of Irving Layton 1936–1959* (1976), edited by W. David John.

886. Bemrose's review of *Bursting into Song: An Al Purdy Omnibus* (and of *The Collected Poems of Raymond Souster*) appeared in *The Globe and Mail* (18 Dec. 1982). He wrote that "Purdy is a personality as granrled [*sic*] and surprising as the eastern Ontario landscape he knows so well."

887. The letter was typed on an order form for recordings by Nexus (including the three albums made by EB).

To Birney (Toronto) from Purdy (Fort Pierce)
January 10, 1983   TL

Dear Earle,

Greeting. Arrived here three weeks ago. Sun and rain, rain and sun. But warm.

I think I am quite "granrled" at my age. (Hope you are not the same.)

I gave you a copy of the book reviewed at the Can. Po. League benefit reading in early summer of 1982. (Did you sell it already?) However, I'd be glad to trade another copy of the book for the album you mention with the cagey percussionists, etc. My book contains mostly old poems, and I presume you haven't read the copy I gave you since you may possibly think they're not old. (It does contain five new ones, at least unpublished in a book.) But you may wish to look around before going on with the proposed trade.

How are you? Doing what? Well and healthy, etc.?

I am groaning and continuing autobio, since I can't get used to not writing anything — anything I like in the way of poems, that is.

Have finished editing Acorn for McStew (the job courtesy of Dennis Lee), blessing my stars he's in PEI so he can't afford to phone me every night. That was for money. But I've taken on, in a weak moment, Ron Everson's poems for Oberon, if if if Macklem says okay.[888] And a burst of five or six poems in the last two months, which has now ended. Tried to write a poem in last few days and can't. Lose interest too soon. Very odd. You've no doubt felt the same mysterious abortive impulses.

Write me here.

Much good writing to come, I wish for you this year and others, Earle; but more, I wish you the feeling of worth and pride that is the most of any of us at our best — (and to Wailan),

Al

To Purdy (Fort Pierce) from Birney (Toronto)
February 7, 1983   AL

Dear Al

Got yr Jan. letter fr Flah. It leaves me still mystified. On Oct. 2 I mailed you no. 3 of the album set I did with Nexus. On 29 Dec. not having heard from you, I sent you a "dodger" that describes the 3 records, with a note on it asking if you got it (it was sent to yr Ameliasburg address). Now yr Jan. letter offers to trade me "another

---

888. *Everson at Eighty* was published by Oberon Press in 1983. Michael Macklem (b. 1928) is the founder and publisher of Oberon Press.

copy" (of your *Bursting* — which I admired and thanked you for in a letter I sent you on June 11) — for "the album" I mentioned — what's happening? Is yr mail not forwarded from Ameliasburg? Did you not get my June & Oct letters? Did you not get the record? Please let me know where to mail you another one — are you settled in Florida now? (Yr letter makes no reference to returning to Canada.) I'll be in England for 2 weeks beginning Feb. 19, but back on Balliol for the spring —

Best to you & Eurithe from us both.

Earle

To Purdy (Fort Pierce) from Birney (Toronto)
March 21, 1983   APC

Dear Al —
Good to know you are doing Ron's *Sel* — he deserves the best! — Also that your own writing goes well — I seem to write nothing but letters-in-support of other writers now, but I'm glad to be alive enough to write anything — London was its predictable damp dark traffic-snarled self, but with some good plays, music, art shows — we saw old friends, got bad colds, wrote nothing, gardened & generally enjoyed ourselves. Come back safe, you 2.

[Unsigned]

To Purdy (Ameliasburgh) from Birney (Toronto)
October 13, 1983   TL[889]

Dear Al
I suppose nostalgia is always a state of weakness but I liked yours re. Vancouver (maybe all poettree's nostalgic).[890] How long since you were there? When I was there in August it was more like "Granville seems to have moved stumped on stone legs to the mountain tops." And the traffic lights are spawning in the harbour … but that same sun is dodging around the highrisers (that's a great sunsetpiece). In Coal Harbour I don't think they allow vulgar fishing boats any more. Just yachts.

& I like your fog. Tho of course being old now as Methuselah I remember (what else have I got to do but?) I remember my first winter in Vanc. in '22–23, when the fog was so incredibly black that drivers would get lost between corners & walk away from their cars in midstreet & pedestrians (which I was when not

---

889. EB addressed the envelope to "Al Purdy, Bird-Watcher." He gave his own name as "Earle Birney, Word-Botcher." The letter was postmarked in Windsor on 17 Oct.

890. The subject of EB's commentary was AP's "Vancouver." The poem was included in *Piling Blood* (1984).

on my bike) had to keep count of blocks or get lost because the street signs, when there were any, were 10 ft high & you couldn't read them even with a flashlight.

I *hope* there are still "a million black suns growing wild at False Creek mouth" but I doubt there's even a single Himalaya bush or whatever they call the black-berries Out There (where my "ex-" lives in a low-riser maze, where once there were giant sawdust-burners & cedar-sweet lumber-yards — v. Anne Marriott's "Woodyards in the Rain").[891]

Why don't you give us a ring when you're in town?

When do you go south? Wailan flies to West Palm Beach tomorrow for 5 days — sounds ritzy but it's just because she has clients down there — they pay her way, of course, but so far she hasn't found clients willing to pay mine too. Not sure if I'd go to West Palm Beach even if my way was paid. (Sour grapes?)

The best to you both from both

Earle

Pome for a Reedin

The secret of my fan-
tastic success as a poe-
tree reeder is my poems
have no humour
so when I give readings
everybody keeps her or his
face straight because he
or she knows ime not trying
no funny business

in any case guffaws
are dangerous   people
have gone into convulsions
of glee and died
laughing at layton and when
purdy reeds women have split
their sides and been rushed
to hospital and expired
in stitches

---

891. From the last section of AP's "Vancouver": "City of the great trees / metropolis of sawdust / and blackberries growing wild / a million black suns / at False Creek mouth" (*BR* 380).

so i'me always careful to be
deadly serious   that way
no one's going to sue me
for reckless writhing without
a license because nobody ever
got arrested for boring
an audience to death

url birney

To Birney (Toronto) from Purdy (Ameliasburgh)
October 23, 1983   TL

Dear Earle,

That poem is "reckless writhing" since you've never bored an audience to death, which includes this poem as well.

The Vancouver piece is now slightly revised, for the better I hope. I'm wondering where to send it — probably Vancouver if there's anything there except *Prism* these days. I'd like it to have a little wider circ. than some. Do you know any places?

No fishing boats? Just shows you, I ain't up to date. No black suns either. I used to pick em by the pail full years back. And yeah, that fog was something; my revision included a line about "the invasion of the grey flowers." It seems your memories [are] somewhat similar to my own with, of course, more female company. I will not forget soon how you talked that gal who was in bed with her boy friend — talked her outa bed and onto your knee in middle of the room, while I watched awe-struck. Remember that? Chiding her gently for not being faithful to you. You didn't bore her to death I'll warrant. I'd write a poem about that, but doubt if the principals involved would waive court action.

Wartime memory: I'd be on guard duty at Hastings Park, come out of the huge storage building yawning, to see fresh snow on the mountains opposite. At night, and then this morning vision. I worked in a lumber yard on Second Ave — Sigurdson's, when we went there in 1950. I stole a lot of mahogany boards from there, stored em at the house we bought, and someone stole them in turn from me when we rented the house.

We intend to go to Europe in the next few weeks if we can find a suitable excursion — Spain or wherever. I've been having a very productive period — for me, that is. Have a hundred pages for new book. Anything new I write, I'll delete weaker poems and sub. For a while everything was a poem; now I'm probably back into a dry period. (Hope you are not the same.)

Best to both of you,

Al

To Purdy (Ameliasburgh) from Birney (Toronto)
October 27, 1983   AL

Dear Al

Good you've got that century of pages ready & able to think of castles in Spain — Wailan has 2 weeks hol. coming up in Jan. & we're thinking of getting to Italy if we can afford it — yes, yes, we bought a sports car, & the bloody thing drinks gas the way I drink water (& you, wine — you & those friends of Jesus in Cava) — also Wailan bruised the corner of 1 fender, & the bill will be $375. So maybe we'll just holiday in Hamilton, Ont., or nearer.

An old friend (une belle québécoise) has sent me a copy of the New Orleans *Outsider*, issue #2 — full of the young upcoming geniuses of 1962, including A.W. Purdy, in company with Miller, Patchen, Burroughs, Finlay, Genet, Kerouac, & ... & ... (you name 'em) — handprinted — (but no doubt you have half a dozen copies, in mint condition) — I shall treasure it & hope for your autograph when next we meet.[892]

Where to send your Vancouver pome? Any mag. would be lucky & grateful to get it — but I wouldn't advise *Prism*, which is in the temporary & faltering hands of obnoxious undergrads, for whom it would be the greatest of triumphs if they could boast they rejected a Purdy — why not *Can. Lit.* (Bill New pays a little) — there's also, in the Vanc. area, *Capilano Rev.* (mark yr. submission for attention of Eve Whittaker — one of the eds. & a great gal — tell her I persuaded you to honor the mag. with a submission) — or *Event* (though neither of the very smart ladies who were its editors are now editing it — some male on the Kwantlen Coll. staff now, I think) (Box 9030, Surrey, B.C.) — I doubt if they pay, however — but I think *Malahat* does, though personally I wouldn't be caught dead in it (nor in *West Coast Review* anymore).

If I had something half as good as yr Vancouver piece I'd try to sell it dear (to maybe Q [*Quill*] & *Quire* or *Sat. Night* — ask $500 at least. But then you're so rich now, price is no matter — — right?

Still hope to see you again before death do us part.

Earle

Just heard from Geo. Johnston (who's still recovering from an operation) that

---

892. The authors listed were rebellious figures indeed and somewhat odd company for AP to keep. Henry Miller (1891–1980): American novelist (*Tropic of Cancer*, 1934). Kenneth Patchen (1911–72): American poet and novelist (*The Collected Poems of Kenneth Patchen*, 1968). William S. Burroughs (1914–97): American novelist (*Naked Lunch*, 1959/62). Ian Hamilton Finlay (1925–2006): Scottish poet (*The Dancers Inherit the Party*, 1960, 1969) and artist. Jean Genet (1910–86): French novelist (*Journal du voleur*, 1949), poet, and playwright. Jack Kerouac (1922–69): American novelist (*On the Road*, 1957) and poet.

Frances Horovitz has died of cancer — perhaps you didn't know her (Mike's ex-wife)[893] — not only a good poet but a beautiful sweet lady — aye aye, timor mortis conturbat me,

Earle

Had a long talk with Ted Hughes last week & learned the whole story of Assia (did you ever know her? — Sylvia's rival).[894]

To Purdy (Fort Pierce) from Birney (Toronto)
December 28, 1983   AL

Dear Purdys

Got Al's card from Spain in Nov. Hope you enjoyed it & that you're managing to survive the weather in Fla. Up here, -18°C + 40 kph winds. Write lotsa pomes. We'll be here till late Jan, when I go to Alaska for 2 wks. Later in Feb. we'll be in San Miguel A. Keep in touch. Healthy survival in '84.

Earle

To Birney (Toronto) from Purdy (Fort Pierce)
January 13, 1984   TL

Dear Earle,

You're a travellin man. Alaska, San Miguel — the last I expect at Leonard Brooks'.

At Toledo we stayed in a hotel where El Greco was supposed to have painted his *View of Toledo*. And thinking of your "El Espolio" writing my own poem on Domenico Theotocopoulos.[895] Litigious guy, as John Glassco said about M. Atwood.

Many poems in last year, a few of them seeming to me worthwhile. Perhaps the enclosed.

Ron Everson and Lorna here for a coupla days. Bill Percy and Vina. We visited the "Lion Safari" (or whatever the name) at Palm Beach yesterday. Sorta place where you're cautioned to keep the car windows up and then drive among the beasts. We hit a sexual time, two ostriches fucking, likewise an elephant with

893. Michael Horovitz (b. 1935) and Frances Horovitz (1938–83): English poets.

894. Ted Hughes (1930–98): English poet and translator (*The Hawk in the Rain*, 1957; *Collected Poems*, 2003). One of the leading poets of the postwar period, he become the Poet Laureate in 1984. The American poet and novelist Sylvia Plath (1932–63; *The Colossus and Other Poems*, 1960), Hughes's first wife, committed suicide, as did Assia Wevill (1927–69), his lover.

895. EB's "El Greco: *Espolio*" was published in *Ice Cod Bell or Stone* (1962). AP's "There Is of Course a Legend" was published in *Piling Blood* (1984). His "Stop Watching," from *Sundance at Dusk* (1976), also refers to the painter.

six-foot dong pursuing a reluctant female with a slippery backside. "The elephant is slow to mate" was not so slow on this occasion.[896] Impressive to see the several tons of elephant rear on hind legs ... And the poor female ostrich came out of it looking bedraggled and mussed ...

Best to you and Wailan,

Al

To Purdy (Fort Pierce) from Birney (Saskatoon)
February [2?], 1984   APC

Dear Al —

Too damned cold, no caribou, no polar bears, but lots of doggy wolves & wolvish dogs — temp at Delta Ju [Junction] yesterday was -60° F. Went out on the tundra a way with a poet[897] & his 5 sled-dogs — wd. like to see this country in July, after-mosquito time, they say is best — everybody loves your pome about shitting among huskies ["When I Sat Down to Play the Piano"] , also your willow one ["Trees at the Arctic Circle"], though of course it was my own golden (24 K.) lyrics that brought out the Aleut girls.

Back today to Saskatoon (Canada's Miami?) — will be in San Miguel in mid-Feb — hope to see you both when we get back from there.

Cheers

Earle

Good dinosaur pome but I got lost with that shapeless shape.

To Purdy (Ameliasburgh) from Birney (Toronto)
April 12, 1984   AL

Dear Al

I'm grateful you (or a publishing company moved in on your Ameliasburgh hide-away) sent me *Morning and It's Summer*. Physically an overpowering book. The huge repulsive front-cover by your three sadistic designers; the RAFish back-cover Purdy with his already beautiful & courageous wife, surmounted on the incontestable tributes from incontestable authorities — overpowering indeed but justified entirely by the contents.[898] I've read them too fast, greedily, but will return, digest, ruminate & — who knows — I may see you in the flesh, to repeat these congratulations, before — — — —

---

896. AP's reference was to "The Elephant Is Slow to Mate," a poem by D.H. Lawrence.

897. Here EB was interrupted by words — "Alaska Joe" — printed on the postcard.

898. The designers were John Sims, Veronica Soul, and Andy Wheatley. The "tributes" were from Dennis Lee and Kildare Dobbs.

Wailan, whose wisdom requires simplicities, says "it's very good — I *like* it."
This ancient waves, with arthritic care, both hands in salutation.

Earle

Don't criticize this mountain scene — did you ever write a good poem with your foot?[899]

To Purdy (Ameliasburgh) from Birney (Toronto)
April 26, 1984   AL

Dear Al

Had time now for a second look @ *Morning & ...* — enjoying the parallels to my own memories — early hockey, chasing cans on the river ice (in Banff, on the Bow, it was puck-size pine knots from Old Man Standish's lumber yard — looking through ice @ "monsters waiting" (we kept thinking we had spotted the team of horses that had fallen through a hole during block ice-cutting) — & out on First Lake (Vermilion) moonlit nights with fires on shores, marshmallows (but this was before hotdogs) — but it was generally too cold to skate for long, as your toes would freeze (as ears, cheeks & nosetip already had) ... watching summer clouds — I liked to think they were pillows I could jump on if I had a balloon to get up above them (in the first 10 yrs of this century, airships were just damfool contraptions back in the U.S., but balloons were what Jules Verne used).

Your grandfather — a great portrait — said "turn up my toes" — my father would say "cash in my chips" — but he was a poker-playin cowpuncher in his youth — as a schoolboy I'd have said "croaked," my mother "gone to my reward" — early movies: yes, we too exploded brown paper bags — my favorite serials were *Perils of Pauline* & *The Iron Claw* ... & I too was "a prisoner of religion, ... hardwood benches" ... but I didn't read from "Genesis & the New Testament" but right through to the end of *Revelations* (but maybe that's what you meant). But where in either the Old or New T. did you find the word "fuck"?? Early reading (p. 25) — yes *Chums* — did you also get the *B.O.P.* [*Boy's Own Paper*]? (A small puzzle near the top of that page: "When I was six and eight years old" — what happened to the "shipyard and drydock" when you were seven?[900] What you say about your mother I too could have written about mine (p. 28) — ah, mothers![901]

---

899. The notecard in which the letter was written is illustrated by "Southern Fiords," "From an Original, footpainted by J. Duncan."

900. From *Morning and It's Summer*: "Beyond the limestone gothic post office in Trenton, there was a shipyard and drydock [*sic*] — when I was six and eight years old."

901. AP's description of his mother in *Morning and It's Summer* is highly self-critical: "There is no excuse for me that I didn't respond to her requests, importunities and demands for love, even if they were unspoken."

When are you coming to town? Joe Rosenblatt the Roseleaf is in town propping up the moribund LCP — the same old endearing Joe.

Best to you & Eurithe.

[Unsigned]

Still Life near Bangalore
for Al

The painter quiets all but his busy brush.
The writer is obsessed to ask: what then?

My train creeps blindly through this canvas
toward Bangalore. Nearest my window,
right, an oxcart moves (or stops?)
on a pinched black road where jacarandas
leave magenta bruises, and a pair of women
stand face to shadowed face beneath tiered baskets.
They are compositions of sky-blue shawls
and sable braids aslant down chalky saris.
Merchants' wives, I'd guess, with time to gossip.
Left, the road elbows, vanishes with palms.

Beyond the oxcart the emerald paddyfields
submit to yoked brute buffalo.
Indifferent geometrists they draw in ochre mud
their sinuous counter-patterns.
Behind each slatey team an almost naked
human beast — bareheaded, breached with rags,
is ploughing (with a stick, is it?, clutched
in raddled hands) while a companion guides
their Shivas by a rope. It threads the sacred
nostrils. They steer around the corpse-like
sleeping cows and boulders huge as bones
of longdrowned mastodons.

The background, between bamboo strokes
and breadfruit blobs, is giving glimpses
of lizard-tawny thatch (the village
of those still, still-talking matrons?)

Near a splash of wall where a flamboya burns
dim figures walk with trays, perhaps of frangipani
for an unseen temple. Or of sandalwood?
(My window cannot smell).

And what now on that dire horizon
explodes from jungle, billows into sky?
What's happening? My window cannot
see, my frame has slid forever past
as round the bend to Bangalore
comes sudden mounting filling the road
a ten-ton oil-truck — it is surely
roaring, blaring, screeching its warnings?
(My window cannot hear).
Did the women leap away? ... the cloud subside?

e. b. '84[902]

To Birney (Toronto) from Purdy (Ameliasburgh)
April 30, 1984   TL

Dear Earle,

Quite right: a sadistic, revolting and altogether uncalled for front cover. I have no wish to dwell on this painful subject (of Lord Fauntleroy and his misbegotten children), but I wish to assure you that you will not be subjected to such mental agony again.

No, never writ a good pome with foot; some say with hand either. I hope the guy washed his feet in that lake.

Have now added sinus trouble to list of ailments. But I won't dwell on that either.

Am now going thru contract discussions with both Oxford [University Press] and McStew, playing them off against each other. Surprisingly, they let me get away with it, knowing the other might not be sincerely in earnest. If you follow me? McStew has to equal or surpass the Oxford deal, and whether they can or really want to is up in the air. This of course is confidential. We shall see.

Turns out that, following your financial advice, I have but two readings this summer. When I receive a letter mentioning a reading and I rebut with the $500. asking price, I see the requesting person actually gulp painfully by return mail.

---

902. The poem was published in *Canadian Literature* 100 (Spring 1984) and was included in *Last Makings* (1991).

Still, I don't really give a shit that there are few readings, tho I do like to have my ego stroked by people asking.

Hope to see you sometime this summer, altho given my ailments … George, Johnston, incidentally, was going to stop at Belleville twice for lunch with Eurithe and I. (We'd have reinstalled him and his wife on a later train.) But had to cancel both times.

All best, and to Wailan,

Al

To Birney (Toronto) from Purdy (Ameliasburgh)
May 3, 1984   TL

Dear Earle,

That's a marvellous poem, takes you right to Bangalore. I think you're amazing to write that. And dire is a Birney-word that seems exactly right for this poem. It is, of course, a still life with a difference: things do move in it. Jesus Christ, Earle, you're passing the goddam genius stage into what? That's just about the most beautiful description of a place I've ever seen. Thank you.

Before I left Florida, Ron Everson sent me perhaps the best poem of his I had ever seen (I am not comparing it to yours in any way), about a Canadian flying squirrel, which he called a "fairy diddle" — which sounds like obscene sex. Almost like something he'd got out of a zoology book, except the book was his mind. Must be something about reaching 80. I may never get to find out.

Yeah, I had those thoughts about clouds too, something so solid up there, one couldn't believe them only mist. Those horses — I expect they drowned, couldn't be got out? "Spooked them" — isn't there a poem there?

Yeah, my grandfather was a continual poker player too — had a little box where the other players stuck in a percentage of the pots in order to pay rent for the venue. I once swiped some silver from it, and got caught, with terrible consequences.

No, of course, didn't find the word fuck, but certainly gathered that "lay with her" meant the same thing. Yeah, got some of those English school papers, *Wizard* — was it?, and several others. But *Chums* was the one I loved.

I never did find out when the drydock at Trenton disappeared. Is there a contradiction involved? I had a passage earlier about the "leaners on the Gilbert House" which I deleted, and later there was still a reference to the leaners which is unexplained. Yeah, mothers! I suppose we all have our illusions, and I think hers made her more comfortable than otherwise. I hope so.

Joe phoned me, wanted to get me back in League, same as you. Said I'd get more readings. Told him I didn't give a damn if I got more readings. Which I suppose is not precisely the truth, since I like to be asked for ego's sake, even if I don't accept. That reply seemed to surprise him a little. No, I'm finished with the League. That bit about the women not thinking they got enough attention pissed me off too. I can't believe anyone would turn down a woman's poem because it was by a woman.

I don't know when Toronto, sooner or later of course. I have a med. apt. later in month.

Thanks again, much, for the poem. I feel like putting it under glass, but then I'd have to take it off the wall to read. I shall wait and see it in print.

luv to both of you,

Al

To Purdy (Ameliasburgh) from Birney (Toronto)
July 4, 1984   AL

Al

You're so appreciative! I had to read that Bangalore thing over again — but it didn't sound as good as your letter, though I decided not to tinker with it any more or you'd give me hell like you did about "Mappemounde." Don't know if you'll like the enclosed — it's not as good but it should "swell a progress" — I'll need it by Oct., when Russell Brown thinks he can start moving my "last pomes" into the McStew assembly line — how good an editor is he?[903]

Wish you'd been at my birthday binge, — but there were too many people for the size of the flat, & you wouldn't have been able to smoke. You can now it's summer & the balcony isn't in deep-freeze (that is, if you haven't still quit) — Your Costa del Sol card was a happy surprise — are you back home yet? ... I got D.Littered again — great intro. by Jamie Reaney, to my surprise, as I thought he disliked me — I certainly can't stand his hypomanic wife — but perhaps he can't either — There were the usual tuck-outs & speeches — I enclose my "address" to the post-graduate school & other oddities.

Love to Eurithe too.

E

Hope you enjoyed Spain — it's where people are still real & themselves.

---

903. "Swell a progress": EB's allusion was to T.S. Eliot's "The Love Song of J. Alfred Prufrock" (1915, 1917). Russell Morton Brown (b. 1942): Professor of English at the University of Toronto, scholar of Canadian literature, and editor and anthologist. Brown succeeded Dennis Lee as poetry editor at McClelland and Stewart; he held the position from 1983 to 1988. He edited *The Collected Poems of Al Purdy* (1986).

To Birney (Toronto) from Purdy (Ameliasburgh)
July 10, 1984   TL[904]

Dear Earle,

Thank you much for the sheaf of stuff and poems. I have so many comments and thoughts about it, I'd probably bore the shit outa you if I say it all. (Which I won't.)

But it's a great address to Grad School. And the bit about watching clouds is fine, an activity-lack-of that I indulged in so much myself as a child! It strikes me as just right, the ego submerged, not in humility exactly but by comparison perhaps with the many more important things than oneself. One point does make me a little puzzled: what are the "earned bottom rungs of academia"? "Solidest" because one is then enabled to climb with stronger underpinning?

The new poem is also fine. You're having a renaissance of some kind. I'm sure you know that the cry you heard joins with your own and Wailan's "wanton cries" — But the fear of the cry contrasts strongly with the cries of love and passion. The poem all fits together well, language and incident warm into the cold "brief day."[905]

I always thought that Reaney disliked me too. He's such an odd little bugger and difficult to read — his character I mean, and his seemingly deliberately odd poems too. But I don't think he's a liar, and when he says you gave him the feeling of being able to write about mosquitoes and poker, it has to be truth. Which makes me wanta write a poem about Birney making me able to write poems about all the Birney-mosquitoes and Birney-royal grand-flushes atop Mt. Assiniboine that I almost stop this letter and do it — (just wait) —

"Ellesmereland" has become, in totality, both a moving and chilling poem. And "[Canada:] Case History."[906] What is a "decapodal turkey"? Sends me to the dictionary. Of course, ten-footed provinces. Yes, Uncle has the cutlery.[907]

I'm still annoyed at you making "Mappemounde" so all-inclusive with *all* as I remember.[908] "it hems heart's landtrace" was enough (I had to go back to the poem to quote that). Reminds me of Auden knocking out some of his best passages in his Yeats poem, about Kipling being pardoned by this strange excuse. What was

904. *YA* 379–81. EB's handwritten note on the letter: "answered in conversation with Al @ Ameliasburg July 13."

905. "The new poem" was "Cry over Aswan," which was eventually published in EB's *Last Makings* (1991).

906. Three versions each of "Ellesmereland" and "Canada Case History" were published in *Last Makings*. AP also wrote about the Arctic island, as in "In Ellesmereland," included in *The Blur in Between: Poems 1960–61* (1962), and "The North West Passage," from *North of Summer: Poems from Baffin Island* (1967).

907. "Uncle": i.e., Uncle Sam. In EB's first "Case History," "Uncle spoils him with candy, of course, / yet shouts him down when he talks at table" (*OMH* 52). In the new "Case History," Uncle "has the cutlery."

908. In the version of "Mappemounde" to which AP referred, the line is: "it hems all hearts' landtrace." (See *OMH* 46.) See AP's second letter dated "April 1955."

it? "Time that with this strange excuse / Pardons Kipling and his views / And will pardon Paul Claudel / Pardons him for writing well."[909] You're gettin me all literary like. Your own sin was much less flagrant. I was annoyed because I loved/love that poem.

I don't know this Brown guy at McStew. Dennis Lee says he's good of course. I somehow feel that a younger generation is fucking me up with strangers in the metrics. But I give the conventional thought, he must be good or else — Or else what? Of course of course. "Send me your credentials, Mr. Brown."

What was Keats' line, about the oncoming generations which "tread me down"?[910] Or like that.

You wanta echo Housman with "Last Pomes"?[911] The romantic view being that they don't end (and I don't mean Frye), that little trickles of jagged music whisper around gravestones.

I kept lookin for Cervantes' ghost in Spain, but all I saw was Quixote iron-cut-outs pluggin hamburgers. But the flowers, migawd the flowers, roadside red poppies like sunken flags of the Armada.

I have a book myself this fall which, perhaps wrongly, I think my best, and probably also my "last pomes" —[912]

Whyn't you come down here with Wailan and we'll toast Wassail, you in tiffin tea and me in beer? Eurithe has fixed up a room with queen-size bed beneath the garage, and a single bed in my work room. We now have a Belleville cop livin next to us replacing LaGuff. Gives one such a sense of insecurity, when said he leaves his lights on all night and if I hear a gunshot not to worry, just some revengeful con that he's sent down.

I copy the only poem in last few weeks below.

On the Planet Earth

> She was lovely as sunrise
> meeting sunset at the world's edge
> without a chaperone and blushing
> I mentioned this to her
> mentioned also Jungian theory
> of the unconscious

909. AP quoted lines from "In Memory of W.B. Yeats" (1939) that were ultimately suppressed by Auden. The quotation is inexact: the first "Pardons" should be "Pardoned," for instance.

910. From John Keats's "Ode to a Nightingale": "Thou wast not born for death, immortal Bird! / No hungry generations tread thee down."

911. The allusion was to A.E. Housman's *Last Poems* (1922).

912. The book was *Piling Blood* (1984). On his copy of the letter, EB underlined AP's "perhaps wrongly" and wrote "It *is* his best! A *great* book! EB."

I said
"All your life there will be
visitors in your mind
you don't know about
and I am there too
when for no apparent
reason you blush
that's me kid —"[913]

love to both of you
Al

To Birney (Toronto) from Purdy (Ameliasburgh)
July 14, 1984   TL

Dear Earle,

I am thinking — have been thinking — of that book of yours. I read some of the stuff twice, last night and again this morning. However, I would not wish to comment on it as an integrated book unless you asked, which you did. Therefore, I take it that an outside look at the manuscript might just be a little helpful.

As I said earlier, I think that long poem is the centerpiece.[914] You thought it might seem boastful. That didn't occur to me as I read it, since it seems to me entirely natural that you might write/talk about the difficulties of a writer getting a hearing. Leonard's experiences and your own fall in with that, his as painter, yours as writer. You mention that the poem has little point, with which I would disagree. In the first place, it's the record of a friendship and as such is worthwhile in that area alone. Personally, I found it very interesting, and was slightly surprised that it was so, despite my knowledge of your ability to make almost any experience interesting. As I recall, at the end you were wishing Leonard well, long life etc. Well, the ending might call for a bit more of a bang than that, which you can surely provide.

And I did not think the poem too long. I read it twice, cursorily last night because of the wine, and more attentively this morning. There are one or two spots in it where you can make it a little more understandable, but that's minor. There's no doubt in my mind that you can do it.

As for the limericks, they are virtuoso stuff I suppose. I think you can do virtually anything in the way of form you choose. If I had written those limericks,

---

913. "On the Planet Earth" appeared as the first poem in *Piling Blood*.

914. "Letter to Leonardo" was not included in *Last Makings* (1991), although it was part of EB's manuscript (1985).

I would have employed them as a break from the seriousness of poems adjacent. However, I'm not sure they work effectively as said breaks. How about a dead serious limerick, the sort of thing that is seldom done? Who ever heard of a serious limerick? Still, why not?

Also, I think some of the poems fall too far short of your best, which makes them stand out unfavourably by comparison.

But what I'm saying, I think this manuscript of yours is the basis of a very fine book. "The Cry" ["Cry over Aswan"] especially is fine, and your "Ellesmereland [III]" is now doubly, triply effective. So is the "Canada: Case History" [1985] poem.[915] And there are other good ones. My memory won't bring them back to me without the manuscript.

All the best,

Al

PS. Good to see you & Wailan

To Purdy (Ameliasburgh) from Birney (Toronto)
July 25, 1984   AL

Al,

You are right — You confirm my own stubbornly-rejected self-criticisms — & thank you, friend, you confirm them with mildest & kindest words — the long poem has to be clearer *throughout*, the limericks go out (there's only three! all of them leaden) (*only*?! one, like these, was too many). The "Commonwealth Arts Festival" is obscure, dated, superficial — out! The "epigrams" either get scattered or disappear — the "Meeting of the Students' Committee" is also dated & superficial & is OUT. The "Threw Daw Kissed" is too much-of-a-much, & I've done it better before, & is OUT — the "To Cumrad Bert" is of dubious value & too personal & so is "To Sarge Robertson."[916] I may also cut down on the number of luv-pomes.

Where then's the book, the 64 pp at least? It will come, I hope, by extending the "Limey Tramp" to a group of about 30 fairly or very short pieces, a sequence over the 40 days I kept a diary on that ship. I've begun work on it, but only in stolen moments as I'm still doing an 8 to 5 researching, with Lan's nephew, in the Fisher, for vol. 2 of *Spreading Time*.

You are a kind man & a longtime friend, & I think you sensed at once that I was impatiently shovelling gravel into a small pan of cement, instead of more cement — cement it will be now, or I'm only a prose s.o.b.

---

915. Three poems called "Ellesmereland" and three poems called "Canada: Case History" were eventually included in *Last Makings*.

916. "THREW DAW KISSED ASS TRIAL YAH!" was in fact included in *Last Makings*, as was "Commonwealth Arts Festival Week, 1965, Cardiff, a Collage."

Love to you both — we sure enjoyed being with you — the Queen's reading was a shambles of unorganization, but the view of the yacht harbor was sumptuous — we got away early Sun & drove north almost to Pembroke & then W. on #7 — a beautiful day.

I hope to hell your back's better, Al. Eurithe, every time he contradicts you, massage him — that way he may get better both in body & soul — but make it a gentle pummelling —

Earle

Al — please send me that speech I gave at UWO [University of Western Ontario] so I can make copies — I've lost my only copy — I'll send you back a Xerox.

To Birney (Toronto) from Purdy (Ameliasburgh)
July 27, 1984   TL

Dear Earle,
Your address to the nobs enclosed.

Please thank Wailan for her note. First letter from her ever?

Back to your manuscript: only two places in Brooks pome I thought needed a little more explication. And I reject entirely your thought that pome might not be of interest or too much about yourself, or too boastful or whatever. I think it among your best.

I agree with the principle for which you included those limericks (lighten up the high seriousness of some of the poems, a bridge or something — at least I think that was your intent), but the limerick form in their case makes them seem *too* trivial. I think it a good idea to write serious limericks, which of course would not serve your intent. Or is it even possible to write serious limericks?

I think of something like the 23rd Flight for a bridge just far enough.[917]

How about *80 Year Old Orgasm* or is that going too far? What we do, I think, is write about our own weaknesses and fallacies and things we dislike saying about ourselves. We self-deprecate to cool down our own plunging egos? But at this point, I remember the poems of yours I think best, such as "The Cry" ["Cry over Aswan"] and the Brooks pome ["Letter to Leonardo"], and the slighter ones fly outa my head.

My own book, from which you read some stuff, and as I said, seems my best to me. Quite possibly I am wrong. But it is a change of direction for me, not so navel-centred, and yet paradoxically quite introspective. You remarked that it

---

917. "Twenty-Third Flight" was published in EB's *Ice Cod Bell or Stone* (1962).

would win the GG. I do not feel that myself. All I can do is write the best I can and let others judge.

My big mistake was not to go with Oxford, tell Bill Toye I wouldn't go back to McStew.[918] But fuckit, we all live with our mistakes.

Love to both of you,

Al

To Purdy (Ameliasburgh) from Birney (Toronto)
August 24, 1984   TL

Dear Al

I return your much-travelled envelope. It reached me today. I kept wondering why you wouldn't send my speech back. Thought maybe you'd liked it so much you couldn't part with it. Thanks for encouraging comments about *Just To Wave* (or *Last Orgasm*?).[919] Will be back Sep 12. When are you coming up to TO again?

Love to you & your longsuffering spouse

Earle

In haste. Taxi to airport in 2 hrs, & not yet packed!

To Purdy (Ameliasburgh) from Birney (Toronto)
November 20, 1984   AL

Dear Al,

I missed seeing you after my Kingston reading — I hope you weren't annoyed by my reading that piece of foolery about "reedin pomes" — maybe you had somewhere else you had to go — anyway by the time I'd signed the last book & autographed the last grubby piece of paper for an oughtagraph, I was tired & headed for bed & an early train back to TO. Wonder are you in Flah now, soakin up sun.

At last I got a chance to read through *Piling Blood* — some of your best, for sure — here's my favorites: the first 2, then (in order of order of contents only) "In the Beginning [Was the Word]," "Adam & No Eve," "There Is of Course a Legend," "Man without a Country," "The Blue City," "Eleanor & Valentina," "Double Focus,"

---

918. William Toye (b. 1926): Influential Canadian literary editor (Oxford University Press), anthologist, and general editor of *The Oxford Companion to Canadian Literature* (1983).

919. The proposed title, *Just to Wave*, was not used. The phrase appears in "Ave Atque Vale," a poem eventually published in EB's *Last Makings*: "Over the hill and / sinking fast in the bog / i've time just to wave // one muddy hand" (*OMH* 182). In *Last Makings* and *OMH* the poem is dated 1986; EB's letter suggests that it existed in some form at least two years earlier.

"For Eurithe," "Museum Piece," "The Strangers," "Dog Song 2," "The Tarahumara Women," & "Choices" — well so whaddyoucare I dint list them all — someday I'll tell you why the others aren't as good if someday you wanna know. Only review I've seen is Fraser Sutherland's — & I agree with much of what he says, especially when he is liking you — hope you get lots more writing done this winter & no more bloody backaches.[920]

I would write more but am in a turmoil of moving the "office" part of my belongings down to Alexander & Church.

Love to Eurithe & to you from us both
Earle

To Birney (Toronto) from Purdy (Ameliasburgh)
November 24, 1984   TL

Dear Earle,

I had a mob of student teachers with me, bound elsewhere (to a pub), and you were surrounded by admirers. I thought it'd be some time before either of us could escape.

Thank you for your good word on *Piling Blood*. Your "best" list parallels my own very largely. I might have added "Birds & Beasts." Re why others aren't as good: would one want everything to be good so there'd be no basis of comparison, all equally homogenous [*sic*]? Or is that a good argument.

We are off to south in two days, and as you say "in a turmoil of packing" — with Eurithe, as you might expect, doing most of the work. I'm catching up on last minute stuff.

Re F. Sutherland's review: it was good, except that I think there should be valuation and placement of the writer under review. Was it a good book, and how does it rank generally? Since it may well be my last, I'd like to know how people think. Oh yeah, I know the review was favourable, but there's a little more could be said besides that.

Our address south will be: J19 Plantation Blvd., Fort Pierce, Fla. 33450.

The Queen's stint was good. And the student teachers bright and sharp and likeable. I was slightly surprised that this was so, and that I liked the experience. Perhaps I am a thwarted academic. I also sold a lot of my own once-about-to-be-remaindered books which I rescued for a price, but whose bulk still bugs me in a

---

920. Fraser Sutherland reviewed *Piling Blood* in *The Globe and Mail* (17 Nov. 1984). The review ("Little Oink Sounds and Pterodactyls") was fairly critical. It prompted a letter to the editor from AP (3 Dec. 1984), who corrected three spelling mistakes. "A subject truly loyal to the Chief Magistrate should not submit to arbitrary typos or incorrect spelling," he wrote, alluding to the motto that appears on the newspaper's editorial page.

corner of the living room. An enduring monument to my own basic unsaleability, despite dribs and drabs here and there.

Al

To Birney (Toronto) from Purdy (Fort Pierce)
November 27, 1984   TL

Dear Earle,

Two day transition from A-burg to Fla., which feels like jet lag to me. One is transported, literally, and figuratively reaches another world.

Thank you for your letter re *Piling Blood*. It means something to me that you think it worthwhile. So little in life is worthwhile, or so it seems at times when one feels down about oneself. Incidentally, a short pome, the only one in some time:

Paranoid Lament

The hardest thing of all
to admit is that
there is at least one other person
in the world as intelligent
as you are —

I'm not sure that works, perhaps "just as intelligent"? Anyway ...

Since I don't feel like writing poems, even tho another part of my mind wants to write them badly, I'm writing a critique of CanPo, and wondering if it's possible to tell the truth. But I shall get back to poems I expect, despite the boringness of this place.

We are both well — and hope you and Wailan are the same — despite our rapid transit. At least the new car is comfortable. It achieved, incidentally, the abstemious consumption of 25 miles per Cangal.

We phoned Ron Everson on passing New Smyrna, and will be seeing him in due course.

How are your own memoirs coming? I "look forward" to them, and hope to see in them some of the Birneys I have known across the years.

Al

To Purdy (Ameliasburgh) from Birney (Toronto)
December 21, 1984   AL[921]

Got your 2 November letters (one of them just a few days ago!).

A footnote to your "short pome":

> It's even harder to admit
> (if merely to myself)
> that there are other people
> smarter than I am.

Tomorrow Wailan starts her festive holiday — almost 5 days (a lot for a lawyer) — & we take night train to Ottawa, to keep Bruce Nesbitt's new house warm in Rockcliffe while he & Vivianne spend their five days with relatives in Montreal.[922] We're taking our skates — for the Rideau — and hoping to see the National Whatsits (Gallery? Ballet? Opera? Theatre? — They're probably all on tour in Lloydminster, Sask., Alta.).

Give our best to Ron & Lorna & tell him I can't find his Florida address (he didn't put it on his envelope) so will write him to Montreal.

The past 5 weeks have been lost from writing ("always scribble, scribble, scribble," as the Duke of Gloucester said to Gibbon) by reason of moving my entire "office" — books, mss, files, desk, etc — to a flat at 484 Church St. (opp. CBC).[923] I had a chance to sublet it very cheaply. This allows Wailan more freedom, & me too — but so far we spend the nights together, here or at Balliol. But the disruption from packing — unpacking — reshelving — etc. was horrendous & still hasn't ended, what with Xmas Mail to cope with. In Jan. I *must* write a 6,000-word article on Lowry for *Sat Nite*, & a 10,000-word "brief autobiog" for the Gale Publishing outfit in Chicago, & a poem for Norman Jeffares' *Festschrift*.[924] In Feb. my radio-plays-coll. comes out from Quarry, & in April my coll. of essays on Chaucer.[925] Otherwise I'll be working on a new book of makings, if alive. Cheers & love to you both from us.

E & WL

921. The letter has no salutation. The date provided is the postmark date.

922. Bruce Nesbitt (b. 1941): Professor of English at Simon Fraser University and the University of Ottawa and commentator on Canadian and Commonwealth literature.

923. Edward Gibbon (1737–94): English historian (*The History of the Decline and Fall of the Roman Empire*, 6 vols., 1776–88).

924. EB's "A Hailing" (dated May 1985) was included in *Literature and the Art of Creation: Essays and Poems in Honour of A. Norman Jeffares* (1988), edited by Robert Welch and Suheil Badi Bushrui.

925. *Words on Waves: Selected Radio Plays of Earle Birney* and *Essays on Chaucerian Irony* were both published in 1985.

I couldn't draw as well as Mr. Schricker, even if I had 4 arms & 2 mouths. I suppose that you, Purdy, paint poems with your mouth, on them readin tours you make, but me, I'm just an earwig.[926]

To Birney (Toronto) from Purdy (Ameliasburgh)
May 10, 1985   TL

Dear Earle,

Would you be kind enough to support a CC [Canada Council] senior grant application? Sorry to be so abrupt, but the forms came in several days ago; but we've had guests and I couldn't get at the typer. Plan to get back to Greece and visit Troy, etc. Details on form, but will wait to hear from you before sending.

Bill Percy and Vina here, he off on CC work, GG [Governor General's] awards etc. And young poet and his wife. Rather hectic.

Two apartments, you said on the phone. Must be great to be rich like that! I hope to get up there in the next month or so.

All best,
Al

To Purdy (Ameliasburgh) from Birney (Toronto)
May 16, 1985   APC

Al,

Got 2 missives from you, both to old address, so I banged off all the grapeshot (shit?) on hand to Council. — Said that you were the greatest, etc. (next to me, of course). — But you sure left it late! — The 2 apts. we have now are for the price of one — come & try them soon!

Earle

To Purdy (Ameliasburgh) from Birney (Toronto)
May 28, 1985   APC

Al,

Your letter addressed to "114C" instead of Apt. 414 has just been delivered. So I waited-in, all Thurs, expecting you, & phoning your Ameliasburgh # & getting no answer. Meantime Eurithe phoned me, thinking you were with me. I hope she reached you eventually. I was relieved you hadn't landed in a hospital somewhere

---

926. The letter was written on a notecard illustrated with a "Clematis … From an Original, mouth-painted by I. Schricker."

from a highway accident ... I wrote CC that you are "the outstanding living Canadian poet & at the height of his powers, but still in need of financial support from the CC. He will write well, wherever he is, but perhaps writes best under the stimulus of foreign travel. I can't think of a better way to support poetry in Canada." OK?

Earle

To Birney (Toronto) from Purdy (Ameliasburgh)
May 31, 1985   TL

Dear Earle,

Sorry I couldn't thank you in person for your CC support. I phoned several times between 3.30 and 4.30 that day (Thurs), then again later, tho I forget what time later. Anyway, some pills and I felt better, but too late to get on the road by that time. I went out to the work room here, to type some more at this bio-crit stuff I'm workin on.

Somebody at CC wrote and said my application would have to wait until next Oct. competition. So what the hell, at least it isn't wasted entirely. Besides you, I have George Woodcock and Northrop Frye, which ain't a bad bunch of supporters. I had to get all three of you in a panicstricken rush when I found I was late with my application.

And yeah, I think you're right about travel: it kinda puts the onus on me to produce, like a deadline, a climate and geography of writing.

And I note that you were mistaken about the GG award. I see they are limiting the short list to new writers, old codgers like me ain't eligible. In the *TorStar* story it quotes the GG jury: which wishes "to draw attention to major new voices." So the short list: [Roo] Borson, Marilyn Bowering, Paulette Jiles, [David] McFadden, Sharon Thesen and Peter Van Toorn. Interesting idea to limit it like that. I presume Joe Rosenblatt had a hand in it, since he was on the jury last year. Dennis Lee said the same as you, that *Piling Blood* deserved the award. However, I console myself with the thought that writing those poems was very rewarding; I would also have liked more tangible rewards.

But I am not writing now, poems I mean. That bothers me more than not getting the GG. I have this odd ambivalence — I want and yet don't want to write poems. I want to want to, that is. I could, of course, sit down and struggle with poems, perhaps turn out something. But I don't like it that way. The poems should take me, not me them. And it's depressing when they don't.

Eurithe is still out west, near three weeks now, and I'm a little stir crazy here alone.

By the way, I heard a nice story re Layton. Seems his biographer dug up a spare wife for him in Halifax. Elspeth Cameron did, that is.[927] That would be his first wife, but also his sixth? Seems also Irving was an insurance salesman and jeweller while supporting the lady, who is now 70 and healthy. Irving is now said to be writing his autobio in order to refute Elspeth Cameron, which must be quite difficult a refutation. And he is also disagreeing strongly with the guy who's helping him with the autobio. And I'm sure Irving loves it. I lose count of his wives, but if you do it like we used to do Henry VIII's in school — how did it go, divorced, beheaded, died for the first three ...

So I don't hear if I get any CC money until January, '86.

Did you get any more copies of that book of yours? Radio plays, I think you said.

How are you? Chirpy and healthy? Ron Everson was writing like hell before leaving Fla. then shut down when he got to Mtl. One terrific poem about flying squirrels ... Me, I'm drinking cheap French wine on Tony Aspler's (*Star* wine columnist) say so, and morosely struggling with prose. No wonder stomach trouble occasional ...

Thanks again for good words, I'm grateful ...

And to you both,

Al

To Purdy (Ameliasburgh) from Birney (Toronto)
October 15, 1985   AL

Dear Al

I owe you an apology. As you've seen I've grown old & crotchety, and get upset by trifles. I'd looked forward to your company in TO last week but I found myself listening to you and two fellows I'd never met all talking a bit maliciously (I thought) about other writers (or whatevers) in TO, people I felt friendly to. It made me uncomfortable to be included in the hostility — but I got hostile myself, which was damned silly, because it made me say nasty things to you, my old and dear friend. You are worth all these other poets & poetasters put together. I had hoped you would stay the night at my place & we could talk without quarrelling, but you were determined to drive back to Ameliasb. Hope you got there safely. Hope also very much that you can forgive me. We have been friends & fellow-writers far too long to be at odds.

Peace to you, love to Eurithe. Write me.

Earle

---

927. The biography is *Irving Layton: A Portrait* (1985), by Elspeth Cameron.

I found the radio-play book I inscribed for you. Will you pick it up next time you're in town or shall I mail it?

Earle

To Purdy (Ameliasburgh) from Birney (Toronto)
August 11, 1986   AL

Dear Al

Sorry I couldn't make it to have beer or supper or whatever with you when you phoned a while back from some hotel on Sherbourne. I've written Bernice too, in case she was anyway miffed.[928] It was a poor day for me. Lan has been suffering from a nerve ailment, very painful, requiring heavy pain-killers (with the usual side-effects that seem to accompany any pill these days). I have had to be a part-nurse, making sure she gets home from work OK & properly fed. She is entirely off alcohol & so now am I, not even beer, because of my own various ailments. Getting old, man, getting old. So please don't cast me off — try me next time you're in town & give me a day's warning so I can fix up a bedroom to put you in, & save yourself the exorbitant prices hotels in TO charge.

I had a heavy session at Harrison Hot Springs — 3 days working 12-hour days, advising writers, holding workshops, attending other people's events, giving 1½-hour nightly readings — & then off in a 2-seater monoplane to catch my Seattle plane back home. Back to a desk-mountain of mail.

And how are you? & Eurithe? Send me words, or bring some.

As ever,
Earle

To Purdy (Ameliasburgh) from Birney (Toronto)[929]
October 13, 1986   AL

Dear Al

You didn't put your Victoria address on your August letter, only the address of a Dutch motel I have no wish to engage as an intermediary, but it could be that Purdy letters are rushed by courier to the Pacific the moment they show up in Ameliasburghhh — we will see.*

Wailan had a *tic douloureux* attack in August, was advised to quit all work for at least 3 weeks — the pains were controlled by heavy drugs of some sort & a

---

928. Probably Bernice Lever (b. 1936): Canadian poet (*Excuses for All Occasions*, 1979) and literary editor.

929. AP was in Victoria but EB sent the letter to Ameliasburgh.

2-week stay on the West Coast (Victoria mainly) got her back into working shape, but she has, I hope, learned there is a limit even to her endurance of law courts & lawyers' clients — she is now working only about eleven hours a day.**

We economized on plane-fares by booking a prepaid return on United from here to Seattle & back — from Seattle we took a remarkably cheap round trip on ferries to Victoria – Nanaimo – Vancouver, stayed with Lan's family in Vic., & friends in Vanc. — in between, we borrowed Lan's brother's car & drove up the new road to Port Hardy — that north tip of V.I. [Vancouver Island] has scenery as spectacular as Alaska's — in Vanc., saw Lionel Kearns & the Woodcocks — also my son, but Bill was recovering from an appendectomy & not very conversational (he's O.K. now) ... After Lan flew back to TO to work again, I went to Harrison Hot Springs & worked my ass off for 4 days giving readings, interviews, tapings, workshops, etc. — then found I was marooned there (having given my bro-in-common-law his car back) — the Vanc. Expo had bought up all the bus seats, there was no train, etc. So the Harrison Festival people found a 20 year old bush pilot to fly me from Chilliwack direct onto the United runway at Seatac [Seattle-Tacoma] airport — great way to travel (a 2-seater, skimming the glaciers on the sides of Mt. Baker & the fresh ash on St. Helens).

So now I'm back trying to start writing my autobiog (got a CC grant) & answering letters from a retired poet basking on the sands of Sooke or Manzanillo or Crete or wherever. I hope he continues to send them.

Your smell pome reminded me that cancers indeed do have smells — my mother's had but I doubt she could smell it; but it's nothing compared to a week-old human corpse — there were some around Nijmegen in '45.[930]

I enjoyed your (second?) preface to a Pete Trower's book (the new selected he just sent me) [*The Slidingback Hills*, 1986] & I enjoyed the one to an earlier book of his — thanks for "A Small Town in Mexico" — I committed a similar undetected crime one night in a flat on Toronto's Hazelton St., back in the 30s — I put out about one square mile of Toronto lights just trying to repair a short in a vac. cleaner ... 2 years ago I set out with Lan from Guadalajara to show Lan the beauties of Lake Chapala — but there were so many "deviaciones" I got lost & drove all the way past the lake (about 150 kms) without ever seeing it, because of the huge dirt-hills the highway repair crews had erected. Reading your description of Ajijic, I'm glad we never found it. We drove on to San Miguel Allende & had a great time ... By the way, next time

---

930. AP's "The Smell of Rotten Eggs" appeared in *The Collected Poems of Al Purdy* (1986). It begins: "The cancer had taken both breasts / and I got the strange impression / that what was left of her / was not really sentient" (*BR* 441).

you quote (& misquote) Longfellow's "Excelsior," don't let Whittier spring into your head. (It happens to all of us.)

Earle

* Sorry about the illegibility of this — Typewriter on the blink, & it's a weekend holiday.

** Great relief when we learned it wasn't, as first suspected, a brain tumor!

To Birney (Toronto) from Purdy (Victoria)
April 8, 1987   TL

Dear Earle,

Now that you're recovering, I want to wish you a speedy one, and remember, you still have the motives and impetus — after showing off your physical prowess in that fruit tree — that years ago enabled you to recover from the original fall, or was it original sin? I really didn't know how I could finish the foregoing sentence, and it would cause madness in any high school grammar teacher.

And of course, this is in lieu of a "Get Well" card.

It appears that you recommended me for a creative writing instructor and performer at Harrison Hot Springs, the which I've accepted. But accepted with the proviso that I'm not Birney, despite the names' similarity. So thanks: altho, when I look at the schedule, I may have to call for Birney desperately, to help me out with all the talking. As you know, I don't talk much or well.

One surprising bit: Phyllis Wilson, the Festival coordinator, tells me you put away your share of booze. Shame! Was this because you were away from Wailan and the tie that binds didn't? Next you'll be taking up smoking cigars.

It turns out Eurithe and I will have several things to do this summer. I have a day at Bayside (near Trenton, my hometown, where I've never read on accounta my plethora of four-letter words), both reading and one-day workshops for the fee you recommended to me once (500 bucks). Also Halifax, for the C.A.A. [Canadian Authors Association], to my shame; but Bill Percy and his wife Vina are my excuse (friends).

To my shame also, I haven't written much here. Still haven't figured out how to write a poem, which so many people keep asking both of us. (I tellem I don't know, but if I did I'd try to forget right away so I could surprise myself with my own continual stupidity.)

We leave here end of April for the drive east. And U. of T. in the fall, when we hope to see something of the Birneys.[931] And I'm still trying to outwit myself and write something unexpected to me. Which leaves me a bit morose. I get flashes and streaks of light re poems in my head, then when I try to write em all they are is cobwebs … You know, of course. I refuse to knowingly repeat myself; but haven't the equipment to explore unknown territory. But to hell with that, it's depressing.

Get outa that place as soon as you can. And Eurithe and I will see you in the fall, or perhaps this summer. And Wailan.

Al

To Elspeth Cameron from Purdy (Sidney, British Columbia)
March 23, 1994   TL

Dear Elspeth,

I'd like to explain a little more fully why I don't want *all* of those quotes from my letters embodied in your bio [*Earle Birney: A Life*, 1994].

First, *I don't think Birney is a great poet*. At his best, he is a *very fine poet*, one of the finest or something similar in Can. lit. history. But not great or even close to it.

Second, I was much too effusive in my praise in those letters. Undoubtedly I wanted to meet him at the time, and later we became fairly close friends, which could be counted among the reasons for my praise. But then, at that precise time, he did seem very very good to me. Perhaps I've mentioned that I converted "David" into a half hour play for CBC?[932] That shows you what I thought of him, very highly.

Also, my praise seems to go on ad infinitum, and gets tiresome. Haven't you anyone else you can use to praise Birney?

Having some regard for you, Elspeth, quote other praise as well. Over-quoting me looks kinda bad. There must be others — ?

[…]

Anything else I can do to help you with the book, I'll be glad to; altho I can't think of anything.

Al

---

931. AP was writer-in-residence at the University of Toronto in 1987–88.
932. See the letters of 5/6 Oct. 1961, 13 Oct. 1961, 19 Oct. 1961, 3 Dec. 1961, and 1 Feb. 1962.

To *The Globe and Mail* (Toronto) from Purdy (Sidney)
December 23, 1995   TL[933]

The Editor,

I note that prostitute "The Contessa" [Elizabeth Spedding] was honoured in your "Larger Lives" feature today (Dec. 23); whereas poet Earle Birney was omitted entirely.[934]

Presumably this indicates the *Globe and Mail*'s opinion of Canadian poetry?

Sincerely,

Al Purdy

933. *YA* 511. The letter was published with minor changes in *The Globe and Mail* (12 Jan. 1996).
934. The newspaper did not include EB in its account of notable deaths in 1995.

Al Purdy
EARLE BIRNEY IN HOSPITAL

He knows me and does not
know me and the fatal
facility for transposing
myself into another someone
ends with me peering out
from his eyes into my eyes
and dizzily thinking
My God! My God!
I have stopped being Me!

But calmer now:
he knows me and does not
know me and I am a coloured
shadow in sunlight
his brow furrowed and puzzled
with the effort of not knowing
poems he's written and not written
yet that will never be
and he smiles in memory
what might be memory
of whatever smiling was
and it is somehow left for me
to write them remembering pain
of not writing beyond
this grey land of nowhere
forgetting the pain before
beautiful verb and handsome noun
agreed to live together
for better or worse somehow
and kicked their heels
in the printed word
while the shadow stranger waits
the strange shadow
watching and ill at ease
and a little afraid:

as he questions himself
asks himself: *Who is this guy?*
Why is he here?

At that very moment
when the puzzlement is greatest
I smile at him
and the *why* and the smile together
glow just beyond the poem
and shine on his face and his face shines
and for that one moment
my friend remembers
among the multiple choices
of his lost remembering
he chooses
and the poem blossoms[935]

---

935. The poem was published in AP's *Naked with Summer in Your Mouth* (1994) and was included in *BR* (486–87).

Appendix 1: Undated Letters and Fragments

Two Early Poems by Purdy

Version

If it hadn't been for Ariadne's wheedling, cheek
and bosom pressing against him when
they walked, and Pasiphae's innocent sort of look,
as if she'd like to make him happy,
but really shouldn't —
the wandering tinker, the great mechanic,
might never have watched his island-hopping son
sink like a stone. True the wings were a copy,
and chancy things at best.
But Icarus was a laconic
youth who hated his father and wouldn't
admit that Minos hated HIM,
flew at the sun and shook his fist
at the dwindling world and the anxious man below;
hesitated, and cursed himself for a yellow
coward: after that the slow
man-fall to the sea's pillow.
The old perfectionist
sighed helplessly and went on.

Everybody knows what happened,
a cause célèbre for a time.
Of course the courts took no action
against the father, called it an accident.
Faulty materials, it seems
to me they said. The crops ripened
much as before; Poseidon's ocean
found a place for the new chum
in a basement room; and Daedalus,
the old roué, appears
sometimes to be a little glum,
is staying with Cocalus,
working on the drafting table, one hears.

And Ariadne in the family way somewhere in the Medit
erranean area smiles at the sea, and continues her slow audit.[936]

Invocation[937]

To be spoken aloud in a land without snow

Mourn for snow: the sun-staring, the blue-memory
Of hip-high drifts and town mirage;
The shading, the symmetry of trees beneath slow
Flakes, flowers in a lonesomeness of young age.
And morning, white morning after the windy
Yesterdays in the forest of always Sunday.

Roads in white nowhere on strange errands.
Only wire-hum, foot-heart-beat audible
And terror-telling: the steady sky-falling torrents,
As a woman should be, a woman most beautiful.

The horse-clopping, the bell-ringing time of earth,
The cloud-beaten, wind-bullied hammers of blood
Bursting in noiseless thunder — no sound heard —
Only the sky emissaries slow going to bed.

Send snow! Send it white in this land of green trees
And small brown people — comptroller of all my days.

---

936. As AP probably knew, EB referred to Ariadne in "Within These Caverned Days" (in *Now Is Time* and *The Strait of Anian*). AP referred to Ariadne in "The North West Passage" ("dead sailors / suspended from Ariadne's quivering cord" [*BR* 98]), from *North of Summer: Poems from Baffin Island* (1967), and in "Vestigia" ("slim Ariadne under the multiple petticoats"), from *The Crafte So Longe to Lerne* (1959) and *Love in a Burning Building* (1970). "Version" contains a strong echo of the final lines of W.H. Auden's "Musée des Beaux Arts" (1938), a poem that AP knew well and to which he sometimes alluded: "and the expensive delicate ship that must have seen / Something amazing, a boy falling out of the sky, / Had somewhere to get to and sailed calmly on." AP omitted the accents from "cause célèbre" and "roué."

937. The poem was published (without the directive "To be spoken ...") in AP's *Emu, Remember!* (1956).

To Birney from Purdy
December 10   TL

Dear Earle,

Just a note to repeat again — be sure and drop down here fore dryness I mean Christmas sets in. Beds for all, and, if you can, let me know so I can get something besides the home made wine I have.

Have the feeling I may not be here long after new year, and these concatenations of circumstance and synchronizings of separate necessities don't occur too often — I mean, after spring you go to London, and where the hell I go is puzzling. I've often wondered — you know?

Anyway, shout me a give when you time have.

Best,
Al

Tell Esther I'm saving her a sleeping bag near the fire.

To Birney from Purdy
December 17   TL

Dear Earle,

Well I have put my foot in it badly this time. When Callaghan phoned I didn't have the brains to ask to see your letter before I gave him permission to publish. And despite saying you personally had changed etc., I disagreed with you on points that I wouldn't have if I'd known. If I'd known? Well, I should have.

If I were you I'd be mad as hell at me, and I expect you are. All I can do is apologize, and that isn't enough. I feel badly, but that isn't enough either. I hate to lose a friend, but I don't seem to have the sense to keep my mouth shut at the right or wrong time. It was just stupid on my part.

Al[938]

Note, left for Purdy when Birney stayed at Ameliasburgh

Dear Al

A thousand thanks.

Missed you — really.

How the hell do you turn off the kitchen light, except by unscrewing it, the way I have?

Earle

---

938. EB's note: "replied by ld tel. … — nothing to apologize for."

To Purdy from Birney
Mon morning   AL

Dear Al
I was waiting for you to ring again but now have learned you have departed —
here's a letter that came this a.m.

Also, Ron Everson in a letter to me says to tell you he has "a photo of your
backhouse to send.

Note written by Birney

Here I sit beside Purdy & Everson
Something that's seldom or never don [*sic*]
by any bugger not in the League
of Canadian Poets
even by friends of Farley Mowat's

Jeez it's great to be
an LCP-
er
sitting here
& just sitting
& sitting
while others do
all the shitting

by Earle Birney

To Purdy from Birney
AL

Al —
We're despatching publicity. — Copy of your tape off to you very soon.

Best!
Earle

To Purdy from Birney
AL

Dear Al,

Here's the house (but the former owners took the big dish. I think they could have left the dog, a silly beast whom I sternly ordered to decamp to his rightful master — instead, as you can see, he went off to drown himself in that trout pond — all this was in Dec. — come Jan., masses of snow buried, & still buries, the scene — I now spend my weekends shovelling, sawing, axing, splitting, or driving thru blizzards on Hwy 47. Hope Eurithe is quite recovered. I'll be in Vancouver Mar 4 to 7 (UBC Alumni Celebration) & again Mar 12–14 & again May 24 to 30 (Victoria 24–26). Any chance of seeing you? Back in TO on Mr [?] 30th — When you comin here?

xxx to both from both

"In the Desert" *good*. [The poem was published in *The Woman on the Shore*, 1990.]

— E

Appendix 2: Purdy on Birney

To John Glassco, October 20, 1964

Birney assailed me for review — for saying poets 20 years ago imitated Carman in Canada.[940] Challenged me to name one. I did. Myself. Perhaps I was the only one who escaped (eventually) his influences unharmed. Birney had a graph made out with all the 20-years-ago poets, giving their ages then, and their influences. Made a good case too. And I grant him much validity, but I still think the old-lady poets, those who submerged and were never seen again, that many of them at least, were Carman worshippers. But he, apparently, will give no ground ...

To George Woodcock, April 6, 1966

I didn't do any more on the Birney.[941] He's very busy — has a book of prose coming with CBC pub. A thought on that: why not review both his *Selected*, which is due shortly and the prose articles in the CBC book at the same time — One ought to throw some light on the other. And seems to me Birney deserves large treatment. Don't know exactly how you feel about his work, but I'm admiring, with a few reservations. Seems to me also the prose book would do away with any need to tape-record anything and the whole call for a full-length article. I doubt my capability in any such assessment, and maybe one of the more prominent critical figures like [A.J.M.] Smith or Milton Wilson would be better. As you know, they have far more all-round erudition and general knowledgeability of such things as literary inter-relations, influences etc.

To Woodcock, August 1966

Got your Birney review in *Forum* along with other mail at Deer Lake [Newfoundland], where it was sent on. I'm rather fond of Birney personally, but apart from that I do agree with you. Particularly on the point: (paraphrase you) he doesn't reveal himself. He doesn't even if you know him well either. But then, the person you can figure out really well is a distinct minority. A unicellular creature maybe, and there do seem to be such in the world.

---

939. See *YA* 94–95, 117, 120, 122, 139, 155–56, 186, 231, 252, 253–54, 304, 389. 446, 447.
940. See the letters of 15 and 19 Oct. 1964.
941. "The Birney" was AP's abandoned critical study of EB's poetry.

To Woodcock, October 12, 1966

Also dissatisfied with the Birney piece, which Inge [Woodcock] mentioned you had. It doesn't really get at Birney. But I'm sure there's another Birney, very different than the one in his poems and these essays on writing. The submerged Birney that I get hints of every now and then rouses my extremest curiosity.

To Woodcock, March 1, 1968

I'm definitely, now, doing a book on Birney, and looking toward it with foreboding. Have made tapes with him, but got nowhere close to what I was looking for. I wanted to relate changes in his own life with his poems — you know, suddenly he discovers Sartre and how does this affect his poems? But like I said, got nowhere on this tack. There must be another Birney somewhere, dammit, for if there isn't I'm chasing nothing. Of course he's a damn impersonal poet, says really very little about himself, only gives his reactions to situations and conditions.

To Margaret Laurence, February 1, 1970

So what else is new? Birney I sympathize with, for he is a friend, tho I can't talk to him the way I do in letters to you, or in person. I do agree that he's a phony Lothario, whether he realizes this or not. But in a way, perhaps unexplainable, I do sympathize with his wish to stay young thru others. In another way I do not, for it makes him a phony if he knows it, an idiot if he doesn't. I think a lot of men — at a certain more youthful age than him — have the wish to fuck every beautiful woman in the world. Some women perhaps too, vice-versa. It's not altogether silly, perhaps has to do with one world psychologically, one human world etc. But really, the only important women are those with whom there is some kind of rapport, whether instant or developing. And beyond that again is death.

To Laurence, November 2, 1971

Birney telling me he sends his books to the US mag hoping for a review, finally gets the mag and thinks AHA, this is it. Then sees a review of Purdy and thinks Oh shit what do I hafta do??[942] The review ends: "These are the two most essential Purdy books to own & Purdy, whether he is Canadian or not, it doesn't matter, is a most essential poet to read." Now isn't that sweet? Makes me feel great, read me

---

942. See EB's letter of 22 Aug. 1971.

because the curse of Canadian might never have descended and I might even be American if no one says different.

To Jack McClelland, June 29, 1973

I'm told Birney has a new girl friend (add gossip): so I wrote to Earle and said please, boy, give me some hint how you do it. Can I put a bug in your foreskin, Earle?[943] May I marinate you for an aphrodisiac?

To Woodcock, September 6, 1974

Thinking about my last letter to you: I don't really want to review Birney's *Collected*. I'm by far the most interested in young poets, whose talent you can't entirely predict. I'm editing another anthology of them [*Storm Warning 2*], collecting the material now. I guess the deadline will be about April of next year. I might write a piece on all these poets later, at least the most interesting ones? I suppose a thing like this is bound to reflect my own tastes, as such books always do. And I have no defense for them at all.

To Robin Mathews, September 27, 1974

Re Birney, I didn't do the book on him because I was in Greece on a CC award at the time, and it would have been too much work. I didn't read the book Davey did until I started work on an article for *Weekend* about Birney.[944] (It's now finished and ready to go.) I don't have a very high opinion of the Davey book, on accounta when you start to do a book of this nature on a Canadian writer it isn't worth doing if you intend to make it partly a put-down. I know Earle feels this very strongly. I've recently seen some of his letters (carbons) to Davey, and if I'd gotten letters like that I'd probably shrivel into the size of a coconut.

To Frank Scott, August 3, 1979

I remarked a while back in a letter to Birney that older people were much more likeable to me. He said something to the effect that they learned something over the years. He said "of course — older people, like me, are wiser, better-natured, funnier — there have to be *some* dividends to go with arthritis, insomnia and

---

943. See AP's letter of 26 June 1973.
944. See the letters of 24 Dec. 1974 and 3 Jan. 1975.

forgetfulness"[945] ... Which is partly facetious, but not inaccurate. I couldn't have written "Fathers" a while back. I had this great period where you dash off six or seven poems in a week. Then subside, or lie fallow, or whatever.

To George Galt, December 21, 1984

Just occurred to me I could include personal and unprintable anecdotes about Birney, especially, and others in the CanPo piece, which would make it much more interesting to and for me. And some of Birney's own stories about Bliss Carman and Roberts are very good. And he himself is (he himself?) is so prickly and bright that he's better than any character in his writings.

To Sam Solecki, November 8, 1989[946]

Have you seen the blooper at the end of my Afterword for Birney's *Turvey*? [1989] They omitted the "w" of "now" which fucks up the whole piece. The typesetters, I mean. Who else?[947]

To Solecki, December 22, 1989

I was afraid to say much to [Elspeth] Cameron about Birney, after her Layton book [*Irving Layton: A Portrait* (1985)]. I think she was looking for something disgraceful. Did I mention: George Woodcock wouldn't see her at all.

---

945. See EB's letter of 20 July 1979.

946. Sam Solecki (b. 1946): Canadian literary critic (*The Last Canadian Poet: An Essay on Al Purdy*, 1999; *Ragas of Longing: The Poetry of Michael Ondaatje*, 2003), professor at the University of Toronto, and editor of several volumes of AP's poetry, prose, and letters. Solecki and AP were regular correspondents in AP's later years.

947. The last paragraph of the afterword follows a recollection of the depression that attended AP during his military service: "But Colonel Bogey sounds in my ears. What an irony for me to have all my blood stir with music as I read the book. No birds build their nests in springtime. The world renews itself annually. And "DAH-DAH" goes that music, as it will again and again, as Birney and Turvey knew it would." AP would have been dismayed to know that the misprint — "No birds" instead of "Now birds" — remains uncorrected in a recent edition of *Turvey* (2008). Cf. *SA* 288.

Glossary of Selected Names

Abrahams, Cecil: Canadian professor, activist.

Acorn, Milton (1923–86): Canadian poet.

Ahvenus, Martin (1928–2011): Canadian bookseller.

Aiken, Conrad (1889–1973): American novelist.

Albee, Edward (b. 1928): American playwright.

Allen, Rita Greer (1918–2010): Broadcaster, writer, artist.

Allen, Robert Greer (1917–2005): Playwright, television and radio producer for the CBC.

Almey, Kerrigan: Trenton-based printer of works of Purdy's.

Amiel, Barbara (b. 1940): British-Canadian journalist.

Anderson, Patrick (1915–79): Canadian poet, editor.

Arnett, Tom (1935–2008): Canadian newspaper editor, writer.

Atsumi, Ikuko (b. 1940): Japanese poet and translator.

Atwood, Margaret (b. 1939): Canadian poet, novelist, essayist, critic.

Auden, W.H. (1907–73): English poet, playwright, critic.

Avison, Margaret (1918–2007): Canadian poet.

Bailey, Alfred (1905–97): Canadian poet, historian.

Barbour, Douglas (b. 1940): Canadian poet, critic, professor.

Barker, George (1913–91): British poet.

Barrett, David (b. 1930): Premier of British Columbia, 1972–75.

Bates, Ronald (1924–95): Canadian poet, critic, professor.

Baudelaire, Charles (1821–67): French poet.

Beaver, Bruce (1928–2004): Australian poet.

Belford, Ken (b. 1946): Canadian poet.

Bennett, W.A.C. (1900–79): Premier of BC, 1952–72.

Bentley, Roy: Professor of English at UBC.

Berryman, John (1914–72): American poet.

Berton, Pierre (1920–2004): Canadian writer, journalist, television personality.

Betjeman, John (1906–84): English poet, journalist, architectural preservationist.

Birney, Esther (1908–2006): English-born Canadian social worker; EB's wife.

Birney, William (b. 1941): Son of EB and Esther Birney.

Bissell, Claude T. (1916–2000): Canadian biographer, president of the University of Toronto.

bissett, bill (b. 1939): Canadian poet, artist, publisher.

Blaser, Robin (1925–2009): Canadian poet, editor, professor.

Blazek, Douglas: (b. 1941): American poet, small-press publisher.

Borden, Carl (1905–78): Canadian archaeologist, professor.

Bowering, Angela (1940–99): Canadian writer, professor.

Bowering, George (b. 1935): Canadian poet, novelist, essayist, professor.

Bradstreet, Anne (c. 1612–72): American poet.

Brewster, Elizabeth (1922–2012): Canadian poet, novelist, professor.

Bridie, James (Osborne Henry Mavor) (1888–1951): Scottish dramatist.

Bromige, David (1933–2009): Canadian poet.

Brooke, Rupert (1887–1915): English poet.

Brooks, Leonard (1911–2011): Canadian painter.

Brown, Russell (b. 1942): Canadian professor, editor, literary critic.

Browning, Robert (1812–89): English poet, playwright.

Buckley, Joan: Editor of the *Vancouver Sun*'s poetry section when AP was a beginning poet.

Buitenhuis, Elspeth: See Cameron, Elspeth.

Bukowski, Charles (1920–94): American poet.

Bunting, Basil (1900–85): English poet.

Burles, Gordon (b. 1949): Canadian poet.

Burroughs, William S. (1914–97): American novelist.

Byron, George Gordon (1788–1824): English poet.

Callaghan, Barry (b. 1937): Canadian author, editor, journalist.

Cameron, Elspeth (b. 1943): Critic, literary biographer, professor.

Campbell, Roy (1901–57): South African poet.

Carman, Bliss (1861–1929): Canadian poet.

Carr, Emily (1871–1945): Canadian painter, writer.

Carruth, Hayden (1921–2008): American poet, anthologist, editor, critic.

Cary, Joyce (1888–1957): Anglo-Irish novelist.

Cather, Willa (1873–1947): American novelist, writer of stories.

Cervantes, Miguel de (1547–1616): Spanish novelist (*Don Quixote*, 1605), poet, playwright.

Chatterton, Thomas (1752–70): English poet, forger.

Chaucer, Geoffrey (c. 1343–1400): English poet, courtier, diplomat.

Chesterton, G.K. (1874–1936): English novelist, poet, essayist.

Christy, Jim (b. 1945): Canadian author.

Ciardi, John (1916–86): American poet, translator.

Claudel, Paul (1868–1955): French writer, diplomat.

Cogswell, Fred (1917–2004): Canadian poet, professor.

Cohen, Leonard (b. 1934): Canadian poet, novelist, and singer and songwriter.

Cohen, Nathan (1923–71): Canadian theatre critic, broadcaster.

Coleridge, Samuel Taylor (1772–1834): English poet, literary critic.

Colombo, John Robert (b. 1936): Canadian writer, anthologist, translator.

Conard, Audrey (b. 1943): Canadian poet included in *Storm Warning 2*.

Cook, James (1728–79): British explorer, cartographer.

Copithorne, Judith (b. 1939): Canadian poet.

Coulthard, Jean (1908–2000): Canadian composer.

Coupey, Pierre (b. 1942): Canadian poet, visual artist.

Creeley, Robert (1926–2005): American poet, editor, professor.

Crosland, Margaret (b. 1920): English author, translator, biographer.

Curnow, Allen (1911–2001): New Zealand poet, critic, anthologist.

Daniells, Roy (1902–79): Canadian poet, professor of English.

Dardick, Simon (b. 1943): Publisher, Véhicule Press.

Davey, Frank (b. 1940): Canadian poet, critic, professor.

Davidson, Claude (1924–91): Haida artist.

Davidson, Robert (b. 1946): Haida artist.

Day Lewis, Cecil (1904–72): English poet.

De la Mare, Walter (1873–1956): English poet, novelist.

De la Roche, Mazo (1879–1961): Canadian novelist, short-story writer.

Dennison, William (1905–81): Mayor of Toronto, 1967–72.

Dickey, James (1923–97): American poet, novelist.

Dickinson, Emily (1830–86): American poet.

Diefenbaker, John (1895–1979): Prime minister of Canada, 1957–63.

Dobbs, Kildare (1923–2013): Canadian essayist, editor, autobiographer.

Donne, John (1572–1631): English poet, priest, religious writer.

Douglas, James (Jim) (b. 1924): Canadian editor, publisher.

Drainie, John (1916–66): Canadian radio and television actor.

Dudek, Louis (1918–2001): Canadian poet, critic, editor.

Duncan, Robert (1919–88): American poet.

Dwyer, Peter (1914–73): British spy, director of the Canada Council.

Eaton, John (1909–73): Canadian businessman.

Eberhart, Richard (1904–2005): American poet.

Eliot, T.S. (1888–1965): American poet, playwright, literary critic.

Empson, William (1906–84): English literary critic, poet, professor.

Engel, Howard (b. 1931): Canadian writer, producer for the CBC.

Epstein, Jason (b. 1928): American editor, publisher.

Everson, Ronald Gilmore (1903–92): Canadian poet, public-relations executive.

Faber, Geoffrey (1889–1961): English publisher.

Farrell, James T. (1904–79): American novelist.

Fawcett, Brian (b. 1944): Canadian journalist, writer of poetry and fiction.

Fetherling, Douglas George (b. 1949): Canadian author of poetry, fiction, and biography.

Fiamengo, Marya (1926–2013): Canadian poet.

Finch, Robert (1900–95): Canadian poet, professor.

Finlay, Ian Hamilton (1925–2006): Scottish poet, artist.

Finlay, Michael (b. 1949): Canadian poet, journalist.

Fischman, Sheila (b. 1937): Canadian journalist, translator.

Ford, R.A.D. (1915–98): Canadian poet, diplomat.

Fraser, Dana (b. 1944): Canadian poet included in AP's *Storm Warning*.

Freuchen, Peter (1886–1957): Danish explorer, anthropologist.

Frost, Robert (1874–1963): American poet.

Frum, Barbara (1937–92): Canadian journalist.

Fry, Christopher (1907–2005): English playwright.

Frye, Northrop (1912–91): Canadian literary critic and theorist, professor of English.

Fulford, Robert (b. 1932): Canadian journalist, broadcaster, and author.

Fulton, E. Davie (1916–2000): Member of Parliament, justice of the Supreme Court of BC.

Galt, George (b. 1948): Canadian writer, editor.

Garneau, Hector de Saint-Denys (1912–43): Canadian poet.

Garner, Hugh (1913–79): Canadian writer of fiction and autobiography.

Geddes, Gary (b. 1940): Canadian poet, editor, critic.

Genet, Jean (1910–86): French novelist, poet, playwright.

Gervais, Marty (b. 1946): Canadian writer, publisher.

Gibbon, Edward (1737–94): English historian of Rome.

Gibbon, John Murray (1875–1952): Editor of *Canadian Poetry Magazine*, musicologist, author.

Gibbs, Robert (b. 1930): Canadian poet, professor.

Gilbert, Gerry (1936–2009): Canadian poet, visual artist.

Ginsberg, Allen (1926–97): American poet.

Glassco, John (1909–81): Canadian poet, memoirist, translator.

Godfrey, Dave (b. 1938): Canadian novelist, publisher.

Godwin, William (1756–1836): English philosopher, novelist.

Gotlieb, Phyllis (1926–2009): Canadian poet, science-fiction writer.

Graham, Billy (b. 1918): American evangelist, author.

Graves, Robert (1895–1985): English novelist, poet, autobiographer, mythologist.

Gray, Thomas (1716–71): English poet.

Greene, Graham (1904–91): English novelist.

Guest, Edgar (1881–1959): American poet, newspaper columnist.

Guevara, Che (1928–67): Marxist revolutionary.

Guillén, Jorge (1893–1984): Spanish poet.

Guillén, Nicolás (1902–89): Cuban poet.

Gustafson, Ralph (1909–95): Canadian poet, professor.

Gzowski, Peter (1934–2002): Canadian broadcaster, radio personality.

Haig-Brown, Roderick (1908–76): Canadian conservationist, author.

Haley, Alex (1921–92): American author.

Hambleton, Ronald (b. 1917): Canadian poet, novelist, editor.

Hardy, Thomas (1840–1928): English poet, novelist.

Harlow, Robert (1923): Canadian novelist, professor at UBC.

Harris, David W. (1948–94): Canadian poet.

Harris, Frank (1856–1931): Irish-born American journalist, publisher, autobiographer.

Hebb, Marian (b. 1939): Canadian lawyer who worked with The Writers' Union of Canada.

Herbert, Walter (1901–98): Canadian public-relations worker, director of the Canada Foundation.

Herrick, Robert (1591–1674): English poet.

Hill, Douglas (1935–2007): Canadian writer of science fiction.

Hindmarch, Gladys (b. 1940): Canadian writer.

Hine, Daryl (1936–2012): Canadian poet, editor.

Hood, Hugh (1928–2000): Canadian novelist, short-story writer.

Hopkins, Gerard Manley (1844–89): English poet, priest.

Horovitz, Frances (1938–83): English poet.

Horovitz, Michael (b. 1935): English poet.

Housman, A.E. (1859–1936): English poet, classical scholar.

Houston, James (1921–2005): Canadian artist, author.

Howe, Tom (b. 1952): Canadian poet included in *Storm Warning 2*.

Howith, Harry (b. 1934): Canadian poet, professor, publisher.

Hughes, Ted (1930–98): English poet, translator.

Hunt, Alison (b. 1930): Canadian schoolteacher, lover of EB's.

Hurtig, Mel (b. 1932): Canadian publisher.

Huxley, Aldous (1894–1963): English novelist, essayist.

Huxley, Julian (1887–1975): English biologist.

Inkster, Tim (b. 1949): Canadian publisher, printer.

Iremonger, Valentin (1918–91): Irish poet, translator, diplomat.

Jackovich, Jack: Canadian painter, fishing guide, friend of AP's.

Jeffares, A.N. (1920–2005): Irish literary critic, professor.

Jeffers, Robinson (1887–1962): American poet.

Jensen, Jack (d. 1997): Friend of EB's and AP's who held various jobs in Canadian publishing.

Jewinski, Ed (b. 1948): Canadian poet, professor, critic.

John, Augustus (1878–1961): Welsh painter.

Johnson, Pauline (1861–1913): Canadian/Mohawk writer and performer.

Johnston, George (1913–2004): Canadian poet, translator, professor.

Jung, Carl Gustav (1875–1961): Swiss psychiatrist, author.

Kain, Conrad (1883–1934): Austrian mountaineer.

Kearns, Lionel (b. 1937): Canadian poet, professor.

Keats, John (1795–1821): English poet.

Keeler, Wally (b. 1947): Canadian poet.

Kerouac, Jack (1922–69): American novelist, poet.

Kilgallin, Tony (b. 1941): Professor at UBC, commentator on Lowry's works.

Kipling, Rudyard (1865–1930): English poet, novelist, short-story writer.

Kirk, Downie (1910–64): Schoolteacher, friend of Malcolm Lowry's in Vancouver.

Kirkconnell, Watson (1895–1977): Canadian poet, anthologist, translator, professor.

Kizer, Carolyn (b. 1925): American poet, diplomat.

Klein, A.M. (1909–72): Canadian poet, novelist, lawyer.

Kunitz, Stanley (1905–2006): American poet, translator, professor.

Lambeth, Michel (1923–77): Canadian photographer.

Lamming, George (b. 1927): Barbadian novelist.

Lampert, Gerald (1924–78): Canadian arts administrator, novelist.

Lampman, Archibald (1861–1899): Canadian poet.

Lane, Patrick (b. 1939): Canadian poet, novelist.

Lane, Richard (Red) (1936–64): Canadian poet.

Lang, Curt (1937–98): Canadian poet, friend of AP's.

Laurence, Margaret (1926–87): Canadian novelist, short-story writer.

Lawrence, D.H. (1885–1930): English poet, novelist, essayist, critic.

Layton, Irving (1912–2006): Canadian poet.

Leacock, Stephen (1869–1944): Canadian satirist, political scientist, professor.

Lee, Dennis (b. 1939): Canadian poet, essayist, editor, critic.

Lehmann, John (1907–87): English literary critic, editor.

Lemieux, Jean Paul (1904–90): Québécois painter, professor.

LePan, Douglas (1914–98): Canadian novelist, poet, diplomat, professor.

Lever, Bernice (b. 1936): Canadian poet and literary editor.

Levertov, Denise (1923–97): English-born American poet.

Lévesque, René (1922–87): Founder of the Parti Québécois, premier of Québec, 1976–85.

Livesay, Dorothy (1909–96): Canadian poet, critic.

Logue, Christopher (1926–2011): English poet, translator.

Low, Wailan (Lily) (b. 1950): Canadian lawyer, judge, EB's companion 1973–95.

Lowell, Amy (1874–1925): American poet.

Lowry, Malcolm (1909–57): English novelist, writer of stories, poet.

Lowry, Margerie (1905–88): American writer, Malcolm Lowry's second wife and literary executor.

Ludwig, Jack (b. 1922): Canadian novelist, sportswriter.

Lytton, Edward BulwerLytton (1803–73): English novelist, playwright, poet.

MacCaig, Norman (1910–96): Scottish poet.

MacDiarmid, Hugh (1892–1978): Scottish poet.

MacDonald, Wilson (1880–1967): Canadian poet.

MacKay, L.A. (1901–82): Canadian poet, professor of classics.

Macklem, Michael (b. 1928): Founder and publisher of Oberon Press.

MacLean, Sorley (1911–96): Scottish poet.

MacLeish, Archibald (1892–1982): American poet, playwright, essayist, critic.

MacLennan, Hugh (1907–90): Canadian novelist, professor.

Mac Low, Jackson (1922–2004): American poet.

MacNeice, Louis (1907–63): Irish poet, playwright, critic.

Macpherson, Jay (1931–2012): Canadian poet.

Major, Leon (b. 1933): Canadian opera and theatre director.

Mandel, Eli (1922–92): Canadian poet, critic, editor.

Marlatt, Daphne (b. 1942): Canadian poet, novelist.

Marriott, Anne (1913–97): Canadian poet, journalist, scriptwriter.

Marshall, Tom (1938–93): Canadian novelist, poet.

Marty, Sid (b. 1944): Canadian conservationist, park warden in the Rockies, writer.

Marvell, Andrew (1621–78): English poet, satirist.

Maschler, Tom (b. 1933): English literary editor.

Mathews, Robin (b. 1931): Canadian writer, professor.

Mavor, Ronald (1925–2007): Scottish drama critic, playwright, physician.

Mayakovsky, Vladimir (1893–1930): Russian playwright, poet.

Mayne, Seymour (b. 1944): Canadian poet.

McCarthy, Bryan (b. 1930): Canadian poet.

McCartney, Linda (1944–2000): Canadian literary agent.

McClelland, Jack (1922–2004): Canadian publisher.

McClure, Michael (b. 1932): American writer.

McDermid, Anne: Canadian literary agent.

McKuen, Rod (b. 1933): American songwriter, poet.

McLuhan, Marshall (1911–80): Canadian professor, critic, theorist of communications.

McNeil, Florence (b. 1937): Canadian poet.

Melville, Herman (1819–91): American novelist, poet, writer of stories.

Miller, Arthur (1915–2005): American playwright.

Miller, Henry (1891–1980): American novelist.

Milton, John (1608–74): English poet, dramatist, political writer.

Moore, Marianne (1887–1972): American poet, essayist.

Mowat, Angus (1892–1977): Librarian who worked in Trenton and Belleville.

Mowat, Farley (b. 1921): Canadian writer, conservationist.

Muir, Edwin (1887–1959): Scottish poet.

Murphy, Richard (b. 1927): Irish poet.

Murray, Rona (1924–2003): Canadian writer, teacher of writing, EB's student.

Musgrave, Susan (b. 1951): Canadian poet, novelist.

Neruda, Pablo (1904–73): Chilean poet.

Nesbitt, Bruce (b. 1941): Canadian literary critic, professor.

New, W.H. (b. 1938): Canadian professor, literary critic, poet, editor.

Newbolt, Henry (1862–1938): English poet.

Newlove, John (1938–2003): Canadian poet, editor.

Newman, Peter C. (b. 1929): Canadian journalist, editor.

Nichol, Barrie Phillip (bpNichol) (1944–88): Canadian poet.

Nietzsche, Friedrich (1844–1900): German philosopher.

Nowlan, Alden (1933–83): Canadian poet, playwright, writer of stories and memoirs.

O'Brien, A.H. (1865–1957): Lawyer in Toronto, business manager for *Canadian Poetry Magazine*.

Ondaatje, Michael (b. 1943): Canadian poet, novelist.

Owen, Wilfred (1893–1918): English poet.

Pacey, Desmond (1917–75), professor, commentator on Canadian literature and culture.

Page, P.K. (1916–2010): Canadian poet, painter.

Papadopoulos, Georgios (1919–99): Greek military dictator.

Parrot, Jean-Claude (b. 1936): President of the Canadian Union of Postal Workers.

Patchen, Kenneth (1911–72): American poet, novelist.

Peale, Norman Vincent (1898–1993): American religious figure, author.

Percy, H.R. (Bill) (1920–97): Canadian novelist, short-story writer, literary biographer.

Persky, Stan (b. 1941): Canadian writer.

Peyto, Bill (1869–1943): Canadian mountaineer, park warden.

Plath, Sylvia (1932–63): American poet, novelist.

Porter, Anna (b. 1944): Canadian editor, publisher, author.

Pound, Ezra (1885–1972): American poet.

Powell, Craig (b. 1940): Australian poet.

Pratt, E.J. (1882–1964): Canadian poet, professor.

Priestley, J.B. (1894–1984): English novelist, playwright, critic.

Proust, Marcel (1871–1922): French novelist.

Purdy, Eurithe (b. 1924): AP's wife; they were married in 1941.

Purdy, Jim (1945–2012): Son of AP and Eurithe Purdy.

Ransom, John Crowe (1888–1974): American poet, literary critic, professor.

Reaney, James (1926–2008): Canadian poet, playwright.

Reeves, John (b. 1926): English-born Canadian composer, CBC radio producer.

Reid, Bill (1920–98): Haida sculptor, jeweller, writer.

Richler, Mordecai (1931–2001): Canadian novelist, essayist.

Rilke, Rainer Maria (1875–1926): German poet, novelist, noted writer of letters.

Rimanelli, Giose (b. 1926): Italian professor, novelist, poet, anthologist.

Roberts, Charles G.D. (1860–1943): Canadian poet, writer of stories.

Roberts, Dorothy (1906–93): Canadian poet.

Robinson, Brad (1942–2009): Canadian journalist, poet.

Rosenblatt, Joe (b. 1933): Canadian artist, poet, editor.

Ross, John (1777–1856): Scottish explorer of the Arctic.

Ross, Sinclair (1908–1996): Canadian novelist, short-story writer.

Ross, W.W.E. (1894–1966): Canadian poet.

Russell, Bertrand (1872–1970): English philosopher, historian, essayist.

Safarik, Allan (b. 1948): Canadian poet, publisher, memoirist.

Schliemann, Heinrich (1822–90): German archaeologist.

Schroeder, Andreas (b. 1946): Canadian writer, professor.

Scobie, Stephen (b. 1943): Canadian poet, critic, professor.

Scott, F.R. (1899–1985): Canadian poet, editor, professor.

Sedgewick, Garnett (1882–1949): Professor of English at UBC, Shakespearean scholar.

Shakespeare, William (1564–1616): English playwright, poet.

Silcox, David (b. 1937): Arts Officer for the Canada Council, scholar of Canadian art.

Sinclair, Lister (1921–2006): Canadian broadcaster, playwright, writer for the CBC.

Sitwell, Edith (1887–1964): English poet.

Skelton, John (c. 1460–1529): English poet.

Skelton, Robin (1925–97): Canadian poet, critic, anthologist, editor.

Smith, A.J.M. (1902–80): Canadian poet, critic, anthologist.

Smith, Denis (b. 1932): Editor of *The Canadian Forum,* professor of political science.

Smith, Iain Crichton (1928–98): Scottish poet, novelist.

Smith, Sydney Goodsir (1915–75): Scottish poet.

Solecki, Sam (b. 1946): Canadian critic, professor, editor of works by Birney and Purdy.

Sommers, Robert (1911–2000): Minister of Forests in BC.

Souster, Raymond (1921–2012): Canadian poet.

Spender, Stephen (1909–95): English poet, critic, editor.

Spenser, Edmund (c. 1552–99): English poet.

Spicer, Jack (1925–65): American poet.

Stanfield, Robert (1914–2003): Canadian politician.

Stevens, Peter (1927–2009): Canadian literary critic, biographer, poet, professor of English.

Stevenson, Robert Louis (1850–94): Scottish novelist, poet.

Stewart, Douglas (1913–85): Australian poet, critic, anthologist.

Suknaski, Andrew (1942–2012): Canadian artist and poet.

Sutherland, Ronald (1933–2013): Canadian critic, novelist, professor.

Suttles, Wayne (1918–2005): American anthropologist, professor.

Sylvestre, Jean-Guy (1918–2010): Canadian critic, anthologist, National Librarian 1968–83.

Symons, Scott (1933–2009): Canadian novelist.

Tallman, Ellen (1927–2008): Canadian professor at UBC.

Tallman, Warren (1921–94): American critic, professor at UBC.

Teunissen, John (b. 1933): Canadian novelist, professor.

Thibaudeau, Colleen (1925–2012): Canadian poet, writer of short stories.

Thomas, Clara (1919–2013): Professor, scholar of Canadian literature.

Thomas, Dylan (1914–53): Welsh poet.

Thurber, James (1894–1961): American humorist, cartoonist.

Tolstoy, Leo (1828–1910): Russian novelist.

Town, Harold (1924–90): Canadian painter.

Toye, William (b. 1926): Canadian literary editor, anthologist.

Trotsky, Leon (1879–1940): Russian revolutionary, military and political leader.

Trower, Peter (b. 1930): Canadian poet, novelist, logger.

Trudeau, Pierre Elliott (1919–2000): Prime minister of Canada, 1968–79, 1980–84.

Turner, W.J. (1889–1946): English music and theatre critic, novelist, poet.

Twigg, Alan (b. 1952): Literary journalist, historian of literature in British Columbia.

Ustinov, Peter (1921–2004): British actor, dramatist, filmmaker.

Vancouver, George (1757–98): British explorer, navigator.

Voznesensky, Andrei (1933–2010): Russian poet.

Waddington, Miriam (1917–2004): Canadian poet, writer of stories, professor.

Wagoner, David (b. 1926): American poet, novelist.

Wain, John (1925–94): English novelist, poet, critic.

Watson, Wilfred (1911–98): Canadian poet, playwright, professor.

Watt, F.W. (b. 1927): Canadian literary critic, professor.

Waugh, Evelyn (1903–66): English novelist.

Wayman, Tom (b. 1945): Canadian poet, anthologist, professor.

Weaver, Robert (1921–2008): Canadian broadcaster, literary editor.

Webb, Phyllis (b. 1927): Canadian poet.

Webster, Jack (1918–99): Radio and television broadcaster and reporter in BC.

Welles, Orson (1915–85): American film director, actor.

Wenner-Gren, Axel (1881–1961): Swedish industrialist.

Whalley, George (1915–83): Canadian poet, professor.

Whitman, Walt (1819–92): American poet.

Whyte, Jon (1941–92): Canadian poet.

Wieners, John (1934–2002): American poet.

Wilbur, Richard (b. 1921): American poet, translator.

Wilkinson, Anne (1910–61): Canadian poet, biographer, literary editor.

Williams, David (b. 1945): Canadian novelist, professor, critic.

Williams, Tennessee (1911–83): American playwright.

Williams, William Carlos (1883–1963): American poet.

Wilson, Milton (1923–2013): Professor of English at the University of Toronto.

Wolfe, James (1727–59): British general.

Woodcock, George (1912–95): Canadian poet, critic, professor, editor.

Woods, John (1926–95): American poet.

Wordsworth, William (1770–1850): English poet.

Wreford, James (James Wreford Watson) (1915–90): Scottish geographer, poet.

Wright, Charles (b. 1935): American poet, professor.

Yates, J. Michael (b. 1938): Canadian poet, professor, memoirist.

Yeats, William Butler (1865–1939): Irish poet, playwright, essayist.

Yeomans, Ed (1927–2009): Canadian professor of English at UBC, poet.

Yevtushenko, Yevgeny (b. 1933): Russian poet, novelist, essayist, film director.

Bibliography

Listed below are significant works by Birney and Purdy discussed in the letters and notes, as well as works quoted in the introduction. Basic bibliographical details of other works by or pertaining to Birney and Purdy are included in the notes as required.

Works by Earle Birney

Alphabeings & Other Seasyours. London, ON: Pikadilly, 1976.

The Bear on the Delhi Road: Selected Poems. London: Chatto and Windus, 1973.

Big Bird in the Bush: Selected Stories and Sketches. Oakville, ON: Mosaic/Valley, 1978.

The Collected Poems of Earle Birney. 2 vols. Toronto: McClelland and Stewart, 1975.

Copernican Fix. Toronto: ECW Press, 1985.

The Cow Jumped over the Moon: The Writing and Reading of Poetry. Toronto: Holt, Rinehart and Winston, 1972.

The Damnation of Vancouver. Toronto: McClelland and Stewart, 1977.

David and Other Poems. Toronto: Ryerson, 1942.

Down the Long Table. Toronto: McClelland and Stewart, 1955.

"E.J. Pratt and His Critics." *Our Living Tradition* (Second and Third Series). Edited by Robert L. McDougall. Toronto: University of Toronto Press, 1959. 123–47.

Essays on Chaucerian Irony. Edited by Beryl Rowland. Toronto: University of Toronto Press, 1985.

Fall by Fury & Other Makings. Toronto: McClelland and Stewart, 1978.

Ghost in the Wheels: Selected Poems. Toronto: McClelland and Stewart, 1977.

Ice Cod Bell or Stone. Toronto: McClelland and Stewart, 1962.

Introduction. *Selected Poems of Malcolm Lowry*. By Malcolm Lowry. Edited by Earle Birney. San Francisco: City Lights, 1962. 7–10.

Last Makings. Edited by Marlene Kadar and Sam Solecki. Toronto: McClelland and Stewart, 1991.

Memory No Servant. Trumansburg, NY: New Books, 1968.

Near False Creek Mouth. Toronto: McClelland and Stewart, 1964.

Now Is Time. Toronto: Ryerson, 1945.

One Muddy Hand: Selected Poems. Edited by Sam Solecki. Madeira Park, BC: Harbour Publishing, 2006.

The Poems of Earle Birney: A New Canadian Library Selection. Toronto: McClelland and Stewart, 1969.

Pnomes, Jukollages & Other Stunzas. Toronto: Ganglia, 1969.

Rag & Bone Shop. Toronto: McClelland and Stewart, 1971.

The Rugging and the Moving Times: Poems New and Uncollected. Coatsworth, ON: Black Moss, 1976.

Selected Poems 1940–1966. Toronto: McClelland and Stewart, 1966.

Selected Poems of Malcolm Lowry. Edited by Earle Birney. San Francisco: City Lights, 1962.

Spreading Time: Remarks on Canadian Writing and Writers. Montreal: Véhicule, 1980.

Spreading Time: Remarks on Canadian Writing and Writers, 1904–1949. Rev. ed. Montreal: Véhicule, 1989.

"Struggle against the Old Guard: Editing the *Canadian Poetry Magazine*." *Essays on Canadian Writing* 21 (Spring 1981): 9–31.

The Strait of Anian. Toronto: Ryerson, 1948.

Trial of a City and Other Verse. Toronto: Ryerson, 1952.

Turvey: A Military Picaresque. Toronto: McClelland and Stewart, 1949.

Twentieth Century Canadian Poetry: An Anthology. Edited by Earle Birney. Toronto: Ryerson, 1953.

What's So Big about Green? Toronto: McClelland and Stewart, 1973.

Words on Waves: Selected Radio Plays of Earle Birney. Kingston, ON: Quarry, 1985.

Works by Al Purdy

At Marsport Drugstore. Sutton West, ON: Paget, 1977.

Being Alive: Poems 1958–78. Toronto: McClelland and Stewart, 1978.

Beyond Remembering: The Collected Poems of Al Purdy. Edited by Al Purdy and Sam Solecki. Madeira Park, BC: Harbour Publishing, 2000.

Birdwatching at the Equator: The Galapagos Islands Poems. Sutton West, ON: Paget, 1982.

The Blur in Between: Poems 1960–61. Toronto: Emblem, 1962.

"Canadian Poetry in English since 1867." *Journal of Commonwealth Literature* 3 (July 1967): 19–33.

Bursting into Song: An Al Purdy Omnibus, Windsor, ON: Black Moss, 1982.

The Cariboo Horses. Toronto: McClelland and Stewart, 1965.

The Collected Poems of Al Purdy. Edited by Russell Brown. Toronto: McClelland and Stewart, 1986.

Cougar Hunter: A Memoir of Roderick Haig-Brown. Edited by Alex Widen. Vancouver: Phoenix, 1992.

The Crafte So Longe to Lerne. Toronto: Ryerson, 1959.

Emu, Remember! Fredericton, NB: Fiddlehead Books, 1956.

The Enchanted Echo. Vancouver: Clark and Stuart, 1944.

Fifteen Winds: A Selection of Modern Canadian Poems. Edited by A.W. Purdy. Toronto: Ryerson, 1969.

A Handful of Earth. Coatsworth, ON: Black Moss, 1977.

Hiroshima Poems. Trumansburg, NY: The Crossing, 1972.

In Search of Owen Roblin. Toronto: McClelland and Stewart, 1974.

Introduction. *Last Makings.* By Earle Birney. Toronto: McClelland and Stewart, 1991. xi-xvii.

Love in a Burning Building. Toronto: McClelland and Stewart, 1970.

The Man Who Outlived Himself: An Appreciation of John Donne. By Doug Beardsley and Al Purdy. Madeira Park, BC: Harbour Publishing, 2000.

Morning and It's Summer: A Memoir. Dunvegan, ON: Quadrant Editions, 1983.

Moths in the Iron Curtain. Sutton West, ON: Paget, 1979.

Naked with Summer in Your Mouth. Toronto: McClelland and Stewart, 1994.

The New Romans: Candid Canadian Opinions of the U.S. Edited by A.W. Purdy. Edmonton: M.G. Hurtig, 1968.

No Other Country. Toronto: McClelland and Stewart, 1977.

North of Summer: Poems from Baffin Island. Toronto: McClelland and Stewart, 1967.

On the Bearpaw Sea. Burnaby, BC: Blackfish, 1973.

Piling Blood. Toronto: McClelland and Stewart, 1984.

Poems for All the Annettes. Toronto: Contact, 1962.

Poems for All the Annettes. Rev. ed. Toronto: Anansi, 1968.

The Poems of Al Purdy: A New Canadian Library Selection. Toronto: McClelland and Stewart, 1976.

Pressed on Sand. Toronto: Ryerson, 1955.

The Quest for Ouzo. Trenton, ON: M. Kerrigan Almey, 1970.

Reaching for the Beaufort Sea: An Autobiography. Edited by Alex Widen. Madeira Park, BC: Harbour Publishing, 1993.

Rooms for Rent in the Outer Planets: Selected Poems 1962–1996. Edited by Al Purdy and Sam Solecki. Madeira Park, BC: Harbour Publishing, 1996.

Selected Poems. Toronto: McClelland and Stewart, 1972.

Sex & Death. Toronto: McClelland and Stewart, 1973.

Starting from Ameliasburgh: The Collected Prose of Al Purdy. Edited by Sam Solecki. Madeira Park, BC: Harbour Publishing, 1995.

The Stone Bird. Toronto: McClelland and Stewart, 1981.

Storm Warning: The New Canadian Poets. Edited by Al Purdy. Toronto: McClelland and Stewart, 1971.

Storm Warning 2: The New Canadian Poets. Edited by Al Purdy. Toronto: McClelland and Stewart, 1976.

Sundance at Dusk. Toronto: McClelland and Stewart, 1976.

To Paris Never Again: New Poems. Madeira Park, BC: Harbour Publishing, 1997.

Wild Grape Wine. Toronto: McClelland and Stewart, 1968.

Yours, Al: The Collected Letters of Al Purdy. Edited by Sam Solecki. Madeira Park, BC: Harbour Publishing, 2004.

Bukowski, Charles, and Al Purdy. *The Bukowski/Purdy Letters: A Decade of Dialogue 1964–1974.* Edited by Seamus Cooney. Sutton West, ON: Paget, 1983.

Laurence, Margaret, and Al Purdy. *Margaret Laurence-Al Purdy: A Friendship in Letters: Selected Correspondence.* Edited by John Lennox. Toronto: McClelland and Stewart, 1993.

Purdy, Al, and George Woodcock. *The Purdy-Woodcock Letters: Selected Correspondence 1964–1984.* Edited by George Galt. Toronto: ECW Press, 1988.

Selected Works by Other Authors

Atwood, Margaret. *Second Words: Selected Critical Prose.* Toronto: Anansi, 1982.

Auden, W.H. *Collected Poems.* Edited by Edward Mendelson. New York: Vintage, 1991.

—. *Forewords and Afterwords.* Selected by Edward Mendelson. New York: Random House, 1973.

Bentley, D.M.R. "Unremembered and Learning Much: LAC Alfred W. Purdy." *The Ivory Thought: Essays on Al Purdy.* Edited by Gerald Lynch, Shoshannah Ganz, and Josephene T.M. Kealey. Ottawa: University of Ottawa Press, 2008. 31–50.

Bishop, Elizabeth, and Robert Lowell. *Words in Air: The Complete Correspondence between Elizabeth Bishop and Robert Lowell.* Edited by Thomas Travisano with Saskia Hamilton. New York: Farrar, Straus and Giroux, 2008.

Bowering, George. *Left Hook: A Sideways Look at Canadian Writing.* Vancouver: Raincoast, 2005.

Cameron, Elspeth. *Earle Birney: A Life.* Toronto: Viking, 1994.

Cavafy, C.P. *The Complete Poems of Cavafy.* Translated by Rae Dalven. New York: Harvest-Harcourt, 1976.

Djwa, Sandra. "A Developing Tradition." *Essays on Canadian Writing* 21 (Spring 1981): 32–52.

Dragland, Stan. "Al Purdy's Poetry: Openings." *Al Purdy: Essays on His Works.* Edited by Linda Rogers. Toronto: Guernica, 2002. 15–57.

Kertzer, Jon. "Teasing Birney." Rev. of *Earle Birney: A Life*, by Elspeth Cameron. *Canadian Literature* 150 (Autumn 1996): 154–56.

Kittredge, William. "Introduction: What Thou Lovest Well: Richard Hugo." 2007. *Making Certain It Goes On: The Collected Poems of Richard Hugo.* 1984. New York: W.W. Norton, 2007. xxvii–xxxii.

Larkin, Philip. *Selected Letters of Philip Larkin 1940–1985.* Edited by Anthony Thwaite. London: Faber and Faber, 1992.

Lee, Dennis. Introduction. *The New Canadian Poets 1970–1985.* Edited by Dennis Lee. Toronto: McClelland and Stewart, 1985. xvii–liii.

—. "The Poetry of Al Purdy: An Afterword." *The Collected Poems of Al Purdy.* By Al Purdy. Edited by Russell Brown. Toronto: McClelland and Stewart, 1986. 371–91.

Logan, William. *Our Savage Art: Poetry and the Civil Tongue.* New York: Columbia University Press, 2009.

Low, Wailan. "Biographical Note." *One Muddy Hand.* By Earle Birney. Edited by Sam Solecki. Madeira Park, BC: Harbour Publishing, 2006. 14–18.

Lowry, Malcolm. *Sursum Corda! The Collected Letters of Malcolm Lowry.* Edited by Sherrill E. Grace. 2 vols. London: Jonathan Cape, 1995.

Lynch, Gerald, Shoshannah Ganz, and Josephene T.M. Kealey, eds. *The Ivory Thought: Essays on Al Purdy.* Ottawa: University of Ottawa Press, 2008.

McDonald, Larry. "Earle Birney." *Encyclopedia of Literature in Canada.* Edited by William H. New. Toronto: University of Toronto Press, 2002. 118–20.

Motion, Andrew. *Philip Larkin: A Writer's Life.* London: Faber and Faber, 1993.

New, W.H. *A History of Canadian Literature.* 1989. Montreal: McGill-Queen's University Press, 2001.

Pacey, Desmond, *Ten Canadian Poets: A Group of Biographical and Critical Essays.* Toronto: Ryerson, 1958.

Rexroth, Kenneth. *Classics Revisited.* Chicago: Quadrangle, 1968.

Solecki, Sam. "Chronology." *Yours, Al: The Collected Letters of Al Purdy.* Edited by Sam Solecki. Madeira Park, BC: Harbour Publishing, 2004. 11–17.

—. "Editor's Foreword." *One Muddy Hand: Selected Poems.* By Earle Birney. Edited by Sam Solecki. Madeira Park, BC: Harbour Publishing, 2006. 9–13

—. *The Last Canadian Poet: An Essay on Al Purdy.* Toronto: University of Toronto Press, 1999.

—. "Materials for a Biography of Al Purdy." *The Ivory Thought: Essays on Al Purdy.* Edited by Gerald Lynch, Shoshannah Ganz, and Josephene T.M. Kealey. Ottawa: University of Ottawa Press, 2008. 13–30.

St. Pierre, Paul Matthew. "Al Purdy." *Encyclopedia of Literature in Canada*. Edited
by William H. New. Toronto: University of Toronto Press, 2002. 914–16.

Twigg, Alan. *For Openers: Conversations with 24 Canadian Writers*. Madeira
Park, BC: Harbour Publishing, 1981.

Ware, Tracy, ed. "The Lives of a Poet: The Correspondence of Earle Birney and
Desmond Pacey, 1957–58." *Canadian Poetry: Studies, Documents, Reviews* 56
(Spring/Summer 2005): 87–119.

Woodcock, George. *Northern Spring: The Flowering of Canadian Literature*.
Vancouver: Douglas and McIntyre, 1987.

Acknowledgements

Madam Justice Wailan Low and Mrs. Eurithe Purdy graciously provided permission to publish the letters and to quote and reprint poetry and other published works by Earle Birney and Al Purdy. I am grateful to them and to the staff of Harbour Publishing for their support of this project.

I was assisted generously by the librarians at the following institutions: The Thomas Fisher Rare Book Library, University of Toronto; Queen's University Archives; Special Collections, Libraries and Cultural Resources, University of Calgary; the Lilly Library, Indiana University Bloomington; Special Collections Department, University of Saskatchewan Library; and Special Collections, McPherson Library, University of Victoria. Support from the Social Sciences and Humanities Research Council of Canada and the University of Victoria made possible the research necessary to complete this book.

I am indebted to Melanie Hibi for administrative help and to Jonathan Olaf Johnson for expert assistance with research and editorial matters. Elaine Park was an assiduous copy editor. Many of my colleagues in the Department of English at the University of Victoria answered obscure questions; I must thank in particular Gordon Fulton, whose knowledge of Prince Edward County surely rivals that of Al Purdy.

We Go Far Back in Time is dedicated to three great editors, whose contributions to Canadian writing serve as models, and to whom I am most deeply beholden.

— Nicholas Bradley
Victoria, British Columbia
March 2014

Index of Titles

Works that appear in this book are listed in **bold**.

WORKS BY EARLE BIRNEY

"Adagio," 293n626

"Ajijic," 363n806

Alphabeings & Other Seasyours, 41

"Anglosaxon Street," 64, 64n111, 72n134, 76, 83

"Atlantic Door," 70, 70n124–27

"Ave Atque Vale," 423n919

"Bear on the Delhi Road, The," 100n215

Bear on the Delhi Road, The: Selected Poems, 41, 249n537, 279

Big Bird in the Bush: Selected Stories and Sketches, 26n43, 42, 333–34n720, 364n808, 370n818

"Billboards Build Freedom of Choice," 153

"Bushed," 58, 76, 107, 109

"Can. Lit.," 324n698, 344n752

"Canada: Case History," 99, 210, 294n629, 418, 421, 421n915

"Cartagena de Indias," 69n122, 72n137, 100n215

"Christchurch, N.Z.," 248n528

"Climbers," 22, 238n510

Collected Poems of Earle Birney, The, 41, 298nn642–43

"Commonwealth Arts Festival Week, 1965, Cardiff, a Collage," 421, 421n916

"Conrad Kain," 298n642

Copernican Fix, 42

Cow Jumped over the Moon, The: The Writing and Reading of Poetry, 41, 72n133, 240n513, 249n536, 252n541, 266n570, 277n588

"Cry over Aswan," 418n905, 421, 422

"Cucarachas in Fiji," 288n610

Damnation of Vancouver, The, 41, 58n88, 302

"David," 12, 22, 38, 49, 49n58, 54, 55n74, 107n245, 109n251, 195, 238n510, 240, 251, 308, 310, 324, 331, 343, 353, 353n781, 369, 401

"David," *cont.*
Dorothy Livesay review of, 81n161, 309n669
dramatization of, 107–8, 108n248, 109, 433
on rejections of, 57, 57n85, 64

David and Other Poems, 14, 38, 49n58, 55n74, 60, 64n111, 72n134, 104–5n235, 197, 242, 320

"Dear Biographer," 21

Down the Long Table, 13, 39, 56n81, 83, 86, 326

"Dusk on English Bay," 49n56, 109

"Ebb Begins from Dream, The," 58, 61, 71n130, 76

"E.J. Pratt and His Critics," 101

"El Greco: *Espolio*," 411n895

"Ellesmereland," 418, 418n906, 421, 421n915

Essays on Chaucerian Irony, 42, 87n175, 426

"Excelsior on the Prairies," 311n672

"Fall by Fury," 352–53, 353n781, 357, 382

Fall by Fury & Other Makings, 11n12, 42, 360n796

"Flight across Canada," 61

"For Maister Geffrey," 88n177

"From the Bridge: Firth of Forth," 294n627

"From the Hazel Bough," 58, 61, 76

Ghost in the Wheels: Selected Poems, 41, 347, 348n762

"Hailing, A," 426n924

"i should have begun with your toes," 127n304

"i think you are a whole city," 127n304

Ice Cod Bell or Stone, 40, 54n72

"imageorge," 224n477

"Images in Place of Logging," 58

"In Purdy's Ameliasburg," 44–47, 47n54, 133
"Introvert," 58, 58n87, 76
"Invasion Spring," 72n134

Last Makings, 11n12, 15, 17n28, 23, 43, 127n304
"Laurentian Shield," 71n129, 77, 78n150
"Leavetaking," 364, 364n810, 368, 369
"Letter to a Cuzco Priest," 315n678
"Letter to Leonardo," 420n914, 422
"Loggia dell' Orcagna," 248n528

"Macchu Picchu," 313n676
Mammoth Corridors, The, 42, 353n785, 391
"Mammoth Corridors, The," 181, 191, 353, 353n785, 392
"Mappemounde," 55n74, 56n78, 76n146, 81, 95, 277n588, 301n651, 417
    Al Purdy on, 54–55, 61, 71, 72, 76, 80, 418, 418n908
    Earle Birney on, 57–58, 72n133
"Mammorial Stunzas for Aimee Simple McFarcen," 100n215
"Meeting of the Students' Committee," 421
Memory No Servant, 41, 165, 166, 186, 189, 202n428, 205, 268
"Montreal," 58

Near False Creek Mouth, 40, 121n289, 188
"North of Superior," 24–25, 78n152
"November Walk near False Creek Mouth," 93n198, 210
Now Is Time, 38, 50n62, 61, 197

One Muddy Hand: Selected Poems, 22n34, 24nn38–39, 33, 34, 46n54, 56n78, 61n98, 69n122, 70n125, 72n137, 107n245, 109n251, 238n510, 250n539, 314n677, 315n678, 324n698, 341n742, 353nn781–84, 418n907, 423n919
"Our Forefathers Literary," 324n698

"Pacific Door," 58, 70, 70n124, 76, 81n160, 104n232
"plastic plinkles for Gaudy Nite at HMF College, Yule 1966," 250n540
"Plaza de la Inquisición," 314
Pnomes, Jukollages & Other Stunzas, 222, 222n472

Poems of Earle Birney, The: A New Canadian Library Selection, 41, 205n435, 208n441
"Pome for a Reedin," 408–9
"Prairie Counterpoint," 71n131

"Quebec May," 71, 71n128, 77

Rag & Bone Shop, 41, 225, 225n482, 228, 235, 242, 244, 247–48, 250
"Remarks for the Part of Death," 71n130
"Reverse on the Coast Range," 55, 55n74, 58, 58n87
"Road to Nijmegen, The" 58, 58n87, 76
Rugging and the Moving Times, The: Poems New and Uncollected, 41, 320n690, 333n719, 345n756

Selected Poems 1940–1966, 40
"Sestina for Tehuántepec" ("Sestina for the Ladies of Tehuántepec"), 346n758
"Shapers, The: Vancouver," 293n626
"Shotgun Marriage without Shotguns," 333, 333n720, 334n721
"Six for Lan," 333, 334
"Skier's Apologies," 72n137
"Slug in Woods," 54, 55n74, 58, 64, 64n111
"Small Faculty Stag for the Visiting Poet, A," 249, 249n537, 288, 293n626
Spreading Time: Remarks on Canadian Writing and Writers, 42, 50n62, 114n264, 364n808, 370, 370n817, 371, 372, 384, 384n846, 385n850, 387, 387n858, 388, 421
    Douglas Fetherling review of, 388n859
    William French review of, 389n862
"St. Valentine is Past," 58
"Still Life near Bangalore," 414–15, 415n902
Strait of Anian, The: Selected Poems, 38, 54n71, 55n74, 58, 58n87, 72n124, 78n150, 79, 79n155, 104n232, 296, 438n936
    Al Purdy on, 54, 54n72, 61, 70, 71, 72, 75, 76, 80, 104, 397
    Malcolm Lowry review of, 62–63n106
"Struggle against the Old Guard: Editing the *Canadian Poetry Magazine*," 50n62, 204n433

"Tavern by the Hellespont," 292, 292n623
"there are delicacies," 127n304
"Three for Alison," 127n304
"THREW DAW KISSED ASS TRIAL
  YAH!," 421, 421n916
"Time-Bomb," 106n240
"To Cumrad Bert," 421
"To Sarge Robertson," 421
"Trawna Tuh Belvul by Knayjin Psifik,"
  217n459
Trial of a City and Other Verse, 22,
  22n34, 39, 55n76, 58, 58n88, 79, 82, 87,
  143n338, 238n510
  Al Purdy on, 54n72, 55, 61, 64, 75–76,
  94, 111
Turvey: A Military Picaresque, 14, 38, 61,
  61n100, 92n194, 197–98, 326
  adapted as a play, 122n290, 123, 126
  Al Purdy Afterword for, 445, 445n947
  Arnold Edinborough review of, 327n709
  George Woodcock introduction to, 249,
  249n538, 251
  Malcolm Lowry review of, 62–63n106
  Robert Fulford review of, 327, 327n708

*Twentieth Century Canadian Poetry: An
  Anthology*, 108, 238n510
"21st Century Belongs to the Moon, The,"
  293n626
"Twenty-Third Flight," 422n917

"Ulysses," 58

"Vancouver Lights," 54, 55n74, 58, 60,
  77n149, 95
"Villanelle," 288n611

"Waiting for *Queen Emma*," 364n810
"War Winter," 58
What's So Big about Green?, 41, 288n609,
  293nn626–27, 294n628
"Wind through St. John's, The," 354n788
"Winter Saturday," 71
"Within These Caverned Days," 438n936
*Words on Waves: Selected Radio Plays of
  Earle Birney*, 42, 364n808, 426n925

"Young Veterans," 58, 341n742

WORKS BY AL PURDY

A Splinter in the Heart, 23, 43
"About Pablum, Teachers, and Malcolm
  Lowry," 63
"Adam & No Eve," 423
"Air Force Discharge," 269
"Along the Ionian Coast," 349n766
"Ameliasburg Stew," 14n18
**"And We Shall Build Jerusalem — in
  Montreal,"** 96–97, 96n209
"Angus," 295n631
"Antenna," 342n743
"Arctic Romance," 293, 293n625
"Armistice Poem," 186, 186n408
"At Lenin's Tomb," 336, 336n729, 338
At Marsport Drugstore, 41, 170n388,
  319n687, 342n743, 358n789
"At Paricutin Volcano," 365, 370, 370n816
"At the Athenian Market," 292, 306,
  306n660
"At the Quinte Hotel," 11, 57n84, 171
"At the Yacht Club," 97–98
"Athens Apartment," 292

"Atomic Museum," 253, 253n545

"Ballad of the Despairing Wife," 228n491,
  231n498
"Battlefield at Batoche, The," 254, 254n548,
  290, 291
"Beat Joe McLeod," 262–63, 262n563, 272,
  291
"Beavers of Renfrew, The," 292, 295n632
Being Alive: Poems 1958–1978, 42, 337n731,
  345n755, 358n789, 359, 360n798, 371,
  383, 395, 397, 400
"Bestiary," 59n94
"Bestiary [II]," 11n9, 59n92, 59n94
*Beyond Remembering: The Collected Poems
  of Al Purdy*, 11n9, 25n40, 34, 43, 54n69,
  55n77, 59n92, 59n94, 68n121, 86n172,
  132n312, 137n324, 167n384, 226n485,
  256n551, 292n621, 306nn660–61,
  321nn693–94, 326n706, 341n742,
  345n755, 365n812, 372n822, 408n891,
  431n930, 436n935

Beyond Remembering (cont.)
    Margaret Atwood foreword for,
    119n284
"Beyond the Mountains of Heaven,"
    335n727
"Birds & Beasts," 424
"Birdwatching at the Equator," 386n855
Birdwatching at the Equator: The Galapagos
    Islands Poems, 42, 397n872
"Bits and Pieces," 148n343
"Blue City, The," 423
Blur in Between, The: Poems 1960–61, 40,
    83n166, 94n203, 129
"Bored with Ruins," 306n661
"Buddhist Bell, The," 253n545
Bukowski/Purdy Letters, The: A Decade of
    Dialogue, 1964–1974, 29n52, 170n388
"Bums and Brakies," 14n18
Bursting into Song: An Al Purdy Omnibus,
    320n690, 400, 400n879, 401, 407
    John Bemrose review of, 405n886

"Canadian," 144n339
"Canadian New Year Resolutions," 88,
    88n176
"Canadian Poetry in English since 1867,"
    150n350
"Cancel All My Appointments"
"Cantos," 67–68, 67n120
"Cariboo Horses, The," 107n243
Cariboo Horses, The, 14, 40, 107n243, 129,
    145, 188, 228n491
    Earle Birney to Guggenheim Foundation
    on, 21, 130
"Cave Man," 268
"Cave Painters, The," 82
"Chiaroscuro," 56n80
"Children, The," 341n741
"Choices," 424
"Chronos at Quintana Roo," 293, 293n624,
    306n661
"Coffee with René Lévesque," 291,
Collected Poems of Al Purdy, The (1986),
    13n16, 42, 56n80, 167n384, 335n727,
    417n903
"Colombo Was Here," 336, 336n728, 338
"Correspondence," 129
"Country North of Belleville, The," 24
"Coyotes in Merida Zoo," 341

Crafte So Longe to Lerne, The, 18, 39,
    63n107, 83, 83n168, 88n176, 91, 91n188
    David Bromige review of, 217n456

"Darwin's Theology?," 386, 386n855
"Dead Girl, The," 69–70
"Dead March for Sergeant MacLeod,"
    353n786
"Dead Poet, The," 380–81, 381n842, 383
"Death Mask, The," 349n766
"Death of a Friend, The," 352n777
"Departures," 148n343
"Depression in Namu, BC," 306n661
"Deprivations," 341, 341nn741–42
"Detail," 136n320
"D.H. Lawrence at Lake Chapala," 361n800
"Dogsong," 256n551
"Dog Song 2," 424
"Double Focus," 423
"Double Shadow, The," 292
"Driving the Spanish Coast," 362n802
"Dutch Masters, The" 88
"Dust," 49n56, 268

"Earle Birney in Hospital," 435–36
"Eleanor & Valentina," 423
"Elegy," 231n497
"Embarkation," 268
Emu, Remember!, 18, 39, 81, 81n159,
    82n162, 82n164, 341
Enchanted Echo, The, 14, 15n21, 18, 38,
    57n84, 268
    Watson Kirkconnell review of, 268n575
"Ephesus," 306n661

"Fathers," 217n459, 373, 373n827, 374–75,
    277, 445
"Fiddleheads," 350
Fifteen Winds: A Selection of Modern
    Canadian Poems, 139n332, 191,
    192n416, 193, 221, 221n467, 245,
    247n527
"Flat Tire in the Desert," 292
"For Ann More (1584–1617)," 55n77
"For Eurithe, " 424
"For Her in Sunlight," 290, 291
"For 'Richard Hakluyt and Successors,"
    61–62
"For Robert Kennedy," 167, 167n384, 168
"For Steve McIntyre," 276n586

"Fragmentary," 349, 350n770
"From the Wisconsin Glacial Period," 342n743
"Funeral," 349, 351

"Great Man, The," 84–85

"Hallucinations of a Tourist," 292
"Handful of Earth, A," 347
Handful of Earth, A, 41, 345, 345n755, 349, 351, 358n789
"Hands," 292, 294
"Hazelton, B.C.," 107n243
"Hellas Express," 183, 293, 295, 305, 305n659
Hiroshima Poems, 41, 249, 249n533, 250, 262, 264, 265, 266, 268, 291, 292
"Hombre," 372n822
"Home-Made Beer," 11, 173, 176
"Horseman of Agawa, The," 11, 221, 221n465, 221n468, 222, 224
"Hub-Cap Thief," 349, 349n767
"Hunting Season," 166n383

"If Birds Look In," 86, 86n172
"Iguana," 235n504, 292, 292nn621–22, 294
"In Ellesmereland," 418, 418n906, 421, 421n915
"In Mid-Atlantic," 81
"In Peace Memorial Park," 253, 253n545
"In the Beginning," 423
"In the Desert," 441
"In the Foothills," 293, 295n632
"In the Fourteenth Century," 335n727
"In the Garden," 367–69
"In the Pope's 1968 Encyclical," 293
In Search of Owen Roblin, 41, 216n451, 259n557, 283–84, 283n599
"Indictment," 81
"Infra-Red," 350, 350n770
"Inside Gus," 378, 378n836
"Inside the Mill," 341, 343
"Invocation," 438

"Jackovich and the Salmon Princess," 352n777
"Joe Barr," 149n346, 151–52, 151n352
"Johnston's on St. Germain," 290, 290n620

"King Tyee and the Salmon Princess," 352n777
"Kispiox Indian Village," 107n243

"Lament," 60, 319, 321, 321n693, 342, 342n747
"Lament for Robert Kennedy," 167n384, 168
Last Makings
introduction to, 15, 16n23, 17n28, 23
"Llama," 350
Love in a Burning Building, 10n7, 41, 86n172, 113n261, 181n397, 203n431, 216n453, 228n491, 231n498, 438n936

"Make Watermelons Not Love," 335n725
"Man Who Killed David, The," 308, 308n667, 310
Man Who Outlived Himself, The: An Appreciation of John Donne, 55n77
"Man without a Country," 423
Margaret Laurence–Al Purdy: A Friendship in Letters: Selected Correspondence, 29n52
"Marius Barbeau: 1883–1969," 104n233
"Meeting," 362n802
"Mr. Greenhalgh's Love Poem," 113, 113n261, 116
"Monastery of the Caves," 337–39, 337n731
"Moonspell," 386n855
Morning and It's Summer: A Memoir, 42, 397, 397n873, 412, 413n900, 413
"Moses at Darwin Station," 386n855
Moths in the Iron Curtain, 42, 335n725, 335n727, 336nn728–29, 339n735, 358n789, 364
"Museum Piece," 424

Naked with Summer in Your Mouth, 43, 117n280, 436n935
"Names the Names, The," 148n343
"Near Pátzcuaro," 365–67, 368
New Romans, The: Candid Canadian Opinions of the U.S., 163, 164n376, 167, 172–74, 176–77, 179n395, 195, 235, 335
"News Reports at Ameliasburg" 186, 186n407
"Night Errant," 268, 268n576, 272
"Nine Bean-Rows on the Moon," 203, 203n431

No Other Country, 41, 319n688, 247, 351, 354, 356, 358n789
   Jim Christy review of, 354n787
North of Summer: Poems from Baffin Island, 21, 25, 40, 125, 130, 171, 180, 256n551
"North West Passage, The," 137n324, 142, 326n706, 418n906, 438n936
"Notes on a Fictional Character," 132n312
"Notes on Painting," 134n317

"Observing Persons," 293
"Ode to a Wornout Electric Stove in the Snow," 341n741
"Of Course You Can't," 350
"Old Man and the Boat, The," 295n631
"On a Park Bench," 113
"On Bliss Carman," 116n278
"On the Altiplano," 345n754, 350, 350n772
"On the Avenida Juarez," 158n365
On the Bearpaw Sea, 41, 310, 310n670
"On the Planet Earth," 419–420, 420n913
"One Thousand Cranes," 253n545

"A Pair of 10-Foot-Concrete Shoes," 121n289
"Palimpsest," 85, 85n171
"Paper Mate," 342n743
"Paranoid Lament," 425
"Peaceable Kingdom, The," 221n465
Piling Blood, 42, 139n330, 419, 419n912, 423–25, 428
   Fraser Sutherland review of, 424n920
"Poem" ("Here am I at six o'clock"), 81, 82n162
Poems for All the Annettes, 14, 40, 67n120, 83nn167–68, 113n261, 132n312, 145, 161, 163, 167–69, 171, 173, 176, 186n407, 231n497, 252, 252n542
Poems of Al Purdy, The: A New Canadian Library Selection, 41, 319–20, 319n685, 324, 360, 360n798
"Portrait," 268
"Portrait of Herman," 292
"Possession of Monsters," 336n730
"Postscript," 68–69, 68n121
"Power Failure in Disneyland," 291–92
"Pre-School," 341, 341n741
Pressed on Sand, 18, 39, 56, 56n80, 82n164, 217n456

"Prince Edward County," 351
"Proust," 246n525
Purdy–Woodcock Letters, The: Selected Correspondence, 1964–1984, 29n52, 402n881

Quest for Ouzo, The, 41, 208n440, 221n465, 224–25

"R.C.M.P. Post," 290–91
Reaching for the Beaufort Sea: An Autobiography, 14, 14n18, 16, 23, 34, 43, 51n64, 54n69, 57n84, 58–59nn90–92, 63n107, 104n235, 127n302, 216n453, 217nn456–57, 231n498, 239–40n511, 276n586, 296nn635–36, 313n675, 316n680, 320n690, 328n710
"Recipe," 341n741
"Ritual," 342n743, 343, 343n748
"Roblin Lake," 186n407
Rooms for Rent in the Outer Planets: Selected Poems 1962–1996, 43
"Running," 345n754

"Sadness," 341
"Sailor Legend," 268
Selected Poems (1972), 41, 248, 248n531, 254–55, 257–58, 329, 329n713
Sex & Death, 41, 249n533, 262n563, 271, 290, 291–94, 296
   G.S. Kaufman review of, 289, 289n615
   Gary Geddes review of, 295n632
"Shout, The," 349
"Small Town in Mexico, A," 431
"Smell of Rotten Eggs, The," 431n930
"Sorrow for Tom, A," 148n343
"South of Durango," 362n803
"Spinning," 373–78
"Starlings," 345n754, 351–52
Starting from Ameliasburgh: The Collected Prose of Al Purdy, 34, 43, 57n84, 116n278, 127n302, 205n436, 217n457, 220n464, 259n556, 295n631, 300n648, 303n655, 329n713, 339n735, 347n759, 352n777
"Still Life in a Tent," 256n551
Stone Bird, The, 42, 392–93, 395, 397, 402
"Stop Watching," 342n743, 411n895

Storm Warning: The New Canadian Poets, 153n355, 164n378, 174n389, 221, 221n465, 221n467, 225, 227n488, 228n489, 235, 237, 243–44, 247, 247n527, 320n690

Storm Warning 2: The New Canadian Poets, 306, 312, 319, 325, 325n702, 332, 345n757, 444

"St. Paul to the Corinthians," 181

"Strangers, The," 424

"Street Scene," 293

"Subject/Object," 242n743

Sundance at Dusk, 41, 319n683, 321n693, 341–43, 343n748, 411n895

"Survivors," 253n545

"Syllogism for Theologians," 122n291

"Tarahumara Women, The," 424

"Temporizing in the Eternal City," 248

"There Is of Course a Legend," 411n895, 423

"Time of Your Life, The," 293

"To —," 68

"To Candace," 73–74

To Paris Never Again, 43, 104n233

"Touchings," 117n280

"Tourist Itinerary," 226n485, 295n632

"Transient," 14n18

"Transvestite," 341n741

"Trees at the Arctic Circle," 256n551, 412

"Uncertainties," 342n743

"Vancouver," 408n891

"Version," 437

"Vestigia," 438n936

"Visiting Tolstoy," 335n727

"West of Summer: New Poets from the West Coast," 183n400

"What Do the Birds Think?," 125, 125n298

"When I Sat Down to Play the Piano," 412

"Who's Got the Emphasis?," 113n263

"Whoever You Are," 86n172

"Whose Mother?," 253n545

Wild Grape Wine, 41, 156n362, 161n372, 161n374, 163, 173, 176, 204, 252, 252n542, 326n706, 350n771

Yours, Al: The Collected Letters of Al Purdy, 29–31, 29n49, 33–34, 49n55, 53n68, 56n78, 73n139, 114n268, 117n281, 136n322, 149n346, 149n348, 216nn452–53, 231n498, 246n525, 260n560, 284n602, 300n649, 336n728, 343n749, 378n837, 385n853, 390n865

Index of Names

Abrahams, Cecil, 277, 277n587
Acorn, Milton, 83, 83n167, 103, 103n229, 105n236, 109–10, 129, 143, 147–48, 164–67, 170, 174, 191, 199–202, 202n429, 204, 204n434, 206, 217, 217n457, 218, 222, 222n469, 237, 269n577, 369, 402–3, 406
Ahvenus, Martin, 168n385, 189, 189n411, 217
Aiken, Conrad, 114, 114–15n270
Albee, Edward, 138, 138n327
Aldington, Richard, 392
Allen, Rita Greer, 143, 143n338, 163, 169, 291, 393, 395
Allen, Robert (Bob) Greer, 143, 143n338, 163, 291, 393
Almey, Kerrigan, 208n440, 221n465
Amiel, Barbara, 365, 365n811
Anderson, Patrick, 73, 73n138, 114–15, 191, 196
Arnett, Tom, 248, 248n530
Aspler, Tony, 429
Atsumi, Ikuko, 26n43, 120n286, 122
Atwood, Margaret (Peg/Peggy), 10, 10n7, 40, 119, 119n284, 120n287, 136, 137n323, 141, 144, 191, 198, 216n451, 263, 265, 269n577, 271, 295, 297, 297n640, 315, 323, 326, 343–44, 360, 365n811, 384, 411
Auden, W. H., 9, 9n1, 9nn3–5, 10, 10n6, 10n8, 11, 11n9, 12, 12nn13–14, 26, 39, 57, 57n84, 64, 76n147, 113–15, 113n263, 115n271, 117–18, 118n283, 343, 383, 418, 419n909, 438n936
Avery, Denise, 333, 342–44
Avison, Margaret, 40, 114, 114n266, 185, 191
Bailey, Alfred, 114, 114n265, 263n564, 339n735, 400n877
Ball, Nelson, 141, 141n336, 148
Barbour, Douglas, 264, 264n566
Barker, George, 100–1, 100–1n216, 115
Barrett, Dave, 300, 300n647, 302–4
Barton, Edith, 239, 241
Bates, Ronald, 219, 219n461, 226
Baudelaire, Charles, 80, 80n157
Beardsley, Doug, 55n77, 59n94
Beaver, Bruce, 311, 311n673

Belford, Ken, 243, 243n518, 269n577
Bellow, Saul, 180
Bemrose, John, 405, 405n886
Bennett, W.A.C., 88n176, 237, 237n507, 261
Bentley, D.M.R., 15n21
Bentley, Roy, 240, 240n513
Berg, Kathy, 355
Berryman, John, 202, 202n427, 271, 271n584
Berton, Pierre, 27, 179, 179n395, 225, 347, 376
Betjeman, John, 92, 92n193, 96
Betts, Lorne, 108n248
Bevan, Alan, 140, 140n333, 170
Birney, Esther, 14, 18, 18n29, 33, 36–41, 43, 123–24, 128, 138, 148, 159–60, 166, 168, 173, 176, 179, 182, 187, 194, 201, 205, 209, 216, 219, 233, 236, 241, 245, 257n552, 281–82, 299, 439
Birney, William (Bill), 36
Bissell, Claude T., 86, 86n174, 319, 319n684, 339n735
bissett, bill, 140n334, 160, 160n370, 161–62, 164, 168, 170, 172, 182–84, 186, 188, 190–92, 205, 228, 263, 266n569
Blaser, Robin, 183, 183n400, 185n403, 229, 229n493, 231, 231n498, 340n739
Blazek, Douglas, 170n388, 252, 252n542
Borden, Carl, 102, 102n223
Borson, Roo, 428
Bosch, Hieronymus, 314n317
Bowering, Angela, 224n477, 398
Bowering, George, 25, 25n41, 52n66, 106n242, 153n355, 154, 154n356, 185n403, 191, 201, 208, 208n442, 211, 217, 217n458, 222, 222n469, 224n477, 260n560, 269n577, 278, 391, 398
Bowering, Marilyn, 428
Bradstreet, Anne, 200, 200n423, 202, 202n427
Braymer, Marjorie, 234
Brett, Brian, 310n670
Brewster, Elizabeth, 264–65, 264n565
Bridie, James, 88, 89n179, 90
Bromige, David, 217, 217n456, 219–20, 289, 289n616
Brooke, Rupert, 175

Brooks, Leonard, 210, 257, 257n552, 280, 314, 345, 352, 361, 364, 411, 422
Brooks, Reva, 257n552, 280, 345, 361
Brown, Doug, 307, 310
Brown, Jim, 205, 205n436
Brown, Peter, 397
Brown, Russell, 13n16, 417, 417n903, 419
Browning, Robert, 57–58, 57n84, 64, 78, 164
Bruce, Phyllis, 246n523
Buckle, Daphne (*see* Marlatt, Daphne)
Buckley, Joan, 50, 51n64, 64
Buitenhuis, Elspeth (*see* Cameron, Elspeth)
Bukowski, Charles, 29, 29n52, 170, 170n388, 228–29, 252
Bunting, Basil, 229, 229n492, 231
Burles, Gordon, 325, 325n703, 327
Burroughs, William S., 410, 410n892
Byron, George Gordon, 178
Cage, John, 185n403, 405–6
Callaghan, Barry, 164, 164n377, 179, 439
Cameron, Elspeth, 18n29, 21, 29, 33, 278, 278n592, 327, 449, 429n927, 433, 445
Campbell, Joseph, 78n151
Campbell, Norman, 122n290
Campbell, Roy, 16, 63, 63n109, 80
Camus, Marcel, 270n581
Cantor, Aviva, 217n459
Carman, William Bliss, 104n235, 113–17, 113n263, 114n264, 116n278, 146, 384n846, 442, 445
Carr, Emily, 317, 317n682
Carruth, Hayden, 101n216, 133–35, 133n315
Caruso, Barbara, 141, 141n337
Cary, Joyce, 60, 60n96
Cather, Willa, 53, 53n67
Cervantes, Miguel de, 33, 419
Chatterton, Thomas, 58, 58n90
Chaucer, Geoffrey, 13, 37, 42, 56n78, 58, 87, 87n175, 88n177, 92–93, 93nn195–96, 101n221, 105, 115, 202–3, 253, 342, 384n846, 385n853, 426, 426n925
Cherry, Zena, 352, 352n779
Chesterton, G. K., 78n152, 117, 117n280, 296n635
Christmas, Pat, 127
Christy, Jim, 354, 354n787, 356
Chute, Robert (Bob), 123, 124n294
Ciardi, John, 99, 99n211, 101
Claudel, Paul, 419

Cogswell, Fred, 150, 150n350
Cohen, Leonard, 39, 54n71, 140, 140n335, 145, 201n426, 264n566
Cohen, Nathan, 126, 126n301
Coleman, Victor, 306, 127n306
Coleridge, Samuel Taylor, 143, 146
Collins, Aileen, 370, 370n819
Colombo, John Robert, 108, 108n246, 110, 135–36, 141, 143–44, 170–72, 174, 189, 194, 202, 205–7, 207n439, 211–13, 336, 336n728, 338
Conard, Audrey, 325, 325n702, 327
Constant, Benjamin, 246n524
Cook, James (captain), 79, 175
Copithorne, Judith, 185, 185n405, 188, 205, 244, 266n569
Corkett, Anne, 327n707
Cottrell, Leonard, 178, 180
Coulthard, Jean, 77, 77n149
Coupey, Pierre, 183–84, 183n400
Cowley, Liz, 187, 196
Crane, Hart, 392
Creeley, Robert, 40, 52n66, 123, 123n292, 126, 185n403, 229, 231n498, 351
Crosby, Caresse, 392
Crosby, Harry, 392
Crosland, Margaret, 186, 187n409, 190, 192, 195, 197
Crossley-Holland, Kevin, 199n421
Cummings, E. E., 191
Curnow, Allen, 106n239, 312n674
Dahlie, Hallvard, 153n355
Daigneault, Robert, 127n304
Daniells, Roy, 114, 114n265, 114n267, 120n287, 159, 339n735
Dardick, Simon, 370n817, 372
Davey, Frank, 27, 52n66, 153n355, 185n403, 211, 211n447, 213–14, 214n449, 239, 256, 277–78, 277n588, 315–16, 315n679, 444
Davidson, Claude, 360, 360n799
Davidson, Robert, 360, 360n799
Davies, Robertson, 201
Day, Douglas, 287, 290, 293n635
Day Lewis, Cecil, 36, 76n147, 114n269
de Bruyn, Jan, 113n262
De la Mare, Walter, 59, 59n94
De la Roche, Mazo, 297, 297n641
De Quincey, Thomas, 361
Dennison, William, 218, 218n460

Dickey, James, 340, 340n740
Dickinson, Emily, 57, 57n84, 64, 115, 271
Diefenbaker, John, 154n358
Djwa, Sandra, 29n50, 120n287
Dobbs, Kildare, 169, 169n387, 172–73, 289, 412n898
Donne, John, 55, 55n77, 117, 121
Douglas, Diana, 182n399
Douglas, James (Jim), 182, 182n399, 233
Douglas, James (governer), 333, 333n720
Dowson, Ross, 128, 123n307
Doyle, Mike, 391, 391n866
Dragland, Stan, 373n826
Drainie, John, 111, 112n256
Dudek, Louis, 39, 52n66, 83, 83n166, 99n211, 103, 105–6, 105n236, 111, 114, 195–96, 211, 333, 370–71, 370n819
Duffy, Dennis, 201n426
Duncan, Robert, 40, 52n66, 101, 101n217, 183n400, 185n403, 229, 229n493, 231, 231n498, 351, 351n775
Durrell, Lawrence, 178, 178n393, 180
Duthie, Bill, 233
Dwyer, Peter, 139–40, 139n330, 154–55, 158, 223
Eaton, John, 225, 225n481
Eberhart, Richard, 100, 101n216
Edinborough, Arnold, 327, 327n709
Eliot, Alexander, 273n585
Eliot, T. S., 11n12, 45, 55, 55n77, 57, 64, 71, 71n132, 80, 104, 104n234, 113–15, 113n263, 114n268, 117, 117n281, 134, 197, 273n585, 296nn634–35, 342n743, 417n903
Ellis, Havelock, 110, 110n253
Empson, William, 54, 54n73
Engel, Howard, 378, 378n835
Epstein, Jason, 266, 266n571
Epstein, Perle, 206, 206n437
Evers, Medgar, 169, 169n386
Everson, Lorna, 217n459, 242, 263, 330, 370–71, 411
Everson, Ronald, 33, 99n211, 217, 217n459, 221, 223, 239, 241–42, 245, 263, 280, 304, 307, 312–13, 315, 319–20, 322–23, 330, 339, 339n735, 351, 358, 360n797, 365, 370–71, 373n827, 389, 400, 406, 406n888, 411, 416, 425, 429, 440
Faber, Ann, 197
Faber, Geoffrey, 101

Farrell, James T., 213, 213n448
Fawcett, Brian, 340, 340nn739–40
Fetherling, Douglas George, 164, 164n378, 209, 269n577, 388, 388n859
Fiamengo, Marya, 184, 184n402, 265, 277
Fiedler, Leslie, 180
Finch, Robert, 62, 62n105, 99n211, 114, 114n265
Finlay, Ian Hamilton, 410, 410n892
Finlay, Michael, 236, 236n506, 242, 242n515, 244
Finnigan, Joan, 191, 191n415, 196, 207
Fischman, Sheila, 146n341
Foley, Jim, 299, 299n645
Ford, R.A.D., 338–39, 338n733
Fraser, Dana, 488, 227n488, 235–36, 242–43
Fraser, Ray, 269n577
Fraser, Sylvia, 302, 302n653
French, William (Bill), 389, 389n862
Freuchen, Peter, 91–92, 91n190
Freud, Sigmund, 111, 287n607
Frick, Alice, 188, 196
Frost, Robert, 59
Frum, Barbara, 326, 326n705
Fry, Christopher, 75, 75n143, 79
Frye, Northrop, 57n83, 219n461, 339n735, 349, 349n764, 351, 419, 428
Fulford, Robert (Bob), 320, 320n689, 324, 324n697, 327, 327n708
Fulton, E. Davie, 384, 384n848
Gadd, Maxine, 391, 391n866
Galt, George, 29n52, 402, 402n881, 445
Garneau, Hector de Saint-Denys, 58, 58n90, 60
Garner, Hugh, 288, 288n612
Gasparini, Len, 191, 269n577
Geddes, Gary, 153–54, 153n355, 156, 169–70, 199–200, 211, 213–14, 239, 246, 246n523, 293, 293–94n627, 295, 295n632, 350
Genet, Jean, 410, 410n892
Gervais, Marty, 320, 320n690, 345, 397, 400
Gibbon, Edward, 26, 116n277, 426, 426n923
Gibbon, John Murray, 387, 387n858
Gibbons, Maurice, 116n277
Gibbs, Robert (Bob), 264, 264n565
Gilbert, Gerry, 113n263, 174, 174n390, 184
Gill, John, 123, 123n293, 165–66, 168, 174, 202n428, 249n533, 265, 265n568, 268–69, 269n577, 270–71

Ginsberg, Allen, 40, 165, 165n382, 185n404, 190, 281

Glassco, John, 124, 124n296, 399, 411, 442

Godfrey, Dave, 160–61, 160n367, 217

Godwin, William, 65, 65n115

Gotlieb, Phyllis, 216n451, 217, 217n459

Graham, Billy, 95, 95n205,

Graves, Robert, 59, 59n94, 64, 92

Gray, Thomas, 78, 78n153, 353n786

Grayson, Ethel Kirk, 51n65

Greene, Graham, 390, 390n865

Grier, Eldon, 191

Guest, Edgar A., 65, 65n117, 92, 352

Guevara, Che, 372, 372n822

Guillén, Jorge, 343–44, 343n749

Guillén, Nicolás, 343n749, 344

Gustafson, Betty, 336

Gustafson, Ralph, 41, 63n107, 114, 114n268, 124, 191, 195–96, 255n549, 264–65, 333, 335n727, 336, 336n727, 343, 378

Gzowski, Peter, 359, 359n794

Haig-Brown, Roderick, 27, 303–4, 303n655, 338, 338n732, 352n777, 376

Haley, Alex, 379, 379n839

Hall, Donald, 200

Hambleton, Ronald, 81, 81n161

Hardy, Thomas, 59, 115, 117, 229

Harlow, Robert (Bob), 112, 112n258, 288

Harris, David W., 140, 140n334

Harris, Frank, 300, 300n650

Harron, Don, 122n290

Harvey, Rolf, 345n757

Hazzard, Russ, 328n711

Hebb, Marian, 389, 389n864

Hemingway, Ernest, 272

Herbert, Walter, 131

Herrick, Robert, 58, 115

Hiebert, Paul, 372n823

Hill, Douglas, 188, 188n410

Hindmarch, Gladys, 185, 185n403

Hine, Daryl, 90, 90n184, 92

Hinz, Evelyn, 328n710

Hood, Hugh, 320, 320n691, 323

Hopkins, Gerard Manley, 114, 114n268, 229

Horovitz, Frances, 411, 411n893

Horovitz, Michael, 411n893

Housman, A.E., 59, 59n92, 59n94, 349n764, 419, 419n911

Houston, James, 404, 404n884

Howay, F.W., 75, 75n142

Howe, Tom, 327, 327n707, 328

Howith, Harry, 237–38, 238n508

Hughes, Ted, 186n406, 411, 411n894

Hugo, Richard, 14, 14n20

Hunt, Alison, 127n304, 212

Hunt, Leigh, 252n543

Hurtig, Mel, 104n233, 156, 156n363, 160–61, 163–64, 170, 173, 177–78, 180, 207, 207n439, 284, 286

Huxley, Aldous, 175, 175n391, 227n487

Huxley, Julian, 175n391

Ingstad, Helge, 127, 127n302

Inkster, Tim, 351, 351n776

Iremonger, Valentin, 64, 64n110

Jackovich, Jack, 352, 352n777, 392

Jackson, A.Y., 125

James, R.S., 107, 109–10,

Jaques, Edna, 191, 191n415, 193

Jeffares, A.N., 372, 372n824, 426, 426n924

Jeffers, Robinson, 13, 14n19, 45, 59, 59n92, 59n94, 78n152, 115, 117, 117n282

Jensen, Jack, 33, 242, 242n514, 249, 276, 316, 321, 330, 347

Jewinski, Ed, 326, 326n704, 327

Jiles, Paulette, 428

John, Augustus, 63, 63n108

Johnson, Lyndon B., 123

Johnson, Pauline, 189, 189n412, 250–51

Johnston, George, 344, 344n753, 410, 416

Johnstone, Sylvia, 37

Jonas, George, 152, 152n354, 191, 269n577, 297n640

Jones, D.G., 137, 137n326, 146–47, 146n341, 191, 196

Joyce, James, 13, 72, 72n137

Jung, Carl Gustav, 104

Kain, Conrad, 298, 298n642

Karchmer, Sylvan, 140

Kaufman, G.S., 289, 289n615

Kearns, Lionel, 157, 158n364, 183, 229, 244, 398, 431

Keats, John, 58, 58n90, 196, 419, 419n910

Keeler, Wally, 231, 231n496

Kennedy, Leo, 54n71

Kennedy, Robert F., 166–68, 167n384, 169n386, 170

Kenner, Hugh, 238n510

Kerouac, Jack, 185n404, 410, 410n892

Kertzer, Jonathan, 29, 29n48,

Ketcham, Ed, 222
Kilgallin, Tony, 215n450, 296n635, 321
King, Martin Luther, Jr., 169n386
Kipling, Rudyard, 117, 418–19
Kirk, Downie, 63n107, 96n208, 296–98, 296nn635–36, 297nn636–37
Kirkconnell, Watson, 49–50, 49nn56–57, 50n62, 268–69, 268n575
Kitto, H.D.F., 178, 180
Kittredge, William, 14, 14n20
Kiyooka, Roy, 113n263, 191, 191n415, 196
Kizer, Carolyn, 101, 101nn219–20
Klan, Yvonne, 403n883
Klein, A.M., 54, 54n71, 56, 99n211, 114, 115n274, 153n355, 183n401, 242, 242n517, 290, 384
Klinck, Carl F., 339n735
Knickerbocker, Conrad, 209, 209n444
Kunitz, Stanley, 343, 343n751
Kurc, Marta, 392, 392n867, 394
Lambeth, Michel, 339, 339n737
Lamming, George, 403, 403n882
Lampert, Arlene, 339, 339n736
Lampert, Gerald, 248–49, 248n530, 267, 279–81
Lampman, Archibald, 104, 104n235, 191
Lane, Patrick, 11n12, 18, 119, 119n285, 149, 149n347, 182–84, 191, 191n415, 201, 205n436, 264–65, 269n577, 307–11, 313, 313n676, 340n740, 385
Lane, Richard (Red), 119n285, 191, 191n415, 193
Lang, Curt, 15–16, 17n27, 18, 39, 54, 54n69, 55n75, 56, 58, 60, 63, 63n107, 65, 67, 72, 82, 87–88, 90, 271, 276n586, 296, 296n635
Lanigan, George T., 191
Larkin, Philip, 26, 26n44
Laurence, Margaret, 27, 29, 29n52, 40–41, 149, 149n349, 150, 187, 189, 200–1, 201n426, 204, 226, 280, 280n595, 284n602, 299, 299n645, 303, 306, 350n771, 376, 443
Lawrance, Scott, 326–27, 326n704
Lawrence, D.H., 23, 59, 59n94, 231n497, 259, 361, 361n800, 363, 390, 392, 412n896
Layton, Aviva, 217, 217n459, 222
Layton, Betty, 103, 103n230

Layton, Irving, 24, 39, 54n71, 63n106, 73, 73nn139–40, 83, 83n166, 95, 95nn206–7, 99, 99n211, 102, 103n230, 104–5, 105n236, 110, 117, 140, 147, 149–50, 153–54, 187–88, 190–91, 193–94, 200, 203, 206, 216n453, 217–18, 217n459, 222, 222n469, 237, 254, 256, 269n577, 270–71, 278n592, 308–9, 324 324n700, 333, 343–45, 356, 360, 365, 365n811, 383–84, 405, 405n885, 429
Leacock, Stephen, 61, 61n101, 191, 370
Leavis, F.R., 392
Lee, Dennis, 13, 13n16, 24n38, 134n316, 160n367, 164, 164n380, 169, 170, 180, 263, 293, 294n628, 295, 329, 351, 359, 383, 397, 406, 412n898, 417n903, 419, 428
Lehmann, John, 58n86
Leishman, J.B., 300, 300n649
Lemieux, Jean Paul, 242, 242n516
LePan, Douglas, 114n269, 191, 196
Lever, Bernice, 430n928
Levertov, Denise, 185n403, 396, 396n871
Lévesque, René, 291, 345n755, 346, 358
Levine, Norman, 395, 395n870
Lillard, Charles, 236n506
Livesay, Dorothy, 49n59, 63n106, 81, 81n161, 114, 116n277, 191, 195, 205, 217, 309, 309n669, 360, 360n797, 395
Logue, Christopher, 90, 90n187, 92–94
London, Jack, 226n484
Longfellow, Henry Wadsworth, 432
Low, Wailan (Lily), 18, 33, 41, 215n450, 284–85, 301, 304–5, 313, 319, 323, 339, 357, 363, 365, 367, 369–71, 375–77, 379, 391, 394–95, 403, 408, 410, 413, 418, 422, 426, 430, 432
Lowe, Frank, 295
Lowell, Amy, 59, 59n92
Lowell, Robert, 15n22, 19, 19n30, 202n427, 311n673
Lowry, Malcolm, 18, 20, 23, 38–39, 45, 54n69, 62–63, 62n106, 63nn106–7, 65n116, 75, 75n144, 78n150, 89n180, 96, 103, 103nn226–27, 105–6, 112, 114, 115n270, 123, 191, 193, 198–202, 204–6, 204nn432–33, 206n437, 209, 211, 215, 215n450, 224, 224n476, 235, 237–40, 239n511, 240n511, 252, 282n597, 287n607, 287–90, 296–98, 296nn635– 36, 297n638, 350n769, 389, 394, 426

Lowry, Margerie, 62n106, 63, 103, 103n227, 162, 204, 204n432, 224, 239, 252, 297
Ludwig, Jack, 179, 179n395, 195, 302, 319, 319n684
Lunn, Richard (Dick), 139, 142, 147
Łysohorsky, Óndra, 179
Lytton, Edward Bulwer Lytton, 297n641
Mac Low, Jackson, 185, 185n403
MacCaig, Norman, 88, 89n179
MacDiarmid, Hugh, 88, 88n178
MacDonald, Wilson, 384, 384n846,
MacEwen, Gwendolyn, 83n167, 127n305, 191, 196, 217n458, 222n469
MacKay, L.A., 115, 115n271, 192–93
Macklem, Michael, 406, 406n888
MacLean, Sorley, 378, 378n837
MacLeish, Archibald, 109, 110n252
MacLennan, Hugh, 106, 106n241, 278n592, 371
MacNeice, Louis, 76n147, 115, 115n271
Macpherson, Jay, 56, 57n83, 90, 92, 94, 104, 191, 196
Major, Leon, 245, 245n520
Mandel, Eli, 57n83, 81n161, 191, 191n415, 196, 211, 217–18, 304, 309n669
Marlatt, Daphne, 52n66, 183, 183n400, 185, 185n403
Marquis, Don, 321n692
Marriott, Anne, 49, 49n59, 53, 191, 196, 408
Marshall, Tom, 148, 148n343, 203, 216n451, 217, 307, 364
Marty, Sid, 221, 221n466, 277, 302, 304
Marvell, Andrew, 110, 110n252, 117
Maschler, Tom, 162, 162n375, 209
Mathews, Robin, 230, 230n494, 232, 351, 444
Mavor, Ronald (Bingo), 88, 89n179
Mayakovsky, Vladimir, 264, 264–65n567, 268, 272–73, 276
Mayne, Seymour, 183–84, 183n401, 205, 205n436, 233, 370
McCarthy, Bryan, 191, 191n415, 196, 233
McCartney, Linda, 315, 315n679
McClelland, Jack, 22, 33, 161, 161n373, 171, 216, 245, 269, 286, 298, 444
McClure, Michael, 185, 185n404
McCullagh, Gale, 293–94, 293n626, 294n629
McDermid, Anne, 236, 242
McFadden, David, 269n577, 428

McIntyre, Steve, 276, 276n586
McKinley, Hugh, 179–80, 179n394, 186, 189–90, 192, 306
McKinnon, Barry, 228, 228n489, 230, 243, 267, 319, 319n687, 400n877
McKuen, Rod, 271, 271n582
McLachlan, Alexander, 192
McLuhan, Marshall, 179, 179n395, 201, 293n626
McNeil, Florence, 183, 183n400
Melville, Herman, 114
Miller, Arthur, 138, 138n328
Miller, Henry, 178, 410, 410n892
Mills, John, 205, 205n436
Milton, John, 33, 58, 78, 95, 377n833
Minushin, Valery, 397
Montgomery, Joan, 359n793
Moore, Brian, 179, 179n395
Moore, Marianne, 114, 114n266,
Moraes, Dom, 186, 186n406
Morrow, Judith, 257n553
Motion, Andrew, 26, 26n44
Moulding, P.J., 161n372
Mowat, Angus, 284, 284n601, 296, 322
Mowat, Farley, 127, 127n302, 179, 216, 284n601, 295–96, 440
Muir, Edwin, 90n186
Murphy, Richard, 348, 348n763
Murray, Rona, 119, 119n286, 183, 195, 398
Musgrave, Susan, 288, 288n613, 332, 393, 393n868
Neruda, Pablo, 11n12, 36, 313–14, 313n676, 365
Nesbitt, Bruce, 305, 305n657, 426, 426n922
New, W.H. (Bill), 24n38, 34, 403, 403n882, 410
Newbolt, Henry, 384n846
Newfeld, Frank, 161, 161n372
Newlove, John, 18, 113n263, 126, 126n300, 139, 144, 192, 205n436, 216n451, 220, 220n463, 235, 242, 248, 261, 265, 269n577, 342–43, 385
Newman, C.J., 144, 144n340
Newman, Peter C., 232, 232n499, 259
Nichol, Barrie (bpNichol), 140n334, 191, 191n415, 196, 222n472, 224, 238, 263, 266n569
Nietzsche, Friedrich, 104, 111
Noel-Bentley, Peter, 154, 154n357, 154n359

Nowlan, Alden, 18, 129, 129n310, 144, 150, 192, 216n451, 263, 269n577, 365n811

O'Brien, A.H., 387, 387n858

Ochs, Phil, 190, 190n413

Olson, Charles, 40, 52n66, 114n263, 123–24, 123n292, 126, 185n403

Ondaatje, Michael, 148, 148n343, 191, 196, 201n426, 264–65, 266n569, 315, 364, 385, 386n854

Ouimet, Alphonse, 155, 155n360

Owen, Wilfred, 115

Pacey, Desmond, 22, 23n35, 29, 29n51, 223, 223n475

Pachter, Charles, 120n287

Page, P.K., 56, 56n82, 62, 81, 115, 191, 196, 264, 364, 385, 391, 391n866

Papadopoulos, Georgios, 305

Parrot, Jean-Claude, 369, 369n815

Parton, Lorne, 194

Patchen, Kenneth, 410, 410n892

Paterson, Sheena, 309–10, 314

Peale, Norman Vincent, 95, 95n205

Pearson, Lester B., 155, 155n360

Percy, H.R. (Bill), 379, 379n838, 411, 427, 432

Percy, Vina, 379, 411, 427, 432

Persky, Stan, 229, 229n493, 340n739

Peyto, Bill, 325, 325n703

Plath, Sylvia, 411n894

Porter, Anna, 307, 307n666

Porter, Peter, 186, 186n406

Pound, Ezra, 11n12, 52, 52n66, 59n92, 71–72, 71n132, 80, 110n252, 114, 229n492, 296n635

Powell, Craig, 282, 282n596

Pratt, E.J., 20, 37, 49n56, 50n62, 54, 54n71, 56, 60, 62, 62nn103–4, 83, 83n169, 86, 94, 99–102, 99nn211–12, 100n213, 101n221, 107–8, 114, 118, 125, 182, 191, 196, 200–1, 204, 206, 263, 263n564, 265, 293

Priestley, J.B., 93, 93n199, 180

Procope, Mervyn, 191, 191n415, 196

Proust, Marcel, 246, 246n525, 246n525

Purdy, Eurithe, 14, 14n18, 18–19, 33, 37–39, 42, 45, 122–23, 136, 138, 150, 155–57, 161, 163–64, 167, 171, 174, 178, 181, 187, 189, 192, 194, 198–205, 207–8, 211–12, 215–16, 222, 222n471, 225–26, 230, 232–35, 243, 245–46, 248, 255–56,

Purdy, Eurithe, *(cont.)*, 260, 269, 271, 277, 280–81, 284–87, 289, 303, 305, 307, 310, 313n675, 314, 322–23, 331, 336, 336n727, 338–39, 341, 343–44, 348–49, 352, 355, 358, 361, 363, 365, 379, 383, 387, 389–90, 392–93, 395–97, 397n872, 405, 416, 419, 422–24, 427–28, 432, 441

Purdy, Jim, 38, 60n97

Ransom, John Crowe, 59, 59n93

Ravenscroft, Arthur, 124, 124n297, 192

Reaney, James, 94, 94n204, 99n211, 100, 126, 297, 373n826, 417–18

Reed, J.D., 124, 124n295

Reeves, John, 91, 91n191, 277–78

Reid, Bill, 102, 102n225

Rexroth, Kenneth, 26, 26n43

Richler, Mordecai, 179–80, 179n395, 201n426, 368–70

Rilke, Rainer Maria, 26, 300–1, 300n649

Rimanelli, Giose, 120, 120n288, 388

Roberts, Charles G.D., 71n128, 104–5n235, 115, 359, 359n793, 360, 387–88, 445, 191, 196, 304

Roberts, Dorothy, 150, 150n350

Robinson, Brad, 244, 244n519

Roedde, Bill, 93

Rosenblatt, Joe, 127, 127n303, 131, 133n315, 139, 164, 182–83, 201–2, 205, 207, 216, 216n452, 277, 288, 318, 324, 340, 358, 391–92, 414, 428

Ross, John, 137, 137nn324–25, 142

Ross, Sinclair, 362, 362n801

Ross, W.W.E., 140, 140n334

Russell, Bertrand, 93, 93n199

Safarik, Allan, 302, 307–8, 307n664, 310, 310n670

Sagan, Carl, 377–78, 377n832

Scarlatti, Domenico, 229

Schliemann, Heinrich, 178, 234

Scholefield, E.O.S., 75, 75n142

Schroeder, Andreas, 236, 236n506, 244, 356

Scobie, Stephen, 264, 264n566

Scott, Duncan Campbell, 191, 200

Scott, F.R., 39, 54n71, 73n138, 99n211, 105, 105n237, 124, 137, 138n326, 146, 156, 171, 180–81, 181n396, 193, 200, 223, 223n473, 264–65, 320, 371, 378n837, 399–400, 400nn876–77, 444

Sedgewick, Garnett, 114n264, 282n597, 384–86, 384n846

Service, Robert, 191

Shakespeare, William, 33, 58, 169, 220n462, 228, 286n605, 377n833

Silcox, David, 267, 267n572

Simon, Kate, 233

Sinclair, Lister, 75, 75n143, 78, 78n151, 81–82

Sitwell, Edith, 59, 59n94, 114–15

Skelton, John, 115

Skelton, Robin, 112, 112n257, 392

Smart, Elizabeth, 101n216

Smith, A.J.M., 54, 54n71, 56, 63n109, 64, 73, 73n139, 76, 76n146, 99n211, 110, 115, 124, 143, 181, 181n396, 208, 212, 217n459, 223, 442

Smith, Denis, 347, 347n760

Smith, Iain Crichton, 373, 373n829, 378

Smith, Sydney Goodsir, 88, 89n179

Solecki, Sam, 11n9, 15n22, 16n23, 23, 24nn38–39, 28n47, 29n49, 30–31, 34, 73n139, 117n281, 149n348, 231n498, 246n525, 336n728, 343n749, 385n853, 390n865, 445, 445n946

Sommers, Robert, 90n182

Souster, Raymond, 83n166, 105, 105n236, 115, 144, 192, 235, 249, 263, 405n886

Spears, Heather, 191, 191n415, 196

Spedding, Elizabeth, 434

Spender, Stephen, 43, 76, 76n147

Spenser, Edmund, 56n78, 58, 78, 88n177

Spicer, Jack, 183n400, 185n403, 229n493, 351, 351n775

Stanfield, Robert, 249, 249n535

Stein, Gertrude, 126, 126n299

Steingass, David, 195

Stevens, C.J., 124, 124n294, 189

Stevens, Peter, 191–93, 311, 311n672

Stevenson, Robert Louis, 175

Stewart, Douglas, 161, 161n371

Stewart, Sam, 285–86, 285n604

Suknaski, Andrew, 210, 210n445, 221, 226, 242n515, 244, 260, 266n569, 268, 304, 307, 330

Sutherland, Betty, 103n230

Sutherland, Fraser (Frank), 424, 424n920

Sutherland, John, 83, 83n169, 86

Sutherland, Ronald, 195, 195n419, 201n426, 373, 379

Suttles, Wayne, 102, 102n224

Swift, Jonathan, 79

Sylvestre, Jean-Guy, 139, 139n331, 159

Symons, Scott, 149, 149n347, 257, 257n553, 268, 271

Szumigalski, Anne, 192, 192n416

Tallman, Ellen, 185, 185n403, 231, 231n497

Tallman, Warren, 101n216, 185, 185n403, 222n469, 229

Tate, Allen, 101n216

Teunissen, John, 316, 316n680, 318, 328n710

Theroux, Paul, 392

Thesen, Sharon, 428

Thibaudeau, Colleen, 373, 373n826, 375, 378

Thoby-Marcelin, Philippe, 123

Thomas, Clara, 350, 350n771

Thomas, Dylan, 38, 57, 57n84, 60, 63–64, 73, 76, 80, 101, 114–15, 117, 229, 293, 296n635, 382, 389

Thoreau, Henry David, 125

Thurber, James, 288n614

Tod[d], John, 333–34, 333n720, 334n720

Tolstoy, Leo, 335

Toms, Mary Lu, 249n534

Toppings, Earle, 158, 158n364

Town, Harold, 179, 179n395, 216, 216n453, 246, 251, 257, 314

Toye, William (Bill), 423, 423n918

Trotsky, Leon, 13, 37, 388

Trower, Peter, 277–78, 277n589, 302, 304, 403–4, 403n883, 431

Trudeau, Pierre, 40, 161, 161n374, 166–67, 203, 261, 289, 294, 405

Turner, W.J., 117, 117n280

Twigg, Alan, 360n797, 374, 374n830

Ustinov, Peter, 90, 90n183

Van Toorn, Peter, 428

Vancouver, George, 79

Verne, Jules, 413

Voznesensky, Andrey, 336, 336n728, 336n730, 340, 343–44

Waddington, Miriam, 115, 115n274, 141, 153n355, 188, 191, 194, 196, 196n420

Waddington, Patrick, 196, 196n420, 334

Wade, John (see Stevens, C.J.)

Wagoner, David, 101, 101nn219–20

Wah, Fred, 52n66, 185n403

Wain, John, 159, 159n366

Walcott, Derek, 135, 136n318

Watkins, Hollis, 169, 169n386

Watson, James Wreford (*see* Wreford, James)
Watson, Wilfred, 99n211, 255n549
Watt, F.W., 245, 245n521
Waugh, Evelyn, 371, 371n821
Wayman, Tom, 160, 160n368, 163, 191
Weaver, Robert (Bob), 91, 91n189, 169–70, 172–73, 255–56, 267
Webb, Phyllis, 57, 57n83, 92, 102, 191, 196, 216, 385, 393
Webster, Jack, 237, 237n507
Welbank, Mike, 178
Welles, Orson, 277
Wenner-Gren, Axel, 88–89, 88n176
Wevill, Assia, 186n406, 411n894
Wevill, David, 186, 186n406, 188
Whalley, George, 115, 115n273
White, Howard, 182n399, 302, 302n654
White, Mary, 182n399
Whitman, Walt, 115, 260, 260n560, 373n828
Whittaker, Eve, 410
Whittier, John Greenleaf, 432
Whitton, Charlotte, 155, 155n360
Whyte, Jon, 304, 304n656
Wieners, John, 351, 351n775
Wilbur, Richard, 246, 246n526
Wilkinson, Anne, 115, 115n275, 191, 193
Williams, David, 316–18, 316n681, 322, 327–28, 332
Williams, Tennessee, 138, 138n328
Williams, William Carlos, 52, 113–14n263, 116–17, 117n279

Wilson, Edmund, 16
Wilson, Milton, 94, 94n202, 111, 154, 201n426, 442
Wilson, Phyllis, 432
Winkler, Donald, 394, 395n869
Wolfe, James, 353, 353n786
Woodcock, George, 24n38, 26n43, 29, 29n52, 43, 129, 129n309, 149, 153n355, 201n426, 248–49, 248n531, 249n538, 251, 296n635, 329, 329n713, 398–99, 399n876, 402n881, 428, 431, 442–45
Woodcock, Inge, 443
Woods, John, 160, 160n367
Woodward, Pauline, 182
Wordsworth, William, 78, 78n154, 175, 293
Wreford, James, 115, 115n272, 118
Wright, Charles, 160, 160n367
Wright, S. Fowler, 392
Wright, Theon, 106n242
Wright, Wayne, 325n701
Yates, J. Michael, 236n506
Yeats, W.B., 13, 57n84, 58, 58n91, 76, 76n145, 80, 95, 114–15, 115n271, 117, 203n431, 267n573, 317, 348, 372, 372n824, 418, 419n909
Yeomans, Ed, 351, 351n774
Yevtushenko, Yevgeny, 290, 290n617, 336, 336n728, 344
Young, Ian, 269n577
Zilber, Jake, 112, 112n258
Zuckerman, Dick, 120, 125